Teaching Reading: Selected Materials

Teaching Reading: Selected Materials

EDITED BY

WALTER B. BARBE

Highlights for Children, Associate Editor,
and University of Pittsburgh, Adjunct Professor

New York   Oxford University Press
1965

To Dr. and Mrs. Garry C. Myers

Introductory Statement

by PAUL A. WITTY

In this book of selected readings Dr. Walter Barbe has sought to offer the student a comprehensive overview of the reading process and an understanding of the principles underlying effective reading instruction. Examination of the selections will show that he recognizes the importance of the sequential development of basic habits and skills, and the significance of interests and needs in a balanced reading program. That Dr. Barbe is an advocate of individualized or personalized reading and a follower of the developmental reading approach is also evident from the readings chosen.

Teachers concerned wth reading instruction sometimes assert that most textbooks provide an inadequate and meager background for understanding the many important contributions found in the constantly expanding professional literature. To extend the textbook approach some teachers find it desirable to assign additional readings in various sources. This practice becomes very difficult when large numbers of students are enrolled in a single class. Often there are only single library copies of articles dealing with important recent developments and contributions of various kinds. Some teachers therefore utilize books of readings to offer students the materials they consider indispensable in encompassing the most significant aspects of effective reading instruction.

In order to present an overview of the extensive literature, the compilers of books of readings have typically included a large number of *very short* articles. It is sometimes asserted that these excerpts fail to do justice to the topics and result in partial understanding or confusion on the part of many students.

Perhaps the greatest contribution of Dr. Barbe's book is found in his utilization of a limited number of longer articles than are usually found in similar books (only fifty-three articles as compared with about twice that number in other books of readings). Unique among his selections are entire chapters from some outstanding books, as well as several articles by an author on a single topic. As a result, this book provides a comprehensive, well-rounded treatment of reading instruction. Although it contains a relatively small number of selections, it does treat the most significant aspects of effective teaching. Notable also are complete articles presenting pointed criticism of practice. Most of the selections are current and are long enough to present the author's view validly. This departure from the usual practice has resulted in a book that has marked continuity and unity. The presentations are further unified by introductory statements to various sections of the volume. This book should be welcomed by teachers of large classes. And it should enable students and teachers generally to gain an understanding of the reading process and of procedures of great value in fostering efficient instruction.

Preface

The contents of this book have been selected to provide materials about teaching reading. Research reports are included on the process of learning to read and methods by which the learning environment is improved. The wide variety of new methods and programs for more effective teaching of reading is demonstrated by the abundance of recent articles. An attempt was made to present some of the best materials, with the realization that not all outstanding contributions could be included. Materials concerning teaching reading at different grade levels, research reports, reviews of research on reading, and discussions of topics currently of major concern in the teaching of reading are included.

The materials in the present book were selected on the basis of their significance to the problem of teaching reading rather than on their recency of publication. New ideas in the teaching of reading are given relatively more attention than more established practices in order to introduce them to the reader. The length of an article was not the prime factor considered in its selection. Certain important materials have been included even though they are longer than the usual readings in other books.

The editor believes a book of readings has particular value in teacher training programs today. Without replacing the student's need to pursue specific areas further, it does bring together for him some of the most important ideas in the field. Moreover, where library resources are limited, a book of readings meets the specific need of assuring the student that he has available a large amount of the significant literature.

Any book such as this owes a major debt of gratitude to the authors of the original articles and their publishers for granting permission to have them reproduced, in many instances without charge. Frequently, the only reward they receive is the satisfaction of knowing that their contribution has been of influence in improving reading instruction. The list of contributors to this book is not limited exclusively to the "names" in the field of reading but contains a number of "one-time" authors. To all the contributors, the editor wishes to express his appreciation.

The planning for this book began many years ago when the editor was director of the Junior League Reading Center in Chattanooga, Tennessee. The workers in the Center provided encouragement not only in his work in reading, but also in bringing together this collection. To Mrs. Evelyn Orr, Mrs. Jewell Rudicil, and Mrs. Louise Tone of the Junior League Reading Center the editor will forever be indebted. Those who assisted in collecting the materials and preparing the manuscript include the Rev. Herbert Neff, Mr. John Guidubaldi, Mrs. Katherine Steiert, and Mr. Walter Brown. Mrs. Margaret Betzhold not only typed, filed, and sorted the materials for this book, but managed at the same time to run a busy office efficiently. Mr. Paul Whitfield of Oxford University Press provided valuable encouragement and assistance. Kent State University provided the time, through a research grant, to prepare the materials which finally resulted in this publication.

Honesdale, Pennsylvania   **W.B.B.**
October 1964

Contents

Teaching Reading: Selected Materials

PART ONE

Teaching and Learning To Read

INTRODUCTION

The teaching of reading has never held a more prominent place in the school curriculum than it does today. The reasons for this are many; but probably most important is the new emphasis on "quality" education. Public reaction to entrance into the space age has been a demand for more and better education of all children. The degree of success in this goal will be reflected by how well our children learn to read.

The goal of reading instruction should not be defined in terms of quantitative factors. How early a child learns to read, how well he calls words, how fast he reads them, or even the scores he receives on standardized reading tests are only quantitative factors, relatively unimportant when not accompanied by an interest in reading. Schools have too frequently relied heavily upon the graded school, the assignment of specific marks for performance, and the belief that chronological age is the best indicator of the child's reading instructional level.

There is little likelihood of any improvement in methods of teaching reading or in the reading ability of children if we do not carefully distinguish between quantitative and qualitative goals. "What I think and feel about what I read is more important than what I read," is the statement of the goal of the reading program for gifted children in the Cleveland public schools.[2] The final goal of reading instruction must be to teach each child, by whatever means necessary, the skills of reading, and concurrently to develop permanent interests in reading for pleasure and continued learning.

Reading is not a single act, and it is more than just a process. Reading involves numerous physiological, neurological, and psychological processes. "The Process of Reading" described by Buswell in the selection that follows leads logically into the concept of reading by Buswell that "the teaching of reading is basically a problem of visual perception." [3] Reading is further explained by Anderson and Dearborn in the next selection by the statement that "learning to read is primarily a process of associative learning." [1] Reading, as a physiological process, primarily involves visual perception, but associative learning must occur if reading is to be more than mere word-calling.

Any consideration of learning or teaching reading must include a discussion of learning as a product, process, and function.[4] When the end result or outcome of learning is emphasized, the learning is product-directed. When learning is considered a process, concern is directed toward "what happens during the course of a learning experience in attaining a given learning product or outcome." [5] The point of view that describes learning as a function emphasizes "certain critical aspects of learning which presumably make behavioral change in human learning possible." [6] Much of today's disagreement about the teaching of reading is on whether learning to read is a process, function, or product. A definition of reading as solely a perceptual process would direct attention to what happened perceptually as the child learned to read, while being concerned only with whether the child could read, would be product learning. Defining reading as a perceptual-conceptual function recognizes reading interests, attitudes, and needs, while minimizing the product or end result of word-calling as being the sole purpose of teaching reading.

HISTORY OF READING INSTRUCTION

A knowledge of the history of reading instruction is important for teachers in order that they may understand present practices and philosophies. The importance of reading instruction throughout the past two hundred years is noted by Smith, who states, "Reading was the most important subject in our early American schools and it has continued to be the most important subject all through the years of our national growth." [7]

The early history of reading instruction in America provides valuable insight into some of today's problems. The *New England Primer,* published about 1683, reflected not only the content of what children were taught to read, but indicated the method by which it was believed children best learned how to read. The *New England Primer* contained the alphabet, the Lord's Prayer, and the Creed, as well as lists of words of increasing length. Primarily by a visual recognition method, beginning with the alphabet and progressing increasingly to longer words, children were taught to read material of a religious nature.[10]

By about 1790 the emphasis was on *The American Spelling Book,* better known as the Blue-back Speller. The method of teaching reading in this period was through the use of a spelling approach. The alphabet was taught first, followed by syllables. The materials were highly moralistic, but less religious than in earlier readers.

From 1836 to about 1920 the *McGuffey Readers* were the most influential materials being used to teach reading. A phonetic approach was stressed, although the alphabet approach was still in use. The *McGuffey Readers* were the first carefully graded readers, with one book for each grade.[8]

The word method was introduced into American reading instruction at about the same time as the *McGuffey Readers,* and in some instances was taught exclusively without teaching the individual letters within words. Phonic methods were developed to counteract this deficiency. Phrase, sentence, and story approaches to reading, emphasizing thought-getting rather than word mastery, were stressed along with phonics and oral reading.[11]

A review of the recent history of reading instruction, by Smith, the fourth selection in this book, presents a follow-up to her thorough presentation of the history in *American Reading Instruction.*[9]

GOALS OF TEACHING READING

Today, education has assumed a magnitude undreamed of only a generation ago. Far greater numbers of children enter school and remain there longer, and the amount of knowledge to be imparted has vastly increased. The result is an educational program that must constantly be improved to provide for an increasingly better-educated populace.

The nature and types of reading described by Gray serve as a base for the discussion by Krippner relating reading instruction and existential philosophy. The ultimate goal of reading instruction must be the development of both the skill of reading and the desire to read. The only limitation to the acquisition of knowledge for the child who has learned to read well is his inherent mental capacity.

REFERENCES

1. Anderson, Irving H., and Dearborn, Walter F., *The Psychology of Teaching Reading.* New York: The Ronald Press Company, 1952, p. 138.
2. Barbe, Walter B., and Norris, Dorothy E., "Reading Instruction in Special Classes for Gifted Elementary Children," *The Reading Teacher,* Vol. 16, No. 6 (May 1963), p. 425.
3. Buswell, Guy T., "The Process of Reading," *The Reading Teacher,* Vol. 13, No. 2 (December 1959), p. 114.
4. Harris, Theodore L., and Schwahn, Wilson E., *Selected Readings on the*
Learning Process. New York: Oxford University Press, 1961, pp. 1-3.
5. Ibid. p. 1.
6. Ibid. p. 3.
7. Smith, Nila B., *American Reading Instruction.* New York: Silver, Burdett and Company, 1934, p. iii.
8. Ibid. p. 105.
9. Ibid.
10. Witty, Paul A., *Reading in Modern Education.* Boston: D. C. Heath and Company, 1949, p. 3.
11. Ibid. p. 6.

CHAPTER I

The Reading Process

1: The Process of Reading *

GUY T. BUSWELL

When children first enter school they have already learned to communicate through speech. The process of learning to read can best be understood by relating it to the nature of speech and to the experiences which children have had in learning to speak. Psychologically, the processes of speech and reading are quite similar, the difference being mainly in the sense avenue through which the verbal stimuli are received. When children enter school they have an oral vocabulary of several thousand words, they have learned to distinguish very small differences in word sounds, they have learned that the ideas expressed in speech depend on the serial order in which the words are spoken, and they have attained a degree of skill in listening that enables them to understand speech at the usual rate of adult conversation. The essential difference between knowing how to read and how to understand oral speech is the substitution of visual preception of printed verbal symbols for the auditory impression of the same symbols when spoken. The thoughts expressed are the same, the vocabulary is the same, and the word order is the same. The new problem in reading is to learn to recognize the visual symbols with accuracy and reasonable speed.

WORD RECOGNITION

The unit in reading material is the same as the unit in speech, namely, the word. The first problem in learning to read is to recognize these printed symbols and to relate them to the corresponding speech symbols. The early American schools failed to see this essential relationship and instead introduced reading by teaching first the letters of the alphabet, then syllables, regardless of whether or not they were meaningful, and finally whole words and phrases. However, studies using a tachistoscope have shown that familiar words can be recognized about as quickly as individual letters or syllables, and that short phrases of familiar words can be recognized almost as readily as single words.

The effect of the extensive research of this type has been to emphasize that reading deals with word patterns rather than with individual letters or syllables. To be sure, in the initial learning of new words attention may need to be given to the sequence of certain letters and syllables, but when the child has learned

* Reprinted from *The Reading Teacher*, Vol. 13, No. 2 (December 1959), pp. 108-14, by permission of the author and the publisher.

thoroughly to recognize a word, the relationship of length of word and difficulty disappears. Learning a word is not a matter of getting the meaning from the sum of the letters or syllables, but rather from learning to recognize it as a whole much as one learns to recognize a person. The appearance of words should be learned so thoroughly that, during the process of reading, only a minimum of attention needs to be given to these details. One should, however, distinguish between this process of recognizing words as wholes while reading from the process of first learning words before they are used in reading. Research on this latter point will be noted in the section which deals with phonetics.

Tachistoscopic research has shown that it is easily possible to recognize a familiar word in one hundredth of a second. But it does not follow that a person can recognize one hundred words in one second. Reading is not a process of rapid recognition of one word after another. Rather, it is a process of fusing the meaning of single words into a sequence of meaning. The total act of reading is, therefore, a combination of the visual recognition of words and the central thought processes that are stimulated by them. This complex is sometimes separated into the mechanics of reading and comprehension. This may be a convenient way to analyze the total reading process provided one understands clearly that both are necessary for the complete act of reading. Several studies of oral reading in the first grade have shown that pupils sometimes carry on a process of word-calling without any apparent comprehension of the fused thought content.

FUNCTIONAL READING

In contrast with the tachistoscopic techniques which have dealt chiefly with the static recognition of words and phrases, the technique of eye-movement photography has been employed in studying the functional processes that are carried on during actual reading. There are now well over a hundred substantial studies of eye-movements in reading and they provide a valuable body of objective data for understanding the process of reading. Four particular contributions of this kind of research will be noted.

Span of Recognition. Several studies have covered the school grades from the first through high school. They show a steady increase in the number of words perceived during a single pause of the eye. In grade one there are generally more pauses, or fixations, of the eye than there are words. This reflects the perceptual behavior of a child in trying to recognize words. As the child learns to read, the span of recognition increases up to the high school level, although the rate of increase is less after the middle grades. However, even for adult readers, the average span of recognition is usually not more than two words per fixation. It used to be common to print beginning readers in so-called "eye-fulls," phrases of two, three, or four words per line. Actually, no primary children have eye spans of that width.

Speed of Recognition. As words become more familiar, the duration of eye pauses in reading becomes shorter. Here, as in span of recognition, the research shows a steady increase in speed of recognition from grade to grade. When new or difficult words are encountered, the number of eye pauses and the duration of eye pauses both show an increase. The average duration of a pause of the eye for an adult reader is about one-fourth of a second, whereas in the first grade it is more than twice this long.

Irregular Eye-Movements. The beginning reader's eyes make many back and forth movements in reading a line of print, whereas a mature reader's eyes move forward very regularly as they cover the lines. For the highly competent reader the eye-movement pattern shows great regularity from line to line.

These three characteristics, (a) span of recognition, (b) duration of fixations, and (c) regressive eye movements provide objective evidence of difficulties in the reading process and are also excellent measures of level of maturity in the perceptual aspects of reading. They show the devastating effect of unfamiliar words on the smoothness of the reading process. They show the effects of difficulty in content on the perceptual habits of the reader. They show the very heavy load of eye-muscle work for the first grader, which is one of the main reasons for his fatigue in reading. If a teacher is familiar with the eye-movement studies, she can understand much better the nature of the difficulties that are encountered in learning to read.

The Eye-Voice Span. Another of the useful findings of the eye-movement studies is the relation of the eye and the voice in oral reading. The beginner looks at each word as he pronounces it and then moves on to the next. This produces a mechanical, word-calling type of reading. The mature reader lets his eye travel a considerable distance along the line of print before he begins to read orally. This lag of the voice behind the eye gives him an opportunity to grasp the meaning and to organize his vocal expression in terms of the content of what is read. This looking ahead provides the flexibility that characterizes effective oral reading.

Eye-movement habits are directly influenced by the degree of difficulty of what is read. While it is obviously necessary to push ahead into more difficult material year by year, it would also seem to be desirable to develop increased speed and smoothness of perceptual habits by providing much prac-

tice in reading material that is at a level of difficulty a year below the present grade location of the pupil.

PHONETICS

Teaching reading by analyzing words into their sound, or phonetic, elements has been a controversial matter for many years. The research literature at present is not adequate for a final solution of the problem. Much of the data from research relates to the value of phonetics for pronunciation and spelling, and is of little value for understanding the reading process. Curiously, there is far more discussion than research being carried on at present.

The case for phonetics rests basically on two sets of facts. The first of these has to do with the nature of language. The number of distinct vocal sounds that man can utter is small, probably about fifty. The English alphabet has twenty-six letters. With this small number of sounds and letters, English words to the number of more than 300,000 can be spoken and written. To learn to recognize each of these words as an independent verbal symbol is too great a task for the school to attempt. But if systematized by learning the phonetic elements of which words are made, a small amount of teaching would cover the *pronouncing* of a large number of words.

As a matter of fact, it is not this simple. The English alphabet is not a phonetic one and there are many nonphonetic elements in English words. Although the pronunciation of many words can be covered by a small amount of phonetic instruction, there are many irregular words for which such instruction only results in confusion. To provide the necessary instruction for learning to read by the sole and consistent use of the phonetic method would spread the method over the entire elementary school period and would necessitate impossible restrictions in the use of words prior to the time their phonetic elements could be taught. Furthermore, at best the phonetic method teaches only the *pronunciation* and not the *meaning* of the words.

The second set of facts on which phonetic instruction rests is that, on entering school, children know both the sounds and the meanings of several thousand words, but do not know their visual appearance in print. Since they already know the meanings of these words, it is pointed out that a limited use of the phonetic method would be highly advantageous in helping them recognize the printed symbols by "sounding" the phonetic elements of the words. This method works well with such words as "telephone" since a child already knows what a telephone is and he recognizes the visual symbol when he hears himself say it. But if the word were "phlobaphene" the sounding of its elements would be of no help in reading because he would still be ignorant of its meaning.

From the evidence at hand it would be difficult to support either a program of all phonetics or of no phonetics. A combination (which is now the rule in many schools) seems to have more support than either extreme. There is some evidence from research to support this view. First, while the unabridged dictionary does contain more than 300,-000 words, no one uses all of them. Of the common non-technical material read by adults, more than 98 per cent of the words are found in a basic vocabulary of 4,000 words. Furthermore, it has been shown that 75 per cent of such reading matter makes use of no more than 300 different words. If the schools that use the word-recognition (non-phonetic) method were to teach words selected at random from the unabridged dictionary the task would indeed be hopeless. But if they use the data from

vocabulary research and teach the commonest words first, the task is by no means impossible. By using a combination of common sight words plus some phonetic analysis for other words whose meanings are already known through use in speech, the school may develop a very workable method. However, the case for phonetics should not be dismissed, and better research on the problem is certainly warranted.

ORAL READING

In the early American schools reading and spelling were taught together. In fact, the most widely used textbook in reading in the 1800's was Noah Webster's Blue Backed Speller, which is also the best example of a one-hundred-per-cent phonetic reader. Also, in the early American schools, oral language and reading were tied together for purposes of instruction. The oral reading method was quite universally used throughout the entire elementary school period until the second decade of the twentieth century. At that time Judd called attention to differences in oral and silent reading as revealed through eye-movement research. He noted that in oral reading the span of recognition was narrower and the duration of fixations longer than in silent reading. Other evidence showed a superior rate for silent reading. One of the clearest examples of the influence of research on a school subject is found in the shift of major emphasis from oral to silent reading in the 1920's and 1930's. In some cases, as in the McDade method of non-oral reading, there was an extreme one-hundred-per-cent shift to silent reading. The recent popular demand, mainly outside the schools, for a return to the phonetic method would reverse the shift by an equal amount in the direction of an oral method.

The research evidence indicates that

children will learn to read regardless of the degree of emphasis on oral or silent reading methods. The question of emphasis resolves itself into a sensible appraisal of the values inherent in each. The strongest case for oral reading as the basic method of instruction comes from the eminent linguist, Leonard Bloomfield, who holds that reading should be keyed to the oral language already mastered at a functional level when children enter school. He would use oral language through the medium of phonetic instruction as the sole method for learning to read. The opposing position which leans to major emphasis on silent reading is defended on the basis of psychological rather than linguistic evidence. This position is that reading is essentially a process of communication from the printed page to the child, resulting in the transfer of information and ideas to the mind of the child. Oral reading, they hold, is simply a modification of the basic act of reading by which meanings received may, quite properly, be expressed to others when the occasion demands but that it is better to stress from the beginning the idea that reading is, at heart, a thought-getting process.

Some of the conflict between oral and silent reading methods might be resolved by separating instructing in oral language from reading, as at an earlier time spelling was placed in a separate program. No one denies the importance of training in oral language. The phonetic method would quite properly be applied to learning pronunciation of words. Oral expression, including much of the oral reading, could be taught with audience situations that are genuine. The most important objection to mixing oral and silent reading is the carryover of subvocalization or inner speech into the silent reading process. When this is done the rate of silent reading is held down by the muscular limits of inner articulation, and the resulting product is a slow reader.

RATE OF READING

The fact that an increasing number of young people continue their education beyond high school is focusing new attention on rate of reading. In spite of the wide interest in reading during the last thirty years there is little evidence of increase in the usual rate of reading. Yet, the demands of college programs put an ever greater strain on the slow reader. The usual rate of reading nontechnical material at the end of the elementary school is about 250 words per minute, while for college students the average rate is about 300 words. The smallness of the increase beyond the rate of the elementary school is a cause of much concern, particularly in view of the selective character of the college population.

There has been a great deal of research on methods of increasing rate of reading. One method has been to use flash cards or tachistoscopes to induce quicker perception of printed words. By and large, the results have been disappointing. In an attempt to deal with rate of reading in a more functional situation, various methods have been devised to stimulate and control rate. Of the different methods used to present successive parts of a line at controlled rates, the Harvard reading films are perhaps the best known. More recently, attention has shifted to methods of exposing, or covering, successive lines on a printed page by mechanical devices which make possible the exposure of material to be read at whatever rate is desired. The results from these methods have indicated that rate, without loss of comprehension, can be increased far beyond the rates usually obtained in school classes. Evidence from eye-movement records taken at the end of such training shows that the principal change has been in span of recognition rather than in duration of fixations. A gain of 50 per cent in span of recognition is usually accompanied by gains of no more than 10 per cent in speed of recognition. There have been extreme claims for gains in rate of reading that go quite beyond the credulity of serious researchers, but there is well substantiated evidence from research on rate of reading that leaves little room for doubt that a sizable increase in rate without loss in comprehension could be achieved if schools were to attempt it seriously. There is no support in research for the popular notion that the slow reader is superior in comprehension.

An increase in rate by even 25 per cent by the end of high school would be of incalculable value to those who go on to college and would make possible increased breadth of information and ideas for those who leave school. More serious research on rate is needed, but studies now available indicate that, at the college level, rate of reading may be forced from 100 to 300 words per minute above the reader's present rate without a break in level of tested comprehension.

RESEARCH IN READING

In the writer's view, the teaching of reading is basically a problem of visual perception. The first goal is to enable the child to derive meaning from printed verbal symbols at the same level of functional efficiency that he has already attained in getting meanings from spoken words. The child has learned to interpret speech at a functional level before entering school. The first obligation of the reading class is to produce this same efficiency with respect to the visual perception of print. There is no substitute for this ability; this is a first obligation. The process of learning to read is the process of doing just this.

Other aspects of reading are less important until basic reading ability is achieved. The school has often so cluttered its program of reading with secondary objectives, some of them of admitted value, that the primary objective of teaching reading is not achieved. The writer has had in his college classes students of unquestioned intelligence who were slow, clumsy readers because their basic reading ability was permitted to level off too soon. On tests of basic reading they scored below sixth grade norms.

Learning to read a foreign language is a parallel case of perceptual learning. If I want to learn to read the Russian language, my first task is to learn the words when they are printed in Russian and to associate them with their meanings. My goal is to learn these words in their various forms so well that I can read them at the same rate as I read my vernacular. I do not need to be taught how to think, or how to solve problems, or how to spell, or how to improve my personality by reading Russian, or what the great classics of Russian literature are. These may be good, but they do not teach me to read Russian. I already know how to read, but not in the Russian language.

The reading process is basically this kind of perceptual learning. The school needs to know how to accomplish it more effectively. The present intellectual climate is more favorable to basic research on methods of teaching reading than has been the case for three decades. Reading would be served by some singleness of purpose.

2: The Psychology of Learning To Read *

IRVING H. ANDERSON and WALTER F. DEARBORN

INTRODUCTION

When it comes to teaching reading, teachers naturally want to know what method to use. This is a fair question, and it calls for a fair answer, but it cannot be answered through a study of methods alone. In fact, there is only one way in which it can be answered, and that is to first ask another question which has to do not with the teacher but with the child. Specifically, the teacher must first ask: By what process does the child learn to read? On the answer to this question the method to use always depends. In other words, the teaching process must take its cue from the learning process, and the rule to apply is simply as follows: *Having found out by what process the child does learn, select the method which best sets the conditions for that type of learning.* The object of the present chapter is to develop a methodology of teaching reading in terms of this principle.

LEARNING TO READ AS A PROCESS OF ASSOCIATIVE LEARNING

Learning to read involves what is perhaps the oldest concept of learning in psychology. Aristotle recognized it first, and almost every writer on psychology since has had something to say about it. We refer, of course, to the concept of associative learning. As ancient as it is, there is none that better explains the case at hand. Learning to read is primarily a process of associative learning.

The association in learning to read is that between the sight of the word and the child's response to the sound of it. That is, the child may be said to have learned to read when he makes the physical, mental, and emotional responses to the printed word that he would make upon hearing the word spoken in an oral context identical with the printed one. This concept of learning to read is obviously related to the order of development of the language-related skills. Learning to respond appropriately to spoken language comes first. The child next learns to say the words himself. Then he learns to read. Reading is a controlled form of talking in which the words on the page are substituted for the usual stimuli for speech. Teaching a child to read consists mainly in setting the conditions for this stimulus substitution.

THE "LOOK-AND-SAY" METHOD

Learning by association requires the presentation of the new stimulus simultaneously with the response to the old. In teaching reading, these conditions can be met by showing the word to the child and pronouncing it for him. After some repetition, the response to the sound of the word will become associated with the sight of it. The oral stimulus can then be omitted, and the sight of the word alone will carry the response or recognition. During the early stages of learning to read by this method, the response includes the saying of the word. For that reason, the procedure

* Reprinted from *The Psychology of Teaching Reading,* New York: The Ronald Press Company, pp. 138-52, 162-75, by permission of the publisher. Copyright 1952 by The Ronald Press.

has been described as the "look-and-say" method of teaching reading, nowadays a standard approach.

The conditions of the "look-and-say" method are plotted on the diagram of Figure 1. The reader will doubtless recognize the diagram as the same as that for the conditioned response. That is as it should be. Conditioning is the modern nomenclature for associative learning. Learning to read by the "look-and-say" method is an example of conditioning. Book [6] has skillfully related learning to read to the process of conditioning and has demonstrated how both are a process of association.

To the Russian physiologist Pavlov, of course, belongs the credit for demonstrating the phenomenon of conditioning in a carefully controlled laboratory situation. The concept of conditioning makes possible a restatement of association in terms of stimulus and response, and thus a better description of the learning process and one susceptible to better control and measurement. Pavlov's experiments, as is now generally known, were made on the salivary reflexes of dogs. The natural or adequate stimulus to the functioning of the salivary gland is the presence of food in the mouth. In human beings, the mere sight or smell of food or the ringing of a bell at dinner time will also produce a watering of the mouth, but these are doubtless all acquired reactions. In the case of the dog, however, the ringing of a bell at least will ordinarily have no such effect. It does cause a tension or perking of the ears as in listening. If, however, a bell is rung regularly when the dog is fed, this sound of the bell will soon have an effect on his feeding responses. After a time, even if no food is presented, the sound of the bell will produce a flow of saliva. The bell may be called an acquired or substitute stimulus for one of the responses of eating, or if one thinks of the response, one may speak of an acquired response to a given stimulus. In learning to read by the "look-and-say" method, the sound of the word may be regarded as the old or adequate stimulus, and the sight of the word as the new or substitute stimulus.

It should be emphasized that learning by association or conditioning ideally requires the occurrence of the new stimulus *simultaneously* with the response to the old stimulus. In the case of the "look-and-say" method, this requirement means that the eyes should be on the word at the exact time the response is made to the sound of the word. "Look at the word before you say it," the teacher admonishes the pupil. This is good advice because children do not always look at the word before they say it. As Guthrie notes, "many nonreaders among children foil our efforts because they have established habits of looking away from the printed word to which

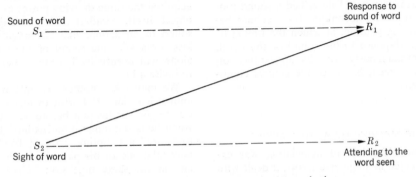

Fig. 1.—Conditions of the "look-and-say" method.

we point." [15] The following is a situation which frequently occurs when the teacher is seated beside the child, listening to him read orally. The child comes to a word which he does not know, so he turns to the teacher for help. She proceeds to supply it for him, but the child repeats the word while still looking at the teacher or while in the act of turning his eyes back to the page. Sometimes the children do not even bother to give the word a second look, but go right on to the next. One child had the habit of covering the word with his finger as a means of keeping his place when he turned to the teacher for aid. He would then say the word upon being told what it was, but he kept his finger riveted to the word until he was ready to go on. Failure to retain words under any of these conditions is not surprising. Seeing the word merely in the mind's eye is an all too fleeting stimulus. It is better if the word is plainly in view *at the time* the response is made. This may seem like a small point, but the writer has observed teachers having to supply the same words over and over again for what seemed like a failure to keep it in mind. The occurrence of the new stimulus simultaneously with the response to the old is *the* desideratum of good learning. One of the reasons why Fernald's kinesthetic method may be effective in individual cases is that it virtually compels the child to look at the word simultaneously as he utters it. We have elsewhere [1] described a sound motion-picture technique for teaching beginning reading, in which the timing of the response to the sound of the word, simultaneously with its appearance on the screen, is one of the central conditions.

THE MEANING OF WORD SYMBOLS

The older law of association was expressed in subjective terms; it dealt with the connection of ideas in the mind. In that sense, learning to read has often been described in terms of an association between the visual symbol and the sound of the word. This is something of an error: the association is not between stimuli but between stimuli and a given response. In handling and eating an apple, the taste of the apple, the feeling of its roundness, the sight of its redness are associated through the act of handling and eating. Stimuli affecting the organism while a response is in progress all *tend,* on their reoccurrence, to elicit that response. Two or more stimuli are thus associated only in the sense that they become possible activators of the same response. Printed words acquire meaning through association with the same reactions which first attach to the word sounds. The visual symbol is not connected with its sound except as both are associated with common reactions.

The Meaning of Word Sounds

The way in which word sounds first acquire meaning is, of course, well known. It is another example of the operation of our old friend, the principle of conditioning. If, when a child is handed an apple, he is regularly told the fruit's name, sooner or later the youngster will make the connection between the object and its name. The sound of the word alone may then provoke a glance or set toward the bowl of fruit on the table which contains an apple. The name has acquired the same drawing power as the object itself. Similarly, if a word is suited to an action, like exchanging a kiss for a kiss, the sound of the word alone will eventually become sufficient to invite a kiss.

We may take another example from animal learning: If I wish to teach my dog to give me his paw before he is fed, when he is standing up on his hind legs to "noze" a tempting plate of food, I may take one of his paws in my hand, and at the same time say: "Give me your paw." For a time he may stretch himself, stand up, partially projecting his paw, and make many other responses and then only when the *tempting* food is held up (he may be rather indifferent to canned food if his responses are being conditioned on fresh beef steak). After many repetitions of this situation the dog will however learn, when standing, even without the presence of food, to hold up his paw at the command "Give me your paw."

Here we see a new (auditory) stimulus being added to the previously existing pattern of stimuli—to wit, the sight or smell of food and the *gnawings* of hunger—which produce the diffuse responses of standing up, stretching, jumping, etc. With repetition, the new stimulus alone, even when the dog is not hungry, will be sufficient to release these responses. Even the month-old infant may exhibit sucking movements at the sound of its mother's voice. To begin with, the touch of a nipple on the infant's lips may have been needed to set off the sucking movement, but soon any sounds or sights which regularly accompany the feeding time may set off feeding responses. Other sights and sounds become stimuli or signals for going out to play or for going to bed. The learning of a language is thus the associating, in the first instance, of a word sound with an activity, a situation, or with just some thing. The sounds acquire meaning (or become a part of language) simply by occurring at the time an activity is in process, that is, when we are responding to some situation or thing. Thus John Locke in 1690, in his *Essay Concerning Human Understanding*, writes: "If we will observe how children learn languages, we shall find that to make them understand what the names of simple ideas or substances stand for, people ordinarily show them the things whereof they would have them have the idea; and then repeat to them the name that stands for it, as white, sweet, milk, sugar, cat, dog. . . ." Locke speaks of the connecting of the

name with the thing or the idea, whereas we have preferred to speak in terms of stimulus and response; but this is a difference which we have already resolved. Without response there is no association.

The First Steps in Learning To Read

In a like manner, we may describe the initial steps in the child's learning to read as a process of adding new stimuli to old responses. If we wish to give meaning to the printed word "father," we (or the first-grade teachers) talk about "father" so as to reinstate in the child's mind the attitudes and ideas which go with father. We say the word "father," and he repeats it. We may then show him a picture of father at home, and at the same time show the printed symbol. Soon the sight of the word "father" will lead to much the same incipient responses as the saying of the word "father" or perhaps even the presence of the father. So the most effective method of teaching a foreign language is through the associating of the foreign word with an actual activity. This is the so-called "direct method" of foreign-language instruction. Instead of first associating the foreign word with the word in the vernacular, the word is associated with an activity by being presented when the activity in question is in progress. If the child hears the words "ferme la porte," as he is performing the act of closing the door, these words when repeated, will be found to have become the stimuli for the act of closing the door.

THE RELATION OF READING TO ORAL LANGUAGE

When is a child ready to read? One capable teacher of primary reading has in effect answered: When he begins to take an interest in words by noting the name on the street sign, on the "stop" and "go" signs, or on the "hot" and "cold" water faucet; by asking how to write his own name, or what that word in the funnies is, or what a poster announcing a new movie says. In a word, when he once gets the idea that those black marks on white surfaces actually say something and he wants to know what, he is then ready for learning to read.

Since children normally learn to talk before they learn to read, they can learn to read by learning to say the words from the printed symbols. If the word is a familiar one, the saying of it will arouse its meaning because the child will respond to the sound of his own pronunciation of it, much as if he heard someone else say it. This is obviously the *modus operandi* of the "look-and-say" method. As Harris expresses the matter:

In its beginning stages, learning to read means that queer-looking marks stand for speech. The child "reads" when he is able to say the words which are represented by the printed marks. The child may say the words out loud, or he may say them to himself; in either case, reading means saying the correct words. If the child says the right words, they fall into a familiar sequence whose meaning is apparent to him because of his previous acquired facility in comprehending speech. If he says the wrong word, if he has to leave out too many words because he does not recognize them, or if his recognition is so slow and halting that the words are not heard as coming in the meaningful sequences that we call phrases and sentences, the approximation to heard speech will not be sufficiently good to convey the correct meaning. The discovery that printed words "talk" is the first step in learning to read.[16]

The reason why the visual symbol of the printed word is first associated with the spoken word is, then, that the spoken word already carries meaning for the speaker. This may not, however, always be the case. The language used in the school may not be the child's own method of expression, and therefore the child may not get the meaning expected. We are all familiar with children who have learned to "talk" words parrot fashion, without the words having much if any meaning or significance to them. The teacher must then find out "for sure," quite apart from the visual symbol, whether the children sense and can or do express orally what the matter is all about. The visual symbols must then be associated with the child's (not the teacher's or anyone else's) way of expressing the idea. If the language which the child understands is not that of the school, then things must be talked over until his own language becomes suited to school learning.

The point to be emphasized here is neatly illustrated by an incident described by Browne [7] in a doctoral dissertation submitted to the Harvard Graduate School of Education. It is one of those rare theses in which the author managed to introduce a bit of humor. As the incident is described, a boy in the first grade was reading aloud monotonously and without any show of interest or concern about the sentence: "Johnny does not have a dog." The situation suddenly took a turn for the better when the teacher explained that what the sentence meant was "Johnny done got no dog." Now that *was* too bad, he *should* have one, and there were plenty of overt expressions of sympathy and general agreement that under the circumstances Johnny should by all means have a dog. The authors of instructional material for the training programs of the armed forces during the last war were encouraged to get down to the level of the enlisted personnel. The writer of a handbook on radar operation had included in his copy the sentence: "On certain nights reception is awful." The typist questioned whether the word "awful" was good usage. The author of this frightful blunder exclaimed: "You're right, change it to, 'On certain nights the reception is lousy.' " Youngsters learn to respond to the language they have heard, and they pick up the speech habits of their surroundings. The easiest words for children to learn to read are those which occur in their conversations.[17] We are not proposing that beginning materials be written in the vernacular of the Dead-end Kids, although it helps to write material in the way that children talk, so long as the style is reasonably standard.

How speech serves to arouse meaning is convincingly revealed by the failure of the word to make sense when it is mispronounced. A common example is that of a child working on a word by the phonetic method. Every teacher of reading is aware of the trial and error that often goes into the process. The child may be observed to mouth the word first in one way, then in another way. Nothing seems to work. Suddenly he hits upon just the right combination of speech movements and just as suddenly the word registers. It registers because it now sounds and feels right. It is an example of the "Aha" phenomenon (the token of insight of the Gestaltists). Rogers[30] administered a word-pronunciation test to 72 poor silent readers among college freshmen, and found that of the words which were mispronounced, 78 per cent were also missed in meaning. For the same reason, little is gained at the start by teaching the child to read words, the correct pronunciation of which is unfamiliar to his ears. One school which has come to the writer's attention takes great pride in teaching its first-grade youngsters to read and spell such words as "quintessence," "homogenize," and "jurisdiction." Such accomplishments are offered as proof of the superiority of the phonetic method, which is the method employed by this school. The teachers admit that the children do not always know the meaning of the words. One wonders, therefore, what purpose is served. Meaning

is the *sine qua non* of learning to read. The most common cause of failure to retain words is that the words have no meaning for the child. The results of Ebbinghaus applied the clincher to that. Every student of the first course in psychology will be reminded of the form of his forgetting curve for nonsense syllables. Words which are not already a part of the child's meaning vocabulary amount to nonsense syllables. The thoughtful teacher of reading will accordingly resort to a vocabulary which is rich in meaning and which rings true to the ears.

The relation of reading to *oral* language background is clearly brought out by studies which have been made of the relationship between hearing vocabulary and comprehension and reading vocabulary and comprehension. These studies have shown that the relationship is extremely close. Anderson and Fairbanks[2] obtained a correlation of .80 between the hearing and reading vocabularies of 220 college freshmen representing all degrees of reading achievement. The poorest readers in the group had small hearing as well as reading vocabularies. By the same token, the best readers ranked high on both counts. In a study in which elementary school pupils were used as subjects, Young[34] found a correlation of .80 between hearing and reading comprehension of paragraph material. Larsen and Feder[23] have similarly reported positive and substantially high correlations between hearing and reading vocabulary and comprehension scores. The intimate relationship which exists between reading and oral language has also been effectively demonstrated by Hildreth.[18] Knowledge of the spoken word comes first and sets the standard of reading achievement that can be reached. Reference has already been made to the difficulties which children encounter in learning to read when they have not had the support of a good language atmosphere at home. It can hardly be otherwise. Hearing vocabulary constitutes the major source of words that the child can and does learn to read.

Durrell and Sullivan [11] have devised a set of reading capacity and achievement tests based on the relationship between hearing and reading vocabulary and comprehension. The capacity test is simply a standardized measure of hearing vocabulary and comprehension. High scores on this test are taken to indicate good capacity for reading, low scores, poor capacity. The reading achievement test which Durrell and Sullivan have included provides a means of estimating whether the child is reading up to capacity as measured by the other test. The two tests together make for some interesting comparisons and analyses. In general, scores on the two run fairly close together. Children with high scores on the one are likely to have high scores on the other, just as children with low scores fall in double trouble. Exceptions occur. The results quite often turn up children who have conspicuously higher scores on the capacity test than on the reading test. Such cases are said not to be reading up to capacity, and remedial measures may be indicated. The reverse can also happen, in which the reading test yields the higher score. It perhaps can be said of those children that they make skillful use of the context in their reading. The unfortunate ones are those who have neither the capacity nor achievement. For such cases a wealthy program of oral language activities is recommended as preparation for reading.

The importance of speech—of both hearing oneself speak as well as of listening to the speech of others; of learning to discriminate between words of similar sounds; of vocabulary building; of getting the precise meaning of words; of increasing in general one's powers of oral expression—is such that this phase of readying the child for reading can scarcely be overdone. The same cannot be said, at least with equal assurance, of the exercises for visual discrimination and training which are commonly employed in the reading readiness workbooks. Matching similar objects and discriminating between different objects may not help as much as thought in recognizing similar elements in and noting differences between words. Recognizing, for example, a not-even ugly baby duckling in a brood of baby chicks, and vice versa, a baby chick in a brood of ducklings, may not help in the differentiation of "horse" from "house"—even though the "context clues" may be equally pointed!

A young child's powers of observation and of visual discrimination for matters in which he is interested and has some background of experience may be extraordinarily good, and he may need only to have them directed (through arousing his interest and extending his experiences) to where he can use them. To give an example: In the primer or preprimer of a currently used series of readers, there is a picture of a toy airplane caught in the branch of a tree. Unfortunately for one young reader, the artist in his sketchy fashion had left a small gap between the branch and the trunk of the tree. Only after persistent inquiries as to why the airplane (and presumably the branch) didn't fall down was the teacher led to examine the picture carefully enough to discover what she then explained as the artist's mistake. The young observer, however, was not otherwise given credit for what in another setting (say print) would have been regarded as acumen.

It should be said in passing that the method which Durrell and Sullivan have employed to measure capacity for reading serves the same purpose as an intelligence test. It has the advantage over most intelligence tests in that it entails no reading at all. This characteristic of the test makes it especially appropriate for poor or retarded readers who are likely to be rated unfairly by any mental test that requires reading.

THE SILENT OR SIGHT METHOD

It is possible, of course, to teach reading without involving the spoken word. Printed symbols are really twice removed from their meaning, since they represent speech sounds, which in turn usually stand for objects. The child can get the meaning from pictures as well as from the spoken word. Another way of setting the conditions for learning to read, therefore, is to present the word, together with a suitable picture. In this case the child associates his response to the picture with the appearance of the word. The conditions of this method are diagramed on Figure 2. No overt pronunciation of the words is necessary either on the part of the pupil or the teacher, which is why the procedure is often referred to as the silent or sight method of teaching reading, as contrasted with the "look-and-say" method. Incidentally, the method is in the nature of an adaptation of Pestalozzi's famous method of object teaching. There would be nothing wrong with pairing the word with the child's response to the actual object. This is essentially what is done in the common kindergarten practice of labeling familiar objects around the room. If the children are already familiar with the objects, however, pictures of the objects serve the same purpose and may be a bit more convenient.

Any argument regarding the relative merits of the "look-and-say" procedure as compared with the visual or silent approach is likely to be of small practical importance. Each has its place, and virtually all beginning programs use a combination of the two anyway. Most of the points which can be made are minor and hardly more than notes of caution. To begin with, the "look-and-say" method does not absolutely guarantee that the child will know the meaning of the word after he has learned to pronounce it. Children can repeat words through sheer imitation, which is what the "look-and-say" procedure amounts to when the words are not already a part of the pupil's meaning or hearing vocabulary. Supplying words when youngsters are reading orally is essentially the same method. The point we are laboring is that, even though the children may be able to repeat the words after the teacher, they may or may not know what the words mean. Learning to pronounce the words by the phonetic method suffers the same limitation. Dewey [10] found that children can often pronounce words correctly without being able to identify from pictures or a collection of objects what the word stands for. Many of the words in textbooks are alien to the children. Learning to read such words implies more than mere pronunciation.

The word-picture approach is more likely to assure the meaning of the word,

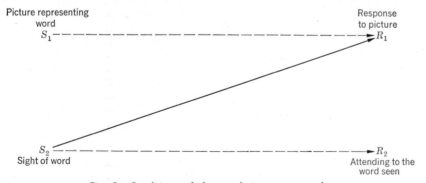

Picture representing word

S_1 - →R_1

Response to picture

S_2 - →R_2

Sight of word

Attending to the word seen

Fig. 2.—Conditions of the word-picture approach.

for if the child can name or identify the picture, it is almost a sure sign that he has had the experiences, language and otherwise, to give meaning to the word. The dark side (shall we say of the picture?) is that not all words can be easily depicted in pictures, which is to say nothing about the difficulty of portraying relationships between words. Pictures, moreover, do not always control the child's response in the way that was intended; that is, the child may misname the picture. A picture of "Puff," for example, may be called "cat" or "kitty." Misnaming pictures may have an inhibiting effect when it comes to learning to read the words correctly. Children can get into trouble on the same basis while responding to test materials making use of pictures. A good example is the word recognition section of the Gates Primary Reading Tests.[13] As the reader may know, each item of this test presents a picture together with four words, one of which names or labels the picture correctly and the child is instructed to mark the right word. It is the familiar type of multiple-choice test device. Often, however, the child cannot find the word he is looking for, the reason being that he calls a picture of a copper coin, "penny," instead of "cent," the picture of a rocking horse, "horse," instead of "toy," the picture of a barking dog, "dog," instead of "bark," and so forth. We can say of the "look-and-say" approach that it does control the child's response with a high degree of accuracy. The child is not going to say "cat" or "kitty" for "Puff," when "Puff" is what he hears.

. . .

THE CONCEPT OF CUE-REDUCTION

Buswell's finding that there is almost as much evidence of vocalization among children taught by McDade's [25] nonoral method as by methods which incorporate oral reading can probably be

explained in terms of just such implicit language behavior as Jacobson [21] and Max [24] have demonstrated in their studies. The presentation of the word, together with a picture, for example, does not automatically rule out speech. Speech manifests itself in the naming of the picture, which is the clue to the word. The child, it is true, may "mouth" or say the word to himself, but implicit though his response may be, it is speech for all that. Speech may thus remain a part of learning to read by the nonoral method as well as by the "look-and-say" method.

Even when a child learns to read by the "look-and-say" procedure, the overt responses of saying the words aloud gradually give way to implicit speech movements. This abbreviation of the speech responses is covered by the concept of cue-reduction, which is one of Hollingworth's [19] favorite notions. Cue-reduction refers to the refinement of a skill and to the elimination of waste motion. In the case of reading, the concept of cue-reduction applies not only to the motor side of the performance but also to the sensory side, in that, with time, fewer cues from the printed page or less of the original pattern of stimulation is required to get the meaning. The efficiency of the eye movements which characterizes skillful silent reading is a function of cue-reduction.

The response of saying the word is not the only response to the visual symbol, and at the start especially, if there were not other responses, much of the meaning would be lost. If the teacher shows the phrases "Clap your hands," "Close the door," and at the same time gives these commands orally and the children obey, and if later, when she shows the cards, the children perform these acts, they may be said to have learned to read. Doubtless the "hearing" child will say these words either aloud or to himself and will *feel* his own vocal response, and later these may become his chief responses (in some abbreviated form), but he will also sense the incipient responses of clapping his hands and moving (or at least experience a muscular tension) in the direction of the door, and these responses, too, are the *meaning* of the visual symbol.

Again, if the teacher shows an appropriate picture with the words, "Father is at the door," and so says, then the child may experience withdrawing reactions (for fear of the punishment which mother has promised when father gets home) or the joyous experience of running to the door to welcome him, and for the rest of his life the word "father" will arouse some attenuated emotional responses which will, however vaguely, reinstate the gist of his experiences with "father." This is as much a part of reading as the response of speaking the words, although in time the subvocal responses may be the part which is substituted for the whole or "stands for" it in the sense that it "heads up" or summarizes all these previous experiences.

The way in which speech may seize control of the total pattern of response to the word has been neatly demonstrated by Hudgins [20] in his interesting experiments on the conditioning of the involuntary movements of the contraction and dilating of the pupil of the eye. In one experiment, at the same time that a light was suddenly made brighter and the pupil of the subject's eye was seen to be contracting, a buzzer was sounded. After a time the sound of the buzzer caused the pupil to contract, even though the light was unchanged. In a further experiment, the experimenter and the subject both said "contract," the buzzer was sounded, and the intensity of light increased all at the same time. After a large number of repetitions of this combination of stimuli, the saying of the word "contract" by either the experimenter or subject caused the pupil to contract with no sound of buzzer or change in intensity of light. Menzies [27]

has described a similar experiment, in which the subject's whispering of the nonsense word "prochaska" was substituted for a cold-water stimulus in bringing about a vasoconstriction of the small arterial blood vessels of the skin. How one's own saying of the word operates these wonders to perform can be explained in terms of the fact that speech is not only a response but also a stimulus. It is a stimulus in the sense that the individual can hear himself talk and feel himself talk. The feel of talking results from the stimulation of sense organs located in the speech muscles themselves. These sense organs, which are called "proprioceptors," are imbedded in the muscles, joints, and tendons. Whenever a muscle contracts, the proprioceptors located in the muscle are stimulated by mechanical pressure. Such stimulation forms the basis of the kinesthetic sense. As Hudgins and Menzies have demonstrated, the self-stimulation of which speech consists can serve to condition a response.

In the early stages of reading, the child's response of recognition normally includes the saying of the word aloud or subvocally, and at times the hearing and always the feeling of saying it (or the awareness of the incipient movements of speech). This speech stimulation may establish ties with the total pattern of response to the printed word, after the fashion of Hudgins and Menzies. In learning to read, the situation is considerably simplified by the fact that the responses of recognition are already conditioned by the sound of the word. The child needs only to hear himself say the word from the printed symbol to get the same meaning. The feel of saying the word is part and parcel of the same pattern of speech stimulation, and shortly it may be all that remains of a speech influence. Alexander Bain once said that *"Thinking is restrained speaking and acting."* This is an equally good definition of reading, although in time the incipient movements of speech may come to "stand for" or symbolize the whole pattern of responses to the printed word. There are words for everything, and no other mechanism is so readily capable as speech of organizing the enormous variety of response patterns which the interpretation of the printed page demands.

The habit of vocalization probably depends more on the individual than on the method of teaching. Most if not all children go through a stage when they move their lips while reading silently. Some children grow out of this stage more rapidly than others, just as some children stop counting on their fingers sooner than others. In this connection it is of interest to note that Anderson and Swanson [3] found a closer relationship between oral and silent reading in the case of poor readers than in that of good readers. It is doubtful that this finding can be attributed to the idea that the poor readers had been taught to read by an oral method and the good readers by a silent method. Buswell's own results show that the method does not make as much difference as might be expected. Individual differences are bound to occur under any method. The better the reader, the less chance that he will vocalize (the farther removed the silent reading from oral reading). Buswell's results throw light on this point, too. His data show that the pupils who remained vocalizers, whether in the oral or nonoral group, tended to be less intelligent than the average of all his cases. In view of the relationship which exists between reading achievement and intelligence, it is likely that these children also tended to be the less able readers in both groups.

As for overcoming the habit of vocalization, Pintner [29] once proposed that the individual practice reading while repeating a series of digits. Pintner reasoned that if the individual engaged in counting, he could not enunciate the words at the same time. Secor [32] recommended whistling or repeating the alphabet as a means of preventing an articulation of the printed matter. Such methods are unnecessary. The condition for cue-reduction is practice, and there is no substitute for practice. A lot of reading of a wide variety of easy and interesting material will help as much as anything else to reduce the vocal element. Too difficult material tends to make vocalizers of all of us. As a means of drawing attention to a problem and motivating the individual to do something about a skill which he ordinarily neglects, even freakish methods have their place. Otherwise it is a case of practice and more practice. It is hard to better the advice of an early New England settler who offered the following recipe for improving reading ability:

1. Read.
2. Read.
3. Read some more.
4. Read anything.
5. Read about everything.
6. Read enjoyable things.
7. Read things you yourself enjoy.
8. Read, and talk about it.
9. Read very carefully some things.
10. Read on the run, most things.
11. Don't think about reading, but
12. Just read.

In the sense that the response to the printed symbols does not include the saying of the word, "purely visual reading" is possible. Cases of "motor" aphasia (speechlessness due to brain damage) who were able to read have been reported. Woodworth cites one of Head's cases, of whom Head has said, "All power of reading aloud was abolished. ... There was not the slightest doubt, however, that he understood much of what he read to himself." [33] This individual, according to Woodworth's report of the case, could execute simple printed directions. And it is true that deaf-mutes can learn to read. In fact, the easiest vocabulary for the deaf to acquire is the reading vocabulary. However, people who have lost their speech, or who have no speech, or whose speech is imperfect, cannot learn to read as easily as the person with normal speech. In view of this fact, one may question whether it really is an advantage to try to learn to read without so much as even saying the words silently. It would appear that in learning to read, speech is more of a blessing than a curse. The best readers in the first and second grade are generally the pupils who are the most advanced in speech.[31] Why bite the hand that feeds one? Recent research findings [9] indicate that a certain aid to meaning or comprehension may be sacrificed by the prevailing efforts in the early grades to suppress inner speech. Saying the words to oneself undoubtedly makes for slower reading but may make for better comprehension. Speech has a dimension, namely, of stress or emphasis which can be only partially indicated in print. It has been found, experimentally, that there is a close relationship between this oral stress and meaning, and that an excellent measure of a reader's comprehension of a passage is the extent to which he can indicate the words which should or should not be stressed were he to read the passage aloud. As a measure, it correlates as well with the results of standardized tests of reading comprehension as they correlate with one another.

In reading readily comprehended materials, inner speech may well be at a minimum, but in efforts to get the meaning of printed materials, which the reader finds difficult, he should be free to call on the deeper reservoir of meaning of spoken language. Under some such circumstance, who of us adult readers has not found himself *saying* the words to himself? Oral reading *with expression* should not lose its rightful place in the curriculum.

Of course, when auditory and speech handicaps are present, methods must be employed which minimize or neutralize these conditions. Deaf-mutes can only learn to read by so-called silent or sight methods. The finding, however, that deaf-mutes engage in implicit finger and hand movements in their abstract thinking is suggestive in this connection. Apparently, even deaf-mutes fall back on some substitute for speech when it comes to such "mental" activities as reading.

THE RELATION OF MEANING TO ORAL READING ERRORS

The finding that oral and silent reading are related has a practical aspect. As Swanson's results strongly suggest, many of the errors which an individual makes when he reads orally probably also occur when he reads silently. The practical difficulty is that these errors cannot be discovered by means of a silent reading test. The concept that silent reading is an implicit form of oral reading provides an easy solution; that is, we can turn to an oral reading test instead. Oral reading will operate to make errors explicit so that they can be recorded and analyzed. This approach has been widely applied. Errors are recorded by means of a test like Gray's Standardized Oral Reading Paragraphs. Elaborate methods have been developed for classifying the errors into types. Monroe and Backus,[28] for example, offer the following error categories: faulty vowels, faulty consonants, reversals, addition of sounds, omission of sounds, substitutions, repetitions, addition of words, omission of words, and refusals or words aided. After the errors have been classified according to some such scheme, the usual procedure is to compute the percentage for each type of error from the total error score. The same line of reasoning is then applied to the correction of difficulties. The argument here is that, if the errors are first cleared up in oral reading, they will also vanish from silent reading because of the relationship which exists between the two types of reading. Errors which need attention are identified from an error profile based on the percentage scores, and specific remedies are prescribed for the most troublesome errors. Thus Monroe and Backus recommend tracing and writing methods for errors of reversal, word discrimination drills for additions and omissions of sounds, choral reading for repetitions, insertions, and omissions of words, and so forth. The advantage of the oral approach again is that it is explicit and offers objective evidence for the evaluation of pupil progress. These practices should be looked into from the standpoint of the underlying causes of the errors.

It is true that poor readers make more oral reading errors than good readers, and that the errors have a bearing on silent reading. In his study of the oral reading of good and poor readers at the college freshmen level, for example, Fairbanks [12] found that the poor readers made an average of 5.8 oral errors per 100 words, and the good readers an average of only 2.1 errors per 100 words on the same material. However, there is another difference which is even more important; namely, the mistakes which poor readers make tend to change the meaning, while the errors of good readers do not alter the sense. This is another fact that was brought out in Fairbanks' study. Substitutions of words were found to be the most frequent type of error for both the good and poor readers, but there was a great difference in the seriousness of the errors. Thus while 51 per cent of the substitutions made by the poor readers seriously changed the meaning, not one of the good readers' substitutions was of that type. Furthermore, good readers correct their errors more often than do poor readers. In this connection Fairbanks found that the poor readers in his study corrected only 7 per cent of their errors, while the good readers corrected 19 per cent. In other words, poor readers are often unaware that their mistakes change the meaning. It follows that they are probably not

getting the meaning to begin with. Otherwise they would sense that something was wrong and correct their mistakes. It seems doubtful, therefore, that the errors constitute the real problem. It appears, rather, that the crux of the matter is related to the question of comprehension. If material is used which the pupil can read with understanding, oral errors will largely disappear as a problem.

Yet the method usually employed to help children with their reading remains directed at the oral errors themselves. As we have noted earlier, some of the poorest teaching at times passes for remedial reading. It consists of sitting down with the child, listening to him read orally, stopping him when he makes a mistake, and asking him to try it over but to get it right this time. Here is a typical scene, complete with sound effects: "All right, start here," says the teacher, getting the lesson under way. The child reads a word or two and then makes a mistake. No sooner does he make his first mistake than the teacher exclaims, "Uh-uh! Look at that word again. What did you say it was?" The child looks and discovers the error of his ways. "All right, that's better," nods the teacher. "Now, start over, and read it that way this time." Another word or two, and another mistake. "Uh-uh, there you go again!" interjects the teacher as before. "You'll just have to learn to look at these words more carefully. Now, what was it?" The child, subdued, calls the word correctly on his next attempt. He is then told to start from the beginning again, and to get *all* the words right this time. The rest of the script can be filled in from imagination. The process is one of constant interruption. The child cannot keep the train of thought intact under these conditions. The process operates only to make the child hyperconscious of individual words, and the real purpose of reading, which is to get the meaning, is destroyed. The teacher would do better to supply the words outright. There is nothing wrong with telling children what words are. A word to the wise now and then saves unnecessary interruption and urges the thought along. Furthermore, one of the ways that children learn to recognize words in the first place is by being told what they are.

The practices described above are a survival from days when methods of teaching reading were mainly if not exclusively oral. The accuracy and the expression with which children read aloud were at one time virtually the only means used for gauging progress in reading. In many schools, the reading period still consists chiefly of the pupils' taking turns reading orally. This practice is aided and abetted by many parents who believe that children should have a whirl at oral reading each day in school. Oral reading is the means that they use at home to check up on their own children, and, incidentally, to check up on the school. Letter-perfect oral reading is often a false guide. In their endeavor to read without error, the children may become so preoccupied with the articulation of the words that they lose sight of the meaning altogether. No child is a better oral reader because he does not get the meaning, but oral reading does tend to divide attention between the mechanical process of articulating the words and the thought process of getting the meaning. The former can go on without the latter. One child, when asked to state the substance of a passage which he had read aloud to perfection, lamely replied, "I didn't know I was supposed to." In other words, even when the child recites his piece perfectly, we cannot always be sure that he is taking in the meaning. One wonders what purpose is achieved in that case.

The intelligent way to solve these reading problems is to place the emphasis on meaning. This is largely a matter of using material which is easy enough for the child and encouraging

him to read it for meaning. Errors will still occur, but what if the child does omit a word now and then, add one here and there, reverse the position of a few words, or even occasionally substitute words, so long as the meaning remains unchanged? Most authorities agree that errors which do not change the meaning can be safely ignored. Many errors of that type result from filling-in from the context; that is, the child understands so well what is coming next that he does not even bother to check the words but reads the rest of the sentence in his own way. Calling attention to each error in this case would amount to sheer meddling. The whole object of using material which is easy enough for the child is to make it possible for him to profit by the context. It is mainly important in this connection that the child reads enough of the words correctly that he can supply the rest from the context. The power of context to suggest words was vividly brought to the writer's attention recently in the case of a boy who has had a long history of reading disability. This boy is nineteen years old and has a perfectly good mind, but to this day he cannot read primer material with security. He is interested in athletics and is a good performer in a number of sports. The writer had an extra ticket to one of the Michigan football games and offered it to the boy, partly in payment for a guest performance which he had put on before one of the writer's classes. A doubt arose, however, as to whether the young man could locate his seat in the stadium from the information on the ticket. Before the ticket was turned over to him, therefore, he was put to the test. He identified the section, row, and seat numbers without difficulty. He read the date of the game correctly, identified the kickoff time, and recognized the names of the contending teams—word recognition which he had never equaled before. The power of suggestion of the ticket did the trick. It is a great advantage to have printed context so strongly suggestive of words.

The writer has often felt that he would like to try teaching reading, especially in the upper grades, by surrounding the children with a wide variety of reading material, permitting each pupil to select a book according to his own interest and ability, and then just letting the children sit back and read. This approach would free the teacher to circulate among the group, giving individual help as needed. There are teachers who are already employing this method successfully. It would be an interesting experiment for other teachers to try out. A good book is like good music—the child needs a certain amount of freedom from distraction to enjoy it. Of course, if the child is not up to reading even the easiest of material, something else must be tried. However, there would still be no justification for hacking material to bits. Even the first words can be taught in a meaningful setting, but that's something that we shall look into later.

RAPPROCHEMENT BETWEEN ORAL AND SILENT METHODS

The relationship between oral and silent reading is not perfect, and one factor which may operate to reduce the relationship is the method of teaching. Oral reading can be overdone, and it is a good guess that, if pupils receive nothing but a diet of oral reading, they will become better oral than silent readers. It is perhaps a joker in Buswell's experiment that he did not have a group of children who had been taught by a method which was as extremely oral as the method employed with the experimental group was purely silent. A comparison of the performance of such groups on the silent reading tests might well have changed the complexion of the experiment.

Much the same argument applies when the bill of fare is confined to silent reading. In this instance the children should become better silent than oral readers. They get the meaning from context clues and from the pictures in the book, but they have difficulty reading the material orally so that it makes sense. It would have been interesting to compare the oral reading ability of Buswell's two groups, but oral reading was not included in an evaluation of the methods used. It is a reasonable conjecture that a test of oral reading would have reversed the picture for silent reading, especially if the test had been given during the primary period. Children who have been taught to read chiefly by silent means are prone, during this stage, to read inaccurately both orally and silently, although they may often read very fast silently. Pupils who are low in comprehension and high in rate of reading should stress accuracy through oral reading. Oral reading slows the pupil down and promotes accuracy. Children who suffer speech defects also do not as a rule read as well orally as silently. Care should be taken not to force children who have speech defects to read orally before the class. Such children are likely to be emotionally disturbed by audience reactions to their speech, and serious personality problems may result. Children with speech defects need much the same methods as the acoustically handicapped child.[5]

One extreme method is as unnecessary as the other, and most teachers of primary reading use a combination of oral and silent methods which probably helps to account for the relationship which has usually been found between oral and silent reading. The beginning is most often made by oral means. In one survey [4] of the practices of 288 successful teachers of beginning reading, every teacher in the group reported using oral reading in the first grade. Oral reading, moreover, received the chief attention of these first-grade teachers. The advantage of the oral approach is, of course, that the spoken word already carries meaning for the child. The whole object of learning to read is to get the same meaning from the printed symbols. Ruling out the oral cue, as McDade has done, does not jibe with the normal course of language development, which is from the oral to the silent. For this reason, Judd [22] and others have described the oral approach as the natural one.

Meaning ultimately rests on the experiences which the children have had. The job of the school is to make these experiences "verbal," first by talking and then by reading. One reason why children have difficulty learning to read is that they have not had necessary experiences and that their "verbal" level is low. The teachers will, therefore, from the moment their new charges enter school, expect to "talk things over with them." They will expect to listen to what the children have to say, even before they expect the children to listen to them. They can thus find out what the youngsters are interested in; what sort of experiences they have had or haven't had; something of what they understand or don't understand; what things have meaning for them, etc. They can then capitalize on these interests and experiences in their later efforts at associating the printed words with the spoken word until the one acquires the same meaning as the other—and thus the first steps on the road to reading have been taken. Pictures, however, will constantly be used to reinforce the response to the spoken word. Action sentences and dramatizations are always good, as giving meaning to the printed symbols. Oral discussions preceding the reading lesson, as in McDade's method, are an excellent means of preparing the child for the vocabulary of a story. These discussions should introduce words and expressions which appear in the story. Later, when the pupils turn to the story, these words and phrases

will still be "ringing in their ears," which should make the reading of the story just that much easier and meaningful.

After the first grade, silent reading should receive an increasing amount of attention. Silent reading naturally follows from oral reading and in most cases the transition from oral to silent reading presents no problem. The mechanism of cue-reduction takes care of the matter, and the pupils tend to drop out the voice of their own accord. After the children have learned to read on their own, which is the ultimate objective, most of their reading will be silent. Oral reading at this stage should always be preceded by silent study and it should involve a natural audience situation. Dialogues and simple plays provide excellent material for oral reading, and McGann [26] has demonstrated the value of such materials in remedial reading.

The contention that teaching silent reading through an oral approach makes for inefficient eye movements and the habit of vocalization has not been convincingly demonstrated in the literature. As we have already reported, Buswell's study of the nonoral method revealed that lip movement was almost as common among his experimental cases as among his control cases. In an earlier investigation, Buswell [8] showed that in the first grade the eye movements in silent reading are no more efficient than the eye movements in oral reading. During the first grade, whatever the method of instruction, the response of the pupil to the printed symbol is chiefly oral, whether he is reading to himself or reading aloud, and his rate of silent reading is accordingly no more rapid than that of his oral reading. Gray [14] and Judd [22] demonstrated that the rate of articulation increases rapidly until roughly the fourth grade, and then begins to level off. Meanwhile the child's rate of reading usually overtakes his rate of talking. After the child learns to read as fast as he ordinarily talks, oral reading should be definitely curtailed and the scales tipped far in favor of silent reading.

SUMMARY

Learning to read, then, is an aspect of total language development. The child first learns to respond to the speech of others. He next learns to speak himself. Then he learns to read. Learning to talk subserves learning to read. Finally, the child learns to write and spell. Writing and spelling lag behind reading in the language sequence. The process of learning to read is a case of associate learning. The association is that between the sight of the word and the child's response to the sound of it, although the same results may be obtained from an association of the visual symbol with the response to a picture. Teaching a child to read consists essentially in setting the conditions for the formation of these associations. Two methods for meeting these conditions have been described, the "look-and-say" method and the so-

called silent or sight method. Except possibly for such a "completely nonoral" method as McDade's, the general practice is to use a combination of both methods, which for convenience we may characterize as "word" methods. What we have built up to so far *is* the word method. This, however, does not end the story of learning to read. The object here has been merely to describe what is the essence or main business at the *start* of learning to read. Learning to read at the start *is* a matter of learning to recognize most of the words, but reading is also a process of getting ideas from printed matter. Sometimes all the words may be familiar, but no meaning results. This problem has often been attributed to the idea that too much attention was given to individual words early in the grades. Obviously we cannot settle for the word method alone. Other methods exist. All should have an equal hearing. Some attention should be given to phrases. The dangers of word-for-word reading must be met. There are other complications. . . .

REFERENCES

1. Anderson, Irving H., and Dearborn, Walter F., "A Sound Motion-Picture Technique for Teaching Beginning Reading," *School and Society,* LII (October 19, 1940), 367-9.
2. Anderson, Irving H., and Fairbanks, Grant, "Common and Differential Factors in Reading Vocabulary and Hearing Vocabulary," *Journal of Educational Research,* XXX (January 1937), 317-24.
3. Anderson, Irving H., and Swanson, Donald E., "Common Factor in Eye-Movements in Silent and Oral Reading," pp. 61-9 in *Studies in Psychology of Reading,* I, University of Iowa Studies in Psychology, No. 21. Psychological Monographs, XLVIII, No. 3. Princeton, N. J.: Psychological Review Co., 1937.
4. *Better Reading Instruction—A Survey of Research and Successful Practice,*

Research Bulletin of the National Education Association, XLLL, No. 5. Washington: Research Division of the National Education Association, 1935, 273-325.
5. Bond, Guy L., *The Auditory and Speech Characteristics of Poor Readers,* Teachers College Contributions to Education, No. 657. New York: Teachers College, Columbia University, 1935. 48 pp.
6. Book, William F., "Various Methods of Mastering New Words While Learning To Read," *Journal of Educational Research,* XXXI (February 1930), 81-94.
7. Browne, Rose Butler, *A Critical Evaluation of Experimental Studies of Remedial Reading and the Report of an Experiment with Groups of Backward Readers,* Unpublished doctor's dissertation, Harvard University, 1939.

8. Buswell, Guy Thomas, *Fundamental Reading Habits: A Study of Their Development,* Supplementary Educational Monographs, No. 21. Chicago: University of Chicago Press, 1922. 150 pp.

9. Dearborn, Walter F., Johnston, P. W., and Carmichael, L., "Oral Stress and Meaning in Printed Material," *Science,* CX (October 14, 1949), 404.

10. Dewey, Joseph C., "A Case Study of Reading Comprehension Difficulties in American History," pp. 26-54 in *Doctoral Theses in Education,* III, University of Iowa Studies in Education, X, No. 1. Iowa City: University of Iowa, 1935.

11. Durrell, Donald D., and Sullivan, Helen Blair, *Reading Capacity and Achievement Tests.* Yonkers: World Book Co., 1937.

12. Fairbanks, Grant, "The Relation Between Eye-Movements and Voice in the Oral Reading of Good and Poor Silent Readers," pp. 78-107 in *Studies in Psychology of Reading,* I, University of Iowa Studies in Psychology, No. 21. Psychological Monographs, Vol. XLVIII, No. 3. Princeton, N. J.: Psychological Review Co., 1937.

13. Gates, Arthur I., *Gates Primary Reading Tests.* New York: Bureau of Publications, Teachers College, Columbia University, 1943.

14. Gray, Clarence Truman, *Deficiencies in Reading Ability.* Boston: D. C. Heath & Co., 1922. 420 pp.

15. Guthrie, Edwin R., "Conditioning: A Theory of Learning in Terms of Stimulus, Response, and Association," pp. 17-60 in *The Psychology of Learning,* Forty-first Yearbook of the National Society for the Study of Education, Part II. Bloomington, Ill.: Public School Publishing Co., 1942, p. 25.

16. Harris, Albert J., *How To Increase Reading Ability.* New York: Longmans, Green & Co., 1947 (revised), p. 7.

17. Hildreth, Gertrude, "An Individual Study in Word Recognition," *Elementary School Journal,* XXXV (April 1935), 606-19.

18. ————, "Interrelationships Among the Language Arts," *Elementary School Journal,* XLVIII (June 1948), 538-49.

19. Hollingworth, H. L., *Educational Psychology.* New York: Appleton-Century-Crofts, Inc., 1933. 540 pp.

20. Hudgins, Clarence V., "Conditioning and the Voluntary Control of the Pupillary Light Reflex," *Journal of General Psychology,* VIII (January 1933), 3-51.

21. Jacobson, Edmund, "The Electrophysiology of Mental Activities," *American Journal of Psychology,* XILV (October 1932), 677-94.

22. Judd, Charles Hubbard, *Reading: Its Nature and Development.* Supplementary Educational Monographs, No. 10. Chicago: University of Chicago Press, 1918. 192 pp.

23. Larsen, Robert P., and Feder, D. D., "Common and Differential Factors in Reading and Hearing Comprehension," *Journal of Educational Psychology,* XXXI (April 1940), 241-52.

24. Max, Louis William, "Experimental Study of the Motor Theory of Consciousness: IV. Action-Current Responses in the Deaf During Awakening, Kinaesthetic Imagery and Abstract Thinking," *Journal of Comparative Psychology,* XXIV (October 1937), 301-44.

25. McDade, James E., "A Hypothesis for Non-Oral Reading: Argument, Experiment, and Results," *Journal of Educational Research,* XXX (March 1937), 489-503.

26. McGann, Mary, "Dramatic Dialogues for Simultaneous Treatment of Reading and Personality Problems," *Journal of Educational Psychology,* XXXVII (February 1947), 96-104.

27. Menzies, Roderick, "Conditioned Vasomotor Responses in Human Subjects," *Journal of Psychology,* IV (July 1937), 75-120.

28. Monroe, Marion, and Backus, Bertie, *Remedial Reading.* Boston: Houghton Mifflin Co., 1937. 171 pp.

39. Pintner, Rudolph, "Inner Speech During Silent Reading," *Psychological Review,* XX (March 1913). 129-53.

30. Rogers, Maurine V., "Phonic Ability as Related to Certain Aspects of Reading at the College Level," *Journal of Experimental Education,* VI (June 1938), 381-95.

31. Rossignol, Lois Josephine, *The Relationships Among Hearing Acuity, Speech Production, and Reading Performance in Grades 1A, 1B, and 2A,* Teachers College Contributions to Education, No. 936. New York: Teachers College, Columbia University, 1948. 50 pp.
32. Secor, W. B., "Visual Reading: A Study in Mental Imagery," *American*

Journal of Psychology, XI (January 1900), 225-36.
33. Woodworth, Robert S., *Experimental Psychology.* New York: Henry Holt & Co., 1938. p. 718.
34. Young, William E., "The Relation of Reading Comprehension and Retention to Hearing Comprehension and Retention," *Journal of Experimental Education,* V (September 1936), 30-39.

3: Eye Movements in Reading *

ROBERT S. WOODWORTH and HAROLD SCHLOSBERG

It will be recalled that Javal [16] observed that the eyes, far from sweeping smoothly across a line of print, executed a series of saccadic movements, fixating at several different points along each line. In the chapter on Attention it is shown that the practiced reader can "take in" several words at a time. Obviously these two facts belong together, and the eye movements in reading should throw light on the reading process and on the operation of eye movements as well. Dodge's corneal reflection method furnished a practical method; since then there have been many investigations aimed at finding general principles, and a host of applied and clinical studies. The equipment has been improved and modified for special purposes. Perhaps the extremes are represented by Tinker's [22] permanent installation, built on a 70-inch camera barrel, and the neat portable ophthalmograph usable in a clinician's office. Either instrument will yield good records of both eyes. . . .

The average reader shows pretty good coordination of his eyes. They follow the horizontal line pretty well, with lit-

tle vertical movement. Inaccuracy and loss of convergence in return sweeps are fairly common, but moderate amounts of such anomalies seem to have no clear-cut effect—although bad muscular imbalance, with excessive convergence strain, may be fatiguing.[11]

DEVELOPMENT OF READING SKILL

Reading is a complex skill, and like all skills, it develops gradually, improving in both precision and in speed. Pencil and paper tests are useful in measuring progress, but eye-movement records are of value in analyzing the details of what is happening. By comparing samples of students at various grade levels (see Table 1) we see that improvement occurs in three ways. In the first place, there is a steady decrease in the number of fixations per line. This holds true even though the reading material increases in difficulty at each grade. Thus the college student is taking in at least three times as much reading matter per fixation as is the beginning reader. Secondly, the fixations grow shorter as academic

* Reprinted with slight abridgement from *Experimental Psychology,* revised edition, New York: Holt, Rinehart & Winston, pp. 504-10, by permission of the publisher. Copyright 1954 by Holt, Rinehart & Winston.

level increases; the advanced reader takes in the material faster. Finally, there is a very marked decrease in regressive movements. This means greater regularity in progressing along the lines of print. It is natural to conclude that the ideal reader would have no regressive movements. Actually, a few regressive movements show that the reader is alert to what he is reading, so that he goes back to clear up an obscurity.[3, 7] Sometimes the regressive movement should be blamed on the author, rather than on the reader!

FIXATIONS

All the reading is done during the fixational pauses, for there is no clear vision during the intervening saccadic movements. Hence, the number and duration of the fixational pauses have received considerable attention. The number of fixations per line depends on the difficulty of the material as well as the habits of the reader. One of the authors (H.S.) once took eye-movement records of a half dozen visitors who attended an "open house" at the laboratory. Since he agreed to report the results, he kept names and addresses of the Os. When the records were developed, he was shocked to see that several showed more fixations per line than the average third-grade student. More careful examination showed surprisingly regular movements, with no regressions. A check on the addresses showed that these particular visitors were judges; in legal documents every word is important, and these Os had carried over their habit of meticulous reading to the laboratory test. The moral of this tale is that there is no single rate or style of reading that is appropriate to all types of reading material. The good reader is the one who adjusts his speed to the material of the moment. Failure to recognize this rule has led to much faulty advice in remedial reading classes.

The duration of the fixations, as distinguished from their number, is not closely dependent on the difficulty of the material, at least as far as the mode is concerned.[6, 18] Good college freshmen will average around 210ms, while their slower classmates run around 260ms.[1, 26] These are considerably longer than the exposure needed for perception of dots or letters; the usual

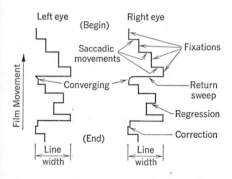

Left eye (Begin)   Right eye
Saccadic movements — Fixations
Film Movement
Converging — Return sweep
Regression
(End) — Correction
Line width   Line width

Fig. 1. A schematic representation of an eye-movement photograph, such as one would obtain from an ophthalmograph. Since the film moves upward, the record progresses downward. Hence, the length of vertical lines gives the duration of fixations, and that of horizontal lines the extent of lateral eye movements. The width and location of the line of reading matter are indicated below the record for each eye. Starting at the top the record shows four fixations and three saccadic movements in the reading of the first line of print. The two eyes give parallel, conjugate records. But they diverge slightly on the first return sweep and slowly slide back into correct convergence at the beginning of the second line. There is a regressive movement further along on this line. The return sweep for the third line failed to bring the beginning of that line into clear view, and so it was followed by a small corrective movement. The record is cut off after the next fixation. (Actually, the eye movements seldom extend to the very beginning and end of a line of print.)

Table 1: Eye Movements in Reading, According to School Grade [6]

A sample of 8-19 children from each grade, of about medium reading ability, had their eyes photographed while reading, and the Mean for each grade is given.

School grade	Fixations per line of print	Mean duration of fixation	Regressive movements per line
I B	18.6	660 ms	5.1
I A	15.5	432	4.0
II	10.7	364	2.3
III	8.9	316	1.8
IV	7.3	268	1.4
V	6.9	252	1.3
VI	7.3	236	1.6
VII	6.8	240	1.5
High School I	7.2	244	1.0
H. S. II	5.8	248	0.7
H. S. III	5.5	224	0.7
H. S. IV	6.4	248	0.7
College	5.9	252	0.5

tachistoscopic exposure is about 100 ms, depending on the illumination. All of these facts indicate that the number and duration of fixations, and hence the speed of reading, are limited by central, rather than by peripheral factors; that is, O moves his eyes only as fast as he can absorb the material.

The saccadic movements themselves take very little of the total time. They average around 22 ms for the short jumps and 40 ms for the return sweeps. If we read a line of print with four fixations, there will be three short jumps and one long return, totaling about 100 ms of actual movement. The four fixations will total about 900 ms, indicating that about 90 per cent of the total reading time is spent in fixation pauses.[12, 19] In slower reading, with longer and more numerous fixations, the total fixation time may be as high as 95 per cent.[23] In one way, this is a measure of efficiency since it gives the proportion of the total time actually devoted to seeing. As a matter of fact, the perceptual

processes undoubtedly go on during the saccadic movements, even though retinal stimulation is not effective with the moving eye. Reading is a continuous process in that the perceptual development of meaning goes on steadily. Perhaps one can think of it as a continuous production process, a machine into which the raw material is tossed by the shovelful. The output will be continuous, as long as there is some raw material in the works. This analogy has another similarity to reading; the rate of input will usually be limited by the rate at which the machine processes the raw material, and not vice versa. In a similar fashion, the eye movements adjust to the rate at which O is digesting the sensory input.

THE EYE-VOICE SPAN IN ORAL READING

Following our analogy, we can raise the question as to how long it takes O to "process" the sensory input. But how can we tell when the process of perceiving is complete? One way is to make O read aloud, recording eye movements and speech sounds on the same film. It is relatively simple to determine when a given word was fixated, when it was uttered, and the length of the delay.

Buswell[5] has made fairly extensive studies of the eye-voice span. It varies with the skill of the reader, as the following results indicate.

School grade	Average eye-voice span in letter-spaces	
	of three good readers	of three poor readers
II	11.0	5.4
VI	11.9	11.2
IX	15.8	11.5
XII	15.9	12.4

There is considerable variation from these average values. In the first place, the oral output goes on at a relatively constant rate, consistent with the proper speed for expressive speech. If O hits a difficult spot in the written text, his eye movements slow up, and there may be regressive movements to develop the meaning. Thus, his output tends to catch up with the input, and the eye-voice span drops almost to zero. Once the difficulty is overcome, the eye runs ahead rapidly, until it is again well ahead of the voice. With experienced oral readers the span is as long as eight words, 2 seconds, or a line of print, depending on which unit of measurement one prefers to consider.

This estimate of the "processing time" is based on oral reading in which O must develop a word in the context of those that come before and after. The minimum time for perceiving and responding to an isolated word is shorter; reaction time experiments put it at about $4/10$ second. But such measurements are misleading when applied to reading, which is a continuous process. The reader does not respond to each word as a new one, just flashed before

his eye. He has been prepared for it by earlier words in the sentence, and has seen it in peripheral vision. His response is more than merely shouting the word; he must integrate it into the sentence as a whole. Probably the overlap between visual and vocal processes is our best measure of processing time.

Overlapping processes can be demonstrated in other similar performances such as typing from copy and taking down a telegraphic message from the sounder. The ear-hand span in receiving a telegraphic message is specially long because of the amount of organization needed to reduce a series of clicks to a meaningful message. In typing from printed copy, the eye-hand span averages only about 5-6 letter spaces, or about a second. In space it is much shorter than in oral reading, but in time it is about the same—typing being the slower motor process. The number of fixations is much greater in typing than in oral reading, and is least of all in silent reading. When the motor process is necessarily slow, the eyes have to put in the time somehow. (For determining the eye-hand span, the carriage of the typewriter made an electric contact at every tenth space, and these contacts were recorded on the film along with the eye movements.[9])

ORAL VERSUS SILENT READING

The overlap or processing time must not be confused with the speed of reading. As we have indicated, the speed of oral reading is largely set by the demands of speech. The eyes normally go only fast enough to maintain a comfortable lead over the voice. But if O reads silently, the limiting effects of speech drop out. For example, Huey[14] studied the speed with which 20 university students read an interesting novel. The ordinary oral reading ranged from 2.2 to 4.7 words per second; if they tried to speed it up, the oral range shifted to 2.9-6.4. But their ordinary silent rate was between 2.5 and 9.8 words per second. Note that the slower silent readers are little, if any, faster than they were at oral reading. It is possible that these readers were doing what might be called "silent oral reading" —that is, making actual speech movements as they read silently. Many adults have carried over this habit from their early reading lessons; watch people reading, and see how many of them move their lips. This habit acts as a drag on reading rate in two ways. In the first place, it limits reading speed to speech speed. In the second place, it discourages or prevents the integration of material into larger wholes. A skilled reader perceives the words, not singly, but in meaningful phrases. In very rapid reading these units of perception may be quite large. Dearborn [12] found a professor whose average rate for *Robinson Crusoe* was 11 words per second.

There is some question as to whether such rapid reading picks up all details, or just the general sense of the passage. This is particularly true when we do the kind of reading called "skimming." A person who is thoroughly familiar with a subject can get a pretty good idea of what the author of a new textbook says by glancing at key sentences. It is hard to draw the line between actual reading and such skimming. At the other extreme is the slow and detailed reading of the lawyer or of the student working on an unfamiliar technical subject. We see again that there are as many appropriate rates of reading as there are classes of material and purposes in reading.

Training Eye Movements. While we are on the subject of individual differences in reading behavior, we might as well say a few words about remedial reading. Considering the importance of reading in school work, one is not surprised that the slow reader has been a challenge to psychologists. With the development of the eye-movement camera, the psychologist had a tool for comparing slow and rapid readers. As one might expect, the slow reader has a relatively large number of fixations and regressive movements per line, and his fixation pauses are long. The obvious remedy was to speed up the eye movements so that they would be smooth and regular. All sorts of methods were tried. The simplest way is to get the pupil to make three regular fixations per line, perhaps in time with a metronome. Another is to use the *Metronoscope,* a gadget which exposes lines of print in successive thirds, forcing O to make the desired pattern of eye movements.[21] Dearborn and Anderson [13] have developed a moving picture film which simulates the reading situation a little better; it has a moving clear region that passes along the line in regular jumps. The eye follows this region, but it has the advantage of some peripheral vision of the rest of the line. There have been a number of careful experiments, with control groups who get no training, all groups being tested before and after the training (or no training) period. There is usually a pronounced gain in the experimental group. But where other control groups have been used, such as a group of children who did motivated library reading while the experimental group practiced with the Metronoscope, *both* groups showed gains.[10] The answer seems to be that any method which arouses an interest in greater reading speed will probably work.

Many experts feel that emphasis on training eye movements is tackling the wrong end of the process. As we have indicated above, eye movements are only one link in the chain; the limiting factor is central. Hence, what is necessary is to improve perceptual skills directly and let the eye movements follow.[8]

Does this mean that one should forget about eye-movement cameras in the reading clinic? In the first place, it has been shown that the typical short test with a camera like the ophthalmograph yields unreliable results.[2, 4, 15] This is probably due to the short sample furnished with the instrument, for Tinker [24] found that the reliability went up to .80 when samples of 20 to 40 lines were used instead of 5 to 15. In the second place, the eye-movement camera encourages too much attention to eye movements instead of a more

```
1       2       3       4       5 8 7 9 6   10
•       •       •       •       • • • • •   •
A common violation of this rule is illustrated by the sentence,
20      24      20      24      16 24 24 36 16   12

1   2    4 3   5             6 8 9 10 7    12 11
•   •    • •   •             • • • • •     • •
"Every one started at the same time."   The expression Every one
32   12    24 x    36            40 32 28  28 20    24 24

2  1 3    5 4    6    7 9 10 8    11 12
•  • •    • •    •    • • • •     • •
is singular.   The predicate expresses an idea of comparison.
40  16 16   28 x    24    20 52 x 32    20 16

2   1    3   4   5    6    7    8
•   •    •   •   •    •    •    •
Two persons might start at the same time, but one person could
24  12   24  12  24   20   28     x
```

Fig. 2. (From Judd & Buswell.[17]) Fixations in four lines of reading. The dots indicate the location of the fixations. The numbers above the dots give the order of fixations in each line, while the numbers below show the duration of each fixation in hundredths of a sec. Where an x occurs, the duration could not be made out from the record. The reader was a university student. Plots of this type are prepared by projecting the eye-movement photographs onto the original reading material, and noting where each fixation falls. To aid in lining up the image, O, fixates each of two dots (not shown here) at opposite edges of the reading matter before he starts to read.

thorough analysis of the reading skill as a whole. Hence, the camera should be used only by experts with a good psychological training.

This book is not the place to go too deeply into a specialized topic like reading, much less the improvement of reading skills. The student who wishes to study further will find an excellent summary in Tinker's [25] review. He lists 126 references, mostly from the decade 1935-1944. Many of them were concerned with limited practical problems. The more general problems had already been covered in the widespread exploratory activity that characterized the first quarter of the century as eye-movement cameras became available. Experimental psychologists were intensely interested in such problems as the following:

1. *Does the fixation favor any particular parts of words, or any particular sorts of words?* The answer seems to be that O is nearly as likely to fixate a space between words as a letter, to use an extreme example. There is, however, some question as to whether the usual record is accurate enough to locate fixations so precisely.

2. *What part of a line gets the most fixation time?* The answer is that about 30 percent goes in the first quarter, with the rest evenly divided over the other three quarters. It is possible that the need for corrective movements after the return sweep makes up the excess.

3. *How does the eye behave in reading music, foreign languages, mathematical formulas, adding, etc?* The answers come out about as one who knew the task would anticipate. One interesting point came out from a study of reading Chinese.[20] The pattern of eye movements was very different from that used in reading English, as one might expect from the form and direction of Chinese printing. But the reading rate, if scored in terms of content, showed about the same amount of thought taken in per second in both languages. Again we find an emphasis on central, rather than on peripheral limitations.

REFERENCES

1. Anderson, I. H., "Studies in the Eye-Movements of Good and Poor Readers," *Psychological Monograph*, No. 215, 1937.

2. ———, "The Ophthalm-O-Graph and Metron-O-Scope Evaluated in the Light of Recent Research on the Psychology of Reading," *Teachers College Journal*, Vol. 12, 1941, pp. 60-63.

3. Bayle, E., "The Nature and Causes of Regressive Movements in Reading," *Journal of Experimental Education*, Vol. 11, 1942, pp. 16-36.

4. Broom, M. E., "The Reliability of the Reading Graph Yielded by the Ophthalmograph," *School and Society*, Vol. 52, 1940, pp. 2-5, 208.

5. Buswell, G. T., "An Experimental Study of the Eye-Voice Span in Reading," *Supplementary Educational Monograph*, No. 17, 1920.

6. ———, "Fundamental Reading Habits: A Study of Their Development," *Supplementary Educational Monograph*, No. 21, 1922.

7. ———, "How Adults Read," *Supplementary Educational Monograph*, No. 45, 1937.

8. ———, "Remedial Reading at the College and Adult Levels," *Supplementary Educational Monograph*, No. 50, 1939.

9. Butsch, R. L. C., "Eye Movements and the Eye-Hand Span in Typewriting," *Journal of Educational Psychology*, Vol. 23, 1932, pp. 104-21.

10. Cason, E. B., "Mechanical Methods for Increasing the Speed of Reading," *Teachers College Continuing Education Bulletin*, No. 878, 1943.

11. Clark, B., "Binocular Anomalies and Reading Ability," *American Journal of Ophthalmology*, Vol. 23, 1940, pp. 885-91.

12. Dearborn, W. F., "The Psychology of Reading," *Archives of Philosophy, Psychology and Scientific Methods*, No. 4, 1906.

13. ———, and Anderson, I. H., "A New Method for Teaching Phrasing and for Increasing the Size of Reading Fixations," *Psychological Record*, 1, 1937, pp. 459-75.

14. Huey, E. B., *The Psychology and Pedagogy of Reading*, New York: Macmillan, 1908, pp. 494-508.

15. Imus, H. A., Rothney, J. W. M., and Bear, R. M., "Photography of Eye Movements," *American Journal of Optometry*, Vol. 20, 1943, pp. 231-47.

16. Javal, L. E., "Essai sur la physiologie de la lecture," *Annual d'Oculistique*, Vol. 82, 1878, pp. 242-53, 493.

17. Judd, C. H., and Buswell, G. T., "Silent Reading: A Study of Various Types," *Supplementary Educational Monograph*, No. 23, 1922.

18. Robinson, F. P., "The Role of Eye Movements in Reading, with an Evaluation of the Techniques for Their Improvement," *Iowa State University Aims Prog. Research*, No. 39, 1933.

19. Schmidt, W. A., "An Experimental Study in the Psychology of Reading," *Supplementary Educational Monograph*, No. 2, 1917.

20. Shen, E., "An Analysis of Eye Movements in the Reading of Chinese," *Journal of Experimental Psychology*, Vol. 10, 1927, pp. 158-83.

21. Taylor, E. A., *Controlled Reading*, Chicago: Chicago University Press, 1937.

22. Tinker, M. A., "Apparatus for Recording Eye-Movements," *American Journal of Psychology*, Vol. 43, 1931, pp. 115-18, 495.

23. ———, "Time Taken by Eye Movements in Reading," *Journal of Genetic Psychology*, Vol. 48, 1936b, 468-71.

24. ———, "Reliability and Validity of Eye-Movement Measures of Reading," *Journal of Experimental Psychology*, Vol. 19, 1936c, pp. 732-46.

25. ———, "The Study of Eye Movements in Reading," *Psychological Bulletin*, Vol. 43, 1946, pp. 93-120.

26. Walker, R. Y., "The Eye-Movements of Good Readers," *Psychological Monograph*, No. 199, 1933.

History and Philosophy of Reading Instruction

4: What Have We Accomplished in Reading?—A Review of the Past Fifty Years *

NILA BANTON SMITH

This last half-century stands out as a truly golden period in the progress of reading instruction. More innovations have been effected in reading during the last fifty years than during the entire three hundred years antedating this period of American history. I am sure that progress has been equally notable in the other phases of the language arts constellation. It is most appropriate that accomplishments in all of the language arts areas be reviewed upon this momentous occasion—the Golden Anniversary of The National Council of Teachers of English!

Progress in reading instruction has been marked by a succession of turning points. For a period of years reading methods and materials all over the country are quite similar—so similar, in fact, that an unbiased examiner might arrive at the conclusion that all had been turned out of the same mold, with just a slightly different crimp here and there in the contour of the pan. Then, rather suddenly, a new plan becomes popular, and we teach reading in this manner until another turning point arrives. Thus, epoch after epoch of reading instruction passes.[12]

Fortunately printed records are available to which we can turn in delineating these epochs and ascertaining their characteristics. In attempting to obtain information to bring to you about reading epochs during our recent half century the following source materials, published between 1910 and 1960, were explored: prominent educational magazines that usually contain reading articles, yearbooks of learned societies, summaries of published investigations in reading, lists of unpublished master's and doctoral researches completed or under way. More than 300 pieces of materials were surveyed for the purpose of picking up the sequence of events and trends which marked the pilgrimage of reading in its upward march from 1910 to the present time. This information will be presented to you by decades.

ACCOMPLISHMENTS FROM 1910 TO 1920

The dramatic decade beginning with 1910 ushered in the first truly great break-through in reading progress. This was the birth of the scientific move-

* Reprinted from *Elementary English*, Vol. 38, No. 3 (March 1961), pp. 141-50, by permission of the National Council of Teachers of English and the author.

ment in education. In 1909 Thorndike made the initial presentation of his
handwriting scale before a meeting of
the American Association for the Advancement of Science, and in 1910 it
was published.[14] Generally speaking, the
publication of the Thorndike scale has
been recognized as the beginning of
the contemporary movement for measuring educational products scientifically.
In the immediately ensuing years scales
and tests appeared rapidly. Courtis
arithmetic tests, Hilligas's Composition
Scale, Buckingham Spelling Scale—and
then a reading test—The Gray Standardized Oral Reading Paragraphs.[2] This
test was published in 1915. Other reading tests followed shortly.

As a result of the strong new surge
of interest in placing education on a scientific basis together with its correlative
motives for developing instruments of
measurement, we would naturally expect that the scientific study of reading
problems would take a vigorous spurt.
And this it did.

Through all the years up to 1910
only 34 studies had been reported in
reading. During the 1910-20 decade,
200 accounts appeared, about six times
as many as had been reported during
the entire history of reading preceding this time. These studies had to do
mostly with tests and school surveys as
would be expected.

As for method: the most revolutionary thing happened that had happened
since clergy began to teach reading in
churches, and dames began to teach
reading in kitchens. "For hundreds of
years oral reading had maintained a
supreme and undisputed claim on teaching methods." [11] During this decade,
however, the concept of teaching *silent*
reading burst into our slumbering com-
placency like a bombshell. It came suddenly and in the midst of a period in
which school people were serenely content in the use of sentence-story methods applied to the oral reading of selections in literary readers. For the most

part they continued to use these practices to the end of the decade but the
startling new idea was at least launched.
Discussions of the advantages of silent
reading appeared for the first time in
the Sixteenth [4] and in the Eighteenth [5]
Yearbooks of the National Society for
the Study of Education. Speakers at
educational conventions began to talk
about it, magazine articles began to discuss it. The idea had been born.

To sum up: developing the concept
of applying scientific techniques to the
study of reading, devising standardized
instruments to measure reading achievement, increasing the number of studies
tremendously, initiating the silent reading idea. These seem to have been the
major accomplishments from 1910 to
1920.

ACCOMPLISHMENTS FROM 1920 TO 1930

The period extending from 1920 to
1930 is perhaps the most golden decade
in this golden era of progress in so far
as fundamental changes in reading practices are concerned. These changes were
largely due to the scientific movement
which had shaped up during the preceding period and which now was opening up fresh wells of information with
improved and extended applications.

The new studies conducted during
this decade carried with them three distinct earmarks of progress: the number
increased tremendously; they covered a
wider scope of problems; many of them
were conducted in classrooms by teachers and other school personnel, rather
than being confined to the laboratory.

As to the number of investigations:
Gray's summaries reveal that 763 were
reported as compared with 200 during
the preceding decade. This unprecedented increase reflected the zeal and enthusiasm with which school people were
searching for more information about
the important subject of reading.

The studies of this period probed
a variety of problems, but there were

three problem areas which were most highly significant. They were significant because they resulted in sweeping changes in practice. These three areas were: (1) silent reading, (2) individual differences, and (3) remedial reading. The first half of this decade might well be called "The Age of Silent Reading." "These years were marked with an exaggerated, often exclusive emphasis on silent reading as opposed to the traditional oral reading techniques." [11] As previously mentioned, the concept of teaching silent reading was initiated during the latter part of the preceding period, but it didn't really take hold as a nation-wide classroom practice until during the years of 1920 to 1925. This sudden and widespread reversal in practice was largely due to two influences: the development of tests which revealed that silent reading was superior to oral reading in speed and comprehension; and the publication of The Yearbooks of the National Society for the Study of Education. As already indicated, one article each appeared in the Sixteenth [4] and the Eighteenth [5] Yearbooks. The climax, however, came with the publication of the Twentieth Yearbook, Part II [7] of which was devoted entirely to the report of the "Society's Committee on Silent Reading." Following the appearance of this Yearbook, "textbook writers began to produce readers based on silent reading procedures; other authors prepared professional books on silent reading; teachers busied themselves in preparing exercises that would check comprehension of silent reading by means of drawings, true-false statements or completion sentences and so forth. The whole country for a time seemed to be obsessed with the idea of teaching silent reading." [11]

This extreme emphasis, however, was soon balanced with other factors. By 1925 the novelty of the new idea had worn off, somewhat; investigations revealed some unique uses of oral reading, school people discovered that there

still were some special needs for oral reading in the school program. Perhaps, the culminating influence came with the publication of the Twenty-fourth Yearbook, Part I [8] which appeared in 1925. This Yearbook advocated a broader program of reading instruction which among other things recognized both oral and silent reading. New courses of study, professional books and readers immediately reflected the broadened objectives of this Yearbook and methods during the years 1925-1930 were shaped largely by its contents. So during the first two decades of the last fifty years we progressed from extreme oral reading to extreme silent reading to a broader program which recognized both. In my opinion, this was an indication of real accomplishment.

As for individual differences: with the administration of the newly developed tests, a very great fundamental truth became apparent with a violent impact— the realization that there were wide individual differences in the reading achievement of children, in the same grade and in the same classroom. This discovery spurred school people to experiment with a variety of adjustments in classroom organization and instruction, designed to cope with this newly revealed variation in the learning rate of children.

There were reports of adjustments made in classrooms which maintained the regular organization such as ability grouping, flexible promotions, and differentiated assignments. But the pulsating new idea was that of breaking up class organization entirely to permit of individual progression. This plan of organization received as much attention at this time as it is receiving at the present moment. Speeches, articles, and Yearbooks dealt with the subject. San Francisco; Los Angeles; Detroit; Winnetka; Madison, Wisconsin; and other school systems reported [9] results they had obtained by individual instruction. The states of Connecticut and Illinois reported [9] experiments in individualizing instruction in rural schools.

The various plans, on the whole, were patterned after the Winnetka or the Dalton ideas, in both of which individual progression in reading and other subjects was made possible by means of assignments in which the child worked through subject material that increased in small increments of difficulty. The important point to note is that attention to individual differences in reading received its first great impetus during this decade of remarkable progress.

The concept of *remedial* reading was launched from its small island of study during this period and sent out over unexplored seas in quest of answers to disability problems. The movement was spurred on by the use of standardized tests. These tests revealed that thousands of boys and girls were failing each year to make normal progress in reading. Published reports of work in the reading disability field indicate that the chief interest at this time was in diagnosing individual cases. As for method, it was during this period that Fernald evolved her kinesthetic method, and that Orton expounded his theory on mixed dominance and the treatment that accompanied it. Remedial reading did get under way during this period.

In beginning reading there were also innovations. Experience charts first came into use. The Nineteenth Yearbook,[6] published in 1920, dealt with reading materials. In it examples were given of charts based on children's experiences, and the practice of introducing children to beginning reading through the use of such material was advocated. This practice was not widely accepted until much later, but progress had been made in evolving the idea.

And last but not least, mention must be made of another mark of progress which clearly stamped itself into the later annals of this decade. The reading readiness concept began to take shape at this time.

In 1926 the International Kindergarten Union in cooperation with the United States Bureau of Education conducted an investigation of "Pupils' Readiness for Reading Instruction upon Entrance to First Grade." The first articles on this subject were published in Childhood Education in January, 1927. Two of these articles used the term "reading readiness." In so far as I am aware, this was the first time that this phrase crept into our reading vocabulary.[13] In Gray's summaries published in 1928, he reported for the first time three studies on reading readiness. A few master's theses and a trickling of articles on this subject also appeared before the close of the decade. The new concept, however, was still in the formative stage, and little was done about it in a practical way until the following period, but the movement was on its way.

Much more could be said about the accomplishments made during this unprecedented period. I should like to dwell longer on the accumulation of information gathered about reading and the auspicious innovations in classroom practice that were inaugurated at this time, but I must pass on to other conquests and other days.

ACCOMPLISHMENTS FROM 1930 TO 1940

This period may be characterized largely as one of extension and application rather than one of revelation and initiation.

Investigations continued at an accelerated pace. In round figures about 1200 studies were reported between 1930 and 1940. Not only were these studies greater in number, but they were superior in isolation of problems, in designs, and in controls.

Some of the embryo ideas that had sprouted in the preceding decade came into full bloom and fruited profusely at this time. For example: the reading readiness interest reached its zenith in this period.[13] Published investigations on this topic increased steadily during each successive year of this decade,[1] reaching their climax of frequency in 1940 when Gray reported 22 studies relating to this topic in one year. Since that time the number has decreased steadily.

Turning to unpublished research, this was the hey-day of aspiring masters and doctors in finding problems for research in the readiness area. The first doctoral dissertation on readiness was reported in 1927. From that time on, the number of master and doctoral studies increased, reaching its peak in the years 1937 to 1940. Fourteen such studies were completed in 1937, 15 in 1938, 14 in 1939, and 12 in 1940. Since that time only 2 or 3 academic studies on readiness have been reported each year.

A similar trend is seen in published articles on reading readiness. Periodicals abounded with discussions on readiness topics from 1930 to 1940. Articles on this subject rarely appear in present-day literature.

In the light of this evidence, it may be concluded that this was the period of most vigorous emphasis, both on investigations of reading readiness and applications of the readiness theory. The concept has been accepted now and we hear little about it at the present time.

Remedial reading, which had experienced a touch-and-go recognition during the preceding period, now became established and gained stature. Many significant studies were conducted in the remedial reading areas: causes of difficulties, diagnosis, and corrective procedures. Professional books devoted exclusively to remedial reading were first published. Some laboratory studies were still made but the majority of studies now were conducted in schools. Remedial reading, which had started in laboratories, now became a topic for practical experimentation in the public schools themselves.

A new trend that began to emerge was that of giving beginning attention to high school, college, and adult reading. Studies made at these levels, however, were mostly concerned with interests in, and uses of reading, rather than with reading achievement and teaching procedure.

Every decade reviewed so far has been characterized by one or two events of great distinction. In the 1910-1920 decade, it was the application of scientific measurement and investigation to reading, in the 1920-'30 era, it was the startling innovations of silent reading and of individual progression. What was the spectacular event in the nineteen-thirties?

The Activity Movement swept the country during these years, and the startling new idea in reading was to teach this skill as a part of the Activity Program. In such a program children worked freely and spontaneously and actively in following their own interests; and teachers were intrigued with the new "game" of trying to get all of their subject matter across through "Units of Work."

In so far as reading was concerned, pupils had access to a considerable number of books bearing largely on the topic of their "Unit of Work." This was the first big impetus for bringing a quantity of books into the classroom for reading. There was a profusion of charts and school-made booklets growing out of children's interests. Pupils read functionally from their co-operatively prepared materials and out of many books in doing research in connection with their Units. In a word, this was how reading proceeded in the Activity Program in the thirties.

We no longer hear of the Activity Program at this time nor of the teaching of reading in connection with this program. The Activity Movement, however, made a vigorous impact on the teaching of reading and other subjects at this time—an impact so strong that its influence still continues. The Activity

Movement distracted the school public from its age-old concept of schools centered almost exclusively on subject-matter goals to schools in which consideration is given to the child, himself, his stage of development, his interests, his activities, his choices and his decisions.

In summary, we may say that progress in this decade was characterized by continuing investigations, greater in number, higher in quality than in the preceding decade; intensive application of the readiness concept; transfer of remedial activities from laboratory to classroom; beginning attention to reading at higher levels; and wide-spread interest in teaching reading as an integral part of the Activity Program.

ACCOMPLISHMENTS FROM 1940 TO 1950

An event resulting from progress in science overshadowed all other indications of progress during this period. The "birthday of the atomic age" is officially set as December 2, 1942, when Dr. Enrico Fermi turned on the first successful nuclear energy machine in Chicago. The first atomic bomb destroyed Hiroshima on August 6, 1945. On the face of things this terrifying discovery with its possibilities for good or for evil reduced to comparative insignificance our little scientific achievements in reading. Yet, could this achievement have been possible without reading? Can we cope adequately with its future destructive or beneficent effects, as the case may be, without more efficient reading skill and a wider reading citizenry? The atomic age and reading immediately become interactive.

But we didn't realize this at the time. We were too close to this earth-shaking event to sense its import for reading instruction. The war probably only had two *immediate* effects on reading. One of these was a diminution in the number of reading investigations. This was probably due to the fact that many of the psychologists and educators who conducted research in reading, or stimulated others to do so, were in the armed services.

The other major effect of the war was the shocking discovery that at this day and age thousands of young men in the military service could not read well enough to follow the simple printed instructions for camp life. Coupled with this discovery was the revelation that reading could be taught to these young men in army camps in an amazingly short time. Concurrently, several new investigations disclosed reading deficiencies in large numbers of high school and college students. These several influences combined to produce a spurt in attention to reading at these higher levels. Immediately following the war, a great deal of professional literature on reading emerged and among these publications several bulletins and one Yearbook appeared dealing with high school and college reading. Chief among these publications was a bulletin of the National Education Association titled *Reading Instruction in Secondary Schools*,[3] and the Forty-eighth Yearbook, Part II of The National Society for the Study of Education, titled *Reading in High School and College*.[10] The actual teaching of reading at these levels had not progressed far at this time but the idea was vigorously expanding.

During this period, reading in the content subjects also became a matter of wide discussion and the subject of a few investigations. The studies at this time pointed to the general conclusion that while good readers can read well in all subject fields, special practice in reading in particular subject areas is helpful to average and poor readers.

In the forties, wide recognition was given to the interrelationships amongst the language arts. Studies, articles, speeches were concerned with the relationship of reading to spelling, handwriting, vocabulary, and composition. As a result we came to recognize that reading was not an isolated skill independent of other skills used in the interchange of ideas, but that it was just one aspect of the total language arts constellation mutually dependent upon and interactive with all other skills in the communication dimension.

A strong new concern also sprang up in regard to the effects of three of the newer media for mass communication: comics, movies and radio. Television did not come in for much attention until the next decade but during this period wide dissemination of entertainment through the first named agencies stirred up worry on the part of school people and parents. They feared that interest in listening to radio, looking at comics, viewing movies would reduce interest in reading and thus decrease the amount of reading done. Numerous popular articles bemoaned the situation and pointed out its dangers. Several studies were conducted directed toward the exploration of students' interests in this area and finding out how much time they devoted to the offerings of these types. Thus initial steps were taken in obtaining information to combat what was thought to be the first threat to reading.

Remedial diagnosis and treatment continued to claim a large segment of the spotlight. Mechanical instruments and devices which had been introduced during the preceding period increased in numbers and use. There were fewer studies reported on psychological factors such as dominance, handedness, eyedness, and reversals. An increasing number were devoted to personal factors as related to reading: personal interests and attitudes, personal status in social, emotional, and experiential maturity. This attention to other growth and development factors as related to reading was certainly one of the most notable advances made during this period.

To sum up: the chief points of progress during this decade were: increased attention to teaching reading at the higher levels; growing attention to reading in the content subjects; concerns about mass communications; attempts to find relationships between reading and handwriting, spelling, vocabulary and composition; and perhaps, most important of all, a growing consciousness of the profound truth that reading doesn't develop in a vacuum by itself, but that it is part and parcel of general child development and is affected by all other aspects of child growth.

ACCOMPLISHMENTS FROM 1950 TO 1960

A most exciting decade! For one thing, interest in reading instruction became almost universal during this period. There was a time when primary teachers were the only people interested in the teaching of reading. Now teachers of all subjects and at all levels want to know more about reading. Parents are asking questions, pursuing books and articles on reading. Students at high-school and college levels and adults beyond college are flocking to reading centers. Slick magazines and laymen are discussing reading freely. A great conflagration of interest has been ignited amongst teachers and students, and more especially amongst the lay public. And this is good.

During this period, however, for the first time in history, reading instruction in American schools underwent harsh and severe criticism by laymen. School people maintained that the criticisms were unfair and rose to the defense of their methods through articles, speeches, discussions, and investigations. Several comparative studies of "Then and Now" were made. These studies, on the whole, showed that we were teaching reading as well as or better than in preceding years.

Insofar as progress is concerned the criticism by laymen probably had three good effects: it caused school people to examine their present methods more carefully; it stimulated the interest of parents and other laymen in reading instruction; it offered motives and opportunities to school people to explain the research, psychology, and philosophy on which present methods are based. So in this situation, as is often the case in other situations, even criticism caused reading to move forward.

Perhaps as an off-shoot of interest and criticism, coupled with a growing awareness of the complexity of the reading process, there has been a spurt of activity in the re-instatement and increase of reading courses in the curriculums of teacher-training institutions. Concurrently with this interest in adding more courses, standards are being raised in regard to the qualifications of teachers of reading and of reading specialists. This movement toward better-trained teachers in reading is a big step forward.

As for the number of investigations: studies during this period reached incredible proportions. Gray reported over 1,000 studies in his 1960 summary, but in his introduction he said for the first time in his thirty-five years of annual summarizing, "The number of studies are increasing so rapidly that it is no longer possible to report all of them in this annual summary. Those referred to this year represent either a new or distinctive approach to a problem or suggest significant issues in need of further study." Not only was this increase apparent in the published reports of reading investigations, but it also was reflected in the reports of dissertations completed or in progress which soared to new numerical heights, the number reported averaging about 90 per year as compared with about 50 in the preceding decade.

Advance is shown in the subjects of investigation. Reading in the content fields, adult reading deficiencies, and television as related to reading came in for strong additional attention. The most gratifying trend revealed, however, is that we are at present delving more deeply into the reading process and more broadly into the factors that affect it. The former popular topic of phonics now seems to have been replaced with studies of perception. Comprehension is no longer treated as a lump sum; the emphasis at present is upon the higher thinking processes of interpretation and critical reading. The old readiness studies are replaced with investigations of prediction and expectancy. Remedial reading is not so much concerned now with studies of gadgets and specific teaching remedies as it is with organismic and personality factors. Parental personality, attitudes, and interactions with the child as related to reading entered the research scene for the first time during this period, and many reading investigations concerned with parents and their children are now being reported. Studies are made in regard to the climate of the classroom and its effect on reading. This mere glimpse at some of the subjects of the most recent studies is indicative of a trend toward probing to greater depths and in wider breadths than was evident in most of the studies preceding this period.

Special mention should be made of a clearly discernible advance in regard to reading and the other language arts. In the preceding decade we became strongly concerned about the relationships of reading to the subjects of spelling, handwriting, vocabulary, and composition. During this decade we have moved on to a concern about aspects of the language arts which perhaps are less tangible than the subject matter areas but more inclusive in their application to the entire block of communication skills. Listening studies have increased by leaps and bounds. Some of the most recent dissertation topics have to do with semantic studies of reading content, multiple meanings, figures of speech in reading, and the linguistic approach to reading. Is it not an accomplishment to have moved on from subject interrelationships to relationships dealing with listening and the various aspects of linguistics?

The innovation in reading method which has loomed large on the horizon of late is the plan known as *individualized instruction*. The amount of attention given to this plan in this decade is comparable to that given to individual instruction in the nineteen-twenties. It probably is the most popular topic of discussion at present in educational magazines and often at teacher gatherings.

This individualized plan of the present is different from individual instruction which was popular in the twenties. The earlier plan was subject-matter oriented. Each child was given subject matter assignments divided into small increments of difficulty and he was permitted to progress as fast as he, personally, could complete each successive increment. The present plan is child-psychology oriented utilizing particularly Dr. Williard Olson's theory of *seeking, selfselection,* and *pacing* in that the child seeks that which stimulates him, selects the book he desires to read, and proceeds at his own rate.

This plan has been used too recently for research reports to have crept into published summaries of investigations. Most of the research on this topic at present falls into the unpublished category of theses, dissertations, or mimeographed reports of experiments carried on in certain school systems. An examination of the most recent sources listing dissertations completed or under way indicates that a quantity of research is now taking place in regard to this topic. Much of it will undoubtedly find its way into print in the near future.

Much more could be said about this period, but because of lack of time we now shall let the curtain fall over the last scene in fifty years of reading accomplishment. As we review the stirring events of the past, we have a right to feel cheered, grateful, proud. In looking back in retrospect we might wonder whether another fifty years could possibly bring about so many changes. This was the first period in which experimentation could be conducted scientifically. In consideration of the newly developed tools, our eagerness to learn, and studies conducted, we might reason that practically all facets of reading instruction have been explored and thus another era could never be so great as this.

If we do reason to this conclusion, we probably are wrong. We pioneered during this period in unexplored territory. We chopped down and cleared away the large virgin trees, but perhaps some of the humble shrubs or creeping vines or fragile mosses may hold even more significance for us than the strikingly obvious, first-sight timbers. But these more obscure growths won't yield their significance with the use of heavy saws and axes. We shall need fresh, piercing insights in choosing which of these to select for dislodgment, and then we shall need unique, delicate tools to pry them loose from their tangled environment and to test the potency of their effect.

What I am trying to say is that while our accomplishments have been very great, indeed, it may be that we have only penetrated the first layer, the troposphere, so to speak. Undoubtedly, brilliant new insights will be revealed, ingenious new techniques of experimentation will be evolved. Possibilities of such developments portend opportunities for unlimited achievement in the future.

Most assuredly, we shall not rest complacently in the glory of achievement during this past golden age. Rather shall we look forward to still greater accomplishments in reading. Let us push on and on with more and more vigor in the next decade and the next decade, and in all of the other decades ahead!

REFERENCES

1. Good, Carter V., "Doctoral Studies Completed or Under Way," *Phi Delta Kappa*, 1923-53; (Separate publications) Lyda, Mary Louise; Jenson, Glenn; Brown, Stanley; Anderson, Harold, Phi Delta Kappa, Bloomington, Ind.: 1954-59.
2. Gray, William S., *Oral Reading Paragraphs Test*, Public School Publishing Co., Bloomington, Ind.: 1915.
3. National Education Association, *Reading Instruction in Secondary Schools*, Research Bulletin, Vol. 22, No. 1, 1942.
4. National Society for the Study of Education, *Sixteenth Yearbook, Part I*, 1917.
5. *Eighteenth Yearbook, Part II*, 1919.
6. *Nineteenth Yearbook, Part I*, 1920.
7. *Twentieth Yearbook, Part II*, 1921.
8. *Twenty-fourth Yearbook, Part I*, 1925.
9. *Twenty-fourth Yearbook, Part II*, 1925.
10. *Forty-eighth Yearbook, Part II*, 1949.
11. Smith, Nila Banton, *American Reading Instruction*, Silver Burdett, New York: 1937.
12. ———, "Historical Turning Points in Reading," *National Education Association Journal*, 280-82, May 1952.
13. ———, *Readiness for Reading and Related Language Arts*, National Council of Teachers of English, 1950.
14. Thorndike, E. L., *The Thorndike Scale for Handwriting of Children*, Bureau of Publications, Teachers College, Columbia University, New York: 1910.

5: The Nature and Types of Reading *

WILLIAM S. GRAY

I RELATION OF READING TO LEARNING

Children learn specific facts and extend their experiences in many ways. They observe what goes on about them; they listen to the conversation or reports of others; they engage in constructive activities that stimulate thinking and provide motives for learning; they listen to the radio and follow the presentation of sound-motion pictures; they experiment, explore, and investigate with or without guidance; they go to museums and art galleries, or wherever their interests direct; they read widely in school, at home, or in the library. In these and other ways they continuously gain new insights, broader understandings, and deeper interests.

As an aid to learning, reading possesses unique characteristics. Of special significance is the fact that it utilizes printed or written words as symbols of meaning. For this reason it is often called an indirect form of learning. Through the associations aroused when symbols are recognized, experience is extended, new concepts developed, and thinking clarified. Thus it is possible for one to learn about or gain understanding of persons, places, or events that he has never seen or witnessed. The extent, however, to which meaningful associations are aroused depends in large meas-

* Reprinted from *The Teaching of Reading: A Second Report*, The Thirty-sixth Yearbook of the National Society for the Study of Education, Part I, Guy Montrose Whipple, editor, Bloomington, Ill.: Public School Publishing Company, 1937, pp. 23-38, by permission of the publisher.

ure on the background of related experiences that the reader possesses. In this respect, the interpretation of printed and of oral symbols is quite similar. Furthermore, the mental processes involved in interpretation are identical. In fact, the fundamental difference between reading and listening lies in the sense avenue through which the stimuli are received.

Various advantages attach to reading as an aid to learning. Its most obvious value arises from the fact that many of the experiences that children should acquire cannot be gained directly. The vast majority must be learned indirectly, as children look at pictures, listen to oral presentations, or read well-written accounts prepared by others. In the case of those who have acquired reasonable fluency, reading is a more rapid method of learning than is listening to an oral report of the same content. Furthermore, reading is admirably adapted to differences in rates of learning, since each child may proceed at a rate most suitable to himself. It also stimulates the development of habits essential in independent learning; if the materials read are properly prepared, they may greatly facilitate self-learning.

Reading is also subject to serious limitations as an aid to learning. The fact is well known that both the printed and the spoken word fail at times to convey to the learner as clear and vivid concepts as does direct contact with reality. Far too much of the material placed in children's hands today presupposes a broader background of related experiences than they possess; consequently readers are often unable to comprehend or interpret the author's meaning. Furthermore, the printed page is often ill-adapted to the varying individual experiences and reading abilities of the pupils and, therefore, contributes less to some than to others. Not infrequently, the ideas that the page is intended to convey are inadequately expressed and, as a result, cannot be readily understood. Teachers should be conscious of these limitations and take such steps as may be necessary to avoid or overcome them.

In view of the considerations presented, reading and other aids to learning should be used as they best serve the needs of pupils. The basic problem we face is not to determine whether a specific method of learning should be used to the exclusion of others, but rather the conditions under which each may be employed to greatest advantage. The answer, as it relates to reading, depends in part on the function of reading in child life.

II   READING DEFINED BROADLY

Reading has been variously defined by different writers and at different periods in history. At one time, a narrow conception of reading prevailed. Not infrequently, it was defined as the process of recognizing printed or written symbols, involving such habits as accuracy in recognizing the words that make up a passage, span of recognition, rate at which words and phrases are recognized, rhythmical progress of perceptions along the lines, and accurate return sweep of the eyes from the end of one line to the beginning of the next. The proponents of this view maintained that the comprehension and interpretation of meaning were not a part of the reading act, but involved supplementary thought processes. No one questions today the need for accurate, fluent habits of recognition. However, programs of teaching based upon the foregoing definition would be very narrow and provide primarily for the mastery of the mechanics of reading.

A broader view of the nature of reading is that it involves the recognition of the important elements of meaning in their essential relations, including accuracy and thoroughness in comprehension. This definition, while implying a thorough mastery of word recognition, attaches major importance to thought-getting. Those who hold this view believe that reading involves both the recognition of the meaning of words and phrases, and the fusing or organization of the various elements of meaning into a chain of ideas or an integrated system of thought. The need is urgent today for greater accuracy, precision, and thoroughness in comprehension among both elementary- and secondary-school pupils. It is imperative that teachers of the content fields, as well as of reading, devote themselves with increased vigor to the exacting obligations involved in promoting efficient habits of comprehension. The fact should be pointed out, however, that comprehension, as the term is used here, provides merely for a grasp of meaning in the form in which it is presented. It does not include the reader's reaction to the facts or view apprehended nor the discovery of their value or significance. It follows that a definition of reading limited to desirable habits of recognition and comprehension is inadequate to meet current needs.

A third definition implies that reading is a much more inclusive process than either of the preceding. It assumes that the reader not only recognizes the essential facts or ideas presented, but also reflects on their significance, evaluates them critically, discovers relationships between them, and clarifies his understanding of the ideas apprehended. In reading for a particular purpose, such as to determine the relative merits of the views presented by two authors, the reader may select and organize pertinent facts as he reads and may weigh values carefully. The superior quality and unique advantage of reading of this type have been discussed pointedly by Wheat:

The active selection, organization, and assimilation of thought from the printed page in terms of the author's purpose is coming to be recognized as a mental activity that is not only more important but also of a higher order. In the former activity, the writer controls the thinking of the reader; in the latter, the reader controls his own thinking.[8]

The Yearbook Committee believes that any conception of reading that fails to include reflection, critical evaluation, and the clarification of meaning is inadequate. It recognizes that this very broad use of the term implies that reading includes much that psychologists and educators have commonly called thinking. The Committee does not object if anyone wishes to make a distinction between securing ideas on the one hand and using them in thinking on the other. It takes the position, however, that since efficient readers do think about what they read while they are reading it, the teacher should provide needed stimulus and guidance both in securing ideas from the page and in dealing reflectively with them.

The implications of the foregoing discussion are quite clear. During the next decade, teachers should increase their efforts to guide pupils in the deliberate study of the meaning and significance of what they read. Related concepts, experiences, and principles should be recalled and the facts apprehended should be interpreted in the light of them. As Pyle [6] has aptly pointed out, it is not what is presented to the child that promotes growth but rather the reaction that he makes to what is presented. It follows that, beginning in the earliest grades, there should be much clear thinking and weighing of values during the act of reading as well as subsequent to it. This may result at times in reducing the speed of reading. However, the content of what is read should be more fully apprehended because its value, significance, and implications are understood. In this connection, the teachers of various other fields, as well as of reading, have heavy responsibilities. Only as adequate guidance is provided in all fields will reading serve most effectively in promoting broad understanding and social enlightenment.

But it is not sufficient that pupils merely recognize the words of a passage and comprehend and interpret their meaning. If they are aided through reading in acquiring adequate power of self-direction and ability to solve personal and social problems, they must learn to apply successfully the ideas gained from the printed page. As pointed out by Book,[1] "No one has really learned to read aright who does not apply to his own problems and work the thoughts which he has acquired from his reading." Desirable results are attained most economically when pupils make application of what they learn from the page while in the act of reading. It follows that reading, as here conceived, includes not only recognition, comprehension, and interpretation, but also the application of the facts apprehended in the study of personal and social problems.

Some of the reading activities to which reference has been made are often referred to as "study." According to Webster's International Dictionary, *study* is a setting of the mind with "absorbed or thoughtful attention" to some task or purpose. The source of information, or the materials studied, are not only books, but in addition, laboratories, people, nature, and things. The steps or processes involved include, in addition to reading, observation, discussion, and inquiry, the recording and interpreting of the findings, and oftentimes their organization for presentation to others. Reading becomes an essential part of a study situation when books and other printed materials form a valuable source of information and help. The purpose of reading in a study project and the steps that are involved depend upon the reader's needs. On some occasions, he may engage in general assimilative reading; on other occasions he may read rapidly to locate specific items of information or proceed very deliberately in order to apply the ideas apprehended to a problem situation. Whatever demands are made upon the pupil while engaged in the act of reading are here conceived as contributing to the total problem involved in teaching reading.

Inherent in the foregoing discussion is the conception that reading is also a form of experience that modifies personality. As pupils comprehend accurately, interpret broadly, and apply what they learn wisely, they acquire new understandings, broader interests, and deeper appreciations. Thus, personality is continually modified and enriched through reading. Furthermore, the fact is well known that reading, as well as other forms of experience, may produce various kinds of reaction—fear, ambition, appreciation, happiness, illness, action, critical thinking. Teachers should realize that such emotional responses are often aroused without adequate understanding on the part of the reader and that there may be decision and action without due consideration of all the facts involved. A properly conceived and intelligently directed reading program should reduce such responses to the minimum and should aid materially in developing a generation of citizens with social, stable, and enriched personalities. The fact is recognized that all children and young people will not rise to equal heights. It is essential, however, that everyone receive appropriate stimulus and guidance.

In adopting the broad conception of reading that has been discussed, the fact is recognized that many of the mental processes included are not confined to reading. In this report, therefore, reading is not conceived as a psychologically unique mental process but rather as a complex of mental activities having much in common with other complex operations and also some elements that are unique. The inclusion of the whole group of associated processes is justified by the fact that they make up an educationally coherent unit of organization.

The attainment of reading attitudes and habits, appropriate for contemporary needs, requires a much more comprehensive program of reading instruction than has been provided in the past. It will not be sufficient to plan merely for the development of habits that underlie accurate recognition, speed, and comprehension in silent reading, and fluent oral reading. Equally, if not more, important is the need for the development and refinement of habits of interpretation, critical evaluation, and the application of the facts apprehended. Since these processes are of primary importance in all curricular fields, appropriate guidance should be provided wherever reading aids in enriching experience, in stimulating thought, and in modifying personality.

III IMPORTANT TYPES AND PURPOSES OF READING

The nature of the instruction provided in reading depends not only upon the basic conception of reading adopted, but also upon the types and purposes of reading in which children and adults engage. Experiments show clearly, for example, that the specific habits involved in reading vary with such factors as the kinds of material read, their difficulty, and the reader's purpose. Furthermore, classroom studies justify the conclusion that where as some transfer of training occurs from one type of reading situation to another, the best guarantee of efficient reading habits lies in the provision of specific guidance in each. As an aid in identifying the major types and purposes of reading for which provision should be made in teaching, the results of a four-fold analysis will be presented.

1. Types of Reading with Respect to Its General Form

Two types of reading are easily distinguished; namely, silent reading and oral reading. Their general characteristics are so well known that they do not require a detailed description here. Both involve the recognition of symbols and the comprehension and interpretation of meaning by the reader. In addition, oral reading involves the interpretation to others of the thoughts, sentiments, and ideals expressed. Obviously, the oral interpretation of a given passage is a more complex process than the silent apprehension of its meaning. As revealed by laboratory studies, good oral reading utilizes all the basic attitudes and habits involved in efficient silent reading and, in addition, those that are essential in interpreting the content of a passage to others.

The life situations in which need arises for silent reading and oral reading are numerous and varied. Unfortunately, a scientifically derived list is not available. Use has been made, therefore, of a very suggestive list prepared recently by McKee.[5] Examples follow:

1. Situations in which one reads silently:

   a. Reading the newspaper to keep informed about current events.
   b. Reading a magazine or book of current fiction to idle away time or to relieve the strain of the day's work.
   c. Reading a book that has suddenly captured public interest.
   d. Reading excellent character portrayals to be better able to interpret human life and motives.
   e. Reading cartoons, jokes, and comical short stories for fun.
   f. Reading to understand a situation, such as why Brazil is the leading country in the production of coffee.
   g. Reading to secure information that will aid in the solution of a problem.
   h. Reading to form an opinion concerning a program or issue.

i. Reading to guide action; for example, what to do to cure a cold in the head.

j. Reading to become acquainted with the best work in a field, such as modern plays, or short stories.

2. Situations in which one reads orally:

a. Reading passages to others to support a position taken in class discussion.

b. Reading to give directions or instructions, such as the steps to be taken in reporting a fire.

c. Reading to provide general information, such as an illuminating news item.

d. Reading to recall past action, such as the minutes of a meeting.

e. Reading magazines or books to or with others for pleasure and enjoyment.

f. Reading a poem aloud to enjoy its rhythm more fully.

The foregoing list, which is far from complete, shows that both silent and oral reading meet vital needs in the lives of children and adults. *The Twenty-fourth Yearbook* rightly emphasized the importance of the former because of its greater social value, economy, and efficiency. As a result, increasingly wide provision for silent reading has been made during recent years in most school systems. The enthusiasm for it has been so great in many centers that provision for oral reading has been neglected, particularly above the primary grades. As a result, pupils have often been deprived of various values inherent in a well-conceived program including both silent and oral reading.

The great social value of silent reading has become more and more widely recognized during the last decade. Accordingly, the Yearbook Committee has endeavored in subsequent chapters to suggest ways and means of increasing the breadth and value of the guidance provided. The Committee is aware also that oral reading serves many practical needs both in and out of school and

that it possesses distinct possibilities in broadening the appreciational and cultural life of a people. In order to provide teachers with specific suggestions for improving oral reading, Chapter X has been prepared. The advisability of such a chapter lies in two facts; namely, the neglect of oral reading in many centers during the last decade, and the inadequacy of traditional methods of teaching it. The need is urgent today for an enriched reading program that retains and further emphasizes all the values inherent in intelligent silent reading and in addition secures economically and effectively the unique values that oral reading may contribute.

2. Types of Reading Based on the Reader's General Attitude

Two types of reading that are determined by the reader's general attitude were identified by the National Committee on Reading [7] in 1925; namely, "work-type" and "recreational." They were emphasized vigorously in the *Twenty-fourth Yearbook* on the assumption that they had either been neglected or sadly confused. As a result, rapid progress has been made during the last decade in providing appropriate emphasis on each. In retaining the distinction in this Yearbook no claim is made that work-type and recreational reading are mutually exclusive. As a matter of fact almost any book or selection may be read with different purposes by various readers or by the same reader on different occasions. Indeed, a reader's purpose or attitude may change during the course of the reading of a given selection or book. The distinction between "work-type" and "recreatory" reading, as presented in the 1925 report, may be reviewed here to advantage.

a. Work-Type Reading. "The work-type of reading is associated with the demands of our vocations, civic duties, and other phases of daily life. Such reading, it should be noted, is directed most often by relatively conscious and practical purposes. Thus, adults turn to professional, trade, or home-making journals to discover new and important items of information. Most people read news items, advertisements, editorials, and notices purposively, to direct action, to study current problems, and, if possible, to arrive at principles of conduct in civic and personal affairs."

Similarly, children engage in much the same sort of reading. Boys read and follow directions in the *Scout Manual* and books on radio, and girls read about campcraft, cooking, and sewing. "Children's magazines abound in puzzles, construction problems, and directions for various activities. Moreover, since schools are organized, in large part, for definite increase of knowledge, a great deal of the reading assigned there belongs primarily to the work type. Most lessons in history and civics, geography and other sciences, mathematics, and language require this kind of reading."

Typical situations that lead children and adults to reading of the work type are:

1. Crossing streets, finding stores and houses, and making longer journeys; reading signs, railroad folders, maps, road guides.
2. Understanding assignments and directions in both school and life activities.
3. Working out complicated problems or experiments: reading scout manuals, materials on radio, cookbooks, problems in arithmetic, or other textbooks and science manuals.
4. Finding or verifying spelling, pronunciation, meaning, use of words; using the dictionary, encyclopedia, and other reference books.
5. Gathering material for fuller understanding, for talking or writing on one's hobby, for assigned papers and discussions in school or club, and for experiments.
6. Informing or convincing others; reading aloud.
7. Finding out what is going on.

8. Deciding how to act in new situations.
9. Reaching conclusions as to guiding principles, relative values, or cause and effect.

b. Recreational Reading. Recreational reading "is associated with the wholesome enjoyment of leisure time." Two varieties of recreational reading are quite familiar.

One of these grows out of natural and useful curiosity about human nature and the condition of our lives. "Such curiosity begins with the child's first interest in stories and pictures, and continues increasingly through life. We want to know about the ways of animals and about strange countries and stars and times different from our own. A parallel concern is with pictures of things and happenings that are most familiar to us. Following on a quite opposite recreational track, we often seek mere enjoyment and rest through getting away from reality. Children's engrossment in fairy tales and tales of wonderland and nonsense is an example of this enjoyable kind of recreational reading. It is wholesome and harmless for all of us so long as it is not taken for reality."

Typical situations that lead children and adults to reading of the recreational type are:

1. Reliving common everyday experiences.
2. Seeking fun or sheer enjoyment during leisure time.
3. Enjoying sudden changes or sharp contrasts.
4. Getting away from real life.
5. Enjoying ready-made emotional reactions.
6. Satisfying natural and valuable curiosities about human nature and motives.
7. Giving pleasure to others.
8. Reading aloud parts of plays and dramatic dialogue.
9. Satisfying curiosity about animals, strange regions and times, and current happenings away from one's own environment.
10. Pursuing a hobby.

The importance of both work-type and recreational reading has increased conspicuously during the last decade. The enrichment of the course of study and the growing complexity of social life have greatly enlarged the demand for reading of the study type. Likewise, the need for diversion, enjoyable pastime, and the satisfaction of interests and curiosities has stimulated greater interest in recreational reading. By and large, the more versatile and broad one's interests, the more frequent the occasion for recreational reading. It is obvious that any reading program organized at this time should make adequate provision for both types of reading. In view of the fact that reading is described in this Yearbook under four classifications rather than one, the distinction between "work-type" and "recreational" reading does not receive so much emphasis in this report as in the 1925 report.

3. Types of Reading Based on Specific Purposes of the Reader

Types of reading can be classified, not only with respect to form and the reader's general attitude, but also with respect to the specific purposes that lead to reading on given occasions. For example, children read to find information relating to a problem or to follow detailed directions; adults read to understand a situation better or to determine the validity of arguments relating to a social issue. When the steps or processes involved in such reading activities are analyzed, significant differences are noted. It is obvious, for example, that the mental processes involved in reading to answer a question involving judgment are much more elaborate than in reading to answer a factual question. In the latter situation, one recognizes the various elements of meaning in a passage and identifies the particular word or phrase that answers the question. In reading to answer a question involving judgment, a greater amount of analysis, reflection, and organization of ideas is essential.

Such differences as the foregoing may be rapidly explained. When one reads for a given purpose, his attention is directed to certain meanings more than to others; furthermore, he is stimulated to use the facts apprehended in a particular way. On one occasion, for example, he merely remembers the facts apprehended well enough to report them in class. On another occasion, he reflects on the meaning of the statements read or applies them in the solution of problems. As revealed by laboratory studies made by Judd and Buswell,[4] changes in the purpose of reading result in differences in the mental processes involved in reading. The records they secured showed that many pupils are relatively unprepared to engage effectively in reading for various purposes. They rightly concluded that if the school is going to hold the pupil for specific responses to the printed page, it should "train him in methods of meeting its demands."

The number of specific purposes for which pupils read is surprisingly large. In perhaps the most elaborate study reported thus far, Hathaway[3] identified 1620 purposes of reading, which were classified under nine major headings; namely, "to gain meanings," "to gain information," "to guide activity," "for social motives" (that is, to influence or entertain others), "to find values," "to organize," "to solve problems," "to remember," "to enjoy."

When the specific purposes were ranked for usefulness by twenty-five judges, the following were among those ranking highest:

To satisfy an eagerness for knowledge.
To compare views on a subject.
To find illustrations of an idea.
To discover relationships.
To note the degree to which a thing is true.
To view two sides of a question.
To seek advice.

To attain an attitude of open-mindedness and ability to form a tentative judgment.
To entertain children.
To learn the opinions of a district upon a political issue.

The foregoing list has value only in suggesting the wide variety of purposes that were identified.

Studies of the purposes for reading in classrooms are equally illuminating. An effort to identify those which have been emphasized repeatedly in recent reports and investigations resulted in the following interesting list:

1. To find answers to specific questions.
2. To determine the author's aim or purpose
3. To find the central thought of a selection.
4. To follow a sequence of related events.
5. To enjoy the facts or story presented.
6. To find the most important points and supporting details.
7. To select facts which relate to a problem.
8. To judge the validity of statements.
9. To find facts supporting a point of view.
10. To draw valid conclusions from materials read.
11. To discover problems for additional study.
12. To remember what is read.
13. To determine the essential conditions of a problem.
14. To follow directions with reasonable speed and accuracy.

When the results of various studies are combined, three conclusions stand out clearly: first, reading is used for a surprisingly wide variety of purposes; second, the purposes of reading in one curricular field vary to a considerable extent from those in other fields; and third, the purposes change from one level of scholastic advancement to another. In view of the facts presented earlier, it is evident that teachers of all subjects from the primary grades to the university face a major responsibility in training pupils to engage effectively in the various types of reading activities in which they should participate.

4. Types of Reading Based on the Relation of the Ideas Involved

Types of reading may also be identified in terms of the relation of the ideas involved. For example, geography is often defined as the relation between natural environmental conditions and human activities. To read geographically, according to this definition, involves the interpretation of facts in terms of such relations. It follows that a child or an adult might read a geography merely for the facts presented; in that case he would not be interpreting its content geographically. It also follows that he might read and interpret geographically a newspaper article or a passage in a popular novel. Obviously we are thus brought to deal with types of reading that are determined by facts and by relations inherent in the materials read. Such reading can be cultivated best under the expert guidance of teachers in the various curricular fields.

In order to exemplify further important differences in the relations involved in reading material, reference will be made next to the fields of history and sociology. In discussing these two fields, Fling [2] points out that "all past social facts are not necessarily historical facts." A social fact becomes "an historical fact when it has been made a part of an historical synthesis." . . . As limited to human affairs, history concerns itself with the "unique evolution of man in his activities as a social being." It follows that one who interprets historically is concerned with specific kinds of relations between the facts presented and must carry on corresponding chains of thinking while reading. If, on the contrary, "we are interested in *what past social facts have in common,* in the way in which *social facts repeat themselves,* if our purpose is to form *generalizations,* or *laws* concerning social activities, we employ another logical method, the method of the natural sciences. . . . The result of our work is sociology, not history." Specialists in these fields may take exception to the definitions quoted. The purpose here is not to defend the validity of a specific definition. The examples quoted serve their purpose if they indicate that the two fields involve different kinds of relationships and therefore require different modes of interpretation.

Distinctions similar to those already pointed out may be made in the case of most curricular fields. Not infrequently, as in the case of English, various types of interpretation are required in the materials studied; for example, fiction, argumentation, drama. Furthermore, the material presented in one field should often be interpreted in the light of the relationships emphasized in other fields. For example, the facts presented in a history should often be interpreted geographically or mathematically, and the facts presented in a geography should be interpreted in terms of their economic or historical significance. Teachers should identify the types of relations that are involved in specific fields and should provide guidance in developing appropriate habits of interpretation.

We are now prepared to point out a major difference between the responsibilities of the teacher of reading and the teacher of the content fields in promoting desirable reading habits. The teacher of reading is responsible for developing the basic attitudes and habits that underlie all reading activities or are common to the various curricular fields. The teachers of the content fields are responsible not only for guidance, as needed, in applying basic reading habits to their respective fields, but, in addition, for developing and refining the various modes of thinking and interpretation involved in these fields. Only through a clear recognition of such responsibilities will adequate guidance in reading be provided during the next decade.

IV CONCLUDING STATEMENTS

The facts presented in this chapter show clearly that reading is a varied and highly complex process. In order to provide adequately for the needs of child and adult life, the definition of reading adopted by the Committee includes not only the processes involved in recognition and comprehension, but also those involved in interpretation and application. The analysis of types of reading in which persons engage both in and out of school shows that reading assumes different forms and that it varies with the reader's general attitude, with specific purposes for reading, and with the kind of material read. Its varied nature has been described in impressive terms by Judd and Buswell [4] as a result of a detailed laboratory analysis of silent reading. The printed page is the source, according to them

of a mass of impressions which the active mind begins to organize and arrange with reference to some pattern which it is trained to work out. If the mind is fitting together the impressions so as to bring into high relief grammatical distinctions, the grouping of words and the distribution of emphasis will be according to one pattern. If the mind is intent on something wholly different from grammar, as, for example, the experiences which the author is trying to picture, the whole mental and physical attitude of the reader will be very different. . . . The grammatical attitude is not the same as the attitude of reading for understanding a scene; nor are the grammatical attitude and the drama attitude interchangeable parts of a single mental complex. . . . Mental life is a complex of organized attitudes, not a collection of mechanical associations.

One of the important conclusions the foregoing explanation justifies is that the task of teaching reading is by no means a simple one. It involves not only vigorous effort on the part of teachers of reading but also of teachers of every curricular field. The fact is also apparent that satisfactory results cannot be attained easily or quickly. It is true that maturity in basic habits of recognition and comprehension is often acquired by the end of the sixth grade. However, the attainment of the necessary background and the mental habits involved in reading different kinds of material for different purposes comes only as a result of wide experience and carefully planned guidance extending throughout the elementary, secondary, and college periods.

The problem of helping pupils attain an adequate grasp of the meaning of given passages is complicated by a series of factors or conditions, such as: (1) the inherent nature and difficulty of the concepts with which the passage deals; (2) the adequacy with which the concepts are presented through the language of the text; and (3) the reader's ability, including his intelligence, experience, interest, and command of reading habits. Such factors merit intensive study in every classroom in order that necessary adjustments may be made and conditions favorable to rapid progress established.

In adopting the broader conception of reading that has been outlined, the Committee recognizes that it is impossible at present to provide a complete and detailed program for realizing all the values suggested. It is willing to accept the criticisms that arise from such limitations. The Committee is unanimous in its judgment, however, that a broad definition of reading should be adopted if instruction is to provide adequately for contemporary needs. In the chapters that follow, numerous constructive suggestions are offered that aim to promote the development of desirable types of reading attitudes and habits. Through creative effort in the classroom and laboratory, the program outlined should be improved and refined rapidly during the next few years.

REFERENCES

1. Book, William F., "Analysis of the Task of Learning To Read," *Journal of Educational Research,* Vol. 21, 1930, p. 2.
2. Fling, Fred Morrow, *The Writing of History: An Introduction to Historical Method.* New Haven: Yale University Press, 1920, Chapter 1.
3. Hathaway, Gladys M., "Purposes for Which People Read: A Technique for Their Discovery," *University of Pittsburgh School of Education Journal,* Vol. 4, 1929, pp. 83-9.
4. Judd, Charles H., and Buswell, Guy T., *Silent Reading: A Study of the Various Types,* Supplementary Educational Monographs, No. 23, Chicago: Department of Education, University of Chicago, 1922, pp. 4-5, 44-5.

5. McKee, Paul, *Reading and Literature in the Elementary School.* Boston: Houghton Mifflin Company, 1932, pp. 48-55.
6. Pyle, William H., *The Psychology of the Common Branches.* Baltimore: Warwick and York, 1930, p. 77.
7. *Report of the National Committee on Reading,* The Twenty-fourth Yearbook of this Society, Part 1, Bloomington, Ill.: Public School Publishing Company, 1925, pp. 4-8.
8. Wheat, Harry G., *The Psychology of the Elementary School.* Newark, N. J.: Silver Burdett and Company, 1931, p. 234.

6: Reading Instruction and Existential Philosophy *

STANLEY KRIPPNER

Being a pragmatic people, Americans are more concerned with how than why—how to teach Johnny to read rather than why to teach Johnny to read. As a result, Americans have devoted more attention to the comparative virtues of the "phonics method" and the "sight method" than to such problems as censorship, propaganda, and the estimate that fewer than one out of every five Americans ever buys a book.[21] Existential philosophy, with its emphasis upon man's attempt to find meaningful purposes in life, can be of great assistance in evaluating and improving reading instruction.

Contemporary educational philosophy is purportedly based upon the writings of William James and John Dewey, who are associated with the "pragmatic" school of thought. Like James and Dewey, the existential philosophers oppose "rationalistic" thinking which equates reality with the object of thought (or "essence") rather than with actual experience. According to Tillich,[29] both the pragmatists and the existentialists regard man's immediate experience as revealing more completely the nature of reality than does his cognitive experience. Kierkegaard,[14] a nineteenth-century existential philosopher, proclaimed that truth exists for the individual only as he himself produces it in action; this stand also characterizes pragmatic thought.

However, existentialism differs from pragmatism in several ways. To Dewey, value dwells within one's experience, while to the existentialist it is the individual alone who creates value. Fact and value are an irresolvable dichotomy.[15] Furthermore, the pragmatic approach allows for individuality, but only insofar as society tolerates individual differences. However, existentialism invariably stresses the individual's transcendence of his culture, not adjustment to it.[1, 15] There is no "group consensus" in existentialism; group dynamics are not used to illustrate the superiority of group decisions over individual decisions.[22] Finally, there is a tendency among pragmatically oriented teachers to view the child in terms of the social or statistical norm, in terms of his place on a normal distribution scale. To the existentialist, such a comparison would be unfair as the child must always be viewed as a completely unique being-in-the-world, as an entity in his own right. When Kierkegaard concentrated on portraying the single phenomenon rather than speculating on the universal, he formed the basis of all existential thinking since his time.[15]

Kierkegaard and his followers were in revolt against many basic characteristics of Western philosophy. May [18] describes the existential approach in this historical setting.

Existentialism, in short, is the endeavor to understand man by cutting below the cleavage between subject and object which has bedeviled Western thought and science since shortly after the Renaissance. . . . Traditionally, in Western thought "existence" has been set over against "essence." Essence refers to the greenness of this stick of wood, let us say, and its density, weight, and other characteristics which give it substance. By and large Western

* Written especially for inclusion in this volume.

thought since the Renaissance has been concerned with essences. . . . The search for essences may indeed produce highly significant universal laws in science or brilliant abstract conceptualizations in logic or philosophy. But it can only do it by abstraction. The *existence* of the given individual thing has to be left out of the picture. . . . And the crucial question which confronts us in psychology and other aspects of the science of man is precisely this chasm between what is *abstractly true* and what is *existentially real* for the given living person.

The fundamental contribution of existential thought to education is its understanding of man as *being*.[1] Our grasping of the being of a child occurs on quite a different level from our knowledge of specific things about him. We might know that the child has a hearing loss, an older sister, and an IQ of 91 on the Stanford-Binet. Yet, these are all facts *about* the child. If we work with him merely on the basis of these isolated bits of data, we overlook the reality of the child as a whole, his uniqueness, and his being. To the existentialist, therefore, the child is a functioning individual, not a statistical norm.

Existentialism stresses the continuous development of the child. What one is today is not what he will be tomorrow. German existential writers use the term "Dasien" which means to stand out, to emerge, to become. Sartre [27] insists that man's existence precedes his essence; man exists before his purpose is achieved. Therefore, man is always free to make choices. With each choice he stakes his future. Education, therefore, should help the child make wise choices so that he can develop his potentialities to their maximum extent. With this in mind, Nietzsche [24] calls upon each individual to ". . . become who you are." For Nietzsche, self-perfection is the highest principle of education.[12] To perfect himself, man must come to terms with himself and his world. To Kneller,[15] the willingness "to face unabashed,

naked if you will, the problem and meaning of human existence as individual existence is the central motive force and allure which characterize existentialist philosophy."

THE CHILD AS BEING-IN-THE-WORLD

Van Kaam [30] sees man as a "relatively free subject-pole which interacts with his culture." Arbuckle [1] also stresses the interaction between man and his phenomenological world; "there can not be one without the other." However, man stands out from his world; the term "existence" comes from the Latin root *ex sistere,* meaning to stand out or emerge. The existential educator must view the child as being; he must understand the child's phenomenological world so as better to encourage the child's emergence and growth.

Some writers have questioned the suitability of many basal readers for children of minority groups or of limited cultural backgrounds. How can a child from this type of background identify with the boy or girl in the basal reader who lives in a single-family home, plays in a spacious backyard, and who has attractive suburban parents who spend considerable time in family recreation, including trips to grandfather's farm?

The staff of the Maury School in Richmond, Virginia, has reacted to this problem by utilizing experience charts as the basis of the instructional program in reading. The author, as a member of the city's special education team, had an opportunity to observe this program in action and saw first-graders from low socio-economic backgrounds transform their experiences into words and paragraphs. Their games, their flights, their triumphs, and their frustrations were all recorded in the huge collection of stories which accumulated during the year. Word-attack and comprehension skills were based on the emerging material. Despite the extremely limited background of these pupils, standardized reading tests showed them to be keeping up with pupils in other schools. In addition, as the Maury staff has emphasized, these children made progress in many cultural and social areas not measured by tests.

The success of the Maury program is due to its concern with the child as being-in-the-world. The child's environment, his reaction to that environment, and his transcendence of the environment are all graphically recorded on the experience charts. To impose a basal reader upon these pupils would be the epitome of an essence-oriented approach, one which is centered not on the child but on the body of knowledge which is to be mastered.

The basic existential condition of pupils has also been perceived by Ashton-Warner,[2] who has worked with lower socio-economic class children in New Zealand. Her program of reading instruction is based on the conviction that ". . . words must have intense meaning for a child. They must be part of his being." [2]

Every day, Ashton-Warner asks each pupil what word he wants to learn, writes it on a large piece of cardboard, gives it to the child for the day, reviews it the next morning, and places it in a box along with other words. Eventually, the box contains enough words so that the child can write his own story. Gradually, his stories accumulate into a book.

. . . these first books . . . must be made out of the stuff of the child itself. I reach a hand into the mind of the child, bring out a handful of the stuff I find there, and use that as our first working material. Whether it is good or bad stuff, violent or placid stuff, colored or dun.[2]

Out push these words. . . . It's a lovely flowering. I see the creative channel swelling and undulating like an artery with blood pumping through. And as it settles, just like any other organic arrangement of nature it spreads out into a harmonious pattern; the fear words dominating the design, a few sex words, the person interest, and the temper of the century. Daddy, Mummy, ghost, bomb, kiss, brothers, butcher knife, goal, love, dance, cry, fight, hat, bulldog, touch, wild piggy. . . . If you were a child, which vocabulary would you prefer? Your own or . . . Come John come. Look John look. Come and look.[2]

Ashton-Warner stores the cardboard words in a large box. Each morning, the children collect their own words and read them to a partner. While they are teaching each other, Ashton-Warner has individual conferences with each child during which he reviews the old words and gets his new word for the day. Soon the children begin to copy their words and before long they are creating stories. The children master their own stories first, then go on to read the stories of other children. If a word causes trouble, it is supplied by the writer of that story. These stories are the basis for spelling, grammar, punctuation, and handwriting, as well as reading.

A transition is eventually made to commercially produced books but creative writing is continued. In this way, each child's own existential situation is at the core of his learning and is the first consideration in constructing the bridges he needs to expand his knowledge.

Ashton-Warner attempts to deal with the total being of the child; although she emphasizes his creative channels, she does not ignore the fact that destructive tendencies exist. Emphasis upon the education of emotions is urged by existentialists. Morris [22] notes that pragmatists stress the inculcation of the scientific method as an approach to problem-solving. "Existentialists, while no doubt providing room for this kind of teaching, will be more interested in developing the effective side of man, his capacity to love, to appreciate, to respond emotionally to the world about him."

To the existential philosopher, man is capable of making personal choices. Although his actions are heavily influenced by heredity and environment, there is always the potentiality of free will—of man choosing a course of action, committing himself to that course, and involving himself in it. To Nietzsche, the schools have no more important task than to teach children to exercise the "will to mastery" through vigorous thinking.[13] This position is reflected in Witty's description of developmental reading.[32]

A developmental reading program will recognize the value of continuous, systematic instruction, utilization of interests, fulfillment of developmental needs, and the articulation of reading experience with other types of worthwhile activity. The chief aim of this program will be to help pupils become skillful, self-reliant, and independent readers, who will continue to enrich their understandings and satisfactions through life by reading. At all stages, reading as a thinking process will be cultivated.

Some writers have seen a "personalized" approach as the best means of implementing a truly developmental reading program. To Barbe[3] a personalized approach encourages the maximum amount of growth for each pupil because the program is adjusted to the child, rather than the child to the program. Personalized reading, therefore, is existence-oriented rather than essence-oriented; existence is solidly placed before essence.

In personalized reading, formal instruction is essential,[3] differentiating it from so-called "individualized" approaches, many of which do away with basal readers and class instruction. The personalized approach is consistent with the existential point of view which stresses mastery of the basic curriculum in order to give the pupil a base for individual creative effort.[15]

Other aspects of the personalized approach are existentially sound. A Socratic encounter is encouraged in frequent one-to-one sessions between the pupil and his teacher. Decision-making is required of each pupil in the self-selection of reading materials. Commitment is necessary as the child announces his favorite stories and even brings books of his own to school to share with others. Progress is at the child's own rate and a natural "seeking" process is allowed to operate.

Skill instruction is provided at the level at which the child is reading. Arbuckle[1] says, "We can both run. But we can not both run as fast or as far. This does not mean that you are any less free to run than I am." The analogy to reading is clear; the less advanced reader is as worthy of our attention as the more advanced reader. Both share the basic freedom to learn, to progress, and to select the reading material that will aid their development.

A non-personalized, essence-oriented approach to reading would invariably present the various skills in a formal setting, would minimize the importance of interest, and would stress *how* to read rather than the immediate, meaningful experience of reading itself. Grouping would be based on such abstractions as IQ or age rather than on such existential conditions as personal interests, deficient skills, and individual choices. In personalized reading, groups must be kept flexible as needs and interests are in constant flux. One week a pupil might be a member of a group reading cowboy stories while the next week his interest might switch to outer space, necessitating a group re-assignment. One pupil might be assigned to a group studying context clues; upon mastery of this skill, at a certain level, the pupil might be shifted to a group receiving phonics instruction.

Abstract labels such as "high," "medium," and "low" would not be applied to groups by an existence-oriented teacher. Even such terms as "robins," "bluebirds," and "sparrows" invite invidious comparisons. Call a child a "sparrow" in the first grade and he may remain a "sparrow" for the rest of his life! The personalized approach to reading groups is described by Barbe.[3]

Personalized reading is essentially a means whereby children read from material which they have selected themselves. Once about every three days, the child comes to the teacher and she checks to see how he is progressing in his reading. If he is having difficulty in attacking certain words, or comprehending the material, the teacher then groups him with other children having the same type of difficulty and teaches them as a group.... The groups are established by the teacher each day, with no group staying in existence for more than two or three days. A group is formed only for a specific purpose and is disbanded as soon as this purpose has been accomplished.

Barbe has presented reading skill check lists to aid the teacher in a personalized situation and has described ways in which basal readers may be utilized in a personalized setting. To Witty,[32] this approach gives an opportunity for "... the creative child or the gifted pupil to explore his interests and to develop his background through reading." The principle of self-selection has special relevance here since its use may permit the expression of the developmental gifts.

The existential emphasis upon freedom of choice is also of importance in understanding certain types of poor readers. A recurring problem in first-grade classrooms is the child who is socially immature and who lacks personal competence. Perhaps the child comes from a home background in which his

parents hang up his clothes, pick up his toys, drive him to school, and make excuses for his shortcomings.[10] This child's basic problems are existential. He is incapable of making decisions, of working independently, of committing himself in the learning situation. This child, perhaps, will never become an independent reader as long as he avoids responsibility and depends upon the decisions of others.

Another type of existential problem is manifested by a number of children who lack conscious control over their actions. The behavior of the brain-injured child is often influenced by his impaired neurological state. The activity of a neurotic or pre-psychotic child is distorted by unconscious drives and forces. The destructive actions of a sociopathic child are often due to a basic character disorder; as a result, he can not enter into an "I-Thou" relationship with other people and can not commit himself to long-range goals. Mentally retarded children sometimes lack the intellectual capacity for decision-making. The brain-injured, emotionally disturbed, and retarded children will often do better in a classroom situation which is highly structured and tightly disciplined as they can not cope with the freedom offered by a more permissive educational setting.

THE EXISTENTIAL ENCOUNTER

To the existentialist, the teacher's role is extremely important. Although the learning experience centers around the child rather than around the teacher, he must always be present to assist the emerging child. The teacher must never forget that his real purpose in the classroom is to educate somebody else.[15] To do this, the existential "I-Thou" relationship is encouraged between pupil and teacher, a relationship in which one person commits himself to the education of another and constantly risks himself as he attempts to achieve this goal.

Gans [6] describes how teachers can capitalize on the existential moment to produce valuable learnings. One teacher placed the names "Barry" and "Benny" on locker doors and used the name similarity as the basis for a lesson in phonics. To an imaginative teacher, names are filled with phonic teaching potentiality because a child not only wants to learn how to read and write his name but also has an emotional investment in it.

Most six-year-olds have a strong interest in their own names. The phonic elements common to several children's names may be the basis for a talk in the first week of school. One first grade had six *J* names: Janey, Jean, Jill, Jimmy, Joan, and John —a bonanza for the alert teacher.

The teacher must always seek ways of stressing immediacy of experience in the existence-oriented classroom. This results from such practices as the writing of experience stories, the sharing of personal books with classmates, the critical analysis of story content, and the adaptation of reading materials in the light of personal interests. Witty [32] insists that the curriculum be developed "in accord with the child's needs, interests, and problems if it is to have maximum significance and application." To provide strong motives for learning, teachers should utilize children's interests. The Witty Diagnostic Record [33] includes an interest inventory which can quickly give a teacher insight into a child's hobbies, collections, travel experiences, favorite games, televiewing habits, and reading preferences.

The pupil's growth in reading results from his existential encounter with reading materials as well as his personal experiences with his teacher and peers. If used properly, programed instruction can serve existential purposes as it permits a direct encounter between the pupil and subject matter. In addition, it emphasizes the process of choice and allows each child to proceed at his own rate. As one part of a balanced reading program, self-instructional devices may be used as independent or supplemental material to reinforce previous learnings or to cultivate a wider range of reading interests and skills.

Programed workbooks permit the young learner to make a response which he can easily check against the correct answer. Word attack and comprehension skills are broken down into small units so that a step-by-step learning process is possible. As each item is built upon what was previously learned, the pupil usually meets with success as he proceeds with the material.

For a true existential encounter to occur in a learning situation, the pupil must abandon the role of spectator. The classroom experience must be so interesting and vital to him that he takes an active part in the process.

The existential world is in fact a stage and all those who really want to know the doctrine for themselves will have to live in this world as players, each with his own entrances and exits, each with his own drama of life to enact.[15]

To encourage an active role for the learner, skills in reading must not be emphasized to the neglect of meaning. It is important that a child master such word recognition skills as phonics, context, structural analysis, visual cues, and dictionary usage. However, many word-by-word readers recognize each word but have little idea of what they have read.

For this reason, expression and intonation should be integrated into oral reading sessions if they are to be made meaningful. McKee [20] states, "Since this problem lies at the heart of ... beginning reading, it is imperative that the child be directed and helped to read lines as he would speak them or as he thinks he would hear them if they were spoken to him."

Without the integration of meaning into the reading process, the pupil's curiosity needs will not be satisfied, reading will lack vitality, and the enjoyment of books will never become a part of the child's behavioral repertoire. If basal material seems too insipid for a child, it should be supplemented by other material. Adventure and fantasy could, perhaps, be given a more significant place in beginning reading; stories about dragons and rocket ships cut across more class-lines than the so-called "real-life" accounts of a suburban Rick, Rose, and Rover. In addition, this type of tale would appeal more strongly to boys, from whose ranks come most of our disabled readers. The existence-oriented teacher subscribes to Woodring's injunction [34] that "Reading should be an elevating experience—one that permits the spirit to soar."

EXISTENCE BEFORE ESSENCE

Arbuckle [1] regrets that our culture has set up essence above existence. "Essence is the emphasis on immutable principles, truth, logical laws, etc., that are supposed to stand above any given existence." Under an essence-oriented teacher, the basal reading program can become the apotheosis of an approach which ignores existence. A teacher who follows lesson-plans religiously, making no adaptation for individual differences, is creating a Procrustean bed, stretching and slicing those pupils who do not fit. In a similar way, programs which utilize one exclusive method (phonics, linguistics, "look-and-say") or device (the film-strip projector, the teaching machine, the controlled reader) are essence-oriented.

An example of existence before essence is Great Britain's celebrated Summerhill School. Neill [23] writes that the main concept behind Summerhill is to make the school fit the child rather than making the child fit the school.

Lessons at Summerhill are optional; children can go to class or stay away. Grouping is based on mutual interests. No tests are given but the required subjects are taught and pupils are prepared for the nationally organized set standard examinations should they want to attend college. Teachers at Summerhill emphasize the child's motivation for learning rather than a specific teaching method.

We have no new methods of teaching, because we do not consider that teaching in itself matters very much. Whether a school has or has not a special method for teaching long division is of no significance, for long division is of no importance except to those who *want* to learn it. And the child who *wants* to learn it *will* learn it no matter how it is taught.[23]

In recent years, an American version of Summerhill has been organized. Named Summerlane, the school utilizes a linguistic approach to reading instruction but emphasizes the importance of "reading to learn" over "learning to read."

General Linguistics is usually reserved for graduate courses in college. We find, however, that children naturally break language down, turn it about, modify it, turn it inside out, and seek ways of arranging it meaningfully. Reading and writing skills are developed as tools with which to handle much more exciting material.[28]

The policy statement for Summerlane emphasizes that the reading material of its pupils should never be regulated or censored. This is in sharp contrast to public school administrators who, in recent years, have banned such books as *Huckleberry Finn, Brave New World, To Kill a Mockingbird,* and *1984.* The censor is necessarily essence-centered as he feels that there is a dividing line between "safe" and "dangerous" books. Furthermore, he feels that he is able to draw that line and that he can predict the appalling results that will follow the reading of "dangerous" literary materials.

The Summerhill and Summerlane approach has aroused great controversy. However, Rogers [26] reminds us that "... the only learning which significantly influences behavior is self-discovered, self-appropriated learning." Rogers admits that the implications of this statement are revolutionary because they include a de-emphasis of examinations, grades, credits, and degrees, but an increased emphasis on direct experience —on *learning* instead of on *teaching*.

THE EXISTING PERSON

May [16] warns the existentialist not to ignore essences completely. They are of extreme importance in understanding logic, mathematics, and other aspects of truth which are not dependent upon individual decision. However, the existing person can never be understood on an essentialist basis. Maximum growth in the classroom does not occur if it is essence-oriented.

If the basic existential situation of each first-grade pupil is to be considered, multiple methods are necessary in reading instruction. A recent study by Durrell clearly demonstrates the wisdom of this position.[25] Durrell compared the results of reading instruction in Lynnfield, Massachusetts, with the results of instruction in "Town X."

In Lynnfield, during the first week of school, every pupil was tested to determine his familiarity with letters, his ability to identify sounds in words, and his rate of learning sight words. Reading instruction was based on these results; readiness work was skipped for children who were ready to read. Pupils were started on library reading as soon as they were ready for it.

In Lynnfield, pupils with poor auditory perception were given ear training; those with poor visual perception were given help in letter knowledge. Phonics were introduced from the beginning as were whole word methods so as to emphasize meaning. A basal reader was used with children being paired into teams for self-directed lessons and mutual aid.

Back in Town X, the children were engaged in reading readiness, following the basal reader lessons at a steady pace, and taking turns in a large group with no provision for mutual aid. The boys and girls were divided into three ability groups: the "robins," the "bluebirds," and the "sparrows."

The teachers in Town X had background and training similar to those in Lynnfield. The average IQ of the 202 Lynnfield pupils was 106 while the average IQ of the 196 children in Town X was 114. Class size was similar in both school systems.

At the end of the first grade, 51 per cent of the Lynnfield pupils were reading above the third-grade level. Only 5 per cent of Town X pupils did this well. None of the Lynnfield children ranked below a 1.5 grade level while 28 per cent of the Town X pupils fell that low. The average reading achievement grade for Lynnfield, as measured by standardized tests, was 3.2 versus 1.9 for Town X. This dramatic study shows the superiority of an approach emphasizing the existential condition of each pupil rather than the essence of the subject matter.

Woodring [34] strikes an existential chord when he states that teachers should feel free to use whatever methods they find most successful—and accept responsibility for the results. For Woodring, there is "no *one* correct or sound method of learning to read. Successful teachers have always employed a variety of methods, children have learned to read in many different ways, and many bright children can read before they enter school."

The existential approach to education takes the child where he is, allowing for the widest possible range of individual differences. For example, Wepman [31] finds that many first-graders are primarily "visual learners" while others are primarily "auditory learners." Visual learners are typified by excellent visual acuity, visual discrimination, visual memory, visual closure, visual-motor coordination, and revisualization skills. Various "sight," "look-and-say," or "whole word" methods work well with these children. On the other hand, auditory learners are predisposed to successful learning experiences through phonics because of their advanced auditory skills.

Ben was seen at the Kent State University Child Study Center when he was in the third grade. Despite above average intelligence, he was not achieving in reading and his teacher had decided to retain him. Diagnostic evaluation revealed that Ben was an auditory learner, with excellent auditory acuity, auditory discrimination, auditory memory, auditory blending, and reauditorization skills. However, the school's reading program stressed "sight" methods; phonics were not to be utilized until the latter part of third grade.

In an attempt to assist Ben, tutoring was inaugurated at the Child Study Center. Phonics was introduced and Ben learned rapidly through the new approach. At the same time, a program of visual training was initiated to improve his poor visual memory and other deficient visual skills. Within six months, Ben's reading ability had improved to such an extent that he was dismissed from the Center.

Ben is an example of a boy who suffered from an essence-oriented reading program. The decision had been made that phonics were not to be introduced in first or second grade, the assumption

being that all pupils would benefit from this decision. No consideration was given to children as they actually exist with different patterns of ability requiring a multiplicity of materials and a variety of techniques.

It comes as no surprise to the existentialist that research demonstrates that auditory learners do poorly in an exclusive "sight" approach to reading.[4] By the same token, visual learners do poorly when phonics are overemphasized.[5] The existence-oriented reading program must utilize several approaches to release the potentialities of young learners. In commenting on this concern with the existing person, Harper [8] states that ". . . no other philosophy has taken the self and its situation seriously enough to make that situation the subject matter of inquiry." As a result, "No philosopher today is more concerned with education . . . than an existential philosopher." [8]

THE INDIVISIBLE CHILD

Tests would be de-emphasized in existential education. Arbuckle [1] feels that testing operates on the assumption that one can cut man into bits and pieces, segregating and isolating parts of him. However, intelligence can not really be isolated from the rest of the person. Nor can interests be isolated, nor school achievement, nor personality traits. May [17] reminds us that existence is indivisible; the human being, to the existentialist, is also indivisible.

Tests often serve a useful purpose in suggesting what reading skills a child needs to master or what reading level he has attained. However, too many teachers give group intelligence tests and, for the rest of the year, think of Joan as "the girl with the 72 IQ" and of James as "the boy with the 148 IQ." Whether or not Joan's test score is valid, the essence-oriented teacher will react to Joan as she would to a hypothetical "72 IQ child." Harper [8] prescribes a corrective to the essentialist view of the child.

Existentialism is concerned about the unfolding of the individual as a whole in the situation in which he finds himself. This implies two things: first, that there is some sense in speaking of the individual as a whole . . . and, second, that individuals cannot be considered independently of their situation.

Many educators claim to consider "the whole child" as they design a program in reading instruction. Yet, how many of them consider the basic psychological and physiological integrities that must be present before reading instruction can be effective? If a child has poor visual or auditory skills, special perceptual training might be in order. If he does not follow reading material from left to right, directional orientation may be needed. If his attention span is short, training in listening may be advisable. If his personal vocabulary is meager, he may need enrichment experiences. Perhaps there is no desire to learn how to read due to social, emotional, or environmental handicaps. Perhaps endocrinal deficiencies have sapped the energy he should be devoting to the learning task. Perhaps a central nervous system problem exists and has never been corrected.

Don had been retained in the first grade before he was seen at the Kent State University Child Study Center. Diagnostic evaluation, including a neurological examination, revealed a desire to learn, adequate mental ability, an absence of brain damage, and a fine cultural background. However, Don had not achieved lateral dominance, could not identify the left and right sides of his body, and made frequent reversals in words and letters.

Don's parents had been giving him extra work every evening with flash cards and phonic records. They were told to stop this practice and to begin a program of neurological training. Under the direction of the Center, Don's parents took him through a series of exercises described by Getman [7] including crawling, creeping, balancing, body image development, dominance training, and directional orientation. Following three months of this work, remedial reading was initiated at the Center with a strong emphasis on perceptual training, visual-motor coordination, and left-to-right progression. The home exercises were continued so as to provide a solid neurological base for the utilization of printed symbols.

Two months later, Don was in the top reading group at his school and was dismissed from the Center. The young boy's success was the result of a diagnostic and remedial approach that considered his neurological being as well as his educational being.

TESTING THE INNER LIFE

For the existence-oriented teacher, reading is basically an existential act. Ideally, the reader will re-create what the author discloses. In so doing, he risks himself; the message of the writer may challenge the reader's beliefs and test his inner life.

To prepare the pupil for a truly existential encounter with reading material, several steps may be taken by the teacher. Initially, the child must understand that he is not "reading" unless he understands the meaning embodied in the group of letters he identifies. The child must realize that a printed word stands for a spoken word and that a spoken word stands for a thing or event. The word is never the thing itself. However, by bringing his own experiences to the printed page, the pupil can, hopefully, re-create the writer's meaning.

The child's desire for books of his own should be encouraged. As he selects a book, he commits himself and reveals himself. Therefore, his personal library should proclaim to the world the individual that he is.

McCracken[19] notes that in classes using his textfilm approach to reading, conversation naturally ensues and "It is common practice in these classes for the pupils guided by the teacher, to arrive at group decisions. This is learning in its finest form." Existentialists would take violent exception to this practice and McCracken's evaluation of it as "learning in its finest form."

The teacher must always attempt a penetration into the inner life of the child in order for growth to take place. In the moment that the teacher encounters the child there should be a merging, a fusion that will permit the greatest possible interplay of ideas. Like the teaching method of Socrates, instruction should be an "I-Thou" affair in which knowledge and wisdom are achieved through mutual interaction.[15]

However, the existentialist also places great importance on the curriculum, on the body of word recognition and comprehension skills that is to be mastered. Not only does the curriculum present the child with a body of knowledge to be explored but it gives him a firm foundation for later creative effort. The creative writer needs to know grammar, the poet must be aware of sentence structure, the orator must have an adequate vocabulary, and the individual who reads and writes for recreation needs a basic background in imagery, spelling, and literary criticism. Kneller[15] sees the existential approach to curriculum as differing from other contemporary approaches.

No matter what the pragmatist, the instrumentalist, or the progressivist does with the curriculum, his point of departure is always a social norm; he constantly bears in mind the psychological order of subject-matter presentation and accepts from sociology and other studies what findings are compatible with his concept of learning through critical experience. His measurement of the learning acquired is based on adjustment to growth norms universally agreed upon.... The trouble with the pragmatic, instrumentalist method is that its progenitors are living denials of what they understand to be the foundation of truth.... Did not Dewey arrive at his understanding of truth through an analysis of a personal crisis?

A child who develops into a capable reader will find that the reading process is a basic part of his phenomenological world. This would be the end result of an education that has stressed not only *how* to read, but *why* to read. Critical reading is indispensable if he is to make decisions concerning political candidates and election issues. Reading for information demands that he understand the author's existential framework while recreational reading requires a personal commitment to certain esthetic values and standards.

If independent reading is a part of the adult's behavioral repertoire, he will reject censorship of reading material as anti-existential in nature and a denial of personal freedom. Rather, he will see the classroom and the home as arenas where the level of personal taste can be raised and where a variety of wholesome interests can be developed.

As the adult reads for a basic understanding of his inner nature, of his fellows, and of his world, he will comprehend, interpret, and react. Reading involves sensing and perceiving printed verbal symbols, achieving meaning from them, and reacting to them.[9] A wise teacher prepares his pupils for these more advanced stages in the reading process. The teacher that is existence-oriented sees reading as an existential act which negates the boundary between subject (the reader) and object (the printed page), enabling something new to emerge from the encounter.

It should not be thought that existential concepts have been universally accepted in this country. Existential philosophy has been welcomed by only a handful of educators, psychologists, and psychiatrists since its introduction to America. It has aroused considerable criticism. Wolstein,[35] for example, believes that it has failed in its attempts to become a philosophy of experience and others have questioned its right to invade the provinces of education.

CONCLUSION

Two recent novels present examples of the existence-oriented and the essence-oriented approaches to education. Aldous Huxley's *Island* [12] describes a modern-day utopia in which the basic educational question is, "What are boys and girls for?" A visitor to the island is told that America sees its children as future consumers while Russia trains its children to strengthen the national state. On the island, children are for actualization, "for being turned into full-blown human beings." The injunction to island children is, "Become what you really are."

The visitor is told that the island's "first business is elementary education, and elementary education has to deal with individuals in all their diversity of shape, size, temperament, gifts, and deficiencies." Sense training is emphasized, talent is identified, and emotionality as well as the intellect is developed. Instruction is based on individual differences.

And how does he do his thinking and perceiving and remembering? Is he a visualizer or a non-visualizer? Does his mind work with images or with words, with both at once or with neither? How close to the surface is his storytelling faculty? Does he see the world as Wordsworth and Traherne saw it when they were children? And, if so, what can be done to prevent the glory and the freshness from fading into the light of common day? Or, in more general terms, how can we educate children on the conceptual level without killing their capacity for intense non-verbal experience?

A different approach is presented in John Hersey's *The Child Buyer.*[11] The representative of a large corporation sets out to buy a bright child who will spend the rest of his life working on advanced scientific projects. Permission for the sale is given by the child's teachers and parents. The process is then described by which the boy will be conditioned to worship the corporation and to forget his past experiences. He will be fed considerable data which he will use in solving the scientific tasks he has been assigned. He then will undergo major surgery which consists of destroying the sense organs.

Since the subject need not take in any more data, he has no further need of sight or hearing. Smell and taste have long since been useless to him, since he regards the intake of food as a mechanical process he carries on only for Her (the corporation's) sake. Only so much sense of touch is left the specimen as to allow him to carry on his bodily functions and "write" on a Simplomat Recorder, a stenographic machine the use of which has long since been a ceremonial rite for the subject.

Both *Island* and *The Child Buyer* take place in the twentieth century. Both reflect patterns of thought and behavior in our culture—one emphasizing existence, the other emphasizing essence. It is not an unlikely possibility that the personal actions of each classroom teacher will take our society in one direction or the other.

To the existentialist, reading instruction is far more than group recitation of words, sentences, and paragraphs. The act of reading is a key to the exploration of a child's inner life, a means by which he can exercise his will and make wise decisions. Therefore, the existence-oriented teacher sees the pupil as unique, as indivisible, as being-in-the-world. The reading program must place the child's existence before the "essentials" of the curriculum and encourage encounters between the child and his teacher, his classmates, and the learning materials that will involve him in the ongoing process of life.

To obtain these goals, multiple methods are needed, experience stories are valuable, and a personalized approach is advisable. The wise teacher can utilize basal readers, audio-visual devices, programmed instruction, and skill-building lessons without letting any of them overshadow the child and his needs. The teacher must always ask himself *why* he is teaching the child to read as well as *how* he is teaching. Existential philosophy stresses the emergence of the child, the cultivation of his talents, and his potentiality of involvement in life's creative opportunities.

REFERENCES

1. Arbuckle, Dugald S., "Existentialism and Counseling." A paper presented at the Kent Area Guidance Council Meeting, Kent, Ohio, April 24, 1963.
2. Ashton-Warner, Sylvia, *Teacher.* New York: Simon and Schuster, 1963, pp. 30-40 *passim.*
3. Barbe, Walter B., *Educator's Guide to Personalized Reading Instruction.* Englewood Cliffs, N.J.: Prentice-Hall, 1961, pp. 22-3, 229.
4. Bond, Guy L., *The Auditory and Speech Characteristics of Poor Readers.* New York: Bureau of Publications, Teachers College, Columbia University, 1935.
5. Fendrick, P. A., *Visual Characteristics of Poor Readers,* ibid.
6. Gans, Roma, *Common Sense in Teaching Reading.* Indianapolis: Bobbs-Merrill, 1963, pp. 76-9.
7. Getman, G. M., *How To Develop Your Child's Intelligence.* Luverne, Minn.: Author, 1962.
8. Harper, Ralph, "Significance of Existence and Recognition for Education," Fifty-fourth Yearbook of the National Society for the Study of Education, Part I, *Modern Philosophies and Education,* Nelson B. Henry, editor. Chicago: University of Chicago Press, 1956, pp. 215-58.
9. Harris, Albert J., *Effective Teaching of Reading.* New York: David McKay, 1962.
10. Heilman, Arthur W., *Teaching Reading.* Columbus, Ohio: Charles E. Merrill, 1961, p. 78.
11. Hersey, John, *The Child Buyer.* New York: Alfred A. Knopf, 1960.
12. Hillesheim, James W., "Nietzsche on Education," *Education,* 84, 1963, 226-30.
13. Huxley, Aldous, *Island.* New York: Harper and Row, 1962.
14. Kierkegaard, Soren, *Stages on Life's Way.* Princeton: Princeton University Press, 1940.
15. Kneller, George F., *Existentialism and Education.* New York: Philosophical Library, 1958.
16. May, Rollo, "The Emergence of Existential Philosophy," *Existential Psychology,* Rollo May, editor. New York: Random House, 1961, pp. 11-51 *passim.*
17. ———, "The Existential Approach," *American Handbook of Psychiatry,* Vol. II, Silvano Arieti, editor. New York: Basic Books, 1959, pp. 1348-61 *passim.*
18. ———, "The Origins and Significance of the Existential Movement in Psychology," *Existence: A New Dimension in Psychiatry and Psychology,* Rollo May, Ernest Angel, and Henri F. Ellenberger, editors. New York: Basic Books, 1958, pp. 3-36 *passim.*
19. McCracken, Glenn, *The Right To Learn.* Chicago: Henry Regnery, 1959.
20. McKee, Paul, *The Teaching of Reading in the Elementary School.* Boston: Houghton Mifflin, 1948.
21. McMahan, Allan, "Make Friends with Your Bookseller," *The Wonderful World of Books,* Alfred Stefferud, editor. New York: New American Library of World Literature, 1952, pp. 226-9 *passim.*

22. Morris, VanCleve, "Existentialism and Education," *Educational Theory,* 4 1956, 255-6.
23. Neill, A. S., *Summerhill.* New York: Hart Publishing, 1960.
24. Nietzsche, Friedrich, *Joyful Wisdom.* New York: Frederick Ungar, 1960.
25. "Reading in Lynnfield—and in 'Town X,'" *Education U. S. A.,* January 10, 1963.
26. Rogers, Carl R., *On Becoming a Person.* Boston: Riverside Press, 1961.
27. Sartre, Jean-Paul, *Existentialism and Human Emotions.* New York: Philosophical Library, 1957.
28. *Summerlane,* Bismarck, N.D.: Conrad Publishing, 1962.
29. Tillich, Paul, "Existential Philosophy," *Journal of Historical Ideas,* 5, 1944, 44-70.
30. Van Kaam, Adrian, "Existential Psychology as a Comprehensive Theory of Personality," *Review of Existential Psychology and Psychiatry,* 3, 1963, 11-26.
31. Wepman, Joseph, *Manual of Directions, Auditory Discrimination Test.* Chicago: Language Research Associates, 1958.
32. Witty, Paul, "Reading Instruction—A Forward Look," *Elementary English,* 38, 1961, 151-64.
33. ———, *et al., The Witty Diagnostic Record.* Kent, Ohio: Kent State University, 1963.
34. Woodring, Paul, "Can Johnny Read?" *Saturday Review,* January 20, 1962.
35. Wolstein, Benjamin, *Irrational Despair.* Glencoe, Ill.: Free Press, 1962.

PART TWO

Initial Stages of Learning To Read

INTRODUCTION

The best single indicator of a child's future academic potential is the extent of his initial success in reading. Initial success or failure in reading is not an indicator of an unchangeable inherent ability factor. The child who encounters undue difficulty in his initial reading attempts frequently complicates the problem by developing negative attitudes toward reading so that there is little chance for him to use what inherent ability he has. Rather than "growing out of the problem," as it was popular to believe at one time, the problem becomes more and more serious.

The importance of success in the initial stages of learning to read has long been recognized by educators. Monroe, in selection seven, develops the stages of book behavior prior to the time when the child begins formal instruction. It is true that critics have argued against delaying instruction, protesting that many children are ready to read long before the school will allow formal instruction. Cases are frequently cited where children were not only ready before the usual school age, but actually learned at a phenomenally early age. Parents have even been encouraged to undertake the teaching of reading to their children, sometimes even years before the usual age at which the teaching of reading is recommended.[3] But there is reason to believe that for the vast majority of children the time best suited for formal reading instruction is when they are in the first grade.

READINESS FOR READING

Those language activities in which a child engages before formal reading instruction begins are known as reading readiness activities. These are discussed in detail by Kottmeyer. Whether these activities are a part of the normal, everyday environment of the child, such as talking to those around him, looking at pictures and books, or listening to others talk, or whether they are formally provided in nursery schools and kindergartens, following prescribed procedures and using specially prepared materials, they are nevertheless all reading readiness activities. Predicting success in achievement and improving achievement as a result of readiness activities are the concerns of two of the articles in this section.

A first concern about readiness is whether it is a prerequisite to learning. It is popular today among critics of educational methodology to deny the need for readiness. If the word "set," used psychologically to mean a predetermined conditioning of the individual for a particular activity, were substituted for the word "readiness," it is doubtful that there would be so much opposition. Readiness is a necessary prerequisite for all learning, not just on the part of the young child but also on the part of all human beings at every age level.

A second and far more legitimate concern today about readiness is whether or not *formal* readiness programs are necessary. Hymes [6] insists that "you do not have to 'build' readiness." His point is that there are no "programs" for such activities as "pre-crawling, or pre-standing, or pre-walking, pre-talking, or pre-dating," for adults work at what the child needs now, at that point in his development, rather than artifically building a foundation for tomorrow's activities.[7] This argument is not against readiness, but is directed against the artificial readiness program aimed at the child's future needs, rather than his needs at that particular time.

A third concern about readiness is whether there is a point in the child's development when formal reading instruction should occur, and concomitant concerns of the age at which this occurs and how this point can best be determined. As with any other learned activity, reading can most likely be taught earlier to many children, just as the same children could be taught to walk at an earlier age, talk at an earlier age, or do any of the other complicated learned activities. One question must be asked, however, and this is not, "Can it be done?" for there is ample demonstration that with many children the function of reading can be mastered at an earlier age than six, and in some instances as early as two.[8] The all-important question is, "What is gained and what is the price of formal reading instruction for children at ages of two to five?" The facts, as one popular journal [4] reports them, are that tiny children want to learn, can learn, are learning, and should learn. There is no denying that for some children the first three are facts, but the reasoning that because some tiny children want to, can, and are learning to read, they therefore "should" learn to read does not follow. Merely because some children want to do a certain act, are able to do it, and are even doing it does not mean that they necessarily should do it. The explanation that "tiny children should learn to read (because it is good to be able to read)" [5] can hardly be accepted as more than an expression of civilization's belief in literacy. No one would deny that it is "good" to be able to read, but the question remains unanswered as to what is gained and at what price by learning to read at age two.

Frequently concern is expressed about those children who learn to read before entering school, without the benefit of formal instruction. Some studies of gifted children have reported that up to half of them learned to read before entering school.[1] Children who can learn to read *without* the benefit of formal instruction should be encouraged to do so. The school can and must adapt its program to provide for these exceptional children. It is most likely, however, that children who learn to read without a formal program are demonstrating an inherent ability far above that of the average child. The high I.Q. may produce the early reader; early reading does *not* produce a high I.Q.

INTEREST VERSUS SKILLS APPROACH

Two distinct approaches in teaching reading are apparent, although even a cursory examination of current literature would lead one to believe that the list was unlimited. Referred to sometimes as "schools of thought," one is the school of skills and the other the school of interests.

Buckingham [2] explains these two positions clearly:

The school of skills minutely analyzes a pupil's reading disabilities and seeks a remedy—largely through drill—for each of them. It has faith that when the pupil needs these skills he will put them together in the total reading act. The school of interests considers what a pupil likes, or admires, or wishes to become, and gives him adjusted reading material which will serve these interests. It relies on the drive of emotionalized effort along paths of least resistance. The school of skills does not discard interests, nor does the school of interests ignore skills. The distinction is one of emphasis.

The term "school," of course, does not mean that all writers and practitioners of remedial reading stand apart in two groups. Rather by their theory and practice they place themselves along an S-I (Skills-to-Interests) scale with the pronounced drillers upon skills well over toward the S end, with the unwavering supporters of interests at the I end, and with a host of others in between.

Currently there is a wide variety of adaptations on the skills approach, with less attention in methodology toward the interest approach. However, publishers of children's books have clearly recognized the value of the interest approach and are producing children's literature of both quantity and quality undreamed of only a few years ago.

Much attention has been directed in recent years toward methods of teaching reading, as well as toward understanding how children learn. The most effective teacher of reading most certainly needs to know "how" to teach reading, but equally important is an understanding of how children learn. Improving methodology alone will not succeed in improving reading instruction unless it is accompanied by an increased understanding of how children learn. The assumption that any single method will work with all children could only be explained by the erroneous assumption that all children learn in the same way.

Perhaps the adaptability of children has been the cause of some of the difficulty, for if children were less adaptable they would have failed completely to learn from a preconceived procedure that failed to take into account their particular nature and needs. Their adaptability has resulted in a modicum of success from methods and procedures unsuited to them, so that no changes were made, while if they had been less adaptable and had failed completely, the need for another method of teaching reading to them would have been more apparent.

But the mere fact that children can adapt to a single method of teaching does not justify this procedure, if the teacher is concerned with promoting the maximum development of every child. The extent of research in reading is astounding, but if the results are to be given no more attention in the classroom than has too often been true in the past, continued efforts will be hard to justify. As teachers of reading, one of our greatest concerns must be to use what is already known about the most effective methods of teaching reading, as well as what is known about how children learn.

REFERENCES

1. Barbe, Walter B., "A Study of the Reading of Gifted High-School Students," *Educational Administration and Supervision,* Vol. 38, No. 3 (March 1952), p. 149.
2. Buckingham, B. R., Foreword in Paul Witty and David Kopel, *Reading and the Educative Process.* Boston: Ginn and Company, 1939, pp. ix, x.
3. Doman, Glenn, Stevens, George L., and Orem, Reginald C., "You Can Teach Your Baby To Read," *Ladies' Home Journal,* Vol. 80, No. 4 (May 1963), pp. 62-3, 124-6.
4. Ibid. p. 62.
5. Ibid.
6. Hymes, James L., Jr., *Before the Child Reads.* Evanston, Illinois: Row, Peterson and Company, 1958, p. 17.
7. Ibid. pp. 17-18.
8. Pines, Myra, "How Three-Year-Olds Teach Themselves To Read—and Love It." *Harper's Magazine,* Vol. 226, No. 1356 (May 1963), pp. 58-64.

Getting Ready for Reading

7: Typical Book Behavior Develops by Stages *

MARION MONROE

Gesell and Ilg [1] have studied the behavior of large numbers of infants and children, and have described what they call a typical "behavior-day" from birth to five years and older. Book activities are mentioned as a part of the typical behavior-day of infants as young as fifteen months. "Looking at colored pictures and turning pages while sitting on the lap of an adult" is recorded as a part of the normal day of an infant of this age.

From the studies of Gesell and other investigators there appears to be a normal drive toward book activities from infancy on that culminates in the recognition of the meaning of printed symbols at approximately six years of age. Reading has its roots deeply imbedded in the child's total growth process. How well a child, at the age of six, is prepared to look at a printed word and associate its meaning depends largely upon the early experiences he has had, his rate of physical, mental, and emotional maturation, and the extent to which he has developed the basic pre-reading skills and understandings.

Pre-reading book behavior may be divided roughly into eight stages that

follow a definite sequence. The rate and age at which each stage appears depend upon the interests and abilities of the individual child, upon the richness of his environment in books, and upon adults who take the time to read books and talk to him about them.

STAGE ONE: MANIPULATION

Most infants give only fleeting attention to books at twelve months of age, except to regard the book as one of the many fascinating objects in the environment to be mouthed, manipulated, dropped, and regained. Paper is crumpled, torn, brought to the mouth. Books are pushed through the bars of a play pen and the problem of getting the book again occupies more attention than the book itself. Old magazines are enjoyed for the fun of tearing paper. A year-old infant spends many happy moments of the day in his play pen tearing out magazine pages, crumping, mouthing, stamping them with his feet until he has surrounded himself with a litter of shredded paper. During such activity he may give momentary attention to a

* Reprinted from *Growing Into Reading*, Chicago: Scott, Foresman & Company, pp. 7-21, by permission of the publisher. Copyright 1951 by Scott, Foresman & Company.

portion of a picture, attracted primarily by its brightness.

Concepts Developed at Stage One

The Book as an Object. Books are made of interesting material having certain distinctive textures (tactile sensations) and qualities (can be torn, crumpled, or otherwise manipulated).

Content of Book. Books contain bright-colored patterns that are part of the paper. A few twelve-month infants appear to recognize pictures of simple, familiar objects, especially if the picture is photographic in detail and colored accurately.

Printed Symbols. No notice is given to printing.

STAGE TWO: POINTING

At fifteen months or thereabouts, the infant develops a growing interest in the pictures in books. He enjoys sitting on his mother's lap, looking at colored pictures while she turns pages. He may become absorbed in the page-turning activity and try to turn the pages himself. He still lapses frequently into the tearing and manipulating activities of the twelve-month infant, especially if he has not had ample opportunity for this type of exploration in the past. He becomes attached to a cloth, cardboard, or plastic book that will stand up under the battering he gives it, and carries it around at times just as he does other favorite toys. Tactile books interest him and help him make a transition from perceiving a three-dimensional object to perceiving a two-dimensional representation of the object. Patting a tactile bunny distracts the infant from tearing, as his hands are occupied in patting and feeling, and he is able to give more prolonged attention to the pictures. He shows recognition of pictured objects, for he will sometimes, on demand, pat or point to the ball, the cup, the doggy, or other familiar objects.

Concepts Developed at Stage Two

The Book as an Object. Books contain pages to be turned. Books which survive destruction may become well-loved objects.

Content of Book. Pictures resemble familiar objects. Pictures are identified in response to adult naming, although a few fifteen-month-old infants will name pictures if they have the oral vocabulary to do so.

Printed Symbols. No notice is given to printing.

STAGE THREE: NAMING

When the child is about eighteen months, great strides are made in book activities. Spontaneous oral language is now used with the pictures, and the pictures help to increase vocabulary. At this stage of growth an infant likes to crawl up on the lap of an adult with a book or magazine and have the adult say "Show me the kitty," and "Where's the duck?" letting the infant point. Then, reversing the process, he likes the adult to point to a picture, asking "What's this?" and letting the infant do the naming. The eighteen-month-old child likes a picture-dictionary that contains many little pictures on every page. Books become an avenue of information, and the child seizes upon them as he does on every other opportunity for finding out about the world. He learns to name a pictured tiger or giraffe (animals he has never really seen), and he astonishes his parents later by naming them correctly when the family takes a trip to the zoo.

At this stage, the child goes beyond simple naming of pictures, and may answer questions about them. To "What is the baby doing?" he may reply with a verb, "Eating." Also, he not only applies to the picture the name of an animal but often gives the animal noises, "Bow-wow," or "Moo-moo," while looking at the pictures. He enjoys the repetition of these sounds and may "read" an animal book by himself by making appropriate noises for each picture.

He begins to notice orientation of pictures. Although he may crawl around on the floor to the opposite side of a book in order to look at a picture right-side-up, he seldom turns the book around.

Concepts Developed at Stage Three

The Book as an Object. Books are to be taken care of; tearing is usually due to lack of motor control.

Content of Book. Pictures represent objects both familiar and unfamiliar. Pictures of unfamiliar objects arouse curiosity. A few children begin to notice that pictures have a top and a bottom. Pictures of familiar objects are named spontaneously. Pictures of unfamiliar objects are noticed and serve as a means of vocabulary building. Pictures are interpreted in a very simple way in terms of action or in terms of the sound the object makes. For example, a child may say *z-z-z-* while looking at a picture of an airplane, or *bye-bye* while looking at a picture of a go-cart.

Printed Symbols. Very rarely is notice given to printing.

STAGE FOUR: SIMPLE NARRATIVE

By the time they are two, some children in book-loving homes have become devoted book addicts like their parents. In homes of average cultural standards, two-year-olds have usually received several books as gifts, and show considerable interest in book activities. A two-year-old will frequently leave more strenuous activities for a few minutes of rest with an adult if the prospect of looking at a book is used for bait. Most parents have discovered the quieting effect of books on an active child, and a story time before sleep is a frequent American custom with little folks.

The two-year-old calls the process of looking at books "reading," and he enjoys the activity both with an adult and alone. He continues to build his vocabulary by learning the names of unknown objects in pictures. He is becoming aware that pictures have a deeper meaning than just to resemble objects. He wants to have something happen in each picture, and is beginning to listen to a story read or told by the adult while looking at a sequence of related pictures. He likes repetition rather than plot, with the action in each picture repeated, but the character performing the action changed—"A dog said, *Bow-wow, I want something to eat,*" "A kitty said, *Mew-mew, I want something to eat,*" ending with a climax of "A baby said, *Mommy, Mommy, I want something to eat.*" Or he likes to have the same character in each picture doing various acts, such as "Billy got up," "He washed his face," "He combed his hair," "He put on his clothes," "He ate his breakfast." If the two-year-old's own name can be substituted for the name of the child in the book, the story goes especially well.

The child at Stage Four prefers to have each new book read and reread, until he masters the vocabulary and sentence patterns before another book is added to his collection. He becomes confused and careless if too many new books are given to him at one time. It is wise, therefore, for the parents to withhold new books, if the child is fortunate enough to receive several at once, and to bring out the new ones at judicious intervals. Often the first reading of a book presents the child with new language forms that are meaningless, but that gradually take on meaning as he studies the pictures and listens to the language patterns repeated again and again.

During this time, from two to about three years of age, the child becomes aware that books have titles. He may even coin his own title for some books. He begins to develop awareness of the front of the book, especially if the front has a picture while the back is plain. He also notices orientation of pictures and begins to adjust the book so that he will see the pictures right-side-up. A few children may notice the printing under the pictures.

Concepts Developed at Stage Four

The Book as an Object. The child continues to develop concepts of good care of books. He does not tear them, and turns pages carefully. He realizes that the book has a front and back.

Content of Book. Pictures have a top and a bottom. Pictures do more than represent objects; they also suggest action and events taking place in sequence—they tell a story. Adults tell stories about the pictures. The same language is used with reference to each picture. The events portrayed by pictures are continuous from one picture to the next. The process of looking at books is called "reading."

Printed Symbols. Two-year-olds begin to show an awareness of print—they notice that there is something else on a page besides the pictures.

STAGE FIVE: INTERPRETATION

At two and a half, the pictures and stories grow very real to a child. He may pretend to "pick up" an object from a picture; he loves and kisses a pictured baby; he slaps the picture of the villain of a story; he makes clucking noises of sympathy over a pictured calamity— "Poor Jack and Jill fell down—don't cry." He talks to the pictured characters, and if he lacks sufficient normal social contacts he may even create an imaginary playmate or companion out of a book character.

At this age the child pays increasing attention to the oral language that accompanies the pictures and he tends to memorize verbatim from frequent repetition of stories. He likes very much to have the adult stop for him to give a word or complete a sentence. He enjoys participating in the reading in this way.

As he develops interest in listening to the language of books he also develops interest in catchy sounds and jingles. This is the age when Mother Goose rhymes are remembered.

He enjoys not only storybooks, but also books that give him information, such as train books or airplane books or fire-engine books, in which he can learn to identify the various kinds of trains or airplanes or fire-engines.

The child at this stage is increasingly aware of orientation and may adjust a book for another person while showing him a picture, so that it will be right-side-up for the other person. The child also likes to experiment with pencils and crayons and often marks in his books, perhaps stimulated by the bright colors he sees in the pictures.

Alphabet books are often given to little children because of the lovely pictures and colors. A few children of two and a half notice the large printed letters, but most children of this age ignore the letter names even in alphabet books.

By two and a half years of age, the child has usually acquired a number of books of his own and has a book shelf or some place to put the dog-eared favorites of previous months and the fascinating new books that arrive.

Concepts Developed at Stage Five

The Book as an Object. Books are to be put away after use. Books are decorated with color.

Content of Book. Pictured characters often seem as real as actual people. The events pictured or told about can make one feel happy or sad or angry. Books give information about things one needs to know, like trains and airplanes. The language adults use in reading books is constant for each page or picture. This language can be remembered and retold to one's self, especially if the language contains catchy sounds and jingles and is very simple and repetitive.

Printed Symbols. Some children notice the capital letters in alphabet books, but rarely attempt to name them.

STAGE SIX: STORYTELLING, NOTICE OF PRINT

By the time a child is three years of age, his book activities are diversified. If the child attends nursery school, he is able to share his book experiences with a group, sitting around the teacher with others of his age, listening while she reads a story and shows the pictures. At home he may share his story time with brothers or sisters. Three-year-olds begin to dramatize stories and jingles by imitating actions suggested by adults; for instance, "This is the way we wash our clothes, wash our clothes." The three-year-old can tolerate longer language content with each picture and will listen while an adult reads an occasional passage without a picture. This is a distinct gain over the younger child, who can hear only a brief sentence or two before turning the page to see the next picture.

The three-year-old develops rapidly in ability to interpret pictures and stories. He often makes spontaneous comments that show anticipation of outcome and simple reasoning. He has developed enough language to describe as well as identify objects in pictures, as "nice little kitty." Some three-year-old children can retell a simple story of two or three episodes, if the episodes are well linked and the lead into the second or third episode is very evident in the pictures, or if an adult gives the lead by starting each succeeding episode.

At this stage of growth children who have developed considerable interest in books may learn to name four or five capital letters in their alphabet books. Usually a letter in the child's name will be learned, and *O, S,* or some other letter having distinctive appearance. Equally bright children whose book interests are not developed and who prefer more vigorous activities usually continue to ignore the printed symbols in books and give attention chiefly to the pictures and stories as told by adults.

Concepts Developed at Stage Six

The Book as an Object. Concepts of book care are extended and put into practice more effectively with the child's increasing motor control. There is still a tendency to add to the decoration of books by marking and coloring.

Content of Book. Language content of books is now almost as interesting as the pictured content. Sharing a story with other children is fun. Story episodes can be remembered and retold in sequence with some help. Picture-stories and verbal stories suggest related ideas of one's own (what happens next, simple reasoning).

Printed Symbols. Many children notice the capital letters in alphabet books, and a few children learn to name four or five letters.

STAGE SEVEN: DIFFERENTIATION OF REAL AND FANTASTIC

A four-year-old child enjoys companionship. He seeks out other children in the neighborhood to play with and is anticipating kindergarten. For this reason book activities may lag while social skills develop.

At this stage the child begins to differentiate better between reality and fantasy and to like books that are definitely one or the other, either very realistic or very fantastic. He enjoys the ludicrous, particularly humorous pictures, and silly language in stories and nonsense rhymes. He enjoys looking at books and hearing stories read in groups of children, and he will pore over books alone, if he cannot find someone to play with. He readily memorizes stories and insists on their being reread verbatim. He will correct an adult who substitutes a word or condenses the content of a paragraph into a sentence. Imaginative stories are favorites for the story hour and he likes to dramatize these stories. He also likes books that give him accurate information, and he wants the pictures to be exact in detail.

Many of the four-year-old's questions begin with "Why?" or "What for?" He wants explanations of everything that he sees or hears; a picture or story may set off a train of questions and interpretations. Thus, instead of interrupting the reader to go on to the next picture or episode as before, the child himself sometimes needs to be interrupted so that the book may be finished in a reasonable time.

Many children of four and five realize that there is a relationship between the printed text and the story. They understand that the reader gets his cue from the text as to what to say. They refer to the printed text as "some reading"—"There's some reading on this box." They also distinguish printed text from handwritten text, which they call "writing." Many four- and five-year-olds try to "write" by drawing crude letter forms, often reversing or inverting the forms. They are not aware of printed words within a text, but select letters here and there to copy, rather than words. Usually capital letters stand out prominently in a text and are chosen for reproduction. Also, capital letters are used decoratively in A-B-C books and on blocks, so that capital forms are more impressive to the child than small-letter forms. The book-loving child at four or five, may learn to identify a number of letters by name.

Concepts Developed at Stage Seven

The Book as an Object. Concepts of book care are extended. The tendency to mark in books is decreasing.

Content of Book. The language value of books now comes to the foreground and begins to rival the picture to some extent, especially if the child has good verbal ability. Pictures and stories stimulate an abundant flow of ideas and expression from the child, usually of the "why" or explanatory type. The child likes to have a clear distinction made between fantasy and reality, since he is still not too sure of the difference himself. Language used in books is often memorized and repeated.

Printed Symbols. The child begins to recognize that the printed text tells the reader what to say. Printing is differentiated roughly from writing. Little notice is taken of the orientation of a letter—letters are frequently drawn or copied in reverse as well as in correct orientation.

READING READINESS AT SCHOOL

It sometimes happens that parents or teachers, seizing on a child's developing interest in letters and printing, attempt to teach the child to read at the first sign of letter recognition, usually during the developmental Stages Six and Seven. Such premature attempts are often not fruitful because the child must mature a great deal more before he can grasp all the parts of the reading process. He must develop an appreciation of the spoken word as a unit of oral language and of the printed word as a unit of printed language. He must have an awareness of the point-by-point correspondence between oral and printed language and become accustomed to the conventional left-to-right sequence of printing. Moreover, he must attain sufficient emotional stability to sustain and direct his attention while forming the correct associations between oral and printed symbols.

An infant exhibits a desire for locomotion when he pushes out toward objects, yet he must learn to pull up, stand alone, and walk with support before he is ready to take his first unaided step. Even after he has achieved all the necessary physical coordinations, he must screw up his courage to a certain level of confidence before he can step out completely on his own. He cannot be rushed from pushing out to walking without progressing through the steps of intermediate development in physical, mental, and emotional control. Similarly, after a child first understands vaguely what reading is and wants to read, he needs a period of time to organize his thinking and extend his preschool concepts to the level necessary for successful learning.

REFERENCE

1. Gesell, Arnold and Ilg, Frances L., *Infant and Child in the Culture of* *Today*. New York: Harper and Brothers, 1943.

8: Readiness for Reading *

WILLIAM KOTTMEYER

Throughout the nation, the problem of improving reading instruction continues to be of primary concern to educators. The repeated testimony of the literature in the field, however, shows that determined and aggressive attempts to increase instructional efficiency almost invariably yield gratifying results

The problem is most serious, perhaps, in the large urban communities. Large school systems are naturally unwieldy units and reflect wide variations among teachers in philosophy and techniques. The close co-ordination of effort, the personal contact, and unanimity of purpose which are possible in small school systems are far more difficult to achieve in systems of several thousand teachers.

Furthermore, the alarming increase of blighted areas within the limits of most large cities has had great influence on their educational programs. For example, a large segment of public school population which in former years came to city schools from middle and upper-middle class homes has been seriously diminished. Such families normally have a tendency to migrate to suburban communities. As the residential city areas are thus slowly depleted and deteriorate with the years, they are occupied by lower-income and transient groups.

This changing school population has made its influence felt particularly in the primary grades. In recent years educators have been increasingly conscious of the need to provide reading readiness programs for the considerable number of first-grade entrants who demonstrate their inability to benefit from formal reading programs as traditionally administered in the schools.

* Reprinted from *Elementary English*, Vol. 24, No. 6 (October 1947), pp. 355-66, by permission of the National Council of Teachers of English and the author.

Children who come from economically deprived homes are usually handicapped with regard to growth in three great conditioning areas of readiness: language skills, experiential backgrounds, and physical and sensory health. Simply stated, the city systems have increasingly large numbers of children entering first grade, who are, as a group, less ready to learn to read than formerly. The need for strong readiness programs felt in all communities is accentuated in the large cities, where rapid adaptation to changing conditions comes sluggishly. The literature and research in the field of readiness is and has been far ahead of common school practice. These are melancholy facts.

The efforts of Superintendent Phillip J. Hickey to deal with the reading problem in the St. Louis schools has been reported upon previously.[4]

Recent efforts to improve the program have stressed the importance of prevention. *The St. Louis Public School Journal* of January, 1946, was devoted largely to the problem of reading readiness in the St. Louis Public Schools. The testing and examination results of September, 1945, were presented and analyzed. Briefly, the important findings were that:

1. Children entered the first grade of St. Louis Public Schools in September, 1945, at these mean chronological ages: White, 6 years and 4 months; Negro, 6 years and five months.

On September 17, 1945, the following school entrance regulation was made effective:

———Children whose fifth birthday occurs on or after August 1 and before the first day of the second semester may enter at the beginning of the first semester or any time during the first semester.

Children whose fifth birthday occurs on or after the first day of the second semester and before August 1 may enter at the beginning of the second semester or any time during the second semester.

It was expected that the age of first-grade entrants would be lowered in the future. Implications of lowered chronological ages for first-grade children with respect to reading readiness are evident.

2. Using the criterion of a mental age of 78 months on the Detroit Beginning First-Grade Intelligence Test, 34.4 per cent of beginning first-grade children in white schools and 55.5 per cent in Negro schools were apparently not ready for reading instruction.

3. Using the criterion of a critical score of 69 on the Metropolitan Readiness Test, 29 per cent of the beginning first-grade children in white schools and 64 per cent in Negro schools did not have one chance in two of making one year of progress in reading in the first grade, as measured by a standardized silent reading test.

4. The physical and sensory tests given by the Division of Health and Hygiene showed that approximately 10 per cent of first-grade entrants failed the Snellen Chart Vision Test, approximately 5 per cent had seriously handicapping hearing losses; approximately 60 per cent needed dental attention; approximately 40 per cent had other physical defects which might interfere with their learning efforts in school.

HOW MUCH YOUNGER ARE FIRST-GRADERS IN ST. LOUIS NOW?

All primary teachers are probably aware of the assertion commonly made by researchers that a minimum mental age of 78 months is a desirable requisite for formal instruction. In the past, St. Louis children have customarily entered the kindergarten at the age of five. Thus, the minimum entrance age to the first grade was usually six years. Most children were older than six years and no months, of course.

In September, 1945, the mean chronological age of 3,444 white low-first-graders was 6 years and 4 months, of

1,172 Negro low-first-graders, 6 years and 5 months. Since the lower age entrance regulation was issued on September 17, 1945, it is probable that these figures do not deviate significantly from the mean chronological ages of other groups of first-grade entrants in the recent past.

Apparently the effect of the lower age entrance regulation has been to reduce the central measure of chronological age of first-grade entrants two to three months. It does not appear likely that the chronological ages will deviate significantly from these figures so long as the present regulation is in effect. It is possible, of course, that larger numbers of children are now being retained longer than a year in the kindergarten. There is no evidence at hand to show that this is or is not true.

Children traditionally are eligible to enter the first grade in American schools at the age of six, largely because they have been doing so for years. The evidence has shown that sometimes half or even more of the children of such a group cannot successfully follow a formal reading program. If this is true—and there appears to be little doubt about it—there are two courses open to the schools.

One is to admit children at more mature ages. Of course, this will probably never happen. Parents generally would be displeased to the point of indignation. Furthermore, most large city systems are under pressure or have succumbed to pressure to continue or to duplicate the child care centers popularized during the war. Certainly many children have excellent conditions for growth, particularly in the areas of language development, social adjustment, and physical care in such institutions. The enthusiasm of educators for these opportunities for underprivileged children is natural and laudable. But the natural extension of this program will ever be downward, to include younger children. There is apparently no general agreement as to where it will eventually stop.

The other course open to the schools is to make serious and vigorous efforts on a far broader scale to develop readiness, or pre-reading programs. Our apathy and indifference in this field has been one of our serious educational tragedies.

HOW WELL ARE ST. LOUIS FIRST-GRADERS READING?

In May, 1946, Form 2 of Types 1 and 2 of the Gates Primary Reading Tests were given by the first-grade teachers. It was assumed that a reading grade of 1.8 would constitute normal progress in reading as measured by the test. In order to use the data for further analysis, only those children who had taken the initial intelligence and readiness tests in September, 1945, were considered. The number in this group totaled 3,115, of whom 822 were Negro children and 2,293 were white children.

The mean score for the white children was 1.89 for Type 1 (Word Recognition), and 1.91 for Type 2 (Sentence Meaning). The mean score for the Negro children was 1.85 for Type 1, and 1.85 for Type 2.

For all children in the testing program, the mean was 1.88 for Type 1 and 1.89 for Type 2. Thus, these first-grade children of St. Louis for the 1945-46 school year were approximately one month ahead of the national norms.

Of the 3,115 children, 50 per cent made a score of at least 1.8. In the white schools, the range of the mean scores for Type 1 was from 1.32 to 2.88 and for Type 2, from 1.41 to 2.80. For Negro schools, this range of means extended from 1.44 to 2.31 for Type 1 and from 1.53 to 2.20 for Type 2. Of the eighty-three white schools considered, forty-seven scored at least 1.8 on Type 1 and fifty-two on Type 2. Of the twenty-one Negro schools, eleven scored at least 1.8 on Type 1 and thirteen on Type 2.

In May, 1947, Form 2 of Types 1 and 2 of the Gates Primary Reading Tests were given by the first-grade teachers again. It was assumed that a reading grade of 1.85 would represent normal progress in this instance. Again, in order to use the data for further analysis, only those childhen who had been rated for readiness by the teachers in September, 1946, were considered. The number in this group totaled 3,219 pupils, of whom 876 were Negro children and 2,343 were white children.

The mean score of an average of Type 1 and Type 2 for the white children was 2.06. The mean score for Negro children was 2.00.

For all children in the testing program, the mean was 2.05. Thus, the first-grade children of St. Louis for the 1946-47 school year were approximately two months ahead of national norms. Of the 3,219 children, almost 62 per cent made a score of at least 1.85, or normal progress as measured by the tests.

Under the increasingly difficult conditions of large city school systems, these figures appear to be comforting. Mean scores for large groups often appear so. We must bear in mind that the mean score is slightly beyond the point of normal expectancy only because many individual school means are well into the second-grade level. There are many groups of children whose mean scores are considerably below the expected 1.85. These figures represent *children*—they are not things in themselves. Let us remember that over a thousand *children* will come back to school in September to St. Louis Public Schools without the skills that a basal reading series assumes for them at the second-grade level.

It will be easy to cause further harm through the delusion that there is really something which we call the second grade and, under the convenience of large group instructional techniques we

violate for these children a fundamental principle of reading instruction: to provide reading material and reading activities at the level at which the child is and not beyond it.

PREDICTIVE MEASURES FOR SUCCESS IN READING

Intelligence Tests

In addition to the subjective measures employed by teachers to predict success in reading for first-grade entrants and to guide them in making decisions as to the optimum time to begin reading instruction, the group intelligence tests and readiness tests have been widely used. The literature in the readiness field has popularized a minimum mental age of 78 months as one criterion for reading readiness.

The Detroit Beginning First-Grade Intelligence Test was administered to 3,307 white and 999 Negro children, or to a total of 4,306 children in Grade I-Low in September 1945. The mean score for white children showed a mean mental age of approximately six years and eight months. This figure, incidentally, is probably too high. The mean score for Negro children showed a mean mental age of approximately six years and three months. The mean score for all St. Louis children was equivalent to a mean mental age of approximately six years and seven months. A total of 2,699 or some 63 per cent of all children, made a mental age score of six years and six months or better.

The Detroit Test was administered in January, 1946, to 2,212 white and to 793 Negro children. Mean mental ages and percentages of children with a mental age lower than the generally recommended criterion of 78 months were almost identical with the September results.

If the Detroit Test is a valid measure of mental age, the results seemed to show that about 37 per cent of St. Louis first-grade entrants who remained in school throughout the year did not have sufficient mental maturity to guarantee a reasonable chance of success in learning to read.

Readiness Tests

The Metropolitan Readiness Tests were administered to the same group of 4,306 children in September, 1945. The mean score on the test for white children was 77.42 and for Negro children, 61.42. The mean score for all St. Louis children was 73.69. A total of 2,702 children, or 63 per cent, made a score of 69 or above on the test. A score of 69 is given by the test authors as assuring a child one chance out of two of attaining a grade status of 1.9 at the end of the school year.

The Metropolitan Test was again administered in January, 1946, to 2,241 white and 780 Negro children. The white mean score varied only .3 from the September results, whereas the Negro mean varied 5.25.

If the Metropolitan Readiness Test is a valid measure of readiness for reading, it may be said that some 37 per cent of first-grade entrants who remained in the first grade in the Public Schools of St. Louis had less than one chance in two of making normal progress in reading during their first year.

It is interesting to note here that 37 per cent of the St. Louis children scored below the critical points on both Detroit and Metropolitan tests. Of the 4,306 children, 1,827 white children and 282 Negro children, or a total of 49 per cent had a mental age of six years and six months and had made a score of at least 69 on the Metropolitan test.

CORRELATION OF READINESS AND INTELLIGENCE TESTS

The correlation between the Detroit and Metropolitan tests was .77 ± .004. The correlation of mental age as found on the Detroit test and reading readiness as predicted by the Metropolitan test is similar to results found in other investigations involving smaller numbers. Senour,[8] with eighty cases, using the same tests, found a correlation co-efficient of .80. Wright,[10] using the same tests with 203 cases, reported a correlation of .73. The authors of the Metropolitan test [5] cite a correlation of .70 based on thirty-four cases for these two tests. Briefly, the results merely confirm a conclusion reached years ago on fewer cases: That, generally, readiness tests and intelligence tests are very similar and measure much the same thing.

CORRELATION OF INTELLIGENCE TESTS AND READING ACHIEVEMENT TESTS

The correlation, for 3,115 children, of mental age on the Detroit test and an average of the Gates Word Recognition and Gates Sentence Reading tests was .423 ± .01. This correlation co-efficient is lower than in almost all similar studies. With some variation in the selection of tests, similar studies show the correlation co-efficients: Senour,[8] 80 cases, .534; Wright,[10] 203 cases, .547; Grant,[3] 260 cases, .63; Dean,[2] 116 cases, .62; Seavy,[7] 31 cases, .7838; Willmore,[9] .65. Lee, Clark, and Lee [6] report correlations of .40 and .39.

The correlation between Detroit mental ages and reading achievement as measured by the Gates tests appears to be too low to warrant confidence in prediction of success in reading for individual cases.

CORRELATION OF THE READINESS TESTS AND READING ACHIEVEMENT TESTS

The correlation for 3,115 children, of the readiness test scores and an average score on the two Gates tests was .461 ± .01. Again, although the results obtained were close to those obtained in several other studies, they were lower than in related studies. With some variation in the selection of test combinations, similar studies show these results: Senour,[8] 80 cases, .538; Craig,[1] 63 cases, .57; Willmore,[9] 82 cases, .49;

Lee, Clark, and Lee,[6] .49; Dean,[2] 116 cases, .59.

The results are similar to the findings with the use of the Detroit test.

COMPARISON OF TEACHERS' ESTIMATES OF READINESS WITH INTELLIGENCE AND READINESS TESTS ESTIMATES

The intelligence and readiness tests were administered to first-grade entrants in September, 1945, and some measure of their predictive value was approximated by correlating the scores with reading achievement in May, 1946. In September, 1946, St. Louis Public School teachers made subjective estimates of readiness for reading for each individual child of the new group of first-grade entrants. An estimate of readiness or unreadiness was counted as accurate or inaccurate if the child made an average score above or below 1.85 on the Gates tests administered in May, 1947.

A total of 142 first grade teachers made estimates of readiness for reading of 3,156 children as individuals. One hundred and eight white teachers made 2,280 estimates and thirty-four Negro teachers made 876 estimates. The percentage of accuracy of prediction for the 142 teachers was 71.4 per cent, with percentages for white and Negro teachers being practically identical. White teachers predicted that 17.6 per cent would fail to make a year's progress, whereas 36.7 per cent actually did fail to do so. Negro teachers predicted that 22.7 per cent would fail; 41.4 per cent did so.

In order to make some estimate of the value of teaching experience at the low-first-grade level as far as accuracy of prediction is concerned, teachers who made the estimates were classified in three categories: Those having less than five years of experience, those having five to ten years, and those having more than ten years. The thirty-three white teachers who had less than five years of experience had a prediction percentage of 65.9 per cent. The nineteen having

five to ten years scored 67.8 per cent. The fifty-six having more than ten years scored 75.7 per cent. Among Negro teachers the fifteen having less than five years of experience scored 61.1 per cent, the seven having five to ten years, 73.9 per cent, and the twelve with more than ten years had 78.8 per cent. It appears to be probable that, generally, teachers with more than ten years of low-first-grade teaching experience can predict reading success noticeably better than can teachers with less experience.

Thus the crude evidence shows these facts:

1. That 67 per cent of first-grade children made a score of 69 or above on the Metropolitan Readiness Test, indicating that they had at least one chance in two of making normal progress in reading. Sixty-two per cent of this group did make the normal progress tentatively expected. Therefore, when predicting success for children, the Metropolitan test had an accuracy index of 62 per cent. The total prediction accuracy, including successes and failures, was 66.6 per cent.

2. That 66 per cent of the first-grade childern had a mental age as measured by the Detroit test of at least six years and six months, indicating that, as far as this aspect of readiness is concerned, they might be expected to make normal progress. Sixty per cent of this group did make normal progress. Therefore, when predicting success for children, the Detroit test had an accuracy index of 60 per cent. The total prediction accuracy, including successes and failures, was 63.3 per cent.

3. One hundred and forty-two St. Louis first-grade teachers, when predicting success for children, had an accuracy index of 76.6 per cent. Their total prediction accuracy was 71.4 per cent. The tentative conclusion appears to be that low-first-grade teachers can predict reading success about 5 per cent better than the Metropolitan test and about 8 per cent better than the Detroit

test. However, these facts do not obviate the usefulness of the tests.

A combination of the intelligence and readiness tests does not appear to increase the prediction index of the tests—a fact which has been intimated previously by the relatively high correlation between the two tests. Some 57 per cent of the total number of children taking the tests scored 69 or better on the Metropolitan and made a mental age score higher than 78 months. Of this 57 per cent of all children, 65 per cent attained a grade status of at least 1.8. If the predictive index of percentages of success is a reasonable measure of test efficiency, the use of both tests shows comparatively little gain over the use of either one alone.

It must of course be borne in mind that prediction accuracy of both objective tests and subjective judgment of teachers will be decreased by children's illness or physical and sensory handicaps, absence from school, transferring from one school to another, unpredictable emotional blocks, inadequate teaching materials, poor teaching and similar factors.

From the available evidence, it appears that large city systems with some concern for their teaching budgets will get fairly accurate results in predicting readiness for first-grade entrants by relying upon subjective judgment, particularly of experienced teachers. Worthy of particular attention, however, is the fact that teachers seem to make most of their errors of judgment in assuming readiness on the part of children who are not ready for reading. This is precisely what the schools have been trying to prevent. It therefore appears to be reasonable to suggest that the best compromise at present is still a combination of teachers' judgment with either an intelligence or a readiness test. The slight increase of prediction accuracy by using both a readiness and an intelligence test is apparently not justified.

REFERENCES

1. Craig, James Calvin, "The Predictive Value of Reading Readiness Tests," Unpublished Master's Thesis, Graduate School, University of Pittsburgh, 1937, p. 42.
2. Dean, Charles D., "Predicting First-Grade Reading Achievement," *The Elementary School Journal,* Vol. 29 (April 1939), p. 612.
3. Grant, Albert, "The Comparative Validity of the Metropolitan Readiness Tests and the Pitner-Cunningham Primary Mental Test," *The Elementary School Journal,* Vol. 38 (April 1938), p. 602.
4. Hickey, Phillip J., *The Elementary School Journal,* Vol. 45, No. 1 (September 1944); *Colliers* (November 30, 1946).
5. Hildreth, Gertrude H., and Griffiths, Nellie L., *Metropolitan Reading Tests.* New York: World Book Co., 1939, p. 3.
6. Lee, J. Murray, Clark, W. W., and Lee, D. M., "Measuring Reading Readiness," *The Elementary School Journal,* Vol. 34 (May 1934). p. 658.
7. Seavy, Donald, "A Study of Comparative Predictive Value of Certain Measures of Reading Readiness in Predicting Success in Reading in First Grade," Unpublished Master's Thesis, Department of Education, State University of Iowa, 1943, p. 42.
8. Senour, A. C., "Comparison of Two Instruments for Measuring Reading Readiness," *Official Report of the American Educational Research Association,* No. 3 (February 23, 1937), p. 180.
9. Willmore, Waldo W., "Relative Validity of Three Group Tests in Predicting Reading Achievement" Unpublished Master's Thesis, Kansas, University, 1939, p. 67.
10. Wright, Wendell W., "Reading Readiness—A Prognostic Study," *Bulletin of the School of Education,* Indiana University, Vol. 12 (June 1936), p. 14.

9: The Metropolitan Readiness Tests as Predictors of First-Grade Achievement *

BLYTHE C. MITCHELL

Purpose. The purpose of this study was to investigate the predictive validity of the *Metropolitan Readiness Tests* against the 1959 Revision of the *Metropolitan Achievement Tests* as the criterion measure.

Predictor variables. The six subtests of the Readiness battery, with the number of items indicated, are as follows: 1.Word Meaning (19), 2.Sentences (14), 3.Information (14), 4. Matching (19), 5.Numbers (24), and 6.Copying (10). The validities of Tests 1-4 combined (66 items), of Test 5, and of the Total test (100 items) are reported. Tests 1-4 are generally considered as predicting readiness for reading; Test 5, readiness for arithmetic.

Criterion variables. The Primary I Battery of the *Metropolitan Achievement Tests* is designed for use at the end of the first grade. Four separate measures are provided: 1.Word Knowledge (35 items), 2.Word Discrimination (35 items), 3.Reading (45 items), and 4.Arithmetic Concepts and Skills (63 items). An assessment of total reading achievement is provided by the average of Tests 1-3.

Subjects. Complete results on predictor and criterion tests were available for 1170 pupils in the white and negro schools of an entire Virginia county for the school year 1959-60. In order that observed correlations between predictor and criterion would not be affected (raised) by the greater variability of a combined group, results were obtained separately for white and negro schools. This report is concerned largely with the 919 pupils in the white schools of the county.

Procedure. The Readiness tests were administered during the month of September, 1959. Performance was expressed in raw score terms and, for the total of Tests 1-6, as Readiness Status categories E (low) through A (high). These categories are set up to contain successively 7 per cent, 24 per cent, 38 per cent, 24 per cent and 7 per cent of the distribution of scores for the national standardization group.

The Achievement tests were administered the following May (1960), with results expressed in terms of grade equivalents.

Results. The predictor-criterion rela-

Table 1: Reliabilities of the Predictor and Criterion Instruments

Metropolitan Readiness Tests (Alternate-form)		Metropolitan Achievement Tests (Split-half)	
Tests 1-4	.83	Test 1. Word Knowledge	.90
Test 5	.84	Test 2. Word Discrimination	.87
Total, Tests 1-6	.89	Test 3. Reading	.92
		Test 4. Arithmetic Concepts & Skills	.93

* Reprinted from *Educational and Psychological Measurement*, Vol. 22, No. 4 (Winter 1962), pp. 765-72, with permission of the author and the publisher.

tionships are shown as product-moment correlation coefficients (Tables 2-4) and as bivariate charts (Tables 6-9).

Table 1 gives reliability data on the two instruments as reported in the respective test manuals. Each of the values shown for the *Metropolitan Readiness Tests* represents the median of alternate-form determinations for six separate groups averaging 195 pupils each. The reliabilities for the *Metropolitan Achievement Tests* were obtained by the split-half method (raised by Spearman-Brown) and represent the median of determinations in four school systems, with 100 cases in each sample.

Table 2 gives the correlations between the September readiness scores and achievement as measured in May. Means and standard deviations for all variables are also shown.

Tables 3 and 4 compare the validities of the Total Readiness score for boys and for girls (white), and for the white and the negro pupils in the county. The coefficients are shown to be almost identical for the four groups. The greatest difference is between the white and negro pupils when Word Discrimina-

tion is the achievement criterion. This difference of .091 is not statistically significant.

Sex difference in readiness. The usual relation between the readiness of boys and that of girls is reaffirmed by the present data for the pupils in the white schools of the County. The mean Total Readiness score of the 488 boys was 73.92, while that of the 431 girls was 76.42. This difference of 2.5 in the means is significant at better than the .05 level, indicating that the entering girls are more ready for formal learning than are the entering boys. The difference, though statistically significant, would appear to be of minor practical significance, however. The boys' mean score of 73.9 would have a percentile rank of 58, and the girls' mean of 76.4 one of 64, in the distribution of individual scores for the combined boy-girl national standardization group. The standard deviation of the Total score distribution for boys was 15.82, that for girls 15.14.

Readiness and achievement vs. CA. In contrast to the correlations of .51 to .63 between Readiness test scores

Table 2: Predictive Validity of Metropolitan Readiness Tests as Found for the 919 First-Grade Pupils in the White Schools of a County System

	Correlation with *Metropolitan Achievement Tests* (1959 Edition, Primary I Battery)						
Metropolitan Readiness Tests	1. Word Knowledge	2. Word Discrimination	3. Reading	Average Reading (Tests 1-3)	4. Arithmetic Concepts & Skills	Mean [1]	S.D.[1]
Tests 1-4	.467	.462	.427	.482	.544	53.4	9.3
Test 5	.563	.581	.512	.589	.622	15.1	5.1
Tests 1-6 (Total)	.558	.557	.511	.578	.632	75.1	15.6
Mean [2]	1.87	1.99	2.01	1.96	2.31		
Standard Deviation [2]	.44	.61	.59	.52	.61		

[1] In terms of raw score.
[2] Grade equivalents. Norm for date of administration is 1.8.

Table 3: Boy-Girl Comparisons for Correlation between Total Score on Metropolitan Readiness Tests (September) and Grade Equivalents on Metropolitan Achievement Tests (May) for the 919 Pupils in the White Schools of a Virginia County

		Metropolitan Achievement Tests (1959 Edition)				
Group	Number of Pupils	1. Word Knowledge	2. Word Discrimination	3. Reading	(Average Reading) Tests 1-3	4. Arithmetic Concepts and Skills
Boys	488	.559	.535—	.494	.565+	.635—
Girls	431	.551	.576	.524	.587	.627

Table 4: White-Negro Comparisons for Correlation between Total Score on Metropolitan Readiness Tests (September) and Performance on Metropolitan Achievement Tests (May) for the 1170 First-Grade Pupils in a Virginia County

		Metropolitan Achievement Tests (1959 Edition)				
Group	Number of Pupils	1. Word Knowledge	2. Word Discrimination	3. Reading	(Average Reading) Tests 1-3	4. Arithmetic Concepts and Skills
White Pupils	919	.558	.557	.511	.578	.632
Negro Pupils	251	.553	.466	.475+	.583	.617

Table 5: Correlation between Chronological Age and End-of-First-Grade Performance on Metropolitan Achievement Tests for the 919 Pupils in the White Schools of a Virginia County

	Correlation with Chronological Age	
Metropolitan Achievement Tests (1959 Edition)	For entire CA range, 5-11 through 7-11 ($N = 919$)	For CA's 5-11 through 6-11 only [1] ($N = 862$)
Test 1. Word Knowledge	−.016	.077
Test 2. Word Discrimination	−.023	.084
Test 3. Reading	−.001	.091
Test 4. Arithmetic Concepts and Skills	−.001	.087

[1] The correlations are positive when only those cases within this modal-age range are included. For *all* first-grade pupils, as shown in the preceding column of the table, however, the correlations are affected by the inclusion of 57 repeaters, pupils who are over-age but are at a low level of achievement.

and achievement, as shown in Table 2, Table 5 shows the relation between chronological age and end-of-first-grade performance on the *Metropolitan Achievement Tests*. The highest *r* for the modal-age group (.091) just reaches the .01 level of significance. It appears that *within the twelve-month age range for first-grade entrance* achievement is only very slightly related to age differences.

The relation between CA and the October score on the *Metropolitan Readiness Tests* was .126 for the entire age range, .146 for the modal-age range 5-11 through 6-11 only. Thus CA dif-

ferentiation within the year's span of normal entrance age is shown to be a relatively poor measure of the degree of readiness for learning, and of little use as a predictor of first-grade achievement.

In Tables 6 through 9 the relation between Readiness Status, as determined by Total score on the Readiness tests, and end-of-the-year achievement is shown in the form of bivariate distributions. The first-grade "success" of pupils in each September Readiness Status category is shown by the frequencies (and percentages) at each 3-month grade-equivalent interval. In the lower

Table 6: Distribution of May Grade Equivalents on Test 1, Word Knowledge, for Pupils in Each September Readiness Category

Grade Equivalents on *Word Knowledge* (Metropolitan Test 1)	Readiness Status in September of First Grade										Total
	E Poor Risk		D Low Normal		C Average		B High Normal		A Superior		
	f	(%)	f	(%)	f	(%)	f	(%)	f	(%)	
3.0-3.2					1		9	(3)	14	(10)	24
2.7-2.9					2	(1)	17	(6)	33	(23)	52
2.4-2.6			4	(2)	19	(7)	30	(11)	25	(18)	78
2.1-2.3			1	(1)	8	(3)	30	(11)	14	(10)	53
1.8-2.0	1	(4)	25	(14)	93	(32)	118	(42)	40	(28)	277
——————————————————————————————————————											*
1.5-1.7	5	(19)	98	(56)	146	(50)	73	(26)	14	(10)	337
1.2-1.4	15	(56)	35	(20)	20	(7)	7	(2)	1	(1)	78
Below 1.2	6	(22)	12	(7)	3	(1)					20
Total	27	(101)	175	(100)	292	(101)	284	(101)	141	(100)	919
Median Grade Equivalent	1.3		1.6		1.7		1.9		2.4		1.8
Per Cent Reaching (or Exceeding) Norm	4%		17%		42%		72%		89%		52.7%

* This dotted line divides those who scored at or above norm (1.8) from those who failed to reach the norm on the May achievement test.

Table 7: Distribution of May Grade Equivalents on Test 2, Word Discrimination, for Pupils in Each September Readiness Category

Grade Equivalents on *Word Discrimination* (Metropolitan Test 2)	Readiness Status in September of First Grade										
	E Poor Risk		D Low Normal		C Average		B High Normal		A Superior		Total
	f	(%)	f	(%)	f	(%)	f	(%)	f	(%)	
3.9 and over							1		2	(1)	3
3.6-3.8					3	(1)	10	(4)	18	(13)	31
3.3-3.5											
3.0-3.2					8	(3)	11	(4)	23	(16)	42
2.7-2.9			1	(1)	6	(2)	20	(7)	21	(15)	48
2.4-2.6			6	(3)	21	(7)	69	(24)	28	(20)	124
2.1-2.3			7	(4)	31	(11)	53	(19)	20	(14)	111
1.8-2.0	2	(7)	34	(19)	73	(25)	62	(22)	18	(13)	189
* — *											
1.5-1.7	3	(11)	39	(22)	83	(28)	38	(13)	6	(4)	169
1.2-1.4	20	(74)	82	(47)	65	(22)	19	(7)	5	(4)	191
Below 1.2	2	(7)	6	(3)	2	(1)	1				11
Total	27	(99)	175	(99)	292	(100)	284	(100)	141	(100)	919
Median Grade Equivalent	1.3		1.4		1.7		2.2		2.6		1.9
Per Cent Reaching Norm	7%		27%		49%		80%		92%		59.6%

* This dotted line divides those who scored at or above norm (1.8) from those who failed to reach the norm on the May achievement test.

rows of the table, the average achievement (median grade equivalent) for each readiness category and the proportion reaching the grade norm of 1.8 are shown.

The five Readiness Status categories, E through A, correspond successively to the Total score ranges 0-39, 40-64, 65-79, 80-89, and 90-100.

The significant information to be gained from each table is illustrated by the following statements regarding Table 6, in which the criterion is the Word Knowledge subtest:

Of the 27 pupils who made a Total Readiness score below 40 and were thus classified as "Poor Risks" for learning, only one reached the national norm of 1.8 at the end of year. Of the 175 with Readiness scores classified as "Low Normal," 30, or about one out of six, reached or exceeded the national norm. Of the 292 with "Average" Readiness scores, 42 per cent achieved at 1.8 or above; and for the 284 "High Normal" and the 141 "Superior," the per cents were 72 and 89, respectively. The median May grade equivalent of the cases classified by the Readiness tests as "Poor Risks" was 1.3, with the successively more "ready" pupils averaging 1.6, 1.7, and 1.9 and 2.4 (middle second grade), respectively.

Summary. Test results for 1170 first-grade pupils in a county school system show the *Metropolitan Readiness Tests* to be good predictors of first-grade learning. Correlations of Total Readiness score as a predictor with achievement on each of the four subtests of the *Metropolitan Achievement Tests* as the criteria range from .51 to .63. No significant differences in validity between boys and girls or between white and negro pupils were found.

Bivariate charts show a considerable degree of relationship between the five Readiness Status categories and end-of-year grade equivalents. Less than 10 per cent of the October "Poor Risks" reached the grade norm in May, and less than 10 per cent of those of "Superior" readiness status failed to reach it.

The Readiness tests would appear to be a useful instrument in determining the degree of readiness for first-grade learning. The results may serve (a) as guides in homogeneous grouping for differentiated instruction, and (b) as suggestive of the types of readiness development needed by various pupil groups.

Table 8: Distribution of May Grade Equivalents on Test 3, Reading, for Pupils in Each September Readiness Category

Grade Equivalent on *Reading* (Metropolitan Test 3)	Readiness Status in September of First Grade										Total
	E Poor Risk		D Low Normal		C Average		B High Normal		A Superior		
	f	(%)	f	(%)	f	(%)	f	(%)	f	(%)	
3.9 and above					1		4	(1)	6	(4)	11
3.6-3.8					3	(1)	5	(2)	10	(7)	18
3.3-3.5					1		2	(1)	12	(9)	15
3.0-3.2			1	(1)	5	(2)	12	(4)	18	(13)	36
2.7-2.9			3	(2)	6	(2)	23	(8)	29	(21)	61
2.4-2.6			6	(3)	12	(4)	27	(10)	7	(5)	52
2.1-2.3					16	(5)	54	(19)	21	(15)	91
1.8-2.0	2	(7)	34	(19)	102	(35)	98	(35)	24	(17)	260
— —											*—*
1.5-1.7	16	(59)	103	(59)	128	(44)	57	(20)	11	(8)	315
1.2-1.4	4	(15)	22	(13)	16	(5)	1		3	(2)	46
Below 1.2	5	(19)	6	(3)	2	(1)	1				14
Total	27	(100)	175	(100)	292	(99)	284	(100)	141	(101)	919
Median Grade Equivalent	1.5		1.6		1.75		2.0		2.8		1.8
Per Cent Reaching Norm	7%		25%		50%		79%		90%		59.2%

* This dotted line divides those who scored at or above norm (1.8) from those who failed to reach the norm on the May achievement test.

Table 9: Distribution of May Grade Equivalents on Test 4, Arithmetic Computation and Skills, for Pupils in Each September Readiness Category

Grade Equivalent on *Arithmetic Computation and Skills* (Metropolitan Test 4)	Readiness Status in September of First Grade										
	E Poor Risk		D Low Normal		C Average		B High Normal		A Superior		Total
	f	(%)	f	(%)	f	(%)	f	(%)	f	(%)	
3.9-3.9+					1		3	(1)	6	(4)	10
3.6-3.8			2	(1)	2	(1)	7	(2)	17	(12)	28
3.3-3.5											
3.0-3.2			2	(1)	16	(5)	42	(15)	41	(29)	101
2.7-2.9			1	(1)	20	(7)	26	(9)	22	(16)	69
2.4-2.6			12	(7)	53	(18)	69	(24)	33	(23)	167
2.1-2.3	2	(7)	39	(22)	83	(28)	92	(32)	16	(11)	232
1.8-2.0	1	(4)	34	(19)	68	(23)	37	(13)	5	(4)	145
* — *											
1.5-1.7	4	(15)	33	(19)	21	(7)	7	(2)	1	(1)	66
1.2-1.4	8	(30)	35	(20)	22	(8)	1				66
1.0-1.1	12	(44)	17	(10)	6	(2)					35
Total	27	(100)	175	(100)	292	(99)	284	(98)	141	(100)	919
Median Grade Equivalent	1.2		1.8		2.1		2.4		2.8		2.2
Per Cent Reaching Norm	11%		51%		82%		96%		99%		81.8%

* This dotted line divides those who scored at or above norm (1.8) from those who failed to reach the norm on the May achievement test.

10: Improving First-Grade Achievement by Readiness Instruction *

R. W. EDMISTON and MRS. BESSIE PEYTON

Three years ago there was published in this journal the report of a study by the late Miss Hollahan which indicated some measures to be used to predict first-grade school achievement.[1] She verified her findings by repeating her studies and then turned to the discovery of some means of lessening the predicted deficiencies in achievement. Miss Hollahan had provided a separate first grade for those pupils whose lack of success was predicted by the measures

* Reprinted from *School and Society*, Vol. 71, No. 1842 (April 8, 1950), pp. 230-32, by permission of the senior author and the publisher.

reported, but her death came before any report of her work on improving first-grade achievement was made available.

Mrs. Bessie Peyton,[2] of the Willard School of the Dayton, Ohio, city system, a colleague and fellow student of Miss Hollahan, became interested in procedures to improve first-grade achievement. She used readiness, intelligence, and personality tests as described by Miss Hollahan to locate the weaker entrants. She then set up a program of readiness instruction to determine the possibility of improving the pupils' achievement. The Willard School is a school for colored children and the principal, W. E. Wiley, was both interested and co-operative.

Fifty-four children whose test scores indicated definite possibility of poor achievement were placed under Mrs. Peyton and Willetta Chavous to provide two first-grade groups for the study. Dolch's *Readiness for Reading*[3] was used as the basis of instruction. The organization of this book permitted the completion of the first unit of readiness training in one month. Readiness scores were then obtained as a basis for determining which children could proceed with the regular first-grade instruction. Clark's *Reading Readiness* was used in selecting the pupils for the groups and the Metropolitan *Reading Readiness* for indications of readiness at the end of the instruction periods. The *California Mental Maturity* and *Personality* measures were administered with Clark's *Readiness* in selecting the group but were not repeated. Three four-week periods of readiness training were provided using the Dolch book.

At the end of the first period of readiness instruction, 32 of the 54 pupils obtained satisfactory reading readiness scores as per test standards. These pupils then proceeded with the regular first-grade reading program. Twenty-two pupils remained in the group and received further readiness instruction. Fifteen of these entered upon the regular first-

grade program after another four weeks; a total of eight weeks' readiness instruction.

The reading achievement was measured by the Metropolitan Achievement Test in April when the grade equivalent should have been 1.8. Of the 32 who entered the regular program after four weeks of readiness instruction, five fell below 1.7 in grade achievement and two of these were more than one standard deviation below the 1.8 norm. Neither the original intelligence nor the personality scores offered any reason for these two low achievements. Of the fifteen pupils with eight weeks' readiness training, only five obtained Metropolitan grade equivalents of 1.7[4] or better and five were more than one standard deviation below the 1.8 test norm. Of the seven in the group with three months' readiness instruction, only five showed progress in reading and three of these were a standard deviation below the 1.8 test norm. The three groups had three, two, and one months, respectively, less regular first-grade training due to the periods spent in readiness training. None of this third group had final satisfactory reading achievement by the end of the school year.

The critical ratios among the means of readiness, mental maturity, and personality-tests scores for the three groups formed from the 54 pupils studied showed the definite superiority of the first group in the three factors as did the critical ratios of the means of the Metropolitan achievement-tests scores. These comparisons of means indicated that the scores were indicative of reading attainment.

The two children with no reading progress had speech difficulties and mental ages of 2-10 and 4-0, the lowest of the 54. These children were transferred to special schools at the end of the year. They are not included in the following comparisons of the groups from the two studies.

Mrs. Peyton's group was selected on

the basis that all had reading-readiness scores below the 39 figure established by Miss Hollahan as the lowest score indicative of success in first-grade work. The correlations of the scores of reading achievement with the scores of mental age, reading readiness, and personality were .57, .59, .50, and .50, .52, .55 for the Hollahan and Peyton studies respectively. The means and ranges of the (1) reading readiness, (2) mental age, and (3) personality scores were (1) M = 39, Range = 14 to 58, (2) M = 77, Range = 66 to 88, (3) M = 69, Range = 35 to 92, respectively, for the Hollahan study, and (1) M = 32, Range = 7 to 38, (2) M = 65, Range = 51 to 96, and (3) M = 46, Range = 14 to 75 for the Peyton study. The correlations were similar for both studies while the means indicated the lower capacities and achievements of the Peyton group.

The differences between the low scores of pupils attaining satisfactory achievement as established by the two studies indicated that, while a mental age of 5-6 was the lowest appearing with successful first-grade achievement with no readiness instruction, a mental age as low as 5-0 appeared with successful achievement after 4 weeks' readiness instruction, and a second mental age of 5-0 succeeded after 8 weeks of readiness instruction. While Miss Hollahan established 39 as the desirable readiness score, a pupil with original readiness score of 25 did successful work after 4 weeks of readiness instruction as did 29 others with scores from 26 to 38 in readiness. One pupil with readiness score of 20 succeeded in attaining a 1.7 grade achievement after 8 weeks' readiness instruction, but the three others with 8 weeks of readiness instruction and readiness scores below 25 did not achieve above 1.5. The low achievement of those with readiness score below 25 was also maintained by those with 12 weeks of readiness instruction.

Miss Hollahan found 59 as the highest personality score of a first-grade failure and no one passing with a score below 37. Mrs. Peyton had two successful pupils with personality scores of 30 in the group with 4 weeks of readiness instruction, and, while one with 24 in the group with 8 weeks of readiness instruction attained success, eight others with scores of 30 or below had low reading achievements.

The above data indicated that, with readiness instruction of the type provided, only those pupils with mental ages below 5 years, California personality scores below 30, and Clark reading-readiness scores below 25 had little or no chance to attain satisfactory first-grade reading achievement. There was little value in the third four weeks of readiness instruction since all the pupils who obtained above 1.5 reading achievement had attained successful readiness scores at the end of eight weeks. However, the added instruction might have been desirable for those finally unsuccessful in the group with eight weeks of readiness instruction. It is recommended that a readiness score of 70 rather than 60 be required after the second 4 weeks of readiness instruction. This would have retained in the special group all but one of the pupils from the second group who obtained a final unsatisfactory achievement score. Perhaps a different readiness test rather than repetition of the Metropolitan was indicated. An extra period of school to replace the period of regular instruction lost by the readiness instruction is also recommended.

Twelve of the 52 normal pupils in the Peyton study group did not succeed in attaining the achievement considered desirable for placement with the regular second-grade groups. If one can assume that the 52 pupils would not have made satisfactory attainment, 42 were brought to the necessary achievement to proceed with their school group by the readiness instruction. A saving of 80 per cent seems worth while and commendable.

The data suggested the further conclusion that at least two types of difficulties which affect the success of first graders were amenable to rather rapid improvement. One was adjustment and the other readiness. Just what features of adjustment and readiness were not designated, but further research to determine these features and procedure to bring improvement was indicated.

REFERENCES

1. Edmiston, R. W., and Hollahan, C. E., *School and Society* (April 13, 1946), p. 268. *Education Digest* (November 1946), pp. 52-4.
2. The data for the computations reported can be found in Mrs. Peyton's thesis, "Preparing Below Average First Graders To Do Effective Reading," which is on file in the library of Miami University.
3. Dolch, E. W., Dolch, M. P., and Jackson, B., *Readiness for Reading,* Champaign, Ill.: The Garrard Press, 1942, pp. 1-64.
4. The figure 1.7 was used because it was considered as expressing reading achievement indicative of probable success in the second grade.

CHAPTER IV

Word Perception and Meaning

11: Sequence in Word Perception *

DOROTHY J. NEWBURY

Word perception is defined differently by various authorities in the field of reading. In this paper, it is defined as the ability to identify words and understand their meanings. This definition has a solid foundation in the psychological research dealing with visual perception.

The perceptual process, according to Vernon,[3] involved three stages. The first is described as a *vague awareness* that there is something in the visual field. The second—the stage of the *generic object*—involves awareness that the stimulus is connected with an existing object. The third stage is that of identifying the visual stimulation and attaching meaning to it. A fourth stage reported by some investigators, involves *naming* the object, or making some other appropriate response to it. This definition of the perceptual process provides a theoretical framework for the definition of word perception for this paper, and, to some extent, for the broad framework of sequential development of the skills.

WORD-PERCEPTION SKILLS

The first two stages in word perception, awareness of a vague form and identification of it as something (perhaps

a word), characterize the earliest stages in learning to recognize words. With specific training, naming of these words, even without meanings, can be developed. Indeed, the history of teaching reading reveals that these steps were long considered to be the major goals of reading instruction. Today, however, we recognize these stages only as a means to an end: the stage of understanding meaning of a passage and making appropriate responses to it.

In order to name a word and know its meaning, the child must have the essential readiness skills such as: ability to see total configurations and their components; ability to hear and discriminate words; sufficient background of experience to interpret words when they are identified; and associated facility in language to name the words. Furthermore, if interpretation, rather than mere naming is the goal of instruction in reading, then at the pre-reading levels pupils must develop the ability to interpret materials similar to those expected in the reading selections. Perhaps of greatest importance is the development of an attitude of demanding meaning, beginning with the earliest stages in learning to read, and continuing through all others to maturity.

The foregoing explanation sets the

* Reprinted from "Sequential Development of Reading Abilities," Helen M. Robinson, editor, *Supplementary Educational Monographs,* No. 90, Chicago: The University of Chicago Press; (December 1960), pp. 25-30, by permission of the publisher.

stage for identification of the word-per- ception skills. First is readiness, with emphasis on the attitudes and skills of obtaining meaning from what is seen and heard. To develop readiness in this area, good teachers help boys and girls to "read" picture stories without the printed word. Pupils learn to identify characters, to see time and place rela- tionships, to follow the thread of the story, to recognize emotional reactions, and to infer behavior and incidents in and later between pictures.

A second general approach involves listening to stories which the teacher tells or reads. Here, too, the emphasis is on developing interpretation. Later, or perhaps concurrently, children listen to the author's words and follow the se- quence of the pictures as the teacher reads interesting stories accompanied by pictures.

Then comes the talking picture-story of the preprimers, where action is sup- plied by the pictures and is basic to what the characters say in the text to be read. At this level, children interpret the pictures and words, the former be- ing a powerful stimulus to the later.

WORD FORM AND CONTEXT CLUES

Sight words are recognized as meaning- ful wholes fitting into a context sup- plied by pictures and words. By using the same words in different contexts, the words become familiar units and are recognized by their form and configura- tion. Familiar words may then be used to build larger units such as the sen- tence, the paragraph, the story and the book.

But form and configuration are insuf- ficient when picture clues are reduced, so that gradually the child is taught to scrutinize the word, noting the details of form within it. Through repetition in meaningful context, accurate memory of many word forms, associated with mean- ings, is achieved. This is called a sight vocabulary. Developing this stock of sight words is one of the major tasks of the primary teacher, and, to some ex- tent, of teachers at succeeding levels. By the end of first grade a child should have a stock of about 300 sight words and by the end of fourth grade, about 3000 sight words have been taught.

Memory for word form is no longer left to the ingenuity of each young child. Instead, exercises in workbooks and directions in guidebooks accompanying basal readers offer a wide variety of suggestions for aiding memory of word form.

A word-perception program, however, is not dominated by memory of each word. Instead, perception of words is enhanced by the use of context begin- ning at the pre-reading levels. Context helps to insure the complete cycle of perception. Context enables the child to infer the meaning of an unfamiliar word among several possibilities and from the inference, the pupil calls forth the proper word, or one with a similar meaning. For example, the primary pupil who does not recognize the word "red" in the sentence "He had a big red car," may refer to the context of the picture to determine the color of the car in the picture, to infer the meaning, and the word.

By fourth grade, pupils have learned to use additional types of context clues. For example, the word "traffic" may be inferred from summary clues in: "There were many cars, taxicabs, busses and trucks on the road. He had never seen so much *traffic.*" Comparison and con- trast might lead to identification of "seacoast" in: "Some birds like to live on dry land, but pelicans like the *sea- coast.*"

The ninth-grade student should be able to use all types of context clues. Examples are: "James heard the *ap- plause* but noticed that the man in the front row was not clapping." "The writer was guilty of plagiarism because he copied from Dickens and presented the writing as his own." At this level it is often necessary to use one or several paragraphs to determine the meaning of a word.

The college instructor of writing calls his student's attention to a selection entitled "Right Words." McCrimmon states that "since the relation between a word and its referent is a mental one, we can think of different referents for the same word. . . . In practice we learn the meanings of words by their context. . . . This is exactly how the writers of dictionaries get their definitions." [1] Then the student may be asked to define from context the word *disparity* in the sentence "There was an obvious disparity in the size, the one being more than double the size of the other." [2]

Context clues are used very widely by mature readers and are usually the first means for attacking unfamiliar words. Consequently it is essential that both the use and limitations of context clues be clearly understood as pupils progress in reading. [4]

In a sequential reading program it is difficult to separate the use of word form and context clues because they are so closely interrelated. However, the sequence of each adopted by most basal readers may be determined by consulting the index of skills in the accompanying guidebook.

STRUCTURAL AND PHONETIC ANALYSIS

Since there are many referents for the same word it is also obvious that one must choose among words for a single referent. Consequently additional means of independent analysis of words are needed.

Since words are usually first learned as meaningful wholes, the first stage of analysis is that of the structure. In the first grade, pupils learn about inflected endings. By the end of the second grade, they usually recognize syllables and are aware of accent. By the end of third grade, the average pupil can visually analyze three-syllable words into their components and know some of the principles of accent. He is beginning to recognize prefixes and suffixes too.

The middle-grade pupil adds other principles of accent. Combining these with what is known about syllabication, he must choose among them as he deals with more complex words. This process continues into high school and college.

Concomitantly, pupils learn phonetic analysis of words. As a rule, the beginnings occur in the reading readiness period when pupils learn to distinguish similarities and differences in speech sounds in words. Once this step is mastered, pupils are ready to note that changing the first consonant in a word makes another word. So he begins the association between spoken and written sounds, which continues to grow throughout his school years. After learning to substitute initial consonants and their sounds comes substitution of final consonants and then vowels. The principles for the changing sounds of vowels and some consonants are gradually understood. With attention directed to meaning the pupil accepts variations in sounds because he combines phonetic analysis with context clues. He remembers principles for attacking new words because he uses them in many different meaningful selections.

The sounds of the letters are changed by the accent in words of more than one syllable. For example, by the fifth grade, a pupil can usually divide an unknown word into syllables, determine which one is accented, and choose the proper vowel sound for the accented and unaccented syllables. He begins to associate the use of words, such as nouns and verbs, with their accent.

In the junior and senior high schools, comes the study of etymology. Students learn that a language changes and grows. Part of this change is achieved through the use of foreign words, so students learn common pronunciations for words borrowed from other languages. They also recognize some Greek and Latin roots and verb forms. For example, *vista, supervise,* and *visualize* are derived from the Latin root *visus.*

Thus the gradual and continuous introduction and mastery of the phonetic-analysis skills as they are needed in the selections from which pupils read lead to maturity in phonetic analysis of word forms. At all times it is recognized as a means to an end—not an end in itself.

words are encountered in materials read, the simpler dictionaries are gradually replaced by those that are more complicated and more complete.

Thus the major means for promoting a well-developed sight vocabulary is wide reading in which words are repeated until they are thoroughly familiar and accurately recognized instantaneously. This sight vocabulary is acquired gradually. To develop independence, each learner must become proficient in the use of context clues, structural analysis, phonetic analysis, and the dictionary.

DICTIONARY SKILLS

In some programs, the picture dictionary is used as early as the first grade, but it usually offers only a picture and a word. The use of even a simple dictionary requires familiarity with the alphabet in order, the ability to use diacritical marks (based on knowledge of sounds of letters and phonemes), and the ability to use context to determine the proper meaning among the many supplied. It is obvious that many of the word-perception skills necessarily precede the use of the dictionary.

As in all of the other aspects of word perception, attention is directed toward meaning, and as a rule the pupil turns to the dictionary when context clues combined with structural and phonetic analysis fail to provide the pronunciation of a word; or when successful pronunciation does not supply the proper meaning to secure complete understanding of the selection.

In many programs pupils begin, in the middle grades, to place known words in alphabetic order, using the first letter, then the first two, and so on. As pupils need to turn to their first dictionary, they learn about guide words at the top of the page. Continuously they are learning to use pronunciation keys. As more technical and unusual

WORD MEANINGS

Visual perception is incomplete until the percept fits into some framework of experience and yields meaning. Likewise word perception has little value if the words are merely named without meaning attached to them.

In the early stages of learning to read, words which are already a part of children's speaking vocabularies are used. This is done to simplify the complex process of reading. Gradually, as pupils become proficient in the other aspects of word perception, unfamiliar words are encountered. In the process of identifying, or naming the word, context clues, based on the broader meaning, are used both to identify and determine the meanings of new words. Furthermore, familiar words take on new and varied meanings in different selections, or in different content areas.

At the upper grade and secondary levels, students learn to make use of explanations in the selection to illuminate word meanings; to refer to illustrations, glossaries, and footnotes; and finally to turn to the dictionary.

The basis for acquiring word meanings is experience accompanied by conversation and discussion. The reading materials provided for young children are selected to be within the range of their experiences. As children progress in school the words they encounter move further from their realm of direct experience. At this time vicarious experiences such as pictures, filmstrips, films, charts, and diagrams are often used to develop an expanding fund of word meanings. New meanings are learned by establishing relationships to known concepts. For example, the concept of the term "glacier" may be based on experience with ice and snow, or even on experience with ice in a skating rink. Concurrently, words become more abstract and concepts must be built from description, and discussion. Such words as *democracy, civil rights,* and *freedom* serve as illustrations. Words also become more abstract as they represent increased generalizations, and students must go through the inductive steps to acquire these meanings.

Approaching maturity, students should know several words which represent a single meaning and be aware of the particular shade of meaning which the author wishes to express by his selection of a particular word.

Early in the school years, teachers usually identify words which are likely to have inadequate meanings prior to assigning a selection. Later, children must learn to encounter new words and determine the meanings if they are to become independent readers.

LEVELS OF INSTRUCTION

Although several of the major word-perception skills have been isolated for discussion, in practice they are interdependent. As pupils mature, the different skills supplement each other quickly and smoothly. In fact, the mature reader often finds it difficult to determine which techniques he is using.

In the early school years, teachers give conscious attention to developing word perception. Gradually, as children develop independence, they are given more responsibility for learning on their own. But guidance on the part of teachers is needed throughout the school years. A common belief that word perception is taught mainly in the elementary school and interpretation in the high school and college is no longer tenable. Each stimulates, supplements, and enriches the other.

At the elementary level the teacher systematically directs students in the acquisition and use of word-perception skills. By the high school years, some teachers continue to present concepts and identify words to be read in lessons. In college, courses in writing are most likely to give attention to word perception.

Word perception is a complex aspect of reading in which the different skills are introduced gradually, practiced in a meaningful context, and mastered. For this reason, it is important to have proper vocabulary control and repetition. Publishers of basal readers usually take careful account of these skills. However, the order of introduction and sequence of development vary somewhat from one series to another. This is the reason I recommend following a single series in the elementary school rather than moving from one to another.

CONCLUDING STATEMENT

Word perception is basic in obtaining the meaning, reacting to what is read, and learning through reading. Therefore, it is not reading but only an essential ingredient. An attitude of demanding meaning from written and printed material enhances the development of all of the word-perception skills. Likewise, acquisition of the skills of word perception frees the reader to give his full attention to the ideas presented by the writer. Therefore, sequential development of word-perception skills lays the foundation for maturity in reading.

REFERENCES

1. McCrimmon, James M., *Writing with A Purpose: A First Course in Composition*. Boston: Houghton Mifflin, 1957.
2. Ibid. p. 157.
3. Vernon, M. D., *A Further Study of Visual Perception*. London: Cambridge University Press, 1954, pp. 20-23.
4. For a discussion of different techniques see *The Reading Teacher*, Vol. 11 (April 1958), entire issue.

12: A Core Vocabulary Study in the Elementary Grades *

GLENN R. JOHNSON

This is a study of the reading vocabulary used in the reading program of seven series of basic readers for grades one through six.

The basic reading series used in the study were: American Book Co., 1953; Ginn and Co., 1953; Houghton, Mifflin Co., 1957; Lyons and Carnahan, 1949; Macmillan Co., 1951; Row, Peterson & Co., 1947; Scott, Foresman & Co., 1955.

The basic reading series were selected for the study because they represent the majority of series used in the Euclid City Schools as basic texts and supplementary readers.

The complete study was undertaken by ten teachers and ten parents, with the author as chairman. The study was started during the school year 1956-57 and was completed during the school year 1957-58.

The committee's purpose was to compile a list of words believed to be the central core vocabulary used in the reading program for each grade level, to determine the overlap of vocabulary between publishing companies and to present any recommendations resulting from the study.

Since the committee was to compile a list of words believed to be the core vocabulary used in the reading program

for each grade level, they defined core vocabulary as: "Those words found in the lists of new words introduced in each of the seven basic series and which are common to at least five of the seven series."

The committee began its study by tabulating the words listed as "new words" in each of the basic reading series books. Each "new word" was placed on a 3" x 5" card along with the grade level and a code letter for the publishing company. Well over 15,000 cards were alphabetized by grade levels. The results of the tabulations for the first, second and third grades are as follows:

1st Grade. 727 different words were introduced on the first grade level by the entire seven basic reading series used in the study.
56 new words appeared in all seven series
81 new words appeared in only six series
58 new words appeared in only five series
52 new words appeared in only four series
67 new words appeared in only three series
118 new words appeared in only two series
295 new words appeared in only one series

2nd Grade. 1,289 different words were introduced on the second grade level by the entire seven basic reading series used in the study.
6 new words appeared in all seven series

* Reprinted from *Elementary English*, Vol. 39, No. 5 (May 1962), pp. 470-73, by permission of the National Council of Teachers of English and the author.

25 new words appeared in only six series
78 new words appeared in only five series
127 new words appeared in only four series
184 new words appeared in only three series
270 new words appeared in only two series
599 new words appeared in only one series

3rd Grade, 2,272 different words were introduced on the third grade level by the entire seven basic reading series used in the study.
20 new words appeared in all seven series
47 new words appeared in only six series
105 new words appeared in only five series
194 new words appeared in only four series
292 new words appeared in only three series
465 new words appeared in only two series
1,149 new words appeared in only one series

Because so few words appeared in five or more series on the fourth, fifth and sixth grade levels, they were not listed. However, it is interesting to note that less than fifty words appeared in five or more series on each of the upper elementary grades even though 2,790 different new words were introduced on fourth grade, 3,693 different new words were introduced on fifth grade and 4,584 different new words were introduced on sixth grade.

Only root words, proper nouns, compound words, hyphenated words and onamatapoetic words were included in the tabulations.

Those words appearing in five, six or seven basic series were then listed by grade level as "core words." This was only done for the first three grades since so few words appeared in the other grades as "core words."

Core lists for the first three grades were made available to classroom teachers. Tachistoscopic strips using the core words were also developed for use in the classroom.

The study was able to show that there was very little overlap of vocabulary between publishing companies. The vocabulary of basic reading series varies widely even though they are published for the same grade level.

The committee made the following recommendations:

1. Teachers use the core lists to help children develop common words they will come in contact with in their various reading experiences.
2. Teachers use the core lists as a method of evaluating the difficulty of various books (the committee realized this would be but one method of evaluating books and recomended the use of other methods in addition to the core list comparison).
3. The core lists be used by teachers in developing charts, teacher made tests, in teaching opposites and similarities, and in teaching prefixes and suffixes.
4. The core lists be used as an additional check list in teaching spelling.

The following conclusions are submitted for consideration:

1. There was very little overlap of vocabulary between publishing companies. This has implications for classroom teachers when they consider approaches to use in helping children read. Does the predetermined control of vocabulary used by any one basic reading series tend to limit a pupil's vocabulary instead of extend it? Is the basic series approach to reading best for pupils when we consider the extreme differences in the reading ability of children for any one classroom? Would individualized reading be more in keeping with what we know about children's interests and abilities?
2. If teachers are involved in an individualized reading program, perhaps the "common word list" could be used in checking and measuring the vocabulary development of the pupils, especially during the primary grades.
3. The "common word list" could be used as ONE method of evaluating various books children read.
4. In some cases a "common word list" could be used as a guide in the development of teacher made tests. A study by the author indicates that many children are handicapped by the vocabulary words used in test items supposedly developed to test comprehension ability.[1]

5. If a basic reading series approach is used, the "common word list" could be used in reading readiness, experience chart making, and vocabulary preparation for pre-primers, primers, and first readers.
6. The "common word list" can be used as a supplementary spelling list.

APPENDIX

FIRST GRADE
CORE VOCABULARY

Words that Appear

7 times

1. a
2. all
3. and
4. are
5. ask
6. back
7. be
8. big
9. blue
10. do
11. down
12. farm
13. fast
14. from
15. funny
16. go
17. had
18. have
19. here
20. him
21. house
22. I
23. is
24. like
25. little
26. look
27. man
28. may
29. mother
30. must
31. my
32. no
33. not
34. one
35. other
36. over
37. play
38. red
39. paid
40. sat
41. see
42. something
43. stop
44. the
45. them
46. there
47. time
48. to
49. up
50. want
51. we
52. were
53. what
54. when
55. work
56. you

6 times

1. about
2. am
3. as
4. at
5. baby
6. basket
7. began
8. Bill
9. boy
10. brown
11. call
12. can
13. car
14. come
15. could
16. day
17. did
18. dog
19. egg
20. find
21. fish
22. for
23. fun
24. get
25. girl
26. go
27. good
28. green
29. he
30. help
31. her
32. his
33. home
34. how
35. in
36. it
37. jump
38. just
39. kitten
40. know
41. let
42. long
43. made
44. many
45. me
46. name
47. night
48. now
49. of
50. old
51. on
52. pretty
53. put
54. ran
55. ride
56. road
57. run
58. saw
59. she
60. snow
61. so
62. some
63. soon
64. street
65. thank
66. that
67. they
68. thing
69. this
70. three
71. too
72. two
73. under
74. us
75. went
76. where
77. who
78. wish
79. with
80. yes
81. your

5 times

1. after
2. again
3. airplane
4. apple
5. around
6. away
7. before
8. bird
9. black
10. boat
11. but
12. by
13. came
14. door
15. eat
16. far
17. father
18. feet
19. four
20. give
21. happy
22. has
23. head
24. hill
25. horse
26. if
27. into
28. laugh
29. leave
30. make
31. morning
32. Mr.
33. Mrs.
34. new
35. next
36. oh
37. our
38. out
39. party
40. pig
41. rabbit
42. school
43. sleep
44. store
45. take
46. then
47. think
48. Tom
49. took
50. toy
51. tree
52. very
53. wagon
54. walk
55. water
56. white
57. will
58. would

SECOND GRADE
CORE VOCABULARY

Words that Appear

7 times

1. beautiful
2. care
3. front
4. left
5. kitchen
6. real

6 times

1. always
2. another
3. been
4. bell
5. burn
6. carry
7. caught
8. city
9. even
10. ever
11. eve
12. field
13. hand
14. happen
15. himself
16. keep
17. knew
18. light
19. listen
20. live
21. through
22. until
23. watch
24. wife
25. world

5 times

1. any
2. better
3. both
4. bright
5. bring
6. brought
7. clean
8. climb
9. deep
10. did
11. dig
12. drink
13. drive
14. end
15. fence
16. fine
17. flew
18. four
19. give
20. glad
21. gray
22. great
23. hard
24. hide
25. hole
26. hot
27. hurry
28. hurt
29. knock
30. learn
31. leg
32. letter
33. men
34. more
35. mouth
36. move
37. need
38. noise
39. nothing
40. paper
41. park
42. people
43. pick
44. piece
45. place
46. plant
47. policeman
48. puppy
49. queer
50. quick
51. right
52. river
53. sad
54. seen
55. should
56. side
57. sign
58. small
59. smell
60. start
61. still
62. strange
63. summer
64. sun
65. supper
66. sure
67. than
68. their
69. tie
70. tire
71. top
72. try
73. turn
74. uncle
75. wait
76. wash
77. while
78. wide

THIRD GRADE
CORE VOCABULARY

Words that Appear

7 times

1. breath
2. built
3. circle
4. danger
5. draw
6. fright
7. hang
8. hundred
9. instead
10. log
11. meat
12. month
13. much
14. mud
15. settle
16. sharp
17. star
18. teeth
19. woman
20. worry

6 times

1. adventure
2. arrow
3. beat
4. below
5. between
6. blanket
7. bow
8. bowl
9. break
10. cabin
11. chase
12. chief
13. child
14. company
15. dry
16. during
17. excited
18. felt
19. free
20. gun
21. heart
22. held
23. herd
24. hid
25. interest
26. jar
27. kick
28. life
29. lose
30. market
31. matter
32. mind
33. moment
34. notice
35. pile
36. save
37. set
38. shore
39. skin
40. stove
41. stretch
42. slow
43. smoke
44. thick
45. trade
46. trail
47. wall

5 times

1. act	26. either	51. low	79. silver
2. against	27. explain	52. luck	80. since
3. already	28. feed	53. meet	81. spoil
4. among	29. fierce	54. middle	82. spoke
5. angry	30. fight	55. mine	83. swift
6. bang	31. final	56. narrow	84. stir
7. become	32. finger	57. needle	85. stone
8. begin	33. fog	58. nod	86. straw
9. born	34. forest	59. ocean	87. sudden
10. cattle	35. forgot	60. plain	88. slip
11. chain	36. forth	61. plan	89. smooth
12. claw	37. forward	62. post	90. taste
13. cliff	38. Friday	63. pound	91. themselves
14. close	39. fur	64. prairie	92. though
15. cloud	40. gather	65. promise	93. tool
16. course	41. half	66. queen	94. toss
17. creep	42. hour	67. quick	95. tough
18. crowd	43. howl	68. race	96. toward
19. different	44. indeed	69. rather	97. trap
20. disappear	45. Indian	70. reply	98. vegetable
21. drop	46. lake	71. ribbon	99. village
22. drove	47. lambkins	72. root	100. weather
23. dust	48. led	73. sea	101. whole
24. eager	49. line	74. shape	102. wild
25. earth	50. load	75. shine	103. wool
		76. shook	104. worse
		77. shoot	105. worth
		78. should	

REFERENCE

1. Johnson, Glenn R., *Differences in Scores When the Comprehension Section of a Silent Reading Test Is Given Silently and Orally,* Unpublished Master's Thesis, Ohio State University, Columbus, Ohio, 1960, 70 pp.

13: The Problem of Vocabulary in Reading *

EDGAR DALE

In his *Defense of Poetry,* published in 1821, Shelley wrote: "We have more moral, political, and historical wisdom than we know how to reduce into practice; we have more scientific and economical knowledge than can be accommodated to the just distribution of the produce which it multiplies." He went on to say that we lacked the creative faculty to imagine that which we know, the generous impulse to act that which we imagine, that our calculations have outrun conception, that we have eaten more than we can digest. We are living circumscribed, enslaved lives. We lack the poetry of life. Shelley was talk-

* Reprinted from *Educational Research Bulletin;* Vol. 35, No. 5 (May 9, 1956), pp. 113-23, by permission of the author and the publisher.

ing, I assume, about the creators of excellence, the dreamers of dreams, the poets with bold conceptions described by Shakespeare

... as imagination bodies forth
The forms of things unknown, the poet's pen
Turns them to shapes and gives to airy nothing
A local habitation and a name.[24]

We cannot all be creators of excellence, but we can be purveyors of excellence. We can spend our time bringing the best to the most. Indeed, the essence of today's world-wide struggle is the desire of about two billion people in this world to share the good things that the other half-billion have. Such sharing in the past has been confined to a small number. Illiteracy is as high as 90 per cent in some undeveloped countries.

The sharing process has moved ahead in the United States under a philosophy of democracy aiming at the greatest possible growth of the common man. The American common school was founded with the goal or ideal of the diffusion of information. In the last century we had the sharing of ideas among adults through the press, through the Mechanics Institutes, Chautauquas, Lyceums, business colleges, Granges, Unions, and other groups. All aimed in some way to share insights, distribute knowledge and skills, to let the ordinary man in on things. The great growth of our elementary schools came after 1850, of our high schools after 1900, of our junior colleges after 1950—much of it is yet to come.

How does all this relate to the problem of vocabulary in reading? Certainly, in preparing reading materials for all levels of ability, we need to have information about the experiences, the interests, the needs, the background, the information already possessed by these readers. All suggest the need for vocabulary study. Words, after all, are the deposit of experience—the result of

what we have done or are thinking. They are the bearers of meaning—the symbols which represent experience.

To have data on the vocabulary of individuals whom we are trying to teach is imperative. Let us not call such data "mere words." Words represent the concepts, the distillate of previous experience.

What data on vocabulary in reading and writing do we now have? What do we need? We already know the words that adults and children are most likely to use when writing letters and thus to read. Here we have studies by Ernest Horn, [14] by Henry D. Rinsland, [26] by Frederick S. Breed, [2] and many others. Their studies have proved useful in eliminating from spelling instruction the words only rarely used.

From these studies we can predict that about 50 simple words will make up about half of the total words used in writing or reading. These studies also disclose a basic difficulty found in all frequency studies of vocabulary. The prediction of the additional words beyond the 50 commonest which an individual will write gets progressively poorer and the usefulness of additional words diminishes rapidly. Horn points out that "two thousand words with their repetitions make up 95.05 per cent of the running words in adult writing; 3,000, 96.9 per cent; 4,000, 97.8 per cent; and 10,000, 99.4 per cent." [15] This means that it is hard to predict the words which a person will write once he has gone beyond 2,000 words. You would have to add 8,000 words to a common spelling list to increase the vocabulary from 95.05 to 99.4 per cent.

We also know the words and the frequency of their appearance in a wide variety of reading materials. Thus we have Thorndike and Lorge's study of the most frequently appearing 30,000 words, [21] as well as their studies of semantic frequencies; the Buckingham-Dolch list which combines several lists, [3] and the Gates list of 1,500 common words.[13]

We have studies of the spoken vocabulary of young children, notably the International Kindergarten Union List compiled by Madeline Horn and her collaborators.[16] One of these studies appeared in this magazine in 1935. The report, based on a series of dictations to a dictaphone plus a check list used by the parents, shows that a five-year-old girl had learned over 3,145 words for she used them in conversation.[29] This would be about 800 words learned a year for four years or around two a day.

Studies in vocabulary frequently have served, and continue to serve, a useful purpose, but such studies have certain weaknesses which make them not as useful in preparing reading materials as we once hoped. E. W. Dolch concludes that

... word counts [of children's speech and writing] are useful and desirable. They "stake out" areas of word knowledge. They tell us what children may know about by discovering use of words by a few children. Beyond that point, however, they are hopelessly unreliable because of the factors of opportunity and emotional set.... As a result, though we may use word counts, the only source of genuine knowledge of children's word knowledge is systematic testing procedure.[10]

The difficulty with such frequency studies of reading materials is similar to the one that Horn has noted about spelling words. A limited number of words—1,000 or 2,000, certainly not more than 3,000—give us the easily predicted words. From then on we have moved beyond the words of common experience—the structural words in the English language, the household words, the words of time, place, direction, parts of the body, and the like.

Can we use these frequency data and predict the words that children will know grade by grade? Thorndike and Lorge set up certain suggestions for the use of their frequency data.[22] They suggest that during each successive grade the following number of words selected from their list should be taught "for permanent knowledge":

	Number of Words
Grades I and II	1,069
Grade III	952
Grade IV	1,864
Grades V and VI	1,867
Grades VII and VIII	1,896
Grade IX	1,574
Grade X	1,064
Grade XI	1,442
Total	11,728

They conclude that graduation from high school "may be made conditional upon knowledge of at least 15,000 words." Assuming that he came to school with 3,000 words, this would mean adding about 1,000 words a year or three words a day. This is a sensible goal and probably accords well with actual vocabulary growth and possibilities.

Unfortunately, however, there are many discrepancies between frequency of occurrence of words and their familiarity. The correlation is not high—perhaps somewhere between .40 and .50. Kirkpatrick and Cureton found a correlation of .47 with a multiple-choice test and the Thorndike-Lorge frequency. However, the estimates of five judges correlated .71 with the same test. The correlation increased to .81 by combining both methods.[20] Note the following words which Thorndike and Lorge found occurring four times or less per 18,000,000 running words. Statistically, then, youngsters should not be expected to know words like these:[23]

accompanist	astigmatism
adorably	avoidable
aflutter	backache
airdrome	backbite
air-mail	backdoor
anklet	bedbug
asterisk	beefy

black-list	faultfinding
bluegrass	firebrick
bootee	flagman
bucksaw	flare-up
bunghole	floodlight
butterfat	furthermost
cashew	get-together
clubman	goody-goody
clubroom	grandaunt
cowbell	greyhound
crossways	handhold

According to their scheme, words having ratings of less than three are for twelfth-graders. Yet this includes words like *abbreviate, abbreviation, able-bodied, ably, abolitionist, absent-minded, abusive, accelerate, acceleration, accelerator, accordion, acrobat, adenoids, adrift, advertiser, aflame*—words known by two-thirds of sixth- or eighth-graders.

The word lists noting frequency of word counts are helpful in preparing reading materials. But, as I noted earlier, the frequency score does not correlate highly with familiarity. Is there a better approach to the problem?

The difficulty with sampling millions of running words is that we are sampling nothing really homogeneous. I suggest, therefore, that further studies of general frequency are not likely to be very fruitful. What we especially need are studies of specialized areas—technical fields—and the like.

Some of the earliest studies in technical vocabulary were done by Luella Cole and Sidney Pressey. In 1923, Mr. Pressey with Bertha Lively reported a study entitled *A Method for Measuring the Vocabulary Burden of Textbooks*.[25] Luella Cole, in *The Teacher's Handbook of Technical Vocabulary*,[5] lists words from her own studies combined with words from the studies of others. She also presents the Thorndike ratings of these words. However, since these are not semantic counts one can hardly assume that such words as *bond, note, check, balance,* are appearing frequently because of their technical meanings.

Luella Cole's lists of social-studies terms are quoted by Kelley and Krey in *Test and Measurements in the Social Studies*. There was usually a steady gain from grade to grade; some words, however, showed a loss. These tended to be words where the test itself was inadequate or where the words were no longer studied in the school.[17] From Luella Cole's study we can conclude that there is a mean growth of about 8 per cent a year with greatest growth in the junior high and less in the upper years of the high school.

This may be because the ceiling kept getting closer and closer. My own study of the growth of understanding of technical terms in business from Grades VII to XII showed an average gain of 6 per cent a year with a big gain in the seventh or eighth grade. Luella Cole thought that growth in the senior high school was below normal expectancy and suggested that it might be due to lessened attention to the vocabulary problem in high school.[18]

I have previously reported a technique for vocabulary control in preparing reading materials in health, and the article is briefly summarized here. The directors of the National Tuberculosis Association thought that their materials for the layman were inadequate and launched a careful study of these pamphlets. A readability analysis showed that their materials were averaging around ninth and tenth grade when the average reading level of the persons who are most likely to get tuberculosis is probably around Grade VI—the poorer people, the less-schooled people living in crowded conditions. Next, experts in the field of tuberculosis were asked to underline all the technical terms in ten of their key pamphlets. My collaborator and I found 715 different technical health terms with the word, *tuberculosis*, used 103 times and one appearance only for words like *arrested disease, congestion,* and *lymph canals*. About 62 per cent of the words appeared only once, 19 per cent twice, 9 per cent three or four time, 6 per cent from five to nine times, 2 per cent from ten to twenty-four times, and 2 per cent from twenty-five to over one hundred times. This is a typical pattern of a situation in which specialists, unaware of the difficulty or complexity of a technical vocabulary, prepare reading materials for the public. Next, we asked tuberculosis specialists to list the terms most important for health education and added to it the highly frequent health words from this source and others.

Then 550 pupils in Grades VII to XII checked whether they knew the meaning of each of these 476 important health terms. We also had a number of the pupils write out definitions for some of these words. We then compared the two tests and found that for almost every word, a larger percentage had checked it as known than had actually defined it correctly on the definitions test. The average discrepancy for a small sample of words was 11 per cent. The tendency to overestimate was greater on words which were not widely known.

A third study of technical terms in health was made with adults who had about six years of formal education. Fifty of these terms were tested by a multiple-choice test, with the remaining 328 words tested by checking as known or not known. These words are presented in five categories of ascending difficulty.[4]

Other studies of technical terms are going forward. Lloyd Bostian and Bryant Kearl, University of Wisconsin, have reported their findings in the pamphlet *"Frequency of Economic Terms and Concepts in Farm Magazines."*[1]

Much fruitful information is likely to come in studies of familiarity of technical terms in areas important for the lay reader. But there are also general words used in such communications. We have seen that their level of familiarity can be roughly gauged by their Thorndike score but that this is an inadequate measure. Is there some way of testing all these words so that we can get a score on some 20,000 different words? I have made that attempt and

I shall describe here what my collaborators and I have done.

My first approach was to test some 8,000 different words—words in the first 10,000 of Thorndike using a simple check as to whether or not words were known to the person seeing the word either in a list with no context, or with a phrase context if the word had several meanings or its spelling—appearance—was likely to be confusing. The validity of this method had been noted by Washburne and Morphett, [30] Curtis, [6] and Tilley, [28] who had reported correlations of the order of .80 and .90. My own studies showed correlations between the two.[7]

I early discovered, as had Whipple [32] and Kirkpatrick, [19] that there was a tendency to overestimate knowledge and that confusion due to spelling caused errors in judgment. We were not certain that a child was checking an unfamiliar word as known merely because it looked like a word he did know. Interviews showed, for example, that *unique* was thought to be a man who lived in a harem; *belie* was defined as stomach; and *abominable* was defined as stomach trouble. Dolch found that if a pupil says the meaning of a word is unknown, a suitable test usually confirms his judgment. He suggests a combination of checking words for familiarity and objective tests saying that each one acts as a check upon the other.[11] But when asked to identify unknown words in reading materials, Elivian found that pupils omit more than half of the unknown words as disclosed by a later test.[12]

We did, however, use the method for our earlier studies and got scores on 8,000 words in Grades IV, VI, and VIII. The data were useful and publishers and writers made some use of our data. When preparing graded reading materials, the writer needs greater exactitude. The 3,000 Word List used with the Dale-Chall formula [8] was developed in this way (with additional data) and it has proved to be a usable list.

We later tried a number of devices to see if we could get an inexpensive method of testing general, non-technical words. I had children in the fourth grade read *Black Beauty* and underline words not known to them. We had Freshmen at Ohio State University and at Stephens College work with an open dictionary and check the words they did not know. This has given us scores on several thousand words likely to prove of difficulty to college Freshmen. It is a rough but useful check. It showed, for example, that over one-half of these persons checked as unknown words: *abacus, aberration, abettor, abeyance, aborigines, abrogate, abscond, absinthe, abutment, acetanilide, acetic, acrimonious, acrostic, actinism, accouchement, accrue, acerbity, actuary, adamant,* and *addenda.*

When we concluded that there was not any "easy" way to check on familiarity with words and get an exact and dependable score, we began testing in the sixth grade some 2,000 words which were less familiar than the 3,000 already tested in the fourth. We have used a three-choice multiple-choice test. I shall not describe here the problem of constructing valid test items. The test deviser must use effective distractors and avoid clues which will enable pupils to guess the correct choice when they do not know the meaning of the word. Our testing, although nation-wide, is concentrated in large towns and cities. Miss Beverly Bennett is reporting the sixth-grade study as her Master's thesis, and Miss Bertha Jacobs has completed the eighth-grade list, and will soon finish the tenth-grade list.

We have been testing lowest grade levels first thus making it unnecessary to re-test familiar words. We can thus be certain that the alternate phrases in the tests are expressed in familiar words. Some vocabulary tests use definitions that are as hard as the word itself.

These studies will enable a writer of expository material to get a grade-score for each word used—4, 6, 8, or 10. He will know which terms are already understood and which ones are so unfamiliar that they ought to be defined directly or in context. He can thus write with his eyes open and control more effectively the number and nature of his explanations.

Why bother with all this vocabulary control? Is it not true that Seashore discovered that a first-grader knows 16,900 basic words, plus 7,100 derived words, a total of 24,000; that an eighth-grader knows 62,500 words, a twelfth-grader 80,000? [27] There are several implications in these questions which need clarification.

First, there is confusion about the definition of *know,* and also about the definition of a *word.*[9] Assuming that we can agree that responding to a certain test is a pragmatic test of knowing, we still must define a *word.* The *Webster's New International Dictionary* presents 43 meanings of the word *make.* The editor, P. B. Gove, informed me in a letter, dated October 23, 1955, that these are all counted as one word, but the 196 compound words formed by using *maker* are all counted as separate words, starting with *anvil maker* and ending with *wine maker.* If you compare an abridged dictionary with an unabridged, you will note in the latter the sharp increase in the number of words that are variant forms of the same root.[31]

Second, there are likely sampling errors and testing errors of significant size. For example, the sixth-graders in Seashore's study knew fewer words than the fifth-graders.

Third, the gain of some 10 new words a day suggested by the Seashore study does not fit the known facts about vocabulary growth. In the free-association word study carried on by Buckingham and Dolch, they found 9,520 different words and assumed that the vocabulary of children grows at the rate of about 1,000 words a year. If we think in terms of root meanings, not derived forms which can be regularly constructed from these roots, I believe that this is a pretty sound figure. Obviously, for some children it will be less, for some it will be more.

Fourth, if the twelfth-grader has a vocabulary of 80,000 words, he knows as many words as are in the 896-page Thorndike-Barnhart dictionary which includes 80,000 entries.

Fifth, even if a pupil does know a larger number of words than we previously assumed (and this is probably true), we still cannot abandon vocabulary control of expository materials which most pupils in a grade level have to read. For example, here are familiarity scores on social-studies terms obtained by Luella Cole testing eighth-grade pupils: *Whig* 35, *primary* 59, *suffrage* 58, *conservative* 31, *partisan* 52, *radical* 31, *lobbying* 24, *patronage* 26, *spoils system* 26, *commodity* 18, *competition* 48, *consumer* 72, *exploit* 19, *rebate* 35, *inflation* 38, *primitive* 43, *precedent* 23.

But even when figures for size of vocabulary or rate of growth are stated, we must begin to hedge. We have no data on slang, semi-vulgar expressions (the word *snot* does not appear on any published list of words written by children in literature as far as we can discover). Many words are metaphorized: *wolf, dog, cat, peach, banana, tree, rose, book*—and thousands of others. Are they to be considered as separate words? What about the 43 different senses of the word *make* which the dictionary maker counts only as one? Are some of them so highly uncorrelated in meaning as to make them, in fact, different words?

Shall we then throw up our hands and exercise no vocabulary control? I think not. Rather we ought to get scores on the familiarity of these terms, rate their importance perhaps, and then write as needed. We shall, of course, not avoid hard or unfamiliar words

since they may be rich bearers of meaning. But we should know that they are hard or unfamiliar.

Here are some words on a single page of a junior-high school textbook noted as hard in context by some seventh-grade children who were studying it. I give our eighth-grade score on these items. The seventh-grade score is probably 10 points lower: *manor* 60, *implements* 67, *wheelwright* (no score), *conquests* 69, *self-sufficient* 67 (*sufficient* is 35 in Grade VI), *loyalty* 82, *missionary* 82, *primitive* 77, *encourage* 80, *thorough(ly)* 81. The writer of this book should know that for some of his readers this page has a heavy vocabulary burden and either reduce it, define these words, or use them in a more revealing context.

Further, since wide reading is the chief method by which we learn to read, we ought to be able to make available to children and adults a wide variety of material two or three grades below their top level of ability—material like *Harper's* or *Time* or the *Atlantic Monthly* for the readers of this article.

Finally, when we study vocabulary, we do not assume that words are like bricks—each having an independent, unrelated entity, a meaning that can be stored in the dictionary and used on a somewhat mechanical basis. Technical terms, of course, have much more restricted meanings—have less elbowroom. But the essence of language is fluidity, not rigidity.

But because language has a growing edge, does not mean that it lacks solidity. If there were none, we could not communicate with each other. It is this solid core of relatively permanent meaning that we have been trying to measure. And I believe that intelligent use of such data would make more readable books and magazines, would help us to better distribute the moral, political, and historical wisdom that Shelley talked about.

REFERENCES

1. Bostian, Lloyd, and Kearl, Bryant, *Frequency of Economic Terms and Concepts in Farm Magazines.* Madison, Wisconsin: University of Wisconsin, 1956. (Bulletin No. 25, Department of Agricultural Journalism, College of Agriculture.)

2. Breed, Frederick S., "What Words Should Children Be Taught To Spell? Vocabularies of Various Types," *Elementary School Journal,* Vol. 26 (November 1925), pp. 202-14.

3. Buckingham, B. R., and Dolch, E. W., *A Combined Word List.* Boston: Ginn and Company, 1936.

4. Chall, Jeanne S., and Dale, Edgar, "Familiarity of Selected Health Terms," *Educational Research Bulletin,* Vol. 39 (November 15, 1950), pp. 197-206.

5. Cole, Luella, *The Teacher's Handbook of Technical Vocabulary.* Bloomington, Illinois: Public School Publishing Company, 1940.

6. Curtis, Francis D., *Investigations of Vocabulary in Textbooks of Science for Secondary Schools.* Boston: Ginn and Company, 1938.

7. Dale, Edgar, *Familiarity of 8,000 Common Words to Pupils in the Fourth, Sixth, and Eighth Grades.* Unpublished.

8. ———, and Chall, Jeanne S., *A Formula for Predicting Readability.* Columbus, Ohio: Bureau of Educational Research, Ohio State University, 1948.

9. Dolch, Edward W., "Implications of the Seashore Vocabulary Report," in *Methods in Reading.* Champaign, Illinois: Garrard Press, 1955, pp. 260-69.

10. ———, *Methods in Reading.* Champaign, Illinois: Garrard Press, 1955, p. 258.

11. ———, "Testing Word Difficulty," *Journal of Educational Research,* Vol. 26 (September 1932), pp. 22-7.

12. Elivian, Jeannette, "Word Perception and Word Meaning in Silent Reading in Intermediate Grades," *Education,* Vol. 59 (September 1938), pp. 51-6.

13. Gates, Arthur I., *A Reading Vocabulary for the Primary Grades.* New York: Bureau of Publications, Teachers College, Columbia University, 1935.

14. Horn, Ernest, *A Basic Writing Vocabulary.* Iowa City: University of Iowa (First Series, No. 4), 1926.

15. ———, *Teaching Spelling.* Washington, D.C.,: American Educational Research Association, National Education Association, 1954, p. 6.

16. Horn, Madeline Darrough, *et al., A Study of the Vocabulary of Children Before Entering the First Grade.* Baltimore, Maryland: International Kindergarten Union, 1928.

17. Kelley, Truman L., and Krey, A. C., *Test and Measurements in the Social Studies.* New York: Charles Scribner's Sons, 1934.

18. Ibid. p. 166.

19. Kirkpatrick, E. A., "A Vocabulary Test," *Popular Science Monthly,* Vol. 70 (February 1907), pp. 157-64.

20. Kirkpatrick, James J., and Cureton, Edward E., "Vocabulary Item Difficulty and Word Frequency," *Journal of Applied Psychology,* Vol. 33 (August 1949), pp. 347-51.

21. Lorge, Irving, and Thorndike, Edward L., *The Teacher's Word Book of 30,000 Words.* New York: Bureau of Publications, Teachers College, Columbia University, 1944. See also *Semantic Count of English Words,* prepared with the assistance of the Institute of Educational Research, Teachers College, Columbia University, 1938.

22. Ibid. p. xi.

23. Ibid. p. 242.

24. *A Midsummer-Night's Dream,* Act 5, Scene 1, Lines 14-17.

25. Pressey, Sidney L., and Lively, Bertha, "A Method for Measuring the Vocabulary Burden of Textbooks," *Educational Administration and Supervision,* Vol. 9 (October 1923), pp. 389-98.

26. Rinsland, Henry D., *A Basic Vocabulary of Elementary School Children.* New York: Macmillan Company, 1945.

27. Seashore, Robert H., "How Many Words Do Children Know?" *Packet,* II (November 1947), pp. 3-17.

28. Tilley, Harvey C., "A Technique for Determining the Relative Difficulty of Word Meanings Among Elementary School Children," *Journal of Experimental Education*, Vol. 5 (September 1936), pp. 61-4.

29. Uhrbrock, Richard Stephen, "The Vocabulary of a Five-Year-Old," *Educational Research Bulletin*, Vol. 14 (April 17, 1935), pp. 85-97.

30. Washburne, Carleton, and Morphett, Mabel Vogel, "Grade Placement of Children's Books," *Elementary School Journal*, Vol. 38 (January 1938), pp. 335-64.

31. *Webster's New International Dictionary*, 3rd edition, see vocabulary entry, p. 2854.

32. Whipple, Guy Montrose, "Vocabulary and Word-Building Tests," *Psychological Review*, Vol. 15 (January 1908), pp. 94-105.

14: Teaching Word-Meaning Through Context *

A. STERL ARTLEY

MEANING OF CONTEXT

Teachers of reading have for years made use of context clues, along with configuration clues, picture clues, and word analysis, as a means of developing independence in word recognition. In this sense context clues refer to what might commonly be called "hints" that lie within a sentence, which are used as a means of aiding the child in recognizing the meaning of a new or unfamiliar word. If, for example, in the sentence, "The boy stumbled and seemed about to fall," *stumbled* should be a word with which the child is unfamiliar, he is encouraged to read the remainder of the sentence, omitting the difficult word, while logically "guessing" as to what the word might be. In this sense context is defined by Perrin [2] as "the discourse that surrounds a word or passage that is being separately discussed."

In a broader sense, however, context clues refer to much more than merely the clues to meaning afforded by the other words that are closely associated with an unknown word. Let us take, for example, "We were unable to complete the job, for after several revolutions of the wheel, the dog broke." For our purpose let us assume that the child knows the meaning of every word in the sentence; that is, the common, every-day meaning. In spite of this the sentence might not convey sense, especially as it involves the unusual meaning of "dog." It simply doesn't make sense to say, "the dog broke." Yet, if the child had seen his father reassemble a lawnmower wheel and had heard him refer to the "dog" as the device which regulated the action of the cutting blades, he would immediately have an idea of the full meaning of the sentence. One must get the full interpretation *through experience* with the thing in question. In other words, context clues may be experiential as well as verbal.

To the two types of context aids to meaning already mentioned, there might still be added a third, namely, that which is expressed in the author's tone, mood, and intent. Although one might be able to comprehend a paragraph or stanza of a poem on the basis of the

* Reprinted from *Elementary English Review*, Vol. 20, No. 1 (February 1943), pp. 68-74, by permission of the National Council of Teachers of English and the author.

objective sense-meaning alone, a complete, appreciative interpretation of the whole rests upon those subtle, subjective factors, the clues to which exist in the tone, mood, and intent of the writer.

EXAMPLES OF CONTEXTUAL AIDS

It is important that the classroom teacher be able to recognize the various types of contextual clues as a means of guiding the child to a full interpretation of meaning. Moreover, it is more important that the child himself be able to recognize the various types of aids to meaning, so that he may use them independently and automatically to interpret the full sense-meaning of the sentence or paragraph, as well as the subtle implication.

It must be pointed out that the following classification of contextual aids to meaning is purely an arbitrary one containing a great deal of overlapping. The purpose of this grouping has been merely to organize context in such a way that they might be presented systematically to the child. The teacher must realize, however, that rarely will a particular clue exist in complete isolation.

1. Typographical aids
   a. Quotation marks—The "minutes" of a meeting are usually written by the secretary.
   b. Italics—The *minutes* of a meeting are usually written by the secretary.
   c. Bold face type—The **minutes** of a meeting are usually written by the secretary.

It is obvious that these three devices are inadequate in providing a meaning for the word "minutes." They do, however, point out the word and emphasize the fact that here is a new word, or a common word in an unusual setting, which needs to be studied or looked up in the glossary or dictionary. Gray and Holmes point out [1] that unless these

devices are paralleled by illustration, explanation, or definition, as a means of satisfying the child's curiosity, they are of little value.

   d. Parentheses—The minutes (a written record) of a meeting are usually written by the secretary.
   e. Footnotes or glossary references—The minutes * of a meeting are usually written by the secretary. (At bottom of page) * minutes—a written official record of the proceedings.

These two devices are particularly valuable since a definite reference is made to the particular word. Not only do we have a direct reference to the word, but the explanation is usually superior to a dictionary definition since it refers to the word in the particular context in which it is used.

Little needs to be done by the teacher in teaching the use of context clues as expressed in parentheses and footnotes, since the meanings are so obvious. In respect to the first group of typographical aids mentioned, the teacher needs to capitalize upon the child's curiosity as aroused by the word, and supply the necessary meaning. These devices should be taught as "stop signals," or as a means of informing the child that here is an unusual use of a familiar word, the meaning of which must be secured through inference, or by the use of the dictionary.

2. Structural aids
   a. Appositive phrase or clause—The fertilizer should supply plenty of vegetable matter, which by decaying furnishes *humus,* the food for plant life.
   b. Non-restrictive phrase or clause—The decaying vegetable matter of the fertilizer will furnish *humus,* which is food upon which plant life depends.
   c. Interpolated phrase or clause—*Humus*—the food for plant life—comes from the decaying vegetable matter of the fertilizer.

Structural or grammatical elements furnish very useful clues of meaning. In fact, grammar takes on meaning to children when they see that it has a definite function in aiding interpretation as in the sentences above. Sentences having troublesome words should be analyzed for these structural aids, and the children led to see that commas and dashes are often helpful warnings to go slowly for meaning. Again, practice exercises might be constructed, containing elements like the above, and be used as the basis for class discussion.

3. Substitute words
   a. Synonyms—The fertilizer should supply plenty of vegetable matter, which by decaying furnishes *humus* or vegetable mold. (The word *"humus"* is explained through the use of the phrase, "vegetable mold," which has similar meaning to the original word.)
   b. Antonyms—There is a great difference between the important and the *trivial* in what he has said. (The meaning of "trivial" is expressed through the opposite of "important.")

Synonyms and antonyms are very important aids, and for skillful readers, furnish almost unconscious clues to meaning. The teacher might devise exercises somewhat like those above where similar and unlike words are used that directly or indirectly give clues to meaning.

4. Word elements
   a. Roots—John was successful in the *aquatic* event. (Meaning of the word derived from the knowledge that the root, *aqua,* means water.)
   b. Prefixes—After numerous tests, the inspector found the milk to be *substandard.* (Meaning derived from knowledge that prefix, *sub,* refers to under, below.)
   c. Suffixes—The attorney was well versed in *criminology.* (Here the meaning may be derived from the knowledge that the suffix *ology,* means the science or knowledge of.)

Knowledge of common roots, prefixes, and suffixes are valuable aids to meanings of new words, and in this connection the knowledge of foreign languages has value in the building of English word meanings. A valuable exercise consists of studying word families, or words related in meaning to a particular word element. This might be done by suggesting a word element; root, let us say, and having the pupils suggest all the words that are related, pointing out in each case the relationship. The pupils should be cautioned however, that due to the devious history of many words, the present meaning may be only indirectly related to the original element, or vice versa. Witness for example, the word *pew* from the root *pod.* In this case both the present day word and its meaning are only indirectly related to the original element, and one can only in a very indirect way get a hint as to the meaning of the word.

5. Figures of Speech
   a. Similes—The old car *lurched* forward like an anxious dog released by its master. (Meaning of "lurched" expressed in the simile "like an anxious dog released.")
   b. Metaphors—You dare not *evade* the responsibility, for the promise you gave is binding. ("Evade" is subtly explained in the metaphorical use of "binding" in relation to promise. If you are "bound" to a promise you then dare not step aside or get away from (evade) the responsibility.

Figures of speech may be referred to as particular types of inferential clues. The contextual use of the simile, usually expressed after the words "like" or "as," is very easy to understand and usually requires only incidental mentioning by the teacher. Unless children have had instruction in the use of metaphor, it is usually best to treat clues to meaning that lie in that particular figure of speech as inferential clues (No. 7).

6. Pictorial Representations
   a. Pictures—Egypt is often called the land of the *pyramid*. (Picture of pyramid at side of page.)
   b. Diagrams—The *superheterodyne circuit* resulted in a great improvement in radio reception. (Schematic diagram in text.)
   c. Charts, graphs, maps—Learning will take place effectively until a *plateau* is reached. (Graphs at side of page illustrating a learning plateau.)

Valuable and obvious clues to meaning lie in pictorial representations which accompany the text. It is generally sufficient to point out to the child that a clue to the meaning of a troublesome word may be found in a chart, diagram, or picture. In science, particularly, the parts of an object, a flower, for example, are often designated by dotted lines connecting the parts and words. Every opportunity should be taken to utilize this device as a valuable aid to word meaning.

7. Inference
   Sunlight is an accepted germicide, for even the most hardy bacteria will die in a short time under its direct rays. Not only will the sunlight kill germs, but it will prevent them from growing. (Meaning of "germicide" inferred from the rest of the sentence and following sentences through such words as "die," "kill," "prevent.")

Of all the contextual aids to meaning, those secured through inference are perhaps the most helpful. Inferential aids are particularly helpful since there are so many times where no typographical aids, punctuation, or familiar word elements offer help in giving an interpretation of the word and sentence. Though inference is most helpful in securing meaning, it is perhaps the least used. Hence, the teacher should give it special attention. In teaching its use, actual class texts in geography or history should be utilized from which the children are privileged to suggest words,

the meanings of which are not entirely clear. They should then be encouraged to omit the word temporarily and see whether the meaning, or a close meaning, might not be extracted from the rest of the sentence. Children should form the habit of inferring the meanings of words as a time saver rather than referring to the dictionary. There will be words, naturally, where the remainder of the sentence will give no help in meaning. In this case one will then refer to the dictionary.

8. Direct Explanation
   Many objects are *buoyant* which simply means that they will float on the surface of the water. As you already know, cork or pine float about readily, and even a steel ship will not sink. (In this case the author is directly attempting to make clear the meaning of the unfamiliar word by explaining it and giving examples.)

9. Background of Experience
   The *lumberjack* skids the logs on the *bobs* with the use of a *cant-hook*.

In the above example it is apparent that a background of experience is necessary on the part of the reader for a full and complete interpretation of meaning. Where direct contextual aids are not given, the teacher should supply the basis for understanding through excursions, field-trips, pictures, films, slides, museum exhibits, models, and the like.

10. Subjective Clues
    a. Tone—
       Such a poor, old, gray-haired man as leader! To ask him to serve us again is to murder him. How can we impose ourselves as his worthless children upon such a paternal creature?

This statement, uttered by one who is upholding the virtues of a veteran leader with a record of honorable public service, but who, in the interests of health, should be permitted to retire, would possibly draw forth sympathetic assents from the audience. If, on the other hand, it were made by a politician in a sarcastic tone of one who should be forced to retire to give way to himself, it might be met with laughter. One can interpret the meaning only through the context of the *tone* in which the utterance was made.

    b. Mood—

All day she sits behind a bright brass rail
Planning proud journeyings in terms that bring
Far places near; high-colored words that sing,
"The Taj Mahal at Agra," "Kashmir's Vale,"
Spanning wide spaces with her clear details,
"Sevilla or Fiesole in Spring.
Through the fiords in June." Her words take wing
She is the minstrel of the great out-trail.
At half past five she puts her maps away,
Pins on a gray, meek hat, and braves the sleet,
A timid eye on traffic. Duly gray
The house that harbors her in a gray street,
The close, sequestered, colorless retreat
Where she was born, where she will always stay.
("The Travel Bureau"—Ruth Comfort Mitchell)

This sense meaning of this poem is incidental to the mood which the author is trying to express, and one can interpret it properly only through that context of mood—in this poem the mood of one living a common-place life, but dreaming of doing great things and seeing fine places.

    c. Intent—

The final score with 509 softball players showed that 3 out of 5 preferred the flavor of Flavor-last gum. The purpose of the writer of this

quip is obvious, even without the phrase which might follow—"Get a package today."

In this last group of context clues one sees *meaning* as much more than that which lies within the pale of sense-meaning. To read even a simple newspaper account—especially today when propaganda is rampant—requires much probing below the surface if one desires a full interpretation. It is the prime responsibility of the teacher to make the pupil aware of all the subtle implications found in news accounts, advertisements—in fact, in writings of any kind. Such questions as the following might be asked of the pupils to help them get below the surface to the real heart of the meaning. "How do you think the author would have *spoken it?*" "Is what he said what he obviously wanted to say?" "How do you think the author felt; what mood was he in?" "What can you read between the lines that wouldn't be apparent to the casual reader?" "What do you think the author would like to have us do after reading his paragraph?"

USE OF CONTEXT CLUES

One of the most practical uses of context clues is that of helping the child extend his present vocabulary. The dictionary has a place in helping the children to a meaning of unfamiliar words, but teachers would do well to recognize dictionary limitations and to teach their children of them. It is an interesting and instructive exercise to take a text book that the children are using, or even the daily paper, and on a particular page have the children suggest words with which they are not entirely familiar. With the list on the blackboard, and the magazine or text at hand, the teacher should carefully read the sentence aloud, asking the pupils to note any clues within the sentence, or in those nearby, that might suggest the meaning of the unknown word. Where the children experience difficulty the teacher should furnish help by pointing out familiar word elements, structural aids, the use of synonyms, and the like. In this manner the pupils will become less dependent on the dictionary, using it only where contextual aids are not available, or where a more precise definition is desired.

Mention was made of the limitation of the dictionary in supplying word meaning. This should have further consideration. Were the meanings of words in a sentence separate and distinct like the posts in a fence, it would be possible to take the definition of each of the words, put them together, and arrive at the meaning. In this case *"fresh peach pie"* and *"fresh* peach *pie"* would add up to the same meaning, in spite of the fact that in one we are emphasizing the fresh peaches as distinct from canned ones; while in the other, a fresh pie as distinct from the one of a day-old, soaked crust. In this simple illustration it is apparent that the meaning *intended* by the author is more significant than the definition of the words. To put it another way, the meaning of a sentence is the result of the relationship, the interplay, that exists between the words, as well as the mood, intent, and tone of the author.

From this one can see that the sheer dictionary definitions might be inadequate to a full meaning that the author is trying to express. But surely a dictionary has some purpose, some value. What is it? Zahner in *Reading in General Education* [3] states the value and limitation of the dictionary well in the following words:

... The dictionary lists the literal sense-meanings of the word and some of the metaphorical-sense-meanings which have got into common use. It indicates the present boundaries of the sense-meaning, and within that field drives in several fixed stakes, useful as guide-posts. But it does not exactly place in this field the sense-meaning of the word in any given passage; nor can it give any hint at all of the other kinds of meaning the word may convey— tone, mood, or intent. The common idea that it is the dictionary that "defines" a word, or that gives it its meaning; that the dictionary is the one and final authority as to what in any given instance the word is being used to say; that the matter of understanding and comprehension can be settled by reference to the dictionary, is a common error, and one that is directly or indirectly responsible for some of the common blocks and imperfections in communication and for questionable practice in general education.

True, the dictionary will continue to be a valuable reference book, but its many limitations should be recognized and the pupils led to see that the sentence context itself is at times the best clue to a full and complete meaning.

In spite of the fact that word relationships and, in some cases, the dictionary itself may be utilized as aids to meanings, it must be pointed out that neither the context nor the dictionary *gives* a particular word *meaning*. In the final analysis "meaning" comes only through the combined experience of the writer and the reader. As Zahner points out [3] "The narrow use of 'context' as other words printed in the passage ... is simply the clue to the present situation." This makes apparent the responsibility of the teacher in supplying a background of experience as a basis for complete understanding, in other words, supplying referents. Though teachers of primary grades have utilized direct and vicarious experiences to a certain extent, teachers on the upper levels have by no means made sufficient use of them, with the result that much of the learning is sheer verbalism.

As was implied at the outset, the term context clues has been extended to include not only the words that surround a given word, but also those clues to meaning that exist in the past experience of the writer and reader, and those subtly expressed in the tone, mood, and intent of the writer. Moreover, it is not only imperative that children know of the existence of context clues, but that they utilize them auto-matically in their everyday reading. Only by so doing will they be able to transcend ordinary sense-meaning, and come to a complete understanding and full interpretation of what is being read.

REFERENCES

1. Gray, W. S., and Holmes, Eleanor, *The Development of Meaning Vocabularies in Reading.* Chicago: University of Chicago Press, 1938, p. 83.
2. Perrin, Porter G., *An Index to English.* New York: Scott, Foresman and Company, 1939, p. 163.

3. Zahner, Louis, "Approach to Reading Through Analysis of Meanings," *Reading in General Education,* W. S. Gray, editor, Washington, D.C.: American Council on Education, 1940, p. 89, 91.

15: Development of Word Meaning Through Verbal Context: An Experimental Study *

HEINZ WERNER and EDITH KAPLAN

A. THE TEST

In the main, a child learns the meaning of a word in two ways. One way is direct and explicit, i.e., the adult names a thing or defines a word for the child. The other way is indirect and implicit, through experience with concrete and/or verbal contexts.

This study is concerned with the acquisition of word meanings through verbal contexts. The children participating in this investigation ranged from 8½ to 13½ years of age and were divided into five age groups with 25 children at each age level. The interquartile *IQ* range was from 101 to 111.

The test was as follows: The child's task was to find the meaning of an artificial word, which appeared in six different verbal contexts. In all, there were 12 sets of six sentences each. The 12 artificial words denoted either an object or an action. For example, the artificial word in the first set of six sentences was CORPLUM, for which the correct translation was "stick" or "piece of wood." The contexts for CORPLUM were as follows:

1. A CORPLUM MAY BE USED FOR SUPPORT.
2. CORPLUMS MAY BE USED TO CLOSE OFF AN OPEN PLACE.
3. A CORPLUM MAY BE LONG OR SHORT, THICK OR THIN, STRONG OR WEAK.
4. A WET CORPLUM DOES NOT BURN.
5. YOU CAN MAKE A CORPLUM SMOOTH WITH SANDPAPER.
6. THE PAINTER USED A CORPLUM TO MIX HIS PAINTS.

* Reprinted from *The Journal of Psychology,* Vol. 29, Second Half (April 1950), pp. 251-7 by permission of the senior author and the publisher. This study was carried out under a grant from the Social Science Research Council.

B.   PROCEDURE

The experimental procedure was as follows: After the child was made thoroughly familiar with the task, he was presented with a card on which Sentence 1 of Series I was printed. After the child responded to the first sentence, he was asked how and why the meaning he gave for the word fit into the sentence. He then was presented with the second sentence while the first context was still in view. After having given his interpretation of the word as it appeared in the second sentence (which may or may not have differed from his first response) the child was again asked how and why it fit and also whether it could be applied to the preceding sentence. This procedure was carried out until all six contexts had been presented to the child. The child's responses were carefully recorded.

C.   ANALYSIS AND RESULTS

Although correctness was not the major aspect of the study, it may be briefly mentioned that correctness of responses increased significantly from age level to age level.

Our main concern was with the ways children gave signification to the artificial words; we were especially interested in the development of the signification process. For the purpose of analysis, three judges derived 60 criteria from a preliminary inspection of the protocols. These criteria, pertaining to linguistic as well as semantic characteristics, were then employed by the three judges in the final analysis.

Studying the protocols one is impressed with the great variety of processes by which children acquired and generalized word meanings from verbal contexts. Many responses of the younger children indicate a *lack in the differentiation between the meaning of the word and the given verbal context.* Instead of conceiving the word as referring to a circumscribed meaning, many of the younger children regarded the artificial word as carrying the meaning of the whole or part of the context in which it appeared. We may call this type of conception a *sentence-core concept.* For instance, one sentence, containing the artificial word, BORDICK (faults), was the following: PEOPLE TALK ABOUT THE BORDICKS OF OTHERS AND DON'T LIKE TO TALK ABOUT THEIR OWN. One child, dealing with this sentence, remarked: "Well, BORDICK means 'people talk about others and don't talk about themselves,' that's what BORDICK means." That this child seriously thought that BORDICK meant the whole sentence became clear when he tried to fit this meaning into the context: PEOPLE WITH BORDICKS ARE OFTEN UNHAPPY. The child fitted his sentence-core concept into this context as follows: "People talk about others and don't talk about themselves—they are often unhappy." To the question: "How does this meaning fit?", the child had this answer: "Say this lady hears that another lady is talking about her, so she'll get mad at her and that lady will be very unhappy."

A frequent method of fitting a sentence-core concept, formed for one sentence, into another context was by a process we have termed *assimilation.* The child interprets the context of a new sentence as the same or similar to the context of the previous sentence. Through such assimilation, the concept for the previous sentence now fits into the new sentence. To illustrate, in one series the artificial word is HUDRAY (for which such concepts as "increase," "enlarge" or "grow" are adequate). Sentence 6 of this series read: YOU MUST HAVE ENOUGH SPACE IN THE BOOKCASE TO HUDRAY YOUR LIBRARY. One child said: "Hudray means 'to have enough space.'" He took a part of the context as the referent for HUDRAY. Returning to the previous sentences, he said that the concept, "to have enough space," fit all six sentences. For example, it fit

Sentence 1 (IF YOU EAT WELL AND SLEEP WELL YOU WILL HUDRAY): "If you eat well, that is, if you do not overeat, you will have enough room in your stomach and won't get too chubby; if you sleep well, but not too much, you don't get overlazy; so you leave some room for more sleep—so you leave space—like."

Not infrequently, the child derived two independent sentence-core concepts pertaining to two successive sentences. In attempting to apply the second solution to the first sentence, he often combined the two solutions. For instance, for the two sentences:

JANE HAD TO HUDRAY THE CLOTH SO THE DRESS WOULD FIT MARY.
YOU HUDRAY WHAT YOU KNOW BY READING AND STUDYING.

one child gave as respective solutions: "Jane had to 'let out the hem' of the cloth" and "You 'learn by books' what you know." Coming back from the second to the first sentence the child said, " 'Learn by books' fits here. Jane had to 'learn by books' how to 'let out the hem' in the cloth. Jane used an encyclopedia of sewing." For this girl, the first solution "let out the hem" was so completely embedded in the sentence context that it became a part of the sentence and no longer a substitute for HUDRAY. The child could now introduce the subsequent solution ("learn by books") above and beyond the first, original solution. At times, we obtained as many as three independent solutions combined in one sentence.

Another indication that word and sentence were not clearly differentiated at the earlier levels was the frequent manifestation of what we have called *holophrastic gradient*. Here, the concept was not limited to the unknown word, but spread to neighboring parts, thus carrying pieces of the sentence with it; e.g., for the word, LIDBER (collect, gather), one child stated for the sentence: JIMMY LIDBERED STAMPS FROM ALL COUNTRIES, "Jimmy 'col-

lected' stamps from all countries." The concept was extended from "collect" to "collect stamps." Thus the concept, "collect stamps" was applied to another sentence: THE POLICE DID NOT ALLOW THE PEOPLE TO LIDBER ON THE STREET, in the following manner: "Police did not permit people to 'collect stamps' on the street."

Thus far, we have considered only those forms of signification of a word which are based on an intimate fusion of word and sentence (or sentence-parts). In our analysis, we found other forms of signification, in which the concepts, though they did not display sentence-word fusion, were still lacking the circumscribed, stable character of the more mature concepts. We called such products *simple contextual or simple holophrastic concepts*. Here the word meaning was definitely set apart from the context of the sentence; nevertheless, it differed from conventional word meanings in that it bore a wide situational connotation rather than a circumscribed, stable one. The artificial word did not refer, for the child, to a single object or action, but to a more inclusive context. Sometimes the broad situational connotation of the word was explicitly stated by the child, i.e., he employed a whole phrase to express the meaning of the word. In other cases, the child used a single word, seemingly delimited in its meaning, which on probing was found to be far more inclusive than it appeared on the surface. The following may serve as examples of explicitly stated holophrastic concepts.

The artificial word, ASHDER (obstacle), appears in the sentence, THE WAY IS CLEAR IF THERE ARE NO ASHDERS. One child responded: "The way is clear if there are no 'parts of a radio that don't fit in right' (together)." In the mind of this child, the word, ASHDER, referred to a radio-repair situation.

In the case of the sentence: THE POLICE DID NOT ALLOW THE PEOPLE TO LIDBER ON THE STREET, one child's translation of LIDBER was "throw paper around" (i.e., cluttering up the street by throwing paper around).

An illustration of implicit holophrastic concepts is the following, involving the word ONTRAVE (hope): ONTRAVE SOMETIMES KEEPS US FROM BEING UNHAPPY. A child substituted for ONTRAVE the seemingly circumscribed word "want." However, on probing, it became apparent that "want" referred to a broad contextual situation: "If you 'want a bow and arrow set and you get it,' that keeps you from being unhappy."

For this same sentence, another child came to the solution, "mother." " 'Mother' keeps you from being unhappy." However, "mother" actually meant "mother when she gives you things you want."

One may note an important characteristic attached to such situational word meanings; the word has not only a broad situational content, but this content is fluid and lacks closure: i.e., the concept may change in range from sentence to sentence, elements being added or subtracted etc. This can be seen from the way children quite typically expanded a concept in order to fit it into another sentence. This process of expansion, denoting fluidity of conceptualization, we have termed *contextual* or *holophrastic expansion.* An example of this holophrastic expansion is the following: One child had developed the concept "books to study" for HUDRAY. "Books" became expanded to "throwing books" when the child attempted to fit the concept into the sentence: MRS. SMITH WANTED TO HUDRAY HER FAMILY. The child stated: "Mrs. Smith wanted to 'throw books,' at her family."

Another child, who had arrived at the concept "long" for one sentence, expanded it to "get long hair" in another: THE OLDER YOU GET THE SOONER YOU WILL BEGIN TO SOLDEVE, ". . . the sooner you will begin to 'get long hair.' "

On occasion the contextual expansion was more systematically employed.

The child formed a conceptual nucleus, which remained constant throughout the six contexts; and added to this nucleus elements varying with each sentence. We have termed this procedure *pluralization.* For example, one child formed a nucleus for all the sentences of one series containing the artificial word, LIDBER. This nucleus was "collect." In one sentence LIDBER meant "collect ribbons" (ALL THE CHILDREN WILL "collect ribbons" AT MARY'S PARTY); in another sentence, it was "collect autographs" (THE PEOPLE "collected autographs" from THE SPEAKER WHEN HE FINISHED HIS TALK); in a third sentence, it meant "collect information" (PEOPLE "collect information" QUICKLY WHEN THERE IS AN ACCIDENT), and so on.

We should like to mention two other forms of signification of a word, that were essentially based on contextual or holophrastic conceptualization. One we have termed *generalization by juxtaposition;* the other *generalization by chain.*

In the case of juxtaposition, a concept of an object *A* obtained in one sentence is applicable to a second sentence through the mediation of a concept of an object *B* that is spatially contiguous to the object *A*. For instance, a child gave the solution "plaster" for CONTAVISH in the sentence: BEFORE THE HOUSE IS FINISHED, THE WALLS MUST HAVE CONTAVISHES. "Plaster" also fit into the sentence, A BOTTLE HAS ONLY ONE CONTAVISH. Here the child used "label" for CONTAVISH, saying, "A bottle has only one 'label.' " Nevertheless "plaster" was retained as the solution bcause "plaster," as the child explained, "is used to put on the 'label.' " In other words, the concept of an object such as "plaster" could be used as an overall solution because the juxtaposed object ("label") fit into the sentence. Most likely, the concept was contextual: not just "plaster" but "plaster +."

A similar mechanism seemed to be operative in generalization by chain.

This type of generalization probably differs from juxtaposition only insofar as the two objects in question are conceived of as temporally rather than spatially connected (e.g., cause and effect). As an example, "honor" was substituted for SACKOY in one sentence: WE ALL ADMIRE PEOPLE WHO HAVE MUCH SACKOY. In the next sentence, "guts" was the meaning attributed to SACKOY. "You need 'guts' to fight with a boy bigger than you." But "honor" still fit because, as the child explained, "If you have 'guts,' you are 'honored' aren't you?"

Finally, the two main groups of immature signification discussed in this paper may be briefly compared statistically. As will be recalled, in the first group, the word carries with it the whole or parts of the sentence context; in the second group, the word is clearly differentiated from the sentence context, though it still possesses a broad contextual meaning. Table 1 summarizes the occurrence of these two types of contextual word meanings at the various age levels.

The figures represent the mean occurrence per child at each age group. Both forms of word meanings decreased as age increased; however, there is a clearcut difference between the two developmental curves. Signification based on sentence-word fusion (Type I) decreased most sharply between the second and third age levels (around 10-11 years), with practically no occurrence after the third age level. The other type of contextual signification (in which there is no fusion of word meaning and sentence) showed an entirely different developmental trend: it gradually decreased, and even at the 13-year level there were as many as 3.3 such solutions per child.

The abrupt decrease of Type I, the most immature form of signification, around the 10- to 11-year level suggests a rather fundamental shift in language attitude, toward a task, which, as in our test, is on a relatively abstract verbal plane. This points to important implications which will be treated at greater length in a future paper.

In closing, we should like to mention briefly that there are aspects of language development other than semantic, discussed in this paper, which showed similar abrupt changes at the same age levels. This is particularly true with respect to grammatical structure. The data indicate that there is a growing comprehension of the test sentence as a stable, grammatical structure. Younger children manipulated the sentence as a fluid medium, lacking closure; that is, in the case of giving meaning to the artificial word they frequently altered the grammatical structure of the test sentence. The frequency of such manipulation showed an abrupt drop at the end of the second age level with practically no occurrence at the fourth and fifth levels.

One of the most significant and little explored problems of language development concerns the relationship between the semantic and grammatical aspects of language. The close correspondence of the developmental curves, indicated by our data, between two seemingly independent aspects of language lends support to those theories that assume a genetic interdependence of meaning and structure.

Table 1

Age	8½-9½	9½-10½	10½-11½	11½-12½	12½-13½
I Sentence-contextual	11.9	9.2	1.8	0.2	0.5
II Non-sentence-contextual	11.7	10.8	7.9	4.6	3.3

CHAPTER V

Primary Grade Programs and Methods

16: Whose Brand of Reading Methods Is the "Best Buy"? *

DELWYN G. SCHUBERT

When the numerous methods and techniques of teaching reading to the disabled reader are pondered, many teachers are in a quandary. Each specialist—Gates, Monroe, Dolch, Fernald, etc., all renowned in the reading field—advocates a different method. What is the answer? What should be used? Is there a best method?

Basically, there are three methods for teaching words to disabled readers: the visual, the phonic, and the kinaesthetic. There is no best method *per se*. Only when a remedial program is based on individual needs can any method be cited as superior.

For example, Marion Monroe [2] tells of a seven-year-old boy who suffered from a severe reading disability of a neurological origin. No matter how hard the child tried, he was unable to remember words when the usual sight method was employed. As soon as the cause was uncovered, he was taught by tracing large models of words while saying them out loud. This was a kinaesthetic approach. And it worked! Soon he was able to recognize words and began to show definite and competent progress.

Bond's research [1] shows that children suffering from hearing losses are at a marked disadvantage in learning to read when a purely phonetic method is employed. On the other hand, he found that the look and say method does not penalize the child who has an auditory loss. It is evident that if a child suffers from auditory or visual deficiencies, it is wise to choose a method of instruction that minimizes the handicap as much as possible.

It is a mistake to assume that just because children are free from discernible sensory impairments that they will learn as easily when one method is employed as another. Any teacher can convince himself of the falsity of this belief by checking the auditory and visual memory spans of a group of children. Not infrequently does one find that students with fine visual memories have much poorer auditory memories or vice versa. For seemingly inexplicable reasons some children have great difficulty in making visual associations but show excellent phonic aptitude. In such cases, Monroe's phonetic approach of blending and forming word elements into whole words is to be recommended.

* Reprinted from *The Clearing House*, Vol. 27, No. 5 (January 1953), pp. 266-7, by permission of the author and the publisher.

For the child who is adept at making visual associations but shows ineptitude when phonetic approaches are employed, Gates' method of stressing the general configuration of words as a basis for recognition is appropriate. Since it is not possible to tell which method will work best in an individual case, the teacher must be flexible and versatile. If Harry doesn't respond favorably to one method, another method must be tried.

In final analysis, if there is a best method, we are forced to term it an eclectic one. When an individual method is used to the exclusion of others, some children are doomed to failure regardless of how sincere, competent, and enthusiastic the teacher. Today many teachers use the popular flash method. It is true that most children learn easily and quickly when this method is employed. But still there are needless fatalities. The number of failures could be reduced markedly were the teacher to use several avenues of approach so that the student could choose the particular method or combination of methods that seem to be best suited to his individual needs.

REFERENCES

1. Bond, G. L., *The Auditory and Speech Characteristics of Poor Readers,* Teachers College Contributions to Education, No. 657. New York: Teachers College, Columbia University, 1935.

2. Monroe, Marion, *Growing Into Reading.* Chicago: Scott, Foresman and Company, 1951, pp. 63-5.

17: The Relationship Between Reading Achievement and the Method of Teaching Reading *

IRVING H. ANDERSON, BYRON O. HUGHES, and W. ROBERT DIXON

What is the best method to teach reading? No one knows the answer to this question, but the present paper is concerned with a contribution to our knowledge about the matter. We take our cue from a discovery that we have made regarding the age at which children learn to read in the University School at the University of Michigan. For the business at hand, we have defined age of learning to read as that chronological age at which a reading age of 84 months is reached on the *Gates Primary Reading Tests.* These are the tests used in the University School to assess growth in beginning reading and we have found that an age score of 84 months best represents the point at which, on the Gates tests, the child can first be said to be firmly established on the road to reading. The exact time at which this standard is met is identified by noting the chronological age at which the child's longitu-

* Reprinted from *The University of Michigan School of Education Bulletin,* Vol. 27, No. 7 (April 1956), pp. 104-8, by permission of the senior author and the publisher.

dinal growth curve in reading intercepts a reading age of 84 months.

The "normal" child, of course, achieves a reading age of 84 months at a chronological age of 84 months, but we found that the average child in the University School did not attain this standard until he was 86 months old— a delay of two months. This is a surprising discovery, especially since a superior group of subjects was involved. The average [1] IQ of children in the University School is about 120. Reading and intelligence are closely related and children who have IQ's above average typically get off to a fast start in reading. Why should children who attend the University School prove an exception to this rule? The same problem does not appear in a neighboring public school, where children with better than average IQ's tend to learn to read early and to reach a reading age of 84 months sooner than the "normal" child. The data reported in the accompanying table expose the problem in full.

The table is concerned with a detailed comparison of the distribution of age of learning to read between the University School and the public school. The subjects number 109 boys and 102 girls from the University School and 223 boys and 211 girls from the public school. These samples include only children who had continuous records of reading achievement through the sixth grade. Such records are needed in order to obtain a complete distribution of age of learning to read. It has already been explained that age of learning to read in this instance refers to the chronological age at which a reading age of 84 months is reached on the *Gates Primary Reading Tests*. Scores on the Gates tests were on record for the children from the public school as well as for those from the University School—a happy coincidence for the present purpose.

As the table shows, 66.8 per cent of the boys and 86.3 per cent of the girls from the public school [2] achieved a reading age of 84 months at or before a chronological age of 84 months. The same can be said for only 44.9 per cent of the boys and 60.8 per cent of the girls from the University School. The table also reveals a notable difference between the schools in the overall distribution of age of learning to read. Notice the number of University School children who did not learn to read until after they were 119 months old. None of the public school children learned to read at an age later than 119 months. For all of the present subjects from the public school, the average age of learning to read was 81.1 months. We have

Age of Learning To Read in the University School and in a Public School

Age of Learning to Read (in Months)	University School				Public School			
	Boys		Girls		Boys		Girls	
	Number	Per Cent	Number	Per Cent	Number	Per Cent	Number	Per Cent
Below 85	49	44.9	62	60.8	149	66.8	182	86.3
85- 95	27	24.8	20	19.6	63	28.3	25	11.8
96-107	21	19.3	15	14.7	9	4.0	4	1.9
108-119	6	5.5	3	2.9	2	0.9	0	0.0
120-131	5	4.6	2	2.0	0	0.0	0	0.0
Above 132	1	0.9	0	0.0	0	0.0	0	0.0
Total	109	100.0	102	100.0	223	100.0	211	100.0

previously reported that the average child in the University School does not learn to read until he reaches an age of 86 months.

It is apparent from the table that girls tend to begin their reading earlier than boys and that they also show less variation in age of learning to read. The average girl in the University School learns to read at an age of 83.1 months, the average boy at 89.6 months. The average age of learning to read of the present sample of girls from the public school was 79.9 months, of the boys 82.3 months. These sex differences are perhaps best explained by the fact that girls mature more rapidly than boys and hence become ready for reading sooner than boys.

The differences which the table reveals between schools cannot be attributed to differences in intelligence. If anything, the children from the University School held the advantage in mental-test performance. According to the *Revised Stanford-Binet Scale,* the average IQ of the girls from this source was 121 and of the boys 120. These averages are based on IQ's obtained in the first grade. The Standford-Binet is not included in the routine testing program of the public school, but scores on the *Kuhlmann-Anderson Intelligence Test* were contained in the records. On this test, the average IQ of the girls from the public school was 111 in the first grade and of the boys 110. Research has shown that Stanford-Binet and Kuhlmann-Anderson IQ's are distributed alike, at least at the primary level. These results, therefore, may be interpreted to mean that the children from the University School were slightly brighter than those from the public school, even though different mental tests were involved.

If differences in intelligence are not a factor, how else can the results shown in the table be explained? The most likely hypothesis is that they involve a difference in the method of teaching reading. A description of the difference in method will set the stage for a further consideration of this hypothesis.

In the University School, children are introduced to reading according to their readiness for it. Since children differ widely in their readiness for beginning reading, it follows that instruction is highly individualized. Material is suited to the individual and each child advances at his own rate and pattern of growth. Promotion is automatic and individual needs are met within age groups. Basal readers are employed, but they are not pursued systematically. The children are permitted a choice of basal readers and they frequently switch from one set of readers to another as they advance through the grades. Reading is not formalized in the usual sense. Those children who have already learned to read are encouraged to read independently. The rest continue to receive individual help.

The public school, for its part, employs a systematic approach to reading. Beginning reading classes are given a planned program of instruction to develop readiness, which lasts from one to two months. Children are classified basically according to chronological age and individual instruction is given by the teacher to children having reading difficulties. Each class is organized for formal reading and basal readers are used systematically year by year as the basis of reading instruction. The basal reader used with a class is selected from among three basal reader series, the choice being made by the teacher and the principal. Basal readers not currently being used by a class as the basic series are used as supplementary readers. Beyond the classwork in formal reading, pupils are encouraged to engage in independent reading of their own.

The fact that we find these differences in practice establishes a strong presumption that they are responsible for the differences shown in the table. In other words, it appears that the systematic approach employed by the public school enables the children to learn to read early and reduces the individual variation in age of learning to read. Conversely, the informal practice pursued by the University School apparently delays the age of beginning reading and maximizes the individiual variation which occurs in this connection.

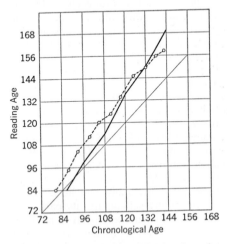

Fig. 1. Average Progress in Reading for Children in a Public School (dotted line) and in the University School (solid line).

A question remains regarding rate of reading development after the age of learning to read. Do children in the University School continue to lag behind children in the public school or do they eventually catch up? We have already reported that longitudinal records of reading achievement were available on all of the present subjects through the sixth grade. These records were used to produce the accompanying figure. This figure compares the average growth in reading between schools after the children have learned to read. Boys and girls were treated together in this instance, because no significant differences in rate of reading development after the age of learning to read were found between boys and girls in either school. For the public school, the curve was obtained by plotting the average chronological age of the children at each test period against the average reading age achieved at each test session. For the University School, the plotting was done by taking children at exact year points and finding what the average reading age was at these points. We have already stated that the *Gates Primary Reading Tests* were used to measure progress in beginning reading for all children in this study. In the later grades, the University School changes to the *Stanford Reading Achievement Tests* and the public school to the *California Reading Test*. No significant differences in the continuity of the results can be attributed to the change in tests either within or between schools.

The figure shows that the initial difference between the groups is not sustained indefinitely. Once the children have learned to read, a more rapid rate of gain is revealed for the University School group than for the public school group. As a consequence of this difference in rate, the initial delay on the part of the University School group is gradually overcome. The curves meet at an age of about 132 months. At this point, both groups have an average reading age well above the line of "normal" development, represented by the straight diagonal line. It is evident that the difference in method does not have a lasting effect and that reading can be taught successfully either way.

REFERENCES

1. The average used throughout is the mean.
2. Data from Margot L. Balas, "Progress in Reading Growth." Unpublished Master's Thesis, University of Michigan, 1953.

18: A Modern Systematic versus an Opportunistic Method of Teaching: An Experimental Study *

ARTHUR I. GATES   Assisted by

MILDRED I. BATCHELDER and JEAN BETZNER

This study, conducted in the Horace Mann School during the school year 1923-24, was designed to disclose, in some measure, the outcomes in the form of significant information, skills, habits, and attitudes of a year of school work carried on in one group by a modern systematic method and in another by what we have decided to term an "opportunistic" method. The experimental plan called for two groups equivalent in all pertinent respects: age; intelligence; previous school experience; home surroundings and training; social, moral, and emotional qualities; physical fitness and maturity; and other personal traits. During the work of the year, all relevant factors, such as attendance, time allotments to scholastic work, recesses, materials and equipment, individual attention in school and out, outside study, teacher assistance, etc., were to be kept as nearly equal as possible. For each group, one teacher only was provided. These two teachers, according to a composite of judgments of several experts in education who knew them both well, were exceptionally, and about equally, able. They were allowed no assistance in coaching or teaching their pupils inside the classroom or out; the only help they secured was clerical and mechanical, in the preparation of apparatus, materials, reports, and the like. The end sought was the equivalence of all factors except the methods of teaching and, necessarily,

the particular curriculum materials required to put the methods into effect.

The methods of selecting the pupils for the two classes should be described in some detail, since without equivalence of the groups an appraisement of the methods of teaching is quite impossible.

SELECTING PUPILS FOR THE TWO GROUPS

From the large number of candidates for the first grade in the school, pairs of pupils, who were as nearly as possible alike in all the respects considered, were selected, one pupil for each of the experimental classes. Twenty-five such pairs completed the year's work satisfactorily. How nearly equivalent the two groups were is indicated in the following averages and distributions of ability—in terms of the average deviations from the average.

In the measurable traits given in Table 1 the two groups are substantially equivalent. In sex, age, Stanford-Binet mental age and intelligence quotient, writing, drawing a man, and drawing designs, the group are almost exactly equivalent. In the Detroit Intelligence Test, a general information test, an alphabet, a word pronunciation, a word selection, an oral spelling, and an oral arithmetic test made up for the purpose, the differences are negligible, as may be observed by comparing them with the

* Reprinted from the *Teachers College Record*, Vol. 27, No. 8 (April 1926), by permission of the author and the publisher. This study is from the research department of the Horace Mann School.

Table 1: Mean (M) and Mean Deviation (MD) in Various Traits at the Beginning of the School Year *

	Total Number	Number Boys	Age M	Age MD	Mental Age M	Mental Age MD	Intelligence Quotient M	Intelligence Quotient MD
Systematic Group	25	12	6.3	.29	7.3	.55	116.3	.97
Opportunistic Group	25	12	6.3	.31	7.3	.60	117.6	1.11

	Detroit Intelligence M	Detroit Intelligence MD	General Information M	General Information MD	Alphabet Test M	Alphabet Test MD	Pronunciation Word Test M	Pronunciation Word Test Failures
Systematic Group	37.8	15.5	37.12	9.08	129	48	1.3	20
Opportunistic Group	35.8	16.1	37.04	8.38	122	50	2.7	17

	Speed of Reading Words Failures	Oral Reading Paragraphs Failures	Word Selection Test M	Word Selection Test MD	Oral Spelling M	Oral Spelling MD
Systematic Group	all	all	5.2	2.8	0.9	0.8
Opportunistic Group	all	all	5.0	2.9	1.6	1.8

	Oral Arithmetic M	Oral Arithmetic MD	Writing M	Writing MD	Drawing a Man M	Drawing a Man MD	Drawing Designs M	Drawing Designs MD
Systematic Group	18.0	7.6	3.6	1.7	13.8	3.3	17.2	3.1
Opportunistic Group	16.6	7.9	3.7	1.7	13.7	3.5	17.2	2.9

* Sometimes the number of total failures is indicated.

average deviations. In some of the tests, such as speed of reading words, oral reading of passages, pronunciation of words, and oral spelling, all, or nearly all, of the pupils in both groups failed completely. In other words, they began the work of the first grade uninfluenced by previous instruction in these functions. In sum, the two groups were equal in sex, age, mental brightness, mental maturity, general information, and scholastic equipment.

As far as possible, equivalence in other traits was secured. About twenty of the pupils came from the junior primary division of the Horace Mann School. For these children, the combined estimates of several teachers for (1) physical maturity and fitness, (2) mental maturity and common sense,

(3) social maturity and adaptability, (4) emotional maturity and stability, and (5) educational maturity and fitness for scholastic work were available. The children were matched individually in these traits and assigned to the two groups in equal number. The pupils appearing at the school for the first time were appraised as well as possible in the same traits during the first two weeks and rearranged to yield equivalent pairings. For all children, the measures of height, weight, strength, and physical fitness made by the school physicians were taken into account. We believe that, on the whole, the two groups were as nearly equivalent in traits related to possibilities for educational achievement as can be obtained at the present time.

THE METHODS OF TEACHING

Each of the two methods, the "modern systematic" and the "opportunistic," was followed by an exceptionally able teacher who was experienced in the method and believed it to be, on the whole, the best one. Both teachers were interested in the project as an experimental study; both, understanding that the results would in no way reflect upon their professional reputation, taught their pupils as under ordinary circumstances except for certain imposed limitations and regulations which were cheerfully accepted and faithfully observed. Both teachers followed the same general schedule, the same time assignments to different phases of the work, recesses, lunch periods, assembly music, gymnasium work, etc. Neither teacher gave any out-of-school time to individual pupils nor allowed others to do so; neither suggested home work and each as far as possible, prevented it. Neither was given any assistance in teaching; neither enjoyed any advantage in clerical or other help, in funds for materials, in special demonstrations, etc.

Each teacher drew up her plans at the beginning of the year and carried them through. In addition to the general plans, detailed records of much of the work, as it actually occurred, were made. On certain occasions, visitors, whose purposes were unknown to the teachers, observed and compared the work of the two rooms and, on occasional days, verbatim reports of all that was said and detailed accounts of all that was done by both teacher and pupils were recorded by an expert stenographic reporter. From these sources the differences in the teaching methods were discerned.

The two methods seem most adequately described by the terms "modern systematic" and "opportunistic." The term "project method" we have avoided partly because "projects"—if we mean thereby "a unit of educative work in which the most prominent feature is some form of positive and concrete achievement"—such as the making of a table or the installation of an electric bell outfit (as the term was first used by Snedden [1])—were used in both groups. It seemed inadvisable, furthermore, to use the term because it has come to be applied to several methods of education that differ in important respects.

The Systematic method and the Opportunistic differed primarily in these respects: The former adopted a course of study that was more definitely determined, outlined, and organized beforehand than the other. The daily lessons were more definitely arranged, periods for study of definite lessons more rigidly prescribed, the accomplishment of these particular assignments more strictly required, and the order of the development of topics more fully determined by the nature of the subject matter and more rigorously adhered to. The Opportunistic method utilized a less definite program of studies and activities while aiming more to conform to the inclinations and interests of the pupils. To a greater extent the teacher awaited, and attempted to utilize, the self-initiated urges of the pupils to learn to read, write, spell, etc. To a smaller extent were set up lessons and projects which the pupils were encouraged or required to attack; to a greater extent the policy of awaiting special incentives or opportunities which provided a "need" for certain information or skill was followed. Given the ripe opportunity the facts or abilities were furnished as the occasion demanded. Under such a procedure, the words to be read were those found in an invitation to a party from another grade; the words to be spelled and written were those required to answer the invitation, etc. The subjects were, consequently, taught less systematically and more in accordance with the demands of such opportunities as occurred or were provided. The Systematic teacher did not, of course, disregard special opportunities for motivating the teaching, although she depended less on them, but, on the contrary, availed herself of them. The differences between the two methods were of degree, but they were appreciable. The Systematic group were not required to adhere slavishly to particular texts with daily assignments of so many pages; but, nevertheless, they were expected to master certain materials and skills which the teacher had herself arranged in a developmental order. The comparison, then, is not between the extreme traditional daily-lesson-in-the-book-plus-recitation method and an extreme do-as-you-like procedure, but between what, for want of better terms, may be called modern systematic teaching with considerable emphasis on pupil initiative and a considerably less systematic procedure in which the pupils control the amount, kind, and order of learning, with the teacher taking advantage of opportunities for instruction as they are afforded.[2]

The general schedule of exercises, followed throughout the year, was substantially the same for both classes.

THE MEASUREMENT OF ACHIEVEMENT DURING THE YEAR

The achievements of the pupils during the year in information and skill were measured by a battery of tests, many of them given individually and most of

Table 2: Initial and Final Scores and Gains of Each Group and the Differences in Gains Between the Two Groups

		1.	2.	3.	4.	5.
		Reading * Capital Letters	Reading * Lower Case Letters	Reading * Digits	Word Selection	Word Pronunciation
Systematic Group	Initial Score	129	127	77	5.2	1.3
	Final Score	60	73	37	14.1	27.5
	Gain	69	54	40	8.9	26.2
Opportunistic Group	Initial Score	122	120	76	5.0	2.7
	Final Score	62	72	49	11.2	17.7
	Gain	60	48	27	6.2	15.0
Difference in Favor of Systematic Group		9	6	13.0	2.7	11.2
P.E. Difference		5	5	3.2	0.55	2.0

Table 2: (cont.)

		6.	7.	8.	9.	10.	11.
		Oglesby Silent Reading	Horace Mann Oral Reading	Haggerty Reading Test I	Haggerty Reading Test II	Spelling	Writing Quality
Systematic Group	Initial Score	—	—	—	—	—	—
	Final Score	21.3	7.2	7.9	4.5	8.9	3.8
	Gain	21.3	7.2	7.9	4.5	8.9	3.8
Opportunistic Group	Initial Score	—	—	—	—	—	—
	Final Score	12.2	2.8	3.8	2.9	6.2	4.2
	Gain	12.2	2.8	3.8	2.9	6.2	4.2
Difference in Favor of Systematic Group		9.1	4.4	4.1	1.6	2.7	−0.4
P.E. Difference		*1.1*	*0.4*	*0.85*	*0.5*	*0.6*	*0.25*

		12.	13.	14.	15.	16.	17.
		Writing Speed	Drawing a Man	Drawing Designs	Arith. Problems	Perception of Numbers	General Information
Systematic Group	Initial Score	—	13.8	17.2	—	—	37.1
	Final Score	30	16.3	20.0	24.9	14.0	44.8
	Gain	30	2.5	2.8	—	—	7.7
Opportunistic Group	Initial Score	—	13.7	17.2	—	—	37.8
	Final Score	36	17.3	19.3	21.8	12.1	44.4
	Gain	36	3.6	2.1	—	—	7.4
Difference in Favor of Systematic Group		−6.0	−1.1	0.7	3.1	1.9	0.3
P.E. Difference		*4.2*	*0.8*	*0.8*	*1.2*	*0.9*	*2.0*

* Tests marked with an asterisk are scored in number of seconds; hence the smaller the figure the better the score.

them constructed specially for the purpose.

All of the tests in which any of the pupils might score at all were given at the beginning of the year and utilized in equating the groups; most of them were repeated near mid-year, and all, together with additional ones, were given at the end of the year. In many of the functions tested the progress during the year was determined by subtracting the initial scores from the final scores; in others, the initial score was demonstrably, or assumed to be, zero and the final scores were taken as representing the gains in ability. Table 2 shows the results in terms of average gains during the full year; the results of the mid-year tests are not included.

Achievement in Reading. The difference in particular methods in reading used by the two groups is suggested in the following data provided by the teachers. To the question, "Did you make it clear to the pupils that you expected them to learn to read?" the Systematic teacher answered, "Yes," and the Opportunistic, "No. The majority expressed a wish to read (home influence). I showed them attractive books, read to them, set the stage for reading." To the question, "Did you ever or often insist on efforts to learn to read?" the Systematic teacher replied, "Yes, with two children I did insist through social pressure that they learn to read. This only lasted until they had some control of the material; then there was no need of insistence." The Opportunistic teacher answered, "Never. As a matter of fact insistence was unnecessary. The few who lacked interest had been 'nagged' at home." In answer to the question as to how much time per day was spent in activities arranged to provide opportunities to read, the Systematic teacher reported, "Never more than fifty minutes a day, but as nearly fifty minutes as possible"; the Opportunistic teacher reported, "At least an hour." The detailed procedure in daily work otherwise is sufficiently suggested in the general comparison of the two methods given above.

The first nine tests measure various phases of silent and oral reading ability. The first test consisted of the letters of the alphabet printed twice in irregular order in large capitals; the second was similar, except that lower case letters were used. The pupils, in individual tests, read the letters aloud. Both time and errors were scored. Table 2 gives the results for speed only. The Systematic group shows slightly higher average scores and in the results for errors,

slightly fewer mistakes. The differences in gains are larger than the probable error but less than twice as large. They are, therefore, neither very great nor very reliable.

The third test required the oral reading of 40 digits, 0 to 9 inclusive, irregularly arranged on a printed form. In this test, both in time and in number of errors, the Systematic group showed some superiority—the difference in time amounting to four times the P.E.

The fourth test was designed to measure the speed and accuracy of recognizing words. It consists of a printed form of exercises, such as:

| hat | sat | pot | rat | bat | hat |

the words increasing in difficulty. The pupil encircles the word in the series which is identical with the one at the left. Score is the number of exercises right. The Systematic group showed some superiority—amounting to about five times the P.E.—in this form of word recognition.

The fifth test was a form of the Gates Pronunciation Test [3] which requires the oral reading of 100 words which range from short and easy words, such as *to* and *it,* to longer and harder ones, such as *handkerchief* and *affectionate.* The score is the number of pronunciations correct. The Systematic class averaged 27.5 words; the Opportunistic, 17.7. The difference between the groups was here considerable—five and a half times the P.E.

The sixth test was the Oglesby Test of Silent Reading.[4] It begins with words, such as dog and chair, and later introduces phrases, the longest of which is: "a mother giving her little girl some water." The pupil reads silently, marking a picture to demonstrate his comprehension of the text. In this text the Systematic group showed a clear superiority—the difference being more than eight times the P.E.

Test seven was a Horace Mann oral reading test patterned after Gray's Oral Reading Test, which consists of a series of passages ranging from very easy to very hard. The Systematic group was clearly far more advanced in this type of oral reading.

Tests eight and nine were Parts 1 and 2, respectively, of the Haggerty Silent Reading Scale, which consists of sentences of increasing difficulty to be read silently. In both, the Systematic group excelled.

In all nine tests of reading skills, then, the Systematic group surpasses the Opportunistic. It may be noted, also, that the superiority is greater in word pronunciation, in silent reading of words, phrases, and sentences, and in oral reading of passages than in the simpler tests of recognition of letters or words.

The most interesting results appear, not in the averages shown in Table 2, but in the records of the particular individuals in the two groups. For example, in the oral reading test—in which the scores are given in terms of "reading ages"—the distributions of abilities in the two groups were as follows:

cant result was the greater spread of abilities in the Systematic group and the relatively large number making very high achievements—five exceeded the norms for average nine-year-old pupils. It will be recalled that the average I.Q. of these groups was about 117, and the range was considerable. The Systematic method achieved some reading ability with all pupils, without holding the more able to a common level. In the silent reading tests the results were similar.

Achievement in Spelling. In both groups, the training in spelling and writing was one and the same; no drills in silent or oral spelling were conducted. The differences in the methods appear in the teachers' descriptions. The Opportunistic teacher gave no specific drill in spelling: only "toward the end of the year" were the words which the children could write listed, noted, checked up, and compared with "the second grade list in Pearson and Suzzallo"; "the children learned to spell certain words because of their zeal in writing." The Systematic teacher selected the word

Reading Age

	Failures	6-7 Years	7-8 Years	8-9 Years	9-10 Years	10-11 Years
Systematic	0	16	4	0	4	1
Opportunistic	15	5	4	1	0	0

"Failure" meant inability to read the following passage in 40 seconds or less and with 6 errors or less:

A boy had a cat.
He did not feed his cat.
The cat ran away.
A little girl found the cat and fed him.
Etc., 21 more words.

Fifteen of the Opportunistic group failed in this test; whereas all of the Systematic group succeeded well enough to secure some score. Another signifi-

"needed for a chart or sign or some other purpose," wrote it on the board twice, and required trials at writing it from memory. "The Pearson-Suzzallo list for Grade I guided me but did not limit what the children needed to write." Children were thus given a method of mastering the spelling; spelling was required since the teacher "scarcely ever let children *copy* any word during the first semester."

The test in spelling, given at the end of the year, consisted of words taken

from the Ayres-Buckingham list. All of
the words selected were taken from a
longer list that had been approved by
both teachers as containing no words
incompatible with the verbal experiences of first grade children. The list
follows:

me, go, it, is, the, man, bad, red, him,
book, school, street, home, white, sister,
brother, summer, railroad, teacher, uncle.

Needless to say, the teachers did not
know in advance what words were to
be used, and the words were selected
by a person who did not know what
words either teacher had taught. Tests
were given to the pupils one at a time;
the examiner pronounced the word and
recorded the oral spelling.

Table 2 shows that the average score
of the Systematic group exceeds that of
the Opportunistic by an amount equal
to 4.5 times the P.E. The distribution of
scores, grouped by two's, is also given.

As in reading, the Systematic group
shows no complete failures; whereas the
Opportunistic group shows failure in 20
per cent of the cases. The Systematic
group again shows a large number
achieving high scores.

Scores	Systematic	Opportunistic
18-19	1	0
16-17	2	1
14-15	0	0
12-13	2	0
10-11	4	6
8- 9	8	6
6- 7	2	1
4- 5	3	2
2- 3	3	4
0- 1	0	5

Achievement in Writing. In writing
is found a characteristic type of difference in teaching which may be expected
from the natures of the two general

methods. The Opportunistic teacher reports: "Writing was a great interest in
this class; from my point of view, not a
great need. However, I followed the
interest and taught writing. The ease
with which manuscript writing is acquired by little children is a great factor
in their interest. They love to illuminate
their capitals with crayons, for instance.
All writing, at first, was on the blackboard or with crayons and large paper.
I wrote the word on the board. They
wrote it from memory. Sometimes we
all had difficulty with the same letter.
Then we had an old-fashioned drill. We
wrote every day after the first six weeks
from 5 to 30 minutes." This description epitomizes beautifully the Opportunistic method, perfectly conducted.
Although the teacher did not see "a
great need" for writing, she seized and
utilized the apparent interest which
resulted in a relatively considerable
amount of training.

The Systematic teacher taught writing definitely in two weekly periods, on
the average, of from 20 to 30 minutes
after the first of December. Words
needed for some purpose or those selected from the Pearson-Suzzallo speller
were used.

The test in writing given at the end
of the year differed from that given at
the beginning, since at the beginning
very few children could write either
words or letters. Both classes had been
taught the printlike or manuscript writing. For the final test, the sentence *The
boy saw a cat* was placed on the board
in manuscript writing. After a half-
minute period, the tests proper—two
periods of one minute each with a rest
interval between—were given. The spec-
imens were graded on a scale corresponding in character to the Thorndike
scale, independently, by two experienced
judges.[5] Not being certain that the
formula for combining speed and quality in script [6] would apply to the manuscript type of writing, these two
measures are given separately. Both tell

the same story—the Opportunistic group is superior by amounts less than twice the P.E. The distributions of scores are nearly identical; no complete failures appeared in either class.

Achievement in Drawing. The procedure in the teaching of drawing in the two classes is, in general characteristics, the same as that of writing and therefore need not be repeated.

Two tests of drawing were used at the end of the year: (1) Goodenough's Drawing Test, in which the children are instructed to draw a man and are thereafter left to their own devices, and (2) an improvised test in drawing from drawn models.

In the first test, the directions used by Goodenough were used here. Pupils were allowed unlimited time. The results were scored by Goodenough's method of giving specified credit for each relevant item included.[7]

For the copying test, large drawings of a circle, a square, and a hatchet were displayed before the class. The pupils reproduced these drawings. There was no time limit. The score combined credits for the separate features of each drawing and a general estimate of quality. In both drawing tests and in the writing test above described, the papers for the two classes were shuffled before they were judged.

Table 2 shows that the Opportunistic group excelled slightly, but scarcely reliably, in the first test; whereas the Systematic group excelled by a similarly small amount in the second test. If the scores for the two tests were equally weighted and combined, the averages for the two groups would be approximately equal.

Achievement in Arithmetic. Neither teacher attempted to teach any considerable amount of arithmetic during the year. Neither used a textbook and neither assigned daily or other regular periods to this subject. Both had in mind

the same objective—to establish ability to use foot rules and yardsticks, to count articles used in work, to read page numbers or dates on the calendar, to understand the calendar and clock, to use familiar coins, etc. The extent of the facts and skills held as desirable differed little between the teachers. The main difference was in the methods of teaching, which need not be reviewed again; the one was more systematic and direct than the other.

The test in arithmetic used at the end of the year was made up without knowledge of what was being done or taught in either class. The test consisted of forty-one problems—grouped under seventeen headings, as shown below—which were given orally by the examiner to each child individually. Answers were oral. The score was the total number correct. The problems were mainly practical and realistic ones concerned with everyday affairs. They are given herewith.

ORAL NUMBER PROBLEMS

1. Count up to 10 as fast as you can.
2. *a.* Now count by 10's up to 100.
   b. Now count by 2's up to 20.
   c. Now count by 5's up to 25.
3. If you made 2 clay dishes to-day and 1 to-morrow, how many clay dishes would you have then?
4. If you brought 2 crackers for your lunch and someone gave you 2 more crackers, how many would you have altogether?
5. *a.* How many are 5 and 5?
   b. How many are 3 and 3?
6. *a.* Give me ½ of this sheet of paper (Examiner shows paper 5 x 8).
   b. Now give me ⅓ of this sheet of paper.
   c. Now give me ¼ of this sheet of paper.
   d. Now give me ⅔ of this sheet of paper.
7. If you made three clay dishes to-day and then broke one and threw it away, how many clay dishes would you have left?

8. If you had four apples and gave three apples away, how many would you have then?
9. Now we will play store. Here are 10 cents and I have some postage stamps to sell. (Examiner has 10 pennies and some one- and two-cent stamps.)
   a. How many two-cents stamps can you buy for 10 cents?
   b. Here are 5 cents and you want a one-cent stamp. Pay me. How many cents will you have left?
   c. Here are 10 cents and you want 3 two-cent stamps. Pay me. How much money should you get back?
   d. Here are 5 cents and you want 3 one-cent stamps. Pay me. How much money should you get back?
   e. Here are 10 cents and you want 3 two-cent and 2 one-cent stamps. Pay me. How many are left.
10. a. Give me 4 of these pennies (Examiner shows 10 pennies.)
    b. Now give me twice as many.
11. If you bought milk with crackers for lunch for 11 cents and gave your teacher 15 cents, how much change would you get back?
12. If you bought cocoa with crackers at 10 cents and bought a sandwich for 7 cents, how much would you pay your teacher?
13. How much are 2 and 3; 3 and 4; 6 and 4; 8 and 2; 8 and 6; 4 and 5; 6 and 3; 8 and 3?
14. a. What time is it now? (Examiner—Adjust your watch.)
    b. eight o'clock.
    c. quarter of 9.
    d. quarter past 10.
    e. half past 12.
    f. 20 minutes to 2.
    g. 10 minutes past 4.
15. If you have 8 blocks and throw 3 away, how many will you have left?
16. John gives me 4 cents and Harry gives me 4 cents and Dick gives me 2 cents. How many cents have I?
17. If you had 6 crackers and wanted to give them to 3 children, how many would you give each?

These problems were given individually and were read as above. The examiner recorded each individual section of a question as + or −. If −, the wrong response was noted. The score was the number of individual parts correct. (Maximum score is 41.)

Table 2 shows the differences between the two groups. The Systematic group excels by a trifle less than three times the P.E.

A second, but minor test in arithmetic, already considered under reading, consisted of the oral reading of a series of digits. In this test the Systematic group proved superior by an amount equal to nearly four times the P.E. A third test measured the rate of perceiving the identity of, or the difference between, pairs of printed numbers, such as 186 186, 127 137, etc. In this test (No. 16, see Table 2) the Systematic group excels by twice the P.E.

On the whole, then, the differences in achievement in arithmetic favor the Systematic group.

ACQUISITION OF GENERAL INFORMATION

A series of questions, designed to measure more or less fully the acquistion of information of a practical and general sort, different, in the main, from what is typically found in Systematic courses in reading, arithmetic, etc., was constructed before the teaching in the groups was far under way. How significant this test is, how practical, how fully it may serve to test the claim, sometimes made, that forms of Opportunistic teaching typically result in the acquisition of more information about people, practical affairs, and the surrounding environment, than systematic teaching, may be judged by the reader after observing the actual questions asked. These questions were given orally by the examiner to each child individually; usually two sittings of twenty minutes each were required.

INFORMATION QUESTIONS

1. Where do you live?
2. What is the name of this building (place) we are in?

3. How old are you?
4. When were you born?
5. When is your birthday?
6. Tell me the name of some part of your body. Another, etc., until 10 are named if possible.
7. The same for tree.
8. The same for house.
9. The same for automobile.
10. Where does the president live?
11. Who is president?
12. Who was president before him?
13. Who was the first president?
14. Who was Abraham Lincoln?
15. Tell me one thing your heart does for your body. Another.
16. How many minutes would you boil an egg?
17. How many minutes would you boil a potato?
18. Tell me the name of a tree. Another, 10 if possible.
19. The same for animal.
20. The same for flower.
21. The same for vegetable.
22. Tell me the kind of a shop where you buy: medicine; postage stamps; writing paper; ice cream; train tickets.
23. Tell me the name of the month when Christmas, Fourth of July, Thanksgiving, Washington's Birthday, April Fool's Day, Memorial or Decoration Day, Columbus Day, New Year's, Hallowe'en, Valentine's Day comes.
24. Tell me the names of the months when we have flowers; when it snows; when we find nuts; when it is hot.
25. Stand up a minute.
How far is it from you to me? (Child stands 3 feet away.)
How far is it from your chair to my chair? (Chairs are 1 foot away.)
How far is it from San Francisco to New York?
How far is it from New York to Albany?
How far is it from New York to Boston?
How far is it from New York to San Francisco?
26. Tell me some way the policeman helps us. Another, another.
27. Where do the birds go in winter?
28. Where does butter come from? What is it made of? The same for: beer, milk, potatoes, coal, eggs, paper, cotton, leather, wool.

29. Now I am going to say a lot of things and you tell me what is right to do. Is it right to whisper, to steal, to be sick, to help, to mark on desks?
30. Suppose you were lost. Tell me one place you would go. Another.
31. Suppose your dog was hurt. Tell me one place you would go for help.
32. Suppose a lady dropped her pocketbook and did not know it. What would you do?
33. Suppose a boy ran away with your hat. Tell me one thing you would do. Then what would you do? Why?
34. Now suppose the grocer boy dropped a nice red apple out of the bag. Tell me what you would do. Why?
35. Suppose a big boy said, "Come along, ———, and we will steal some apples." What would you say? Why?
36. Suppose ——— stole a pocketbook and you saw him. Then a man came along and asked you if you stole it. Tell me what you would say? Why?
37. Is March colder or warmer than, or just the same as, June? Which?
Tell me the names of the cold months.
Tell me the names of the hot months.
38. What do you get jealous of? What does it mean?
Tell me one thing that you are afraid of.
39. How many hours is it from breakfast to lunch? What time is breakfast? Lunch? How many hours is it from lunch to dinner? From lunch to dark? Dinner to dark?
40. Stand in front of your chair.
Stand in back of your chair.
Stand at the side of your chair.
Put your chair opposite that chair.

Table 2 (column 17) shows that the gains of the two groups and their final average scores were almost identical.

ADVANCEMENT IN SOCIAL, EMOTIONAL, MORAL, AND OTHER HABITS AND ATTITUDES

From achievement in scholastic information and skills we turn to acquisitions of personal and social attitudes and habits. To determine what attitudes and

	Opportunistic	Systematic
1. Habits of studying quietly and effectively	6.2	7.1
2. Paying attention during recitations, etc.	4.8	5.4
3. Habits of doing what they are told	5.8	6.3
4. Coöperation in joint enterprises	8.1	7.8
5. Interest in reading, writing, spelling, etc.	6.0	6.3
6. Interest in modeling, painting, drawing	9.1	8.0
7. Interest in constructing things with tools	9.2	8.7
8. Interest in music	9.0	8.5
9. Social and personal manners—courteousness, etc.	8.4	8.0
10. Emotional control—lack of apparent anger, grief, etc.	8.5	9.0
11. Care of desks, materials, etc.	6.3	7.5
12. Enthusiasm in school life in general	9.0	9.0
Average	7.55	7.53

habits the two teachers considered of high importance a questionnaire was submitted which the teachers filled and to which they added items not mentioned. These results are not presented, since they were substantially the same. Each teacher attributed great importance to such factors as: habits of studying quietly and efficiently; paying attention; proper obedience; effective coöperation; interest in "carry on" in school work; persistence in undertakings; social adaptability; emotional control; good manners, etc.

Traits such as these are, at present, much more difficult to appraise than those previously considered. As originally planned, such traits were to be gauged in three ways:

1. By the judgments of competent persons unaware of the nature of the experiment, who visited the classes with purposes unknown to the teachers.
2. By the judgments of competent persons, based on detailed stenographic reports of the activities and discussions in the classes on different days.
3. By observation of the pupils in school during the following year.

The first method was not extensively applied. Four competent persons, after visiting each class one day, graded the two on a chart arranged for the purpose. The composite of these judgments, in which ten is the highest and zero the lowest is listed at the top of the page.

The differences between the groups are very small—unreliably small; in the average of all traits, the classes are identical. Indeed, the inability of the judges to observe differences clearly and to agree in their observations led the writer to pursue this method no further. Either no real differences existed, or, if they existed, they were too subtle to be observable—or, if observed, they were differently evaluated by the observers.

To provide material for the second type of appraisal, an experienced shorthand reporter recorded all words spoken and all group and individual activities observed during eight complete school days, four in each class, near the end of the year. A sample of the reports follows.

Teacher A   Grade I   May 5, 1924
8:45

[Children remove their wraps and select seat for the day. A president is chosen each day to take care of the activities for the day.

On Mondays children report week-end trips which they think will be of interest to the class instead of having usual Fine Arts recitation.]

ELSPETH (president for the day). Will you all get chairs and come and sit over by the piano? [Children move quickly and quietly, and seat themselves in a circle around the president, who is seated upon the piano stool.]

ELSPETH. Roger.

ROGER. On Friday I went to the country, and I bought this flashlight and this bookmark. (Teacher) asked me to show you the bookmark because you might like to make one like it. And I bought this flashlight from a shop somewheres in the village because at night sometimes our lights are burnt out, and we need to take this.

These are some paper Japanese flowers. You put them in water and they open up into all different flowers. I will get a bowl and some water later and show them to you.

CHARLES. You are in my place, Theodore.

THEODORE. No, I'm not.

CHARLES. Yes, you are.

ELSPETH. Theodore, get you a chair and sit over there.

CHARLES. I will sit on the table. That's just as good.

ELSPETH (strikes chord on piano and children get quiet). I would like for you to stop talking before I call on anybody else.

[Teacher is seated at her desk, and leaves management entirely to president.]

ELSPETH. Buddie.

BUDDIE: Yesterday we went out to 96th Street to see the submarines, and Dad took me out on board ship, and then we went on one of the submarines, and then we went on the tug boat. Then Dad and I walked home down by that stone wall, and Dad, etc.

In judging these records for such traits as those listed above, a rating device was supplied to the judges who appraised each of the eight days' records separately. These were later divided into the four for each class and the records averaged. Data from six judges were combined. These results do not agree precisely in detail with those obtained from judges directly observing the classes, but they show the same average trend—a trend indicating equal-ity of the two classes. The scores vary from day to day; the differences between ratings on different days for the same class are quite as great as the differences between the two classes.

The most promising method of detecting differences in these personal and social traits—by observing their operation in the succeeding school year—was thwarted by the departure of a considerable number from the school. For the same reason, other follow-up studies originally contemplated were given up.

SUMMARY AND DISCUSSION OF RESULTS

The results of the study may be summarized as follows:

1. In the objectives of education outside the traditional scholastic subjects, in interests in school activities, in social and personal habits, and in attitudes as they were appraised, in general information of varied types—the groups taught by the Opportunistic and the Modern Systematic methods were substantially equal.

2. Opportunistic teaching, following the special interests of the pupils, resulted in slightly higher achievements in the motor functions, writing (manuscript style), rather certainly, and drawing, less surely.

3. Modern Systematic teaching resulted in considerably greater average achievements in the other school subjects, in arithmetic, spelling, silent and oral reading.

An interesting and significant difference between the outcomes of the two methods appeared in the divergencies in the distribution of abilities in some of the school subjects. In reading, for example, in the Opportunistic group, there was what a standard test in reading of simplest materials designates as "complete failure" in 15 out of 25 cases; whereas in the Modern Systematic group there was none. In the former group there were no exceptionally high achievements; whereas in the latter there were five "reading ages" from 9 to 11 years at the end of this first year.

To ascertain exactly the causes of the failure of children in the Opportunistic group in each school function would, of course, be a most fruitful supplement to the results already given. In the case of reading and spelling, at least, such of these pupils as remained in the school, and many others, are the subjects of further study, the results of which will be presented in other articles. We shall present here merely a few notes concerning some of the difficulties which a clever teacher following the Opportunistic method has encountered. As appraised by the teacher, the main difficulties in the case of reading—those judged to be of pronounced importance in the production of failure—were of the following sort:

Pupil A. "Home nagging. Constant comparison with 'brilliant little sister.' "
Pupil B. "Unfavorable conditions to growth at home. Clever naughtiness (rather than better things) made much of."
Pupil C. "Living under unfortunate conditions with a mother overanxious. Poor health; introspective."
Pupil D. "Hovered over by an unbelievably silly mother and aunt."
Pupil F. "Mother does everything for him; dresses him like a little girl—result—babyishness, immaturity."
Pupil G. "Anxious to appear well; self-conscious about books; no real interest yet; leader in sports."
Pupil H. "Immature—loves to play with dolls and pets."

The factors, inhibitive to development in reading, suggested in these comments by a teacher whose sagacity in judging personal traits and relations is well known, are—as I see them—: (1) Inappropriate habits of work, study, self-management in general. These, the teacher seems to believe, should be remedied before the mastery of reading is stressed. (2) Immaturity, whether native or acquired, in certain traits concerned in learning to read. In

these cases, the Opportunistic procedure would be to await further growth. (3) Specific inhibitive factors, such as Pupil G., who, yearning to excel in unusual degree, found reading distasteful, possibly because in it, unlike sports, he must play a subordinate rôle. These are, of course, not all of the sources of difficulty, but they are representative.

For these same difficulties, the Systematic teacher could adopt different treatments and defend them, arguing by analogy, with other principles of psychology. For inappropriate habits of work she might defend the selection of reading as an activity in which to supplant the undesirable by more desirable habits, on the assumption that the interest might then be intrinsic. Instead of depending on time alone to remedy immaturity, she might insist that it is better to work more actively and specifically for maturity by stimulating development through exercise in reading. As a remedy for specific inhibitive factors, such as the one mentioned, she might attempt, through vigorous teaching, to make reading not an activity which results in disclosing an inferiority but one which provides the expression of mastery. The Systematic teacher did adopt the aggressive rather than the watchful waiting policy with results that are only partly known. It has been demonstrated that the Modern Systematic method produced ability to read; whereas the Opportunistic procedure did not in those crucial cases which numbered over half of the group.

If ability to read—if achievement objectively manifest—were the only criterion, the Systematic method might lay claim to superiority, since it is in connection with such cases—those who do not learn without help but really need a teacher and teaching—that the question of method achieves any significance. Here lies the crux of the matter; here lie the inadequacies of our data. For the development of interest and enthusiasm in reading and other school activities, for the improvement of initiative, determination, and other volitional traits, for the general improvement of inappropriate habit tendencies, immaturity, and the dispositions toward inhibitive mental adjustments, for the stimulation of healthful mental and temperamental growth in general—which is superior, the method which achieves the goal of reading ability by aggressive behavior or the one which lingers to secure it by a smoother, even if delayed, route? This question we cannot fully answer. At the most, we may say that, in so far as we were able to secure evidence concerning interest, character development, and the like, the two methods produced no perceptible differences. We should hasten to admit, however, that our evidence is not as detailed and reliable as we desire. We are, therefore, unwilling to make the statement that our data indicate that one method is *better* than the other in any ultimate sense. The study did disclose certain facts,

certain pertinent and clear differences. These findings pave the way for further, much needed study. This should take the form of much more extensive and detailed study of all relevant factors in the critical cases of children upon whom the two general methods exert a differentiating effect. In other words, we should ascertain by far more searching analyses the influence of the contrasting methods upon all aspects of the maturing personality.

With the last words, we must sound a word of warning concerning the possibility of mistaking the nature of the methods studied, especially what we have termed the "Modern Systematic" method. Let it not be thought that this study justifies the rigidly organized, highly rationalized, or logically systematized textbook or classroom series of lesson assignments, study, and recitation. Such a rigid system of teaching was not followed here.

REFERENCES

1. Snedden, David, in *School and Society,* 1916, p. 420.
2. If it is assumed that the "Modern Systematic" procedure is merely a plan of assigning, studying, and reciting of lessons, the significance of this article will be missed. The method, substantially as it was applied to the teaching of reading, was discussed in an article by Miss Jean Betzner in the *Teachers College Record.*
3. Described in *Teachers College Record,* November 1924.
4. Described in the *Journal of Educational Research,* June 1924.
5. Miss Ella Woodyard and Miss Esther Hemke.
6. Gates, A. I., in *Journal of Educational Psychology,* March 1924.
7. As described by Florence Goodenough in Master's Thesis, Department of Psychology, Columbia University.

19: The New Castle Reading Experiment *

GLENN McCRACKEN

In 1947 plans were established to conduct a long-term experimental program at the Thaddeus Stevens School in New Castle, Pennsylvania, for the purpose of

thoroughly testing the correlated image projected on a screen as a medium for reading instruction at the primary-grade level.

* Reprinted from the *Elementary School Journal,* Vol. 54, No. 7 (March 1954), pp. 385-90, by permission of the author and the publisher.

In light of the obvious values attached to the visual approach to teaching, and in view of the success with which the armed services used film in teaching illiterates to read during World War II, the time seemed long overdue when extended film correlation should be undertaken in the reading area. During the ensuing years this study has come to be known as the New Castle reading experiment. Several interim reports have been published about it, in which techniques have been explained and progress noted.[1,2]

PREPARATION OF MATERIALS

Nearly two years were devoted to the selection and preparation of materials and to the experimental work necessary in the organization of new and effective techniques that would be employed when the program was ready for use and the children would be working daily at a projection screen. One of the current basal reading series was selected as a vehicle for the study. The next step involved the planning of filmstrips (textfilms) which would provide at least one frame [3] of material to accompany every lesson in the textbook series. Each frame was designed to stimulate pupil interest and to present the lesson it accompanied in a vivid and clarifying manner.

The basic principle behind the entire program was the idea that, because of the obvious value of a visual approach, every textbook lesson could best be introduced and taught from a large image projected on a screen with the textbooks themselves serving as testing and practice material. For this reason, the material presented on the film frames was similar to that appearing in the accompanying textbook lessons, the differences being (1) that the detail of the film lesson was slightly rearranged to prevent the pupils from working out the lesson correctly in the textbook because they

had remembered the order of words or images on the screen and (2) that only part of the textbook practice material was included on the film frames so that there would be added interest and additional testing material when the pupils transferred to the books.

NEW TECHNIQUES

In planning for the daily use of the projected image in primary-grade reading classes, it was necessary to work out various techniques regarding room conditions and lesson presentation which would be effective as well as educationally sound. The following are some of those decided upon after careful study and experimentation.

1. If the image is about three feet high by four feet in width, the pictures appear lifelike and can readily be seen by the pupils.

2. The top of the image should be about five feet from the floor for beginning classes (slightly higher in Grades II and III).

3. A wall-type screen is superior to the tripod style because there are no tripods for pupils to bump into, the screen is rolled up and out of the way when not in use, and the fact that it fits closer to the wall when in use gives a few more inches of projection distance, which may be needed in small classrooms.

4. Opaque rather than beaded screens give a somewhat brighter image for the viewers who are sitting at a wide angle with the screen.

5. An eighteen-inch ruler (or half a yardstick) makes an excellent pointer for pupils to use at the screen since it is about the right length with which to reach any part of the image and because its width permits the viewers to follow the pointing readily.

6. Pupils should not be seated closer to the screen than twice the width of the image nor farther away than six

times the image width. Neither should they be seated at an angle wider than 30 degrees from the screen.

7. The room should be dark enough to insure a sharp picture but light enough to permit safe moving about by the pupils and effective class management by the teacher. Room darkening is no longer much of a problem because of the recent improvement in the manufacturing of filmstrip projectors.

The selling price of a filmstrip projector does not necessarily indicate the degree of brilliance the instrument will produce. Prospective users should test the various machines for brilliance and sharpness.

8. In working at the screen, pupils should be taught to approach the image from the side of the room in which the pupils are seated. This prevents their walking through the projector lights. They also should be taught to stand well to one side of the screen while pointing at an image in order to protect the viewing area of other children.

TYPICAL PROCEDURE

At the beginning of any new lesson, a pupil is selected to turn the room lights off and on as needed, while another child is chosen to operate the projector.

Attention is then directed to the screen image. Vigorous discussion follows as various pupils go to the screen to circle choices, underscore words or pictures, point to selections, or play any one of the various games which have been worked out at the screen. When general agreement has been reached on the various problems of the lesson, the teacher then invites the pupils to find the similar lesson in their books, where, she tells them, they may expect to find additional interesting things to do. As the individual work progresses, it readily becomes apparent to the teacher as she walks about the room whether the

pupils have mastered the teaching that occurred at the screen. If various children experience difficulty at this point, the teacher may use the screen again for added practice.

VALUES OF THE VISUAL APPROACH

The values of such a visual program seem evident to the many visitors to the New Castle classes, and they are reflected in the unusual results obtained. Interest among the pupils is greatly improved because they are fascinated by the colorful pictures. Many times during the school year, beginning pupils are heard to ask, "Are we going to have movies again today?" The heightened interest means that attention spans are greatly lengthened. The vivid and clarifying aspects of the projected image seem to fix the learning in the minds of the children so that much less repetition is necessary. The large, lifelike images encourage vigorous discussion among the children. Since all the pupils work with the one attention-compelling image, the slower-learning benefit from all that is said by others. The reticent, backward children are greatly improved socially since they have many opportunities to work at the screen and lead discussions.

The writer is not prepared to document the various values that may be present because of the far-point viewing made possible by the visual approach. It is possible, however, that the great amount of close reading made necessary by the traditional teaching method may be damaging to the eyes of very young children. Therefore, a trend toward large type made possible by the projected image may be highly desirable.

Certain advantages to the teacher seem evident in the visual approach. She has correlated visual material for every day of the school year. The films provide unusual and interesting testing material. Class management, which usually is somewhat of a problem during the early part of Grade I, is greatly simplified since the pictures hold the attention of the children.

RESULTS

It is not surprising that these procedures would produce improved results. But the accumulated data for the four years in which this program has been in use show the improvement in reading achievement, as measured objectively, to be so startling as to appear almost improbable. These data, contained in fifteen tables covering the reading progress of fourteen primary-grade reading classes, are too extensive to be included here, but enough information is presented in Table 1 to show

the unusual consistency of progress at a very high level in the classes involved.

In September, 1949, the program was ready for use at the first-grade level, and it was installed in the three sections of beginning classes at the Thaddeus Stevens School. Table 1 shows the progress of these classes as measured by the Gates Reading Tests. The median intelligence quotient of the pupils in Section 1 in the year 1949-50 was average (101), and the readiness grade-equivalent median also was average (1.8). The median grade equivalents for the three types of the reading tests were 2.30, 2.40, and 2.60, and the median score for the average of the three types was 2.45. While these medians are not unusually high (they are the lowest produced in the experimental classes), some interesting informa-

Table 1: Reading Progress, Measured by Gates Primary Silent Reading Tests, of First-Grade Classes in Two Schools Taught by Projected-Image Technique

School and Class Section	Median Intelligence Quotient *	Median Reading-Readiness Score †	Type 1, Word Recognition	Type 2, Sentence Reading	Type 3, Paragraph Reading	Three Types Median	Range
Stevens School, 1949-50:							
Section 1	101	1.8	2.30	2.40	2.60	2.45	2.13-3.27
Section 2	104	1.9	2.47	2.60	3.10	2.72	2.18-3.41
Section 3	104	1.9	2.60	2.60	3.00	2.70	1.99-3.21
Stevens School, 1950-51:							
Section 1	106	1.9	2.60	2.55	3.35	2.88	2.11-3.47
Section 2	111	2.0	2.60	2.70	3.55	2.88	2.00-3.45
Stevens School, 1951-52:							
Section 1	106	1.8	2.50	2.50	3.30	2.80	2.09-3.43
Section 2	106	1.8	2.30	2.50	3.20	2.70	1.72-3.25
McGill School, 1952-53	108	2.0	3.16	3.00	3.23	3.18	2.08-3.51

Median Grade-Level Score on Gates Tests

* In the Stevens School, intelligence quotient was measured by the Otis Quick-scoring Mental Ability Test, Alpha, Form B; in the McGill School, by the Binet-Simon scale.
† Reading readiness was measured by the American School Reading Readiness Test.

tion was revealed. There were no poor scores; every pupil in the class, regardless of his mental ability or apparent readiness for reading, scored at the second-grade achievement level or better after eight months in a beginning class. Two pupils with below-average mental ability and readiness indications (intelligence quotients of 97 and 74, respectively; reading-readiness score of 1.5) made a grade-level score of 2.61 and 2.24 in achievement and otherwise seemed entirely ready for second-grade reading. In several previous years of testing at this school, no pupil scoring 1.6 or lower in reading readiness had ever been advanced to Grade II after one year in school.

In Section 2 of this first-grade class, the median achievement score was 2.72, with the highest score listed as 3.41 and the poorest as 2.18. In Section 3, the median achievement score was 2.70, with the highest shown as 3.21 and the poorest as 1.99.

In 1950-51 there were two sections of beginning classes at the Stevens School. Summary data of their progress are also shown in Table 1. Note the high median scores and the fact that, again, there were no poor scores (lowest scores, 2.11 and 2.00).

The data for the 1951-52 school year again show high median reading scores (2.8 and 2.7). In Section 2 one child did fall slightly below the norm of 1.8 (1.72), but he attended school less than half the year and was ill during the entire time.

Tables for the second- and third-grade classes are not included here, but they show progress only slightly below that indicated for beginning classes.

At the beginning of the 1952-53 school year, this experimental program was transferred to the Arthur McGill School, which is located in a better cultural area of the city. The Stevens School beginning classes returned to the traditional reading program. It is sig-

nificant that, during the three years the visual program was used at Thaddeus Stevens School, reading-achievement scores in the primary-grade classes were, each year, the highest in the city and that during those three years every beginning pupil learned to read to the entire satisfaction of the teachers and the reading tests. During the 1952-53 school year, after returning to the traditional method, the Thaddeus Stevens beginning classes fell from first and second places to twenty-fifth and twenty-sixth in a city-wide ranking of twenty-eight classes. In these classes, twenty-four of the fifty-five pupils scored below the norm of 1.8 in reading achievement, and nine of them scored below 1.6. The poorest listed score was 1.30, and two other papers were unscorable.

Table 1 shows the progress of one of the classes participating in the experimental program at the Arthur McGill School during the year 1952-53. The median score was very high (3.18), and the poorest score (2.08) again was above the norm. Furthermore, twenty-four of the thirty-five pupils achieved third-grade level on the reading tests. These results were obtained, of course, in a better section of New Castle. The class ranked first in the city.

Parents of the beginning pupils at the Arthur McGill School quickly became aware of the improvement in the teaching of reading. They expressed amazement at the interest and rapid progress of their children. All of them came to see the work, and at the close of the year they voluntarily held a surprise party for the teacher, at which they expressed their gratefulness to her for the outstanding progress of their children and presented her with expensive luggage. This indicates improvement in public relations at the school involved and shows the eagerness with which parents await recognition by school people of the fact that their children can be taught to read.

EFFECT ON CHILDREN

A great many visitors have come to observe the New Castle classes. All have been much impressed with the reading progress of each pupil. But some of our visitors have expressed concern because we were not proceeding in a generally accepted manner. In light of the present emphasis on child development, we have been asked questions such as these: "Are you sure it is always wise to try to teach every child to read?" "Are there other things you might have done for some of these children which would have been more valuable to them than learning to read?" "Have you given proper attention to the mental health and growth of these boys and girls?" "Have you driven the slow-learner to heights he should never have been expected to attain?"

The New Castle experience has shown us that a child's emotional and social growth need not be thwarted at the cost of teaching him to read. On the contrary, these pupils who are experiencing success in reading growth, in a program which thoroughly delights them, *are happier and more socially confident* than are the pupils who are struggling along in a program which is unsuited to their needs and interests and in which many of them cannot be happy because they cannot be successful.

REFERENCES

1. McCracken, Glenn, "Have We Overemphasized the Readiness Factor?" *Elementary English,* Vol. 29 (May 1952), pp. 271-6.
2. ———, "The New Castle Reading Experiment—A Terminal Report," *Elementary English,* Vol. 30 (January 1953), pp. 13-21.
3. A "frame" is one of the series of pictures on a film.

20: How Are Basal Readers Used? *

RALPH C. STAIGER

Millions of copies of basal readers are being used in schools throughout the country. In order to collect information on the attitudes of school people toward some aspects of basal reader use, a questionnaire was sent to teachers, supervisors, consultants, and superintendents in many different types of schools in all 48 states and Hawaii in January of 1957. The findings are reported in this article.

Since the sample of schools was not a random one, it would be unsound to conclude that these proportions are truly representative of practices throughout the country. A sample of 474 responses from all 48 states and Hawaii, however, can be a useful indicator of practices.

The questionnaire was designed to offer as little resistance as possible to the respondent. It contained eleven ques-

* Reprinted from *Elementary English,* Vol. 35, No. 1 (January 1958), pp. 46-9, by permission of the author and the publisher.

tions, ten of which could be answered by check marks. A stamped self-addressed envelope was included. 615 questionnaires were mailed and 474 or 77.07% were returned. This was considered an adequate return.

The questionnaire read as follows:

1. Which plan do you use? (a) One series of readers basally (b) Two series of readers cobasally (c) Three series of readers cobasally (d) More than three series of readers for basal instruction (e) No basal readers (f) Other.
2. Which series do you use in your basal program?
3. When a reading group changes from one series to another, when is the change usually made? (a) At any opportune time (b) After the preprimers (c) After the primer (d) After the first reader (e) After the 2-1 or 2-2 readers (f) After the 3-1 or 3-2 readers (g) Other.
4. Who decides whether a pupil or group changes from one series to another, if a change is made? (a) Teacher alone (b) Teacher and supervisor or consultant (c) Consultant alone (d) Administrator alone (e) Other.
5. Do you use for supplementary reading the basal readers of any publishers other than the above?
6. At the primary grade level, are you satisfied with the two-level (2^1-2^2, 3^1-3^2) editions of the readers?
7. At the intermediate grade level, do you believe that two-level readers (4^1-4^2, 5^1-5^2, 6^1-6^2) are desirable?
8. Did or will the additional expenditure involved in two-level readers influence your adopting them in the primary grades?
9. Did or will the additional expenditure involved in two-level readers influence your adopting them in the intermediate grades?
10. Do you encourage use of the workbook which accompanies the basal reader?
11. How do you recommend use of the teacher's manual? (a) As the prescribed course of study (b) As a guide (c) Useful occasionally (d) Rarely useful (e) Other.

RESULTS

Plan Used. Of the 474 schools in this sample, 69% reported using one series of readers basally. Comments made on the questionnaire indicated that 17.7% of these were varying their procedures so that it was doubtful whether a one-series plan was actually being used. Some of the variations mentioned included different series at the primary and intermediate levels, varying practices in the different schools of one community, or even in different classrooms of one school, and the experimental use of a cobasal series in some classes. Eight percent of the single basal users took the trouble to specify that supplementary readers were an important part of their reading program.

That two series of readers were used cobasally was reported by 20.0% of the schools; 5.7% used three series cobasally, 5.1% used more than three series. We must be careful to interpret the data collected in the light of the foregoing findings, for the sample appears heavily loaded with single basal series schools.

Publishers. The materials used by the schools queried were many and varied, and all of the major publishers were reported, sometimes as single basal adoptions and usually in combination with other materials. Being used as single basic readers were the series of Ginn and Company, Houghton Mifflin and Company, Lyons and Carnahan and Company, Macmillan and Company, Row, Peterson and Company, Scott Foresman and Company, and Silver Burdett and Company. Twenty-nine other combinations were represented, including two, three, four, five, and six series combinations. In these groups were represented the readers of the American Book Company, D. C. Heath and Company, Laidlaw and Company, and the Winston Company, in addition to the readers listed above.

Changing Series. Teachers sometimes find that a group of pupils needs additional instruction at a given level. When a shift is made from one series to another by a reading group within a classroom, the data showed that no particular level is favored for making the change. 40.1% of the respondents indicated that such changes were made at any opportune time, no matter at what level the pupils are reading. The schools which use only one series cannot make such a shift, and therefore 33.1% of the responses showed that no change is made. Other responses showed that 4.6% of the schools favored changing after the pre-primer level; 4.0% after the primer, 3.8% after the first reader; 2.5% after the 2-1 or 2-2 readers, and 5.5% after the 3-1 or 3-2 readers.

Decision To Change. The decision to change a pupil or group from one series to another was apparently considered important enough to warrant the teacher's consulting with a supervisor, principal, or consultant in 51.5% of the schools responding. The teacher alone made the decision in 17.7% of the schools. In no case did the consultant or the administrator alone make the decision.

Perhaps it would be well to recall that most of the returns were from principals and supervisors, and so might be colored according to their beliefs. It is possible that in practice more such decisions are made by the teacher than these results indicate.

Supplementary Reading. An overwhelming proportion of the responses indicated that the basal readers of publishers other than those adopted were used for supplementary reading. Only 5.4% of the respondents said that this was not common practice, while 92.5% approved of using basal readers for supplementary reading.

Two-level Readers. Two-level editions of second and third readers have been on the market for several years. Apparently they have been accepted by a ma-

jority of school people, for 89.9% of the returns indicated satisfaction with the two-level plan at the primary level, while 5.3% did not approve. A small number suggested the need for additional in-between books, even though this question was not asked. When the subject of the increased cost of two-level readers was considered, 85.9% of the returns indicated that cost did not influence their adoption in the primary grades.

One relatively new development in basal readers has been two-level readers at the intermediate grade level (4-1, 4-2, 5-1, 5-2, 6-1, 6-2). Opinions on the desirability of these books were 63.7% in favor, 27.2% opposed, with the remainder not answering directly. Opinions on the influence of the cost factor were somewhat different from those toward the primary level materials; 23.5% believed that the additional expenditure would influence their adoption, while 69.8% did not believe that cost would be a factor.

Workbooks. Workbooks which accompany basal reading programs constitute an important feature of the program, according to publishers. Single basal users are more likely to make use of this part of the program, for 91.4% of single basal reader schools reported using workbooks, while 76.3% of cobasal schools and 49.0% of tribasal and other schools use workbooks. Many of the affirmative answers specified that correct use of a workbook was important to its educational value.

Manuals. Teachers manuals are used in different ways in different schools. In 15.0% of the returns, it was reported that the manuals are recommended as a prescribed course of study, while 68.1% of the returns recommended the manuals as guides. Their usefulness for inexperienced teachers was indicated in some of the responses. Other returns showed that they are recommended both as a guide and as a course of study. This accounted for 9.9% of the returns. Less than 1% of the responses suggested that the guides were useful only occasionally.

CONCLUSIONS

Although it is recognized that the sampling of 474 schools cannot be considered truly representative of all schools, the following conclusions appear valid:

1. While many schools adhere to the single basal series plan, a considerable number is making use of books in other series. These are used as cobasal readers, to be used in conjunction with the basal series, or as supplementary readers, to give pupils additional practice in reading. The great majority of schools use basal readers for some supplementary reading.
2. When more than one series of readers is used for basal instruction, the change is made when it will benefit the needs of the child rather than at any predetermined reader level.

3. The change from one series to another is usually made after the teacher has conferred with a supervisor or principal, although in many cases the teacher alone makes the decision.
4. Two-level readers in the primary grades have won widespread acceptance. At the intermediate grade level they are not so well accepted, although many school people think they are desirable. The additional cost of these materials, while taken into consideration in many cases, has not prevented them from being adopted in most schools.
5. The workbooks which accompany basal readers are more likely to be used when a school adopts a single basal reading series. The likelihood of workbooks being used when two or three series of readers are used is considerably less. The greater the number of basal readers used for instruction, the less likely the students are to use the accompanying workbook.
6. Teachers manuals have been accepted by most school personnel as an aid to teachers. While some schools use the manuals as the prescribed course of study, most consider them a guide.

21: Criticism of the Whole-Word Method.*

GLENN McCRACKEN

Take the whole-word method. The idea was not new with the reading series being discussed. It probably dates back as far as 1850. From that period opinion has differed as to the best method of teaching reading—by whole-word or by phonics. Through the early years of the twentieth century it was phonics. But by 1930 the whole-word method had won the popularity race, and after that time phonics was generally considered an old fashioned teaching method.

The whole-word method sometimes is called the "look-say" idea because in

practice the pupil looks at something and then says what it is. He is taught to learn words in "wholes." He may look at the word itself, or first at the word and then at an accompanying picture, after which he is expected to pronounce the word. There is always help in the background, however. If the child cannot then pronounce the word the teacher will pronounce it for him. It was believed that this new method of learning words would relieve the child of all the drudgery connected with phonetic sounds.

* Reprinted from *The Right To Learn*, Chicago: Henry Regnery Company, 1959, pp. 86-8, with permission of the publisher. Copyright 1959 by the Henry Regnery Company.

The authors of the reading series adopted this new method as the fundamental teaching principle of their books. But it could not possibly be successful because it provided no way to fix the learning in the minds of the learners. In the first place it did not even show the child how to pronounce the word.

In this method the pupil is told that he has several ways of deciphering the pronunciation of a new word. He may be able to tell what it is by noting its association with the other words in the sentence. For example, in the sentence "A *fish* can swim," the child may be able to read the other words, after which *fish* seems like a logical conclusion. The authors of this ungainly plan do not tell us that in order to get the meaning of the word *fish* the pupil has to read the sentence backwards. Then there always is the possibility that the story may be talking about a *duck* or a *dog* or a *swan,* because they too can swim.

But don't worry about this, the "look-say" proponents tell us. There are other ways of figuring out the new word. The child can look at the picture. Picture clues are very helpful. If he sees a fish swimming in the picture, that will help him conclude that *fish* is the new word in the story. But what if there are other things swimming in the picture? What if there is no picture? What if every new word is not depicted by the artist? Oh, well, in that case the pupil should use another method. He examines the *appearance* of the word. That often gives him some information. And that is how the pupil learns to attach the most fantastic pronunciations and meanings you could imagine to the words of our language. In this case he now starts to guess. The word begins something like *frog* so he proudly announces to the teacher, "frog." No, no, the teacher tells him. Look again. Look hard. Well, the child conjectures, the other end of the word looks something like *church.* Is it *church?*

Then, of course, the teacher reveals to the pupil the startling bit of information that a church cannot swim, and they are right back where they started. It is this kind of reading instruction that causes pupils to call *house, horse; on, in,* etc. It also is to blame for children calling *house, village;* and *saw, uncle*—because in the last analysis all the pupil can do is guess.

But in the case above the teacher remains undaunted. She has a final avenue of escape. The authors of the "look-say" method have not forgotten her; when she arrives at that point where all clues have failed, she is given this sage advice: *tell* the child what the word says. Now in actual practice the teacher knows how weak the child is in phonics, how remote picture clues often are, how difficult it is to associate the new word with other words in a sentence, so when a child approaches a word he does not know, she usually just tells him what it is and they go on.

The trouble with this teaching method is that it breaks too many fundamental laws of learning. The child's first impression of the word was that it was *frog.* First impressions often stay with the young mind for a long time. The pupil may go on calling *fish, frog* for years, regardless of what the teacher says. We also have known for a long time that effective learning must be meaningful. How meaningful was the above teaching of *fish?* Such teaching procedure is about as flat and as dead as the fish itself would be after lying on the teacher's desk for a day or two. If the child had known any phonics he very quickly would have noticed that the word began with the *fffff* sound, followed by the *iiiii* sound, followed by *shhhhh.* When these three sounds are placed together *fish* is all he could possibly make of it. But he could not resort to such simple word-solving procedure because phonics was old fashioned. Just nobody used that out-dated method any more.

22: The Future of the Teaching of Reading *

SIR JAMES PITMAN

(This paper is in two sections: In the first section Sir James reports certain findings and experiences of the current researches and suggests ways in which they have a bearing on the assumptions postulated in the second section. In the second section he deals with the future teaching of reading while postulating, for the purposes of argument, that teachers of the initial stages of reading will, in the course of the next few years, generally make use of the new medium known as Pitman's Initial Teaching Alphabet (i.t.a.) instead of Traditional Orthography (t.o.) — to which, however, a transition will be made by the children when fluency has been achieved and when learning success has been assured.)

I

So far there have been two interim reports of the research into the use of i.t.a. in Britain: the first [2] was made in this very room at your Convention last year; the second [3] was presented at Miami Beach to the Convention of the International Reading Association. The author of both reports was Mr. John Downing, the research director, and both have been published and widely read.

The research was planned to cover some 2,500 child beginners. In the event 2,808 i.t.a. children have been recruited and as will be disclosed later a further 1,000 are being recruited.

Thus by the end of July, 1963, the research had recruited 2,808 children between 4 and 5 years old; they were

introduced to the new medium in six termly intakes, the first intake having now completed their second year at school;

Table 1: The number of children included in the schools, arranged according to dates of intake into the schools.

September, 1961	432 *
January, 1962	165
April, 1962	164
September, 1962	1,313
January, 1963	424
April, 1963	310
	2,808

* At the September, 1961, intake sixteen experimental schools and thirty-three control schools were effectively participating in the experiment.

An estimated further 1,000 were recruited to the experiment at the September, 1963, intake, in order to improve the matching between individual children in the i.t.a. group and the t.o. group.

Since the second (Miami Beach) interim report,[4] the relevant children have undergone by October of this year, further tests as shown in Table 2.

Perhaps the most significant indications from those further tests arise from the comparison of the results from the 165 and 164 children in the January and April, 1962, intakes with one another and with the results from the 432 children of the September, 1961, intake, all three groups having been

* Reprinted from *Keeping Abreast of the Revolution in Education,* edited by Arthur E. Traxler, Report of the Twenty-eighth Educational Conference, New York City, October 31-November 1, 1963. Washington, D.C.: American Council on Education, 1964.

Table 2: Tests given between May 4th and October 31st, 1963, to children in each intake in both experimental and control schools

Intake	Group tested	Date of testing	Test
September 1961	All children going up into Junior School	July 1963	Reading Comprehension Test (NS 45) in t.o. (318 i.t.a. children tested)
		July 1963	Raven Intelligence Test (358 i.t.a. children tested)
	Children remaining in Infant School		No test given
January 1962	All children (less absentees) (i.e. 396 t.o. children and 165 i.t.a. children less absentees)	May 1963	Word Recognition Test repeated (Schonell)
April 1962	All children (less absentees) (i.e. 228 t.o. children and 164 i.t.a. children less absentees)	September 1963	Word Recognition Test repeated (Schonell)
	Selected Schools	October 1963	Intensive Reading Test (Neale Analysis of Reading Ability Form C)
September 1962	All children (less absentees) (i.e. 1313 i.t.a. children and t.o. children less absentees)	June 1963	Word Recognition Test (Schonell) first time administered
January 1963	No test given to this intake in the period May 4—October 31, 1963		
April 1963	Selected Schools	July 1963	Intelligence Test (Raven)
		July 1963	Social Adjustment Assessment

tested after completing the first year of being taught with i.t.a. The criterion was provided by the Schonell Graded Word Reading Test, the words being, of course, printed in i.t.a. for the i.t.a. children.

It needs to be pointed out that as yet no wholly satisfactory test has been devised for comparing success with i.t.a. and success with t.o.; though so far as the lowest levels of success are concerned (from the failure to read more than 4 words out of 100 up to being able to read 49 or less), it is probable that the Schonell Graded Word Reading Test furnishes, at any rate in part, a sufficiently reliable measure of reading attainment.

Moreover, children of 5 and 6 are very young for such testing and it needs to be pointed out that just as it is possible that the fact a man knows only 4 men out of a roomful of 100 men is not a measure of how many men he knows in total, and will be an entirely unreliable foundation upon which to infer the degree of his acquaintanceship, so a child's knowledge of 4 words out of 100 on the Schonell will not be an accurate measure of his total reading vocabulary. Caution must be exercised over interpreting the graduations of the Schonell results. They are statements of standards of reading ability, not of the number of words in the child's reading vocabulary. As such a statement, they

are probably very reliable, particularly at the lower levels of achievement.

While in course of time the results of all these series of tests will accumulate to complete the ascertainable facts concerning the child and his progress, the interim results which may most conveniently be ascertained and published, and which are of most value, are those from these Schonell Graded Word Reading Tests.

After eliminating those children in the intake who were found to have a prior ability in reading, and needing to accept a number of drop-outs, the September, 1961, intake of 432 became 345, the June, 1962, intake of 165 became 106 and the April, 1962, intake

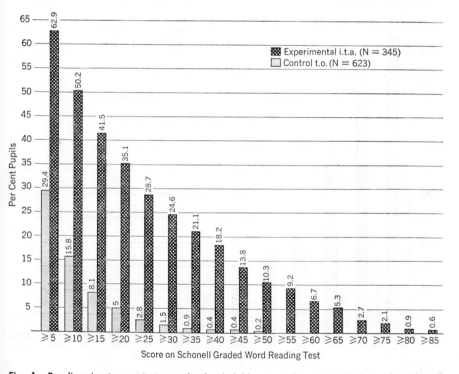

Fig. 1. Reading Attainment in i.t.a. schools of children tested in June, 1962, on the Schonell Graded Word Reading Test transliterated into i.t.a. (All pupils commenced school in September, 1961, at ages 4 and 5 years.)

Each column represents the percentage of children with a score equal to or greater than the one indicated.

of 164 became 143. The total of 761 children thus became 594 who were so tested, all of them after completing the first year of being taught with i.t.a. The similar total of children in the control t.o. classes was 1,073, all similarly tested after the completion of the first year.

If then the results of these three intakes by this Schonell test are merged (total 594) and compared with the 1,073 children tested after the first year of being taught with t.o., the comparison is as shown in Fig. 4 on page 160 (the t.o. children being tested in t.o.).

The results of the intakes of September, 1961, and January and April, 1962, are given in Figs. 1, 2, and 3. These results thus, both when merged and when separate, confirm one another.

The consistency of the results for both the t.o. and the i.t.a. children of all three intakes, as shown in Figs. 1, 2, 3, and particularly 4, is worthy of note. Consideration of Fig. 4 is especially worthwhile in indicating both this consistency and the overall superiority of the i.t.a. results over the t.o. results, and their high degree of superiority at every stage from that of less than 5 to more than 85 but less than 90. It will

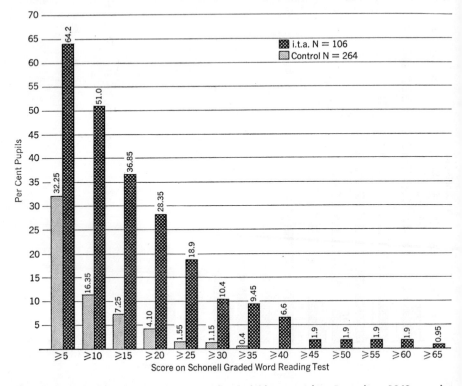

Fig. 2. Reading attainment in i.t.a. schools of children tested in December, 1962, on the Schonell Graded Word Reading Test transliterated into i.t.a. (All pupils commenced school in January, 1962, at ages 4 and 5 years.)

Each column represents the percentage of children with a score equal to or greater than the one indicated.

be seen moreover that the improvement has been at the lefthand side of the scale, where it most matters. Greater earlier success and greater satisfaction at the levels nearest to failure are much more important than the small loss among those who have tasted success and satisfaction—and will read anyhow. (Fig. 5 is, as explained in its caption, a reissue of the results for the September, 1961, intake, but after a further half-year of school.) This, and the consistency of the three groups, provides trustworthy support for both of the propositions advanced by Mr. Downing, and thus for my own assumptions.

I am no scientist. The responsibility of the research is not mine but that of Mr. John Downing, and I would have preferred to contract out of what is his proper territory. However, your most admirable and commanding Dr. Ben Wood has insisted that you should be given some up-to-date facts as a basis for evaluating the most up-to-date results from the British research, and Mr. Downing has very kindly supplied me with the data given above—and helped me with the wording. It is his prerogative to draw, from any presentation of the results of his work, the prestige and honour which he so richly deserves,

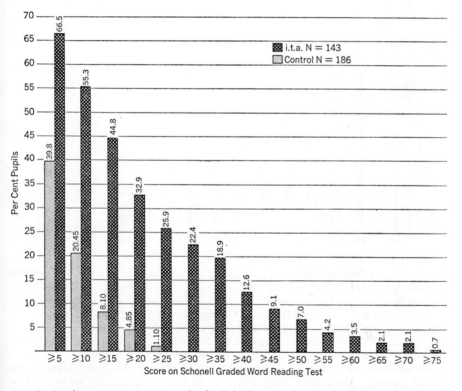

Fig. 3. Reading attainment in i.t.a. schools of children tested in March, 1963, on the Schonell Graded Word Reading Test transliterated into i.t.a. (All pupils commenced school in April, 1962, at ages 4 and 5 years.)

Each column represents the percentage of children with a score equal to or greater than the one indicated.

and so I make no apology for restricting the objective data to that which he has available and has kindly given me.

Yet further data from the more recent tests is not ready and I feel it is reasonable that I should now pass from the objective to the subjective evidence (albeit objectively regarded). But before doing so, you may be interested to have this information about Mr. Downing's plan of testing during the next year or so (*see* Table 3).

The results of all these tests will be released by Mr. Downing in due course.

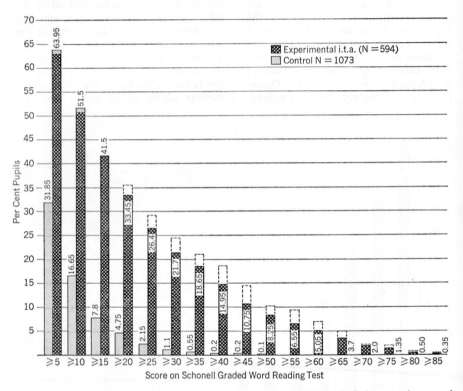

Fig. 4. Reading Attainment in control and i.t.a. schools of children of all three intakes tested respectively in June, 1962, December, 1962, and April, 1962, on the Schonell Graded Word Reading Test. (The standard version of this test was administered in the traditional alphabet and spelling to the control and in i.t.a. to the experimental group.) The results have been merged in a single total covering all three intakes. The graph shows also the changes as between the previously published results for the September, 1961, intake (see Fig. 1) and those for the three intakes (Figs. 1, 2, and 3) thus merged.

The degree by which the percentage of the merged total is higher than the percentage for the September, 1961, intake is indicated, so far as is practicable, by the hatched section: the degree by which it is lower, by the white section. The degree, and the distribution, of the change among the t.o. control children is very similar but cannot be here shown because the proportion is a small one on an already small proportion.

Each column represents the percentage of children with a score equal to or greater than the one indicated.

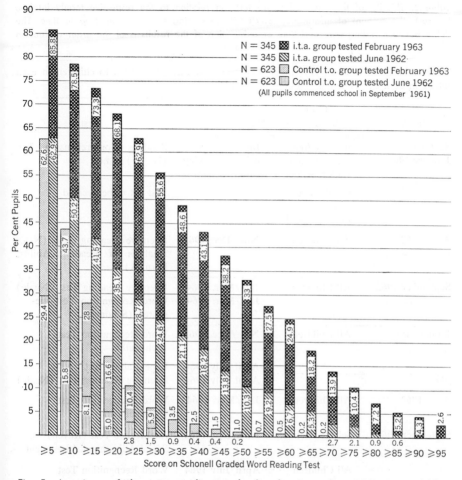

Fig. 5. A re-issue of the corresponding results for the September, 1961, i.t.a. children when tested after a further term-and-a-half—i.e. after four-and-a-half terms. This (Fig. 8 in the Revised Miami Beach report) is reprinted here as a convenient indication of the accelerated progress made by the i.t.a. children of the September, 1961, intake and which the children of the two later intakes may now be expected to have made.

SUBJECTIVE EVIDENCE, OBJECTIVELY REGARDED

During the school year which has just begun, a very considerable number of further i.t.a. classes are being formed by local education authorities on a completely voluntary basis, including classes in areas controlled by authorities which have not hitherto participated or even been invited to do so. These new classes are distinct from the 1,000 children mentioned above, who joined in as final intake in the main research, and will be outside it. So, too, outside the research, will be the new classes in schools which originally participated. They will be conducted as ordinary classes, but using

Table 3: This list of the intended future tests, in relation to the respective termly intakes, forecasts the amount of information which will be coming forward from time to time. The delay between testing time and time of publication of the results is of the order of four to six months.

Tests to be given between November 1st, 1963, and July 31st, 1964, to children in each intake in both experimental and control schools

Intake	Group to be tested	Date of Testing	Test
September 1961 } January 1962 }	All Children going up into Junior School	Immediately prior to leaving Infant School	Reading Comprehension Test (NS 45) in t.o.
	Children re-maining in Infant School		Test yet to be decided
April 1962	All Children	Nov./Dec. 1963	Intensive Reading Test (Neale Analysis of Reading Ability, Form A)
September 1962	All Children	Jan./Mar. 1964 Jan./Mar. 1964	Intensive Reading Test (Neale) Word Recognition Test—re-peated (Schonell)
January 1963	All Children	Nov./Dec. 1963	Word Recognition Test (Schonell)
		April/July 1964 April/July 1964	Repeat above test Intensive Reading Test (Neale)
April 1963	All Children	Jan./Mar. 1964	Word Recognition Test (Schonell)
September 1963	Selected Schools	Nov./Dec. 1963	Intelligence Test (Raven) Social Adjustment Assessment
	All Children	April/July 1964	Word Recognition Test (Schonell)
January 1964	All Children	Jan./Mar. 1964	Intelligence Test (Raven)
April 1964	All Children	April/July 1964	Social Adjustment Assessment
All Intakes	All Children moving from Infant to Junior School	Nov. 1963/July 1964	T.O. Reading Comprehension Test (Neale) Intelligence Test (Raven) Social Adjustment Assessment
All Intakes	All children	Nov. 1963/July 1964 Termly Tests	Maintain record cards of read-ing primer reached

(*Note:* Testing programme from September, 1964, onwards now in course of preparation. This has deliberately been kept fluid as late as possible so that the planners can take advantage of the results of early tests.)

i.t.a. instead of t.o. and adopting the procedures normal for the adoption of a new discovery as part of the day-to-day routine practice.

Some education authorities have even had to be discouraged from yet trying out i.t.a., and in others the number of schools has had to be restricted. This is partly because of organizational difficulties in providing sufficient facilities for instructing practising teachers in the new approach to teaching, and (more limiting still) because of the past-summer shortage of suitable books. Printing numbers of the books designed for the main research were only barely adequate and allowed no margin for the general use of i.t.a. which has now followed. There has also been a delay in the preparation and supply of new apparatus designed specifically to exploit the new teaching situations created by i.t.a.—in which the methods of look-say may be, and indeed ought to be—deliberately combined with those of phonic and syllabic teaching.

It is estimated that 5,000 children will participate in these non-research classes in this school year, of which over 1,000 children actually started in September in England, Wales and Scotland. (This will make a total of 8,800 children since the research began who will have learned through i.t.a.) This estimate of 5,000 children during the current school year has been based upon the thirty-three authorities (and their schools) which have actually applied for books, have nominated teachers and arranged to have those teachers trained in the use of i.t.a., as shown below—

Bedfordshire	Cheshire
Belfast	Dewsbury
Birmingham	Dundee
Blackburn	Exeter
Bolton	Harrow
Brighton	Hertfordshire
Bristol	Keighley
Burton-on-Trent	Lancashire
Caernarvonshire	Leicestershire
Lincolnshire	Stoke-on-Trent
London	Stockport
Newcastle-under-Lyme	Surrey
Oldham	Walsall
Oxford	Wigan
Rochdale	Willesden
Southend	Wolverhampton
Staffordshire	

Most of these authorities have conducted, or will shortly be conducting, lectures and courses for the training of their teachers.

Meanwhile in America, the earlier small beginnings in several private schools have been supplemented by considerable accessions this school year. Six hundred first-grade children in the Lehigh project, under the direction of Dr. Albert J. Mazurkiewicz and supported by a $48,000 grant from the Fund for the Advancement of Education, started this September. So did the ablest 125 children under the Greater Cleveland Educational Research Council. A small remedial class in New York is typical of a number. Some 300 children between the ages of three and six are expected to start shortly under Dr. John Rosenbloom of the University of Minnesota. In addition, small units in Chicago; Akron, Ohio; Media, Pa.; Lompoc, Calif.; and Syracuse, N. Y. and others have started, or will shortly be starting.

In Canada, one major city has already started and at least four of the Provinces, including six other major cities, are considering starting with i.t.a. in some of their schools. In Northern Ireland 50 children are learning to read using i.t.a. In the Republic of Ireland two State E.S.N. (Educationally Sub-Normal) schools and one high-class private school, all near Dublin, have begun to teach with the help of i.t.a.

The spread of the use of i.t.a. and the fact that teachers involved in the research decide freely to go on using it instead of reverting to t.o. is very encouraging. Now that no more children are needed for research purposes, one might imagine that some teachers and authorities would return to the old medium. But they do not. As practical educators they are already convinced. Not only has not a single reversion to t.o. taken place, but many teachers and administrators are making enthusiastic use of their experience gained in the research classes to give lectures and help run courses for those in charge of new i.t.a. classes.

SOME COMPARISONS

Last May at Miami Beach [3] Mr. John Downing reported that, *subject to confirmation by later results,* it would be:

clear that (a) *children can learn to read much more rapidly when their beginning books are printed in Pitman's i.t.a.,* and hence that (b) *the use of the traditional alphabet and spelling for beginning reading does seriously retard children's progress into the world of books.*

Mr. Downing also listed the following five findings of how the i.t.a. children are superior in achievement to the t.o. children:

1. Young children get through their beginning reading program faster when their books are printed in i.t.a.
2. They can recognize more words in print when they are in i.t.a.
3. They can accurately read continuous English prose more readily when it is printed in i.t.a.
4. They can comprehend more continuous English in print if i.t.a. is used.
5. They can read faster when the medium is i.t.a.

He reported too that in the control (t.o.) classes the findings have shown that the conventional alphabet and spellings of English cause reading diffculty and:

1. delay progress in the reading program;
2. frustrate the recognition of words in print;
3. impede the development of skill in reading continuous English prose;

4. cut children off from words within their range of comprehension;
5. reduce their speed of reading.

He further suggested the following:

The impediment caused by the conventional alphabet and spelling appears to go beyond erecting barriers to success in these various aspects of reading. Headteachers of the experimental schools have reported that i.t.a. not only accelerates progress and raises reading standards but it also brings with it certain other advantages:

1. it raises the young beginner's level of self-confidence;
2. it increases enthusiasm for reading and interest in books;
3. it allows children to be more independent in their work;
4. it results in a marked improvement in creative writing;
5. it permits children's thoughts to flow more naturally in writing.

I have Mr. Downing's permission to assure you to-day that all the evidence that has since become available has confirmed what he then wrote, and that not a single piece of evidence has conflicted with it.

THE TRANSITION STATE

Two large questions remain to be discussed: (1) Has the transition to t.o. continued to be made as effortlessly by the "laggards" in the September, 1961, intake—i.e., those who by February, 1963, had not reached the transition stage—as it was made by the quicker learners? (2) When those who still must be considered as laggards eventually do achieve fluency in i.t.a., will the transition be as invariably successful as it has been with the rest of the i.t.a. group?

No further tests of the transition stage have been organized for the September, 1961, intake subsequent to those in February, 1963, which were reported on by Mr. Downing last May. Testing at more frequent intervals has been shown to be superfluous, because doubts about the transition stage have largely disappeared. Whereas at the outset all teachers feared that the transition would present a forbidding hurdle, they are now so confident that fluency in i.t.a. is synonymous with fluency in t.o. (whether upper case, lower case, or cursive handwriting) that additional or intermediate testing of success in the transition no longer seems to be necessary; in any case the progress of the children across the transition stage is indicated by the teachers' records to t.o. books issued to children who have completed the i.t.a. teaching course (see Mr. Downing's report at Miami Beach).*

All the subjective evidence confirms (1) the previous objective findings that the transition appears to be automatic and effortless; and (2) that it is equally true for the laggards when they eventually attain fluency in i.t.a. No evidence at all has appeared to indicate the possibility of the contrary.

I.T.A. AND REMEDIAL TEACHING

When it was originally conceived, the research was concerned with initial teaching only, but the enterprise—and possibly the desperation—of remedial teachers led many to originate their own small experiments or field trials. Indeed, the extent to which this has happened amounts to another unsolicited testimony to the success of i.t.a.

During the School Year of 1962-63 i.t.a. was used in 57 schools and centers for remedial teaching, and there is no doubt that this number will increase to 200-300 during 1963-64 as adequate teaching material becomes available.

The objective data is limited to scattered reports on small groups of children; the information has been passed to the University of London Institute of Education but has not yet been collated. A report, however, by John Downing and Keith Gardner, was published in *Educational Research* [5] in the November, 1962, issue, and was followed up by a further report by John Downing in *The Reading Teacher* of March 1963. If only there had been the money and staff to enable London University's Institute of Education to extend its research to this special field, there would be a great deal more published evidence of i.t.a.'s success in rescuing the apparently hopeless slow-starters and in developing the reading and linguistics of backward readers. Plentiful evidence could also be supplied of the great improvement in attitude to life and to society which follows the mastery of reading—not to mention the change in society's own attitude to its newly literate members.

The reasons which led the committee to limit the research to initial teaching should, no doubt, also apply to my report to this meeting, and therefore the value of i.t.a. must stand or fall on its merits as a medium for initial teaching rather than from remedial teaching. But on this score I have no fears either, that it will, I am confident, prove to offer at least as spectacular and beneficial an improvement for remedial as for initial teaching.

FUTURE PROGRESS REPORTS

It is understandable that teachers and educators generally are impatient to have the results of the research, stage by stage, almost before the statisticians

---

* These results showed that not only those better i.t.a. children, who had "done the transition," could read in traditional orthography at a higher rate, with greater accuracy, and with greater comprehension than could the better children who had been taught in the traditional medium, but also that the less good i.t.a children, who had not yet attempted the transition, at any rate in class, were no less excelling their t.o. control opposite numbers in *all* these respects. A further such comparative test, as indicated in Table 3 has been planned for November-December.

have been able to calculate the percentages! John Downing has met this demand and disclosed his interim findings with commendable promptitude, even though this kind of piecemeal dissemination is clearly not what a research worker normally desires. He has very kindly furnished me with the above important, if limited, third instalment of information. Although your Convention provides a very appropriate occasion for this kind of report, I am sure you will agree that such occasion should not determine a report's precise timing. Moreover, it is only right and fair that the next and most comprehensive release of information should be in Britain, and that our own Minister of Education, with whose sympathetic interest this adventurous research was planned, should be accorded the opportunity to participate in the occasion. He might well decide that this might be the moment for a review of future policy on teaching reading in which might also participate all those in authority over the schools for which he, together with the Secretary of State for Scotland and our 181 educational authorities, are responsible.

DEFENCE IN DEPTH

Throughout my life-time struggle in this field I have become used to opposition which might fairly be described as "defence in depth." The teaching of children's reading is a subject that stirs passion and emotion. Little children and their welfare rightly touch the deepest chords of genuine solicitude. Thus the traditional, both in teaching reading and in the medium in which it is to be taught, is defended to the last ditch—which is reached only after a "phased withdrawal" from previous defensive ditches. Let us examine some of the standard objections to i.t.a.:

Ditch 1. i.t.a. is unnecessary and harmful, because children will find it equally difficult to learn to read in such a novel and obviously imperfect and provisional medium as they do in t.o. If, however, the findings of earlier research are mentioned and if one claims that only by further scientific enquiry will these alleged demerits, or the merits of i.t.a., be disproved or proved, it may or may not produce a concession, but too often it amounts merely to a falling-back, in an orderly withdrawal, to the next ditch.

Ditch 2. That even if it should be admitted that it could be easier for a child to learn in the new medium, it is next argued that the child will then need to *unlearn* the new skill and to learn afresh to read in t.o.; that the process of unlearning will be harmful and that in any case he will lose more time in the lengthy transitional processes than he could possibly have gained earlier in the initial stages. Here again, it may eventually be conceded that *a priori* reasoning, existing evidence, and future research may together be capable of supplying the necessary proof, but should this proof (impossible as it may seem) turn out to be to i.t.a.'s advantage, even then a series of four further defensive ditches are taken up.

Ditch 3. That even if i.t.a.'s success in the transition should be admitted then the damage to the child's spelling would be devastating and permanent.

Ditch 4. That even if good spelling, as well as reading, could be achieved with i.t.a., the child would anyhow have become literate in time and therefore will gain nothing from an easier way of learning, nor by learning to read and write earlier and more effectively by a given age.

Ditch 5. That children who fail to learn to read are anyhow so unintelligent (for how otherwise have they failed?) that reading ability for them would make no real contribution sufficient to justify the great disturbance to the more intelligent majority.

Ditch 6. That the reading ability acquired through i.t.a. may recede at a later stage, or that such children will at least fail to make the further progress which they would have made had they learned with t.o. from the beginning.

Those who have observed children learning with the new medium are convinced that the *a priori* reasoning and the findings of earlier researches have been more than confirmed by their own experiences during the current research;

this is certainly true of the first two of these six defences in depth. Their own experience has also convinced them, even though objective documentation is not yet to hand, that the third line of defence (spelling) has already crumbled.

At what point then does the onus of probability and proof change? At what point should an open-minded neutrality on the remaining points take the place of emotional opposition? Is even one of

accordiŋ too mie calcuelæʃhonſ from uenescœ sorseſ ov informæʃhon, ie reckon ɟhat wiɟh sum 7 million ɟhildren joiniŋ scœl every yeer in ɟhe iŋgliʃh-speekiŋ wurld,[1] and spendiŋ sæ ten yeerſ in scœl, and wiɟh at leeſt 20 per sent ov ɟhem trubld, aſ ie am convinſd, bie reediŋ disabilitiſ whiɟh cœd mœſt speedily bee œvercum, ɟhær muſt-ɟhærfor bee sum 15 million ɟhildren nou at scœl hœ ar in dier need ov help whiɟh cœd bee speedily and ɟheeply given.

ɟhe tiem haſ nou ʃhuerly cum for aull infant scœlſ too acsept and applie in ɟhe classrœm whot haſ been discuverd in ɟhe back-(class)rœm ov reserɟh. ɟhe need iſ eekwally cleer and muɟh mor pressiŋ for remeedial reediŋ in juenior and secondary scœlſ. teeɟherſ ov ɟhe yuŋger ɟhildren mæ pardonably tæk ɟhær tiem, nœiŋ ɟhat remeedial teeɟherſ will læter hav opportuenitiſ too rescue ɟhe fæluerſ. but whot about ɟhœſ yuŋ peepl hœ ar nou in ɟhær fienal yeer at scœl and hœ still cannot reed properly—ɟhæ alœn must amount too sum1.5million out ov ɟhe 15 million? ɯuns ɟhæ hav left scœl ɟhæ ar not liekly too cum back, eeven too niet scœl, and ɟhær remænſ œnly a ʃhort and preʃhius tiem in whiɟh too rescue ɟhem. ie nœ ɟhæ follœ behiend jeneræʃhonſ ov backward reederſ, but ɟheeſ ɟhildren ar yœr and mie responsibility. can wee afford suɟh wæſt ov hueman capasity when wee hav reeſon too beleev ɟhat ɟhe rescue need tæk œnly a fue weeks or munɟhs, sertenly not aſ muɟh aſ a hœl scœl yeer? can wee bee cumfortabl in contemplætiŋ unnesessary hueman sufferiŋ on sœ grand a scæl—rememberiŋ ɟhat from ɟheeſ millionſ will cum (or aulredy hav cum) meny recrœts for ɟhe criminal classeſ, and ɟhat meny uʃherſ will leed inadekwæt lievſ and, too a græter or smauller ekstent, becum a lieability too ɟhe rest ov us?

[1] Source: *Current School Enrollment Statistics,* UNESCO 1962. The figure does not include any English-speaking children in Africa, India, etc.

the three remaining lines of defence tenable? Is it really conceivable that any of the 33 per cent of the i.t.a. children who can read 50 words or more in the Schonell Graded Reading Test will ever fall behind the mere 1 per cent of the corresponding t.o. children who reach the same standard—much less behind the 99 per cent who have not reached it? Is it likely that with their skilled reading in t.o. they will be less, rather than more, amenable to improved comprehension, or faster reading, or both?

II

With the past exciting results, their reiteration and verification now in tests with three successive groups of children, and the growing army of educators who are responding enthusiastically to i.t.a., the happy prognosticiations for the future may be misread. We would be wrong to regard i.t.a. as a wonder drug and cure-all. It is a medium which rationalizes the code-breaking of reading and exploits alphabeticism precisely during that period when alphabeticism is only valuable—the period of learning to read. In so doing, it reinforces the average child's belief in his own rationality, a belief that is sorely buffeted when an arbitrary disorder, such as he finds in our traditional alphabet, is his first window on the literate world.

There are many children, however, for whom even i.t.a. cannot open the magic doors to the real world existing beyond the gates of their own limited experience. These are children with whom you are all doubtless familiar—a portion of that unhappy group said to be suffering from a "reading block." Although, thanks to i.t.a., the proportion of these sufferers is substantially smaller than the percentage usually discovered in a reading program using a traditional orthography, this small stubborn residue exists, and it is to this group that I wish to turn my attention now.

How does it happen that regardless of the better performance in i.t.a. classes, a certain percentage of all children may not become competent linguists in the *visible* versions of *the words we assume they know?* It is possible that they were not competent linguists when admitted to class and still are not competent linguists when spoken to or when speaking. They may, therefore, be misleading those who address them by giving correct responses to spoken messages. They thereby create the false impressions that it is the words, and the words alone, which provide the clues through which their understanding is demonstrated.

How is it possible for these children so to mislead those who address them—to create the impression they are linguistically competent in speech, when, in fact, they are not? To answer this question, we must digress and examine for a moment the process of communication itself.

Reading is a process of being communicated with; writing is communicating; both occur through the medium of visible words. They are skills in the field of sight. Listening and speaking are the corresponding skills in the field of hearing. It is important to differentiate these four separate functions: the receptive and the emissive; the visual, and the audible. We ought never to forget, also, that all four are but secondary aspects of the primary—the God-given gift of language, something unique to man, and the reason for his dominance over the animal kingdom.

THE IMPORTANCE OF "SITUATIONS"

Communication may and often does take place without words, but it is not language. In all communication, "situation" is the essential precondition.

The situation here, while pictorial and thus now imaginary, was at the time real. It helped both the woman and the dog to understand the message.

Fig. 6. A response to a spoken verbal communication does not necessarily imply that the words, as words, have been either heard (in the case of the woman) or understood. (The woman may be non-English speaking and may not understand a word of English even if she did hear them.) Thus, comprehension of a spoken word cannot be safely inferred from a satisfactory response.

Let us begin with the woman. She may or may not have been too deaf to hear at all: moreover she may not have been English-speaking. She may, thus, not have understood the words as words. But, by seeing the man move his lips and by understanding the man's gesture, she was able to apprehend the situation and thus receive the message, "Sit Down."

As for the dog, it is the repetition of situations accompanied by what comes to be the relatable noise which he understands. The words of the man are but a noise, as non-verbal as the differing notes and intervals of the huntsman's horn.

In neither instance—the behavior of the woman nor the action of the dog—was communication achieved by truly linguistic means. But both clearly received the message.

It is important to recognize this potentiality for effective communication and response by means of a symbolism existing apart from language, because it would seem that one of the most serious errors in the teaching of receptive language, whether read or listened to, is the assumption by the communicator that the words have been understood as words, and that it has been the words alone which have carried the message. Moreover, it is in the audible language (speech heard) rather than in the visible (print read) that this error is most likely to lie undetected—and most to be feared. The audible language carries so many more clues than does printed language, over and above the meaning of the words, that it invites opportunities for the hearer to mislead the speaker by seeming to understand his words.

We are all familiar with the weight of communication carried by a speaker's gestures, facial expressions, and tone of voice—aspects of his communication which the speaker himself may neither

Fig. 7. An otherwise incomprehensible verbal communication may become meaningful by reason alone of the urgency of the gesturing and the tone of what appears to be no more than a noise made by another human, if the pedestrian is unfamiliar with the language that creates the noise. This further illustrates that the evidence of linguistic comprehension in any response to speech is much less reliable than a response to print.

intend nor recognize. How often is the listener's response made to these extra-lingual elements rather than to the words themselves.

In the situation in our next picture there are many more such clues to the intention of the spoken message which support its comprehension.

The situation is a real one and was apparent to the eye, without help from the spoken words. Moreover, the noise of the horn, the screeching of the wheels and brakes, the dog's howl, give audible support to the visible message and non-verbal support both to what the eye is seeing and to what the ear is receiving in the verbal message, *Jump for it!* From this we may appreciate that the dangers of crediting a child with a linguistic competence which he does not possess are great indeed in the spoken word—far greater than in the printed word, even though similar dangers exist for the printed word also.

By contrast, cold print is emotionless in its "silent" unhelpfulness (shown in Figure 8). No assistance at all is given to the learner of reading, for even the special form in upper case letters—JUMP FOR IT !—is no more than a conventional device for indicating urgency *to those already literate*. The overtones that can enrich spoken messages are absent and so too, unless there is an illustration, is the situation. In sound, even should the pedestrian be a foreigner and have no inkling of the meaning of the bystander's message, the tone of urgency in the words will carry a clear supporting message. In print there is no help at all. In a real situation the visual message of the situation is so very strong and clear that the verbal message *Jump for it!* is probably superfluous because, unless such a (possibly foreign) pedestrian were blind as well as deaf, he will already have received the non-verbal message. In the unreal

Fig. 8. A response to a printed verbal communication cannot be anything but linguistic. It may, however, be guessed in a very few cases, e.g. if accompanied by an illustration or other assistance giving sufficient situational clues. For instance an instruction on the blackboard may lead to a perfect response by a child—who is no more than copying the action of a neighbour who did comprehend the instruction. A WAY OUT sign with a hand pointing in a direction may be understood in any language.

situation of print there is no situation at all save for those who are linguistic, linguistic *in print,* and have the relevant experience to imagine it.

In the case of print, the situation can be only imaginary. It cannot be observed by any of the senses and is created necessarily as merely a synthetic situation, for which the printed words are the stimulus to the imagination through the sense of sight. Anyone lacking sight, or lacking a knowledge of the language, or lacking the knowledge of that particular visual form of language (the ability to read), will be unable to receive the printed verbal message and will be thus barred from understanding. He will be barred, too, from passing by his own efforts through the portals into that magic world of myriad situations, of the special kind

of unlimited experience which print affords. Such capacity to conjure up situations is, moreover, verbal, and in an "ideal" life is not restricted by time, distance or expense.

Barred from this special world, barred from passing through the gates of print into a new world are those unfortunates, to be found within both conventional and i.t.a. groups, who cannot be taught to read save with special effort and skill.

We can understand failure in the traditional orthography classes. The very magnitude of the superiority demonstrated by the i.t.a. children in the English experiment indicates that the conventionally taught children, even if linguistically competent on admission, have been seriously frustrated by the unnecessary difficulties present in our conventional alphabet.* We can under-

* It would appear that the "slow starters" of the past become identifiable by the use of i.t.a., as two separate groups—those who were adequately linguistic but have been slow, solely because of the mechanical difficulties imposed by t.o., and those who are not adequately linguistic and have been "slow starters" for this reason.

stand, too, that there may have been *some* in both classes who suffer from deficient eyesight or other optical malfunction, but the number will be an insignificant part of the school population. There may be a few, too, who were partially deaf. We may also suppose that there will be others who, because of brain damage at birth or other causes, have been unable to detect, and so discriminate between concepts and between differences in sound upon which communication by speech is based, and are thus not receptive listeners. But the number will again surely be small. There may be some suffering from dyslexia, but they will be relatively few—and may perhaps be found not to exist as a group separate from the others, once the difficulties of learning by a traditional orthography no longer cause failure. There will be yet others, who, because of psychological problems—a need to rebel against authority, parental pressure to read, rivalry with a sibling, emotional immaturity, or some other emotional problem—cannot or will not learn to read.

What then of the others who have thus not begun to read and yet suffer from *no* detectable physical or emotional defect? Could they suffer from another defect—a linguistic one? There are strong grounds for this presumption —for supposing that many of these children come to school with no physical or psychological defect, with no defect other than a linguistic one, and that they are unable, to a far larger extent than has been supposed, to be communicated with, or to communicate themselves, through words. We should, I believe, regard these children as suffering from a misfortune as disabling as deafness. Their home environments have not provided the necessary variety of situations nor has it then exposed them to the appropriate associations of words with such varying conditions and experiences, which have been enjoyed by children who are verbally proficient.

There is undoubtedly scope for the oculist to help the small minority who are linguistically competent (in speech) but cannot see the parallel visual forms. The aurist, too, can help the few with poor hearing discrimination. The psychologist can help the emotionally disturbed child. But there is a far greater, far more difficult field for the skilled language teacher called upon to help children who have come to school without effective competence in language— for whom the task is not one of relating the visible forms to the audible forms of a language they already know—for they do not yet know it!—but one of first learning *language*.

There is every indication that these non-linguistic children form a considerable proportion of reading failures in my country, and we may assume that that constitute a very real problem in teaching reading in classes in other countries of the English-speaking world. In your country, they are frequently described as "culturally deprived"; we shall see, however, that cultural deprivation and linguistic deprivation may very well be the same thing.

These children deserve our best efforts. They come from homes that are truly under-privileged (though not necessarily economically so), in which the parents have neglected to exploit the opportunities presented to teach language or, as language develops, to talk with them about the family and happenings in the neighborhood, to read them stories and, above all, to listen patiently to the children's tentative and improving efforts to convey their own news and the lively imaginings of childhood.[1]

We know very little about how language is learnt by the very young even those who live in linguistically privileged homes.* We know still less about those who arrive at school with virtually no

* See Appendix following references at end of this selection.

linguistic background. It is possible that this second class have, by reason of past failures, not the same aptitudes for learning as they would have had earlier; on the other hand, it may be that with intensive, that is to say skilfully selected and repeated, experiences in language, they will gain the ground they have never won.

CONSCIOUS TEACHING OF LANGUAGE

Such a linguistically deprived child will surely profit greatly from a linguistic exercise which confirms meaning and teaches reading simultaneously. Indeed, he may (as the deaf child frequently will) reverse the usual order, and by means of repetition of relatable situations and their visible symbols, become verbal in print first and then extend his visual language to its "secondary" counterpart in speech. Indeed, this is precisely what all literates experience to some extent, particularly in the higher ranges of their vocabulary. Their reading experience introduces them to new situations and other appropriate words which only then become part of their speech system.

Moreover, a child who has been brought up, for example, to understand and to say *I must of been* (instead of *I must have been*) is made aware of his mis-hearing or mis-learning. The teaching of reading in a medium which closely relates what he reads to what he ought to hear has clearly a linguistic benefit, over and above its benefit thereby, in teaching reading more effectively.

Teaching language as a primary objective, with the teaching of reading being secondary, may thus possibly be the best teaching of reading even for children who are already fully verbal. It will surely be the best, and the *only* effective, approach to the teaching of language (and of reading) to those who have come to school ineffectively verbal.

FORMATION OF WORD ASSOCIATIONS

Is it possible that verbality in print could thus antedate verbality in speech? What are the advantages in acquiring the one before the other? Is learning to speak really easier than learning to read? If so, why? Is it that the ear is a more delicately discriminating sensory organ than the eye? Is there any reason to prefer this supposition to the opposite and more generally held other one? What then are the reasons for the fact, which may be observed that among hearing children listening or talking precede reading and writing and that the ear should thus be made to excel the eye?

May I suggest that the supreme advantage of speech over print in the teaching of language has, heretofore, lain only in the very much greater convenience in uttering speech symbols and the much greater inconvenience of organizing sight symbols and in the reality and immediacy of the situations against which speech can be applied, and in the immediacy with which the effective words can be associated with those situations?

This situation in the illustration is for us imaginary, but for child and mother it was reality. It was one of hundreds of varying situations in which these particular words recurred appropriately. The words were heard by the child *immediately* in relation to the situation. Situation and message in this and all similar situations were immediately associated, and the meaning of the words was thus learned by inference.

The teacher of the deaf child has no such dramatic occasions on which to furnish the opportunities for such inferences.

Apart from the inconvenience, the need for foresight, preparation, special equipment, the necessity to create a suitable statement out of the restricted vocabulary of the card index, and the time taken to display the print-form,

Fig. 9. A situation in which the learning of the words spoken by the mother is helped by:

(a) Noise that compels attention and of itself establishes the communicative situation.
(b) The tone of voice as well as facial expression and gesture which carry a supporting message.
(c) The immediacy of the association of word to concept helps the child to establish the desired relationships.
(d) The ability to speak words instantaneously is conveniently always at call.
(e) The need for effort is minimal and constitutes no deterrent.

the reality has departed with the immediacy. The whole drama and colour have departed because of the delay *and the silence*. Silence, with its inability to convey emotion, urgency, and feeling, is, as we have seen in our earlier illustration, the great defect from which cold print suffers. The very evident distress of the intonation in *Oh Peter, you naughty boy!* . . . conveyed its own support meaning, much as did the urgency of the words *Jump for it!* The emphasis on the word *naughty* in itself fortified the desired association with the meaning of the word which expressed it. By contrast, the mother of the deaf child, limited as she is to the visual, was able, despite her expression and gestures, to inject only part of the emo-

tion and colour, while she conveyed meaning through the visual display of words. Slow, colourless, undramatic, as well as cold, is the product of the printing press. Any warmth comes only later, when words have become clothed in imagery from past associations.

Perhaps when some electronic device uses i.t.a. to show verbal equivalents to a situation instantaneously on a screen this lack of immediacy would be overcome.

An important corollary to this possibility is the implications such electronic developments hold for the teaching of very young, normal children. Such children, if exposed simultaneously to both audible and visible linguistic forms, might learn to read and to

Fig. 10. A situation in which the mother's necessity to communicate only visually (because the child is deaf) imposes great handicaps on her and on the child:

(a) The child's attention will be directed to action on the table and floor and away from *all* other visual interests.

(b) The mother will thus need both to divert visual attention and to maintain it.

(c) Facial expression and gesture must be artificially repeated by the mother in order to support the message.

(d) The "colour" of sound in conveying distress and other situational supporting clues will be absent.

(e) The relevance of the verbal (visual) message to the situation is necessarily stale—immediacy of relationship has been lost.

(f) The material for a wide choice of visual messages needs to be prepared long in advance and, moreover, to be held conveniently accessible.

(g) The task of assembling the words is slow and laborious and will deter even a stout-hearted mother, or teacher.

speak at the same time.* They might even learn to write and to listen at the same time to sounds coming from a specially designed typewriter. Such an approach might be, moreover, a logical extension of the work of Professor Omar Khyam Moore of Yale. The typewriter would certainly facilitate learning of speaking and writing as well as listening and reading. Thus all four could be

---

* It may be significant that two among the most successful i.t.a. children have been two who came to school knowing not a word of English—only Italian and Polish. It is interesting to reflect that the important difference between their situation and that of any non-linguistic children coming from allegedly English-*speaking* homes was that they were fully linguistic in *a* language when they came to school and were thus skilled in those analyses of factors common to varying situations and were furnished with a linguistic "ticket" with which each concept could be and was habitually isolated—which combination is the basis of linguistic perception. These two children would thus seem to have benefited from the contemporary presentation of the visual and new audible "ticket" for the concepts which had already been analyzed and ordered in the linguistic compartment of their little brains. It will be suggested later that such contemporary presentation might carry a particular advantage in teaching language as such.

conjointly presented, just as the two, listening and speaking, alone are today.

I appreciate that Piaget and others have established, apparently to general satisfaction, that young children under the age of five find perception and analysis of the visual (particularly print) more difficult then perception and analysis of sound. It is no doubt rash on my part, but it may possibly be constructive to question whether such concurrent factors as opportunity, reward, satisfaction, motivation, and reinforcement may have been taken insufficiently into account. When considered in the context of suggested lines of further research, it is not, I hope, irresponsible to suggest that motivation, reward, and satisfaction are most relevant; and that if motivation and satisfaction were made as strong when learning *visual* language as they are made when learning *audible* language, and if opportunities to associate the visual word with the situation were as frequent and as conveniently practical, then quite young children might be found to make surprising progress in the visual language and even better progress in the aural.

If this were possible, and it were also practicable to confront the child with both audible and visible forms of the word simultaneously, there might be an advantage in reducing the delay—three or four years—before the child is confronted with the pairing of the visual and the audible.

Please do not misunderstand me. I make no suggestion as to the age at which language should be taught through reading. That must await the investigation which I have deliberately put first on my list of suggested future researches. Moreover, the practical decision in particular cases now rests, as it always will rest, with the parent, the teachers and the authorities responsible. It is not my job to influence any particular decision, only to help insure that unnecessary causes of failure are removed and that lubricants to the wheels of success are available when teaching does begin—at whatever age.

HOW THE GRAPHIC ARTS CAN AID THE TEACHER OF READING

The comparison between teaching language to the deaf and to those who can hear, calls attention to the one great advantage which the teacher of reading enjoys in contrast to the parent who supplies a running, audible commentary upon life's varying realities. The graphic arts, by the very painstaking and time-consuming limitations which we have noted above, afford their own advantages in language teaching.

The synthetic situation presented by the graphic arts is in no way limited and ought never to be accidental. Graphic situations are infinitely variable and the presentation of the desired words is capable of very close control so that the maximum help may be given to the child in creating appropriate situations and in helping the child to isolate and classify the desired common factors. Moreover, the associated word can unfailingly be presented; the delay between reinforcements can be kept to the minimum; and confusion over synonyms can be avoided—e.g. when "uncle" refers to a watch as a *tick-tick* he can be both missing an opportunity to reinforce and undoing previous reinforcements by creating unnecessary confusion. Situations depicted graphically may involve "water" on a scale from Niagara Falls and the oceans to that of the drip feeder for giving water to an ailing chick whether or not the child is near these great falls, or any sea or a farm. No real-life situation can hope to match the limitless *and controlable* potentialities of the synthetic situations which graphic representation makes possible. No real-life situation can thus unfailingly point *le mot juste*, or invariably avoid the confusion of synonyms.

Whenever it is worth talking to a child about an ideal situation in a picture or confronting him with the appropriate printed words, it is sounder and more effective teaching to present the words in a way which, thanks to painstaking design and the provision of the desired key-words in print, shall be consciously directed to helping the child to observe, memorize, analyze and classify the situations and, in learning the appropriate conventional "tickets," to become communicable and communicative. It is only through the graphic arts that this may be guaranteed to happen.

Moreover, it is not in learning by inference the words for the picturable, the demonstrable, the positional and directional, the clearly inferable, that the teaching and learning of language presents its greatest difficulty. The need for help arises when learning the abstractions, the unpicturable, the undemonstrable—those concepts and words which may be learned *only* by a more remote inference and thus only from *a series of a great many situations* and from their verbal associations (*e.g.* concepts such as time-contrasts—*not YET ready, tomorrow;* or values—e.g. *worth twice as much*).

It may be found, now that we have in i.t.a. a medium which enables a relationship to be apparently effortlessly apprehended between words heard and words seen, that for a considerable proportion of young children, the early as well as the more advanced stages of their language will be more easily learned from print and hearing together rather than from hearing alone.

I do not wish to imply that the graphic arts are inherently superior or ought to supersede reality in the development of language or reading skills. Of course, it is most desirable for the child to experience and touch one or more *real* flowers, and desirable, too, that he should have the real experience if possible before the graphic one. But this does not mean that graphic situa-

tions do not present very valuable teaching opportunities to the child to enable him to analyze the general concept and learn the general word *flower*. Naturally, whenever possible the child should be exposed to a direct experience in real life rather than to a paler, more abstract version of this experience graphically presented. However, as I have indicated, exposure to real situations is inevitably limited and haphazard. It is only through the use of graphics that a teacher is able to provide the widest range of simulated experience designed to meet the needs of particular children at a particular time, and may also insure that the associated word is provided, and in the invarying form being taught.

SELECTING THE READING VOCABULARY

I suspect that we shall need to review our existing ideas about reading vocabularies. We may even find that research concerning which words are used by children *who are already competent linguistically* is not of primary relevance for the teaching of language and reading to children who are not.

Of course in our selection of reading vocabularies, it is essential to let the child's interests and needs serve as our guides. No child, however competent linguistically, will care to read about situations which neither interest nor concern him. But the words are subsidiary to the situations, for it is situations which arouse and hold interest. The linguistically deprived child is very hard to reach and must, therefore, require to an even greater degree situations of direct interest to him. I have read that in one school in Chicago, a group of culturally deprived children who could not be interested in the supposedly interesting situations of "pony," "cow," and "farm" (evidently because these words had no relevance to their needs or interests) were quickly alerted by the words "rocket," "space," and "weightlessness." Such words captured their imaginations and delighted their fancy.*

After selecting situations directly related to the child's needs and interests, it may be better, wherever possible, to use *general* words in the initial stages of language instruction rather than specialized ones. For instance, specialist words such as *chased* are full of colour and exciting emotion, *but only to those who already possess some linguistic ability*, and are words which ought to be avoided in the earliest reading material if there is any chance that the child is linguistically deprived. Moreover, general words (*go, run after*, etc.) can be made to recur frequently, and will inevitably tend to recur at short intervals, whereas specialized words like *chase* will not. We may indeed need to return to the study of C. K. Ogden.

The only test for a passage *in these earliest stages of teaching reading* to the linguistically deprived ought to be whether its meaning will be clear and its situations interesting, and whether such words may be expected to provide the best foundation for future repetitive learning and for linguistic reinforcement and progress. The consideration that those who are already linguistic (and literate) would, preferably, express themselves differently, is at this stage irrelevant.

I.T.A. AND THE FUTURE

It now seems to me that we who are interested in the teaching of reading are now like the citizens of a beleagured city whose seige has been raised. The gates stand wide open, and we are free to discover and select from a great many directions where we may each wish to travel.

So far, the researchers have been studying virtually only how well and how quickly children learn to read with i.t.a. I look forward to the long-term, comprehensive, multi-track, adequately-financed research programs (brilliantly outlined a year or so ago by Dr. Eurich, in an analysis which may be obtained from The Ford Foundation Fund of Education) that will be concerned with reading in all of its aspects and in all of its relations with the whole of education. What such research projects are appropriate in such a program? How may early reading be coordinated with other learning, how may early reading provide a base for curriculum reform, and so on? How may we help parents and children to insure that children do not come to school non-linguistic at an age when they may have lost what may be only transient, the optimal aptitudes for language learning? How may we make the learning of reading contribute to the child's all-round verbalism— listening, speaking, writing, as well as reading? In particular, to what extent is non-verbalism in speech likely to be a major factor in causing difficulty in reading, even when the mechanical difficulties of reading and the frustrations of traditional orthography have been removed?

There are many more lines of research. I have some dozen other possible researches listed.† Meanwhile, may

---

* The benefit of television in developing language has been observed. Perhaps the T.V. screen has played a part in creating this new situational interest. The work of Dr. Marion Jenkinson of the University of Alberta, in preceding the T.V. in opening up new areas of Canada's sparsely populated North by linguistic testing and by following it up in due course with post-T.V. testing, will yield interesting and further confirmation.

† The potentialities and the effect of using the new medium upon:
  1. The optimum age for learning to read.
  2. The rate of development and the final level of intelligence.
  3. Emotion and personality—including proneness to juvenile delinquency.
  4. The better development of the physically handicapped (dyslexia, the deaf, speech defectives, E.S.N., etc.)

I suggest one overriding necessity: That our future teaching be *consciously* directed to teaching language through reading. If so, may we not find that the learning of reading will inevitably occur as but one facet of all-round verbalism, rather than as a desirable skill in itself —with improved verbalism a mere by-product.

Parents and teachers must not only establish "the word" in the mind of the child but also teach the relationship between the spoken language on the one hand and the visual language on the other.

These two manifestations of "the word" are linked by meaning and also—thanks to the alphabet—by form. This second relationship must also be made simple and direct and cease to be concealed and disguised by confusion.

Let us then recognize that verbalism is our aim in teaching, and let us plan our future researches around this unique faculty that can justly be termed the quintessence of our humanity.

REFERENCES

1. Bernstein, B., "Some Sociological Determinants of Perception," *British Journal of Sociology*, Vol. 9 (1958), p. 159, is particularly relevant.
2. Downing, J. A., *Experiments with an Augmented Alphabet for Beginning Readers in British Schools*, presented at the 27th Educational Conference sponsored by the Educational Records Bureau in the City of New York, November 1 and 2, 1962.
3. Downing, J. A., *Experiments with Pitman's Initial Teaching Alphabet in British Schools*, presented at the 8th Annual Conference of the International Reading Association, May 1-4, 1963.
4. Ibid.
5. Downing, J. A., and Gardner, Keith, "New Experimental Evidence on the Role of the Unsystematic Spelling of English in Reading Failure," *Educational Research* (November 1962).

APPENDIX

EVOLUTION OF
LANGUAGE AND PASSING IT ON

We do indeed know very little about how language is created or even passed on. Perhaps it may never the less be helpful to consider for a moment an imaginary situation of an artificially non-linguistic group to whom language would not be taught and could only be evolved.

Were a number of dumb children to spend all their lives in a dark room, never exposed to sound or sight but only

---

5. The adjustment of the syllabus to fill the vacuum of time saved in learning to read.
6. Teaching English as a second language.
7. The preservation of common norms in the communicability of English throughout the differing pronunciation groups of the English-speaking world.
8. The place of the typewriter in the early teaching of writing.
9. The application of programmed learning to the teaching of English as a second language—and to the teaching of reading.
10. Social integration of middle-class and working-class sub-cultures.
11. The attitude to, and the means of teaching, comprehension as a formal part of the school curriculum.
12. In delaying—or accelerating—the transition.

The need to prevent overlapping in research and to plan it across the wide English-speaking world is apparent. Educational foundations with the money—universities and others able to carry out the research work, might well create a central source of information, if not also of directional advice, as is being done in the field of programmed learning.

to touch, scent and taste, we may suppose that their needing-to-be-originally created verbalism would be nil—and moreover that any beginnings of embryonic communicative symbols would necessarily be either tactile or by some system of percussion. One of them might, though it is improbable, belong to that body of creative persons who have been in their time the originators of the words of language—a discriminating observer and analyzer of concepts—and may thus have created one of two percussive or directly tactile "words" for his own purposes and thus for the use also of others. With alert observation, with retentive and accessible memory, with a selective input, and with a computer-like analysis of factors all peculiar to common elements in varying situations, he—or shall we not make her she—could evolve a small, no doubt *very* small, but in their time revolutionary, vocabulary of tactile tickets. By passing on these few touch words, she might bring forth from the memories of the other children a realization of some classifiable, peculiar factors which, having existed all along, required only to be so ticketed to become in their world of silent darkness viable as "the word."

I need not point the inference of the duty which falls upon us who are responible for teaching. Our children are not thus in this unnatural condition, nor are they denied a lively variety of situations, nor are they isolated from sound, nor from sight, nor from sound and sight in the form of spoken or printed words related to situational concepts. Words, spoken and printed, are their inheritance. We who have learned "the word" from our preceding generation have a sacred duty to pass it on.

"In the beginning was the Word . . ." God's gift to mankind was to enable each concept to be discovered and attain conceptualization and to be given its peculiar ticket. Each new generation is heir to a truly great treasure—the ac-cumulation of the observation, memory, analyses, classification, and ticketing of our truly brilliant ancestors. To few of mankind is to given to discover, and so to pull from its Platonic heaven, even one such apparently new concept and to name it. To all of us, however, is the opportunity given to "feed My lambs" by ensuring that they shall indeed inherit this vast treasure, this God-given gift of verbalism.

My expectation, my faith, my prayer is that the effect of this exciting work with i.t.a., in which I have been so fortunate in the accident of timing and in my collaborators, may develop over the years, enabling us increasingly to ensure for our little ones that they shall indeed, more and more of them, inherit this their verbal treasure and divine legacy.

After all, reading print is only one of the receptive verbalities. Just as the ear can be verbal in receiving the skill of speech, so too it can be verbal in receiving the skill of morse, or of binary entries on magnetic tape. Just as the eye can be verbal in the skill of reading print and lip movements, so too it can be verbal in the skill of reading static punched card or moving flag signals—or holes in paper tape and even, so I understand, the groove of a gramaphone (phonograph) and the optical sound track of a film. Additionally the eye may become also skilled in reading shorthand and, if they are in circulation long enough, Secret Service codes. Again, just as the fingers may decipher braille, so too, Helen Keller-wise, they may "listen" by touch to the speech organs of a communicator. It is possible to conceive that those who are both deaf and blind could "read" through the sense of touch a new kind of morse, designed to be conveyed by gentle electric shocks of shorter and longer duration. If so, they will be enabled to enjoy the same kind of "talking library" which the blind enjoy from tape recorders and the deaf from the printed page.

Writing is similarly only one of the

emissive verbalities. Just as the hand may be skilful with pen and pencil in writing longhand or shorthand, so it may become differently skilful on the keys of the typewriter and may meaningfully tap the key of a morse telegraph, or punch cards, or play its part in flag-wagging. A blind man's hand becomes skilful in embossing braille.*

In all of these many varieties, it is *verbalism* which is the single common factor. Verbalism is the essence—while the accompanying muscular and nervous skills are no more than its vehicles.

---

* It is a fact that all these, which are alphabetic e.g. Reading, Morse, Braille, Typing, are cross related on the same 26 unit artificial basis: that all which are real, e.g. lip-reading, Helen Keller touching, are also cross related on the same basis but on a real 40 or so unit real basis. Just as it is axiomatic that all which are alphabetic ought to be cross related on the same unit system, so it ought to be no less axiomatic that *all*, both those which are traditionally alphabetic on the basis of the artificial 26 characters and those which are truly alphabetic on the basis of the real 40 or so units of communication, should be related on only one and the same basis, and that the base which is thus to be the same ought to be the 40 real unit one and not the 26 unit artificial one.

Developing Independence in Reading

INTRODUCTION

Through the written word man preserves the knowledge of the past, so that what is learned can be given to succeeding generations without being lost. Unlike other forms of life, which must either depend upon memory for what has been taught or discover for themselves, man is able to add steadily to knowledge. The preservation of accomplishments of previous generations means that man may always be extending this knowledge. Literacy is therefore an absolute necessity for every individual.

The goal of learning to read in school is not merely the accomplishment of the skill itself. Mastering the skill of reading only provides a tool which must be used throughout one's life to continue learning. The ever increasing amount of knowledge necessitates that each individual continue learning, primarily through reading, long after he has completed his formal education.

PREREQUISITE TO INDEPENDENCE IN READING

Beginning with the first-grade teacher and continuing throughout the child's formal education, each teacher must be concerned with aiding the child in developing independence in reading. The specific prerequisites to independence in reading are:

1. Initial success
2. Mastery of sight vocabulary
3. Involvement of the learner
4. Acquisition of word-attack skills
5. Ability to adapt rate
6. Comprehension improvement

IMPORTANCE OF INITIAL SUCCESS

The vast majority of children with reading problems are boys (approximately 90 per cent),[6] and their difficulty in learning to read became apparent in the first grade. Attempts to relate reading problems among upper-elementary-school-age children to lack of readiness, resulting in proposals that reading instruction for boys should be delayed, have not been supported by research.[7] It is very clear, however, that initial success in learning to read is vitally important, for the "blocks" that occur once the child has failed may frequently become so great that future teaching cannot be effective. The problem is much greater than merely providing initial success experiences, but such a step is necessary in avoiding as many problems as possible.

The relationship between interest in reading and the ability to read is worthy of special note. We like to do those things that we do well, and we usually do well, or at least better, in those things that we like to do. A student's interest in reading, both in the process and in the result,[10] is an even better indicator of his ability in reading than scores on a standardized reading test. With the existence of so many uncontrollable factors contributing to reading problems, teachers must be certain not to add to the list improper or inadequate instruction.[2]

MASTERY OF SIGHT VOCABULARY

More so today than ever before, children begin to learn to read long before they enter the first grade. Television has contributed much to the readiness program of children, and this is reflected in better reading among school children. The child's first stage of a formal learning-to-read program is the acquisition of a basic sight vocabulary. Even in the programs that purport to teach first either the names of the letters or their sounds, it is nevertheless likely that the child has begun reading by means of a sight vocabulary, if only his own first name. He makes no attempt to analyze the word or recognize elements within it, but learns its configuration. To this he usually adds the names of his friends and, today, the names of items advertised on television.

There are certain other words that the child learns in much the same way. Many of these are among the 220 words referred to as the Dolch words.[5] They are words that are frequently used but do not necessarily follow any phonetic principle, nor can they be represented by a picture. Formal instruction by other means does not await the acquisition of these basic sight words. Other methods of learning to read will be used concurrently, but some words are best learned by a sight method.

It is popular today for critics of education to condemn the sight word method of teaching reading. The attacks against the method itself are unjustified, for this is clearly *one* method by which children learn to read. The attacks against overuse of this method may have more justification, but less dependency has been placed upon this particular method in recent years.

INVOLVEMENT OF LEARNER

Learning to read is a complicated process. According to Olson, "the involvement of the learner in the decisions affecting his behavior is a fundamental axiom of learning." [8] Perhaps the complexity of the function of reading makes this involvement more necessary than in any other skill area. This same point of view is expressed in the plea for newer approaches to teaching that urge "emphasis upon involvement in the process of learning" as opposed to "emphasis on learning for the product." [3] Clearly, unless the learner becomes involved in the function of learning, which involves so many diversified processes, there is little likelihood that the most effective learning will take place.

Translating the need for involvement of the learner in the process or function of learning to read has been expressed under the headings of "1. seeking, 2. self-selection, and 3. pacing." [9] These are the basic premises upon which the current interest in individualized reading is operating, but it is not necessary that they be limited merely to one teaching approach. Whether the teaching approach is individualized, basal, or any other, the teacher must recognize the need for involvement of the student in the function of learning to read.

Adhering to the principles of the interest approach assures involvement of the learner. The methods of teaching reading and the materials themselves are directly related to the interests of children. How effectively the teacher utilizes an interest approach is directly reflected by the independence in reading that is developed on the part of the students.

ACQUISITION OF WORD-ATTACK SKILLS

The fact that those favoring a sight word method of teaching reading have come into opposition to those who favor word-attack approaches, usually phonic, can be confusing. It is not at all unlikely that either extreme, to the exclusion of the other, would result in children being virtually unable to do any reading. Numerous studies have been made concerning a variety of effective methods of teaching word-attack skills, and in spite of conflicting reports, "all the studies gave some support to the value of direct instruction." [4] There can be no argument but that both approaches must be used, with the only disagreement being the extent to which each is used and perhaps at what point instruction in each begins. There is some evidence that teachers are less familiar with methods of word attack than they should be,[1] but there is reason to believe that this is being rapidly overcome.

The goal of word-attack instruction is to provide each student with the skills of unlocking new words in his reading so that he can read independently. This immediately assumes that once the child has "figured out the word," he will know what it is because it is already in his speaking vocabulary. Methods of word attack are not effective in figuring out new words that are not in his speaking vocabulary. The goal of such instruction is independence in reading, rather than the acquisition of word-attack skills as an end in itself. It must be remembered that reading is a thought-getting process, the sole purpose of which is to prepare the child for the task of reading and understanding independently what others have written.

COMPREHENSION AND RATE IMPROVEMENT

If reading is a function, involving many diverse processes, then it must be more than the process of word-calling. In addition to being able to recognize the words, the student must be able to understand what they mean. If a child is to understand what he reads, he must bring to the reading situation an adequate background of experiences and vocabulary so that the words will go together to have meaning. The word-calling of infants, who do so without any notion that what they are doing is intended to gain either information or enjoyment, should not be referred to as reading.

The past decade has seen a greatly increased amount of attention directed toward rate of reading. Because of the ever increasing demands upon every person, one method of saving time is to read more rapidly. Numerous studies have demonstrated that this can be accomplished with minimum effort and without loss in comprehension. In fact, there is even reason to believe that more rapid reading may improve comprehension, for rapid reading demands the complete attention of the reader and requires him to read in thought units as opposed to isolated words.

Claims that all students should read all material more rapidly cannot be justified, but claims that students need training in adapting their rate to suit the purpose for which they are reading is clearly justified. There can be no reason for reading all material at the same rate, as most frequently happens, for when reading detailed material the rate must be far slower than when reading for enjoyment in non-technical, easy material. Developing proper habits with respect to reading rate is certainly a major part of developing independence in reading, but claims of phenomenally high rates are apparently reserved for a few exceptional individuals. Again, the goal is not merely to see how fast the students can read, but is rather to provide them with the techniques for reading most efficiently.

Comprehension is obviously related closely to the inherent mental ability of the individual. There are limits on the kinds of materials that individuals can understand, and no amount of teaching of any type will enable the student to understand material beyond this level. Better comprehension in more difficult materials can be expected from brighter students than from those with less ability. Comprehension can generally be improved, but it is not intended as a means of increasing inherent ability.

The steps in improving reading comprehension, assuming that one is comprehending below his ability level, as is true in the case of most students, closely follow those procedures commonly referred to as "outlining." The student must learn that before reading particular material he must establish his reasons for reading. This will determine to a large extent the rate at which he reads, as well as some idea of the central theme of the material. He needs to be aware of sub-headings, whether or not they are actually printed, for this is a means of summarizing. Under each of the sub-headings are related ideas which contribute to the main idea. Understanding the proper sequence of events is very important. It is not uncommon to discover that poor readers, when they attempt to relate what they have read, will tell what they read last. In trying to reconstruct what they read beginning at the end, they then jump about so that they remember very few things. The good reader will begin at the beginning and follow a logical sequence of events, allowing each one to remind him of what happened next. By establishing the most important ideas, following each of these by subordinate ideas, and keeping them in their proper order, the student is able to improve his comprehension as well as his memory for material that he has read.

SUMMARY

Developing independence in reading is the goal of all reading instruction. Too frequently overemphasis is placed upon the isolated skills necessary to develop this independence, so that those students for whom the learning-to-read function is difficult frequently give more attention to the technique and sometimes no attention to the major goal of developing independence. More attention is being given today to the methods of teaching reading and the ways in which children learn. The result is not necessarily earlier reading, but it is definitely more independence in reading.

REFERENCES

1. Aaron, Ira E., "What Teachers and Prospective Teachers Know About Phonics Generalizations," *Journal of Educational Research,* Vol. 53, No. 9 (May 1960), pp. 323-30.
2. Barbe, Walter B., "Reading Problems and Their Causes," *The Instructor,* Vol. 65, No. 9 (May 1956), pp. 8-9.
3. ———, and Frierson, Edward C., "Teaching the Gifted—A New Frame of Reference," *Education,* Vol. 82, No. 8 (April 1962), p. 467.
4. Cutts, Warren G., *Research in Reading for the Middle Grades,* Bulletin 1963, No. 31, Washington, D.C.: Department of Health, Education, and Welfare, Office of Education, 1963, p. 12.
5. Dolch, Edward W., *Problems in Reading.* Champaign, Ill.: Garrard Press, 1948.
6. Durrell, Donald D., and Murphy, Helen A., "Boston University Research in Elementary School Reading: 1933-1963," *Journal of Education,* Vol. 146, No. 2 (December 1963), p. 6.
7. Ibid. p. 3.
8. Olson, Willard C., "Child Growth and Development," in *Reading,* 1956-57, Membership Service Bulletin No. 98, Association for Childhood Education International, 1956, p. 4.
9. ———, "Seeking, Self-Selection and Pacing in the Use of Books by Children," *Packet* (Spring 1952), Boston: D. C. Heath and Company, pp. 3-10.
10. Witty, Paul A., *Reading in Modern Education.* Boston: D. C. Heath and Company, 1949.

CHAPTER VI

Word Attack Skills

23: Phonics: Syllables *

EMMETT ALBERT BETTS

Master teachers and practicing specialists in reading have long recognized that efficient reading requires the *automatic* use of phonic and other word-learning skills. When these skills are not taught, the child, left to shift for himself, develops his own system. Unhappily, these haphazard, pupil-developed systems too often are clumsy and ineffective. Hence, there is a need for the systematic teaching of these skills, according to the child's needs.[1, 2, 7, 8, 9, 10]

SYSTEMATIC PREPARATION

One of the first steps in the systematic development of phonic skills is taken before the child is introduced to reading —whether he is in the kindergarten or the first grade. At this time, there are two considerations:

First, there is a need to develop oral language (listening and speaking) skills as preparation for reading readiness activities. For example, the child is taught how to listen to a simple story and how to tell a story in sequence; how to discriminate between simple shapes of pictured things and between sounds in

general; how to think in sentences; how to interpret pictures, etc.

Second, there is a need to develop a readiness for reading, which takes the child into the beginning steps. For example, the child is taught how to discriminate between letters and between word forms; how to discriminate between the rhyming parts of words; how to read from left to right; how to associate names with characters in a book; how to read one-line texts of a picture story; etc.[2]

So far as the school is concerned, systematic, informal, and differentiated preparation for reading begins when the child enters school in the kindergarten or the first grade. This preparation develops [1] interests which take the child to reading,[2] awareness of the sounds of spoken words and of the angles, curves, and vertical lines of written words, and [3] ability to think in his language.[5]

BEGINNING READING

At this point the teacher makes a decision regarding how she will teach the child to tell one word from another.

* Reprinted from *Education*, Vol. 79, No. 9 (May 1959), pp. 557-64, by permission of the author and the Bobbs-Merrill Co., Inc., Indianapolis, Indiana.

She may decide to use the word, or telling, "method" to develop what has been called a sight vocabulary. This telling approach—dignified by the pedagogical term *word method*—is a memory test for the pupil. A child with the necessary attention span may survive this method by working out his own system.[1, 2]

This word "method" has one advantage: the teacher needs no preparation in either phonetics (the science of speech sounds) or phonics (the relating of speech sounds to their letter representatives). Moreover, she can be indifferent to *need, meaning, auditory set, feedback, generalizations, applications,* and other factors in the perception (i.e., knowing) of words.[1,5]

The chief disadvantage of the word, or telling, "method" is that too many children become confused by having to memorize a large number of sight words (i.e., words they can recognize at sight) before they are helped with the relationships between sounds and phonograms representing them.

On the other hand, the teacher may decide to use a phonic method with beginners.[4] In this instance, she helps them to:

1. Associate the first sounds of spoken words with the first letter or letters; e.g., the sound of *m* in the spoken word *me* with the letter *m* in the written word *me;* the sound (blend) of *st* in stop with the letters *st.*

2. Associate the rhyming part of a spoken word with the letters (vowel or vowel-consonant) representing those sounds; e.g., the sound *ook* in the spoken word *look* with the *ook* in the printed word *look;* the sound of *ay* in *play* with the letters *ay.*

3. Blend first consonants of words; e.g., the *b* of the spoken word *big* with the *l* of the spoken word *look* to make the sound of *bl* in the spoken word *blue.* (The next step is the identification of the letters *bl* in the written word *blue,* representing the blend.)

4. Blend the first consonant sound of a known word with the rhyming part (vowel or vowel-consonant) of another known word to make a new word; e.g., the first consonant of (*m*)*y* with the rhyming part of *c*(*an*) to make *man.* (The next step is the identification of the phonograms *m* and *an,* representing the blend.)

5. Check the use (meaning) of the word in its sentence setting.

When the teacher elects to teach phonics to beginners, she assumes that they need as much (or more) systematic help in telling one word from another as they will later. She also takes for granted that learning to know a word calls for a study of (1) the word form as well as (2) its meaning.

SYSTEMATIC SEQUENCES

The foundation for building phonic skills is laid to the language readiness and reading readiness stages of learning. An awareness of the relationship between the sounds of spoken words and the letters representing them in written words is taught as the child meets each new word in a reading situation. In beginning reading, as well as during the latter part of the readiness stage, this phonic learning is reinforced by teaching the child how to use picture clues (e.g., to names or action), configuration clues (e.g., comparing or contrasting lengths and shapes of words), and context clues (e.g., *and* to connect two ideas) to word identification or recognition.

In general, the following sequence appears to have merit:

1. Letter phonics
   a. First consonants sounds of words
   b. Rhyming parts of words
   c. Vowels and final consonants
      (1) Analysis of the rhyming parts
      (2) Generalization regarding the sounds of vowels and consonants in syllables; e.g., one

vowel in a one-syllable word usually has the short sound.

(Note: The child first learns the sounds of letters in words. Later, he studies the different phonograms that represent a sound; e.g., short *e* may be represented by *e* in *red* or *ea* in *bread*.)

2. Phonics of syllables
   a. Syllables
      (1) Hearing number of syllables in spoken words
      (2) Identifying syllables in written words
   b. Inflectional endings; e.g., *ing* as in *working* and *er* in *brighter*
   c. Suffixes; e.g., *ly* in *kindly* .
   d. Roots
   e. Prefixes; e.g., *un* in *unhappy*
   f. Accent (stress)

3. Respellings in dictionary

The above sequence takes the child gradually from letter phonics to syllable phonics to dictionary respellings. There is no need to break this sequence into three different, unrelated parts (i.e., to trichotomize). For example, the child applies his letter phonics to the syllables of words. He applies his letter and syllable phonics to the interpretation of respellings in the dictionary. Therefore, the child's learning sequence is continuous.

GENERALIZATIONS: VOWELS

It is a truism that rote memorization of phonic rules contributes nothing to the child's automatic use of phonic skills. In fact, some pupils are confused because they do not understand how or when to apply a rule. Therefore, the memorizing of rules is a far cry from the making of generalizations (rules) based on personal observations of words.

The problem, then, is to help the child make generalizations based on his own experiences with groups of words. For example, common words include *man, and, at, can, has, hat, ran,* etc. having a short *a* vowel sound. Before the child concentrates on this vowel sound and the letter representing it, he has learned:

1. The sounds of *c* in *can*, *h* in *hat*, etc.
2. The sounds of the rhyming parts (vowel-consonant) in *m(an)*, *h(at)*, etc.
3. The sounds of the last consonant in *ca(n)*, *ha(s)*, etc.

The next step, then, is to help the child tune his hearing to the short sound of *a*. To take this step, it is necessary for him to contrast the short *a* sound with some other sound. Since common words include *big, did, this,* etc., he may be taught to hear the differences between the vowel sounds in *his—has, big—at,* etc. If he has no emotional or hearing handicap to block his learning, he soon learns to hear (to contrast) the sounds of short *a* and short *i*.

After the child learns to hear a given vowel sound, he is taught the letter representing that sound. For example, he generalizes that the letter *a* in *has, hat, back,* etc. represents the same vowel sound. He also generalizes that the letter *i* in *him, his, this,* etc. stands for the same vowel sound.

While words with the short *a* sound are being met daily in the child's reading, words with other sounds of *a* are met. For example, he frequently sees *came, late, make, name,* and other words with the long *a* vowel. Therefore, he is guided in the examination of *man, and, at,* etc., so that he obtains enough related facts to decide that when only one letter *a* is seen in a word, this *a* is usually short.

This same procedure is followed to help the child generalize on short *i* (e.g., *did, big*), short *e* (e.g., *get, yes*), short *o* (e.g., *not, got*), and short *u* (schwa as in *nut, brush*). After he has generalized on three more short vowel situations (e.g., short *a, e, i*), he is prepared to make a broader generalization: one letter in a word may have its short vowel sound. This rule applies to the word *black, best, big, box, but*.

Up to this point the child has been guided through a sequence of generalizations regarding (1) each short vowel sound, (2) the letter usually representing each sound, (3) the sound of a specific vowel letter in word with only one vowel letter, and (4) the short sound of different vowel letters in words. This same procedure is used for long vowel sounds and other vowel situations.

The final step in the teaching of generalizations (rules) regarding vowel letters and their sounds is their application to new words. In first- and second-readers, the pupil is guided into applying the short vowel rule, for example, to *fun, fish*, and many other one-syllable words. However, he is also meeting more and more two-syllable and larger words (e.g., *little, kitten*) to which he can apply the short vowel rule. But first he must be able to hear syllables in spoken words and to see these syllables in written words. Later he learns to hear accented syllables and to decide which syllables of a written word may be accented.

Generalizations, or rules, regarding the sounds of phonograms is somewhat hazardous. For example, there are about 68 chances in 100 that words ending in a final *e* have a long vowel sound as in *take, five, rode*, and *use*. There are 32 chances in 100 that this type of word will have some other vowel sound as in *done, come, some*. Some rules have even fewer applications while others—such as the long *e* sound of *y* in *windy* and *many*—may have more applications. For this and other reasons, the child is taught (1) exceptions to rule and (2) habit of checking the meaning of the word in the sentence or paragraph setting.

Three vowel rules appear to be acceptable:

1. One vowel letter in a word usually is short as is *hat, egg, hit, got*, and *but*. This also holds true for accented syllables as in *att(a)ck* and *att(e)ntion*.

2. A vowel is usually long in a word ending with *e* and the *e* is silent as in *safe* and *ice*. This applies to accented syllables as in *repl(a)ce*.

3. When two vowel letters are side by side, the first is usually long and the second is silent as in *g(oa)t* and *s(ea)t*. This also holds true in accented syllables as in *l(ea)dership*.

GENERALIZATIONS: CONSONANTS

One of the first steps in teaching consonant sounds is to help the child tune his hearing to them. He is taught, for example, to hear the simple sound of *m* in *my* and the blend of *st* in *stop*. Then he is taught to hear, for example, the simple sound of *l* in *tail* and the blend of *lt* in *felt*. In teaching both first and last consonants, the child first learns to hear the undistorted consonant sounds in words before he identifies the letters which stand for those sounds.

It is easy for the child to say the sound of long *a*, the sound of *er*, and other vowel sounds in isolation without distorting them. On the other hand, he cannot say the isolated sounds of *b, p, st*, and other consonants without distorting them. Therefore, it is necessary for him to hear and say consonant sounds in combination with vowel sounds; that is, in syllables and words.

Confusion results when the child is taught that *buh-erd*, for example, is *bird*. *Bird* is a one-syllable word, but the distortion of the consonant sound produces a two-syllable word. This confusion is compounded when an attempt is made to teach him to hear the syllables in *singing, kindly*, and *happen*, and other two-syllable words.

Here are some examples of the types of generalizations regarding consonants that are taught:

1. Consonant letters before the vowel may be blended to make a sound, as in *(st)op*, *(tr)ain*, and *(pr)etty*.

2. Consonant sounds after a vowel may be blended to make a sound, as in *ju(mp)*, *sta(nd)*, and *re(st)less*.

3. The *wh* in *when, what,* etc. stands for the *hw* sound.

4. The *qu* in *(qu)ick*, *s(qu)irrel,* etc., stands for the *kw* sound.

5. The *ck* at the end of a syllable, as in *ba(ck)*, *qui(ck)er,* stands for the *k* sound.

6. The *nk* in *drink* and *bunk* stands for the *ngk* sound.

7. The *c* before *e, i,* and *y,* as in *(c)ent*, *(c)ircus,* and *(c)ycle,* stands for the *s* sound.

8. The sound of *g* before *e,* as in *(g)em* and *(g)eography,* often stands for the *j* sound, (soft g).

GENERALIZATIONS: SYLLABLES

The number of syllables in words tends to increase at successive reader levels. For example, the beginner meets *a, and, the,* and many other common one-syllable words more often than he meets *airplane, something, experiments,* and other words of more than one syllable. This situation makes it possible for the child to make automatic the application of his phonic skills to one-syllable words and to gradually apply these skills to the syllables of longer words.

As the child learns his letter (or phonogram) phonics, he begins to apply his skills to the syllables of words. This application of phonics to the syllables, or pronunciation units, of words is done in four steps:

1. Hearing the number of syllables in common spoken words, as in *singing, farmer, many*

2. Identifying the syllables in writ-

ten words, as the *sing* and the *ing* in *singing*

3. Deciding which syllable is accented, as *cross* in *across* and *gard* in *garden*

4. Applying phonic skills to the syllables of new words, as the *ar* or *er* in *f(ar)m(er)*. (This activity is usually introduced in Step 2.)

The above four steps are used to introduce the child to syllable phonics. They take the child from *hearing* the syllables to *seeing* the syllables. Finally, they help him apply what he already knows about letter phonograms to syllables. This procedure makes the learning of syllable phonics very easy because there is no break in the sequence of learning.[6]

In reading situations, however, the child begins with the unknown written word and applies his phonic skills. Using the learning skills listed above, he can be taken through these steps:

1. In how many places do you see a vowel or a group of vowel letters that has one sound?

In the word *f(a)th(er)*, he would see vowel letters in two places: *a* and *er*. In *explode,* he would see vowel letters in three places. But he knows that the final *e* is usually silent, leaving "sounded" vowel letters in two places.

2. Then how many syllables does the word have?

He soon learns that a word has as many syllables as it has vowel situations. For example, he sees the *e* and the *or* in *r(e)p(or)t* and decides it has two syllables. Or, he notes the two *e's* and the *o* in *d(e)v(e)l(o)p* to decide that it has three syllables. He also learns syllabic *l, m, n, r,* and *y,* as in *nick(el)*, *freed(om)*, *butt(on)*, *rubb(er)*, and *carr(y)*.

When deciding how many syllables an unknown word may have, the child also looks for the *ed* ending. He has been taught to observe that *ed* adds an extra syllable when the root word ends in *d* or *t*, as in *banded* and *hunted*. In other words—such as *begged, cooked, sailed*—the *ed* does not add an extra syllable.

3. Which syllable is accented?

This step is omitted until the child has (1) mastered the first two steps and (2) learned to identify common root words, inflectional endings, prefixes, and suffixes.

First, the pupil learns that many two- and three-syllable words are accented on the first syllable, as in *(fath)er, (happ)en, (gent)le, (luck)y, (fish)ing, (sick)ness, (poss)ible, (med)ium*. His previous experience with syllabic *r, l, m, n, r, y*; with inflectional endings (e.g., *ing*); and with suffixes (e.g., *en* in *golden* and *less* in *restless*) gives him a feeling for the unaccented second syllables.

Second, the pupil learns to identify common unaccented first syllables, as in *(a)bout, (de)scribe, (ex)cuse, (in)-tend, (re)port*. He generalizes that the accent is on the first syllable of a word unless it begins with a common unaccented syllable.

4. What vowel rule will help you with the first syllable?

In accented first syllables of unknown words, a vowel rule may be applied. For example, the single vowel (short) rule may be applied to *(sadd)le, (emp)eror, (blizz)ard, (cott)on, (num)ber*. The rule for two vowels side by side (long) may be applied to *(paint)ed, (dream)-ing, (moan)ing*.

Vowel rules may be applied to other accented syllables, as in the second syllable of *in(vent), ex(plain), be(side)*. Because pupils have already established the habit of left-to-right-word attack, they are taught to quickly identify common unaccented last syllables (e.g., the *er* of *butter*) as well as common unaccented first syllables (e.g., *in* in *invent*). Or, they may rule out the first and last syllables, as in *(com)press(or)*. Developing this type of versatility in the use of phonic skills helps pupils to quickly strip a word down to one unknown syllable which may be quickly analyzed into consonant and vowel phonograms for identification.

5. What is the usual sound of a given phonogram?

To increase the pupil's versatility, he is taught the usual sounds of common phonograms. For example, he learns very early that the usual sound of the last syllable *y* in *many, happy*, etc. is long *e*. The usual sound of *ar* in *farther, charging*, etc. is the sound of the name of the letter *r;* of *oi* and *oy*, as in *app-(oi)nt* and *ann(oy)*, is *oi;* of *ir* and *ur*, as in *bird* and *curtain*, is the *ur* of *hurt;* of *or*, as in *corn*, is the sound of the word *or;* etc. (9, p. G 20).

6. What is the word? What does it mean in the sentence or paragraph?

When the child meets an unknown word in a sentence, he may use the context to identify it. However, when he uses phonic skills to identify the word, he is taught to always check the word in its setting to see if it fits. This attention to meaning develops the automatic use of phonic skills so that the pupil can keep his mind on the thought of the context. Developing phonic skills in isolation from reading situations (1) develops word callers, (2) overemphasizes phonic and other perceptual skills in the reading process, and (3) lowers comprehension. Phonic skills are developed in purposeful reading situations so that they are used automatically in all reading activities—leaving the reader's mind free to think about what he is reading. After all, the materials of reading are concepts rather than word forms.

SUMMARY

For the beginner as well as the more advanced pupil, learning (or knowing) a word requires (1) facility in applying phonic skills to phonograms, including syllables, of written word forms for pronunciation purposes and (2) ability to identify the specific use (or meaning) of the word. In other words, perceptual skills and thinking abilities are inseparable; each is indispensable.

Foundations for word perception are laid in the language readiness and reading readiness programs. On these foundations, the beginner immediately builds his use of letter (phonogram) phonics. These letter phonic skills are gradually and easily applied automatically to the syllables of words. In turn, these letter and syllable phonic skills (including the identification of roots and affixes) are raised to higher levels when the pupil applies them to the interpretation of pronunciation symbols in the respelling of dictionary entries. Hence, the development of word perception skills is continuous from the readiness level through the mastery of dictionary skills.

REFERENCES

1. Anderson, Irving H., and Dearborn, Walter F., *The Psychology of Teaching Reading*. New York: The Ronald Press Company, 1952.
2. Betts, Emmett A., *Foundations of Reading Instruction*. New York: American Book Company, revised, 1957.
3. ———, *Handbook on Corrective Reading*. Chicago: Wheeler Publishing Company, revised and enlarged, 1956.
4. ———, "Phonics," in *Compton's Pictured Encyclopedia and Fact-Index*. Chicago: F. E. Compton and Company, 1958.
5. ———, "Three Essentials in Basic Reading Instruction," reprinted from *Education* (May 1954). Haverford, Penna.: The Betts Reading Clinic.
6. ———, and Welch, Carolyn M., *Teacher's Guide: Fourth Reader Program*. New York: American Book Company, 1959.
7. Durrell, Donald D., *Improvement of Basic Reading Abilities*. Yonkers, New York: World Book Company, 1956.
8. Fernald, Grace M., *Remedial Techniques in Basic School Subjects*. New York: McGraw-Hill Company, 1943.
9. Gray, William S., *On Their Own in Reading*. Chicago: Scott, Foresman, and Company, 1948.
10. Harris, Albert J., *How To Increase Reading Ability*. New York: Longmans, Green and Company, revised, 1956.

24: Phonics in the Reading Program: A Review and an Evaluation *

PAUL A. WITTY and ROBERT A. SIZEMORE

Recently Rudolph Flesch aroused considerable concern among parents and teachers by the publication of *Why Johnny Can't Read*.[12] In this book he contends that Johnny can't read because phonics is not taught in the modern school.

Mr. Flesch, we believe, has oversimplified the problem of reading instruction in a manner similar to that of writers who have sometimes placed the blame for juvenile delinquency on a single factor such as the reading of comic magazines.[29, 33]

* Reprinted from *Elementary English*, Vol. 32, No. 6 (October 1955), pp. 355-71, by permission of the National Council of Teachers of English and the senior author.

Controversy concerning phonic instruction is neither new nor unusual. In other countries as well as in the United States this issue has been debated for a long time. In recent years interest in phonics has centered upon how, when, and by what methods phonics should be presented. It is of special interest to note the intensity with which this issue has been debated in England as late as 1954. Proponents for and against phonics issued some extreme statements and a moderate point was presented by others. Some newspaper writers have presented rather unbiased points of view based on research.

In America, the recent intemperate views have been set forth by some newspaper reporters and by a journalist. However, Dr. John McDowell, the Assistant Superintendent of Schools, Dioceses of Pittsburgh, comments sagaciously

the revival of this strict phonetic approach to reading has been viewed with alarm by some and joy by others; all, however, have shown considerable interest and concern. Some have vigorously maintained that the phonetic method is not only a way of teaching reading, but the way. Some write about it as though it were a new discovery never before attempted, or as if phonetic training has never had any role whatever in primary reading.[18]

In order to clarify certain aspects of this issue, the writers propose in this paper to review available research studies pertaining to the use of phonics in reading programs.

One of the first studies was that of Edmund J. Gill.[16] In 1912, Gill reported in the *Journal of Experimental Pedagogy* that he had studied three groups of children from three different schools. One, group X, consisted of children whose average age was six and one-half years and who had been in the process of learning to read for two years. The second, group Y, averaged seven years, two months of age and had also been engaged in learning to read

for two years. The Y group had been taught by a phonic method while the X group had used a modified "Dale" method of phonics instruction. The third, group Z, had been taught by the method of wholes—a "Thought or Sentence" method, a procedure in which one learned "to recognize the visual wholes of words in meaningful groups." These children had an average age of seven years, three months and had had sixteen months of instruction in reading.

In his experimental procedure, Gill selected "two paragraphs of equal length ... from a reading book used in the upper classes of an infant's school. These were printed separately on cardboard, in type similar to that used in the book from which the extracts were made, but without punctuation or spacing." The pupils read these selections aloud to the experimenter. Gill concluded that:

Comparing the reading times for the three schools, a striking similarity throughout is shown at those two (X and Y) using phonic methods of teaching to read, thus suggesting the two variations of the one method to be of equal practical value. Their reading times are, however, more than double those than the children at Z, who, in fluency and intelligence of reading, also were equally superior. Further, questions which were asked to find out to what extent the extracts had been really "read," i.e., understood, served to confirm the impressions formed by a comparison of the different reading times, of the relative values of word and phonic methods. It is also worth noting that the mean variation in the case of Z is relatively smaller than the mean variation of the other two cases. The shortness of the average time for the class is not due to a few exceptionally good pupils, but the work was very uniform.... The results of the above investigation indicate the greater practical value of the sentence method of teaching to read, as compared with the phonic.[16]

Gill pointed out further than a comparison of the good readers with the poor readers in his group indicated that the former groups tended to read by wholes, attending to the word rather than to parts or to letters.

The results [of Gill's study] confirm the views expressed by Claparéde in the *Psychologie de l'Enfant et Pedagogue Experimentale:* "The mind proceeds from the simple to the complex; the fact that the child sees the whole before perceiving its parts does not contradict this statement. For the child, the whole, not being a collection of parts, but on the contrary a block, a unity, to go from the simple to the complex is to proceed from the whole to its part." [16]

In 1912, Dumville reported in the *School World* on "The Methods of Teaching Reading in the Early Stages." [10] As reviewed by Sister M. Dorothy Browne,[5] Dumville "firmly believed that words should be learned as wholes and not in isolated sound parts." He taught upper elementary and secondary school pupils to read by means of a phonetic alphabet. "The control or 'look-and-say' groups were given complete lists of the words occurring in the test, presented in phonetic transcription and regular spelling. The students in this group were told to learn the words as wholes to prepare for a test. The 'phonic' groups were instructed in the powers or sounds represented by the phonetic symbols and then told to apply these to the lists so as to prepare for a test." Following thirty minutes of study "a prose selection containing the words studied was given individually to each student." The author concluded that "there was little difference in the achievements of the elementary school groups, but the students from the secondary school who received phonic instruction were much superior . . . [and] that perhaps both groups used both methods of word attack while studying."

A year later, in 1913, C. W. Valentine [27] reported a comparison of the "Look and Say" method with a phonic approach. In a preliminary test he selected two classes of twenty-four students each in the Training College, Dundee, Scotland and taught them "a passage of English prose written in Greek characters." One group used a phonic approach; the other, a "look-and-say method." After testing, he concluded that "in every test . . . the Phonic method proved superior."

Following this preliminary testing, Valentine subjected two groups of children—ages six-and-one-half to eight years—to similar but improved experimental procedures. From these experiments he concluded:

There seems to be nothing so inherently difficult, even for little children, in the synthetic work involved by the Phonic method as has been asserted by some of its critics. Such synthesis was done readily by infants of six years of age. . . . Children taught by the Phonic method do better than those taught by the "Look and Say" method, both in reading words previously seen and words previously unseen. . . . There seems to be some evidence, however, that for very dull children the "Look and Say" method is more efficient.[27]

In discussing the two methods of teaching, Valentine questioned the contention that the look-say method "gains and holds the interest of the children more readily." For "interest in the matter is not lost in slowly plodding through the words letter by letter . . . [and] it may be seriously questioned whether such interest in the matter is always essential at the earliest stages of reading. . . . Too great an interest, indeed, in the story which is being read seems undesirable from a psychological point of view, even when the 'look-and-say' method is being used. [A footnote here explains as follows: "I refer, of course, to reading lessons in school where it is desirable that the child shall be storing up a knowledge of words that he will be able to apply when reading alone."] It may tend to divert attention from the words themselves and cause, not only wild guessing and misreading of words, but also such a very fleeting attention even to words properly read that they are not remembered on future occasions. One does not advance one's knowledge of a foreign language best by reading highly exciting novels in that tongue. . . . At the point at which the interest of the child seems to be failing it is doubtless well to seek to hasten the reading. The ideal plan with the average child would seem to be an alternation of the two methods. . . ." [27]

In commenting on his belief that the look-and-say method is better for very dull children, Valentine states that "it may be the only possible method. No doubt it is also the better method for the very dull teacher." [27]

In 1914, Mabel Hassell and Lillian Varley [17] selected two schools—one in which phonic analysis was taught, and another in which the sentence method was employed (a procedure wherein the "words are never taken singly but always in sentences, and the sentence has always a message for the reader"). An oral reading test was given to the one hundred forty-five, seven-year-old children in these schools. The teachers kept records of individual errors and total reading time. The results disclosed that nine boys in the non-phonic school did attempt "phonetic analysis" while thirty-three boys and six girls in the phonics school did not use such analysis when the need arose. Also a phonic attack often caused the reader to lose "grip of the selection." Whole word readers, too, in both schools completed the selection much more quickly.

In another study, the first and second graders of Tilton, New Hampshire public schools were utilized by Lillian B. Currier and Oliver C. Duguid. [7] "Two classes of equal size and equal average ability were formed" in each of the two grades. One class in each grade was given phonetic drills; the other "had no knowledge whatever of phonics. Words were developed by quick-perception and sense-content methods."

As a result of observations made during the year the writers reported:

The phonic classes so concentrated upon letter sounds that the attention was diverted from the sense of the paragraph to word pronunciation. This brought about lack of interest and fatigue and destroyed the pleasure which the story should yield. The reading was generally less smooth, slower, and the idea confused.

The classes having no phonics were found to enjoy reading for the sake of the story. From the story they got the sense-content. They were less careful and less correct than the phonic classes in regard to word pronunciation. Keeping the sense in mind, they often substituted words from their own vocabulary for difficult or unfamiliar words in the text. They read more swiftly and with more expression. Fatigue was reduced, because curiosity in the story held the interest and caused the attention to be focused upon the outcome of the story. [7]

A final test for these classes in June of 1916 indicated there was little difference among pupils in attacking new words whether they were phonetically trained or not. Those who were foreign born or who had speech impediments or poor pronunciation habits were helped by phonetic procedures, while the expressionless, the hesitant, or the habitually slow readers were helped by non-phonetic training.

Seven years later, in 1923, Currier [8] reported that she had continued experimentation with third and fourth grade groups throughout a five-year period. Based upon her observations during this five-year period, she drew the following conclusions:

1. "Phonetic drills have a very real value but are not essential to every child as a part of the daily program in the primary grades."
2. "Phonetic drills should at all times be employed with discretion and adapted to the needs of the individual child or special group."
3. "Word pronunciation drills have proved to be of much value." However, they

may prove to be only a very good device.

4. "Much careless oral reading and failure to get the idea from the printed page come from poorly or carelessly supervised silent reading."

5. "It is of greatest importance to arouse, hold, strengthen, and develop the interest of pupils."

6. A single phonic system should not be used for every pupil. What is food for one may be poison for another. The needs of different pupils should be ascertained and the best method for meeting particular problems should be employed.[8]

During a period of years from 1905 to 1924 experiments were conducted in methods of teaching beginners to read in English schools. W. H. Winch proceeded in the belief that the values of various methods of teaching reading differ.[30] In a monograph, published in 1925, he describes his efforts to determine the relative values of teaching reading by the look-and-say method, by an alphabetic method, by an "ordinary" phonic method, and by a special phonic method called the "phonoscript" method. In the phonoscript method "marks are placed without and within ordinary literal characters which give to every letter a definite and invariable sound. The last proposition is not a reversible one; the same sound is represented, not by one definite shape but by various shapes." Although Mr. Winch set out to "survey the relative success of phonic, look-and-say, and alphabetic methods of teaching reading in its very early stages," his study became "in consequence of the superiority of phonoscript readers in early stages with their own form of print, an evaluation of this system as against an ordinary phonic method." For the early experiments children in the poorer economic levels in London suburbs were chosen. Groups were equated according to their "potentiality to begin to learn to read." The Readiness tests were devised by Mr. Winch. The average ages of the groups of children at the beginning of the experiments were under six years. Mr. Winch concludes:

Phonic and look-and-say methods are put in practice and compared. The result is a victory for the phonic method. A phonic and an alphabetic method are compared. The result is a victory for the phonic method. The most recent phonic system, Mr. Hayes' *Phonoscript,* is compared with an ordinary phonic system; the result is a victory for the phonoscript method.[30]

Winch also comes to the conclusion that "no phonic method (including phonoscript) produces adequate correctness in spelling." He closes with this recommendation:

... English children, under our conditions of school organization, may quite profitably begin definitely to learn to read at an average age of 5 years 3 months the normative age in London for the commencement of the second half of our Grade II educational year. In schools where the children are well-born and of good environment, they may begin earlier; in schools attended by very poor children, later.[30]

Grace Arthur [2] in 1925 reported a study of one hundred seventy-one first-graders in seven public schools of Chisholm, Minnesota. These children were given standardized tests prior to entrance into the first grade and again near the end of the first grade. Arthur concluded:

It would seem from these data that time spent in teaching phonetic methods to children with a mental age of less than five and a half years is largely wasted, since a median score of zero is not impressive as the result of a year's faithful effort. Children with mental ages from 5.5 to 6.4 evidently do gain something from the teaching of phonetics. Yet the increase in efficiency for the next higher mental-age group, 6.5-6.9, is so great as to suggest that age as the better one at which to begin the teaching of reading by this method.[2]

In the *Journal of Educational Psychology* for April, 1927, Arthur I. Gates [14] reported two studies of the results of phonic training in beginning reading. The first study was made in the Horace Mann School. Pupils underwent daily practice in phonics from November, 1923 to May, 1924. In the other study, four groups of New York Public Schools had training from October 1925 to April 1926. These groups were compared with others equated on the basis of CA, MA, IQ, and "abilities shown in several tests of word recognition, word perception, knowledge of the alphabet and reading."

The groups receiving phonetic instruction were provided with materials which "may be considered as representing the superior types in which phonetic analysis and blending are related as closely as possible to real reading situations." The non-phonetic groups used "exercises arranged wholly to stimulate reading to secure the thought . . . to emphasize comprehension . . . to demand accurate discrimination of words and phrases in order correctly to indicate or express the thought." [14]

Gates concluded that:

The results of both studies show slight differences between the two groups in gross achievement in the recognition and in the pronunciation of isolated words although differences in methods of attack were apparent. Both groups showed ability to recognize elements in new words and both showed a degree of independent ability to work out the recognition of unfamiliar word forms. . . . In tests of rate and accuracy of pronunciation in oral reading, the two groups were about equally competent in general, although the non-phonetic pupils in the second experiment had had less oral reading experience than the phonetic and probably less than was advisable. In this work the non-phonetic pupils usually showed a greater disposition to depend on the context and to attack the larger word units or features of configuration; the phonetic groups resorted more to detailed analysis of the new words encountered.

In general efficiency in silent reading comprehension, the non-phonic pupils demonstrated markedly superior attainments. If this type of ability is admitted to be the main objective of reading instruction, the non-phonetic training showed a clear advantage. In the second and longer study, the non-phonetic pupils were superior in silent reading by 35 per cent; in the first study their advantage was also marked.[14]

In 1928 Elmer Sexton and John Herron [23] reported that nearly one thousand pupils took part in a "controlled experiment to test the value of phonics in the teaching of beginning reading." The experiment was started in 1925.

Pupils in eight schools of "various types" from different sections of Newark, New Jersey were divided into phonic and non-phonic instructional groups. At the end of five months of training and again at the end of ten months the pupils were tested by means of a number of reading tests. Results for those children who had had uninterrupted instruction were compared. Further tests were made on four hundred twenty-six pupils who continued in controlled groups through the first half of the second grade.

The results, Sexton and Herron state:

clearly indicate that the teaching of phonics functions very little or not at all with beginners in reading during the first five months. It begins to be of some value during the second five months but is of greater value in the second grade.

Although the experiment was conducted "to test the value of phonics in the teaching of beginning reading," the results show conclusively that there is immeasurably less difference between classes taught with and without phonics than between different schools. Where results were unusually good in a class taught by a teacher using phonics, they were unusually good when the same teacher taught without phonics. On the other hand, poor results were secured in both phonic and non-phonic groups taught by the same teacher. . . . the outcome of the experiment tends to favor some phonic instruction, beginning in the second half of the first year. . . .[23]

Raymond M. Mosher[19] in March 1928 indicated "some results of teaching beginners by the look-and-say method." He had selected previously twenty-six first-graders in the Demonstration School of New Haven State Normal School and employed look-say procedures with them. Vocabulary accomplishments ranging from zero to 1,455 words for different pupils were indicated.

Later, in 1930, Mosher and Sidney Newhall[20] compared a phonics and word approach, using seven classes of first graders in three public elementary schools of New Haven, Connecticut. The children were equated according to intelligence test results. Each group contained children of superior, average, and below average intelligence. After two years' training the pupils were tested for frequency of eye fixations, speed on easy and difficult material, and comprehension.

The authors concluded that:

1. The measures of speed, fixation pauses, and comprehension seem to show, both individually and collectively, no essential difference in the results of the two training methods compared, at least at the end of the second year.
2. If these measures comprise a valid index of reading proficiency then the supposed advantages accruing to phonic training are negated. Look-and-say children under the experimental conditions maintained in the schools are able to read approximately as quickly and effectively as phonic children.
3. In general, our results suggest that added time devoted to phonics would not appreciably increase reading skill, and that therefore phonic training is not especially to be recommended as a device for that purpose.[20]

S. C. Garrison and Minnie Heard[13] began an experiment in September, 1927 which continued through May, 1930. No child was included "who had any knowledge whatsoever of reading or spelling." "Equivalent group techniques ... in regard to children, teachers, and teaching conditions" were used. One hundred eleven children were divided into two groups—those of 100 IQ or more, and those below 100 IQ—and placed in four classrooms. One class in each of the two categories received phonetic training during the first and second year but not in the third. Phonetic training was not given to one class in each of the two categories during the same years.

Every effort was made to keep teaching conditions alike except in a fifteen minute period each day, during which the phonetic group received instruction in phonetics. ...The non-phonetic group during this period used what Gates called the *intrinsic* method—[exercises] arranged to teach children to discriminate accurately between words and to stimulate thought.[13]

At various times during the three-year period the children were checked by standardized tests. Garrison and Heard stated:

From the data collected in this study, the conclusions stated below appear to be indicated; however, it must be remembered that in many cases the P.E. of the difference between the Phonetic and non-Phonetic is not significant.

1. Training in phonetics makes children more independent in the pronunciation of words.
2. Children with no phonetic training make smoother and better oral readers in the lower grades.
3. ... bright children seem to be helped more by training in phonetics than are dull. *For all children phonetic training seems to be more effective in the latter part of the primary grades.* (Italics not in the original.)
4. In the teaching of reading it seems probable that much of the phonetic training now given should be deferred till the second and third grades. It appears that work in meaningful exercises which are planned to increase comprehension and to teach discrimination of words is more important than phonetics.
5. Children who have had training in phonetics have some advantage in learn-

ing to spell over children who have had no such training. Training in phonetics would be well worth while for spelling alone if for no other reason.

6. First grade children with no phonetics training seem to lose less during vacation than do children with such training. Apparently, phonetic training makes a young child, particularly a young dull child, dependent upon a device of word analysis which is more difficult to retain than is his own particular method. With the older children, children at the end of the second grade, phonetic training seems to be an aid in retention during vacation.[13]

Herbert Carroll in 1931[6] attempted to assess "through the medium of spelling, the effect of intelligence upon phonetic generalization." Carroll selected words from a list by Gates and tested bright and dull fourth and fifth grade children in Public School 210 of Brooklyn, New York. The results of his testing indicated that the bright children transferred phonetic generalizations more readily and hence made more misspellings since the rules did not apply to many words. He concluded that "a phonetic-non-phonetic classification of the misspelled words shows that the bright are much more likely than the dull to err phonetically." [6] This study suggests the necessity of stressing the exceptions to phonic rules.

For eight weeks—from March 2, 1936 to April 24, 1936—Harry L. Tate [24] experimented with first grade pupils in the Eli Whitney School of Chicago. Dividing the class of 73 into two groups, Tate subjected one group to a phonetic approach—"both in the supplementary and in the basic reading the emphasis in attacking new words was placed on the phonetic method. However, none of the other elements that enter into proper teaching of reading were neglected." While no phonics instruction was given to the control group, exercises devoted to word and phrase recognition, and recognition of the sense of a selection including exercises requiring dramatic action, completion exercises, and exercises requiring oral response were employed. After standardized tests were given, Tate declared:

Phonics instruction and drill . . . is far superior to the look-and-say method in developing ability to recognize words. The results . . . give a slight indication that the look-and-say method is superior to phonics instruction and drill in developing the ability to comprehend sentences. Results obtained . . . show conclusively that the look-and-say method is superior to phonics instruction and drill in developing the ability to comprehend paragraphs of directions. The use of as many as thirty minutes daily for special phonics instruction and drills leads to an unbalanced development of the abilities to comprehend words, to understand sentences, and to grasp the meaning of paragraphs. Other deductions that do not rest directly on the data and therefore do not have the weight of conclusions are:

1. Regular periods for phonics instruction and drill are not desirable.
2. Phonics should be used by the pupil as a tool and not as subject matter to be mastered for its own value.
3. Overemphasis on phonics hinders rapidity and thoroughness of comprehension.[24]

Edward Dolch and Maurine Bloomster [9] reported in 1937 that they had studied children in the first two grades of a school "in which the teaching of phonics had been uniform for at least two years and in which phonics had had some emphasis, though not an unusual amount." The children were tested in May, 1935 and again in May, 1936 with standardized intelligence tests and a Word-Attack Series of Dolch-Gray. Dolch and Bloomster commented on their measurement of the pupils' mental development and phonic attainment as follows:

When consideration is given to the difficulty of accurate measurement of young children in both the fields concerned, the relation between mental maturity and the use of phonics is remarkably high. The scattergrams made from the scores show a further significant fact: children of high mental age sometimes fail to acquire phonic ability but children of low mental age are certain to fail. The scattergrams seem to show the thing in which we are perhaps most interested, namely, the minimum age for phonics readiness. Children with mental ages below seven years made only chance scores; that is, as far as this experiment indicates, a mental age of seven years seems to be the lowest at which a child can be expected to use phonics, even in the simple situations provided by these two tests.

It has always been known that some first-grade pupils learned to use phonics; but it is also known that many children reach a mental age of seven years before the end of grade I. Most of the others, though not all, reach the mental age of seven years in grade II. These results seem therefore to check with school experience. They do not tell, however, exactly when the teaching of phonics should be started. Ear-training, which is the basis of phonics, may begin early. Children may be taught to notice the similarities between sounds some time before they are expected actually to use sounding generalizations. This study does suggest, however, that the schools are perhaps expecting results from phonic-teaching far too soon.[9]

A research study of college students was reported in 1938 by Maurine Rogers.[21] This investigator attempted to determine the relationship between mispronunciation and comprehension, as well as the effects of phonic training upon certain aspects of reading. Seventy-two poor silent readers of the freshman class at the University of Iowa were divided into two groups. One group was given phonic training (a modification of Anna Cordts' system) while the other served as a control group.

From her results Rogers concluded that

... Mispronunciation of a word and lack of comprehension of its meaning often go together. On the average, 78 per cent of the mispronunciations in this study were accompanied by inaccurate comprehension.[21]

She also found a high frequency of repetitions, substitutions, and omissions in the reading of these freshmen. Thus

any instruction in oral reading should involve training to overcome repetitions and omissions. The high frequencies of these errors justifies more practice in oral reading than in phonics, although the latter should be included if mispronunciations are common in the student's oral reading.

At the college level phonic training is an effective technique for the improvement of pronunciation, oral reading, and reading vocabulary.

The value of phonics in pronunciation in contrast to more sight training lies in the fact that the student is given a tool which will enable him to attack new and unfamiliar words while sight training would improve only the particular words studied. Although it is an aid in oral reading and vocabulary, it should not be used exclusively. Improvement in vocabulary should also include training in suffix and prefix cues, motivation in using the dictionary and any other helpful devices. The value of this research has been to indicate that phonic training is one technique which may be used in the improvement of vocabulary at the college level.[21]

In the *Elementary School Journal* for September and October of 1938, Arthur Gates and David Russell [15] considered the "types of materials, vocabulary burden, word analysis, and other factors in beginning reading."

Three hundred fifty-four pupils, "fairly representative of the population of New York City," in nine classes of four Manhattan schools were equated for mental age and assembled into groups. In one phase of the experiment, three groups were accorded differing types of phonic training. Group D "received the smallest amount of phonics or word analysis." Group E was "given moderate amounts of informal, newer-type word analysis, comparisons, etc." Group F "had substantial or large amounts of conventional phonetic drill."

At the end of the training period, Gates and Russell concluded:

In the case of the scores for the entire groups, although the differences were not marked nor highly reliable, Group E had the highest scores in all the tests of word recognition and comprehension, and Group D exceeded Group F slightly in two of the four, being equal in the other two. The activities used with Group E were, in the main, examples of more recent, informal exercises in comparing, studying, and analyzing word forms. It is significant that the scores of the pupils in that group exceeded those in the groups employing the more conventional or formal phonetic drills by slightly more than one-tenth of a grade in the Gates standardized tests of both comprehension and word recognition. A program including little or no phonetic or word analysis activities in the first year is not as good as the informal program but is at least as good as one containing large amounts of formal phonetic work.

In the case of the group highest in reading—readiness scores, the moderate, modern program of word analysis gave the highest average scores in reading and word recognition, but it barely exceeded the minimum word-analysis program, which in turn had a very slight advantage over conventional phonics. Since the differences have low reliability, the indication is that it matters little which type or how much phonics is taught to the ablest pupils during the first year but that a moderate amount of the newer, more informal types of word analysis is most promising. The average pupils (those of intermediate reading-readiness scores) appear more clearly to secure greater benefit from this type of experience and to profit best from the conventional, formal phonics. The pupils of lowest reading readiness scores show this trend still more clearly. A moderate amount of informal word analysis is helpful; very little of this type seems to be better than large amounts of formal phonetic drill. The latter apparently does not "take" well when taught to children of low readiness scores.[15]

In 1939 Donald Agnew [1] reported the results of another widely-quoted study. He attempted to determine the relative effects of large and small amounts of phonetic training. Two hundred thirty pupils in Grade III A of Raleigh, North Carolina were chosen as subjects. To these pupils were given a number of tests, both group and individual. In order to determine the extent of the phonetic training the subjects had undergone in grades I, II, and III, a questionnaire of twenty-five questions was submitted to each teacher who previously had taught them.

The study of the pupils in Raleigh yielded inconsistent results:

The comparisons made failed to reveal a significant advantage or disadvantage (in terms of reading tests scores) arising from different amounts of phonetic experience. ... [When the subjects had] large amounts of phonetic experiences in grades I and II, [there appeared] to be a tendency [for reading abilities] to be affected adversely [by the training.] [Yet,] large amounts of phonetic experiences in grades I and III [appeared] beneficial. ...[1]

"In order to check the results obtained in the Raleigh investigation," and "to provide new data on the effects of larger and more consistent amounts of phonetic experience than found in Raleigh," Agnew undertook a second investigation. He selected one hundred ten pupils in two schools of Durham as subjects. "In the selection of these schools, two principles were borne in mind: first, it was desirable to obtain subjects who had experienced large amounts of phonetic training; and second, it was desirable to obtain a distribution of subjects comparable to those used in the Raleigh investigation." [1] These children were tested and then eighty-nine from the Raleigh group were compared with eighty-nine from the Durham group.

From the second investigation Agnew concluded:

The comparatively large and more consistent amounts of phonetic training received by the Durham pupils seem to have resulted in greater phonetic abilities. ...

Not only were the Durham pupils "superior to the Raleigh pupils in word pronunciation ability" but also seventy per cent of the Durham pupils "used phonetic methods of word pronunciation," while only thirty per cent of the Raleigh subjects did so. "Comparatively little difference [appeared between the two groups] . . . in the silent reading abilities measured." The Durham group, moreover, had a larger vocabulary, was slower but more accurate in oral reading, and had a greater eye-voice span than the Raleigh pupils. Mr. Agnew inferred that these were the result of the phonic training given the Durham group.[1]

Sixth grade pupils who "had received their early training during a period when phonics were in disrepute and training in them was not generally given" were selected by Sister M. Dorothy Browne as suitable subjects for a remedial program using phonics.[5] Three hundred twenty-six pupils from parochial schools in Chicago, Detroit, and the District of Columbia were divided into four experimental and four control groups. The groups were equated on the basis of reading age and intelligence. For approximately a school year, the experimental groups were given daily ten-minute phonic drills preceding the regular reading lesson. The phonic program followed the approach of Anna Cordts in which "the phonetic elements are studied in words, phrases, and sentences." At intervals during the experimental program the subjects were given standardized reading tests. From these tests, Browne concluded that:

1. Progress in reading in the sixth grade may be aided by a carefully planned series of lessons in phonics.
2. Children with low IQ's are as likely to profit from phonic instruction as those with higher IQ's.
3. Children with IQ's below 100 make more progress in reading as a result of phonic instruction than those with higher IQ's.

4. The study of phonics is helpful not only to the pupil who is deficient in reading, but it is even more effective in stimulating the better reader to further growth.
5. The greatest gain in favor of phonetic training for children with initial reading ability of average and above grade is evidenced in groups with IQ's between 90 and 109.[5]

Sister Browne comments that "the significant progress made by subjects with IQ's below 90 is not a denial of the conclusions drawn by Dolch,[9] but seem to confirm the assumption that the ability to apply phonic analysis depends upon the attainment of a certain mental age, rather than the possession of a particular intelligence quotient. Dolch considers a mental age of seven years as the lowest level for phonic readiness and the lowest mental age in the present study was nine years and five months." [5]

She maintains that:

In general, the findings of this study evidence a specific value to reading achievement in simple systematic phonic lessons when these lessons are used as one of a number of aids to accurate word recognition. This conclusion may be reconciled with the opinions of those who oppose the use of phonics in beginning reading as well as with the opinions of those who reject any but a meaningful analytical approach. Since the study of phonics produced results as a remedial measure in reading, it would seem that they have a proper place in a primary reading program. A timely correction of method instead of the complete abandonment of misused educational practices would do much to obviate the necessity of great amounts of remedial teaching.[5]

In *School and Society,* February 1940, Joseph Tiffin and Mary McKinnis [26] reported their study of one hundred fifty-five pupils from the fifth through eighth grades of the Longlois School in Lafayette, Indiana. In an attempt to determine the relationship between phonic ability and reading ability they gave these pupils Roger's individual phonic ability test of "one hundred nonsense words utilizing most of the letter combinations found in the English language," the Iowa Silent Reading Test, and the new Stanford Reading Test. The following correlations were computed:

Reading Criterion	Correlation with Phonic Ability
New Stanford Reading Test	.70 ± .027
Iowa Silent Reading (Comprehension)	.66 ± .030
Iowa Silent Reading (Rate)	.55 ± .038

"These correlations show with reasonable certainty that phonic ability is significantly related to reading ability among the pupils studied." [26]

Tiffin and McKinnis pointed out further:

For the 155 pupils studied, representing an age range from 9 years 11 months to 15 years 9 months, there was practically no relation between phonic ability and chronological age. The coefficient of correlation was —.08—.055.[26, 191]

In concluding, the authors commented:

Though the present investigation shows that a functional mastery of the isolated principles of phonics is significantly related to reading ability, the authors do not conclude that reading should be taught by drill in the isolated principles of phonics or that drill should necessarily be given in all cases of retarded reading. But it is felt that a program of reading instruction which does not, by direct or indirect instruction, yield a mastery of the principles of phonics is not accomplishing its full purpose. . . . It seems highly probable that cases found to be markedly deficient in phonic ability and not markedly deficient in other important characteristics, may be profitably treated by instruction and drill in the specific principles of phonics. . . . Such cases are obviously rare. It is not often that the source of the difficulty in a retarded reader can be traced so directly to a single causative factor. Yet the existence of even a few such cases,

coupled with the evidence of the present study that phonic ability is related to reading ability, points to the conclusion that the pendulum may have swung too far and that we have been too much neglecting this phase of reading.[26]

David Russell [22] reported in December 1943 a diagnostic study of spelling readiness among four classes of one hundred sixteen pupils when they were in the first grade and early part of the second grade. In two of the classes the teachers employed phonics while in the other two classes little phonics was used in the reading programs. These Vancouver, British Columbia, pupils were tested in May, June, and November of 1941 with seven individual and six group tests.

Russell stated:

The results support the findings of Agnew and others that considerable phonics instruction in the first grade has a favorable influence upon achievement in word recognition and accuracy in reading. They indicate that some of the habits of attention to parts of words, of seeing similarities and differences in words, and of recognizing common phonograms in words, or other habits developed in phonetic analysis, apparently are of value in early attempts at spelling English words. The results do not establish, however, a clear pattern of cause and effect relationships between phonetic instruction and successful visual and auditory perception. It is important to note that the teachers of the "phonics" group used more than a phonetic method with an exclusive reliance on the sound of words. Accordingly it is not possible to say definitely that work in phonics improves visual and auditory perception as measured by the tests used, or that practice in visual and auditory techniques necessarily is the cause of good phonetic analysis and high early spelling achievement. It would seem rather that the visual and auditory techniques are part-and-parcel of the program of phonetic instruction in the classes studied, and that separation into cause and effect is unwarranted. The chief point probably is that primary pupils may acquire a group of basic word skills which are necessary for success in reading, spelling, and other language activities.[22]

In October 1953 The Reverend John McDowell [18] reviewed data from a study of ten parochial schools in the diocese of Pittsburgh. Five schools were recommended by a supervisor as schools in which the phonetic method was in use. The school office of the diocese selected five schools of comparable "intelligence and socio-economic levels" in which a "diocesan-approved" program "included phonetic training, as a subsidiary word-attack skill which is introduced gradually and developed through analysis of meaningful material." [18]

The pupils were given a series of tests during the fourth grade. Ten fourth grades were selected including 550 students. Computation of data, however, included "only those whose entire primary work was uninterrupted in either the phonetic or regular reading programs...." [18]

One hundred forty-two fourth graders who had used the phonetic method and a comparable number who had used the "diocesan" method from the beginning of their entry into the first grade were compared on the results of the Iowa Silent Reading Test. Dr. McDowell concluded:

The group following the diocesan program, ... reads faster, understands words, comprehends paragraphs, uses the index, and, in general, reads better than the phonetic group. The latter, however, is better at alphabetizing.... "On Directed Reading and Sentence Meaning [parts of test] the groups are about the same." [18]

The results of the Metropolitan Reading Test of 128 pupils in each group indicated that "the trend on the reading and language usage tests strongly favors the diocesan program," although the results were not statistically significant:

... on the spelling test, however, those following the phonetic program were clearly superior to the other group and the difference is very significant.... That the phonic group is doing superior work in alphabetizing and spelling should not be surprising. From the very beginning, training in the alphabet and spelling is stressed.... Children who are taught to spell from the beginning should excel in these skills. The strange thing is that they are not better at such skills. The fourth graders following the phonetic method had a 5.4 grade equivalent in alphabetizing and a 5.3 grade equivalent in spelling. The group following the diocesan program had a 4.7 in alphabetizing and a 4.9 in spelling. The norm for both groups is 4.5 since the tests were administered in January of the fourth year.[18]

... for the phonetic group, their word meaning grade equivalent was 4.5 and their grade equivalent for paragraph comprehension and sentence meaning was 4.1. It is not difficult to see what must be sacrificed in a program that is oriented toward pronouncing and spelling skills.[18]

The group following the diocesan program had [a] grade equivalent for word meaning... [of] 5.1; it was 4.6 for Paragraph Comprehension and 4.4 for Sentence Meaning.... There is a more rounded and harmonious development of reading skills and nothing is sacrificed. One can hardly complain about children midway through the fourth grade being able to spell at the level of children who are completing that grade.[18]

McDowell also matched 56 pupils who had missed the first semester (5 months) of the phonetics program with 56 pupils who had had the entire phonetics program. He concluded:

Apparently after three and a half years, it makes little difference whether the child had those first five months of extensive drilling in the mechanics of pronouncing and rhyming. In fact, the Phonics B group [group that missed the first five months] did about as well in alphabetizing as the Phonics A group [group which had the total program.] On those skills so fundamental to reading, Phonics B group is doing slightly better work.[18]

When McDowell compared "the performance of children in the best phonic program [64 pupils]..." with all 142 pupils using the diocesan method, he stated: "The conclusion should be obvious. The phonetic method, even under ideal conditions, is not accomplishing the results that it is said to accomplish." [18]

Three hundred eighteen pupils in five Minneapolis public schools were tested near the end of their fourth grade by Mildred Templin.[25] She reported in February 1954 that her study was

concerned with the relation of phonic knowledge irrespective of how it was acquired, to spelling and reading achievement. [Specifically] it was designed to investigate: (a) the level of phonic knowledge of fourth grade pupils, (b) the relation between phonic knowledge and reading and spelling skill at this grade level, and (c) what differences, if any, exist in the phonic knowledge of good and poor spellers and of good and poor readers.[25]

Phonic tests were constructed and administered over a two weeks period. Reading tests were also given as a part of the regular school testing program.

The tests established that a "substantial amount of phonic knowledge" was acquired by these fourth grade pupils and that phonic knowledge was somewhat more highly related to spelling than to reading. Further, the pupils had higher scores when the test item was a familiar word rather than a sound or nonsense-word. These pupils did not apply phonic knowledge "equally in all of the recognition tests. . . . For the experimental sample there are real differences in the degree of application of phonic knowledge by fourth grade pupils under various conditions." [25]

That the poor spellers and poor readers applied their phonic knowledge less well than good spellers and good readers in the unfamiliar test situations while the difference was not significant when phonic knowledge was measured in familiar words is an intriguing finding. The degree of understand-

ing of sound-symbol association differs for the upper and lower deviate groups although the measured scores show little difference in the familiar test situation. This may indicate a real difference in the ability of children of similar intellectual level to transfer what they know from one situation to another. On the other hand, it may be related to the various methods of teaching used with these children or to the particular testing procedure used in this study.[25]

For a doctoral study at the State University of Iowa, Louise Beltramo [4] formulated an alphabetical approach* "for helping first grade children develop independent word-attack skills useful in identifying words in their everyday reading." An experimental group of five classes of one hundred twenty first grade children received an extra period of "word recognition instruction" for twenty minutes each day during the first semester and twenty-five minutes three times each week during the following semester. The control group of eighty-six children received only the regular program. "The teachers carried on the entire reading program in their usual manner, which it was assumed would exemplify the emphasis and practices provided for fostering independent word recognition in the average classroom."

The groups were tested before and after the experimental training period. From her study, Beltramo concluded that children taught by this experimental procedure made higher reading scores but that the results were not statistically significant. The "children who ranked in the upper third of the class" were definitely helped in reading achievement. Further, she stated, "First grade children can learn the phonic readiness skills as well as the basic phonic skills. For most children, systematic instruction is important for gaining proficiency in these skills." Spelling ability was also

---

* No explanation was given as to the nature of this "alphabetical approach" in the abstract of the dissertation which the writers read. Beltramo does refer to "phonic readiness skills."

helped by the experimental procedures.[4]

Mary Watkins [28] in a recent (1953) doctoral dissertation compared the reading proficiencies of children who were progressing normally through school with children of the same IQ and reading level but who were "retarded readers." She selected "third grade children making normal progress in reading and children of grades 4, 5, and 6, reading at the third grade level." Sixty-four pairs were selected from among these children. Each pair consisted of one retarded and one normal-progress pupil. These were matched for mean reading grade, IQ, and sex. After testing these children with standardized tests, Watkins stated: "Retarded readers seem to possess more phonetic knowledge than the normal-progress group but the retarded readers do not apply this knowledge." [28]

In the spring of 1954, Ralph Bedell and Eloise Nelson [3] reported results of a study involving regularly enrolled fourth, fifth, and sixth graders of the middle school of the National Cathedral School for Girls, Washington, D.C. Working with these sixty pupils of "superior intellectual ability and of high socio-economic level," the investigators gave the experimental group (one-half of the students) instruction in three kinds of word attack—"meaning involving the use of context clues and expectancy of words and concepts; visual, involving visual characteristics of words (identification of known parts within words, use of syllabification, use of prefixes, suffixes, and root words); sound attack, sounding of vowels, consonants, vowel and consonant combinations, and use of other methods of phonetic analysis." Instruction was offered for thirty minutes a day for fifteen days. In all other respects the experimental and control groups had similar training. Tests were given before and after the training period. In addition, pupils in the experimental group wrote daily self-evaluations of each exercise.

Bedell and Nelson state that the experimental group was superior and that "net changes in total scores received by the combined fourth, fifth, and sixth grades on the pre-test and post-test were found to be statistically significant at the .05 level of confidence." [3] They concluded that the procedures used in their study produced superior results and could be used with other elementary school children advantageously.

In 1954 Lloyd Dunn [11] reported a study of certain aspects of the reading of mentally normal and mentally retarded boys of the same mental age. Dunn selected boys of mental age 8-10 and tested them by means of various standardized tests.

From the test results, Dunn concluded that

as to qualitative aspects of the reading process, clear-cut differences appear to exist between mentally retarded and normal boys of the same mental age in ability to use context clues; retarded boys are very inferior in this skill. While reading, they tend to make more faulty vowels and omissions of sounds than mentally normal boys; they make, significantly, fewer repetitions. There would appear to be no differences between the two groups of boys in tendency to make reversal errors, in handedness, in mixed lateral preference, or in speed of recognition of phrases and words.

A number of other factors probably do contribute to the general reading disability of mentally retarded boys. As compared with mentally normal boys of comparable mental ages, they tend to have an excessive number of hearing and vision difficulties. On the basis of teacher ratings, they appear to be more maladjusted, and to come from inferior home backgrounds; parent-child relations in the homes of handicapped children tend to be particularly poor.[11]

CONCLUDING STATEMENT

In this paper the writers have reviewed research concerning the place and value of phonics in a reading program. From this review one may conclude that the nature and amount of phonic instruction to be given is still a debatable question. Adherents to any one of a number of positions may find justification for their views in published sources from the devotees of the doctrine of "no phonics" to the advocates of a highly artificial approach. Despite this fact certain trends do appear and certain recommendations may be made tentatively.

A readiness program for phonics can safely be recommended, since research studies substantiate the need for phonic readiness. Moreover, many phonic systems appear to be difficult for most five and some six year old children. Such children frequently become hopelessly confused and discouraged after exposure to involved systems of phonics instruction. Mental age and other factors are important in determining the propriety of using a phonics approach. Hence phonic readiness should be ascertained before instruction is offered. In this respect, the findings of the research studies are in accord with the experience of teachers.

Phonic systems may develop a tendency in children to recognize words piecemeal. This emphasis results, particularly when the method is used apart from a meaningful approach in very slow reading. The child is often so hampered by his attempts to sound out each part of a word that he fails to react to natural, larger perception units in oral and in silent reading. The research studies indicate this limitation of phonic systems.

Another limitation of phonics instruction is that it does not utilize other techniques that bring about quick, accurate word recognition. Children and adults often recognize words quickly, as wholes, and often recognize groups of words with rapidity too. The good reader does not see each letter or all the letters. He may, for example, respond to the total form of the word and thus be aided in recognition of it.

Accordingly, a soundly conceived program of word recognition is not limited to phonic procedures. Instead, it is a broad program associated with meaningful reading; it utilizes phonics as only one part of the total approach. Again, the research studies point to the merits of this broader program of word recognition.

Many children do need help in the mastery of phonic skills although some appear to have made satisfactory progress in reading without formal instruction. Therefore, a system of careful diagnosis of individual needs should precede the introduction of instruction in word analysis at all levels. Many workers believe that phonic instruction is particularly effective with some disabled or very retarded readers. It is, however, not the only procedure employed nor the sole procedure used with such readers.

The value of phonic approaches with very poor readers is suggested by the work of one of the writers in association with Norma Olson.[32] In this study, work began with experience charts. After a basic stock of sight words was mastered, phonic exercises were introduced. These exercises were designed to give practice in the application of principles formulated by the pupils themselves. With older pupils this approach proved particularly successful. Several of the research studies agree with these findings.

It is well to remember that many basal reading programs give attention to phonics adequate to meet the needs of most children. If children fail to acquire competency under such a program, it is perhaps desirable to introduce some special approach. However, this work should always be articulated closely with the basal program and care should be taken to make the entire approach individually appropriate and meaningful. Phonetic study should begin with known words and an auditory-visual emphasis should be employed.

The research studies do *not* substantiate the contention of Flesch and others that we can have perfect readers by using a phonics approach at an early age. Some shortcomings "in our total instructional program—for which the causes are not in our methods but in our lack of teachers, classrooms and adequate supplies and equipment"[31] affect our teaching of reading. To obtain better results, we need better prepared teachers, more adequate and improved instructional materials, and closer cooperation between homes and schools. There are other needs too. But these needs do not include another system of phonics to be employed by parents with children at age five on the assumption that the use of this system will solve our reading problems.[31]

REFERENCES

1. Agnew, Donald C., *The Effect of Varied Amounts of Phonetic Training on Primary Reading.*, Duke University Research Studies in Education, Number 5. Durham, N.C.: Duke University Press, 1939.

2. Arthur, Grace, "A Quantitative Study of the Results of Grouping First Grade Classes According to Mental Age," *Journal of Educational Research*, Vol. XII (October 1925), pp. 173-85.

3. Bedell, Ralph, and Nelson, Eloise S., "Word Attack as a Factor in Reading Achievement in the Elementary School," *Educational and Psychological Measurement*, Vol. XIV (Spring 1954), pp. 168-75.

4. Beltramo, Louise, "An Alphabetical Approach to the Teaching of Reading in Grade One," *Dissertation Abstract*, Vol. XIV, Part 3 (1954), p. 2290.

5. Browne, M. Dorothy, *Phonics as a Basis for Improvement in Reading.* Washington, D.C.: The Catholic University of America, 1939.

6. Carroll, Herbert A., "Effect of Intelligence upon Phonetic Generalization," *Journal of Applied Psychology*, Vol. XV (April 1931), pp. 168-81.

7. Currier, Lillian B., and Duguid, Oliver C., "Phonics or No Phonics," *Elementary School Journal*, Vol. XVII (December 1916), pp. 286-7.

8. ———, "Phonics or No Phonics," *Elementary School Journal*, Vol. XXIII (February 1923), pp. 448-52.

9. Dolch, Edward, and Bloomster, Maurine, "Phonic Readiness," *Elementary School Journal*, Vol. XXXVIII (November 1937), pp. 201-5.

10. Dumville, Benjamin, "The Methods of Teaching Reading in the Early Stages," *School World*, Vol. XIV (1912), pp. 408-13.

11. Dunn, Lloyd M.C., "A Comparative Study of Mentally Retarded and Mentally Normal Boys of the Same Mental Age on Some Aspects of the Reading Process," *Dissertation Abstract*, Vol. XIV, Part Number 2 (1954).

12. Flesch, Rudolph, *Why Johnny Can't Read and What You Can Do About It.* New York: Harper and Brothers, 1955.

13. Garrison, S. C., and Heard, Minnie T., "An Experimental Study of the Value of Phonetics," *Peabody Journal of Education*, Vol. IX (July 1931), pp. 9-14.

14. Gates, Arthur I., "Studies of Phonetic Training in Beginning Reading," *Journal of Educational Psychology*, Vol. XVIII (April 1927), pp. 217-26.

15. ———, and Russell, David H., "Types of Material, Vocabulary Burden, Word Analysis and Other Factors in Beginning Reading," *Elementary School Journal*, Vol. XXXIX (September and October 1938), pp. 27-35; 119-28.

16. Gill, Edmund J., "Methods of Teaching Reading," *Journal of Experimental Pedagogy*, Vol. I (1911-12), pp. 243-8.

17. Hassell, Mabel, and Varley, Lillian, "A Reading Test," *Journal of Experimental Pedagogy*, Vol. II (1914), pp. 298-301.

18. McDowell, John B., "A Report on the Phonetic Method of Teaching Children To Read," *The Catholic Educational Review*, Vol. LI (October 1953), pp. 506-19.

19. Mosher, Raymond M., "Some Results of Teaching Beginners by the Look-and-Say Method," *The Journal of Educational Psychology*, Vol. XIX (March 1928), pp. 185-93.

20. ———, and Newhall, Sidney, M., "Phonic Versus Look-and-Say Training in Beginning Reading," *The Journal of Educational Psychology*, Vol. XXI (October 1930), pp. 500-506.

21. Rogers, Maurine V., "Phonetic Ability as Related to Certain Aspects of Reading at the College Level," *Journal of Experimental Education*, Vol. VI (June 1938), pp. 381-95.

22. Russell, David H., "A Diagnostic Study of Spelling Readiness," *Journal of Educational Research*, Vol. XXVIII (May 1928), pp. 690-701.

23. Sexton, Elmer K., and Herron, John S., "The Newark Phonics Experiment," *The Elementary School Journal*, Vol. XXXVII (June 1937), pp. 752-63.

24. Tate, Harry L., "The Influence of Phonics on Silent Reading in Grade I," *The Elementary School Journal*, Vol. XXXVII (June 1937), pp. 752-63.

25. Templin, Mildred C., "Phonic Knowledge and Its Relation to the Spelling and Reading Achievement of Fourth Grade Pupils," *Journal of Educational Research*, Vol. XLVII (February 1954), pp. 441-54.

26. Tiffin, Joseph, and McKinnis, Mary, "Phonic Ability: Its Measurement and Relation to Reading Ability," *School and Society*, Vol. LI (February 10, 1940), pp. 190-92.

27. Valentine, C. W., "Experiments on the Methods of Teaching Reading," *Journal of Experimental Pedagogy*, Vol. II (1913-14), pp. 99-112.

28. Watkins, Mary, "A Comparison of the Reading Proficiencies of Normal Progress and Reading Disability Cases of the Same IQ and Reading Level," *Dissertation Abstract*, Vol. XIV, Part Number 4 (1954), p. 644.

29. Wertham, Frederic, *Seduction of the Innocent*. New York: Rinehart and Company, 1953, 1954.

30. Winch, W. H., *Teaching Beginners To Read in England: Its Methods, Results and Psychological Bases*, Journal of Educational Research Monographs, Number 8, Bloomington, Ill.: Public School Publishing Company, 1925.

31. Witty, Paul, "Public Is Misled on the Meaning of Reading," *The Nation's Schools*, Vol. LVI (July 1955), pp. 35-40.

32. ———, and Olson, Norma, "Non-Readers in the High School—Two Case Studies," *Exceptional Children*, Vol. XVIII (March 1952), pp. 161-7, 186.

33. ———, and Sizemore, Robert A., "Reading the Comics," *Elementary English* (December 1954 and January 1955).

25: Phonics for First Grade: A Comparison of Two Methods *

DAVID E. BEAR

For years the place of phonics in the reading program has been a controversial subject. The problem is still with us. But the question is no longer: Should we teach phonics? We are now asking: Which phonics method is most effective?

Many critics contend that the schools should return to the formal phonics drills of earlier reading programs. Actually, over the years many changes have occurred in the teaching of phonics, and many of these changes have been based on insufficient evidence.

Several of the earlier phonic systems

* Reprinted from the *Elementary School Journal*, Vol. 59, No. 7 (April 1959), pp. 394-402, by permission of the author and the publisher. See also, "Two Methods of Teaching Phonics: A Longitudinal Study," by David Bear, which follows.

emphasized the blending of word elements. Teachers began by teaching children the smallest word elements and then used these elements to form larger units. Various techniques were employed, but they all started with sounds of individual letters and proceeded to larger units. That is, the methods were synthetic.

In the early part of this century these highly systematized synthetic methods came under attack. The following criticisms were collected in a survey of the literature:

The methods overemphasize the mechanics of reading.

Phonics is taught as the major method of word recognition.

Phonic elements are taught in isolation and are devoid of meaning.

Overemphasis on phonics slows the rate of reading.

Overemphasis on phonics reduces interest in reading.

Overemphasis on phonics produces unnatural articulation.

Phonics skills do not carry over into normal reading situations.

Because English is an unphonetic language, it does not lend itself to phonetic analysis by beginners.

The usual letter-type phonics instruction fails to carry over to the pronunciation of polysyllabic words.

W. S. Gray wrote in 1948 that the years following World War I ushered in a reaction against phonics.[5] During that period, silent-reading skills received major attention, and phonics instruction was eliminated from many schools. As a result of this practice, Gray believed, many young people came to high school using inefficient methods in reading and spelling.

During the 1920's, several investigators began advocating "intrinsic" phonics. The experiments of Gates[4] during that decade provided the basis for this approach. This type of instruction begins with whole words in a meaningful context. Whole words are compared, similarities in form and sound are pointed out.

Phonics instruction is delayed until the child has acquired a sight vocabulary of about seventy-five words. A phonic element is introduced as a part of the few sight words the child has already learned. After a child has learned two or three sight words that begin alike—such as *ball, bat,* and *boy* —he is taught to notice that the words begin in the same way. In this manner the child makes generalizations that help him identify this sound at the beginning of other words. The sound is never to be learned in isolation from the word. This method is known as an *analytic method.*

Dolch[2] has described three general methods that have been used at different times in the teaching of phonics: the total-memorizing method, the parallel method, and the development, or discovery, method.

In the total-memorizing method, which was used in many early systems, the child begins reading lessons by learning phonic elements. Instruction in reading itself is postponed. During the first few weeks of school, phonic elements are taken up one at a time. After the child has mastered many phonic elements, he reads word lists or specially formed sentences. The next step is the use of books.

In the parallel method, beginning reading is taught with basal-reading books and procedures. At the same time, a phonics workbook or phonics primer is used during a special drill period. The drill is designed to develop a mastery of isolated sounds. The instruction during this period is usually unrelated to other phases of the reading program.

The development, or discovery, method is used in most basal-reading programs today. First, a sight vocabulary is established. After the child has learned a stock of sight words, he develops phonics generalizations by noting likenesses and differences in words. The phonics instruction is integrated into the regular reading lesson, and the generalizations are developed through the analysis of meaningful whole words.

The experimental study reported here compared the results of two methods of teaching phonics in first grade. Fourteen classrooms in the public schools of Alton, Illinois, took part in the study, which began in September, 1956, and continued until May, 1957. Seven classes made up the experimental group, which was taught phonics by a synthetic method. Seven other classes served as a control group, which was taught by an analytic, or whole-word, phonic method.

The popular basal-reader series used in the study had been used in the Alton schools for several years. In both the experimental and the control groups, the basal-reading program was followed with one important exception: the method of presenting phonics.

The control group received phonics instruction according to plans and instructions in the teachers' guide for the basal reader. The method followed the whole-word approach to the teaching of phonics. This phonics instruction was integrated with the regular reading lesson. For instructional purposes each classroom was divided into three reading groups.

In the experimental group the basal-reader phonics material presented in manuals, workbooks, and filmstrips was eliminated. This group received instruction in phonics from a phonics reader during a special period.

The 1954 edition of *Reading with Phonics*, published by the J. B. Lippincott Company, was used for this purpose. This primer was supplemented with three workbooks, phonic picture cards, word-building letters, and a detailed teachers' manual. Pupils began receiving instruction in this material during the first week of school in a special drill period of thirty minutes a day. For this period of phonics instruction, all pupils in the classroom were grouped together. For instruction from the basal reader, however, the pupils were divided into three reading groups.

To match the two groups of pupils, information was obtained on their chronological age, mental age, intelligence quotient, reading readiness, social status, school attendance, kindergarten training, vision, and hearing. This information is presented in Table 1. The *t* test was used to determine the significance of the differences between the

Table 1: Factors Used in Matching 136 Pupils in an Experimental Group and 139 Pupils in a Control Group

| Factor | Mean | | Standard Error | | | |
	Experimental Group	Control Group	Experimental Group	Control Group	*t*	Probability Level
Chronological age	76.94	77.30	.31	.34	.80 *	.42
Mental age (in months)	85.65	87.00	1.15	1.14	.83 *	.40
Intelligence quotient	112.30	113.10	1.26	1.39	.425 *	.67
Reading readiness	55.10	54.66	.70	.71	.445 †	.66
Social status	56.05	57.69	.89	.92	1.33 *	.18
Days attended school	164.55	163.44	.72	.69	1.12 *	.26

* Differences favored the control group.
† Differences favored the experimental group.

means. The experimental and control groups were similar in all factors studied.

Scores on reading readiness were obtained from the Metropolitan Readiness Test, which was administered during the week of September 17-21, 1956. The data on mental ages and intelligence quotients were obtained by using the California Test of Mental Maturity, Primary Form, 1954 edition, during the week of November 12-16, 1956. Social status was determined by using Warner's Index of Status Characteristics.[6] Information on school attendance was obtained from the attendance record of each pupil at the end of the school year.

The fourteen classrooms represented eleven elementary schools widely scattered throughout the district. Three schools had both an experimental and a control group.

Data on pupils who had had a full year of schoolwork in one of the classrooms were included in the final results. Children were eliminated from the study if they were repeating a grade, if they moved away during the year, if they entered one of the classrooms late in the year, or if their test scores were incomplete.

The experimental group finished the school year with 136 pupils eligible to be included in the results. Of this number, 72 were boys and 64 were girls. The control group finished with 139 eligible pupils, 70 boys and 69 girls.

The classroom enrollment in each group was almost identical during the year. The median was about 27 pupils to a classroom. Neither group was favored in this respect.

The two groups received similar results on tests of visual and hearing acuity. About the same number of pupils in each group had attended kindergarten.

An attempt was made to provide the same quality of instruction in each group. Since there are no reliable objective instruments to measure teacher efficiency, ways were devised of arriving at an estimate.

In the spring of 1956, seven teachers volunteered to use the Lippincott phonics primer and supplementary materials and serve as teachers of the experimental group. The background of the volunteers was studied and personnel records were examined to find seven other teachers who closely matched the first group in length of experience, college degrees, college hours in education courses, chronological age, and merit ratings based on the Alton Merit Rating Plan. On the basis of this information, seven teachers were invited to instruct the control group.

Teaching procedures used with the two groups were well defined.[1] The teachers were carefully instructed and supervised. Each classroom devoted 150 minutes a day to reading instruction. It has already been pointed out that the experimental, or synthetic, phonics group used thirty minutes a day of this time for phonics instruction with the phonics primer. The control, or analytic, phonics group had no special period for phonics but received phonics instruction as part of the regular reading lesson. Both the experimental and the control groups followed the plans of the basal-reader manual with one exception: the teachers in the experimental group eliminated all the exercises on phonics and auditory discrimination suggested in the teachers' guides. Each of the fourteen classrooms in the study was divided into three reading groups for instruction in the basal reader.

Achievement tests were used to evaluate results. In January, 1957, after one semester of instruction, the Gates Primary Reading Tests, Form II, were given to measure the effectiveness of the two phonics methods.

The results of the January testing program, reported in Table 2, show that the differences between the means were small and the probability very high that the differences could be due to chance.

Table 2: Mean Scores on the Gates Primary Reading Test in January, 1957, for an Experimental Group and a Control Group *

| | Mean | | Standard Error | | | |
Test Section	Experimental Group	Control Group	Experimental Group	Control Group	t	Probability Level
Word Recognition	11.9	11.43	.71	.75	.73 †	.47
Sentence Reading	13.33	13.21	.64	.66	.15 †	.88
Paragraph Reading	7.22	7.69	.36	.38	1.03 ‡	.26

* 136 pupils in the experimental group and 139 pupils in the control group.
† Differences favored the experimental group.
‡ Differences favored the control group.

The hypothesis that the two methods were equally effective during the first half of the school year cannot be rejected.

The testing program in May, 1957, at the end of the second semester was more comprehensive than the January program. Two silent-reading test batteries were administered—the Gates Primary Reading Tests, Form I, and the Metropolitan Achievement Tests, Primary I, Form R. The Durrell test for hearing sounds in words (or the ear-for-sounds test) and the Durrell test for visual discrimination were also used.[3]

The experimental and control groups were first compared on the performance of each group as a whole. The pupils were then divided into three groups according to intelligence and the scores that corresponding groups made on the achievement tests were compared. The first division included the pupils whose intelligence quotient was below 101; the second, pupils whose intelligence quotient was between 101-120; and the third, those whose intelligence quotient was above 120. When matching variables of chronological age, mental age, reading-readiness scores, and social status were studied, the groups were found to be similar. Differences were not great enough to influence the results.

Table 3 presents the results of the testing program in May, 1957, for the 136 pupils in the experimental group and the 139 pupils in the control group. The three Gates subtests (Word Recognition, Sentence Reading, and Paragraph Reading), the Metropolitan word-pictures test, and the ear-for-sounds test rejected the null hypothesis at the 1 per cent level of confidence in favor of the experimental, or synthetic, phonics group. The Metropolitan word-recognition test rejected the hypothesis at the 5 per cent level in favor of the experimental group. Only two tests—the Metropolitan word-meaning test and the visual-discrimination test—showed differences between the means insufficient to reject the null hypothesis. After two semesters of instruction, the testing program provided evidence that the experimental, or synthetic, phonics method produced significantly higher reading achievement than the control, or analytic, phonics method.

Table 4 presents the results for pupils whose intelligence quotient was below 101. The experimental, or synthetic, phonics group had thirty pupils in this category, and the control, or analytic, phonics group had thirty-two. On all tests there were differences between the means in favor of the experimental group. Four of the eight tests rejected the null hypothesis. The Gates sentence-reading test and the ear-for-sounds test

Table 3: Mean Test Scores in May, 1957, for 136 Pupils in an Experimental Group and 139 Pupils in a Control Group

Test	Mean Experimental Group	Mean Control Group	Standard Error Experimental Group	Standard Error Control Group	t *	Probability Level
Gates Primary Reading Tests:						
Word Recognition	31.90	27.95	.998	1.0	3.1	.003
Sentence Reading	31.55	28.35	.84	.88	3.4	.001
Paragraph Reading	18.13	16.30	.52	.54	3.05	.003
Metropolitan Achievement Tests:						
Word Pictures	32.25	29.40	.87	.86	3.0	.003
Word Recognition	21.25	20.29	.43	.44	1.96	.05
Word Meaning	19.18	17.92	.67	.72	1.63	.11
Ear-for-sounds test	43.05	36.45	1.07	1.18	5.0	.001
Test of visual discrimination	16.96	16.45	.43	.42	1.02	.31

* Differences favored the experimental group.

Table 4: Mean Test Scores in May, 1957, for 30 Pupils in an Experimental Group and 32 Pupils in a Control Group Who Had Intelligence Quotients below 101

Test	Mean Experimental Group	Mean Control Group	Standard Error Experimental Group	Standard Error Control Group	t *	Probability Level
Gates Primary Reading Tests:						
Word Recognition	22.16	17.3	2.28	2.03	2.11	.04
Sentence Reading	24.50	19.50	2.04	1.88	2.33	.02
Paragraph Reading	13.80	10.93	1.23	1.16	2.13	.04
Metropolitan Achievement Tests:						
Word Pictures	23.84	21.55	2.20	2.08	.98	.32
Word Recognition	17.10	15.63	1.14	1.16	1.14	.26
Word Meaning	13.51	10.93	1.53	1.36	1.60	.11
Ear-for-sounds test	33.79	25.10	2.53	2.13	2.63	.02
Test of visual discrimination	14.07	12.30	1.15	1.44	1.2	.23

* Differences favored the experimental group.

Table 5: Mean Test Scores in May, 1957, for 66 Pupils in an Experimental Group and 59 Pupils in a Control Group Who Had Intelligence Quotients of 101 to 120

Test	Mean		Standard Error		t *	Probability Level
	Experimental Group	Control Group	Experimental Group	Control Group		
Gates Primary Reading Tests:						
Word Recognition	32.68	28.10	1.26	1.23	3.42	.001
Sentence Reading	31.77	28.35	1.13	1.10	2.80	.01
Paragraph Reading	18.40	16.05	.70	.66	3.05	.002
Metropolitan Achievement Tests:						
Word Pictures	33.6	29.70	1.08	1.21	3.12	.002
Word Recognition	22.00	20.68	.49	.57	2.27	.03
Word Meaning	20.08	17.83	.87	.91	2.27	.03
Ear-for-sounds test	43.75	36.65	1.3	1.66	4.0	.001
Test of visual discrimination	17.73	16.25	.54	.42	2.66	.01

* Differences favored the experimental group.

rejected the hypothesis at the 2 per cent level. The Gates word-recognition and paragraph-reading tests rejected the hypothesis at the 4 per cent level. The differences between the means on the three Metropolitan tests and the visual-discrimination test were not high enough to be significant.

Evidence indicated that the differences between the means were consistently in favor of the experimental group and that the results of four of the eight tests rejected the null hypothesis; therefore, it seems reasonable to conclude that the experimental, or synthetic, phonics method was superior for the group that had low intelligence quotients.

Table 5 presents a comparison of the test results for the experimental and control groups whose intelligence quotients ranged from 101 to 120. The experimental group was composed of sixty-six pupils, and the control group contained fifty-nine pupils. The results of the testing program in May for this group favored the experimental, or synthetic, group in all eight subtests. Six subtests showed differences between the means that were significant at the 1 per cent level of confidence. The differences between the means on the Metropolitan word-recognition and word-meaning tests permitted the rejection of the null hypothesis at the 3 per cent level.

The third intelligence level included pupils whose intelligence quotient was above 120. The data for this group are presented in Table 6. Forty pupils in the experimental group and forty-eight pupils in the control group were in this category. The differences between the means of the experimental and control groups were smaller than for either of the other two intelligence levels. The ear-for-sounds test is the only one of the eight tests for which differences were as high as the 5 per cent level.

Table 7 shows the mean scores presented in Tables 3, 4, 5, and 6 converted into grade scores. Both the experimental and the control groups achieved well above the national norms. The grade

Table 6: Mean Test Scores in May, 1957, for 40 Pupils in an Experimental Group and 48 Pupils in a Control Group Who Had Intelligence Quotients above 120

Test	Mean		Standard Error			Proba-bility Level
	Experi-mental Group	Control Group	Experi-mental Group	Control Group	t *	
Gates Primary Reading Tests:						
Word Recognition	37.65	34.92	1.41	1.36	1.83 *	.07
Sentence Reading	36.50	34.30	.97	1.18	1.86 *	.06
Paragraph Reading	20.95	20.44	.63	.69	.68 *	.50
Metropolitan Achievement Tests:						
Word Pictures	36.65	35.10	1.00	1.12	1.35 *	.18
Word Recognition	22.99	22.93	.62	.42	.11 *	.92
Word Meaning	21.76	22.69	1.11	1.10	.76 †	.45
Ear-for-sounds test	47.50	43.25	1.44	1.84	2.04 *	.05
Test of visual discrimination	18.18	19.18	.52	.62	1.52 †	.13

* Differences favored the experimental group.
† Differences favored the control group.

scores for the experimental group averaged about two months higher than those for the control group. The experimental groups at all intelligence levels scored above the national norms. The control group in the low-intelligence category scored at the norm on three tests and below the norm on one. The grade scores of the experimental group were higher than those of the control group in all tests except the Metropolitan tests of word recognition and word meaning in the high-intelligence category.

During the first half of first grade, no differences were apparent in the results produced by the two methods. This finding confirms the results of previous investigations in this area. It is possible, however, that certain cumulative changes were taking place that favored the experimental group but did not become apparent until later.

The pupils who used the synthetic method achieved much higher scores after one year of instruction. The dif-

ferences rejected the null hypothesis on both the Gates and the Metropolitan tests. The ear-for-sounds tests also rejected the hypothesis in favor of the experimental, or synthetic, phonics group.

In the total testing program, the t ratios on the Gates tests were slightly higher in favor of the experimental group than those of the Metropolitan tests. This finding might indicate that the experimental group was superior in reading from context, since two of the Gates subtests were concerned with testing this type of skill.

The results of this study reveal that synthetic phonics can be used successfully along with a basal-reading program and serve as a valuable supplement in developing reading skills.

Pupils with intelligence quotients that ranged from 101 to 120 benefited more from the synthetic phonics program of the experimental group than pupils at other intelligence levels. The pupils whose intelligence quotient was below

Table 7: Grade Norms for the Total Group and for the Three Intelligence Groups Converted from the Mean Scores

Test	Total Group		Intelligence Quotient below 101		Intelligence Quotient of 101-120		Intelligence Quotient above 120	
	Experimental Group	Control Group	Experimental Group	Control Group	Experimental Group	Control Group	Experimental Group	Control Group
Gates Primary Reading Tests:								
Word Recognition	2.60	2.43	2.23	2.00	2.65	2.43	3.05	2.80
Sentence Reading	2.50	2.30	2.15	1.80	2.50	2.80	2.80	2.60
Paragraph Reading	2.50	2.30	2.10	1.90	2.50	2.30	2.90	2.75
Metropolitan Achievement Tests:								
Word Pictures	2.50	2.30	2.10	2.00	2.60	2.40	2.70	2.60
Word Recognition	2.30	2.30	2.00	1.90	2.40	2.30	2.50	2.50
Word Meaning	2.50	2.40	2.10	1.90	2.60	2.40	2.80	2.30

101 achieved higher results with the synthetic method than with the analytic method; however, the results were not so significant as for the middle group. The evidence indicated little difference in performance of the two groups whose intelligence quotients were above 120.

Both the experimental and control groups showed gains greater than anticipated by the national norms; the experimental group, however, averaged about two months higher than the control group on grade score norms.

The results of this study were favorable to the synthetic method of teaching phonics. It must be remembered, however, that in this study the synthetic-phonics program was used parallel to a good basal-reader program.

A follow-up study at the end of three years or more of instruction is needed to determine whether the differences in favor of the experimental group persist. Certain factors might be present that would eliminate these differences. On the other hand, after a thorough review of the phonics primer in Grades 2 and 3, the differences might be even more favorable to the synthetic method.

REFERENCES

1. Bear, David E., "A Comparison of a Synthetic with an Analytic Method of Teaching Phonics in First Grade," Unpublished Doctoral Dissertation, Washington University, St. Louis, 1958.
2. Dolch, Edward W., "Phonics in First Grade," *Elementary English*, XXXII (December 1955), 514-18.
3. Durrell, Donald D., *Improving Reading Instruction*. New York: World Book Co., 1956.
4. Gates, Arthur I., *New Methods in Primary Reading*. New York: Bureau of Publications, Teachers College, Columbia University, 1928.
5. Gray, William S., *On Their Own in Reading*. Chicago: Scott, Foresman & Co., 1948, pp. 26-8.
6. Warner, W. Lloyd, *et al.*, *Social Class in America*. Chicago: Science Research Associates, 1949.

26: Two Methods of Teaching Phonics: A Longitudinal Study *

DAVID E. BEAR

There is very little controversy today over the importance of phonics in a well-balanced reading program. Authorities in the field of reading method agree that children need a knowledge of phonics if they are to become independent readers. But authorities disagree on which is the best method to use, how much phonics should be taught, and when phonics instruction should begin.

Phonics programs in use before 1920 were synthetic in nature. Instruction began by teaching the sounds of letters and the blending of these sounds into larger units. These synthetic phonic methods made use of drill on letters and sound units in a special period set aside for this purpose. The actual reading process itself, which dealt with the interpretation of whole words and sentences, was usually delayed until the child had achieved a high degree of mastery of phonics. These early reading programs were highly mechanistic in that great emphasis was placed on phonics and word structure to the neglect of important skills in comprehension.

The programs neglected many important skills needed for efficient reading. Because of the neglect, a few prominent authorities in reading method became highly critical of synthetic phonic methods. Most of these critics believed that synthetic methods over-emphasized phonics instruction and that the over-emphasis resulted in the following:

Word-calling.
Overemphasis on the mechanics of reading to the neglect of reading for meaning.
Lessened interest in reading.
Unnatural articulation.
Little transfer of learning to normal reading situations.
Difficulty in teaching phonics to beginners because of the unphonetic character of the English language.
Lack of carry-over of letter-type phonics to the pronunciation of multisyllabic words.
Poor spelling because of the unphonetic character of the English language.
Retarded development of adequate speed in reading.

The imbalance in the reading programs of this early period and the influence of the critics ushered in a reaction against phonics which almost eliminated it from reading instruction in the United States during the 1920's.[1] Silent reading skills received increased attention during the twenties, and the sight method emerged as the major approach in introducing pupils to reading material in the first grade.

Along with this development, a new method of teaching phonics, known as intrinsic phonics, was introduced. By this method a child acquires a sight vocabulary before he is introduced to phonics. After the child learns a small stock of words by the sight method, he begins to compare these words for similarities and thus builds phonic generalizations.

For instance, after a child has learned two or three sight words that begin alike, such as *bird, ball,* and *boy,* he is taught to notice that the words begin with the same letter and also sound alike at the beginning. In this manner, the child makes generalizations that will

* Reprinted from the *Elementary School Journal,* Vol, 65, No, 5 (February 1964), pp. 273-9, by permission of the author and the publisher.

help him identify this sound at the beginning of other words. This method is known as an analytic method because the identification of a strange word begins with the whole word, which is then analyzed into its pronounceable units.

In describing the phonic methods in use in most basal reading programs today, Emmett Betts made a clear distinction between the synthetic method and the analytic method. He wrote: *"Sounding* methods of phonics have given way to *pronouncing* methods. The *synthesizing* of sounds into words (called the synthetic method) has given way to the *analysis* of whole words (called the analytic method). In recent teacher's manuals, the emphasis has been on the nonseparation, or whole word, method." [2]

The controversy in phonics today centers on these two methods. Each method has its strong proponents, and they are usually quite vocal in their criticism of the method they oppose. Research has failed to give conclusive evidence of the superiority of one method over the other, yet educators continue to take strong positions on the issue.

In the study reported here, a synthetic method of teaching phonics was compared with an analytic method. The study was first reported by Bear in April, 1959.[3] The 1959 report presented test results after one year of instruction of two matched groups of first-grade pupils. This report, which is the second, presents the results of a testing program for the same pupils at the end of Grade 6. The follow-up study was made to determine the long-range effects of two methods of teaching phonics to first-graders. I hoped to learn whether the differences found at the end of first grade were still present at the end of sixth grade.

The orginal experiment began in September, 1956, in fourteen first-grade classrooms in the public school system in Alton, Illinois. The seven classes that made up the experimental group were given instruction in phonics in a special thirty-minute period each day. This group used the phonics primer and workbook material, *Reading with Phonics,* 1954 edition, published by the J. B. Lippincott Company, more popularly known as the Hay-Wingo system.[4] This material is typical of a synthetic method and similar to that used in some of the reading programs in the early 1900's.

Seven other classes known as the control group received instruction in phonics in accordance with the teacher's manuals that accompanied the basal reading series of the Row-Peterson Company which was published in 1954.[5]

In the fourteen classrooms, 136 pupils in the experimental group and 139 pupils in the control group finished the school year. The two groups were found to be equal in intelligence, in reading-readiness scores, and on the Warner Index of Status Characteristics. More details on the experimental design can be found in the first report.[3]

Both the experimental and the control group used the Row-Peterson basal reading program with one major variation: the method of teaching phonics. The control group received instruction in phonics according to the directions in the teacher's manuals accompanying the basal readers. For the experimental group, this instruction in phonics was eliminated. Even the workbook pages dealing with visual discrimination and auditory discrimination were eliminated. Instead, a special thirty-minute period each day was used for teaching phonics using the materials published by the Lippincott Company.

After one semester of instruction in the first grade, the mean scores on the Gates Primary Reading Tests were almost identical. The *t* ratios indicated no differences that were considered statistically significant.

The testing program at the end of

the first grade revealed that the pupils who used the synthetic method achieved much higher scores than those who used the analytic method. The *t* ratios were sufficiently high to reject the null hypothesis on both the Gates Primary Reading Tests and the Metropolitan Achievement Tests. The pupils who used the synthetic method also scored much higher on the Durrell test for hearing sounds in words.[6]

The results of this early study indicated that a synthetic method could be used successfully along with a basal-reading program and serve as a valuable supplement in developing reading skills.

In the 1959 report the writer suggested that a follow-up study should be made at the end of three years or more of instruction to determine whether the differences found after one year of instruction still persisted. The writer also wished to determine the long-range effects of intensive phonics instruction given in first grade. The remainder of this report will present the findings of the testing program for these pupils that was carried out at the end of Grade 6.

Beginning with Grade 2 the Lippincott phonics program was discontinued, and all pupils in the study received reading instruction by the basal-reader approach. During the remaining five years, phonics instruction was given according to the teacher's manuals accompanying the basal-reading series. This report, therefore, is an attempt to measure the long-range effects of an intensive synthetic phonics program in first grade.

In May, 1962, as the pupils were nearing the end of Grade 6, the Gates Reading Survey, Form 2, was administered. In addition, two tests in spelling were given: one was a twenty-word spelling test of a random sample drawn from spelling word lists for sixth, seventh, eighth, and ninth grades; the other was a list of twenty nonsense words that contained syllables that were phonetic. The latter test afforded the pupils an opportunity to apply their knowledge of sounding.

The writer was able to locate 95 pupils of the 136 who made up the original experimental group, and 90 pupils of the 139 who were in the original control group. These two groups were found to be equal on the basis of intelligence as measured by the California Test of Mental Maturity, which was given in first grade, and on socioeconomic status as measured by the Warner Index of Status Characteristics. The *t* ratios indicated no significant differences between the two groups on these two factors.

The results of the Gates Reading Survey, which was administered in May,

Table 1: Mean Scores on the Gates Reading Survey Given in May, 1962, for an Experimental Group and a Control Group

Test Section	Experimental Group *		Control Group †		*t*	Probability Level
	Mean Score	Standard Deviation	Mean Score	Standard Deviation		
Vocabulary	7.27	1.86	6.67	1.7	2.31	.02 ‡
Comprehension	7.42	1.97	7.01	1.86	1.50	.13
Speed	8.50	2.32	8.33	2.16	1.00	.32

* Experimental group of ninety-five pupils.
† Control group of ninety pupils.
‡ Significant at the 5 per cent level of confidence.

Table 2: Mean Scores on the Gates Reading Survey Given in May, 1962, for the Lowest 25 Per Cent of the Pupils in the Experimental Group and the Control Group

Test Section	Experimental Group *		Control Group †			Proba- bility Level
	Mean Score	Standard Deviation	Mean Score	Standard Deviation	t	
Vocabulary	6.24	1.40	5.62	1.04	1.8	.07
Comprehension	5.97	1.46	5.89	1.33	.15	.88
Speed	7.16	2.25	7.08	1.49	.15	.88

* Experimental group of twenty-six pupils.
† Control group of twenty-four pupils.

1962, are presented in Table 1. The differences in the means were all favorable to the experimental group; however, only the differences on the vocabulary test were sufficiently high to reject the null hypothesis at the 5 per cent level. The *t* ratio on vocabulary indicates a difference that is significant in favor of the experimental group.

In addition to tabulating the data on the total number of pupils in the experimental and the control groups, it was thought desirable to compare the reading achievement of the pupils at three different levels of intelligence. For this purpose, the pupils in the experimental and the control groups were divided into the lowest 25 per cent, the middle 50 per cent, and the upper 25 per cent. The pupils in the experimental and the control groups at these three levels were

found to be about equal in intelligence. The *t* ratios indicated no differences that could be considered statistically significant.

The results of the testing program for the lowest 25 per cent are presented in Table 2. For the pupils at this level, the differences in the means favored the experimental group but not enough to reject the null hypothesis at the 5 per cent level of confidence; however, the *t* ratio of 1.8 closely approximated this level.

Table 3 presents the results for the middle 50 per cent of each group. For this middle 50 per cent, the differences in the means on all three tests were favorable to the experimental group. The *t* ratios were high enough to reject the null hypothesis at a point well beyond the 1 per cent level of confidence. The

Table 3: Mean Scores on the Gates Reading Survey Given in May, 1962, for the Middle 50 Per Cent of the Pupils in the Experimental Group and the Control Group

Test Section	Experimental Group *		Control Group †			Proba- bility Level
	Mean Score	Standard Deviation	Mean Score	Standard Deviation	t	
Vocabulary	7.53	1.83	6.5	1.36	3.0	.003 ‡
Comprehension	7.6	1.97	6.62	1.41	2.7	.007 ‡
Speed	8.95	2.15	7.93	1.83	2.4	.016 §

* Experimental group of forty-three pupils.
† Control group of forty-three pupils.
‡ Significant at the 1 per cent level of confidence.
§ Significant at the 5 per cent level of confidence.

Table 4: Mean Scores on the Gates Reading Survey Given in May, 1962, for the Upper 25 Per Cent of the Pupils in the Experimental and the Control Group

| Test Section | Experimental Group * | | Control Group † | | | Proba-bility Level |
	Mean Score	Standard Deviation	Mean Score	Standard Deviation	t	
Vocabulary	7.83	1.57	8.135	1.77	.69	.49
Comprehension	8.525	1.5	8.98	1.56	1.00	.32
Speed	9.25	2.17	10.01	2.05	1.10	.27

* Experimental group of twenty-six pupils.
† Control group of twenty-three pupils.

pupils in this intelligence category apparently benefited more from synthetic phonics than the pupils in the other two categories did. This result is similar to the result obtained at the end of the first grade.

The results for the upper 25 per cent are shown in Table 4. At this level, the differences were sligthly in favor of the control group; however, the t ratios were too low to be considered significant. This result is similar to that found at the end of the first grade: that children of high intelligence learned equally well by both methods.

The results of the two tests in spelling are given in Table 5. The scores indicate a significant difference in the means in favor of the experimental method. The t ratios are well above the result necessary to reject the null hypothesis at the 1 per cent level of confidence. The pupils who received phonics instruction by the synthetic method in first grade made a much higher score on the two spelling tests given at the end of Grade 6.

This follow-up study was made to determine the long-range effects of two methods of teaching phonics. The experimenter wished to determine whether the differences favorable to synthetic phonics found at the end of first grade would persist over a period of several years. From an analysis of the data collected at the end of Grade 6, several conclusions seem justified.

The differences in reading performance between the two groups under study were favorable to the synthetic method which used the Lippincott phonics program. After the comparisons

Table 5: Mean Scores on Two Spelling Tests Given in May, 1962, for an Experimental Group and a Control Group

| Tests | Experimental Group * | | Control Group † | | | Proba-bility Level |
	Mean Score	Standard Deviation	Mean Score	Standard Deviation	t	
Twenty-word spelling test	12.84	3.5	11.1	3.72	3.12	‡
Test of twenty nonsense words	16.7	3.24	14.9	3.7	3.33	‡

* Experimental group of ninety-five pupils.
† Control group of ninety pupils.
‡ Significant at the 1 per cent level of confidence.

that involved all the pupils in each group, the pupils were divided into three categories on the basis of intelligence. It was found that pupils in the middle 50 per cent of the intelligence range received greater benefit from synthetic phonics than the pupils in the highest and the lowest 25 per cent. For the upper 25 per cent of the pupils, the two phonic methods produced almost identical results. For the lowest 25 per cent of the pupils, the results slightly favored the pupils who used the synthetic phonics program.

The differences favoring the synthetic method that were found at the end of the first grade persisted through Grade 6. The results were similar at all three levels of intelligence. These data suggest that in differentiating phonics instruction more attention should be given to the pupils' intelligence.

Pupils taught by the synthetic method scored much higher on tests of spelling ability at the end of Grade 6 than pupils taught by the analytic method. Differences were high enough to be significant at the 1 per cent level of confidence.

In the study reported here, it should be noted that the synthetic and the analytic methods were compared in reading programs that were considered balanced in that attention was given to all the important skills in reading. In some earlier studies that compared these two methods, synthetic phonics was placed at a disadvantage by the fact that it was usually the major activity in the reading program. Proponents of some of these early synthetic phonics programs believed that phonics instruction should constitute the reading program. The lack of attention to other important reading skills caused many critics to condemn synthetic phonics when they should have been critical of reading programs that were imbalanced.

I found no evidence that synthetic phonics as used in this study represented an overemphasis. The nine difficulties listed as typical of synthetic phonics programs of an earlier era were not found to be characteristic of synthetic phonics as used in this study. The test results—which favored the synthetic method on vocabulary, comprehension, speed, and spelling—tend to support this viewpoint.

The results of this study, and of others that have been reported recently, lead me to believe that authors of basal readers should take a more realistic position on the issue of phonics. Recent research has indicated that synthetic phonics is highly beneficial for the average and below average pupil when this instruction is a part of a comprehensive, well-balanced reading program. Synthetic phonics is not incompatible with the word method, since both can be used from the beginning of the first grade for pupils who have developed the necessary readiness skills for beginning reading.

Progress in improving reading programs is likely to be retarded unless educators try to compromise the two extreme positions taken by the adherents of these two approaches to the teaching of phonics. Proponents of synthetic methods should refrain from developing reading programs that place undue stress on phonics to the neglect of other important skills in reading. The authors of basal-reader programs should recognize that many pupils have difficulty in learning to read and that synthetic phonics might make a valuable contribution in this area.

The reading progress of many children would be enhanced by a realistic reappraisal of the phonics controversy.

REFERENCES

1. Bear, David E., "Phonics for First Grade: A Comparison of Two Methods," *Elementary School Journal*, LIX (April 1959) pp. 394-402.
2. Betts, Emmett Albert, *Foundations of Reading Instruction*. New York: American Book Company, 1954, p. 623.
3. Durrell, Donald D., *Improving Reading Instruction*. New York: World Book Company, 1956, pp. 104-7.
4. Gray, William S., *On Their Own in Reading*. Chicago: Scott, Foresman and Company, 1948, pp. 26-8.
5. Hay, Julie, and Wingo, Charles E., *Reading with Phonics*, teacher's edition. New York: J. B. Lippincott Company, 1954.
6. O'Donnell, Mabel, *Guidebooks for the First Grade Basal Readers*. Evanston, Ill.: Row, Peterson and Co., 1954.

27: An Evaluation of Techniques for Teaching Word Recognition *

ROBERT E. MILLS

The teaching of reading has seen the championing of various methods as the most effective for the teaching of word-recognition skills. Reading authorities have used empirical data and their own opinions to promote particular brands of reading without enough objective research data to validate their assertions. Schubert summarizes our present predicament when he comments:

When the numerous methods and techniques of teaching reading to the disabled reader are pondered, many teachers are in a quandary. Each specialist—Gates, Monroe, Dolch, Fernald, etc., all renowned in the reading field—advocates a different method.[4]

Much of the difficulty in determining appropriate methods for the teaching of word recognition comes from confusing the particular reading skill of word recognition with general reading achievement, which involves not only word recognition but comprehension, generalizing, inferring meanings, and the like. Phonics, visual analysis of words, and kinesthetic tracings are techniques which have been developed and used for the specific purpose of aiding the child to identify and recognize the printed symbol. Only after the child has a certain degree of competency in word-recognition skills is he able to read. That is, *the act of reading is different from the act of identifying or recognizing words*. As Dolch might state it, the child has to have a certain number of "bricks" available before the "house" can take shape:

We may say that the understanding of words in reading is basic because without understanding of word meanings there can be no reading. Words are to reading matter what bricks are to a house. When you look at the house you do not think of the bricks; but without the bricks there would be no house.[1]

It is the problem of helping the child secure the "bricks" (words) that has been of concern. Yet most of the researchers have used complicated measures of eye fixations, sentence- and paragraph-comprehension tests, and

* Reprinted from the *Elementary School Journal*, Vol. 56, No. 5 (January 1956), pp. 221-5, by permission of the author and the publisher.

speed of reading in an attempt to ascertain the relative efficiency of a particular method of teaching word recognition. Promotion of generalized plans for developmental reading, such as the "intrinsic method" or the "non-oral method," has become confused with the specific methods of teaching word recognition, namely, the visual or look-and-say, the phonic or auditory, the kinesthetic or tracing, and combinations of these three.

Among the three basic methods there are no clear delineations. Phonic, visual, and kinesthetic elements are involved in all printed symbols of our language. Thus, when we speak of a phonic method, we are simply indicating that stress is being given to the auditory characteristics of the word and that this stress becomes the differential between the various methods.

PURPOSE AND SUBJECTS OF THIS STUDY

The basic purpose of the study reported in this article was to determine the teaching method or combination of methods most effective in teaching word recognition to various types of individuals.

The subjects were thirty-nine boys and nineteen girls in Grades II-IV of five public schools in Pasco County, Florida. These subjects were divided into nine classifications for purposes of treatment. Each of the three age levels was divided into three groups of intelligence levels (low, 65-80; average, 85-100; and high, 105-20) as determined by the Wechsler Intelligence Scale for Children.

PROCEDURES USED

A test instrument, the Learning Methods Test,[3] was specifically devised by the author for this study. Basically this test is a series of standard teaching lessons, accompanied by tests to determine the

efficiency of the various methods for different children. Harris and Roswell [2] have suggested such procedures but with an informal manner of presentation, teaching procedures, and testing. Here we have attempted to standardize an instrument for the specific purpose of determining the most effective method for teaching word recognition to the individual pupil.

The materials for this test consist of four sets of graded picture-word cards; a manual of directions, which provides specific instructions for the four fifteen-minute teaching lessons, each of which stresses a different method (visual, phonic, kinesthetic, or a combination); and record forms.

In order to determine the appropriate level of words to be used in the Learning Methods Test, a pretest of word recognition was necessary. The picture-word cards were administered to obtain forty words that the child could not recognize in five seconds of exposure time. These words were to be used later in the four learning-methods situations. For example, if forty words from the first-grade cards could not be found that the subject did not know, then no words from the first-grade level were used. Instead, a check was made to find forty unknown words on the second-grade level.

The cards were first presented to the child with the word side up. If at the end of five seconds the subject had not responded correctly to the word, this "unknown" word then became one of the training and test words. This process was continued until all the cards on that particular level had been administered. From these unknown words, forty cards were selected at random by shuffling the stack thoroughly and then counting off the first forty cards.

A systematic rotation procedure was used for the order of presentation of the teaching methods. If the visual method was used as the first teaching method with Subject A, then Subject B was presented with the phonic method as the first procedure, and so on.

The pretest and the first fifteen-minute lesson on ten words were administered on the first day. Twenty-four hours later a delayed-recall test was administered to the subject as a check of his recognition of the ten words taught him the preceding day. The total number of correct responses on this delayed-recall test was recorded as his score for that particular method and became a part of the data for this study.

On the same day as the delayed-recall test for the first training session (the second day), a second fifteen-minute lesson using a different method was presented to the subject. This process of individualized lessons and testing at twenty-four hour intervals was continued on consecutive days until all four teaching methods had been utilized. On the fifth day the delayed-recall test for the fourth lesson was administered. Thus each subject had four scores ranging from 0 to 10 for each method.

This study was concerned with four basic methods of teaching word recognition: the visual, the phonic, the kinesthetic, and a combination of the three. In order to obtain specific techniques or steps that would be typical of a particular method of teaching word recognition, six activities were selected for each method on the basis of frequency of mention in the literature. For each method these specific teaching activities were outlined in the manual of directions for the Learning Methods Test. These standard teaching procedures were used so that each subject would have the same variety of activities for each method and in the same order as every other subject.

TREATMENT OF PERTINENT VARIABLES

Because of the many variables of great importance in attempting to evaluate techniques of teaching word recogni-tion, it was necessary to limit the number of variables treated in the research design to those that other research and empirical data indicated as being most significant, namely, sex, chronological age, reading level, and intelligence.

An attempt was made to control the other important variables in the following manner. The teacher variable was controlled by employing only one teacher, the author, to do all the testing and teaching both for the standardizing of the Learning Methods Test and for collecting the data for this study. The race variable was controlled by using only subjects from the white race. A further control of note was that no child from a bilingual home was used as a subject. Visual and hearing efficiency were controlled through administering the telebinocular and audiometer tests; only children who fell in the normal range on both these tests were used as subjects. Reading-achievement level was controlled by the items on the Learning Methods Test. Grade placement was controlled by having all subjects in the seven-year-old group from the second grades, eight-year-olds from the third grades, and nine-year-olds from the fourth grades. Geographical distribution of subjects was confined to a radius of thirty-five miles, with all subjects residing in Pasco County, Florida. This, of course, limits the generalizations that can be made from the findings of this study.

A special research design employing the t test was used to determine the significance of the sex variable. Twenty-four pairs of boys and girls, matched in relation to chronological age, reading level, and intelligence, were used. The results of the t test indicated that there were no significant differences at the 5 per cent level of confidence between the two sexes for any of the four methods. However, the girls tended to score higher on all four methods than did the boys: the girls had a total mean score of 6.39 compared with the boys' total mean score of 5.60. Since there were no significant differences, both boys and girls were used for the study.

STATISTICAL RESULTS

Table 1 indicates means and standard deviations of delayed-recall scores obtained on the Learning Methods Test for all fifty-eight subjects. Because of the high standard deviations for certain groups, a test for the homogeneity of variance was run; the corrected chi square was not significant. Therefore the hypothesis of random sampling from a population with a common variance was accepted.

An analysis-of-variance design was used to determine whether the means of the thirty-six groups differed significantly. (Unequal numbers of cases were used, but there was a minimum of five subjects for each of the thirty-six cells in the factorial design.) The following is a summary of this analysis of variance.

Significant at the 1 per cent level of confidence were intelligence interacting with method, chronological age interacting with intelligence, and intelligence as a main effect. The interaction of chronological age with method was found to be significant at the 5 per cent level of confidence. The interaction of age with intelligence was not of direct importance to this methodology study and, therefore, was not further analyzed. As would be expected, intelligence proved to be the most significant factor in determining the number of words learned in a fifteen-minute teaching session.

After it was found that the over-all F's were significant for the intelligence-method interaction and the age-method interaction, the *t* technique was used to test the significance of the difference between any two of the group means. Using the 5 per cent level of confidence,

the conclusions stated below were reached as a result of this treatment of the data.

CONCLUSIONS

The study showed conclusively that different children learn to recognize words more efficiently by different teaching methods and that no one method is best for all children. Some conclusions about the effectiveness or the ineffectiveness of specific teaching methods were drawn for certain types of children.

1. *Children of Low Intelligence.* The phonic method is least effective for this group. The kinesthetic method is best in the greatest number of cases, but it is not statistically better than the visual and the combination methods.

2. *Children of Average Intelligence.* For the majority of cases in this group the kinesthetic method is the least effective. The phonic method showed no statistical significance in either direction. The combination and the visual methods proved to be about equally good for this group of average intelligence.

3. *Children of High Intelligence.* In this group we are restricted in any conclusions we can draw about the relative effectiveness of methods because all subjects tended to learn words readily regardless of the teaching method used. However, the visual method did prove superior to the kinesthetic method for this group.

4. *Seven-Year-Olds.* The visual method appeared to be best and the kinesthetic method appeared to be the poorest. The other two methods seemed to be neither consistently effective nor ineffective in working with this group.

5. *Eight-Year-Olds.* The kinesthetic method proved to be best for this age group; it is significantly better than the phonic and somewhat better than the other two. This finding may have some possible relation to the fact that eight-

Table 1: Mean Scores and Standard Deviations of 58 Pupils in Grades II-IV on Delayed-Recall Tests of Word Recognition Taught by Four Methods

Age Group and Method	Low Intelligence (65-80)		Average Intelligence (85-100)		High Intelligence (105-20)		All Groups	
	Mean	Standard Deviation	Mean	Standard Deviation	Mean	Standard Deviation	Mean	Standard Deviation
Seven-year-olds:	5 pupils		5 pupils		5 pupils		15 pupils	
Visual	4.0	3.24	7.6	1.14	9.6	0.55	7.1	3.03
Phonic	1.8	3.03	5.2	1.92	8.8	1.10	5.3	3.58
Kinesthetic	4.0	2.86	4.8	2.49	6.4	2.51	5.1	2.63
Combination	3.2	2.77	7.8	1.79	8.6	1.14	6.5	3.09
All methods	..	...	..	...	..	...	6.0	3.14
Eight-year-olds:	5 pupils		6 pupils		5 pupils		16 pupils	
Visual	2.4	1.34	7.5	1.64	9.2	.84	6.4	3.16
Phonic	1.8	.45	7.2	1.94	9.0	1.22	6.1	3.33
Kinesthetic	6.0	.71	7.3	1.96	9.2	1.10	7.5	1.86
Combination	3.8	.84	8.3	.81	9.6	.55	7.3	2.60
All methods	..	...	..	...	..	...	6.8	2.80
Nine-year-olds:	9 pupils		12 pupils		6 pupils		27 pupils	
Visual	6.0	2.78	8.1	1.57	9.2	1.60	7.6	2.34
Phonic	5.1	3.10	7.1	1.97	8.7	1.21	6.8	2.59
Kinesthetic	5.9	2.20	5.9	1.97	8.2	2.14	6.4	2.22
Combination	6.0	3.04	7.4	1.38	9.0	2.04	7.3	2.38
All methods	..	...	..	...	..	...	7.0	2.40
All subjects:	19 pupils		23 pupils		16 pupils		58 pupils	
Visual	4.5	2.93	7.8	1.47	9.3	1.08	7.2	2.77
Phonic	3.4	3.04	6.7	2.03	8.8	1.11	6.2	3.89
Kinesthetic	5.4	2.19	6.0	2.18	7.9	2.20	6.4	2.38
Combination	4.7	2.77	7.7	1.36	9.1	1.39	7.1	2.61
All methods	4.5	2.80	7.1	1.92	8.8	1.57	6.7	2.74

year-olds are usually just becoming proficient in handwriting and show a great deal of interest in related activities.

6. *Nine-Year-Olds.* No one of the four methods was outstandingly effective or ineffective. The visual method did tend to be better than the kinesthetic method for this group of older children.

7. In general, the higher the intelligence, the more readily children learn words. However, there is no consistent relation between age and a child's readiness to learn words for the three age groups studied. This finding has implications for present school practices where chronological age is all too often used as the major criterion in deciding when a child is ready to learn words.

SUMMARY

In any study involving the dynamics of children, some variables are always neglected because of their infinite number and complexity and because of the limitations of research facilities. Therefore more research is needed in this area to validate present findings and to explore other important variables not adequately treated in past research. From this study evolve recommendations of practical application to classroom teachers and remedial-reading clinicians. These include the following:

1. Because different children learn to recognize words most efficiently by different teaching methods, the classroom teacher must be aware of these individual differences when he applies group-instruction techniques. Our research indicates the need for the teacher to familiarize himself with all the various techniques and to be versatile in the use of these if he is to teach *all* the children.

2. In individual cases of failure to make the expected growth in word-recognition skills, our research indicates the need for a diagnostic study of the child to determine the most appropriate method for the particular individual.

In summary, it is believed that this study has far-reaching implications for all those interested in how children learn to recognize words. We have theorized about individual differences for decades, but we have done little to apply this theory in teaching practice. This research indicates the need for the concentration of energies on finding out *which* method is best for *which* children rather than developing a recipe or "a best method" that will serve for all children all the time.

REFERENCES

1. Dolch, Edward W., "The Use of Vocabulary Lists in Predicting Readability and in Developing Reading Materials," *Elementary English,* XXVI (March 1949), 142-9.
2. Harris, A. J., and Roswell, Florence G., "Clinical Diagnosis of Reading Disability," *Journal of Psychology,* XXXVI (June 1953), 323-40.
3. Mills, Robert E., *The Learning Methods Test.* Gainesville, Florida: Reading Laboratory and Clinic, University of Florida, 1954.
4. Schubert, Delwyn G., "Whose Brand of Reading Methods Is the 'Best Buy'?" *Clearing House,* XXVII (January 1953), 266-7.

CHAPTER VII

Developing Rate and Comprehension

28: The Determinants of Reading Comprehension *
PHILIP E. VERNON

Contemporary tests of educational abilities are far more sophisticated instruments than the new-type attainment tests of the 1920's and '30's. At the high school and college levels they avoid questions relating to straightforward factual knowledge and skills, since these have been found to stimulate undesirable methods of study. Instead, as Brownell,[2] Dressel,[7] and Bloom[1] point out, their aim is to elicit understanding of principles, ability to apply knowledge, critical thinking, judgment, and other educationally valuable qualities.

The present writer, however, brought up in a European educational system which still relies primarily on the essay examination for eliciting these higher educational qualities from its students, is inevitably struck by certain weaknesses in such tests. Whatever the subject matter—English, social studies or natural sciences—they tend to take the form of complex reading comprehension tests, and they therefore appear to depend partly on the students' facility in understanding the instructions and coping with multiple-choice items. While admitting that fluency and legibility in essay writing unduly affects

the students' performances in any European examinations, he wonders whether new-type test sophistication does not equally distort assessments of abilities in the American setting.[14] These suspicions are confirmed by a study of the experimental literature and of test manuals, from which it appears that the correlations between tests aimed at different mental functions or different school subjects are extremely high. For example, the mean intercorrelation for five of the Iowa Tests of Educational Development among 9th and 12th grade students is quoted as .716, where the mean reliability is .905; yet these tests are supposed to measure such different abilities as: 1. Basic Social Concepts, 5. Reading in Social Studies, 6. Reading in Natural Science, 7. Interpreting Literary Materials, and 8. Vocabulary. A battery of this kind is highly inefficient for differential predictive purposes, and it is noteworthy that, in Horst's[9] extensive studies of differential prediction, the tests which generally contribute most to the regression equations are the more factual ones such as Scientific Vocabulary, Mathematical Concepts, together with specific high school grades and Strong or Kuder in-

* Reprinted from *Educational and Psychological Measurement*, Vol. 22, No. 2 (Summer 1962), pp. 269-86, by permission of the author and the publisher.

terests. Though several investigations have claimed to show good differentiation among tests in different subjects (e.g., Shores [11]), far too often there is no indication of the extent to which score differences may not be due merely to the imperfect reliability of the contrasted tests.

Evidence regarding the measurement of different levels, or types, of ability is somewhat contradictory. Davis [5] attempted to measure nine skills hypothesized in reading, but Thurstone [13] claimed that all the intercorrelations could be attributed to a single vocabulary + comprehension factor. Derrick [6] suggests that a significant bipolar factor separates these two aspects, and many other studies have shown reading rate, vocabulary, and comprehension to be at least partially distinct. In Derrick's own research, three types of item—factual, inferential and judgmental—(classified by expert judges) and three lengths of reading passage were compared. Factor analysis yielded no reliable differentiation either according to function measured or to length of passage. However, a study of his mean intercorrelations indicate some distinction between factual and more complex items (scarcely any between inferential and judgmental); also between scores on a 50,000 word passage studied beforehand and performance at short and medium passages.

By contrast, Howard [10] extracted five subtests of items representing different levels of complexity (*not* of difficulty) from a 160-item General Science test. The intercorrelations clearly show that the more complex subtests measure a somewhat different ability from the simpler. Again Horrocks [8] describes a test of the ability of psychology students to apply their knowledge of adolescent psychology to the interpretation of case studies, which correlated far below the reliability coefficients with ordinary course marks.

The writer would contend that a major reason for high correlations between tests aimed at somewhat different abilities is their common item-form and their dependence on the students' sophistication. In the same way essay examinations in different subjects, or marked for different qualities, are apt to intercorrelate highly, but to show lower correlations with new-type tests in the same subject. Both test-content or function and test-form or method are highly complex, but a possible analysis (partly derived from Thorndike [12]) is in Table 1.

Table 1: Sources of Variance in Educational Test Scores

CONTENT

Level of integration—interpretation, understanding vs. knowledge of concepts and operations

Different functions at a given level, e.g. evaluation, application to new problems, retention, etc.

Technical bias—scientific, historical, literary, etc.

METHOD

Factors attributable to the medium or material of the test (verbal, symbolic, visual, performance, etc.) irrelevant to its purpose

Type of presentation—oral, visual, verbal; questions asked simultaneously or subsequently

Difficulty level and speed conditions, which may modify factor content

Response-type—multiple-choice, matching, etc.; short-answer (in student's own words), oral, essay (restricted time), dissertation (unrestricted)

Attitudes and motivations induced by the tester and testing conditions

Sophistication—knack in coping with these types of item, recognizing unsuspected clues, guessing and using time wisely, etc.

Sets arising from the student's understanding (or misunderstanding) of the instructions or transferred from previous tests; adaptations in the course of doing the test

Other response sets, e.g., tendency to guess, to choose extreme responses, etc.

Speed and accuracy in recording answers on answer sheets; speed and legibility in written answers

ERROR

Sampling variance between the passages or question set

Fluctuations in moods, attention, fatigue and health of students

Scoring errors in objective tests

Variance between markers in essay or other non-objective assessments

---

Educationists and psychometrists, in their concern over Content and Error, have paid little attention to the Method category; and even if its influence on test or examination performance is small, we should at least attempt to investigate its components more fully. Though correlational factor analysis can help, there is always the danger of interpreting the nature of a factor in terms of content, which really derives more from common method components. (For example, the distinction often drawn by factorists between I—inductive, and D—deductive, reasoning may arise more because most I-tests are based on non-verbal, numerical or letter material, most D-tests on verbal material, than because they involve different kinds of thinking.) A Fisherian type of factorial design would therefore be more appropriate for studying content and method variances simultaneously. The same conclusion was reached by Campbell and Fiske [3] in the field of personality: "Method or apparatus factors make very large contributions to psychological measurements"; and they advocate the Multitrait-Multimethod Matrix to overcome this.

DESIGN OF INVESTIGATION

An investigation was carried out among 108 male students in a British Training College for Teachers. The time available for testing, and the students' patience, permitted the exploration of only a few of the factors listed in Table 1. However, the value of the study was greatly enhanced through its repetition with a group of 75 American college students, for which Dr. W. Coffmann of the Educational Testing Service and Professor D. L. Cook of Purdue University were responsible.*

Several tests were constructed, or adapted, in two parallel forms, to cover various content and method differences in the area of verbal comprehension. Half of each group were given the first form during the first of two 2-hour sessions, the second form at another session a week or two later; half took them in the reverse order. This enabled practice effects, and fluctuations associated with the session or occasion, to be controlled. The order of application was arranged to provide variety. Numbers of items and time limits are listed in Table 2.

TESTS

1. Vocabulary A and B. Definitions to be written by the students in their own words, either synonyms or short phrases.

2. Vocabulary C and D. Multiple-choice.

3. Sentence Completion A and B. Filing gaps in sentences, multiple-choice.

4. Reading Comprehension A and B. Answering questions on 200-400 word passages, in own words.

* The views expressed in this article must not, of course, be attributed to my collaborators. I am further indebted to the Educational Testing Service for the loan of certain test materials and for payments made to the American students; and above all for a grant which enabled me to study current developments in educational testing at Princeton, N.J., during 1957.

5. Reading Comprehension C and D. Ditto, multiple-choice.

6. Reading Comprehension E and F. In each test two passages of 400-500 words were presented, to be read in 3-4 minutes without seeing the questions; thereafter questions were given to be answered without consulting the passages, one lot in own words, the other multiple-choice.

The questions in Tests 4-6 were further cross-classified, half of them being based primarily on factual information given in the paragraphs, half requiring more inference or judgment. Thus each pair of tests could be alternatively scored for factual or inferential abilities.

7. Reading Comprehension G and H. This was a published, multiple-choice test which aims particularly to measure inference from social studies materials.

8. The British group only was given a multiple-choice test of comprehension of tables and graphs, referring mainly to medical and psychological statistics.

9-11. The American group had previously taken the Nelson-Denny Reading Test (Vocabulary and Comprehension) and an Entry English Test, two-thirds of whose items dealt with sentence-structure, punctuation and spelling, the remaining third with vocabulary and reading. The numbers of available subjects dropped to 67 and 62, respectively.

12. An external criterion of intellectual competence, in the form of grade-point averages, was available for the American students. British students wrote essays on educational themes during the year and took an essay examination in education two months later. As their papers were marked by various lecturers, the marks were expected to be weak in reliability. Fourteen months later they took a more thorough, and uniformly marked, examination; but its results were published only in the form of very coarse, and therefore also unreliable, grades.

The scoring of the "own-word" or "creative-response" tests, Nos. 1, 3 and half of 6, was done by the writer alone. However, acceptable and unacceptable answers were listed, and it is believed that no greater subjectivity was involved than in scoring, say, Terman-Merrill vocabulary.

The main hypotheses which can be tested by the above battery are listed in an order following that of Table 1:

I. Tests at different levels (Reading A-H versus Vocabulary A-D) involve partially distinguishable abilities. Sentence completion should be intermediate.

II. Tests of different functions, such as factual versus inferential, will show some distinction, though this may be small. For the classification of items was made by the writer alone, and Derrick [6] has shown that inter-judge consistency is not high.

III. The Table and Graph Reading test involves verbal and numerical questions and responses; but as these refer to visual material, it should measure a somewhat different ability from the verbal tests.

IV. Type of presentation: Reading Tests E and F, in which students cannot search for the answers in the paragraphs, will measure a different ability from conventional reading tests, and will show a higher validity against an examination criterion.

V. Form of response: Tests responded to in own words will correlate more highly among themselves, also multiple-choice tests among themselves, than own-word with multiple-choice.

VI. American students will do relatively better at reading tests, to which they are far more accustomed, than British students, and their responses to multiple-choice tests will be more structured and consistent.

VII. British students, but not American, will improve with practice at these same tests.

VIII. There will be a small but appreciable sessional effect, that is, higher correlations within than between sessions.

RESULTS

Both groups of students were mostly in their early twenties. The British were all male, but the American included 32 men and 43 women. No appreciable difference between the sexes could be observed, except in the Entry English test; thus no distinction was made in analyzing the results.

Table 2 gives the main information about each test in each group. It will be seen that American students were generally allowed longer times since it was thought that they were somewhat less highly selected than the British. Clearly, direct comparisons of means are not legitimate. Nevertheless it is obvious that the British are at least 1σ superior on both vocabulary tests, despite their shorter time, and yet they obtain much the same scores on reading tests. It might conceivably be argued that British students receive much less training in

reading at school, and thus perform less well than might be expected in view of their good vocabulary. But it seems much more likely that American students do relatively well at reading tests because of their familiarity with such tests and their expertise in coping with this item-form. The British would have had virtually no experience of new-type tests (except possibly some eight years earlier when they entered high school). This is confirmed by the fact that the British show larger and more consistent gains in score from the first to the second occasion on all reading tests, but not on vocabulary. On the combined tests the British rise of .30 sigma units is highly significant; the American rise only slightly exceeds its standard error. Hypothesis VII, and the first half of Hypothesis VI, are therefore confirmed.

The low scores, particulary among American students, on creative-response Vocabulary are noticeable. Clearly the

Table 2: Numbers of Items in Combined Tests, Total Times, Means, and Score Increases from First to Second Sessions

Test	Form of Re-sponse	No. of Items in Both Parts	Time (mins) Amer.	Time (mins) Brit.	Mean Scores Amer.	Mean Scores Brit.	Standard Deviations Amer.	Standard Deviations Brit.	Score Gains Amer.	Score Gains Brit.
Vocabulary AB	cr *	40	16	14	6.1	12.7	5.72	6.66	−0.17	+0.49
Vocabulary CD	mc	56	16	12	21.7	31.4	7.69	8.12	−0.05	−0.31
Sentence Com-pletion AB	mc	36	20	20	19.9	24.1	6.40	5.20	+0.02	+0.07
Reading AB	cr	33	34	30	16.5	16.2	4.16	3.88	+0.14	+0.60
Reading CD	mc	32	30	30	20.3	21.6	4.94	4.15	+0.33	+0.28
Reading EF	(i) cr	16			9.6	9.4	2.88	2.39		
			34	30					−0.08	+0.31
	(ii) mc	15			9.0	8.9	2.67	2.51		
Reading GH	mc	34	30	27	23.8	23.6	4.01	5.00	+0.13	+1.08
Tables & Graphs	mc	50	—	40	—	29.7	—	6.09	—	—
N-D Vocabulary	mc	100	10	—	42.2	—	14.15	—	—	—
N-D Reading	mc	36	20	—	45.7	—	10.72	—	—	—
Entry English	mc	225	65	—	78th percen-tile	—	—	—	—	—

* cr = creative response, written in own words. mc = multiple-choice.

test was made much too difficult. How-ever, the four vocabulary lists, A, B, C, and D, were drawn from a common pool of words, and they were known from previous item-analysis data to be of closely similar difficulty. Thus the differences between the means for Vo-cabulary CD and Vocabulary AB pro-vide an indication of how much easier it is to recognize than to formulate a correct concept. Similarly Reading CD is easier than Reading AB, though not so markedly.

Sessional Variance. All 14 part-scores from the seven main tests were inter-correlated in each group by the tetra-choric method, taking splits close to the tertiles and averaging the two coefficients so obtained. Changes from one session to the other in students' motivation, or general adaptation to the testing situation, will be shown by con-trasting the correlations of different tests at the same and at different sessions.

The difference is appreciable in both groups, the average correlation being 5 to 10 per cent higher within the same occasion than between occasions. Doubt-less this difference would increase with a longer time interval. Much the same effect could have been shown by con-trasting the Kuder-Richardson and the

repeat reliabilities of the seven tests. For the British group these averaged .697 and .626, respectively.

There is no obvious technique for testing the significance of differences be-tween mean tetrachorics. However, if the distributions of coefficients them-selves are compared, the American within-session mean exceeds the be-tween-session mean at the .001 level. The British difference is not significant. Over-all, it would seem that Hypothesis VIII is confirmed.

Factual versus Inferential Questions. When the scores on Reading Tests AB, CD, and EF for factual and inferential questions are separated, their tetrachoric intercorrelations yield the means shown in Table 4. Also listed are the correla-tions of both types of score with Read-ing Test GH, most of whose items are strongly inferential.

The American, but not the British, results confirm Hypothesis II. However, in both groups the correlations with Reading GH are confirmatory. Though there is no satisfactory test of the signifi-cance of differences between mean correlations, it would appear that func-tions in reading can be differentiated rather more readily than Derrick be-lieved, and they may contribute some

Table 3: Mean Correlations Showing the Sessional Effect

	Amer.	Brit.
42 correlations within sessions	.534	.427
42 correlations between sessions	.487	.408

Table 4: Mean Correlations Showing Effects of Function Tested

	Amer.	Brit.
6 correlations within factual or within inferential	.535	.385
6 correlations between factual and inferential scores on different tests	.437	.397
3 inferential scores with Reading GH	.563	.415
3 factual scores with Reading GH	.482	.313

10 per cent of variance. But it should be noted that, in this investigation (unlike Davis' and Derrick's), the two types of questions referred to different passages; and it might be argued plausibly that the difference is not so much one of psychological function as of technical bias (cf. Table 1). Thus the passages yielding inferential questions were all of a philosophical, psychological, or aesthetic nature, whereas the passages yielding factual ones were more descriptive—scientific, geographical, or historical.

Retentive Reading versus Immediate Comprehension. The experimental design was inadequate for covering Hypothesis IV. Nevertheless Table 5 provides a little evidence, and more will emerge in Table 10. Here, all tetrachoric correlations are between multiple-choice and own-word scores, that is, item-form is held constant.

Table 5: Correlations Within and Between Retentive and Immediate Comprehension Tests

	Amer.	Brit.
4 correlations within Immediate Comprehension Tests	.485	.328
8 correlations between Immediate and Retentive Tests	.535	.359
1 correlation within Retentive Tests	.60	.47

Table 6: Intercorrelations of All Tests (American Group Above, British Group Below the Diagonal) and Kuder-Richardson Reliabilities

	Voc. AB	Voc. CD	Sent. Comp.	Rdg. AB	Rdg. CD	EF cr	EF mc	Rdg. GH	N-D Voc.	N-D Rdg.	Entry Engl.	Tab. Gra.
Vocabulary AB	.892 / .874	.770	.578	.477	.483	.393	.457	.484	.783	.669	.702	—
Vocabulary CD	.844	.834 / .847	.726	.575	.539	.448	.528	.487	.759	.646	.648	—
Sent. Completion	.702	.687	.826 / .758	.656	.689	.587	.707	.711	.642	.718	.610	—
Reading AB	.488	.406	.591	.626 / .600	.690	.586	.601	.587	.651	.680	.461	—
Reading CD	.498	.434	.621	.504	.785 / .708	.719	.679	.657	.590	.696	.522	—
Reading EF cr	.476	.431	.501	.499	.495	.622 / .490	.568	.572	.531	.641	.422	—
Reading EF mc	.346	.331	.435	.416	.413	.389	.591 / .516	.643	.474	.569	.478	—
Reading GH	.567	.521	.567	.569	.436	.388	.456	.619 / .779	.604	.710	.458	—
N-D Vocabulary	—	—	—	—	—	—	—	—	.899	.737	.678	—
N-D Reading	—	—	—	—	—	—	—	—	—	.867	.569	—
Entry English	—	—	—	—	—	—	—	—	—	—	—	—
Tables & Graphs	.105	.046	.192	.233	.191	.125	.394	.090	—	—	—	.711

The correlations within Immediate Comprehension tests (AB, CD) are no higher than between these and the Retentive tests (EF). However, the single correlation within the two halves of the Retentive test is higher in both groups, indicating that type of presentation may have some influence.

Multiple-Choice versus Creative (Own-Word) Responses. The scores on the two forms of each test were now combined, and the product-moment correlations between all tests are shown in Table 6. The coefficients for American students are above the diagonal. Kuder-Richardson Formula 20 reliability coefficients are shown along the diagonal. Some of these are very low, particularly for Reading test EF, where the creative and multiple-choice scores were based on only 15 or 16 items. But the tests were intentionally kept short to avoid over-taxing the students' patience, and there is no reason to suppose that longer tests, containing more carefully pre-tried items, would not reach acceptable levels of reliability.

A comparison of all the multiple-choice and creative-response correlations does not appear to bear out Hypothesis V. For example, Vocabulary AB does not correlate more highly with Reading AB (both creative) than with Reading CD (multiple-choice). Table 7 shows the mean coefficients.

A further examination was made of the residual correlations after removing the Content factors by factor analysis (see below). A majority of these tended

to be positive for within-item-form coefficients, negative for between-item-form, but not to a significant extent. If any variance is attributable to this difference in item-form, it can hardly amount to more than 1 or 2 per cent. It is unfortunate that a wider difference, as between essay-form and multiple-choice form, could not readily be investigated. Nevertheless some further evidence will emerge in the factor analysis.

Comprehension of Visual Items. The correlations of the Table and Graph Reading test with the seven verbal tests in the British group are clearly very low and irregular (Table 6), thus apparently confirming Hypothesis III that test medium or material makes an important difference. However, it will be seen that the coefficients are highest for Reading tests AB and EF (multiple-choice), lowest for Reading GH and Vocabulary. Unfortunately EF and AB happened to include more passages with a natural science content, whereas GH was based wholly on social science materials. Thus the obtained differentiation probably arises as much, or more, from what was labeled Technical Bias in Table 1, as from test medium.

Level of Integration: Vocabulary versus Comprehension. All eleven verbal tests were factor analyzed by the centroid method in the American group, and the eight tests (omitting Tables and Graphs) in the British group. No significant variance remained in either matrix

Table 7: Mean Correlations Within and Between Multiple-Choice and Creative-Response Tests

	Amer.	Brit.
6 correlations within multiple-choice	.595	.432
3 correlations within creative	.484	.488
Mean	.558	.451
11 correlations between multiple-choice and creative (omitting Vocab. AB with Vocab. CD)	.562	.455

Table 8: Factorial Analysis of Verbal Tests

| | Unrotated Factors | | | | | | Rotated Factors | | | | | |
| | American | | | British | | | American | | | British | | |
	I	II	h^2	I	II	h^2	Voc.	Comp.	Spec.	Voc.	Comp.	Spec.
Vocabulary AB	.771	.503	.847	.829	.364	.820	.916	−.093	.045	.902	.074	.054
Vocabulary CD	.796	.307	.728	.791	.513	.889	.849	.093	.106	.939	−.074	−.042
Sentence Completion	.855	−.083	.738	.840	.030	.707	.722	.467	.088	.752	.374	.051
Reading AB	.763	−.160	.608	.709	−.279	.581	.605	.492	.018	.490	.583	.019
Reading CD	.815	−.299	.753	.677	−.123	.473	.588	.638	.032	.536	.431	.235
Reading EF (cr)	.704	−.290	.580	.628	−.153	.417	.492	.581	.042	.479	.434	.073
Reading EF (mc)	.733	−.254	.602	.554	−.275	.383	.534	.563	−.011	.356	.506	.133
Reading GH	.761	−.252	.643	.698	−.068	.492	.560	.573	−.024	.581	.392	.287
N-D Vocabulary	.839	.275	.777				.871	.140	.122			
N-D Reading	.855	−.038	.732				.743	.427	.135			
Entry English	.714	.290	.594				.767	.070	—			
Percentage Variance		69.1			59.5		50.3	18.8		43.6	15.9	

after two factors had been extracted, hence factorization was stopped and the calculations repeated until the guessed communalities coincided with the obtained values (median discrepancy .002, maximum .006).

As shown in Table 8, the second factor clearly differentiates reading comprehension tests from vocabulary tests, in both groups. Hence rotation was carried out, passing the first axis through the center of gravity of the two vocabulary tests. The second factor then yielded loadings for the Comprehension tests approximately as great as their Vocabulary loadings (cf. Table 9).

This confirms our first hypothesis and thus contradicts Thurstone's verdict on

Davis' tests. Sentence Completion is intermediate between the Vocabulary and the Comprehension tests, and Nelson-Denny Reading shows almost the same composition, presumably because its reading passages are simpler than those used in the writer's tests and it is more highly speeded. The Entry English test, consisting mainly of questions about words or separate phrases, obtains a near-zero Comprehension loading.

In the American analysis almost all the specificities (Kuder-Richardson reliabilities minus communalities) are near zero, except those for the Nelson-Denny tests, which probably results from this test being given several months previously.* The picture is very different in

Table 9: Mean Variances of Five Complex Reading Tests

	Vocabulary Factor	Comprehension Factor	Total Communality
American analysis	31.1	32.6	63.7
British analysis	24.4	22.5	46.9

* Vocabulary CD also shows a suspiciously large specificity. Possibly this arises because the multiple-choice responses were chosen by the writer, and many of them might represent English, rather than current American, interpretations of word-meanings.

the British analysis. The communalities for all Reading Comprehension tests are lower, and the specificity is especially large in the multiple-choice tests, CD, EF (mc), and GH. Clearly the responses of British students to these tests were less organized, more random, than those of Americans, whereas in the own-word or creative tests—Reading AB and EF (cr)—the two groups were confronted with equally unfamiliar forms of response and show much the same specificities. Had the experiment included ordinary written essays, we may infer that the American students would have shown greater specificities on these. A possible alternative explanation might be that the American students are more heterogeneous in reading capacity; but this is contradicted by Reading GH, where the British variance and reliability are higher.

External Validation. The correlations with academic grades, shown in Table 10, are quite low among the British students, partly because of the low reliability of their education marks, but partly also because these grades were based on essay-type examinations,

whereas in the American group objective course examinations would have been generally applied.* Several of the predictors were amalgamated and multiple correlations calculated, with the results shown in Table 11. In the British group, Vocabulary, retentive reading (particularly the creative form), and Tables and Graphs all contribute to the prediction. But apparently the ordinary reading tests, whether in multiple-choice or creative form, are so unlike normal student reading activity that their beta-weight is strongly negative. Even in the American group these reading tests are again the least valid and so yield a negative beta-weight. The objective form of retentive reading contributes most, followed by Sentence Completion, the Entry English test, and Vocabulary. Note that all three creative-response tests are slightly less predictive than their multiple-choice parallels among students who are more accustomed to the latter.

While it would be possible to calculate the validities of Vocabulary and Comprehension factor scores, it is simpler, and as effective, to obtain the combined validities of Vocabulary AB +

Table 10: Correlations with Academic Grades

	American	British
Vocabulary AB	.272	.163
Vocabulary CD	.341	.198
Sentence Completion	.421	.128
Reading AB	.281	.039
Reading CD	.296	.085
Reading EF (cr)	.225	.276
Reading EF (mc)	.434	.203
Reading GH	.295	.081
Tables and Graphs	—	.218
Nelson-Denny Vocabulary	.129	—
Nelson-Denny Reading	.237	—
Entry English	.340	—

* Correlations with the further criterion of achievement, one year later, are not quoted here since they were even lower. However, they followed just the same pattern.

Table 11: Multiple Correlations

American	Beta Coefficients
Vocabulary ABCD	.0259
Reading ABCDGH	−.1672
Sentence Completion	.2332
Reading EF (mc)	.3218
Entry English	.1169
$R_m = .480$	
British	
Vocabulary ABCD	.2017
Reading ABCDGH	−.2682
Sentence Completion	−.0630
Reading EF (cr)	.2924
Reading EF (mc)	.1241
Tables and Graphs	.1847
$R_m = .392$	

CD and of Reading AB + CD + GH by Correlation of Sums, and then to find the partial validity of the latter, holding the former constant. The results are given in Table 12.

We may deduce that the Comprehension factor can make a small but useful contribution to prediction of educational achievement among American students, over and above Vocabulary, but that it actually possesses a small negative validity among British students.

CONCLUSIONS

All our specific hypotheses except V (and possibly III) are borne out. But the general trend of the results goes against our initial argument, in that it suggests that what were called Content factors (particularly "Level" and "Technical Bias") have a much stronger influence than Method factors. Nevertheless, the superior validity of reading tests which employ an unconventional method, that involving retention, suggests that Method variations would be worth further investigation. A similar test, called Directed Memory, was developed by Coffman and Papachristou [4] and is now incorporated in the E.T.S. Law Schools Admission test, where it shows good validity, over and above ordinary reading comprehension.

Although the clearly demonstrated Comprehension factor, orthogonal to Vocabulary, would seem at first sight to

Table 12: Validities of Combined Tests

	American	British
Vocabulary ABCD × Criterion	.326	.188
Reading ABCDGH × Criterion	.333	.083
Vocabulary × Reading	.616	.617
Reading × Criterion with Vocabulary constant	.177	−.042

reflect the difference between comprehending connected arguments and comprehending isolated concepts, it must be viewed with considerable suspicion in view of the British students' weak and poorly organized performance, particularly at multiple-choice tests. Apparently there is an important element of facility or "know-how" in the typical Reading Comprehension test, though presumably the great majority of American students have become so accustomed to it that, in their case, it contributes to the measurement of a valuable study skill. Others who are less sophisticated cannot so readily translate their understandings of the passages into terms of its conventions; hence for them the Comprehension component (as distinct from the Vocabulary component) has no predictive validity whatever.

More generally it would follow that, in the evaluation of complex skills and understandings, it is desirable to employ techniques which will resemble as closely as possible the ways in which these understandings will be ultimately expressed. Neither the objective test, nor the essay examination where the student has to muster all his knowledge and communicate it by answering a few questions in a limited time, much resemble the situation in which he will use his training in professional or in daily life. Probably the oral and clinical examination of the doctor, or the dissertation written and revised by a student in his own time with access to books and notes, both come much nearer to this ideal, since they involve less distortion by Method variance (though admittedly they may be more subject to Error variance). Similarly, in assessing the effectiveness of an educational film, or radio or television program, it is doubtful how far the conventional multiple-choice test of the knowledge retained by the viewer or listener provides an adequate criterion of the total impact of these media on his thinking and behavior.

SUMMARY

1. Assessments of the understanding of complex concepts, whether by objective tests, written essays, oral or other methods, are affected not only by the level and type of concepts tested, but also by many factors arising from the method of testing, and the subject's facility in handling it. Certain weaknesses in current new-type achievement tests, such as their poor differential predictive capacity, may result from neglect of such method components.

2. An investigation was designed to elicit the relative variance of certain test-content, method, and error components, and was carried out among 108 British and 75 American college students. The former group was more highly selected and was much superior in vocabulary tests; but its lack of superiority in reading comprehension tests, and its significant improvement with practice, illustrate the importance of facility or sophistication at such tests.

3. Parallel forms of seven specially constructed tests of vocabulary and reading were applied in two sessions. A sessional or "Occasion" effect was demonstrated by the higher correlations among tests within than between sessions, particularly in the American group.

4. Three reading tests included passages and questions, some of which called for relatively factual, others for more inferential, comprehension. Higher correlations were obtained within than between these types of comprehension, in both groups. However, the difference may reflect the technical bias of the respective passages rather than the psychological functions aimed at.

5. A test in which the questions were not seen or answered until after the completion of the reading of the passages (i.e., involving retention) appeared to measure a somewhat different ability from the conventional immediate-

comprehension test, and it was found to be considerably more valid than the latter in the prediction of academic achievement.

6. The writing of responses to vocabulary and reading questions by students in their own words (creative type) did not, as had been hypothesized, involve a different ability from the objective or multiple-choice type of response. However the scores of British students on multiple-choice reading tests showed very high specificity, reflecting their unsophisticated and relatively unorganized approach to these tests.

7. Centroid factor analyses revealed a strong Comprehension factor, orthogonal to the Vocabulary factor, among both groups in the reading tests. The validity of this factor in predicting achievement among American students is positive (though lower than that of Sentence Completion, Retentive Comprehension, and English Usage tests). Among British students its validity is slightly negative.

REFERENCES

1. Bloom, B. S., *Taxonomy of Educational Objectives.* New York: Longmans, Green, 1956.

2. Brownell, W. A., *et al., The Measurement of Understanding,* Forty-fifth Yearbook of the National Society for the Study of Education. Chicago: University of Chicago Press, 1946.

3. Campbell, D. T., and Fiske, D. W., "Convergent and Discriminant Validation by the Multitrait-Multimethod Matrix," *Psychological Bulletin,* LVI (1959), 81-105.

4. Coffman, W. E., and Papachristou, J., "Experimental Objective Tests of Writing Ability for the Law School Admission Test," *Journal of Legal Education,* VII (1955), 388-94.

5. Davis, F. B., "Fundamental Factors of Comprehension in Reading," *Psychometrika,* IX (1944), 185-97.

6. Derrick, C., *Three Aspects of Reading Comprehension as Measured by Tests of Different Lengths.* Princeton, N.J.: Educational Testing Service, RB 53-8, 1953.

7. Dressel, P. L., *et al., General Education: Explorations in Evaluation.* Washington, D.C.: American Council on Education, 1954.

8. Horrocks, J. E., "The Relationship between Knowledge of Human Development and Ability to Use Such Knowledge," *Journal of Applied Psychology,* XXX (1946), 501-8.

9. Horst, P., *Differential Prediction of Academic Success.* Seattle: University of Washington, 1959, ONR Contract —477(08).

10. Howard, F. T., *Complexity of Mental Processes in Science Testing.* New York: Teachers College, Columbia, Contributions to Education, 1943, No. 879.

11. Shores, J. H., "Skills Related to the Ability to Read History and Science," *Journal of Educational Research,* XXXVI (1943), 584-93.

12. Thorndike, R. L., *Personnel Selection: Test and Measurement Techniques.* New York: John Wiley & Sons, 1949.

13. Thurstone, L. L., "Note on a Reanalysis of Davis's Reading Tests," *Psychometrika,* XI (1946), 185-8.

14. Vernon, P. E., *Educational Testing and Test-form Factors.* Princeton, N.J.: Educational Testing Service, RB 58-3, 1958.

29: Measuring Reading Comprehension *

WALTER B. BARBE

The problem of how to measure comprehension in reading seems to be of major importance for two definite reasons: (1) to determine whether a student understands what is read, and (2) to know what to teach so that comprehension may be improved. In this era of great emphasis on reading problems, attention needs to be turned toward better measurement of reading comprehension.

A definition of comprehension would undoubtedly aid in the measurement; but as with so many such skills, the definition seems to be based upon what the test measures. Almost without exception, standardized reading tests include a section entitled "comprehension," and scores are given to indicate a student's ability in this skill. But unfortunately these scores are often misleading and of little value to the reading teacher who would like to use the scores as a guide for placing children in reading material at their level.

Since some definition of comprehension is essential, perhaps it would be sufficient to say that reading comprehension is understanding the material which is read.

COMPREHENSION OR MEMORY?

One major characteristic of most standardized tests of comprehension is the high value placed upon memory. Instead of measuring how well the student understands what he reads, the test seems to be measuring how well he can remember what he has read. Actu-

ally, memory is not a reading skill as such, and would more properly be classified as a facet of intelligence.

It is possible that the reason for the very high correlations which are reported between the results on group reading tests and group intelligence tests may be partially due to the common factor of memory in both tests. The place of this factor in a reading test is questionable, and certainly it is unacceptable when disguised with the label "comprehension." (Vocabulary is the main factor common to both reading and intelligence tests, and has been used as one explanation for the high correlation between the two types of scores. The presence of memory items on both types of tests may also be another important reason for the high correlation. In this instance, the inclusion of a memory factor may not be justified.)

There can be no doubt that the existing reading tests are little more than checks on how well the child remembers what he has read, and do little actually to determine the level at which the student understands what he has read.

QUANTITATIVE OR QUALITATIVE MEMORY?

The basic problem seems to be whether in the checking of reading comprehension the major concern is over quantitative or qualitative facts. How much? How many? When? Where? These seem to be the usual types of questions on a comprehension check. "Why?" is not a common question, and yet it would

* Reprinted from *The Clearing House*, Vol. 32, No. 6 (February 1958), pp. 343-5, by permission of the author and the publisher.

surely be a better measure of comprehension than those questions which can be answered from memory without any real understanding. The "why?" type of question is not easily prepared. It leaves a greater chance for ambiguity, because the question cannot be stated or answered in so objective a manner as other questions. The student's background of experience is more likely to influence his response, for the question is asking a reaction to something, rather than a rote repetition of what was read.

The method by which a poor reader explained that he took a reading comprehension check is revealing. His comprehension score was always much higher in silent reading than would be expected. When asked why he apparently could "understand" material read silently (a misuse of the word "understand," brought about by the naïve belief that comprehension and understanding were the same thing) whereas he could not read the same material aloud, he answered, "Oh, when I am supposed to read silently I just look for the numbers and dates in the story. Then when I take the test, I mark the answers which have those numbers in them." Unbelievable? Certainly not; it works.

Why must our reading comprehension tests be so concerned with figures and numbers? One possible explanation is given by Saint-Exupéry in *The Little Prince* (Reynal and Hitchcock, Inc.), in which he says, "Grownups love figures. When you tell them that you have made a new friend, they never ask you any questions about essential matters. They never say to you, 'What does his voice sound like? What game does he love best? Does he collect butterflies?' Instead, they demand: 'How old is he? How many brothers has he? How much does he weigh? How much money does his father make?' Only from these figures do they think they have learned anything about him."

Regardless of how much we may deny that this is true, a cursory examination of existing standardized reading tests reveals a preponderance of the "how much—how many?" type of question. An improvement would be to include more items requiring the student to understand and use the material which he has read.

GRADE LEVEL OF COMPREHENSION

Not all reading tests, but certainly many, give a grade level of comprehension in reading. Examining these tests reveals that the level obtained does not necessarily mean that the student comprehends material at that particular level. In many instances it means that he reads at a slow rate and therefore did not finish enough of the material to make a satisfactory score on the comprehension check. Is this poor comprehension? It would hardly seem to be so unless one wished to argue the point that reading comprehension and reading rate cannot be separated. If so, the two scores should never have been separated. Instead of a score in comprehension and a score in other factors in reading, there should have been only a total reading score.

The actual grade level of difficulty of the material which the student can read and understand is what a reading-comprehension grade level should indicate. It should exclude as many other reading factors as possible. It should mean that, given the time, the student can read the material and, without help, understand it. Is this asking too much from a comprehension check? Apparently so, for few tests provide this information.

The grade level at which the child can comprehend material must take into consideration vocabulary, background of experience, concepts, and ability to interpret what the author means.

ORAL AND SILENT READING COMPREHENSION

Reading teachers know well that children have different levels of comprehension for oral and silent reading. In some instances, a child will be unable to read silently and comprehend what he has read. Actually, the child is very likely unable to figure out a word and so does not systematically cover the material beyond that point. Such a child might also vocalize every word, so that he is actually reading aloud, even though he is supposed to be reading silently. Other children will do exactly the opposite. The emotional pressures of reading aloud make comprehension almost nil. Yet our reading tests usually yield one score on comprehension, with practically no indication of what type of reading was required in order to obtain the comprehension level. It is probably safe to assume that the comprehension score was on material read silently, but there is no assurance the child actually read the material in this manner.

LISTENING COMPREHENSION

Of value to all teachers working with children in a reading situation would be a measure of listening comprehension of material read to the child. Merely knowing that the child could understand material if he were capable of reading it would be valuable information to all teachers. Group reading tests give absolutely no indication of the actual comprehension level of the child. The comprehension check, therefore, becomes merely another check on the child's ability to use reading skills, but should not be labeled comprehension.

Of practical value to the person working with a child who is having reading difficulties is to know whether the child could understand the material if he were able to read it. In order to determine this, an individual intelligence test is customarily administered to every child receiving assistance in a reading clinic. But the scarcity of reading clinics and the overcrowded conditions in such clinics clearly indicate that the large percentage of reading problems never reach a reading clinic and therefore probably never have the advantage of individual intelligence testing. Therefore, it would seem logical that a test is needed which would indicate how much the child could understand if he were to learn the skills involved in reading. Such a test should be easily developed, for it would probably be nothing more than a carefully graded series of paragraphs which, instead of being read by the child, are read to him. His ability to understand up to a particular level should indicate how well he is capable of understanding material at any particular level, and might have the practical value of allowing classroom teachers to measure accurately the level at which they can hope to raise the child in reading ability, without having to resort to the unrealistic procedure of calling on outside help for every problem.

HOW ABOUT A NEW TYPE OF CHECK ON READING COMPREHENSION?

If a new type of reading test were developed which actually measured how well and at what level a child truly comprehended reading material, and at what level the child was capable of comprehending, an entire new era of both achievement testing and teaching might evolve. Why do teachers place so much importance on dates and figures in their checks of comprehension? Maybe because the same type of question is asked by the people who prepare reading tests and are supposed to know how to measure comprehension in an accurate manner.

It is only too easy to tell teachers that they should check comprehension in a better way, but until someone can show them how, such suggestions will not have any real meaning.

30: Are Fast Readers the Best Readers?—A Second Report *

J. HARLAN SHORES

Whether fast readers are the best readers depends in large part upon what is meant by reading rate; that is, upon how rate is measured. Reading rate is ordinarily measured as an original reading time (*i.e.,* the words read per minute during a single reading and not including the time taken to answer comprehension questions), or it is measured as a total reading time including both the time for a single original reading and the time taken to answer comprehension questions. Most rate measures either do not permit rereading or discourage this practice even though some reading, such as keeping a long series of ideas in mind in proper sequence or following precise directions, obviously requires rereading even by proficient readers.

It is at once apparent that a single rapid reading for superficial comprehension is a different measure from one that also includes time to answer questions. The question-answering task is often as time-consuming as is the actual reading. It is also apparent that neither of these tests is the same as a measure of the amount of time taken to read and use these materials for whatever comprehension purpose the reader has in mind.

The fact that experiments with reading speed have differed in what is measured as reading rate probably accounts in large part for the somewhat conflicting findings. Realizing that some readers go through the materials once rapidly and then reread all or part of the material for the specific purposes set by the comprehension questions, an adequate measure of reading rate must provide three scores—an original reading rate; a time for reading the questions, rereading the materials, and answering the questions; and a total time which is the sum of the previous two.

The question then, "Are fast readers the good readers?" needs to be broken down into several questions. Defining a "good reader" as one who comprehends well, we need to ask, "Are good readers those who read rapidly during an initial reading?" Do the good readers read rapidly when dealing with the study-type comprehension questions and when rereading to answer the questions? Are the good readers those who take less time in total to read, reread, and answer questions? A single answer is not adequate for these three questions and they in turn give rise to others. Are the fast readers the good readers on each of these measures regardless of the difficulty of the material and the purpose for reading? It is to these questions that this article is directed.

In the January, 1950, issue of *Elementary English* this author and Kenneth L. Husbands reported an investigation concerned with the relationship between reading speed and comprehension.[5] The general conclusion of this study was that there is no relationship between reading speed and comprehension when the task is difficult. The fast reader was not the best reader when he was reading biological science material in order to solve a problem. In fact, under these conditions the efficient

* Reprinted from *Elementary English*, Vol. 38, No. 4 (April 1961), pp. 236-45, with permission of the National Council of the Teachers of English and the author. This study was conducted with the assistance of a research fund provided by Spencer Press, publishers of *Our Wonderful World, Children's Hour,* and *The American Peoples Encyclopedia*.

and able reader slowed his rate to that of the inefficient reader.

STUDENT AND ADULT POPULATIONS

The present study, like the earlier one, was conducted with sixth-grade students. However, in the current study data were also collected from a group of able adult readers, and more adequate instrumentation was employed throughout.

All forty-six sixth graders of a K-12 consolidated school on the Southeastern coast of the United States comprised the student population. Even though the "tourist trade" was the largest industry, each of the children included was a permanent resident of the county. It is apparent from Table 1 that the children were of average age in grade and were somewhat above average in intelligence and reading achievement. In terms of their mental ability the group may have been slightly underachieving. Table 1 also indicates that the two sixth-grade groups reading for different purposes were closely equivalent in chronological age, mental age, and measures of general reading abilities.

The adult group was taken from several advanced undergraduate and graduate university-level courses dealing with the teaching of reading. A few of these were juniors and seniors in the program preparatory to teaching in the elementary grades. The majority were experienced teachers and administrators working toward graduate degrees.

TESTS USED

With the sixth-grade students four reading rate measures provided ten rate scores, and five comprehension measures provided eleven comprehension scores. The Iowa Silent Reading Tests [2] gave one rate score based on a portion of original reading time. Three tests developed by the author, each measur-

Table 1: Equivalence of Groups Reading for Main Ideas and for Ideas in Sequence Expressed in Raw Scores

Measure	Group A (Main Ideas)		Group B (Sequence)		Group A plus B	
	Mean	SD	Mean	SD	Mean	SD
C.A. (months)	137.48	4.28	135.83	6.51	136.65	5.41
M.A. (months)	151.57	26.88	147.61	22.92	149.59	24.78
California Reading *						
Comprehension	29.26	6.80	27.87	6.11	28.57	6.43
Total Score	104.43	14.97	103.65	15.19	104.04	14.92
Iowa Silent Reading **						
Comprehension	69.87	22.88	71.13	21.73	70.50	22.07
Rate	26.70	8.23	26.57	10.16	26.63	9.14
Total Score	122.26	35.23	124.91	36.16	123.58	35.32
Combined Scores—						
California plus Iowa						
Comprehension	99.13	28.53	99.00	26.22	99.07	27.09
Vocabulary	100.43	16.85	103.00	16.67	101.72	16.62

* Ernest W. Tiegs and Willis W. Clark, California Reading Test, Los Angeles; California Test Bureau, 1950.
** H. A. Greene and V. H. Kelley, Iowa Silent Reading Tests, Yonkers on Hudson, N.Y.; World Book Co., 1956.

ing an aspect of the reading of science materials, provided three rate scores each—a measure of original reading time, a measure of rereading and question-answering time and a measure of total reading time.

Each of the rate tests provided one or more measures of comprehension and the California Achievement Tests [7] provided additional comprehension measures. Whenever sub-tests of the Iowa and California tests were measuring in the same area these scores were combined for a more adequate measure. Thus the following scores were available from these two reading tests: California comprehension, Iowa comprehension, combined comprehension, combined vocabulary, combined directed reading, combined references, combined interpretation, Iowa rate (California does not provide a rate score), California total score, and Iowa total score.

Mental ages were derived from the California Test of Mental Maturity, Non-Language Section,[6] and the Sequential Tests of Educational Progress [4] were used to measure achievement in science.

After the standardized tests were administered, three unpublished tests developed by the author of this study were used. One of these, called *Reading for Problem Solving in Science,* is a forty-item test measuring ability to do directed reading for the solution of problems in science. The comprehension reliability of this test with the Kuder Richardson formula is .83. The rate reliability with the split-half method and the Spearman-Brown correction was .56 for original reading time, .43 for question answering time, and .39 for total time.

This was followed by the Directed Reading of Science Materials Tests administered in twenty successive sessions during which the 23 pupils in each sixth-grade group read a science passage of from 200 to 400 words that had been drawn from *Our Wonderful World* [8] and was at that time unfamiliar to them. Group A was instructed to read each passage for the main idea while Group B was instructed to read the same passage to keep the ideas of the passage in mind in their proper sequence. Different passages were employed for the different "tests." There was a total of twenty questions to be answered by those reading for main ideas and eighty questions for those reading for ideas in sequence. Three rate scores (original reading time, rereading and question-answering time, and total time) were taken for each of the twenty "tests." The split-half reliabilities of these tests of rate and comprehension are shown in Table 2.[1]

Fifty-one advanced undergraduate and graduate students read five of the same twenty selections from the *Directed Reading of Science Materials Tests* read by the sixth graders. Twenty-eight read for Purpose A (main ideas) and twenty-three read the same five selections for Purpose B (to keep ideas in mind in sequence). The adults were checked on comprehension and speed for each passage in the same manner as the sixth graders. The difference in the treatment was that the adults responded to all five passages at a single sitting whereas the children responded to only one passage at a sitting.

The adult population was deliberately chosen as a group of able readers. Most of the group were practicing elementary school teachers. A few were administrators and a few were advanced students (juniors and seniors) in a program preparatory to teaching. It may be that success in a field requiring much reading is better evidence of ability to do work-type reading than is any test now available. At any rate successful teachers and good students in teacher education programs probably can offer evidence of adequate reading skills.

As further proof of reading ability the adults scored well on the *Directed Reading of Science Materials Tests.*

Table 2: Reliability of Scores on Directed Reading of Science Tests

Measure	Mean	Standard Deviation	Coefficient of Reliability *
Type A—			
Main Idea			
Comprehension	11.70	4.29	.80
Original Rate	443.74	126.99	.97
Question Rate	119.22	40.62	.82
Total Rate	567.35	138.48	.95
Type B—			
Ideas in Sequence			
Comprehension	36.34	10.73	.90
Original Rate	462.57	159.42	.96
Question Rate	449.87	177.68	.93
Total Rate	916.78	293.54	.98

* The split-half method and the Spearman-Brown correction were used with all scores.

Their average accuracy level was 92 per cent when reading for main ideas, as contrasted with 56 per cent for sixth graders. When reading for the more difficult task of getting ideas in sequence the adult average accuracy level was 80 per cent whereas the sixth grade level was only 42 per cent. On the test of *Reading for Problem Solving in Science* the average adult accuracy level was 90 per cent and the average sixth grade level was only 63 per cent.

It is apparent then that the adult group used in this study are quite effective readers. It is then altogether likely that the relationships between speed and comprehension scores exhibited by this group more nearly represent the kind of relationships that are optimum than do those of sixth-grade students.

Early in the plans for the study serious consideration was given to the question of whether it would be appropriate to use the same measures and materials with able adult readers as are used with sixth-grade students. It is likely that literature or even "story type" material from science or the social studies that would be suitable and interesting to sixth-grade students would have little

appeal for educated adults. However, the descriptive science materials used were thought to be suited to adults and of interest to them. This premise was strengthened by the fact that most of the adults indicated on an anonymous questionnaire that the materials were interesting. There is little question but that the materials made realistic adult demands upon the reading skills.

STATISTICAL METHOD

In order to substantiate that the two sixth-grade groups were not significantly different from one another in chronological age, mental age, science achievement, and general reading ability, the t test of significance of difference between means was used.[1] The values of t ranged from .004 to .222 indicating that the slight differences between the two groups in these characteristics could easily be explained by chance factors.

Analysis of the data was made with product moment correlations [1] between the various rate and comprehension scores. These correlations for the sixth-grade population are set forth in Table 3. For the adult population the corre-

Table 3: Coefficients of Correlation Between Measures of Sixth-Grade Reading Rate and Comprehension *

| | Comprehension Measures | | | | | | | | | | | |
Rate Measures	Calif. Total	Iowa Total	Calif. Compre-hension	Iowa Compre-hension	Combined Compre-hension	Combined Direc-tions	Combined Inter-pretation	Combined Refer-ences	Rdg. Problem Solving Sci.	Directed Rdg. Sci.—Main Ideas	Directed Rdg. Sci.—Sequence	Average Correla-tions **
Iowa Rate	.56	.82	.50	.71	.70	.54	.66	.41	.38	.46	.39	.58
Reading Problem Solving Science												
Orig. Rate	.26	.27	.09	.21	.19	.16	.29	-.09	.20	.19	.19	.18
Ques. Rate	.01	.23	.02	.28	.23	.24	.12	.23	-.28	-.22	.16	.09
Total Rate	.18	.37	.10	.37	.33	.32	.30	.16	-.09	.31	.16	.25
Directed Reading Science (Main Ideas)												
Orig. Rate	.50	.62	.31	.61	.57	.62	.49	.30	-.03	.29		.45
Ques. Rate	-.06	.20	-.10	.19	.13	.04	.17	.08	.07	.07		.08
Total Rate	.41	.57	.24	.57	.52	.52	.45	.30	-.03	.26		.39
Directed Reading Science (Sequence)												
Orig. Rate	.58	.68	.45	.55	.56	.27	.72	.19	.39	.06		.47
Ques. Rate	-.02	.16	-.12	.10	.05	-.15	.23	-.09	-.13	-.46		-.05
Total Rate	.29	.47	.16	.36	.34	.07	.52	.04	.13	-.25		.22

* The signs of all correlations have been converted to a common base. No sign indicates a positive relationship between speed of reading and comprehension.

** Average correlations were calculated in terms of Z equivalents.

253

Table 4: Coefficients of Correlation Between Measures of Adult Reading Rate and Comprehension *

Rate Measures	Comprehension Measures		
	Directed Rdg. Sci. Main Ideas	Directed Rdg. Sci. Sequence	Reading for Problem Solving in Science
Directed Reading of Science Main Ideas **			
Orig. Rate	.03		
Ques. Rate	.10		
Total Rate	.07		
Directed Reading of Science Sequence †			
Orig. Rate		.04	
Ques. Rate		−.13	
Total Rate		−.09	
Reading for Problem Solving in Science ††			
Orig. Rate			.26
Ques. Rate			.14
Total Rate			.23

* The sign of all correlations have been changed. No sign indicates a positive correlation between speed of reading and comprehension.
** N equals 28
† N equals 23
†† N equals 19

lations between rate and comprehension are given in Table 4.

Comparisons between sixth-grade and adult populations were based upon the rate and comprehension correlations and upon mean comprehension and rate scores.

FINDINGS—SIXTH-GRADE STUDENTS

Fast readers are the best readers when rate is measured by the Iowa Silent Reading Test. In Table 3 the correlations between Iowa rate and the various comprehensions range from .39 to .82 with an average correlation of .58, significant at the one per cent level. The Iowa rate score does not correlate as

strongly with the tests of science comprehension as with most of the Iowa and California tests of comprehension.

On the Reading for Problem Solving in Science Test, fast readers are not the best readers. With this type of reading there is little relationship between rate of initial reading and various measures of comprehension. The highest correlation (See Table 3) was .29 with combined interpretation and the lowest was −.09 with combined references. Although most of these show a low positive relationship between rate of reading and comprehension, all of them are low enough to be explained by chance factors.

Those who read rapidly during a single reading of the Directed Reading of Science Materials Tests also comprehend well on tests of general reading abilities. These correlations (See Table 3) were generally significant ones for both the group reading for the main idea and for the group reading for a sequence of ideas. There are, however, notable exceptions for each group. The rapid readers for main ideas are not those who comprehend well when Reading for Problem Solving in Science where a low negative correlation was found. It is also interesting to note that the correlation between speed of reading science materials and comprehension in general reading abilities as measured by the Iowa and California tests is higher than is the correlation between speed and comprehension when reading the science materials for main ideas (.29).

Exceptions to the generality that those who read rapidly during a single reading of science materials for the purpose of keeping a series of ideas in mind in proper sequence are also those who comprehend well on tests of general reading abilities are found with two of the general reading abilities. Positive correlations but low enough to be explained by chance factors are found with the factors of use of references and following directions. Thus those who read science materials rapidly for sequence are not necessarily those who use references and follow directions well. It is rather strange to find a positive correlation at all between any measure of rate of reading and these somewhat meticulous types of reading comprehension, and, at least for use of references, the correlations with rate do tend to be generally low. However, comprehension of combined directions correlates well with original rate of reading on the Iowa test and on the Directed Reading of Science Tests for main ideas.

It is also interesting to note that the fast readers are not the best readers when both speed and comprehension

are measured on the Directed Reading of Science Tests for sequence of ideas. This correlation (.06) is so low that one can say that there is no relationship between rate and comprehension for this relatively difficult reading task.

For both Directed Reading of Science Tests the correlations between original reading rate and the various comprehension measures average in the upper forties (significant at the five per cent level). The average correlation between original reading rate on the Reading for Problem Solving in Science Test and the various measures of comprehension was positive but low (.18) enough to be possibly explained by chance factors.

In view of the generally strong correlations between each of the measures of initial reading time and most of the various measures of general reading comprehension, it is interesting to note that this same result is not found between comprehension scores and time taken to reread and answer questions. Invariably the correlations are low or negative between comprehension and rate of question answering, which includes rereading. In other words those who read general reading test materials rapidly on a first reading also read well, but those who reread and answer questions rapidly are not necessarily those who read well. These correlations between comprehension and rereading and question-answering time ranged from +.24 to −.28 with average correlations for the three measures (See Table 3) of +.09, +.08, and −.05.

The total rate score is a combination of the original reading rate and the question-answering rate, and it really is not as meaningful as is either of the two scores from which it was derived. However, the correlations between the various comprehension measures and the total rate scores were as high as +.57 between the Iowa comprehension test and the Purpose A (main ideas) total rate scores and as low as −.25 between comprehension and total rate on the Purpose B (sequence) test. The average correlation was not significant at the five per cent level with any of the three tests deriving a total rate score.

FINDINGS—ADULTS AND CHILDREN COMPARED

The reader will recall that while the correlations between rates of original reading and comprehension of general reading abilities in the sixth-grade group were generally high, this was not true between rate and comprehension with the measures of the reading of science. While data for adults was not available regarding general reading abilities, it was possible to relate speed and comprehension measures for each of the three measures of the reading of science materials. Each of these correlations (See Table 4) was low—generally somewhat lower than it was with the children. Fast readers, even among adults, are not the best readers when reading scientific materials to solve a problem, to get the main idea, or to keep a series of ideas in mind in sequence.

A case was made earlier for regarding the fifty-one adult readers as a select group of fairly efficient readers on the basis of their professional and academic accomplishments as well as on the basis of their comprehension scores on the Directed Reading of Science and Reading for Problem Solving in Science Tests. How then do these relatively efficient readers differ from the sixth graders? It would seem that the efficient reader would adjust his rate downward, shift gears so to speak, when he was dealing with either more difficult materials or a more demanding purpose. Did the adults slow down for the more demanding tasks? Did the children?

Comparing the average comprehension score of the sixth-graders with that of the adults (See Table 5) the children scored 8.35 to the adults 15.91 (52 per cent as well) on the Purpose B (sequence) task. On the other hand the children scored 2.78 to the adults 4.60 (60 per cent as well) on the Purpose A task, and did 70 per cent as well on the RPSS (Reading for Problem Solving in Science) Test. Using these relative comprehension percentages as an index of difficulty the Purpose B task was most difficult, then Purpose A, and the RPSS Test was the least difficult.

Looking at the Original Rate—Words Per Minute column of Table 5, it is apparent that both groups slowed their rate somewhat for the more demanding tasks. The adults read the relatively

Table 5: Mean Comprehension Scores and Reading Rates for Adult and Sixth Grade Testees *

Group	Compre-hension	Original Rate	Original Rate—WPM	Question Rate	Total Rate
Adult—Purpose A	4.60	73.28	213.15	32.25	105.53
Sixth—Purpose A	2.78	113.04	138.00	37.21	150.25
Adult—Purpose B	15.91	85.56	182.35	126.13	211.69
Sixth—Purpose B	8.35	114.17	136.62	128.30	242.47
Adult—Reading for Prob. Solv. Sci.	35.89	60.63	291.48	207.74	268.37
Sixth—Reading for Prob. Solv. Sci.	25.10	115.58	152.85	267.54	383.13

* Except for Original Rate—WPM (words per minute) the rate scores are in terms of number of five second intervals. Adult and sixth-grade scores are based upon the five passages read by both age groups.

easy RPSS Test at 291 words per minute. They slowed for Purpose A to 213 w.p.m., and for the more difficult Purpose B they read at only 182 w.p.m. The sixth graders also slowed somewhat as the materials became more demanding. They read the relatively easy RPSS Test at 153 w.p.m., for Purpose A at 138 w.p.m. and for the more difficult Purpose B at 137 w.p.m. But note the difference. Where the adults slowed 78 words per minute between RPSS Test materials and Purpose A and slowed another 31 words per minute between Purpose A and Purpose B, the children slowed only 14 w.p.m. between RPSS and Purpose A and only 1 w.p.m. between Purpose A and Purpose B. Even taking into account the fact that the children were reading more slowly and therefore each word per minute slower is a larger percentage of their actual rate, it is readily apparent that the adults are adjusting their rate to the difficulty of the task much more than are the children.

One way of noting this flexibility of rate on the part of the adults is that they read for Purpose A only 73 per cent as rapidly as they read the RPSS Test, and they read for Purpose B only 86 per cent as rapidly as they read for Purpose A. The children, on the other hand, read for Purpose A 86 per cent as rapidly as they read the RPSS Test, and they read for Purpose B 99 per cent as rapidly as they read for Purpose A.

Another way of noting the increased flexibility of reading rate among the adults is by comparing the average reading time for adults and sixth-graders on each of the three reading tasks. The children read the relatively easy RPSS Test materials only 52 per cent as rapidly as did adults. However, they read for the more difficult Purpose A at 65 per cent of the adult rate and for the most demanding Purpose B, they are reading at 75 per cent of the adult rate. It is likely that this trend to read rela-

tively more rapidly as the task becomes more demanding should be reversed for most efficient sixth-grade reading.

This pattern of less difference between child and adult rates with relatively difficult materials than with relatively easy materials is even more obvious with rereading and question answering time than it is with rate of original reading. The children answered the relatively easy RPSS Test questions 78 per cent as rapidly as did the adults, but they answered the more difficult Purpose A materials at 87 per cent of the adult rate and they went through the most difficult Purpose B materials at 98 per cent of the adult rate. The adults are markedly adjusting their rate to the requirements of the task—slowing down and rereading when it is needed—whereas the children are making relatively minor rate adjustments as the reading demands increase.

CONCLUSIONS

1. Fast readers are the good readers when reading some kinds of materials for some purposes. When reading other kinds of materials for other purposes there is no relationship between speed of reading and ability to comprehend. In general the fast readers are the good readers on the reading tasks presented in the standardized tests of general reading ability. There is no relationship between speed of reading and comprehension for either sixth-grade children or well-educated adults when reading scientific materials for the purpose of solving a problem, getting the main idea, or for keeping a series of ideas in mind in sequence.

2. When either adults or sixth-grade children read the same materials for two different purposes and when the purpose for reading is set for the reader in advance of the reading, the purpose for reading influences the speed with which the reading is done. This finding is sup-

ported in Roossinck's study [3] of the reading of scientists and sixth-grade children.

3. There is no relationship for either adults or sixth-grade students between comprehension and rate of the work-study reading involved in responding to the comprehension questions. In other words those who work rapidly on the rereading and question answering are not necessarily the best readers.

4. Efficient adult readers are much more flexible in adjusting reading rate to the demands of the task than are sixth-grade students. In comparison to the adults, the children read relatively more rapidly as the task becomes more demanding with a consequent loss in relative comprehension. The efficient adult slows his rate and rereads as necessary in keeping with the demands of the task. Sixth-grade students need to develop this type of rate flexibility.

5. Inasmuch as there are different relationships between rate and comprehension when rate is measured as an original reading time and when rate is measured to include rereading and question-answering time, it is important to define what is meant by reading rate. This finding also suggests that authorities in the field of reading would do well to attempt to standardize a practice for measuring reading rate. Since rereading and reorganizing what is read is both necessary and time consuming when reading for some purposes, the most meaningful measure of rate would be one which offered both an original reading time and a time for rereading and answering questions. The total time, which is a sum of these two, destroys some of the specificity of the composite parts and is useful only as an indication of the total amount of time taken to complete a work-study reading task.

REFERENCES

1. Downie, N. M., and Heath, R. W., *Basic Statistical Methods*. New York: Harper and Brothers, 1959.

2. Greene, H. A., and Kelley, V. H., *Iowa Silent Reading Tests*. Yonkers, N. Y.: World Book Co., 1956.

3. Roossinck, Esther P., *Purposeful Reading of Science Materials by Scientists and Children*. Doctoral Thesis, University of Illinois, 1960.

4. *Sequential Tests of Educational Progress*. Co-operative Test Division, Educational Testing Service, Princeton, N. J., 1957.

5. Shores, J. Harlan, and Husbands, Kenneth L., "Are Fast Readers the Best Readers?" *Elementary English*, 27 (January 1950), 52-7.

6. Sullivan, Elizabeth R., Clark, Willis W., and Tiegs, Ernest W., *California Test of Mental Maturity, Non-Language Section*. Los Angeles: California Test Bureau, 1951.

7. Tiegs, Ernest W., and Clark, Willis W., *California Achievement Tests*. Los Angeles: California Test Bureau, 1950.

8. Zim, Herbert S., editor-in-chief, *Our Wonderful World*. Chicago, Ill.: Spencer Press, 1961.

CHAPTER VIII

Issues at Upper Elementary Level

31: Studies of Children's Interest—A Brief Summary *

PAUL WITTY and ASSOCIATES [32]

PART I

What do we mean by the term interest? A first approach to an understanding of the term might be for the reader to look back on his own childhood. For most of us there will be a nostalgic glow as we think about interests that led us to collect birds' eggs or stamps, or marbles or dolls. We shall think about the model auto, the play house, or the boat we built. And we shall reflect with great pleasure on the butterflies we mounted, or the animals we hunted and photographed.

The activities cited above were undoubtedly learned, yet they were "freely" chosen—usually just because we wanted to take part in them. They were often unassociated with work and were not usually the result of home or school pressures. In a way, these interests were the result of need for expression although the need was rarely recognized. Elizabeth Hurlock makes the following statement about interests:

An interest is a learned motive which drives the individual to act in accordance with that interest. It is defined as preoccupation with an activity when the individual is free to choose. When the child finds an activity satisfying, it continues to be an interest.[11]

E. K. Strong discusses interest and interests in this way:

Interests possess the four qualitative criteria of interest, i.e., persistent attention, feeling, activity, and direction. Two additional quantitative criteria, namely intensity and duration, could be attributed to interest but it seems more appropriate to attribute them to interests.[36]

Jacob W. Getzels gives a short but useful definition. "An interest is a characteristic disposition, organized through experience, which impels an individual to seek out particular objects, activities, understandings, skills, or goals for attention or acquisition." [9]

For purposes of this article we have described interest and interests similarly: Interest is a disposition or tendency which impels an individual to seek out particular goals for persistent attention. The goals may be objects, skills, knowledges, and art activities of various kinds. The behavior patterns in seeking these goals may be regarded as particular interests such as collecting objects or viewing TV. They should be

* Reprinted from *Elementary English*, Vol. 37, Nos. 7 and 8 (November and December 1960), pp. 469-75, 540-45, and Vol. 38, No. 1 (January 1961), pp. 33-6, by permission of the National Council of Teachers of English and the senior author.

looked upon as acquired, although they are based upon such factors as the constitutional nature of the individual and his personality structure as affected by his unique experiences and his particular environment.

Methods and Values of Studying Interests

Various methods have been used to study or identify children's interests: the questionnaire, the interview, the "log" of activities, the interest inventory, the anecdotal record, and observation under various conditions.

A child-study technique widely used by teachers is illustrated by the Northwestern University Interest Inventory.[6] Guided by the inquiries on the inventory, the teacher and the pupil discuss informally topics such as favorite leisure activities, hobbies, play preferences, movie and reading habits, and familiarity with community places of interest. The inventory also contains questions related to the child's personal and social problems. Included too are lists of play activities and of books to be discussed.

The writer and his associates at Northwestern University recently devised a series of questionnaires to be employed in studying interests.[1] The items were assembled from diverse sources and listed in four questionnaires which deal with the following areas: play and recreational activities; TV, radio, and movie preferences; reading pursuits; and vocational and educational interests.

A first step in the study of interests perhaps involves an examination of the findings of studies in various interest areas. Another step implies consideration of the ways interests can be used to promote growth in and through reading for individuals and for groups. We shall, in this article, summarize studies of activities, interests, and preferences of pupils in play and recreation; TV,

radio, and the movies; reading; and vocations and education.[12]

Play and Recreational Activities

There are many studies now available of play and recreation.[37] The results vary widely depending on the techniques used, the time the studies were made, and the type of groups employed. In a widely quoted study, published in 1927, H. C. Lehman and the writer [17] considered play to be primarily those activities in which children engaged "just because they wanted to." They employed a play quiz which was submitted to thousands of children and youth. Comparable results were reported by Witty and Coomer for boys and girls studied in 1946.[27] In the latter study one may note a persistence of many play activities previously cited. It was found that by the time boys and girls were six years old they began to show differences in their favored pursuits. The six-year-old girl liked to play with dolls and miniature furniture. She enjoyed "playing house" and making things to use in a playhouse. She participated in some group games such as "drop the handkerchief," but she always took part in individual activities such as "jumping rope" and "playing jacks." When boys were six years of age they liked best to participate in more active but relatively unorganized games such as "tag" and "hide-and-seek." Most boys eight or nine years of age found pleasure in spinning tops, flying kites, playing marbles, and building houses. They experienced satisfaction in "playing cowboy" and similar games in which they pretended to be aviators, soldiers, sailors or marines. Other group activities such as playing catch or games the boys referred to as baseball or football, were also popular; but these pursuits were unlike the more formal competitive sports enjoyed by older boys.

By the time the boys were twelve years of age they turned to more highly organized games such as tennis and base-ball. From twelve to fifteen there appeared to be a sharp decrease in the amount of active, spontaneous play, and a tendency developed on the part of both boys and girls to take part to a greater extent in sedentary pursuits. Going to the movies, listening to the radio, riding in an automobile, and watching contests gained favor during this period.

In 1949, Arthur T. Jersild and Ruth J. Tasch cited the results of questionnaires submitted to pupils in grades one through twelve. Among children's interests, the authors stressed the prominence of experiences involving bodily activity:

It is apparent that experiences involving bodily activity, doing something, or going somewhere are much more prominent than activities of a more intellectual or aesthetic character. Many children do mention reading (and other related matters such as going to the library) in describing what they like best, but the youngsters who mention the delights of reading or other intellectual pursuits constitute a small minority. Moreover, it is mainly the girls who mention such intellectual enterprises.[15]

Prior to the advent of television another study revealed a decrease in participation in games with increase in age. Children in grades five through eight in a midwestern community were asked to rank six activities (sports, games, radio, reading, movies, and hobbies) according to the way "they used their spare time." In 1949 it was reported that:

Reading was clearly overshadowed by sports, radio-listening, games, and movie attendance. The pattern of other activities did not vary greatly from grade to grade. Sports were consistently first; hobbies consistently last. Radio-listening stayed near the top, in second or third place for all the grades. Movies seemed to go up somewhat among older children, as might be expected. Games showed the only consistent downward trend with increased age.[18]

Still another investigation emphasized differences between the sexes in favored activities as well as the changing pattern of interests with increase in age. Children ranging in age from four to thirteen were asked to name their favorite play interests and activities. It was reported in 1951 that:

... the boys enumerated 109, and the girls 70 games with an overlap of 42 items. The greatest number of games was obtained from the boys and girls between 7 and 9 years and the smallest number was mentioned by the children between 4 and 6 years of age....[4]

In recent years, TV has been almost invariably assigned first rank among children's preferred activities. A study made in 1954 by Constance M. McCullough in nine Oakland, California, schools clearly revealed this tendency.[20] These schools were located in three distinctly different socio-economic localities. One district was composed "largely of racial minority groups living in low-cost housing and employed as unskilled labor...." Another group included three schools located in a district of native-born skilled laborers of average income. And the third group consisted of schools situated in a district representing upper-middle-class prosperity. Fifth-grade pupils kept a "log" for one week of their out-of-school activities including before-school, after-school, and after-dinner pursuits. Twenty-six "recreational" activities were cited 6,217 times; fourteen "work" activities, 2,922 times. Televiewing was first in popularity among both boys and girls. Next for the boys was active sports, followed by caring for pets, games, doing homework, straightening own room, and visiting friends. The girls mentioned televiewing first; and these activities followed: preparing meals, straightening own room, washing dishes, active sports, doing homework, and games. Reading of books was low on all lists except for the third group in which nearly half the children reported reading books.[20]

Throughout the recent Northwestern University—Office of Education study, the influence of the mass media—with TV first—was evident.[32] There were, of course, other passive activities which were cited at all grade levels. Despite the time devoted to the mass media, boys and girls still found time to take part in outdoor activities. Boys played baseball and football, swam, and rode bicycles; and girls enjoyed skating, jumping rope, building snowmen, and riding on sleds. Certain activities such as playing marbles, fishing, hunting, hiking, flying kites, and picnicking, which formerly enjoyed greater popularity, were less frequently cited.

We may note in these studies a wide range of play activities enjoyed at every level. Of course, some play pursuits are characteristic of younger children while others are followed by older pupils. Moreover, differences in the popularity of play activities depend upon factors such as the location of a school or group studied and the time or season of the year. Marked individual differences too are apparent in play preferences. In order to utilize play interests effectively in motivating instruction, it is desirable for a teacher to investigate the interests of each new group or class he attempts to instruct. Similarly, it is necessary for the teacher to study each pupil individually to ascertain his particular pattern of interests and preferences.

TV—Children's Most Time-Consuming Activity

Diverse opinions have been expressed about the effects of TV upon children. Some writers emphasize the potentialities of TV as a positive force. Others minimize its significance, while still others stress undesirable results. Parents have asserted that TV is affecting adversely children's interest in reading and in other academic pursuits. Some teachers, too, have pointed to certain un-

fortunate features of TV insofar as children's interest and effort in school are concerned. Some have stated that TV is a "time trap for children" and that "TV produces not only idlers, but also bad taste and bad manners."

It is certainly true that TV consumes a great deal of our time. For example, *Time* magazine of October 13, 1958, cited a report showing that 43 million U.S. homes had TV turned on an average of five hours and 56 minutes each day.

In seeking to evaluate the charges made against TV, one may profitably examine the results of investigations made since TV appeared.

In 1949, TV came to the Chicago area. By May, 1950, 43 per cent of the school children reported that they had access to TV. The percentages increased to 68 in 1951, 88 in 1952, and in 1953, to 92. In 1955 and 1956, 97 per cent had TV sets at home. Studies made by teachers in Chicago, Skokie, and Evanston in 1958 also yielded a percentage of 97. [46] In 1959, 99 per cent of the Evanston children had sets; more than one third had two sets or more, and 3 per cent had color TV.

In 1950, the elementary school pupils spent on the average 21 hours each week with TV; and in 1951, the average dropped to 19 hours. There was a small increase during the next two years—to 23 hours in 1953. In 1955, the average was 24 hours, while in 1957, it was 22 hours. In 1958, the average for elementary school pupils was 20 hours, and in 1959, it was 21 hours.

From the first, high school students were found to give less time to TV than did younger pupils. Their average for 1951 was 14 hours per week. In 1958, it was 13 hours, and in 1959, 12 hours.

In 1950, the children's favorite programs were (in order): *Hopalong Cassidy, Howdy Doody, Lone Ranger, Milton Berle,* and *Arthur Godfrey.* In 1952, *I Love Lucy* became the best liked program of boys and girls. *I Love Lucy* continued in first place until 1955, when acclaim went to *Disneyland*. *Rin Tin Tin* and *Lassie* also became very popular. In 1956, *Disneyland* again held first rank with *I Love Lucy*, third. In 1957, the favorites were *Disneyland, Mickey Mouse Club, I Love Lucy*, and *Lassie*. Changes took place rapidly and in 1958 the following favorites appeared: *Zorro, Disneyland, Bugs Bunny, Shock Theatre*, and *Mickey Mouse Club*.

By far the most popular program for elementary school pupils (grades 1-6) in 1959 was a new presentation, *77 Sunset Strip*. Another new program, *Huckleberry Hound* was second on the list of favorites and *Maverick* appeared in third place. In the primary group (grades 1-3), *Huckleberry Hound* won first place in 1959 while *Zorro* fell from first place in 1958 to fifth place in 1959. In the intermediate group (grades 4-6) *Zorro*, which had ranked first among the favorite programs of 1958, was replaced in 1959 by *77 Sunset Strip*. *Shock Theatre*, however, retained second place in 1959.

Maverick and *American Bandstand* were the most popular programs of high school pupils. Although westerns were popular, they appeared as favorites less frequently than in the younger groups.

Writers have asserted that children today tend to spend less time in outdoor play, hobbies, sports, and creative activities than they did in former years. This condition is sometimes attributed to the influence of TV. The studies of 1950-1951 did suggest some reduction in hobbies and in outdoor activities. However, several more recent studies showed a persistence of old hobbies and the appearance of new ones since TV arrived. For example, T. C. Battin found that 57 per cent of the boys and 59 per cent of the girls followed the same hobbies as before TV.[3] Moreover, 38 per cent of the boys and 34 per cent of the girls reported the cultivation of new hobbies, while only 5 per cent of the boys and 7 per cent of the girls indicated less

hobby interest. It is true, of course, that many pupils today cannot recall a time when they did not have TV.

A recent report of high school boys by Joseph K. Balogh shows results somewhat similar to those obtained in the Northwestern University studies.[2] However, in Balogh's study, a sharper decrease in televiewing took place among high school students; the average sophomore spent twice as much time with TV as did the average senior. It was reported also by Lazarus (quoted by Balogh) that with the advent of TV a serious reduction in "creative activities" has taken place; e.g., playing musical instruments, singing, acting, writing, photographing, etc. We have indicated that this finding while holding in some studies is not corroborated by others, as is apparent in the Battin investigation cited above. Our recent studies have revealed that, since the advent of TV, there has been a marked reduction in movie attendance outside the home, in radio listening, and in the reading of comic magazines.[50]

A British study of TV, sponsored by the Nuffield Foundation, reports data for 4,500 English children of ages 10 to 14. According to *Time*, December 29, 1958, this study disclosed that "Even heavy viewing does not necessarily make children more aggressive or listless, or discourage them from reading or studying."

In the Northwestern University— Office of Education studies, both teachers and parents continued to report the following behavior and adjustment problems associated with TV: fatigue, impoverishment of play, lack of interest in school, increased nervousness, reduction in reading, eye-strain, and mealtime disturbance. In recent reports, however, problems are not so frequently cited as in the earlier studies. A relatively small per cent of the parents and the teachers mentioned such problems in 1959.[32]

A few studies have been designed to

disclose the relationship between the amount of televiewing and attainment in specific school subjects. For example, in San Leandro, California, sixth and seventh grade pupils who televiewed the most, 22¾ to 69½ hours a week, were compared with those who televiewed very little, 0 to 9¾ hours a week. Some differences favoring those who televiewed very little appeared in arithmetic and reading, while little difference was found in the language and spelling attainment of the two groups.[30]

In the Chicago area studies of TV, excessive televiewing seemed to be associated with somewhat lower academic attainment.[50] In one early investigation the average time devoted to TV by pupils in the upper fourth of their classes on standardized educational tests was 21 hours per week, while the average for the lower fourth was about 26 hours. Similar results were obtained again in 1957 and in 1959. We should point out, however, that some pupils were led to do better work in school because of interests awakened by TV. Moreover, in the case of an association on TV with poor academic attainment, other undesirable factors, in addition to excessive televiewing were found.

Several other investigators have reported little relationship between televiewing and the marks pupils receive in school. For example, Donald G. Tarbet concluded from a study of televiewing habits of 1,500 sixth graders within a twelve mile radius of Chapel Hill:

It appears that an average of 20 hours of viewing TV per week is not detrimental to pleasure reading or to academic grades. Of course, sectional differences may have affected these results. With proper training in the schools, harmful effects of TV can be diminished or overcome.[38]

Another study now being carried on in California provides relevant data. In May and June, 1958, fifth and sixth grade pupils were divided into heavy viewers (3 or more hours daily) and light viewers (one hour or less daily). Comparisons were made too of the pupils in the first four grades who according to their parents spent more time televiewing than playing. The following conclusions were drawn: "On the basis of data on hand, we cannot say that heavy television viewing, at any stage of elementary school, significantly lowers school grades. What slight difference there was in grades was overall in favor of the heavy viewers." [34]

PART II

Studies of Radio and Movie Interests

Studies concur in showing that prior to the advent of TV, the amount of time spent daily by children in listening to the radio rose to two or three hours. In general, boys and girls were attracted to the same types of programs at the various grade levels.

In early studies boys and girls were found to go to the movies frequently, and some rated this activity above the radio in their leisure preferences. Although the average attendance was once or twice each week there were some boys and girls who went to the movies more often. Children were found to be attracted to the same elements in the movies that drew them to the radio —action, adventure, and excitement.

Studies of the preferred movies showed generally that elementary school children "liked" the current offerings regardless of their seeming suitability or maturity as revealed by topic or subject matter. As has been frequently shown, boys and girls have liked nearly all Disney productions. Films about cowboys and pilots also proved popular. Less favored were pictures of current events, biography and travel, news shorts and commentaries. Jersild stated:

Children's movie interests roughly parallel their reading and radio interests ... although there are exceptions. For example, "comedy" seems to figure more in movie than in reading interests (unless comic strips are so classed). Reports of movie interests at any given time must be taken with a good deal of reservation, just as in the case with radio programs, for the choices depend to a large degree upon what happens to have been available recently and upon the tastes that have been cultivated by the kind of fare offered in the past.[13]

High school boys and girls were found to attend the movies about once each week, and, as in the elementary school, they appeared to "like best" the current movie shown locally. Moreover, there was little change in the popularity of different types of movies. And sex differences in choices were not pronounced.

In 1947, Alice P. Sterner emphasized the appeal of the movies and the value of experiences via the mass media:

Apparently sex, grade, intelligence, and socio-economic status have little influence upon pupils' choices of specific motion pictures. Generally speaking, a teacher can expect that over 50 per cent of the class will have seen the ten most popular films.

The findings of the studies on the kind of material which pupils most often see, hear, or read are amazingly similar. . . .

Without these media to enrich their lives, many adolescents would lead a dull, dreary existence. The escape may seem to an adult cheap and time wasting, but unless something more wholesome can be offered in its place, such entertainment must be recognized as a very important contribution to youthful happiness.[35]

In the recent Northwestern University—Office of Education Study, it was shown that the radio still has a strong hold upon pupils.[32] The average amount of time spent weekly in radio listening was about 8 hours by pupils in grades 3 through 9. In grades 3 through 6 they spent less time with radio than in the higher grades. In some of our earlier studies, radio equalled the popularity of

TV among high school students. But in this latest study, TV was rated first among favored pursuits at all levels. Not only was TV more popular according to pupil statements, but it also offered, they said, greater possibilities than did the radio or movies for fruitful association with schoolwork.

Movies outside the home were found also to attract many boys and girls, who most often attended them once each week or once in every two weeks. It is clear that movie attendance outside the home has been curtailed, as comparison with earlier studies showed. However, the pupils continued to be attracted by, and to find satisfaction in the same types of movies. Moreover, as in earlier studies, their favored movies appeared to be the ones shown at the theatre near their homes.

Thus, in the foregoing studies, we may observe the marked influence of the mass media upon the lives of children and youth. A problem of primary significance in teaching reading implies the recognition of this force as well as the importance of efforts to utilize interests awakened through the mass media. Another problem involves the encouragement in pupils of balanced patterns of interest in which reading, play, as well as response to the mass media find expression.

Reading Activities and Preferences

Perhaps the first study of reading interests was made in 1893, when M. B. C. True reported "What My Pupils Read." From that date to the present time, more than 200 studies have been undertaken. Among the most influential studies was an investigation reported by L. M. Terman and Margaret Lima who concluded that "there are certain well-defined tendencies in reading interests that change as the child's experience grows and as his imagination and reasoning powers develop."[40] They cited several potent factors in the development of reading interests; for example, age, health and physical development, school environment, home training, and differences in mental ability. Few differences in reading choices appeared until age nine "when the divergence is very marked and the breech continues to widen up to adult life. . . ." [41] At every age level, girls read more than boys.

Boys preferred adventure and vigorous action while girls liked fairy tales, poetry, and "sentimental" fiction. Moreover, boys read more nonfiction than did the girls. Both groups liked animal stories. There was an increase in amount of reading from age 6 to 12 or 13 with a later gradual decrease.

May Lazar reported in 1937 "marked sex differences" in the books chosen for reading. Girls read more books than boys. Mystery stories were ranked first by both boys and girls. Boys chose next, in order, adventure, detective, history, invention, science, nature and animal, fairy tales, biography, novels, stories about home and school, and poetry. After mystery stories girls chose and also gave a higher ranking to stories related to activities at home or at school.[16]

In 1944, Marie Rankin studied the circulation of books in eight public libraries located in Illinois, New York, and Ohio. The libraries were chosen to represent "large and small urban and village populations." She found that the most popular books of contemporary fiction that appeal to adolescent or near adolescent-age children were: *Sue Barton, Senior Nurse,* by Helen D. Boylston; *The Good Master,* by Kate Seredy; *Caddie Woodlawn,* by Carol R. Brink; *Silver Chief to the Rescue,* by Jack O'Brien; *Mountain Girl,* by Genevieve Fox; *The Jinx Ship,* by Howard Pease; *Silver Chief, Dog of the North,* by O'Brien; *Who Rides in the Dark,* by Stephen Meader; *Peggy Covers the News,* by Emma Bugbee; and *Sue Barton, Student Nurse,* by Boylston.[25]

Rankin asked the pupils how they selected books and found the theme or specific topic of the book was the most important single factor.[25]

In the spring of 1945, Paul Witty, Ann Coomer, and Dilla McBean surveyed the favorite books of almost 8,000 children in ten elementary schools of Chicago.[44] Choices included stories of the following types: animal, fairy, and humor with a strong preference for animal stories persisting throughout. Sex differences were similar to those reported in other studies.

Alice P. Sterner found in 1947 that "marked" sex differences in reading tastes persisted among high school pupils.[45] Boys preferred adventure while girls chose "modern fiction." A gradual maturation in book taste also transpired during grades 9 to 12.

Herbert Rudman concluded from a recent study, that "children as a group choose mystery, adventure, children, horses, and dogs to read about." [29] From grade 4 through 8 interest in mystery stories and in sports and recreation increased while interest in cowboy stories and fairy tales decreased. A strong interest in animal stories persisted throughout these grades. Action and adventure seemed to be important items in determining the popularity of stories.

In 1955, Marion W. Taylor and Mary A. Schneider studied the book preferences of Chicago public school pupils in grades 5, 6, 7, and 8.[39] They found a "statistically significant difference between boys and girls in their choice of subject interests." Boys chose adventure as their major interest, followed closely by sports and games. The girls chose stories classified as "Teen-age and Romance" more frequently than any other category. In the top seven titles named by girls, five were teen-age stories. Boys showed a more even distribution of choices at all grade levels—among adventure, animal, sports, and humor.

Differences between boys and girls in the amount and nature of magazine reading are revealed in several studies.

Lazar, for example, found that boys more frequently turned to magazines than did girls.[16] Boys preferred detective and mystery stories while girls selected "general story-types."

In a study reported by Paul Witty and David Kopel [47] in 1938, periodicals proved to be popular in every grade above the second in the elementary school. An investigation by Witty and Coomer [43] showed that among high school pupils about four magazines (other than comics) were read regularly, and three, often. The most popular magazines were the *Reader's Digest, Life,* and *The Saturday Evening Post.*

A study by Miriam Peterson, made in 1955 in five elementary schools of Chicago, showed that among the magazines, boys preferred in order: *Life, Look,* and *Boy's Life;* girls chose *Look, Life,* and *The American Girl.*[24] In general girls preferred magazines about home-making and fashions while boys selected those concerned with science and mechanics.

Newspaper reading has also been studied extensively with similarity shown in the findings of investigators. For example, May Lazar found in 1937 that the comic strips constituted the most popular section of the newspaper.[16] Peterson also reported that Chicago pupils in grades 5 through 8 gave top ranking to comic strips. Boys "attributed second preference to 'sports' in contrast with the low ranking accorded it by girls." [24]

Results of earlier studies, showing sex differences in reading interests and the significance of certain elements in determining the popularity of reading materials were largely corroborated by George W. Norvell's extensive investigations of reading interests, published in 1958.[23] More than 24,000 children in grades 3 to 6 throughout the state of New York were studied. Elements favorable to reading for boys included: adventurous action; physical struggle; human characters; animals; humor;

courage and heroism; patriotism. The following unfavorable elements were cited: description; didacticism; fairies; romantic love; sentiment; girls or women as leading characters; and physical weakness in male characters.

Girls favored the following items: lively adventure; home and school life; human characters; domestic animals and pets; romantic love; sentiment; mystery; the supernatural; and patriotism. And the following items were disapproved: violent action, description, didacticism; boys and girls younger than the reader (except babies) and fierce animals.

It was found that many selections classified as juvenile, increased in appeal to a high point and then declined. Moreover, many rhymes from Mother Goose were enjoyed as late as in Grade 6; many others were rejected as early as in Grade 3. It was pointed out the *Aesop's Fables* and fairy tales were especially popular in grades 3 to 5; and myths, legends, and hero and folk tales were most popular in grades 5 to 7. Sex differences in children's choices in reading appeared early, and girls were found to enjoy many boys' books, but boys rejected almost all girls' books. Some adult magazines proved popular with both boys and girls.

In the San Francisco "mass media" study, interviews were employed to yield estimates of the amount of reading among elementary school pupils. Diaries were also utilized:

The amount of book reading increases from first grade through sixth, and girls read more books than boys. On the family interviews, children in the elementary grades could, on the average, give the names of approximately *three* books each which they could recall reading in the last six months. The communication diaries—which in other media tended to give lower figures than did the interviews—showed fifth and sixth graders reading (or reading in) an average of 1.7 books each during the test week. It is probable, therefore, that the average student in the elementary grades, once he has learned the basic skill of reading, reads between one half and one book per month during the school year. (Report 4, pages 1 and 2) [34]

Among the favorite titles, a number of old favorites appeared but the frequency with which they were cited was low.

The favorite books they named in the fifth and sixth grades include some well known titles which have given pleasure to earlier generations, for example, *Black Beauty* (12 votes), *Little Women* (8 votes), *Wizard of Oz, Heidi, Huckleberry Finn, Tom Sawyer,* and *Treasure Island* (3 each). But even these great old favorites attracted only a tiny percentage of the votes. The significant feature of the data on book titles was the spread, rather than the concentration. (Report 4, page 2)

Magazine reading too was limited and comic books were not read frequently. The average child was found to read a little over two comic books each month. The results of the recent Northwestern University—U.S. Office of Education investigation in the field of reading are provocative.[32] The average amount of time devoted to reading voluntarily by the pupils in grades 3 through 9 was 1.1 hours daily. Moreover, the ninth grade pupil appears to read little more than the middle grade child. Compared with TV, reading has relatively small appeal except perhaps for gifted children.

Most of the books reported by these pupils were in the category of fiction. Poetry, essays, and drama were less often read. Stories of famous people were the best-liked nonfiction group. The most popular books fell in the areas of adventure, mystery, and westerns. Many boys were attracted to "science fiction" too. Girls turned more frequently to stories involving romance. *The Landmark* was frequently cited among the series books; there was occasional mention too of paper-back books. However, the results of this study did not reveal wide interest in reading. Like the Stanford study (Report No. 4), this investigation showed that relatively little time is spent on books outside the school. The magazine reading of the older pupils was limited largely to *Life, Look, The Saturday Evening Post,* and news periodicals.

Teachers and parents should attempt to improve the status of reading among children and youth today. For it is clear that a disproportionate amount of time is given to the mass media as compared with that accorded reading. Later we shall suggest some ways by which an improvement might be brought about through the cooperative efforts of parents and teachers.

Vocational and Educational Interests

One of the first studies of vocational interests was reported in 1898 by Will C. Monroe. He presented the following question to 1,775 Massachusetts school children ranging in age from 8 to 16 years: "Tell what you would like to do when you grow to be men (and women) and why."

If this study may be accepted as a probable index of the future activity of our present school population, it indicates that the teaching business will be more largely in the hands of women than it is today. The other professions—the ministry, medicine, and law—are preferred by twenty-one per cent of the boys and eight per cent of the girls.[21]

The need for guidance was suggested by the results of this early study as well as by later investigations. In studies made in 1938, aviation represented the most popular preference of second grade boys.[31] The popularity of aviation was maintained throughout the grades, although in the fifth grade it was outranked by medicine, and in the seventh grade by engineering.

Another investigation which yielded unrealistic or impractical choices was made by Arthur T. Jersild and his associates.[14] Four hundred children, of ages five through twelve were studied:

Almost half of all the children interviewed (47.1 per cent) when asked what they wanted to be when they were grown chose occupations in the professions or as business executive, artist, writer, musician, etc. Nursing, aviation, clerical work, skilled labor, and petty trades comprised 33.2 per cent of the choices; 5 per cent of the children were undecided and did not wish to commit themselves; 6.8 per cent chose semi-skilled and unskilled labor; the remaining choices were scattered among other categories, such as sports, motherhood, unintelligible replies, or general, indefinite answers.

Vocational choices of many secondary school students, like those of elementary school pupils, have been found to be largely the expression of vain hopes.[10] However, the choices at the secondary level are somewhat more realistic than in the lower grades:

Vocational interests change frequently during adolescence. The most frequent and most radical changes occur early in adolescence as there is a shift from unrealistic to more realistic vocational aims.

Two investigators studied the relationship of the occupational choice to the pursuit of occupation by tenth and twelfth grade boys in Wisconsin public schools.[26] More than 45 per cent of the subjects in the two groups were found to enter the occupation chosen in the tenth and twelfth grades.

Two other investigators studied the attitudes of pupils toward occupations. Thirteen thousand former high school and junior college students commented on their needs.[19]

The urgent need for more help in choosing and preparing for an occupation was voiced by large numbers of former students. Youth wanted help with more exploration and preparation for vocations and more vocational guidance and placement.

The pupils in the recent Northwestern University—Office of Education investigation appeared to be more realistic in their choices of occupations than were pupils in studies made a decade or more ago.[32] Their preferred occupations were those in which many might reasonably expect to engage. Girls mentioned such occupations as teacher, nurse, and secretary. The boys chose engineer, scientist, and pilot most frequently. The choices reflect too the present-day demand for airline stewardesses, engineers, and pilots.

These choices, while more realistic than those reported in some earlier studies, are, nevertheless, impractical in many instances. Obviously, guidance is a crucial need which should begin early and should lead to realistic *individual* choice.

These pupils concentrated their participation in a small number of jobs for remuneration. Babysitting was the one most often mentioned. Despite this fact, a few time-honored occupations were in favor. For example, boys continued to have paper routes. But few boys mentioned caddying, running errands, delivering messages, tending lawns and caring for gardens, jobs which were cited more often in earlier studies.

A high percentage, both of boys and girls—82 per cent in grades 7 through 9—stated that they planned to go to college. Moreover, the fact that very high percentages of the parents of these pupils wanted their children to attend college suggests that college education for his children is a goal of the typical American parent today.

We have already indicated that some of the children's vocational choices represented largely illusory hopes. This finding suggests the need for guidance. Certainly it is clear that reading offers a helpful avenue in the cultivation of more suitable choices. It should be noted too that such strong interests may be employed advantageously in motivating instruction.

Educational Implications and Recommendations

Although some parents and teachers continued to indicate that pupils read less now than before the advent of TV, the number of such complaints has decreased. Today, relatively few pupils state that TV has influenced their reading adversely. And many say that televiewing actually has led to an increase in their reading. It has become clear that the average amount of reading has probably increased a little since the advent of TV. This is suggested by reports on the number of books read as well as by statements of boys and girls concerning particular books read. But the small amount of time devoted to reading— about one hour each day—stands out in sharp contrast with the larger amount —three hours daily—given to TV by the younger pupils.

We have already indicated that criticisms of TV were made by a minority only of the parents who stressed the adverse effects on reading as the most undesirable outcome. These protests about children's reading may have been compensations in certain cases for the parents' own failure to read widely.

Gordon Dupee stresses the significance of the home and the attitudes of adults in determining whether children turn to reading:

... ours is a society which does not honor reading.... Forty-two per cent of the houses in America today are without bookcases or bookshelves of any kind.... A survey by one of America's leading encyclopedias revealed that 84 per cent of the families purchasing their encyclopedias had not opened it within one year after purchase. It [the set] was bought as cultural furniture.[7]

It was noted in several recent studies that hobbies, crafts, music, and cultural activities in general were seldom mentioned. However, TV should not be held solely responsible for this condition since Jersild and Tasch described a similar situation in 1949.[15]

Some critics may conclude that the present pattern of interests of boys and girls is too heavily weighted with activities associated with the mass media. They may believe too that the mass media are exercising a restrictive influence upon the recreation, the vocational ambitions, and the reading of too many boys and girls. Certainly the widespread influence of the mass media may be noted again and again in the behavior and attitudes of present-day children and youth. Thus pupils often want to emulate the characters presented in adventurous or glamorous situations on TV or radio or in the movies.

There is a rather widespread concern on the part of parents over the quality of many mass media programs. Parents and teachers alike have repeatedly expressed their desire for programs of higher quality and have voiced again and again their disapproval of presentations featuring crime and violence.

Edgar Dale points out that:

some producers ... have the curious belief that if no proof of harm can be offered, the content under discussion is suitable. Harm, however, has varied disguises. A culture can be drowned in a sea of triviality. A society can prolong into adulthood the film and TV classification of men as either discernibly 'good' or 'bad.'[5]

We might add that children may by too frequent exposure to programs emphasizing violence gradually come to accept crime and destructive acts as almost normal ways of life. Their sensitivity to human suffering may also gradually become dulled. On the other hand, it is generally agreed that a great potential resides in TV and the other mass media for motivating constructive endeavor of many kinds.

For many pupils, and for adults as

well, lack of interest appears to be an outstanding factor in their failure to read widely and well. For such individuals an association of reading with strong interests may have outstanding positive values. Such an association was in part responsible for the remarkable success of the army's program during World War II for functionally illiterate men. Herein was clear-cut unmistakable evidence of the value of a program of group and individual instruction associated with interests and needs.[49]

Case-studies could readily be given to show the value of the use of strong interests to motivate and encourage effective reading.[42] In case-studies one can show too, large gains in reading skills associated with wide reading based on pupil interest. In some cases the establishment of new interests and the redirection of old ones are necessary. But the value of reading experience chosen in accord with interest and need has been shown repeatedly in case-studies to lead pupils to attain a better understanding of themselves and their social environment. It has been shown also to result in the building of a more suitable ideal of self, including attitudes that lead to more realistic vocational and educational choices. [48]

In educational periodicals and books, there are a number of recent accounts in which very successful endeavor is reported in programs based on study of pupil interests. Several are found in the monograph entitled *Developing Permanent Interest in Reading.*[28] For example, an analysis of the responsibility of the teacher in the primary grades is offered by Claribel M. Nayder who stresses the responsibility of the teacher for ascertaining and utilizing interests as well as the necessity of teachers working cooperatively with parents and teachers.[22]

Several articles have cited the use of TV interests to foster improvement in attitude toward reading and to promote skill in reading. In an inspiring article,

Charles G. Spiegler emphasized the potentialities of TV, and stressed the significance of the interest factor.

Beyond a doubt Johnny reads if his interest is stirred, and beyond a doubt, Johnny can be taught reading if interest is the keynote.
... Even with the slowest readers, the teacher makes interest the bridge.[33]

In another article on effective ways to adjust instruction to individual differences in grades 7 to 9, Leo C. Fay states:

Take advantage of interest. A strong interest in a particular topic is often motivation enough for a student to read what for him would be relatively difficult material.[8]

Direct instruction associated with the use of TV or movies in the classroom has proved most effective too in stimulating interest in reading. For example, James Fitzwater and the writer of this article have pointed to some results of the use of films, film-readers, and related language experience in fostering children's vocabulary development and the ability to interpret printed materials.[45] Eight films and eight film-readers were employed in this experiment with second grade children. Data were presented which revealed that great gains in reading skill were made and that desirable attitudes toward reading were developed and maintained. Stressed also was the value of this approach in motivating pupils and in engendering interest. Finally, attention was called to the fact that films may be used to provide a common background of experience and that this experience may be sufficiently varied and vivid enough that every child—the slowest as well as the best in ability within a group—will be led to respond in individually desirable and satisfying ways.

Despite the great potentialities in the use of the mass media, many critics continue to point to undesirable features. The antidote to the undesirable aspects of TV as well as to other standardizing influences lies in the provision of a constructive program of guidance. In such a program the combined efforts of parents and teachers are needed. Working together, they should examine the recreational opportunities of their school and communities. They should try to

offer boys and girls abundant opportunities for varied play activities and creative pursuits of many kinds that will balance their craze for sedentary activities. The development of criteria for the selection of TV and other leisure pursuits is a good way to foster improvement.

REFERENCES

1. *A Study of the Interests of Children and Youth*. A co-operative research project performed (1958-59) in accord with a contract between Northwestern University and the Office of Education, U.S. Department of Health, Education and Welfare. Paul A. Witty, Director of Project (Northwestern University); Robert A. Sizemore, Assistant Director (Toledo Public Schools); Paul Kinsella (Skokie Public Schools); Ann Coomer (Chicago Public Schools); Stanley Krippner (Northwestern University). Report was submitted to the Office of Education, U.S. Department of Health, Education, and Welfare in February 1960. Parts of this article are adapted from this report.

2. Balogh, Joseph K., "Television-Viewing Habits of High School Boys," *Educational Research Bulletin*, Vol. 38, No. 3 (March 11, 1959), pp. 66-71.

3. Battin, T. C., *Television and Youth*. Report published by TV Information Committee, National Association of Radio and TV Broadcasters, Washington, D.C., 1954.

4. Conn, Jacob H., "Children's Awareness of Sex Differences (II), Play Activities and Game Preferences," *Journal of Child Psychiatry*, Vol. 11 (1951).

5. Dale, Edgar, *The News Letter*, Vol. 21, No. 8 (May 1956).

6. Developed from the Witty-Kopel Interest Inventory described in Paul Witty and David Kopel, *Reading and the Educative Process*. Boston: Ginn and Co., 1939.

7. Dupee, Gordon, "Can Johnny's Parents Read?" *The Saturday Review* (June 2, 1956), pp. 5-7.

8. Fay, Leo C., *Improving Reading in All Curriculum Areas*, Supplementary Educational Monographs, No. 76, compiled and edited by W. S. Gray, Chicago: University of Chicago Press, November 1952, p. 36.

9. Getzels, Jacob W., "The Nature of Reading Interests," in *Developing Permanent Interest in Reading*, Supplementary Educational Monographs, No. 83, compiled and edited by Helen M. Robinson, Chicago: University of Chicago Press, December 1956, Chapter I, p. 7.

10. Hurlock, Elizabeth B., *Adolescent Development*. New York: McGraw-Hill, 1949, p. 275.

11. ———, *Child Development*. New York: McGraw-Hill, 1956, p. 440.

12. In Chapter VIII of the forthcoming *Sixtieth Yearbook of the National Society for the Study of Education*, these interests are related to effective reading instruction with examples from case-studies and classroom practice.

13. Jersild, Arthur T., *Child Psychology*, 4th edition. New York: Prentice-Hall, 1954, p. 508.

14. ———, Markay, Frances V., and Jersild, Catherine L., *Children's Fears, Dreams, Wishes, Daydreams, Likes Dislikes, Pleasant and Unpleasant Memories*, Child Development Monographs, No. 12, New York: Teachers College, Columbia University, 1933, p. 36.

15. ———, and Tasch, Ruth J., *Children's Interest and What They Suggest for Education*. New York: Bureau of Publications, Teachers College, Columbia University, 1949.

16. Lazar, May, *Reading Interests, Activities, and Opportunities of Bright, Average and Dull Children, Teachers College Contributions to Education*,

No. 707. New York: Teachers College, Columbia University, 1937.

17. Lehman, H. C., and Witty, Paul, *Psychology of Play Activities*. New York: A. S. Barnes, 1927.

18. Mauck, Inez L., and Swenson, Esther, "Study of Children's Recreational Reading," *Elementary School Journal*, Vol. 50 (November 1949), pp. 148-50.

19. McCreary, William H., and Kitch, Donald E., "Now Hear Youth," *Bulletin No. 9*, California State Department of Education, Sacramento (October 1953).

20. McCullough, Constance M., "A Log of Children's Out-of-School Activities," *The Elementary School Journal*, Vol. 58 (December 1957), pp. 157-65.

21. Monroe, Will C., "Vocational Interests of Children," *Education*, Vol. 18 (January 1898), pp. 259-64.

22. Nayder, Claribel M., in *Developing Permanent Interest in Reading*, op. cit. p. 98.

23. Norvell, George W., *What Boys and Girls Like to Read*. New Jersey: Silver Burdett Company, 1958.

24. Peterson, Miriam, *Reading Preferences and Interests of Pupils in the Chicago Public Elementary Schools, Grades IV through VII*, An Unpublished Ph.D. Study, Northwestern University, August 1955.

25. Rankin, Marie, *Children's Interests in Library Books of Fiction*, Teachers College Contributions to Education, No. 906. New York: Teachers College, Columbia University, 1944, pp. 136-8.

26. Ranstad, Robert, and Rothney, John W. M., "Occupational Classification and Research Results," *Personnel and Guidance Journal*, Vol. 36 (March 1958), pp. 465-72.

27. Reported by Paul Witty, *Reading in Modern Education*. Boston: D. C. Heath, 1949.

28. Robinson, Helen M. (compiler and editor), op. cit.

29. Rudman, Herbert C., "The Informational Needs and Reading Interests of Children in Grades IV through VII," *The Elementary School Journal*, Vol. 55 (May 1958), pp. 502-12.

30. Scott, Lloyd F., "Television and School Attainment," *Phi Delta Kappan*, Vol. 38 (October 1956), pp. 25-8.

31. See studies reported in *Reading in Modern Education*, Chapter II, op. cit.

32. Sizemore, Robert, Coomer, Ann, Kinsella, Paul, and Krippner, Stanley, associates in the Northwestern University —Office of Education Study of Interests. See also "The Role of Interests" by Paul Witty, Chapter VII in *Development In and Through Reading*, Sixtieth Yearbook, Part I, National Society for the Study of Education.

33. Spiegler, Charles G., in *Developing Permanent Interest in Reading*, op. cit. p. 185.

34. Stanford Institute for Communication Research, Preliminary Report No. 2, *Television*, The San Francisco Study of Children and Mass Communication, Palo Alto, California (mimeographed reports, 1959).

35. Sterner, Alice P., *Radio, Motion Picture, and Reading Interests*, Teachers College Contributions to Education, No. 932. New York: Teachers College, Columbia University, 1947.

36. Strong, E. K., Jr., *Vocational Interests: 18 Years after College*. Minneapolis: University of Minnesota Press, 1955.

37. Summaries of studies of interests have been made by Elizabeth Hurlock, *Child Development*, op. cit. and by Irving R. Melbo and John A. Hockett, in *Children's Interests*, 12th Yearbook, California Elementary School Principals, 1940. See also Dale B. Harris, "Interests and Attitudes as Motives," Chapter V in Forty-ninth Yearbook, National Society for the Study of Education, Part I, *Learning and Instruction*. Chicago: University of Chicago Press, 1950.

38. Tarbet, Donald G., "The Televiewing Habits of Pupils," *The Clearing House* (April 1956), pp. 486-7.

39. Taylor, Marion W., and Schneider, Mary A., "What Books Are Our Children Reading? The Reading Interests of Upper-Grade Pupils," *Chicago Schools Journal*, Vol. 38 (January-February 1957), pp. 155-60.

40. Terman, Lewis M., and Lima, Margaret, *Children's Reading: A Guide for Parents and Teachers*, revised edition. New York: Appleton and Co., 1931, p. 131.

41. Op. cit. p. 68.

42. Witty, Paul, Chapter 3 in *Pupils Are People* (edited by Nellie Appy). New York: Appleton-Century, 1941. Paul Witty, "Reading Success and Emotional Adjustment," *Elementary English* (May 1950).

43. Witty, Paul A., and Coomer, Ann, "Activities and Preferences of a Secondary School Group," *The Journal of Educational Psychology*, Vol. 24 (February 1943), pp. 65-76.

44. ———, and McBean, Dilla," Children's Choices of Favorite Books: A Study Conducted in Ten Elementary Schools," *The Journal of Educational Psychology*, Vol. 37 (May 1946), pp. 266-78.

45. Witty, Paul, and Fitzwater, James P., "An Experiment with Films, Film-Readers, and the Magnetic Sound Track Projector," *Elementary English* (April 1953).

46. Witty, Paul, and Kinsella, Paul, "Children and TV—A Ninth Report," *Elementary English* (November 1958). Other studies have been published in former years in *Elementary English*.

47. Witty, Paul, and Kopel, David, *Reading and the Educative Process*, op. cit.

48. Witty, Paul, and Olson, Norma, "Non-Readers in the High School," *Exceptional Children* (March 1952).

49. Witty, Paul, *Reading in Modern Education*, op. cit.

50. ———, "What Children Watch on TV," *The Packet Series Bulletin*, Vol. 14, No. 2, Boston: D. C. Heath and Co. (Winter 1959-60).

32: An Experimental Program in Reading *

WALTER B. BARBE and TINA S. WATERHOUSE

The developmental approach in teaching reading, while it is generally accepted as the "best" method, is difficult to put into practice. Meeting each child at his level, particularly in the upper elementary grades where there is frequently a range of from five to ten years in reading ability, is sometimes impossible. Another problem which is encountered in the developmental program is that many upper elementary teachers know little or nothing about teaching beginning reading, and therefore are unable to cope with the problems of their children who are reading at the primary grade levels.

THE PROBLEM

Recognizing the difficulties in teaching reading at the upper elementary school level, the teachers at Highland Park Elementary School decided to initiate an experimental reading program. The procedure was to group all children in the upper elementary grades by reading level for one period each day. It was the purpose of this study to determine the effectiveness of such a program in teaching reading.

PROCEDURE

During October of the school year, each teacher rated the reading grade level of the children in her room. A standardized group reading test was administered. In addition to these ratings, each child was given an individual informal reading test by the staff of the local reading center. With these three scores, the teachers met and placed each child in a group according to his reading level.

* Reprinted from *Elementary English*, Vol. 33, No. 2 (February 1956), pp. 102-4, by permission of the National Council of Teachers of English and the senior author.

Children included in the program were fourth, fifth, and sixth graders. There are two classes at each grade level at Highland Park. This provided six teachers for the program and approximately 180 children.

Seventeen children were reading on the first and second grade level and so they were all assigned to one reading group. About thirty children were reading at third grade level and were assigned to another reading group. The fourth grade group, numbering about 70 in all, was split into two groups. About 35 children were reading at fifth grade level and were assigned to one group and about 30 were reading at sixth and above level and were assigned to another group.

Following this procedure, it was not necessary to hire any extra teachers. The regular upper elementary grade teachers were then assigned to teach the reading group at the level at which they felt themselves to be best prepared. One of the sixth grade teachers, having formerly been a primary teacher, was assigned to teach the children in the group reading at the first and second grade level.

This division provided for the grouping of upper elementary school children according to their reading level, irrespective of whether they were in the fourth, fifth or sixth grades. The group to which they were assigned, however, consisted of fourth, fifth and sixth graders who were all reading at the same level. The groups were called reading clubs. Most children changed

to another teacher at the time of the club meeting. There were a few children who had their regular teacher, for she was the one who was teaching the reading club at that child's level.

The regular Lyons Carnahan Reading Series was introduced into the school. None of the children were familiar with the books. No mention was made of the grade level at which the children were working even though they could tell the level of the book in which they were reading. Teaching procedures outlined in the manuals were followed.

In November, soon after the program was started, the children in each group were given the Gates Reading Survey, Form I. In May, shortly before the end of school, when the children had been in the program for a six months period, the Gates Reading Survey, Form II, was administered.

RESULTS

In Table 1 the results of testing in reading are presented. In addition to the results obtained by testing before and after the program began, less objective, but equally valuable, information was obtained from the experiment. Reaction to the program by parents, teachers, and children was overwhelmingly favorable. Since grades were not given for work in the reading clubs, no stigma was attached to reading from a book below one's grade level. The children particularly liked the idea of reading clubs, and several stated that they liked

Table 1: Mean Scores on Gates Reading Tests at Beginning and End of Experimental Reading Program

Actual Grade Placement	Mean Grade Level (Nov., 1953)	Mean Grade Level (May, 1954)	Increase Nov.-May
Grade IV (N = 62)	3.9	4.8	+ .9
Grade V (N = 56)	4.9	6.1	+1.2
Grade VI (N = 51)	5.6	6.5	+ .9

the idea of moving to another class "just like they do in junior high school."

The children in the lowest group received far more attention than they could possibly have received in a regular classroom. These children were proud of their success at their own level when they did not have to compete with children reading years ahead of them. Those in the highest reading group were far more enthusiastic about reading because of the absence of the traditional lock-step pace.

The teachers expressed the belief that more material could be covered more effectively when all of the children in the class were somewhat near the same reading level.

Even though the period between testing was only six months, there was a mean increase of .9 of one year in grades IV and VI and of 1.2 years in Grade V. Actually, these data reveal only part of the success of the program, for no effort was made to see how much progress could be made. Instead, each child was taught at his level, and was allowed to progress at his own rate. The greatest amount of individual improvement was noticeable in those children in the groups working at the lower levels.

SOME CONCLUSIONS AND IMPLICATIONS

The purpose of the study was to determine if upper elementary school children could be better provided for in groups in which the children were all reading at the same level. The data collected clearly indicates that a great deal of progress can be made when children are grouped for reading instruction.

The implications of this study are:

1. The traditional lack of attention to reading instruction at the upper elementary level can be partially overcome by grouping the children for one period each day at their actual reading level and instructing them from a textbook at that level.

2. Opposition from parents, teachers, and children to grouping according to reading level can be avoided when the program is clearly defined in terms of purpose and procedures. It is particularly necessary that the teachers themselves believe in such a program and be willing to exert the initial effort to make such a program a success.

3. Teaching according to a developmental philosophy is more feasible when children are grouped according to reading level.

4. Children do not object to reading materials below their actual grade placement, if they are not put in a class with children too far below their own grade placement.

5. Where grouping is employed, more opportunity is available to provide an enriched reading program for children who are advanced in reading.

6. The needs of children can more nearly be met when they are grouped according to reading ability.

While grouping within the regular classroom is accepted as an essential for teaching reading, there is much evidence that teachers in the upper elementary grades do not have sufficient time to give all the attention that is needed to each of the reading groups. By grouping the children by reading level at Highland Park School, it was found that it was possible to give more attention to reading and, at the same time, make the job of teaching reading easier for the teacher.

33: Teaching Critical Reading in the Middle Grades *

JERALDINE HILL

One of the purposes in teaching children to read is that they may ultimately be able to think for themselves. A good reader is not only one who can read, but one who does read, enjoys reading and knows how to use what he has read. A search through literature on teaching reading reveals much written on teaching children to read and to enjoy reading. However, there is very little practical material available on teaching a child how to use what he has read, or, put another way, to do critical reading. Most of the material found has been written on teaching critical reading through the content areas above the elementary school level.

Spache [21] lists six skills necessary for critical reading:

1. Investigating sources
2. Recognizing author's purposes
3. Distinguishing opinion and fact
4. Making inferences
5. Forming judgments
6. Detecting propaganda devices.

These are separate from comprehension skills that require a lower level of inferences and interpretations. These are skills that go beyond the comprehension skills needed. Although you would not expect younger children to think as maturely as those in high school, this does not prove that middle graders cannot be taught to think critically. In fact, middle grade children are at the point in their development when they are questioning. They ask, "Can you prove it?" of their peers, their teachers and their parents. They are skeptical when proof is not available.

Content areas can be used to teach critical reading to these children. Beyond this, the very books read for recreation or as part of an individualized reading program can also be used to teach the skills necessary to do critical reading.

One of the types of books that is of interest to children is biography and biographical fiction. A way to help children grow in their ability to do critical thinking is to compare various biographies and fictionalized stories about one famous person. For example, the life of Benjamin Franklin might be used. The child could read Ben and Me [13] and the one the D'Aulaire's wrote on Benjamin Franklin [5] and use some reference book's account of the life of Benjamin Franklin. The three accounts could be compared as to what phases of the person's life are covered, any bias shown by the author, what is historically true, what is perhaps legend and what perhaps is pure fiction. For the more able readers, adult versions and the children's versions of the biography of a famous person written by the same author can be used. The four-volume biography of Abraham Lincoln by Sandburg [20] and the book he wrote for children, Abe Lincoln, [19] or Esther Forbes' factual account of Paul Revere [9] and Johnny Tremain, [8] the fictionalized account of Paul Revere, can be studied for the author's different purposes in each book, variations in style between adult and children's versions, as well as distinguishing fact, legend and fiction.

Books about families are another kind of book of interest to the middle grade

* Reprinted from Elementary English, Vol. 39, No. 3 (March 1962), pp. 239-43, by permission of the National Council of Teachers of English and the author.

child. These include books such as *The Moffats*,[7] *The All-of-a-Kind Family*,[23] the *Little House*[25] books. Children can discuss the different types of families, their homes, their standards of living, their ideas of discipline, etc. This helps to build the understandings of how families differ and yet are basically alike. Books such as *Elder Brother*,[12] *Thirty One Brothers and Sisters*,[16] *Henner's Lydia*[6] and other De Angeli books give a picture of other cultures, ethnic and social groups and their type of family life. Books such as these also aid in developing more understandings of human interrelations.

Similar to the books about families are books about particular boys or girls. Such books as *Shen of the Sea*,[3] *The Courage of Sarah Noble*,[4] *Caddie Woodlawn*,[2] *Adam of the Road*,[10] *Isle of the Blue Dolphins*,[18] can be used to discuss the problems of the main character, his fears, his dreams and how he shows courage beyond his fears. The personality of the main character can be studied as to his strengths and weaknesses shown in the story, his values and judgments, and whether he is shown to have strong biases or prejudices. Children can consider what they would do under similar circumstances and project what would have happened if the children's suggestions were followed.

Puzzles are a challenge to middle grade children that they find hard to resist. A way to use books to stimulate puzzles is to have children write their version of how a book came to be written, or write how they would have ended a particular book if they had written it. Then the children can go even further and write to publishers and authors and ask about the story behind the books. This would also give children an opportunity to learn more about the publication of books and give them more knowledge of authors as real people. There is, of course, already published, *The Story Behind Modern Books*,[17] but it is quite old. It might serve as a starting point to write about more current books.

Writing to publishers and authors can serve yet another purpose in teaching critical reading. A complete study can develop from writing to various publishers of books that are familiar and favorites of the children. This can take the form of a study of all of the books of a particular author or illustrator. This can lead to a discussion of a particular style of one author, expressions he uses in more than one of his books, similarity of characters or locales. It can be a study of the new books for the year that will be published by one company, their variety, the subject most popular for that year. Sometimes publishers will loan a school original manuscripts, galley sheets or original illustrations. This can lead to an appraisal of the field of publishing, the cost, the way books are advertised, the format, and so forth. The impact that publishers have on what is available for children to read can be discovered from such a study. The people who write books are of much interest to young readers. They enjoy trying to find out as much as they can about the authors' lives and families. *The Junior Book of Authors*[11] and magazines such as *Horn Book* and *Elementary English* can be of much help to them in seeking information about authors. Of course, writing to the author is always a way to learn how he lives, how he chooses his plots, his philosophy of writing, his family and his interests.

The pictures in books fascinate young children. As they grow older they still enjoy pictures, but their books have fewer and fewer illustrations. Children's picture books can be used by older readers for a different purpose. The different styles of various illustrators can be compared. The study of the style and media of one illustrator can be made by collecting as many books as possible and comparing the earlier books of an illustrator with his more recent books. One can never forget the change of style of Robert McCloskey from *Make Way for Ducklings* [15] to *Time of Wonder*. [14] It is very hard to believe that they were done by the same person. Another use of illustration is the comparison of media, color depth and the aesthetic aspects of illustrations. Older readers can appraise the part that the illustrations play in the stories in picture books. A more mature appraisal can be made by a consideration of how illustrators have affected the entire development of children's books.

Many of the basal reader series have a watered down version of famous children's books. Children can read the original books and compare the stories in the readers. They can evaluate the similarities and the differences of the two versions as to simplicity or difficulty, degrees of descriptive language, style and interest. Readers also have simplified versions of folk and fairy tales which can also be compared. Another comparison can be made between the original versions of classics, such as, *Little Women*, [1] *Tom Sawyer*, [24] *Treasure Island*, [22] and series of these that are published in simpler and more attractive form by some book publishers. Don't be surprised if some children do not prefer the original! Studies such as these may include possible reasons for making more than one version, the job of editing, the place of illustrations, differences in cost, and so on.

Children can examine the advantages of various kinds of book clubs in learning how to build up their own personal libraries. Such clubs as the Junior Literary Guild, the Arrow Book Club, the Weekly Reader Book Club, will be good for this. Some readers may move into the adult Book-of-the-Month Club, the Literary Guild Book Club, *American Heritage*. Then there are the scientific types of monthly books, such as *Around the World Program, Know Your America, Nature Program, National Aviation*. The good periodicals for children should be introduced to them, also, for lighter and shorter reading periods. We build discriminating adult readers by helping children to be discriminating in their reading tastes.

One of the many of the mass media that can be used in the classroom to help children develop the ability to read critically is the newspaper. The accounts of important events can be compared in several newspapers. The newspaper can also be used as a spring board into the study of how news is gathered and reported, the effect that the printed words has on the children's lives. More advanced readers may be interested in the *New York Times,* the *Commercial Appeal.*

Poetry is one of the best ways to help children to read critically. For poetry is an abbreviated thought. The poet must leave so much to the reader's imagination. A keen interest in poetry is not developed in a short time. Poetry takes much tasting, much thinking, much time to assimilate the thoughts presented. But for these reasons it must not be neglected. Poetry, as all other reading, should be partly for enjoyment. It should never be presented to young children for analysis of structure, meter or rhyme. It should be presented for the beauty of the thought it brings, the release of emotion through verse. It can be used, without hindering any of these, to discuss and appraise the thought presented and its effect on the reader. Children should be encouraged to see that they, too, can write poetry. However, if we use poetry with children as we should, they will soon discover this for themselves.

There are many sources that a teacher can have in her classroom to help children develop an ability to use and learn more about books, authors and illustrators. Besides many and varied trade books, there are bibliographies put out by the American Library Association, listing books of various age levels and subjects. There are bibliographies of adult books that young people will enjoy. This association also publishes *Libraries Bulletin.* The University of Chicago Children's Book Center publishes an excellent book list about books, their authors and illustrators. The *New York Times* Book Review Section and Supplement has valuable articles, also. The *Saturday Review* and the *Atlantic Monthly* magazines will be of interest to more mature readers. There are many more, but one of the best is a teacher or librarian who tells children of new books, shows them or reads from them to children. This personal appraisal means more to most children than a printed account, no matter how well done the printed account may be. Children, too, can be instrumental in encouraging others to read favorites by preparing bibliographies that they feel other children may enjoy.

The role of a school librarian in helping children grow in interest and ability with books is very important. The public librarian is also important. One who reads and tells stories to children and discusses their reading with them is invaluable. She is the spirit of the library to children. How she helps and guides children with books is one indi- cation of how they will continue their use of libraries in the future. A good librarian will encourage children to feel at home in the library, to enjoy it. She will help children learn the aids the library can give. It is possible for even young children to become acquainted with the card catalog. As they grow older, the librarian can introduce the indexes that are available, and help them to discover aids to their own book needs. If teacher and librarian work together, the ways they can help children keep growing and stretching their abilities to use books are unlimited.

Any one of these suggestions may be used as a starting point to get children to thinking for themselves and interacting with the material that they are reading. There are, of course, many other ways in which this can be done. However, the first step is to begin. The questioning middle grade mind will take up from there. Children will begin to develop better ways to think about what they read if they have the training to do so. Then we have started them on the path toward becoming readers and thinkers who will not be fooled by the language of emotional persuasion. They will be able to recognize propaganda that, unless understood, can result in the enslavement of the minds and enslavement of the people themselves.

REFERENCES

1. Alcott, Louisa M., *Little Women,* (1868). Boston: Little, Brown, 1934.
2. Brink, Carol, *Caddie Woodlawn.* New York: Macmillan, 1937.
3. Chrisman, Arthur, *Shen of the Sea.* New York: E. P. Dutton, 1925.
4. Dalgliesh, Alice, *The Courage of Sarah Noble.* New York: Charles Scribner's Sons, 1954.
5. D'Aulaire, Ingri, and Edgar, P., *Benjamin Franklin.* New York: Doubleday, 1950.
6. De Angeli, Marguerite, *Henner's Lydia.* New York: Doubleday, 1936.
7. Estes, Eleanor, *The Moffats.* New York: Harcourt, Brace, 1941.
8. Forbes, Esther, *Johnny Tremain.* Boston: Houghton Mifflin, 1943.
9. ———, *Paul Revere.* Boston: Houghton Mifflin, 1942.
10. Gray, Elizabeth Janet, *Adam of the Road.* New York: Viking Press, 1942.
11. *Junior Book of Authors,* Kunitz, S. J., and Haycroft, Howard, editors. New York: Wilson and Company, 2nd revised edition, 1951.
12. Lampman, Evelyn S., *Elder Brother.* New York: Doubleday, 1950.

13. Lawson, Robert, *Ben and Me*. Boston: Little, Brown, 1939.
14. McCloskey, Robert, *A Time of Wonder*, New York: Viking Press, 1957.
15. ———, *Make Way for Ducklings*. New York: Viking Press, 1941.
16. Mirsky, Reba P., *Thirty One Brothers and Sisters*. Chicago: Wilson and Follett, 1952.
17. Montgomery, Elizabeth, *The Story Behind Modern Books*. New York: Dodd, Mead, 1949.
18. O'Dell, Scott, *The Island of the Blue Dolphins*. Boston: Houghton Mifflin, 1960.
19. Sandburg, Carl, *Abe Lincoln, The Prairie Years*. New York: Harcourt, Brace, 1928.

20. ———, *Abraham Lincoln*. New York: Harcourt, Brace, 1928. Vols. 1-4.
21. Spache, George, *Toward Better Reading*. Champaign, Ill.: Garrard Press, 1961, Chapter 5.
22. Stevenson, Robert L., *Treasure Island* (1882). New York: Charles Scribner's Sons, 1924.
23. Taylor, Sidney, *The All-of-a-Kind Family*. Chicago: Wilson and Follett, 1951.
24. Twain, Mark (Samuel Clemens), *Tom Sawyer* (1876). New York: Harper and Bros., 1917.
25. Wilder, Laura Ingalls, *Little House* books. New York: Harper and Bros., new uniform edition, 1953.

34: Reading Accomplishment of Gifted and Average Pupils *

SISTER JOSEPHINA, CSJ.

Within the past thirty years various techniques have been presented to try to measure the accomplishment of the gifted pupil in terms of mental ability. Texts in measurement provide a description of these methods, among which are the accomplishment quotient and the education age. Of the many attempts to assess the performance of the gifted, Horn's [1] work was selected because of the consideration of regression in dealing with above average ability. Therefore, the gifted pupil is not penalized because he is compared with other gifted pupils of the same MA and CA.

Correlating the results in reading and IQ for pupils in grades one through eight, Horn's formula resulted in .66 (MA) ÷ .33(CA). The Los Angeles school system uses the method for evaluating the performance of gifted pupils.

In the present study recomputed for-mulae were found because of the limited number of subjects (200), the restricted age range (8.10-11.2), and because the reading and IQ tests differed from those used by Horn. Therefore, prediction formulae were set up for reading vocabulary and reading comprehension, as measured by the *California Reading Test, Form AA*. The IQ's were obtained from the *California Test of Mental Maturity, 1950, Elementary Series, S-Form*.

Fifty boys and girls in grades 5 and 6, classified as average (IQ's ranged from 90-109, with Mean IQ = 101.48, SD = 5.00) and fifty boys and girls in grades 5 and 6, classified as gifted (IQ's ranged from 130-164, with Mean of 137.41, SD=6.52) were given the above tests. The pupils were from five comparably situated schools (middle class), had studied the same cur-

* Reprinted from *Educational and Psychological Measurement*, Vol. 18, No. 4 (Winter 1958), pp. 867-71, by permission of the author and the publisher.

riculum, and used the same text books in reading.

Prediction formulae were found by substituting in Horn's formula the Pearson-Product-Moment Correlation coefficient obtained, when the IQ's were correlated with the raw score data in the reading vocabulary and reading comprehension. The actual score for each pupil was compared with the expected score obtained from the respective prediction formula. Therefore, two scores resulted: one the actual, or obtained score, and the other termed the expected achievement score. The difference between these was called a discrepancy score and was either minus or plus depending upon the size of the expected score. If the expected score was greater than the obtained score, then a minus difference resulted. These discrepancy scores formed the basis of the statistical computation for the study.

The purpose of the analysis was to present objective data to some definite questions. In the research literature the statement is frequently found, yet rarely substantiated by statistical evidence, that the gifted pupil is the retarded pupil in the classroom; that he is not achieving according to his capacity; that teachers neglect him in proportion to the amount of time given him when compared with that given to the slow pupil. To find the answer to the problem of the actual achievement of the gifted in terms of his expected performance these questions are stated:

1. Is the mean discrepancy score difference for gifted and average pupils greater in reading vocabulary or in reading comprehension? In other words, in which of these tests do gifted and average pupils achieve closer to their expected level?
2. Do gifted boys and/or gifted girls achieve their expected level in reading vocabulary and reading comprehension?
3. Do average boys and/or average girls achieve their expected level in reading vocabulary and reading comprehension?
4. Do gifted pupils in grade 5 and/or grade 6, meet the expected level of performance in reading vocabulary and/or reading comprehension?
5. Do average pupils in grade 5 and/or in grade 6, meet the expected level of accomplishment in reading vocabulary and reading comprehension?

Table 1 shows the mean deviation, or mean discrepancy scores, for the gifted and the average groups in grades 5 and 6 in reading vocabulary and reading comprehension.

Discrepancy scores resulted when the difference between the actual and

Table 1: Mean Discrepancy Scores for Gifted and Average Pupils in Reading Vocabulary and Reading Comprehension

Grade	No.	Sex	Reading Vocabulary			Reading Comprehension		
			Gifted	Average	Favors	Gifted	Average	Favors
5	50	B-G	−20.44	−13.98	Average	−18.76	−3.56	Average
6	50	B-G	−18.80	−21.00	Gifted	−24.16	−5.38	Average
5-6	50	B	−21.32	−20.40	Average	−21.08	−8.24	Average
5-6	50	G	−17.92	−14.58	Average	−21.84	− .64	Average
5	25	B	− 8.28	− 9.04	Gifted	− 8.64	−1.64	Average
5	25	G	−12.16	− 4.94	Average	−10.12	−1.92	Average
6	25	B	−13.04	−11.36	Average	−12.44	−6.60	Average
6	25	G	− 5.76	− 9.64	Gifted	−11.72	+ .28	Average
5-6	100	B-G	− 9.81	− 8.75	Average	−10.73	−2.48	Average

the expected level of accomplishment was found. Noting the mean discrepancy scores in Table 1 a minus value was found in all comparisons except one. Girls in grade 6 of average ability achieved up to and beyond that which was expected from them according to their mental ability.

In the eighteen comparisons, the average pupils came closer to their expected accomplishment as observed from the smaller mean discrepancy score in all cases but three. Particularly noticeable are the results when the reading comprehension discrepancy scores were analyzed for the gifted groups. In every case the difference between the mean discrepancy scores for the gifted and for the average groups is large, favoring the average groups. Why gifted pupils deviated so far from their expected level in reading comprehension when compared with a corresponding average group is matter for further investigation.

Examining the results in reading vocabulary according to grade level, gifted pupils in grade 5 showed a larger deviation score (-20.44) than gifted pupils in grade 6 (-18.80). In the same comparison in reading vocabulary, the reverse resulted when average pupils in grade 6, with a discrepancy score of -21.00, surpassed average pupils in grade 5 whose mean score was -13.98.

Smaller discrepancy scores in reading comprehension favored pupils in grade 5 in both the gifted and the average groups. The mean discrepancy scores for gifted and average pupils in grade 6 indicated that their performance deviated to a greater degree from their expected level than pupils in grade 5.

Comparing gifted boys in grades 5 and 6 with gifted girls in grades 5 and 6, the amount of discrepancy for reading vocabulary for the boys exceeded that for the girls. Likewise, in grades 5 and 6 average boys surpassed the mean discrepancy in reading vocabulary score of girls of average ability. The mean discrepancy score in reading comprehension for gifted boys in grades 5 and 6 differed slightly from that for gifted girls in grades 5 and 6. However, boys of average ability in grades 5 and 6 deviated to a much larger degree in reading comprehension than did girls of average ability in grades 5 and 6. The girls showed a mean discrepancy of $-.64$ as compared with that of -8.24 for the boys.

Analyzing the groups by grade level in reading vocabulary, gifted girls in grade 5 presented a larger mean discrepancy score than did the boys in grade 5. The same pattern evolved when the discrepancy scores in reading comprehension were studied.

Summarizing the results the following significant findings are given:

1. Eighteen comparisons were made between gifted and average pupils. The gifted groups surpassed the average groups fifteen times indicating more deviation from expectancy than did the average groups. The gifted then, showed more retardation in reading vocabulary and reading comprehension when their actual score was compared with their expected score.
2. In each discrepancy score in reading comprehension the gifted surpassed the average in the mean amount. The average came closer to their level of expectancy.
3. In only one comparison a plus deviation was reported. This was for the average groups of fifth grade girls in reading comprehension.
4. In reading vocabulary, girls in both the gifted and the average groups were closer to expectancy than were the boys. A slight difference was found in favor of the gifted boys who differed slightly from gifted girls in reading comprehension.
5. Girls of average ability performed closer to their predicted level than did the boys of average ability.

In general it may be stated that pupils of above average ability in this study deviated more than the corresponding group of pupils of average ability when their obtained level was compared with their expected accomplishment. The foregoing data are presented in an attempt to present substantiative evidence to the allegation that the gifted pupil actually is retarded when his actual performance is compared with his expected accomplishment.

REFERENCE

1. Horn, Alice McA., *University Distribution of Effects of Specific Factors*. Los Angeles: University of Southern California Press, 1941, 68 pp.

PART FOUR

Junior and Senior High School Reading

INTRODUCTION

Reading instruction was considered for far too long as the sole responsibility of the elementary school. In far too many instances reading instruction ceased at the end of the sixth grade, and tragically at the end of the third grade in some instances. The great need for continued formal instruction in reading beyond the sixth grade was apparent, but too frequently high school teachers were not trained in even the rudimentary elements of reading instruction.

READING AS AN EVERY-TEACHER—ALL-SCHOOL RESPONSIBILITY

The present philosophy, which may be expected to gain increasing emphasis in the years ahead, considers that not only is the teaching of reading an all-school program from the first grade through the twelfth, and continuing on through college, but it is also the responsibility of every teacher regardless of the specific area in which he teaches. Formal teaching of reading must not stop at any level so long as the individual is in school. While it is likely that the English teacher will be responsible for providing the major part of the formal reading program, every teacher, regardless of the subject he is teaching, must assume responsibility for teaching the specialized vocabulary and reading skills necessary to comprehend the reading material in that particular area.

In earlier years it was believed that all of the necessary formal skills for reading could be taught by the end of the sixth grade.[2] With the ever increasing demand for mastery of more subject-area content as well as mastery at greater depth, this earlier belief that formal instruction could end at the sixth-grade level is no longer held. It is now recognized that there are many types of reading skills that must be taught beyond sixth-grade level. Such factors as rate, comprehension, inferential reading, reading for specific purposes, and specialized vocabulary are only a few of the skills that must be taught beyond the sixth-grade level.

In a report, *The American High School Today*,[3] Conant made twenty-one recommendations. Two of the recommendations dealt specifically with reading: "Recommendation 8: Special Consideration for the Very Slow Readers," [4] and "Recommendation 16: Developmental Reading Program." [5] Essentially, Conant was recommending both a developmental program and a remedial program.

READING IN CONTENT FIELDS

Effective reading in the content fields is obviously the ultimate goal of all formal reading instruction. Any notion that a child can be good in reading class, but be unable to translate this skill into reading in the content field, only points up the inadequacies of isolated skill instruction. How well a child reads in the content areas is a direct reflection of the effectiveness of the formal reading program. It is not enough, however, to assume that each content-area teacher can depend upon the formal reading program to instruct the students in the specific reading skills needed for the content area. There are unique reading skills for social studies, science, math, and literature. Each teacher must first of all know what these skills are and then know the techniques for teaching them.

It has long been popular in the elementary grades to state that although a child is poor in reading, he may be good in arithmetic. Attempts to determine if this is true have indicated that the child is usually poor in both reading and arithmetic, but perhaps somewhat better in arithmetic. This is obviously a reflection of the teacher's honest attempt to develop areas of strength within the child, rather than constantly directing attention toward his area of weakness. Tragically, however, the child who is poor in reading is penalized in arithmetic and all other content areas because reading skill is so essential to each of them.

The specialized vocabulary of each content area is probably the most important reading skill needed. Certainly identifying these words is a first step, but it is erroneous to assume that listing such words and requiring students to memorize them will accomplish the desired results. Methods of word attack such as recognizing prefixes, suffixes, and root words are essential, as is an understanding of phonic elements including initial, medial, and final sounds. Learning certain words that have specialized meaning in a content area is important (that is, the use of the word "of" in an arithmetic word problem in which it acts as a "cue" word meaning to multiply). Materials developed by Smith [5] are specially helpful to junior and senior high-school teachers in content areas who are unfamiliar with the usual techniques for teaching reading.

Directed reading in the content fields, where concern is given to interpretation of meaning as opposed to remembering isolated facts, is very important. Too frequently high-school students believe that reading is intended to serve no other purpose than to acquire isolated facts which are to be "parroted back" to the teacher on a test at some later date. Numbers and dates are given undue attention, while drawing inferences from materials read is frequently entirely overlooked.

Conant describes the developmental program at the high-school level as being intended primarily to:

Helps students acquire skill in different sorts of reading, from close and detailed reading to scanning; to increase reading speed; and to improve comprehension of the material read.[6]

Although Conant stresses the need for developmental reading to be on a voluntary basis at the high-school level, there is ample reason to believe that the values of a required program are sufficiently great to justify its existence.

DIAGNOSING HIGH-SCHOOL READING PROBLEMS

The first major concern in diagnosing high-school reading problems is to determine the level at which students are reading. Unfortunately, standardized reading tests do not always tell the high-school teacher the level at which the child is able to comprehend material in each subject area.

A developmental philosophy "emphasizes the necessity for starting the reading process with materials that are close to the child's own experience and continuing with instruction and subject matter that fulfills his changing needs for reading." [9] The primary emphasis of the developmental approach is that it begins with the student on his level. There is ample evidence that instruction above the child's reading level is notoriously inefficient. In attempting to determine the reading level of the student, it is important to remember that a variety of levels exist. Betts [1] identifies these as: (1) basal level, (2) instructional level, (3) frustration level, and (4) capacity level. The basal level, also referred to as the independent level, is the level at which the student is able to read independently, without assistance. The instructional level is the level at which the child is able to comprehend about 75 per cent. The frustration level is that level at which the child is able to comprehend less than 50 per cent. Too frequently high-school teachers teach at this level. Such teaching is inefficient, for it wastes the time of both the teacher and the student, and frequently results in negative attitudes toward the material. The capacity level is the "hearing or listening level" of the child and indicates the highest level at which the child is able to understand material read to him.

A variety of factors contribute to the reading level of the student. Frequently his interest in the material will directly affect his reading level. For this reason, it is important that the teacher either use material that is of interest to the student, or devote time to developing interest in the subject matter. In addition to the reading level of each student, the high-school teacher must be concerned with comprehension, vocabulary, word analysis techniques, and rate. Although group standardized-test-results are helpful, it is clear that "informal tests based upon the reading material used in the classroom and charts of faulty habits and difficulties observed with the child in reading provide the best basis for planning effective instruction." [7]

READING PROGRAMS IN HIGH SCHOOL

Reading programs at the high-school level should be of two types. The first type, the developmental program, should be part of the regular school program and should be incorporated into instruction in each content area. If the reading program is incorporated into the content areas, there is no problem concerning whether or not it should be compulsory. The second type of program needed is a remedial one. Again, the problem is not one of whether or not the student wants to take it, but of whether or not the student needs this kind of help. It is, of course, true that motivation is considerably higher if the students understand their need for such a program. Rather than ask the students if they want to take it, however, it should be only one more reflection of the total school attitude or philosophy that courses are intended to benefit the students rather than be merely artificial requirements for graduation.

The greatest problem in establishing a developmental reading program at the high-school level is that teachers generally are not trained in the teaching of reading. Only one state, Pennsylvania, requires high-school teachers to have training in reading, and this is limited to one course, which may be insufficient. Another problem, which is diminishing, has been high-school teachers' objection to teaching on different levels (the developmental philosophy) and to concerning themselves with material that they do not see as being directly related to their specific content area.

The remedial program is quite different from that of the developmental program. It is separate from the regular program, may or may not give academic credit, but must not be a penalty on the poor reader who is already heavily penalized in all of his content courses. It will frequently be either small group instruction or individual instruction. The teachers in charge of such a program need to be highly trained in clinical procedures involving diagnosis and remediation. Generally, students reading two or more years below grade level will be referred for such special remedial help.

An adjunct of the remedial program can be speed reading courses. Such training can be performed in large groups, and should be recommended to all college-bound students.

SUMMARY

Junior and senior high schools must assume the responsibility for teaching reading. The greatly increased need for this is not due to any inadequacy in the elementary program, but is rather due to the ever increasing amount of reading material required of students and the higher standards being established. The effectiveness of the new emphasis on quality education may be directly related to the effectiveness with which junior and senior high-school teachers include reading instruction in their program.

REFERENCES

1. Betts, Emmett A., *Foundations of Reading Instruction*. New York: American Book Company, 1954, pp. 445-54.
2. Buswell, Guy T., *Remedial Reading at the College and Adult Levels: An Experimental Study,* Supplementary Educational Monograph No. 50. Chicago: The University of Chicago Press, 1939, p. 6.
3. Conant, James B., *The American High School Today*. New York: McGraw-Hill, 1959, 141 pp.
4. Ibid. p. 55.
5. Ibid. p. 67.
6. Ibid. p. 68.
7. Durrell, Donald D., *Improving Reading Instruction*. New York: Harcourt, Brace and World, 1956.
8. Smith, Nila B., *Be a Better Reader,* Books I-VI. Englewood Cliffs, N.J.: Prentice-Hall, 1958.
9. Witty, Paul A., *Reading in Modern Education*. Boston: D. C. Heath, p. 7.

Reading Instruction in the High School

35: What Does Research Reveal About Practices in Teaching Reading? *

CONSTANCE M. McCULLOUGH

There is no paucity of suggestions for ways of teaching reading. Ideas are free and numerous. One encounters famine only when one asks for methods of scientifically proven worth. The purpose of the present article is to provide a brief summary of practices in teaching reading which research findings support. Armed with this information the secondary school teacher should be able to make wiser judgments about the use of students' time in reading instruction.

Throughout many of the studies consulted there runs the thread that we get what we work for consciously; that if both students and teacher are aware of specific goals, those specific goals are more apt to be reached. Along with this finding, however, runs the danger that narrowly conceived goals produce limited results. We must work for specific goals consciously, but those specific goals need to encompass a broad definition of reading skills if the product is not to be dwarfed and distorted.

DEVELOPING VOCABULARY

Who Should Be Taught?

The idea that we should teach only those students who are below a certain score on a vocabulary test has worn out its welcome. The high school years are years of tremendous vocabulary challenge and a time when all students can benefit by help and encouragement in vocabularly development. However, it does not follow that all students need the same kind of help nor help in the same kinds of vocabulary problems. We need to take an initial inventory of the student's vocabulary development— his knowledge of words and word-relationships, his ability to determine the meaning of a word in context or out of context, his ability to analyze the form of a word by various useful techniques. When we have such an inventory of knowledge and skills, we are ready to determine who shall be taught what.[116]

* Reprinted from *The English Journal,* Vol. 46, No. 8 (November 1957), pp. 475-90, by permission of the National Council of Teachers of English and the author.

Which Words Should Be Taught?

One of the most recent lists of words to be taught is one by Kyte [55] designed for adult illiterates. It contains 663 words derived from a combination of other lists. These should be useful in the preparation of simplified material for seriously retarded students.

Words selected for special study, however, should be drawn largely from material that the students will be reading anyway, and should be taught as the need arises. [44]

What About Word Meaning?

We should use many means of clarifying the meaning or meanings of a given word. We need to discuss with the students not only the technical words peculiar to our fields but the common words which have a different, technical meaning—words such as *consumption* and *demand*. [87] A study of the multiple meanings of words is definitely rewarding. [88] Students should be encouraged to study words in context to determine the particular meanings used. [87] The task of classifying words gives students an increased appreciation of word relationships and a fuller understanding of meaning. [20]

What About Word Form?

Research has pretty conclusively laid to rest the idea that one must study Latin in order to learn English. [75] Indeed, knowledge of root words, while helpful, is not nearly the panacea it was once thought. [9] The study of roots needs to be supplemented by other types of word study, such as the study of suffixes [105] and prefixes. [98] Stauffer has identified fifteen particularly useful prefixes: *ab, ad, be, com, de, dis, en, ex, in* (into), *in* (not), *pre, pro, re, sub,* and *un.* These, of course, would not be the only ones to be studied on the high school

level but might be considered a minimal list. Knowledge of structural elements in words (prefixes, stems, suffixes, compound parts, syllables) is important in the development of vocabulary. [49]

Phonics is also important. The study of the sounds of word elements should employ words the student already knows by sight. [116] To teach phonics through unknown words is to multiply trouble. This fact suggests that phonics drills and pamphlets unrelated to the students' regular reading material probably employ words with which the student is unfamiliar and are therefore not the best materials to use for training in phonics.

Some students on the high school level have a laborious way of figuring out every word they read but are able to recognize very few words at sight. Research shows that words familiar in meaning are more readily learned, and that frequent observation of a word does little good unless meaning is attached to it. [76] In other words, it is good to make a word a part of a student's speaking vocabulary before expecting him to learn it quickly as a sight word. Further, it has been found that the more use a student makes of a word and the more emotion-rousing value the word has (*mother, affection*), the more readily it is learned as a sight word. [31] Of course, we cannot give a clammy word emotion-rousing value if it hasn't any, but those words lacking in emotional meaning can be used in student discussions until they do have substantial meaning and familiarity.

What Methods Should We Use?

The literature on teaching vocabulary is peppered with the controversy over whether a direct approach to word study is superior to a casual approach. The direct approach is one in which lists of words or sentences containing words are studied deliberately for the development of word power, whereas the casual or incidental approach involves the study of words as they happen to occur in material the students are about to read or are currently reading. Both methods have value, and probably neither should be used to the exclusion of the other. The casual learning of word meanings increases vocabulary.[40] But the direct method has been found to be more effective,[67] and especially so with pupils of low ability.[37]

In direct teaching careful pronunciatio of the new word is important.[108] Preferably the teacher should face the class so that the appearance of the lips in forming the word will aid the impression. Since a multisensory impression of the word is more effective, it is desirable that the class repeat the pronunciation of the word as they look at it on the blackboard, in some cases even to trace it with two fingers on the desk as they look at it.[78] It is probably better for the teacher to write the word in front of the students and pronounce it again in syllables as she writes it rather than to have it already written.[2] Wide experiences with the word,[88] including oral activities using the word,[20] reinforce the learning. Seeing the word in many contexts improves recognition.[68]

Word form analysis seems best taught by the inductive method.[116] As students learn or relearn techniques of word study, both of the form and of the meaning, they need to be helped to make systematic attacks on new words.[49, 88] Sometimes a list of things to observe about the meaning of a word (its use in the sentence, the meaning of its prefix, suffix, stem, or compound parts) and about the form of the word (does it have a recognizable prefix, stem, suffix, compound part; does it begin with a letter sound that I know; does it contain a phonogram I know; where are the syllabic divisions) helps the student to go through the inventory of techniques he knows until he finds the methods that work on a particular word.

Such lists breed confidence: I know—things that may work.

DEVELOPING COMPREHENSION

What Kind of Job Are We Doing Now?

There is considerable dissatisfaction (not confined to the United States) with the extent to which schools develop reading comprehension. Test evidence suggests that some schools do not do enough to maintain or develop certain types of reading skill.[94] This may be due to the fact that some teachers teach reading for the main idea for three weeks and then neglect it for thirty, or that some teachers think they have taught it when they teach one lesson, or that others think they have taught it when they have merely required it without explaining *how* to do it, or that teachers actually do not teach comprehension techniques at all.

Some investigations have shown that, while we have apparently developed fact readers, we have failed more or less to develop thoughtful readers. The higher thought processes, such as reading to make comparisons or to draw conclusions or to infer, are influenced by prejudice [65] and emotion.[74] Students are incapable, by and large, of divorcing their own feelings and preconceptions [15] from the content and intent of the article read. College students have been found to be weak in sensing the author's intention, detecting irony, understanding difficult words, interpreting allusions and metaphor, and appreciating the influence of context on word meaning.[15]

While one research study [16] concludes that it is less rewarding to ask intellectually challenging questions of slow-learning students than of bright students of the same mental age, the distributions of achievement overlap so extensively, the number of students involved is so small, and the matching of groups so limited that it would be unwise to generalize. It is probable that slow-learning students can be discouraged into not using their heads when they read, educated to read only facts. Before passing final judgment it would behoove us to give every student material at his level of understanding and experience in attempts at higher thought processes, and continue to ask thought-provoking questions of all students. They will all vote someday. A further criticism is that students have not learned versatility in reading. They tend to develop a habit and read everything in that one way.[19]

What Types of Comprehension Should We Teach?

Davis identifies the following types of comprehension: selecting appropriate meaning for a word or phrase in context, following organization and identifying antecedents and references to it, selecting the main thought, answering questions explicitly answered in the passage, answering questions answered in the passage but in different wording, drawing inferences, recognizing literary devices, identifying tone and mood of the passage, and determining the writer's purpose, intent, or viewpoint.[29] Wishful thinking has been that the elementary school can teach these types once and for all, or that the English teacher on the secondary level can be responsible for the mastery of these types, but the research facts are that these skills have different emphases in different fields [95] and need to be studied in each field [5] as the need arises.[119] Furthermore, although there are high correlations between students' performance on these various types of comprehension, the fact remains that students vary in their mastery of the different types and profit by attention to those in which they are deficient. Therefore, we must test for the different types of

comprehension to find out the kinds students need, and then teach for those specific types.

What Materials Should We Use?

It has long been a cliché that, in order to understand material well, students must be given material "at their level." That is to say, one cannot comprehend something which is written in a strange vocabulary, in sentences too long for one's mind to encompass, in a context that assumes experiences one has not had, and in a complexity of organization that requires a mentality beyond one's own. This has been, and still is, the main support for differentiated reading material—the use of different books for different students studying the same topic and coming together to share impressions. It has long been known also that familiarity with a subject and interest in it make the reading easier. This last fact has given encouragement to people who feel that a student can read anything successfully, no matter how hard, if he is interested in it; but doubtless this is an extreme interpretation which can be believed only if we do not evaluate the resulting comprehension thoroughly.

In choosing materials, we should seek those of high interest value. Intrinsically interesting material yields better comprehension, better speed of reading, and a fuller response to questions about the content.[13] In those instances which allow us no choice, we probably must still depend upon our ability to bewitch and inspire with our own unaccountable enthusiasm.

What Methods Will Prove Productive?

Purposeful listening has a small but significant effect upon reading skill. Students who are read to after being asked to listen for a main idea, for certain kinds of facts, or to decide outcomes of a situation improve in those kinds of thinking when they read something of comparable difficulty themselves.[60] There is probably, therefore, some virtue in having the teacher or student read something aloud if the audience has a specific comprehension task in mind and is held responsible for it in subsequent discussion.

Most of the teaching of reading, however, must involve reading; and, as previously stated, we get what we work for.[12] If we wish students to be able to comprehend graphs, we must teach them how to read graphs related to the material they are studying. If the material is easy enough for the student to comprehend, the graph will be, too.[62] If we wish students to develop the habit of wide, free reading, we shall encourage it; but we shall not expect wide, free reading and discussion of that reading to develop all the types and depth of comprehension for which we are responsible.[11] Believers in wide, free reading and believers in intensive reading must meet on a middle ground.

Literary appreciation does not emerge as a by-product of increased reading skill.[86] If students are to learn appreciation, it must be by direct attention to facets of literary merit.

Vocabulary and comprehension are improved to a certain extent by the use of reading in a core program.[109] However, slow learners do not improve so much in such a program as might be hoped or expected. This fact brings us again to the need for direct instruction to complement such a program, and to the suspicion that it is the low level of our ambition for the better students rather than their ability to grow entirely without direct instruction that makes us think only the slow learners need it.

Because inadequate experience background is a handicap to comprehension,[14] the students can profit by discussion among themselves and with the teacher before they attempt the reading

about ideas, characters, or situations quite strange to them.

Oral reading skill needs to be maintained on the high school level by frequent use, but the passage to be read should be prepared in advance and read to an audience that has a real intellectual reason for listening.[81] Both oral and silent reading benefit by being given a purpose in advance. To teach students to read for different purposes we must set different purposes with them at different times.[19]

DEVELOPING SPEED OF READING

What Is the Nature of Speed of Reading?

Speed in reading is made possible by efficient left-to-right eye movements, few and short fixation pauses,[91] and efficient return sweep down to the next line. But these, in turn, are made possible by reading power,[48] which is composed of the skills that have been previously discussed in this article. Efficiency in reading is more a matter of assimilating material after it gets to the brain than it is of sheer mechanics.[96] It depends more upon vocabulary, ideas, and meanings than upon monocular or binocular vision, perceptual span, or eye movement.[53] This is not to say that the mechanics of reading are not important but rather to say that when we concentrate on the mechanics alone to improve reading speed we are asking the tail to wag the dog.

A student reads material differing in difficulty at different speeds because of comprehension problems.[25] Regressive eye movements over the line of print occur, slowing the reading, when thought is interrupted and the student attempts to re-examine the line for lost meaning.[10] Different types of subject-matter alter both comprehension and speed;[58] a poem tends to decrease the speed and challenge the comprehension more than does an article in the same vocabulary and on the same topic.

Students need to learn to adapt their speed of reading to the type of material and the purpose for which they are reading it.[3] Better readers tend to adjust their rate according to their ability to comprehend, whereas poorer readers read easy and difficult material at the same rate regardless of their purpose.[17] It is true that eye movements are the physical means whereby these adjustments are made; but eye movement patterns in reading are more characteristic of the individual possessing them than they are of the difficulty of material he is reading.[69] For this reason it may be unwise to attempt to alter eye movements directly.[69]

What Kind of Job Are We Doing Now?

The research literature is full of studies showing that groups of students, given instruction to speed their reading, gain in reading speed. Groups are formed in various industries, so that adults dissatisfied with their speed, either in reading on the job or in reading at leisure, may have instruction. A recent survey from fourth graders through adults out of school showed that the ability to skim was not well learned. Wide differences in this ability were found at each grade level.[38] Apparently we could do a better job of teaching our students when and how to read faster.

What Are Artificial Methods of Increasing Speed?

There has been a great debate for many years over whether reading speed may be fostered as well by artificial methods as by natural methods. Artificial methods are those which employ mechanical devices, such as tachistoscopes, metronoscopes, flash meters, films, or other types of rate controllers. Natural methods are those which use books and other

reading material and encourage the students to increase their speed through interest, knowledge of speed techniques, and sheer will-power.

The main concern of the "natural method" enthusiasts seems to be that, when speed is developed artificially, comprehension is neglected. But the Harvard Reading Films, used with comprehension checks, have produced improvement in both rate and comprehension.[90] In other words, perhaps a student, reading as fast as he can with his present comprehension and vocabulary, cannot improve his understanding of a passage by reading it faster; but a student who is reading more slowly than he needs to or can, with his present comprehension and vocabulary, can read faster and still understand. There is such a thing as reading so slowly that connections between ideas are lost. There is a question, however, of whether the greater comprehension gained through emphasis upon speed is really better understanding or simply more ground covered and thus comprehended.

Nelson has claimed that comprehension improves with the use of the metronoscope because the machine forces a reduction in regressive movements and length of fixation.[70] However, Cosper reported one of the few studies to follow up students trained on a mechanical device. He found after two years that a good share of speed gains was retained but that comprehension gains disappeared.[27] A system of underlining parts of a passage to show which portions would be stressed orally (oral peak stress), once reported to be helpful in increasing comprehension, has been unfavorably reported in the past year. Not only did it seem not helpful but experts were unable to agree on the parts to be stressed.[42]

Whatever the fate of comprehension, favorable speed results have been evident in many studies featuring a mechanical approach to reading.[4, 18,72, 103, 113, 117] Opponents of the artificial approach have been equally numerous. Three investigators, two of them reviewing the entire research in this area, concluded that training in eye movements does not seem to aid comprehension.[91, 107, 112] Others have expressed the opinion that there is no exceptional value in the use of mechanical devices to control eye movements during the reading process.[44, 115] It is thought that a large part of the improvement in speed or comprehension is due to motivation.[44] The implication is that if teachers have not broken the handles off their motivators, they should be able to achieve equally good results by a natural method.

What Are Natural Methods of Increasing Speed?

It has been proved that a natural approach to reading, emphasizing comprehension as well as speed, can result in improvement in both speed and comprehension.[21] One investigator, using passages of non-technical prose, timing the students' reading one minute twice a week and counting the words read, found rewarding this pointed attention to reading speed.[3] Speed training seems to be most effective, however, when it is directed toward clearly defined jobs, requiring the students to note the comprehension requirements of the reading job and to determine the speed warranted by them.[32] In a short course of twenty-one hours' duration, a very recent investigation showed that a book-centered course is more effective than a machine-centered course in increasing speed. The mean difference in speed between the two groups was fifty words per minute.[104]

Probably both the artificial and the natural approaches to increasing reading speed have value,[9, 36, 60] but three points need to be made clear: (1) It probably is not necessary to invest in mechanical devices to increase reading speed if we offer students materials in which they can develop it. (2) There is no evidence to support the practice of giving speed exercises solely to the gifted or solely to the slow learners. (3) Training on mechanical devices runs the danger of emphasizing speed for speed's sake, over-simplifies in the students' minds the really complex job of adjusting speed to purpose and material, and reduces the amount of time spent in natural reading situations in which the results are broader. If mechanical devices are used, they should be used with temperance. This has not been typical of their history so far.

DEVELOPING TASTES AND APPRECIATIONS

How Much Voluntary Reading Is Done?

As long as students keep reading, there is hope that their tastes and appreciations will improve. How much do they read? At junior high school ages there is an increase of free reading followed by a decline in the senior high school years.[93] Adult reading habits thereafter seem to follow the patterns established before college is reached. Family patterns, socio-economic status, intelligence, and school experiences are largely responsible for the formation of these habits.[52] As a key person in a student's school experience, the teacher needs to be aware of ways of helping a student to form good habits and to make good choices of his reading matter.

What Do Students Read Voluntarily?

Students tend to be more interested in contemporary and public figures in the sports and entertainment world than they are in the past.[6] Their reading choices tend to be immature.[24, 28, 79, 80] In newspaper reading they prefer sports, comics, and the front page; in magazines their preference is the picture magazines.[7] They read the lighter magazine content,[79] which requires less than their vocabulary development warrants.[1] While some comic books appear to be of good quality,[61] many popular comic books and strips give pat interpretations of life and stereotypes of society.[97] Students appear to be more concerned with such themes as adventure, humor, and love [99] than with the artistry or truth of the writing. Twenty years ago an investigator concluded that little in students' leisure book reading helped to develop judgment, discrimination, or criticism.[26] In some schools little has been done to stimulate wide reading or to improve its quality.[22]

What Procedures Are Useful?

Students do not just happen upon books on topics of interest to them; they must be helped to find them.[41] Certainly it is even less probable that they will happen upon well-written books on those topics. We must take class time to guide book selection.

Students' preferences should be studied for the clues they give to better book selection. For instance, the factors of appeal in a favorite comic strip should be sought in better reading materials, so that the student may be led from the reading of the comic strip to the reading of the better material.[106] In addition, present adolescent interests, such as contemporary events,[83] humor, or vocational values,[83] should be satisfied with books on these topics.[45]

We must make books easily accessible if they are to be read.[56, 61, 66,71,77] Furthermore, we must allow time for reading these books in the classroom.[56] Students of low mentality may prefer reading a whole book, though small, to reading a short article or story, because of the sense of accomplishment it gives them.[39]

Silent reading in the classroom should ultimately be followed by discussion of what was read. Students experience

therapy in discussing objectively some of their own living problems as they are presented in books.[85] Misunderstandings of other cultural groups can be rectified through reading and discussion.[92] At times, a class may decide to pursue a topic through a variety of reading materials. Elements of propaganda, organization, and style can be featured especially well in this way. Activities such as panel discussions, debates, and sharing of parts read aloud for special purposes give vitality to the reading program and help teachers avoid the checking techniques which so often detract from the pleasure of reading.[77]

One of the old standbys in developing appreciation has been oral reading by the teacher or a student of something well expressed. Teachers who have used this method will be glad to know that listening has a place in the reading program. Listening to radio drama, students retain as much of a story as they do by reading it themselves.[43] Participation in choral reading of a selection all enjoy is another helpful technique.

But certainly it should be remembered that taste and appreciation require more than opportunity; they require direct teaching.[86] Students shown, required to find, and encouraged to produce in their own writing examples of good quality will graduate from high school with a better understanding of literary quality than will those who are left to graze at will. Students presented with a good and poor passage and required to explain the differences in quality will be more sensitive to the merits of good writing. Students prodded to think about the deeper meanings in a passage will become dissatisfied with superficial writing.

GROUPING FOR INSTRUCTION

Administrators have attempted to simplify the problems of the high school teacher by homogeneous grouping, putting students of a certain reading ability together in one class. This practice is believed to ease the strain of meeting great differences among students. Parents and students, especially students of superior reading ability, have been favorable toward it.[34] A drawback is that the practice gives the teacher a false sense of security, for differences remain.[84] For instance, the teacher may have fewer reader levels to consider, but may have as great a variety of skills in need of remediation or development. Of course, too, the better the teacher, the greater the differences become; students apparently alike in achievement level at the beginning of the term become more and more disparate as the course proceeds. Therefore, teachers working under the homogeneous grouping system need to appreciate that no one-book, one-method approach is justified.

In every good reading program some of the activities should involve the whole class, some a small group, and some the individual.[33, 46, 101] In each case, individual needs are served;[47] for the individual may need to share something with the whole class, learn something with the help of others in a group, or prove that he knows something by doing it himself.

Grouping, itself, is a method of individualizing, not a way of escaping responsibility. Six types of grouping for reading instruction have been identified:[101] achievement grouping, in which a student reads with others material which is easy enough for him to read but which contains some challenge requiring the help of the teacher; special needs grouping, in which students needing the same kind of skill work on it together with the teacher; team grouping, in which two or more students work on a skill together without the aid of the teacher; tutorial grouping, in which one student who knows a technique helps others who do not know it; research grouping, in which students curious about the same information seek

it together in reference sources; and interest grouping, in which students having the same hobby or preference in recreational reading share ideas. In achievement grouping the teacher provides a systematic, year-long instructional program, reviewing and building important skills.

To determine the achievement groupings and materials to be used, teachers frequently give a test. It is important that the total test score not be used as the measure of reading level, partly because tests do not agree on reading level [73] and partly because it is the difficulty level of material successfully read that most concerns the teacher.[64] Membership in such an achievement group is important for each student, even though some students may spend less time with such a group than others. Gifted students often have been neglected in this respect, with a resultant achievement in skill blow their natural promise.[100]

EVALUATING GROWTH IN READING SKILLS

Popular practice in evaluation has not kept pace with the enlarging concept of the complex of skills and appreciations that reading is. Many schools still measure the success of a reading program with a test of general vocabulary, something called comprehension (usually an over-simplification of the total task), and something called speed—adding to this the number of books read by each student, the width of his smile, and the foot-candles of glint in his eye when reading is mentioned. In fact, the erroneous claims of the virtue of one method of teaching reading over another may well be traced in part to the inadequacy of the evaluation instruments used in the experiments.

To evaluate properly today, the teacher needs to know what he starts with and what he achieves in the end.[23, 110, 111] Evaluation must take place at the beginning of a course, should be informally engaged in during the course,[23] and should be made again at the end. Its scope should include such matters as breadth and depth of vocabulary; breadth, level, and depth of comprehension; study skills; [30] ability to anlyze words in and out of context; reactions to reading; literary appreciation; [50] reading interests; [82] reading habits in and out of school; the adjustment of speed to varied purposes and materials; and self-evaluation in the form of test-analysis, record-keeping, and expressions on the part of the student about his own sense of progress.[15, 118]

Some teachers are fearful of the clerical impossibility of keeping track of the skills of 200 high school students; but if we remember that study of the results of evaluation is learning for the student who does it, and that knowledge of his status in the various skills is the best possible beginning for an intelligent attack upon his own needs, we shall recognize the fact that evaluation is a necessary, worthy use of class time.

The improvement of reading is, throughout, a matter of teamwork. It is promoted best when it is in the hands of educators well aware of the research guideposts and cognizant of the breadth and depth of their responsibility.

REFERENCES

1. Aldrich, Ruth, and Reilly, Marion Stewart, "Student Vocabulary Score— Student Magazine Reading," *College English,* XVI (March 1955), pp. 368-70.
2. Anderson, Irving H., "The Effect of Letter Position on Range of Apprehension Scores with Special Reference to Reading Disability," *The University of Michigan School of Education Bulletin,* XVIII (December 1946), pp. 37-40.
3. Andrews, Joe W., "An Approach to Speed Reading," *English Journal,* XLI (September 1952), pp. 352-6.
4. Apperson, Sarah V., "The Effectiveness of Orthoptic Training as a Means of Remedial Instruction in Reading," *Journal of Experimental Education,* IX (December 1940), pp. 160-66.
5. Artley, A. Sterl., "General and Specific Factors in Reading Comprehension," *Journal of Experimental Education,* XVI (March 1948), pp. 181-6.
6. Averill, Lawrence A., "The Impact of a Changing Culture upon Pubescent Ideals," *School and Society,* LXXII (July 22, 1950), pp. 49-53.
7. Barbe, Walter, "A Study of the Reading of Gifted High School Students," *Educational Administration and Supervision,* XXXVIII (March 1952), pp. 148-54.

8. Barnes, Melvin W., "Root Words and Current Meanings," *School and Society,* LVI (December 19, 1942), pp. 610-11.
9. Barry, Robert F., and Smith, Paul E., "An Experiment in Ninth-Grade Reading Improvement," *Journal of Educational Psychology,* XLV (November 1954), pp. 407-14.
10. Bayle, Evalyn, "The Nature and Causes of Regressive Movements in Reading," *Journal of Experimental Education,* XI (September 1942), pp. 16-36.
11. Bennett, A. L., "An Experiment in Reading," *Michigan Education Journal,* XXX (January 1953), pp. 302-3.
12. ———, "Two Experimental Groups in Reading," *College English,* XV (January 1954), pp. 233-5.
13. Bernstein, Margery R., "Relationship Between Interest and Reading Comprehension," *Journal of Educational Research,* XLIX (December 1955), pp. 283-8.
14. Black, E. L., "The Difficulties of Training College Students in Understanding What They Read," *British Journal of Educational Psychology,* XXIV (February 1954), pp. 17-31.
15. Blayne, Thornton C., "Validity of Self-Evaluation Charts in Developmental Reading Programs," *Elemen-*

tary English, XXVI (May 1949), pp. 279-81, 292.

16. Bliesmer, Emery P., "Reading Abilities of Bright and Dull Children of Comparable Mental Ages," *Journal of Educational Psychology*, XLV (October 1954), pp. 321-31.

17. Blommers, Paul J., and Lindquist, E. F., "Rate of Comprehension of Reading: Its Measurement and Its Relation to Comprehension," *Journal of Educational Psychology*, XXXV (November 1944), pp. 449-73.

18. Bond, Elden A., "The Yale-Harvard Freshmen Speed Reading Experiment," *School and Society*, LIV (August 16, 1941), pp. 107-11.

19. Bond, Eva, *Reading and Ninth Grade Achievement*, Teachers College Contribution to Education No. 756 (New York: Teachers College, Columbia University 1938).

20. Bradley, Martha, Cahill, Loretta A., and Tate, Harry L., "Acquisition of a Reading Vocabulary," *Elementary English Review*, XVIII (January 1941), pp. 19-21, 32.

21. Bridges, Lucile Hudson, "Speed versus Comprehension in Elementary Reading" *Journal of Educational Psychology*, XXXII (April 1941), pp. 314-20.

22. Brink, William, Garfield, Sol, and Witty, Paul, "The Reading Interests of Negro High School Students," *Educational Administration and Supervision*, XXVI (November 1940), pp. 607-13.

23. Broening, Angela M., "Test-Determined Teaching of Reading in the Secondary Schools," *Baltimore Bulletin of Education*, XII (November 1933), pp. 21-3.

24. Burton, Philip Ward, "Newspaper-Reading Behavior of High School Students," *School and Society*, LXIII (February 2, 1946), p. 86.

25. Carlson, Thorsten R., "Effect of Certain Test Factors in Measurement of Speed of Reading," *Journal of Educational Research*, XLIV (March 1951), pp. 543-9.

26. Center, Stella, and Persons, Gladys L., "The Leisure Reading of New York City High School Students," *English Journal*, XXV (November 1936), pp. 717-26.

27. Cosper, Russell, and Kephart, Nowell C., "Retention of Reading Skills," *Journal of Educational Research*, XLIX (November 1955), pp. 211-16.

28. Cuff, Noel B., and Donovan, H. L., "What Freshmen Read in a Teachers College," *AATC Quarterly*, I (September 1931), pp. 8-14.

29. Davis, Frederick Barton, "Comprehension in Reading," *Baltimore Bulletin of Education*, XXVIII (January-February 1951), pp. 16-24.

30. Deer, George H., "The Peabody Library Information Test: A Study of Its Statistical Validity and Reliability," *Journal of Experimental Education*, IX (March 1941), pp. 233-6.

31. DeLucia, Joseph J., and Stagner, Rosa, "Emotional versus Frequency Factors in Word Recognition Time and Association Time," *Journal of Personality*, XXII (March 1954), pp. 299-309.

32. Dolch, Edward W., "Rapid Reading with a Purpose," *School Review*, LIX (October 1951), pp. 410-13.

33. Evans, N. Dean, "An Individualized Reading Program for the Elementary Teacher," *Elementary English*, XXX (May 1953), pp. 275-80.

34. Floyd, Cecil, "Meeting Children's Reading Needs in the Middle Grades: A Preliminary Report," *Elementary School Journal*, LV (October 1954), pp. 99-103.

35. Gilbert, Luther C., "Effect on Silent Reading of Attempting to Follow Oral Reading," *Elementary School Journal*, XL (April 1940), pp. 614-21.

36. Glock, M. D., "The Effect upon Eye Movements and Reading Rate at the College Level of Three Methods of Training," *Journal of Educational Psychology*, XL (February 1949), pp. 93-106.

37. Gray, William S., and Holmes, Eleanor, *The Development of Meaning Vocabularies in Reading*, University of Chicago Laboratory School, Publication No. 6 (Department of Education, University of Chicago, 1938).

38. Grayum, Helen Stolte, "An Analytic Description of Skimming: Its Purpose and Place as an Ability in Reading," *Studies in Education*, 1952, pp. 137-43, No. 4, Thesis Abstract Series

(Bloomington, Ind.: School of Education, Indiana University, 1953).

39. Gunzburg, Herbert C., "The Subnormal Boy and His Reading Interests," *Library Quarterly,* XVIII (October 1948), pp. 264-74.

40. Haefner, Ralph, "Casual Learning of Word Meanings," *Journal of Educational Research,* XXV (April-May 1932), pp. 267-77.

41. Handlan, Bertha, "The Fallacy of Free Reading as an Approach to Appreciation," *English Journal,* XXXV (April 1946), pp. 182-8.

42. Hanitchak, John Joseph, Jr., "Oral Peak Stress: Its Validity and Relationship to Reading Comprehension and Efficiency," *Journal of Educational Research,* XLIX (December 1955), pp. 295-300.

43. Haugh, Oscar M., "The Relative Effectiveness of Reading and Listening to Radio-Drama as Ways of Imparting Information and Shifting Attitudes," *Journal of Educational Research,* XLV (March 1952), pp. 489-98.

44. Henry, Lyle K., and Lauer, A. R., "A Comparison of Four Methods of Increasing the Reading Speed of College Students," *Proceedings of the Iowa Academy of Science,* XLVI (1939), pp. 273-6.

45. Hermans, Mabel C., "Utilizing Adolescent Interests," *Los Angeles Educational Research Bulletin,* X (May-June 1931), pp. 2-29.

46. Hester, Kathleen B., "Every Child Reads Successfully in a Multiple-Level Program," *Elementary School Journal,* LIII (October 1952), pp. 86-9.

47. Hildreth, Gertrude, "Individualizing Reading Instruction," *Teachers College Record,* XLII (November 1940), pp. 123-37.

48. Holmes, Jack A., "Factors Underlying Major Reading Disabilities at the College Level," *Genetic Psychology Monographs,* XLIX (February 1954), pp. 3-95.

49. Hunt, Jacob Tate, "The Relation Among Vocabulary, Structural Analysis and Reading," *Journal of Educational Psychology,* XLIV (April 1953), pp. 193-202.

50. Husband, John D., "A Technique for the Evaluation of Growth in Certain Affective Phases of Reading Among High School Pupils," *Journal of Educational Research,* XXXIX (December 1945), pp. 265-71.

51. Johnson, Marjorie Seddon, "Factors in Reading Comprehension," *Educational Administration and Supervision,* XXXV (November 1949), pp. 385-406.

52. Jones, Harold D., "The Extra-curricular Reading Interests of Students in a State College," *School and Society,* LXXII (July 15, 1950), pp. 40-43.

53. Knehr, Charles Anthony, "The Effects of Monocular Vision on Measures of Reading Efficiency and Perceptual Span," *Journal of Experimental Psychology,* XXIX (August 1941), pp. 133-54.

54. Krathwohl, William C., "The Importance of Acquiring Reading Skills," *National Elementary Principal,* XXV (February 1946), pp. 30-33.

55. Kyte, George C., "A Core Vocabulary in the Language Arts," *Phi Delta Kappan,* XXXIV (March 1953), pp. 231-4.

56. LaBrant, Lou L., and Heller, Frieda M., "Magazine Reading in an Experimental School," *Library Journal* (March 15, 1936), pp. 213-17.

57. Lauer, A. R., "Improvement of Reading Rate," *Optometric World,* XXXVI (May 1948), pp. 34-8.

58. Ledbetter, Frances Gresham, "Reading Reactions for Varied Types of Subject Matter: An Analytical Study of the Eye Movements of Eleventh Grade Pupils," *Journal of Educational Research,* XLI (October 1947), pp. 102-15.

59. Lewis, Maurice S., "The Effect of Training in Listening Upon Reading," *Journal of Communication,* III (November 1953), pp. 115-9.

60. Lewis, Norman, "An Investigation into Comparable Results Obtained from Two Methods of Increasing Reading Speed Among Adults," *College English,* XI (December 1949), pp. 152-6.

61. Malter, Morton S., "The Content of Current Comic Magazines," *Elemen-*

tary School Journal, LII (May 1952), pp. 505-10.

62. ———, "Studies of the Effectiveness of Graphic Materials," *Journal of Educational Research,* XLVI (December 1952), pp. 263-73.

63. McCullough, Constance M., "Learning to Use Context Clues," *Elementary English Review,* XX (April 1943), pp. 140-43.

64. ———, "What's Behind the Reading Score?" *Elementary English,* XXX (January 1953), pp. 1-7.

65. McKillop, Anne Selley, *The Relationship between the Reader's Attitude and Certain Types of Reading Response* (New York: Teachers College, Columbia University, 1952).

66. Milam, Carl H., chairman, *Children's Reading: A Study of Voluntary Reading of Boys and Girls in the United States,* White House Conference on Child Health and Protection (New York: Century Company, 1933).

67. Miles, Isadora W., "An Experiment in Vocabulary Building in a High School," *School and Society,* LXI (April 28, 1945), pp. 285-6.

68. Miller, George A., Bruner, Jerome S., and Postman, Leo, "Familiarity of Letter Sequences and Tachistoscopic Identification," *Journal of General Psychology,* L (January 1954), pp. 129-39.

69. Morse, William C., Ballantine, Francis A., and Dixon, W. Robert, *Studies in the Psychology of Reading,* University of Michigan Monographs in Education No. 14 (Ann Arbor, Michigan: University of Michigan Press, April 1951).

70. Nelson, Eunice, "A Summary of Investigations Dealing with Results Obtained from Teaching Reading with the Metronoscope," *El Paso Schools Standard,* XX (January 1943), pp. 3-21.

71. Persing, Chester L., and Sattley, Helen R., "Discovering the Reading Interests of Maladjusted Students," *Bulletin of the American Library Association,* XXIX (January 1935), pp. 13-23.

72. Peters, Henry B., "The Influence of Orthoptic Training on Reading Ability," *American Journal of Optometry and Archives of American Academy*

of Optometry, XIX (March-April 1942), pp. 95-111, 152-76.

73. Pflieger, Elmer F., "A Study of Reading Grade Levels," *Journal of Educational Research,* XLII (March 1949), pp. 541-6.

74. Piekarz, Josephine A., "Getting Meaning from Reading," *Elementary School Journal,* LVI (March 1956), pp. 303-9.

75. Pond, Frederick L., "Influence of the Study of Latin on Word Knowledge," *School Review,* XLVI (October 1938), pp. 611-18.

76. Postman, Leo, and Conger, Beverly, "Verbal Habits and the Visual Recognition of Words," *Science,* CXIX (May 14, 1954), pp. 671-3.

77. Potter, Robert E., "Reading Unlimited," *English Journal,* XLII (January 1953), pp. 28-32.

78. Pulliam, R. A., and clinical assistants, Delta State Teachers College, Cleveland, Mississippi, "Indented Word Cards as a Sensory-Motor Aid in Vocabulary Development," *Peabody Journal of Education,* XXIII (July 1945), pp. 38-42.

79. Punke, Harold H., "The Home and Adolescent Reading Interests," *School Review,* XLV (October 1937), pp. 612-20.

80. Reinhardt, Emma, "Reading Interests of Freshmen in a Teachers College," *Teachers College Journal,* Indiana State Teachers College, II (November 1930), pp. 57-60, 63.

81. Robinson, Helen M., *Oral Aspects of Reading,* Supplementary Education Monographs, No. 82 (University of Chicago Press: 1955).

82. Roeber, Edward C., "A Comparison of Seven Interest Inventories with Respect to Word Usage," *Journal of Educational Research,* XLII (September 1948), pp. 8-17.

83. Rothney, John W. M., and McCaul, Robert L., "Reading Preferences of High School Boys," *English Journal,* XXVII (October 1938), pp. 650-60.

84. Russell, David H., "Inter-Class Grouping for Reading Instruction in the Intermediate Grades," *Journal of Educational Research,* XXXIX (February 1946), pp. 462-70.

85. ———, and Shrodes, Caroline, "Contributions of Research in Bibliotherapy to the Language-Arts Program," I and II, *School Review*, LVIII (September and October 1950), pp. 335-42, 411-20.

86. Schubert, Delwyn G., "The Relationship between Reading Ability and Literary Appreciation," *California Journal of Educational Research*, IV (November 1953), pp. 201-2.

87. Seegers, J. C., "Recent Research in Vocabulary Development," *Elementary English Review*, XXIII (February 1946), pp. 61-8.

88. Serra, Mary C., "How to Develop Concepts and Their Verbal Representations," *Elementary School Journal*, LIII (January 1953), pp. 275-85.

89. Shannon, J. R., and Kittle, Marian A., "An Experiment in Teaching Vocabulary," *Teachers College Journal*, State Teachers College, Terre Haute, Indiana, XIV (September 1942), pp. 1-6.

90. Simpson, Elizabeth A., "Reading Rate and Its Relationship to Good Reading," *Education*, LXX (May 1950), pp. 565-9.

91. Simpson, Robert G., "The Relationship of Certain Functions to Eye-Movement Habits," *Journal of Educational Psychology*, XXXIII (May 1942), pp. 373-8.

92. Sister Mary Agnes, S. C., "Influence of Reading on the Racial Attitudes of Adolescent Girls," *Catholic Educational Review*, XLV (September 1947), pp. 415-20.

93. Sister Mary Edith, and Sister Mary Amatora, "The Age Factor in Children's Interest in Free Reading," *Education*, LXXI (May 1951), pp. 567-71.

94. Smith, Henry L., and Eaton, Merrill T., *Analysis of the Proficiency in Silent Reading of 11,424 Sophomore Pupils in 234 High Schools in Indiana*, Bulletin of the School of Education, Indiana University, XXII, No. 1 (Bloomington, Indiana: Bureau of Cooperative Research and Field Service, School of Education, Indiana University, 1946).

95. Sochor, E. Elona, "Special Reading Skills Are Needed in Social Studies, Science, Arithmetic," *Reading Teacher*, VI (March 1953), pp. 4-11.

96. Sommerfeld, Roy E., "An Evaluation of the Tachistoscope in Reading Improvement Programs," *What the Colleges Are Doing in Reading Improvement Programs*, Third Yearbook of the Southwest Reading Conference for Colleges and Universities (Fort Worth, Texas: Texas Christian University Press, 1954), pp. 7-25.

97. Spiegelan, Marvin, Terwilliger, Carl, and Fearing, Franklin, "The Content of Comics: Goals and Means of Comic Strip Characters," *Journal of Social Psychology*, XXXVII (May 1953), pp. 189-203.

98. Stauffer, Russell G., "A Study of Prefixes in the Thorndike List to Establish a List of Prefixes That Should Be Taught in the Elementary School," *Journal of Educational Research*, XXXV (February 1942), pp. 453-8.

99. Sterner, Alice P., *Radio, Motion Picture, and Reading Interests: A Study of High School Pupils*, Teachers College Contribution to Education No. 932 (New York: Bureau of Publications, Teachers College, Columbia University, 1947).

100. Strang, Ruth M., "Gifted Children Need Help in Reading, Too," *Reading Teacher*, VI (January 1953), pp. 23-7.

101. ———, McCullough, Constance M., and Traxler, Arthur E., *Problems in the Improvement of Reading* (McGraw-Hill, revised, 1955), Chapter 6, section on "Grouping," pp. 111-18.

102. Stroud, J. B., and Henderson, Margaret, "Rate of Reading and Learning by Reading," *Journal of Educational Psychology*, XXXIV (April 1943), pp. 193-205.

103. Sutherland, Jean, "The Relationship between Perceptual Span and Rate of Reading," *Journal of Educational Psychology*, XXXVII (September 1946), pp. 373-80.

104. Thompson, Warren Craig, "A Book-Centered Course versus a Machine-Centered Course in Adult Reading Improvement," *Journal of Educational Research*, XLIX (February 1956), pp. 437-45.

105. Thorndike, Edward L., *The Teaching of English Suffixes,* Teachers College Contribution to Education No. 847 (New York: Teachers College, Columbia University, 1941).

106. Thorndike, Robert L., "Words and the Comics," *Journal of Experimental Education,* X (December 1941), pp. 110-13.

107. Tinker, Miles A., "The Study of Eye Movements in Reading," *Psychological Bulletin,* XLIII (March 1946), pp. 93-120.

108. Tireman, L. S., "A Study of Fourth-Grade Reading Vocabulary of Native Spanish-Speaking Children," *Elementary School Journal,* XLVI (December 1945), pp. 223-7.

109. Toops, Myrtle Dewey, "The Core Program Does Improve Reading Proficiency," *Educational Administration and Supervision,* XL (December 1954), pp. 494-503.

110. Townsend, Agatha, "Use of the Survey Section of the Diagnostic Reading Tests in the Independent School Testing Program," *1948 Fall Testing Program in Independent Schools and Supplementary Studies,* Educational Records Bulletin No. 51 (New York: Educational Records Bureau, 1949), pp. 42-9.

111. Traxler, Arthur E., *The Nature and Use of Reading Tests,* Educational Records Bulletin No. 34 (New York: Educational Records Bureau, 1941).

112. ———, "Value of Controlled Reading: Summary of Opinion and Research," *Journal of Experimental Education,* XI (June 1943), pp. 280-92.

113. Weber, C. O., "Effects of Practice on the Perceptual Span for Letters," *Journal of General Psychology,* XXVI (April 1942), pp. 347-51.

114. Westfall, Alfred, "Can College Students Expand Their Recognition Vocabularies?" *School and Society,* LXXIII (January 13, 1951), pp. 25-8.

115. Westover, Frederick L., *Controlled Eye Movements Versus Practice Exercises in Reading,* Teachers College Contribution to Education No. 917 (New York: Teachers College, Columbia University, 1946).

116. Witty, Paul A., and Sizemore, Robert A., "Phonics in the Reading Programs," *Elementary English,* XXXII (October 1955), pp. 355-70.

117. Wooster, George F., "An Experimental Study of the Reading-Rate Controller," *Journal of Educational Psychology,* XLV (November 1954), pp. 421-6.

118. Wrightstone, J. Wayne, "Evaluating the Effectiveness of an Integrated Ninth Grade Curriculum," *Teachers College Journal,* State Teachers College, Terre Haute, Indiana, XIX (November 1947), pp. 2-3, 12.

119. ———, *Appraisal of Growth in Reading,* Educational Research Bulletin No. 2, Bureau of Reference, Research, and Statistics (New York: Board of Education of the City of New York, November 1941).

36: High School and College Instructors Can't Teach Reading? Nonsense! *

STANLEY E. DAVIS

Many competent high school and college instructors recognize that they need to be concerned with helping students at all levels of competence to improve their reading skills needed in the various subject areas. But the perennial question that plagues a conscientious instructor is "How can I cover the course con-

* Reprinted from *The North Central Association Quarterly,* Vol. 34, No. 4 (April 1960), pp. 295-9, by permission of the author and the publisher.

tent assigned by the curriculum makers and at the same time teach reading?"

This article is concerned with suggesting ways that may be helpful to the instructor in high school or college who is trying to resolve the conflict between covering assigned subject matter and helping students become better readers.

The realization that learning to read is a life-long process is not new. In recent years, however, there has been a growing uneasy awareness on the part of many workers in secondary and collegiate education that they need to be doing something about helping students to improve the reading skills that are needed in high school, college, and later adult life. But it has not been clear just what should be done.

More and more high school and college instructors are realizing that something more constructive needs to be done than simply blaming the elementary schools for not doing a better job of teaching children to read. Elementary teachers and administrators, as a whole, are the first to realize that improvements in the teaching of reading need to be made, and they are doing an excellent job of making the needed improvements.

But regardless of the caliber of the work being done by the elementary schools in teaching children to read, it is now well known that the art of reading is so complex that no one, not even the brightest child in the best of all possible elementary schools, can learn all he needs to know about reading by the end of six or eight years of schooling.

WHY ELEMENTARY SCHOOLS CAN'T DO THE WHOLE JOB

There are at least two reasons why the elementary schools cannot be expected to do the entire job of teaching students to read, and why high schools and colleges need to take steps to insure continued growth in the reading ability of students.

1. Reading involves interpreting printed symbols and making discriminative reactions to the ideas expressed by them. The processes of interpreting and making discriminative reactions can be taught and learned only in terms of the ideas expressed by the symbols, i.e., the content of the reading material.

The elementary school cannot prepare children to read skillfully in all the different subject areas they will meet in high school, college, and adult life. Many students are able to select from their "bag" of reading skills those that are required for reading any new bit of material, without guidance from the teacher. However, even these students would be able to select appropriate reading procedures more effectively if some guidance were provided. This is certainly not a novel idea, since our whole concept of formal education is based upon the assumption that guided learning is more efficient than unguided learning.

Most students will be more successful in reading in any subject field if they are given appropriate guidance at the appropriate time. Guidance that was given five to ten years earlier may be too remote to be adequate.

2. Individual differences in reading achievement, which have been well documented and discussed in educational and psychological literature,[1] are present at every educational level. The more effective the instruction provided at earlier levels, the greater the range of individual differences will be at the high school and college levels.

Much has been said and done about working with students who are poor readers. Many reading clinics and special reading classes have been established to provide extra help for these students. Much less thought and energy have been given to helping students who are already average or above in reading skill. In many high school and college classrooms it is the students of better-than-average competence who are "short-changed." Too frequently the assumption is made that these students can take care of themselves.

Let's consider some ways in which subject-matter instructors in high school or college can help students become better readers without taking too much of the time needed for covering course content.

HOW SUBJECT-MATTER INSTRUCTORS CAN HELP STUDENTS BECOME BETTER READERS

There are two basic approaches to helping high school and college students to improve their reading skill. One of these involves setting up a special reading improvement program, with a reading specialist in charge. The other involves the provision of guidance in reading improvement by instructors in the various subject-matter classes.

Both of these approaches should be used, since each can accomplish things that the other cannot. The special reading improvement program in a high school or college should be set up to work with competent readers who can benefit from additional guided practice as well as with students who have reading difficulties. The personnel and facilities of this special program should also be available to subject-matter instructors who want to find ways to improve the reading skills of their students in their own classes.

In addition to referring some students for specialized help in reading, or even in the event that no specialized help is available, the subject-matter instructor can do certain things in his own classroom that will be helpful to even the best readers. An instructor does not need to be an expert in the teaching of reading in order to do these six things.

1. Give Attention to Students' Readiness for Reading the Assigned Material

There appear to be three primary factors that determine readiness for reading, or for learning via any other avenue, at any educational level, or in any particular subject field: a) mental maturity; b) background knowledge and skill; and c) motivation for learning.[2]

An instructor can get a reasonably good indication of the mental maturity of his students in several ways: by looking at their recent intelligence or academic aptitude test scores; by looking at their records of past achievements; and by observing the daily behavior of students in the classroom and outside.

In learning about the status of the background knowledge and skill of his students, an instructor can do several things.

1) He can look at the scores made by students on standardized reading tests;
2) He can devise two or three short reading tests of his own to supplement or replace standardized reading tests. This can be done by choosing selections from the textbook(s) to be studied, and composing several comprehension questions on the selections. These short tests can then be used to get an indication of students' rate of reading and comprehension accuracy on material of the kind that they will meet in his course. In making such tests the instructor will need to be careful not to select paragraphs containing technical terms that are not defined within those paragraphs, and that the student could not be expected to know otherwise. Since the material for these two or three tests can be selected from the content of his course, the instructor can get objective indications of his students' reading ability at the same time that he is covering subject matter. By

using two or three short tests on different days, he can be better assured of the reliability and validity of his impressions.

3) An instructor can devise a test on the vocabulary and concepts that students will encounter in a new assignment to determine whether the students have the background knowledge required for understanding the lesson. He can then teach any concepts and terms that may be needed, as indicated by the pre-test.

If students have the mental maturity, the reading skill (and any other required skills), and the understanding of vocabulary and basic concepts required to profitably study the new material, they will be successful readers, *if they are interested.* It is well known that a strong desire to learn will compensate for many background deficiencies. In making any assignment, an instructor needs to seriously consider how he can help students to acquire the interest and drive that will help them to go ahead in spite of obstacles. The problem of motivation is, of course, an age-old one that cannot be easily solved. However, in doing the three things suggested just above, an instructor will be doing a great deal to increase the meaningfulness of reading in his subject for his students. Meaningfulness of activity is one of the major factors in motivation for that activity.

The ideas that follow also bear, at least indirectly, upon motivation.

2. Give Attention to the Readability of Assigned Textbooks and Supplementary Reading Material

Closely related to the problem of determining and increasing students' readiness for learning through reading is the question of the readability of the assigned reading matter. As early as 1923 it was recognized that much textbook material is written at an unnecessarily difficult level.[6] Since that time several "readability formulae"[3, 5, 7] have been devised for estimating the difficulty of reading material. Some of these formulae can be easily applied by an instructor to reading material in his courses to give him a more objective indication of the difficulty of the material than he might otherwise have.

The desirability of providing easier reading material for some students as preparation for successful handling of the normally assigned reading, and of providing more challenging material for others, is obvious. The argument is sometimes heard that providing reading material on different levels of difficulty, particularly easier material for the less competent students, constitutes "spoon feeding" and is not compatible with the goal of maintaining high standards in education. The necessity for maintaining high standards cannot be denied. But it would seem that a good way to help the less competent students to read better and to achieve according to the high standards that we desire, is to let them read easier material on the subject as preparation for successfully handling the more difficult material that is normally assigned. Among other advantages, this would help to decrease the frustration experienced by poor readers when required to read material written in a difficult style, without adequate preparation for it.

Similarly, it seems likely that levels of achievement of the most competent students can be raised by letting them read more difficult material. This attention to readability may enable an instructor to decrease the frustration that hampers a bright student when he has to read material that is so easy as to provide no challenge for him. Even if supplementary reading material of different difficulty levels is not available, an instructor can better help students get ready to do the assigned reading if he knows something about the readability of the material.

3. Show Students How To Preview Reading Material

One of the major premises of many present-day theories of learning is that meaningful material is easier to learn and remember than is non-meaningful material. This principle is highly pertinent to learning through reading. One important way in which a reader can increase the meaningfulness of any material for himself is by previewing the material to be read before reading it in detail. This process will enable him to have some prior understanding of the content and of the major trends in the discussion. He will be less apt to let the appearance of the trees dull his perception of the forest.

Many high school and college students, even among the brightest, have not learned to preview an article, chapter, or book before reading it in detail.[4] In helping students learn how to preview a selection, an instructor should first make clear why such a procedure is helpful. He can help students to realize that it is easier and more enjoyable to learn something when one can see how it is related to the whole. He can then show students how the preface, table of contents, section headings, summaries, footnotes, charts and graphs, topic sentences, index, appendices, glossary, etc., can be used to advantage in studying for this particular course.

The Survey Q3R Method of reading, involving previewing as its first step, is an excellent example of a systematic approach to reading that is based upon experimental findings in psychological studies of learning, perception, retention, motivation, etc.[*][8,9] The few minutes required to explain and demonstrate this method of reading, using the course textbook or comparable material, will be well repaid by the increased effectiveness of students at all levels of reading skills.

4. Help Students Realize the Importance of Varying Style of Reading To Fit Material and Purpose

Many students, particularly the poorer ones, have the misconception that all reading should be done at the same rate and with the same thoroughness, regardless of material and purpose. An extreme example of this misconception may be seen in students who read everything with slow, careful deliberation. At the other extreme are the students who try to read everything rapidly. These students, and others between these extremes, do not realize that the rate and care with which a skillful reader reads a given bit of material depends upon the nature of the material and his purpose in reading it.

An instructor can emphasize two points with students in regard to varying rate and thoroughness of reading according to their purposes and the nature of the material.

1) The skillful reader asks himself, before starting to read, "What do I

---

* F. P. Robinson, who originally designed the Survey Q3R Method, gives the following explanation of it (Pressey, Robinson and Horrocks, *Psychology in Education*, pp. 571-2):

"Survey. The student makes a rapid survey of the headings in the assignment, to find out what major ideas are present and their sequence.

"Question. The student turns the first heading into a question in order to have a seeking attitude and to know what he is reading for.

"Read. The student reads the section under the heading, seeking the answer to his question.

"Recite. Having read the section clear through, the student writes down brief cue phrases *from memory*. (No copying is done, and complete notes are not wanted.)

"Steps 2, 3, and 4 are repeated for each succeeding section that has a heading.

"Review. Immediately after reading the whole lesson in this way, the student tries to recall the points that have been developed in it. This is a second recitation. He glances at his notes only as needed to remind him of points not immediately recalled."

already know about this topic? What do I want to get from this reading—all of the major ideas and their supporting details, or just the main ideas without the details, or am I looking just for some specific items of information?"

2) The skillful reader uses a systematic approach to reading, such as the Survey Q3R Method, varying its application according to the degree of comprehension and retention he desires.

Students who realize the importance of varying their style of reading according to their purposes and the nature of the material can achieve greater mastery of subject matter in a course. They recognize that while the course textbook requires very thorough reading, supplementary readings for additional background can frequently be read less thoroughly, hence more rapidly and in greater quantity. This, of course, presupposes that students know how to find supplementary material on the subject.

5. Help Students To Locate Supplementary Reading Material on the Subject

Wide reading in a subject helps a student to become better informed on the subject, and also helps him to read additional materials in that field more effectively. An instructor can help students to become more skillful readers as well as better informed students by helping them learn to locate reading material in his subject field. He should acquaint them with sources of bibliographies, with indices and abstracts, and with other appropriate guides to reference material.

6. Help Students Improve Their Knowledge of the Vocabulary of the Subject

Since acquaintance with the terminology of any subject is basic to reading skill-

fully in that subject, a major responsibility of an instructor is to help students to acquire the desire and the necessary skills for continued vocabulary improvement in the subject.

An instructor can emphasize that extensive reading constitutes one of the best bases for vocabulary improvement. In addition, he can remind students of certain skills that are useful in deciphering the meanings of strange words. While most students probably learned these skills in the elementary school, many will profit from being reminded of the applications of these skills to the vocabulary of the particular subject being studied. Among the most important of these skills are: [10]

a) using context clues;
b) using phonetic clues;
c) using structural clues—e.g., prefixes, suffixes, roots
d) using the dictionary.

Guidance from the instructor will help students to see how these vocabulary skills may be used in improving knowledge of vocabulary in any particular subject.

SUMMARY

Since learning to read is a lifetime process that cannot be completely mastered by the end of the elementary school, subject-matter instructors in high schools and colleges have a responsibility for helping students continue their growth in reading skill. This article has suggested ways in which a subject-matter instructor can help his students improve their reading skill at the same time that he is covering subject matter. An instructor does not need to be an expert in the teaching of reading in order to help students read better at the same time that he is covering course content.

REFERENCES

1. Anderson, Irving H., and Dearborn, Walter F., *The Psychology of Teaching Reading*. New York: Ronald Press, 1952, pp. 41-8.
2. Cronbach, Lee J., *Educational Psychology*. New York: Harcourt-Brace, 1954, Chapters 4-8.
3. Dale, E., and Chall, J. S., "A Formula for Predicting Readability," *Educational Research Bulletin,* Vol. 27, 1948, pp. 11-12, 37-54.
4. Danskin, D. G., and Burnett, C. W., "Study Techniques of Those Superior Students," *Personnel and Guidance Journal,* Vol. 31, pp. 181-6.
5. Flesch, R. F., "Marks of Readable Style," *Contributions to Education,* No. 897, Teachers College, Columbia University, 1943.

6. Lively, B. A., and Pressey, S. L., "A Method of Measuring 'Vocabulary Burden' of Textbooks," *Educational Administration and Supervision,* Vol. 9, 1923, pp. 389-98.
7. Lorge, Irving, "Predicting Readability," in Hunnicutt and Iverson, *Research in the Three R's*. New York: Harper and Brothers, 1958, pp. 184-94.
8. Pressey, S. L., Robinson, F. P., and Horrocks, J. E., *Psychology in Education*. New York: Harper and Brothers, 1959, Chapter 17.
9. Robinson, F. P., *Effective Study*. New York: Harper and Brothers, 1946, Project II.
10. Spache, G., and Berg, P., *The Art of Efficient Reading*. New York: Macmillan, 1955, Chapters 9-11.

37: Some Research on the Impact of Reading *

DAVID H. RUSSELL

Opinions about the impact of reading materials range at least from the words of Plato to those of Nathalia Crane. Writing in *The Republic* on the importance of impressions on youth Plato said, "We should do our utmost that the first stories that they hear should be so composed as to bring the fairest lessons of virtue to their ears." But the modern young poet says, "Every gaudy color is a bit of truth."

Abraham Lincoln, too, must have believed that the ideas in reading materials have powerful effects. After *Uncle Tom's Cabin* had swept the northern States and he had first met Harriet Beecher Stowe he said, "Is this the little woman whose book made such a great war?" Writers also testify occa-

sionally of the power of good literature in their lives. Autobiographer, critic, and teacher often tell what some piece of literature has meant to them.

From the research point of view, however, the effects of reading are an uncharted wasteland in an otherwise well-mapped territory. We have discovered many facts about eye-movements in reading, reading interests and tastes, and methods of reading instruction—but we don't know much about what reading does to people.

What happens to a ten-year-old who reads a quiet story about a farm boy or one who is gripped by *Treasure Island?* Does the latter, as in Stevenson's superb ending, "start upright in bed, with the sharp voice of Captain Flint still ring-

* Reprinted from *The English Journal*. Vol. 47, No. 7 (October 1958), pp. 398-413, by permission of the National Council of Teachers of English and the author.

ing in (his) ears: 'Pieces of eight! pieces of eight!' " What happens to an adolescent who studies Elizabeth Barrett Browning's "How do I Love Thee?" or J. D. Salinger's *Catcher in the Rye?* Perhaps a hint about the effects of the latter book can be found in the estimates of Holden Caulfield's personality and character made by a group of California high school students. They said such individual things as "Holden is a bum," "He's a crazy mixed-up kid," "He's a sensitive boy," "He's almost like myself," "Holden Caulfield should have minded his parents," and "I can understand how he felt about school." Apparently interpretations, and possible effects, are individual matters. But we can scarcely be content with the generalization that the same story produces different effects in different people.

WHY STUDY EFFECTS OF READING?

First, we need to know about the effects of reading because we need much more information about factors influencing human behavior. Knowledge for its own sake? Perhaps. But books are part of the communication field which includes broadcasts, television programs, comics, advertising, public speeches, all of which may change individuals or groups. We need careful research findings about the effects of these media and the effects of reading, sometimes as a corrective to the opinions about such effects, expressed with the best of intentions and the least of knowledge by censorship and other agencies.

We need to know much more about the specific effects of reading, second, because its effects will influence the amount of future reading the pupil or student does—and this is a laudable concern of every English teacher. One hypothesis is that youth will read, in competition with other activities, only if reading fills some basic needs whether for information, for enjoyment, for escape, or for answers to deep-laid anx-

ieties. Only as reading has some favorable effects on instrumental needs or on personality itself will it be given a place as part of an enduring pattern of activities. Only then will it go beyond the status of the superficial diversion to become a permanent part of the life activities of the individual.

Third, we need to know about the effects of reading so we can do a better classroom job. We need clues to what happens when boy meets book. Then we can go efficiently about the business of making important ideas accessible in many forms to the eight-year-old or the sixteen-year-old. The matching cannot be blind or cannot rely even on the brilliant hunch—it must be based on as many as possible established facts about the effects of books on people. The teacher of English, the compiler of the reading list, or the librarian must go beyond the selection of good-looking titles and themes to much more detailed knowledge of the interaction of young people and books. Part of that knowledge comes in research findings about the effects of specific stories on individual youth.

Perhaps we as English teachers have taken too much for granted in the past. We may have been like the Tibetan monks of whom Marco Polo wrote in his early "travel book." He described how each new Tibetan monk bound a book to his forehead so that he could absorb the wisdom in it. Have we been a bit like the novice monks of that day? Have we merely assumed that young people absorb the good or bad in various types of literature? What of the evidence, rather than hearsay or pious hope?

The established facts about the effects of reading are fragmentary and elusive. It is not enough that some great and good men have testified to the power of books in their lives. We are inclined to agree with Bacon that "Reading maketh a full man." We know that Luther Burbank believed his whole life was changed by the reading of one book, Darwin's *The Origin of Species.* We may not agree with Clarence Day that people "keep on reading, ambitiously, till they have stunned their native initiative, and made their thoughts weak." But these statements, on two sides of the question, do not constitute evidence in the scientific sense. Neither does the skilled analysis of the competent literary critic. We are interested in the insights and reactions of the perceptive critic. We know that he often adds to our own enjoyment and understanding. But the introspective praise of a volume, poem, or passage in an autobiography and the opinions, barbed or bland, of the one critic are conjectures about the effects of literature or personal testimony to its impact on one person. Perhaps the matter should go no further and we should be content with the individual, subjective reaction to a given piece of literature. Perhaps as teachers of English we should merely present the best we know and hope for an occasional gleam in an adolescent eye or brisk discussion in a small student group.

Perhaps, on the other hand, we should examine as much evidence as we have, keeping in mind that some studies labeled "research" may be no more valid than the subtle insights of critic or teacher. For what they are worth, then, let us look at some of the attempts to study analytically the effects of reading. For convenience, the research may be categorized in four overlapping areas:

1. *The characteristics of the material read*
2. *The content of ideas communicated*
3. *The traits of the reader*
4. *Overt responses made*

Readers familiar with communications research will recognize that these categories may be true, not only of reading, but of other communication situations usually described in studies of the mass media and of group persuasion.

CHARACTERISTICS OF THE READING MATERIAL

This section reviews briefly research concerned with the surface aspects of reading materials. It suggests that materials attractively presented, and related to the reader's interests and reading ability, have an initial advantage in producing effects. It suggests a parallel with the findings of the social psychologist who tells us that changes in behavior resulting from communication depend both upon the prestige of the sender and the clarity and credibility of the message.[8, 26, 27]

Studies of children's reading interests such as an early one of Bamberger[3] with young children and a more recent one by Rankin[46] with older girls indicate that people are influenced in their initial choice of reading materials by such factors as theme, format, illustrations, and even size of book. Young children enjoy familiar stories heard in a pleasant setting.[9] Library borrowings are influenced by accessibility, recommendations of others, and previous knowledge of the author.[5] Of scores of studies of reading interest, however, most are content with superficial listings of favorite titles and themes and do not go back of these to reasons for reading. An attempt to get at some underlying motives was made by Rudman[48] in a questionnaire to over six thousand older children and to parents, teachers, and librarians. He found that children's "read-about," "ask-about," and "look-up" behavior do not necessarily coincide. Interests change with age but not with different regions or communities. Parents emphasize the use of reference books and librarians recommend biographies more than children do. Carlsen[10] has also discussed the relationship of reading interests to adolescents' psychological needs such as "assurance of his own normality," but specific evidence is needed.

The effects of reading may be determined also by the difficulty of the materials which the person is attempting to decipher. If you can't read a passage, it probably won't affect you. The exception to this fact is found in clinical cases who can't read but who nevertheless dislike the printed materials. This fact is documented by the reports by workers in reading clinics of hundreds of cases of children, faced by the continual frustration of inability to recognize and comprehend, who have developed negative attitudes toward all print. This effect may be so deep-laid and far-reaching that all reading, or attempts at it, have unfortunate effects on the child's or the adolescent's attitude.[18, 50, 58, 68]

Results of the inability to understand a paragraph or passage have been analyzed in scores of studies of comprehension dating back at least to Thorndike's [63] classic study in 1917. The recent interest and research in readability, ably summarized by Chall,[12] gives many clues to factors in the printed materials themselves, such as hard words, length of sentence, and organization, which cause difficulty and therefore prevent impact. In a study of the interpretation of poetry Richards [47] found two sources of difficulty to be (a) inability to grasp the author's meaning at one or more levels of comprehension such as sense, feeling, tone, and intention and (b) misunderstanding of the author's imagery. Such difficulties in the materials themselves are inevitably tied to the background and personal characteristics of the reader as a person, considered more fully two sections below.

CONTENT OF IDEAS

Recent years have seen a shift in emphases in the study of literature away from the accumulation of historical and linguistic data toward the discovery of qualities and values in writing. As Shumaker [57] put it, "The stress on biography, derivations, influences, successions and so on has been much lightened" and the modern instructor is concerned with "the aesthetic meanings and formal qualities of individual literary works, which he conceives as works of the creative imagination." As a result, Shumaker adds, "Many parents have begun to recognize a puzzling discrepancy between what their children in high school and college seem to know about *David Copperfield* or *Hamlet* and what they themselves remember." This emphasis on the content of ideas may also be noted in a trend toward centering curriculum units around such themes as "Growing Up" or "Interpersonal Relations" and the preparation of book lists such as Kircher's [32] *Character Formation through Books* and Taba's [61] *Reading Ladders for Human Relations*. The first of these attempts to analyze the values found in selected books, such as courage, loyalty, and piety, and the second to suggest sequences of books to be read which center on certain topics such as "Patterns in Family Life" and "How it Feels to Grow Up." The same shift in emphasis may be noted in criticism of books for younger children away from consideration of literary values to explorations of meanings or functions in the life of the child.

Although most teachers would give considerable emphasis to the content of what we teach, one word of warning should be inserted. In a straightforward factual account of the chemical composition of air or of the battle of Gettysburg there may not be too much room for individual interpretation (although there are still disagreements about Gettysburg) but when we come to a work of graphic art or literature, many interpretations may be possible—even about the content. One description of a true work of art, pictorial or verbal, is that it means many things to many men. As Virginia Woolf put it, "There is an ambiguity which is the work of the highest poetry; we cannot know exactly what it means—The meaning is just on the far side of language." Analysis of content has its limitations, then, but this is no reason for omitting it in any study of possible effects of reading. The method used to arrive at the ideas and values in a communication is usually labelled "content analysis" and has been described in sources such as the book by Berelson.[4] In communications research a classic study is Arnheim's [2] analysis of the radio "soap opera" which found, among other facts, that the daytime serial never had skilled laborers or factory workers as heroes and that some eighty-five per cent of human problems were apparently in the area of personal relationships. The method has also been applied to young people's literature in Jacobs' [30] study of thirty-nine books of historical fiction in which he analyzes the materials to determine what concepts of democracy are stated or implied in the stories.

Another example is McConnell's [39] analysis of twenty-four selected biographies for children and young adolescents in which she found that personal achievement was related to (a) individuality, (b) work traits such as persistence, (c) relations with people such as friendliness and kindness, and (d) attitudes towards the self and one's work characterized by modesty, simplicity, and idealism. Jacobs [29] and Fisher [16] discussed respectively cultural patterns and family life in children's literature. Shepard [55] analyzed characteristics of persons treated positively and negatively in popular children's books. Sherwin [56] located no less than 2,300 assumptions in a high school literature curriculum and concluded that these "may either fail to be perceived by students or, what is worse, may be accepted by them uncritically and perhaps unconsciously— we as teachers do not wish to slip ideological 'mickies' to our students."

Similarly, a number of studies have been made of the content of magazines,[6, 19] of comic books,[69, 70] of best-selling novels,[24] and of school readers. In the last category Child and others [13] analyzed the contents of third readers of basic reading series, found a dominance of middle-class values in the books, and suggested an interesting list of possible effects of the reading of the books. Anderson [1] found in another study that modern readers contained more material on "moral and spiritual values" than did the famous old McGuffey readers. Another example of analysis from a specialized point of view is the attempt to analyze nursery rhymes, Christmas stories, and other children's activities in terms of psychoanalytic concepts.[43]

This sampling of studies is perhaps sufficient to show that the content of reading materials is being studied seriously. At first glance it would seem that the ideas, concepts, biases, and prejudices of an author stated directly or indirectly in a story would affect the reader. From the scientific point of view, however, the hypothesis must still be demonstrated. Horror comic books *may* be a cause of juvenile delinquency, or moral tomes produce a virtuous young man, but we can't be sure that content has such a direct effect. As we shall see below, the reader himself, his attitudes and personality, intrude into the picture and affect the impact of the print.

CHARACTERISTICS OF THE READER

Some research has emphasized the active role of the reader and the structural properties of the situation in which he is doing his reading as important factors in determining the impact of print. Sex, age, intelligence, and reading ability of the reader would seem to be important influences on any effects a story or passage may have. In addition, the more subtle psychodynamics of the reader's personality configuration may determine the effects on him. In mass communications Hovland [27] has indicated that effects depend upon (a) the individual's readiness to accept or reject a given idea, (b) his general susceptibility to persuasion and social influence—his "persuasability," and (c) the interpersonal relationships of his group and the individual's conformity or independence in relation to group influences. Some parallels to the act of reading may be drawn. What, then, does research say more specifically about the reading situation? If we turn from the psychological to the literary, can we agree with Cecil: [11]

Every reader is a Lady of Shalott, who, secluded in his secret chamber, forgets the hours as he sits watching the endless procession of human thought and passion and action, as it passes, motley and tumultuous, across the gleaming mirror of literature. (p. 29.)

What are the characteristics that make the reader, like the Lady of Shalott, see his own interpretations in the mirror of his reading? Here research results are of some help. There is considerable evidence, first, that the attitudes the reader brings to the page affect what he gets from it. In an early study Good [20] showed that different types of directions gave different scores on tests of reading comprehension. Jackson [28] showed that the effects of reading on attitudes toward Negroes are influenced by the previous attitudes held by the reader. Crossen [15] showed that attitudes affect critical judgments of passages read. She considered that "the more personal, immediate or intense the feeling, the greater the likelihood that it will prove a barrier between the reader and an accurate interpretation of material read. . . . propaganda contrary to the attitude held by the reader appeared to lead to imitation and confusion rather than to a changed conviction."

McKillop [40] demonstrated that attitudes affect comprehension very little in terms of factual data explicitly stated but are much more influential in answers involving value judgments about the material read. Mannello [41] has shown that attitude affects the acquisition of new facts among eighth-grade pupils. In a recent unpublished study, Groff [23] found that fifth- and sixth-grade children's attitudes toward reading generally, and especially toward certain types of content, were related to their critical reading abilities of the various content types. There were differences between boys and girls in attitudes and in critical reading abilities of the various content types. There were also differences between boys and girls in attitudes and in critical reading abilities in such content areas as stories of sports, airplanes, and interpersonal relationships.

In addition to attitudes, certain experiential factors and personality traits may be associated with results of reading. In the study of Cambridge students mentioned above, Richards [47] spoke of the "mnemonic irrelevancies" of the group —"the misleading effects of the readers' memories of some personal scene or adventure, erratic associations, the interference of emotional reverberations from the past which have nothing to do with the poem." He wrote about (a) the misleading effect of erratic associations and stereotyped responses, (b) confusions caused by doctrinal dispositions of the reader, especially when his beliefs conflict with those presented in the poem, and (c) general critical misconceptions and technical judgments. In a subsequent study Hayakawa [25] also found stereotyped reactions to words, sometimes opposite in meaning to the intent of the passage and spoke of the "intrusion of fixed dogmas." In another related study Cross [14] found causes of misunderstanding in a combination of experience and habit such as (a) too literal interpretation of the printed word, (b) confusions in the meanings of words, (c) erratic associations caused by home or family, and (d) influence of personal experiences.

Recent work has given somewhat more detailed and sophisticated analysis of reasons for private interpretations of passages or stories. Osgood's [44, 45] studies suggest that some of these individual interpretations may be due to the concomitant meanings and feeling tones with which we surround our literal understandings. For example, a person recalls most easily high-value words, and these may be the basis for an autistic response. Put another way, certain high-value words may determine interpretation of a passage, and relevancy of facts is largely fixed by personal values. Such egocentric or need-fulfilling responses have been noted in the interpretation of literature.[25, 33] Apparently interpretations may be a private affair. We need to know more how autistic interpretations of words affect comprehension of passages.

Taba [62] recorded and classified the discussion of books and stories by twenty-five students in an eighth-grade class. She found that projections (attempts to understand and evaluate behavior) accounted for fifty-one per cent to eighty-seven per cent of the statements made by individuals. Less frequent were generalizations, self-references, and irrelevancies. Taba believed that her classification of responses showed four types of readers: (a) those who enter into a story freely and fully without generalizing about it, (b) egocentric readers who find meaning only in light of their own experience, (c) egocentric readers who make prescriptive judgments about story characters, and (d) readers who project or generalize and thus find new experiences in their reading.

Other careful studies have related detailed aspects of personality to reading responses. Foulds [17] found that favorite character choices of children could be predicted from their overt behavior indicative of certain personality traits. Kay [31] obtained evidence that persons with high anxiety levels read predominantly about their own problems in newspaper materials. Loban [35] found that many adolescents miss important implications of stories, feel unable to discuss the literature read, and that those who do respond often do so with superficial concepts. He also found that the adolescents rated as most sensitive have the most to say about a story, and those rated least sensitive tend to attach blame to someone in the story. Adolescents rate as better stories the ones within their intellectual and emotional range, and do not welcome new concepts or different values.

In an important unpublished study which is discussed more fully in the next section Squire [60] found that adolescents reading four short stories containing experiences in personal development gave some six types of reaction to the stories. The frequency of these types was related to personality scores but the relationships were complex and differed for boys and girls. Usually clusters of personality traits rather than single characteristics appeared to be associated with particular types of response. This finding was also made by Wynne [73] in another unpublished study of children in grades 4, 5, and 6. Wynne found only a slight relationship between general personality and reading scores (r's .20−.25) but found that reading scores may be closely related to personality clusters described in such items as confidence, conformity to accepted standards, and good social relationships with peers and adults.

The interrelationships of reading and personality are complex.[49] William Lyon Phelps seems to have been oversimplifying when he stated, "I divide all readers into two classes: those who read to remember and those who read to forget." The effects of reading, like

Cassius' description of our faults, are "not in our stars, but in ourselves." We may hypothesize that impact of reading is determined by the situation in which the reading is done, by the reader's expectations or set, by his overt purpose for reading, by his conscious or unconscious needs, by the personality traits or patterns which affect much of his conduct, and by combinations of these factors.

OVERT RESPONSES AS EFFECTS OF READING

The lack of comprehensive studies of the impact of reading is a curious commentary on fashions in research or on the inability of school people and psychologists to get support for research projects on major topics. In a recent review of reading research Scott[54] concludes that "the most serious shortcomings of research findings are the limited help they give on understanding and influencing the motivation of the reader and the limited evidence they provide that reading produces important changes in individuals." Similarly Russell[52] has indicated the dearth of research in this area and outlined ten topics under the effects of reading on which research is needed.

Despite this paucity in research some leads may be given and a few specific studies cited. Hints at methods of study and of possible results may be found in sociological and psychological research on the effects of mass communications. Two sources by Hovland[26, 27] are useful, the first including a short section on the effects of books, newspapers, and magazines. Schramm[53] has a book dealing with the effects of newspapers, comics, and the comparative effects of the mass media. Lowdermilk[38] compared the effects of listening to radio programs and reading the printed versions of the recordings on pupils' attitudes toward freedom of speech and of assembly. He found that reading was more effective

than listening in changing attitudes, but that the two could be well combined. Witty[67] has discussed possible effects of television along with his surveys of televiewing habits. With some 150 references to all the mass media and discussion of such topics as categorization of types of effects, the Hovland[26] article is required reading for the beginning, serious student of the problem.

A few other reports have indicated the wide variety of possible effects and hence the necessity of varied procedures in studying possible effects. Lind[34] found that college students' reports of the causes and effects of childhood reading could be classified as (a) reading as escape, (b) reading as temporary diversion, (c) reading as an organizing influence on personality, and (d) reading in relation to objective interests. Russell[51] found that beginning teachers reported memories of over fifteen different kinds of effects, the most common of which were identification with character(s), enjoyment of humor and adventure, and enrichment of everyday experiences. Gray[22] summarized some thirty reports to show that reading may have social effects in influencing (a) beliefs, (b) attitudes and morale, (c) public opinion, (d) voting, and (e) crime and other anti-social behavior.

Probably, the greatest need at present is for developmental studies showing comparative effects of reading on young children, older children, adolescents, and adults. An illustration of this type of study in a limited field is the English one by Williams, Winter, and Woods[66] using five tests of literary appreciation. They found for the youngest and dullest children that the subject of the literary work is most important. Up to ten years of age for boys and twelve years for girls the chief criterion in judgment is the ethical intention of the author. About twelve years of age some sense of "literary quality" emerges in such terms as structure, aptness of simile or metaphor, and ingenuity. Because of its methods, such a study illustrates only possible effects, but suggests limits within which effects can be expected.

Studies with young children include those of Wolfenstein [71] who compared effects of a children's story on mothers and children and one by Grace and Lohmann [21] of second-graders' reactions to nine short stories depicting parent-child conflicts. In the latter study, after hearing each story in an individual interview situation the child was asked to pretend he was a story character and to tell what he wanted to do and how he felt "inside." In order of frequency, the commonest reactions were active opposition, simple compliance, constructive behavior, and emotional behavior. Responses did not differ with the sex of the children or of the parent causing the frustration in the story. Wolfson [72] gave an anecdotal account of the use of three books at the third-grade level in having children explore feelings of shyness, relationships of fear and bravery, and fear of the dark. She added a list of thirty books with parallel themes suitable for use in primary grades.

Boyd and Mandler [7] studied the responses of eight- and nine-year olds to stories and pictures of people and animals. Their findings included the following: (a) stories with human characters elicit more personal identification and involvement than animal stories, (b) socially disapproved behavior in the stories elicits expressions of punishment and socially approved behavior more projection of the self, (c) socially disapproved behavior by human characters in the story may arouse anxiety in the subject. Also at the elementary-school level, Smith [59] used the free-response method by having children write about any changes in their thinking or attitudes resulting from reading. Thus prompted, sixty-one per cent of the group told of changes in attitude as a result of reading. Thirty per cent listed changes in concepts, ideas, and understanding, but only nine per cent reported changes in behavior as a result of their reading.

Sister Lorang [37] studied the reading experiences of 2,300 high school students in Catholic and public schools. Her results must be interpreted in light of her use of a questionnaire with leading questions such as "What books or magazines have had a good effect on you; Bad effect on you?" but the report has a useful bibliography of studies up to 1944 of possible effects of motion pictures, reading, and the comics. Sister Lorang concludes that if a book or magazine is classed as good or bad, it will almost certainly have good or bad effects, respectively. The study tabulates emotional responses, imitative behavior, and tendencies toward identification for seventy-five per cent of the material read by the adolesecnt group.

Several other studies of the impact of reading on adolescents are of interest in that they use more intensive techniques than a questionnaire. An early example by Meckel [42] analyzed responses of ninety-six high school seniors to a novel of family life. Although he quotes many positive examples, Meckel warns that "Identification between the reader and a character may be repressed and the reading content criticized or rejected" when the character exhibits "unaccepted" behavior or personality traits or suffers unpleasant experiences. Some sense of caution is conveyed also by the findings of Lodge [36] about the reactions of eighth-graders to biographies. She found little evidence of the influence of carefully selected biographies on the "moral ideology" of the group as reported in essays entitled "The Person I Would Like To Be Like" and in interviews. The group largely wrote about composite or imaginary persons. However, Lodge states that the experiment should continue longer with children more used to applying ideas, and felt that "books are enabling these adolescents to explore, with an undertone of realism, vocational interests and are furnishing relaxation, adventure and romance."

An important study of the reactions of adolescents is that of Squire [60] mentioned above and involving fourteen- to sixteen-year-olds. The group responded to four short stories with themes of personal development in over 14,000 response statements as coded by content analysis. The most frequent response was an interpretational reaction (forty-two per cent), and others in decreasing order of frequency were narrational, associational and self-involvement comments, and literary and prescriptive judgments. Self-involvement and literary judgment responses varied inversely during the reading of the stories. Two major sources of difficulties in interpretation were "happiness binding" and "insistence on certainty in interpretation." At least two types of self-involvement were noted and individual variation in response was clearly indicated.

Older students and adults were involved in a study by Weingarten [65] and in the often-quoted early investigation of Waples, Berelson, and Bradshaw.[64] Weingarten used two questionnaires to get the responses of 1,256 students in seventeen colleges and universities on the personal benefits of their voluntary reading. The average student checked four values but the only one checked by more than half the group was the contribution of reading to "philosophy of life." The benefits of reading in descending order of frequency were: helped understanding of the meaning of life, sixty per cent; changed attitudes, thirty-nine per cent; stimulated imitation in behavior of a character, thirty-four per cent; helped in finding the ideal self, thirty-five per cent; recognized problems similar to their own, thirty-two per cent; tried to develop personal qualities read about, thirty per cent; in-creased self-understanding through identification, twenty-nine per cent; helped in the solution of their own problems, twenty per cent; helped in the selection of a vocation, eleven per cent. The books reported most useful on the second questionnnaire were *The Bible, Seventeen, The Robe, Seventeenth Summer,* and *Of Human Bondage.* Despite these rather optimistic percentages, Weingarten feels that only a small amount of the purposive reading of the group revealed developmental values to them. This conclusion may be a valid one because of a possible tendency to give congenial answers on the questionnaire.

The other study of Waples and colleagues [64] unfortunately gives few solid quantitative data but it does provide a useful categorization of possible effects of reading. These are (a) instrumental —using information in print to help the solution of personal and practical problems, (b) prestige—increasing self-esteem by reading materials favorable to one's own group, (c) reinforcement —of views already held, (d) aesthetic response—appreciation of beauty and other literary qualities in the writing, (e) respite or escape—such as "killing time" or "having a good laugh."

The research studies cited give some clues to the complexity and subtlety of the impact of reading as measured by responses to printed materials. Most reading tests do not get at these deep-laid and wide-ranging responses and, indeed, some researches have shown low correlations between reading achievement scores and interpretation scores. The investigations which are outlined above suggest that effects are often personal and original, that the same passage may produce different effects on different students. As Squire [60] concludes, "The evidence seems largely to support the point of view that readers respond to literature in a unique and selective way." Such a fact need not necessarily discourage further study of the effects of the same material on different persons, or the effects of different materials on the same person. Longitudinal studies of changes in response with age are needed as well as wider samplings of materials and persons at cross-sectional levels.

CONCLUSIONS

The introduction to this research summary stated that it is not enough to say that the same story produces different effects on different people. More detailed knowledge of the interaction between person and passage is needed. The research studies cited mention four variables in the situation: the form of the materials, their content of ideas, the reader himself, and the setting and matrix in which overt responses are made. We have never had a complete demonstration that a story of courage and friendship will communicate ideas of courage and friendship to every reader, much less result in courageous or friendly behavior. In the scientific sense, at least, teachers can no longer talk of "good books for children" as if some books were "good" for all children or adolescents. About the best we can attempt to present is the right book for the right person at the right time.

Lack of research must not be construed to mean that reading has little or no impact on people. Intuitive and stimulating teachers have always transgressed the axioms of little knowledge and rocketed into untraveled space— perhaps with a few satellites attached. The complete evidence does not exist yet in scientific form.

This paper suggests that beginnings in the search have been made in four overlapping areas. We doubt that students acquire knowledge, values, or virtues, as the Tibetan novices hoped, by some process of absorption or osmosis. Instead, we are beginning to get clues about kinds and content of reading materials and the sorts of reactions we can expect from individuals of different backgrounds, interests, and personality patterns. We doubt that the "pleasures of literature" are for everyone, unless "literature" is interpreted broadly. We at least know enough to take care in using reading to help pupils solve their personal problems for often they may fail to understand, they may misinterpret, or they may consciously or unconsciously block the desired responses.

From the research point of view, we suspect that much reading by itself has little effect on a person's deeper layers of feeling and behavior. So far we have been unable to disentangle the influences of reading from the consequences of other activities, and perhaps we never shall. Just as we reject statements that comics or mystery stories are a sole cause of delinquency or crime so we must reject the hypothesis that a book or story usually operates singly to produce favorable effects. We know that the impact of reading is related to constellations of factors in literature, in people, and in the settings in which reading is done. Impact is a resultant of numerous and interacting variables, among them being the nature of the message, the structure of the situation, the reader's previous experiences and expectations, and his personality and value systems. The process of effect is highly complex and not easily predictable.

REFERENCES

1. Anderson, Paul S., "McGuffey vs. the Moderns in Character Training," *Phi Delta Kappan,* 38 (November 1956), pp. 53-8.

2. Arnheim, Rudolf, "The World of the Daytime Serial," in P. F. Lazarsfeld and F. Stanton (eds.), *Radio Research 1942-43.* New York: Duell, Sloan and Pearce, 1944.

3. Bamberger, Florence E., *The Effect of the Physical Make-up of a Book upon Children's Selection,* Johns Hopkins University Studies in Education No. 4. Baltimore: Johns Hopkins University, 1922.

4. Berelson, Bernard, *Content Analysis in Communication Research.* Glencoe, Ill.: The Free Press, 1952.

5. ———, *The Library's Public.* New York: Columbia University Press, 1949.

6. ———, and Salter, P. J., "Majority and Minority Americans—An Analysis of Magazine Fiction," *Public Opinion Quarterly,* 10 (Summer 1946), pp. 168-90.

7. Boyd, Nancy A., and Mandler, G., "Children's Responses to Human and Animal Stories and Pictures," *Journal of Consulting Psychology,* 19 (October 1955), pp. 367-71.

8. Bryson, Lyman (ed.), *The Communication of Ideas.* New York: Harper, 1948.

9. Cappa, Dante, "Reactions of Kindergarten Children to Story Books Read by Teachers," Doctoral Thesis, University of California, Berkeley, 1953.

10. Carlsen, G. Robert, "Behind Reading Interests," *English Journal,* 43 (January 1954), pp. 7-12.

11. Cecil, Lord David, *The Fine Art of Reading.* Indianapolis: Bobbs-Merrill, 1957.

12. Chall, Jeanne S., *Readability: An Appraisal of Research and Application,* Bureau of Educational Research Monograph No. 34. Columbus: Ohio State University, 1957.

13. Child, Irvin L., *et al.,* "Children's Textbooks and Personality Development: An Exploration in the Social Psychology of Education," *Psychological Monographs,* 60, No. 3 (1946), 54 pp.

14. Cross, Neal M., "The Background for Misunderstanding," *The English Journal,* 29 (May 1940), pp. 366-70.

15. Crossen, Helen J., "Effects of the Attitudes of the Reader upon Critical Reading Ability," *Journal of Educational Research,* 42 (December 1948), pp. 289-98.

16. Fisher, Helen, "Family Life in Children's Literature," *Elementary School Journal,* 50 (May 1950), pp. 516-20.

17. Foulds, Graham, "The Child's Response to Fictional Characters and Its Relationship to Personality Traits," *Character and Personality,* 11 (September 1942), pp. 64-75.

18. Gates, Arthur I., "The Role of Personality Maladjustment in Reading Disability," *Journal of Genetic Psychology,* 59 (September 1941), pp. 77-83.

19. Ginglinger, Geneviève, "Basic Values in *Reader's Digest,* 'Selection' and 'Constellation,'" *Journalism Quarterly,* 32 (Winter 1955), pp. 56-61.

20. Good, Carter V., "The Effect of Mental-Set or Attitude on the Reading Performance of High-School Pupils," *Journal of Educational Research,* 14 (October 1926), pp. 178-86.

21. Grace, Harry A., and Lohmann, Joan J., "Children's Reactions to Stories Depicting Parent-Child Conflict Situations," *Child Development,* 23 (March 1952), pp. 61-74.

22. Gray, William S., "The Social Effects of Reading," *School Review,* 55 (May 1947), pp. 269-77.

23. Groff, Patrick J., *Children's Attitudes Toward Reading and Their Critical Reading Abilities in Four Content-Type Materials,* Doctoral Thesis, University of California, Berkeley, 1955.

24. Harvey, John, "The Content Characteristics of Best-Selling Novels," *Public Opinion Quarterly,* 17 (Spring 1953), pp. 91-144.

25. Hayakawa, S. I., "Ways in Which Passages are Misinterpreted and Possible Explanations," *Supplementary Educa-*

tional Monographs, No. 6. University of Chicago, 1944, pp. 58, 84-9.

26. Hovland, Carl I., "Effects of the Mass Media of Communication," Chapter 28 in *Handbook of Social Psychology,* Vol. II (Gardner Lindzey, ed.). Addison-Wesley Publishing Company, 1954, pp. 1062-1103.

27. ———, Janis, I. L., and Kelley, H. H., *Communication and Persuasion.* New Haven: Yale University Press, 1953.

28. Jackson, Evalene P., "Effects of Reading Upon Attitudes Towards the Negro Race," *Library Quarterly,* 14 (January 1944), pp. 47-54.

29. Jacobs, Leland B., "Cultural Patterns in Children's Fiction," *Childhood Education,* 23 (May 1947), pp. 431-4.

30. ———, *Democratic Acculturation in American Children's Historical Fiction,* Doctoral Thesis, Ohio State University, 1945.

31. Kay, Herbert, "Toward an Understanding of News-Reading Behavior," *Journalism Quarterly,* 31 (Winter 1954), pp. 15-32.

32. Kircher, Clara J. (comp.), *Character Formation Through Books: A Bibliography.* Washington: Catholic University of America Press, 1954.

33. LaBrant, Lou, "Personal Factors Influencing Reading," *Reading in an Age of Mass Communication* (W. S. Gray, ed.). New York: D. Appleton-Century, 1949, pp. 39-57.

34. Lind, Katharine, "Social Psychology of Children's Reading," *American Journal of Sociology,* 41 (January 1936), pp. 454-69.

35. Loban, Walter, *Literature and Social Sensitivity,* National Council of Teachers of English, 1954.

36. Lodge, Helen C., "The Influence of the Study of Biography on the Moral Ideology of the Adolescent at the Eighth Grade Level," *Journal of Educational Research,* 50 (December 1956), pp. 241-55.

37. Lorang, Sister Mary C., "The Effect of Reading on Moral Conduct and Emotional Experience," *Studies in Psychology and Psychiatry, Catholic University of America,* 6, No. 5 (1945) pp. 122.

38. Lowdermilk, R. R., *Attitude Shifts from Reading and from Radio Pro-*

gram Listening, Doctoral Thesis, Ohio State University, 1939.

39. McConnell, Gaither A., *An Analysis of Biographical Literature for Children,* Doctoral Thesis, University of California, Berkeley, 1952.

40. McKillop, Anne S., *The Relationship between the Reader's Attitude and Certain Types of Reading Responses.* New York: Teacher's College, Columbia University, 1952.

41. Mannello, George, "Attitude as Conditioner of the Acquisition of New Facts among Eighth-Grade Pupils," *Journal of Genetic Psychology,* 85 (September 1954), pp. 85-103.

42. Meckel, Henry C., *An Explanatory Study of the Responses of Adolescent Pupils to Situations in a Novel,* Doctoral Thesis, University of Chicago, 1946.

43. Mott, Francis J., "Drama and the Evocation of Unconscious Image," *Journal of Clinical Psychopathology & Psychotherapy,* 7 (April 1946), pp. 783-93.

44. Osgood, Charles E., "The Nature and Measurement of Meaning," *Psychological Bulletin,* 49 (May 1952), pp. 197-237.

45. ———, and Suci, G. J., "Factor Analysis of Meaning," *Journal of Experimental Psychology,* 50 (November 1955), pp. 325-38.

46. Rankin, Marie, *Children's Interests in Library Books of Fiction,* Teachers College Contributions to Education, No. 906. New York: Teachers College, Columbia University, 1944.

47. Richards, Ivor A., *Practical Criticism: A Study of Literary Judgment.* Harcourt, Brace, 1930.

48. Rudman, Herbert C., "Informational Needs and Reading Interests of Children in Grades IV through VIII," *Elementary School Journal,* 55 (May 1955), pp. 502-12.

49. Russell, David H., "Interrelationships of the Language Arts and Personality," in *Child Development and the Language Arts,* Research Bulletin of the National Conference on Research in English. Champaign, Illinois: National Council of Teachers of English, 1953, pp. 27-40.

50. ———, "Reading Disabilities and Mental Health: A Review of Re-

search," *Understanding the Child,* 16 (January 1947), pp. 24-32.

51. ——, "Teachers' Memories and Opinions of Children's Literature," *Elementary English,* 26 (December 1949), pp. 475-82.

52. ——, "Unsolved Problems in Reading," *Elementary English,* 31 (October 1954), pp. 335-8.

53. Schramm, Wilbur L. (ed.), *The Process and Effects of Mass Communication.* University of Illinois Press, 1954, pp. 586.

54. Scott, C. Winfield, "A 'Forest' View of Present Research in Reading," *Educational and Psychological Measurement,* 14 (1954), pp. 208-14.

55. Shepard, John P., *The Treatment of Characters in Popular Children's Fiction,* Master's Thesis, University of California, Berkeley, 1958.

56. Sherwin, J. Stephen, "Patterns of Assumptions in a High School Literature Curriculum," *Journal of Educational Sociology,* 29 (April 1956), pp. 321-9.

57. Shumaker, Wayne, "New Emphasis in the Study of Literature," *Idea and Experiment,* 11 (December 1952), pp. 8-11.

58. Smith, Donald E. P., Wood, Roger L., Downer, James W., and Raygor, Alton L., "Reading Improvement as a Function of Student Personality and Teaching Method," *Journal of Educational Psychology,* 47 (January 1956), pp. 47-59.

59. Smith, Nila B., "Some Effects of Reading on Children," *Elementary English,* 25 (May 1948), pp. 271-8.

60. Squire, James R., *The Responses of Adolescents to Literature Involving Selected Experiences of Personal Development,* Doctoral Thesis, University of California, 1956.

61. Taba, Hilda (director), *Reading Ladders for Human Relations* (Rev. ed.), Staff of Intergroup Education in Co-operating Schools. Washington: American Council on Education, 1949.

62. ——, *With Perspective on Human Relations: A Study of Peer Group Dynamics in an Eighth Grade.* Washington: American Council on Education, 1955.

63. Thorndike, Edward L., "Reading as Reasoning: A Study of Mistakes in Paragraph Reading," *Journal of Educational Psychology,* 8 (June 1917), pp. 323-32.

64. Waples, Douglas, Berelson, B. R., and Bradshaw, F. R., *What Reading Does to People.* University of Chicago Press, 1940.

65. Weingarten, Samuel, "Developmental Values in Voluntary Reading," *School Review,* 62 (April 1954), pp. 222-30.

66. Williams, E. D., Winter, L., and Woods, J. K., "Tests of Literary Appreciation," *British Journal of Educational Psychology,* 8 (November 1938), pp. 265-84.

67. Witty, Paul A., "Effective Utilization of Mass Media: Effects on Children," *Childhood Education,* 33 (November 1956), pp. 104-8.

68. ——, "Reading Success and Emotional Adjustment," *Elementary English,* 27 (May 1950), pp. 281-96.

69. ——, and Sizemore, Robert A., "Reading the Comics: A Summary of Studies and an Evaluation—I, II, and III," *Elementary English,* 31 (December 1954), pp. 501-6; 32 (January 1955), pp. 43-9; 32 (February 1955), pp. 109-14.

70. Wolf, Katherine M., and Fiske, Marjorie, "The Children Talk About Comics," in *Communications Research 1948-49.* New York: Harper and Brothers, 1949, pp. 3-50.

71. Wolfenstein, Martha, "The Impact of a Children's Story on Mothers and Children," *Monographs of Society for Research in Child Development,* 30, No. 1 (1946), 54 pp.

72. Wolfson, Bernice J., "Reading About Emotions in the Primary Classroom," *Elementary English,* 31 (March 1954), pp. 146-9.

73. Wynne, Robert L., *The Relationship between Reading Ability and Personality Inventory Responses in Elementary School Children,* Master's Thesis, University of California, Berkeley, 1955.

38: Skills Related to the Ability To Read History and Science *

J. HARLAN SHORES

INTRODUCTION

The statement that "every teacher should be, to a significant extent, a teacher of reading" has gained wide recognition and has led to considerable controversy.[3] The statement assumes that reading instruction must continue beyond the reading period and beyond the elementary school. If this is true, teachers in the content fields must sacrifice time formerly spent on their content subjects to instruction on the reading abilities essential to effective reading of the materials employed in these subjects. If every teacher must teach reading, it follows that the reading requirements of the materials in a given content field are, at least in some respects, unique to that field, and that these more or less unique skills would be more effectively taught by a person well acquainted with the materials and requirements of the content field. In other words, if the teacher of science in the ninth grade must teach the ability to read science materials, there must be reading skills essential to effective reading of science that are not essential to good reading of literature, history or other content materials. If the skills all had general application it seems that they could be well-taught in a general reading period.

PROBLEM

The purpose of this study was to determine the relationships among ninth-grade pupils, between certain study and

reading skills and reading comprehension of scientific and historical materials. An attempt was made to (1) study the relationship between each of the measured reading and study skills and reading comprehension of historical material; (2) to determine the relationship between each of the measured reading and study skills and reading comprehension with scientific material; (3) to better understand the relationship between both scientific and historical reading comprehension and a sampling of vocabulary from diverse fields; (4) to further explore the relationship between a vocabulary of words frequently found in historical and scientific materials and reading comprehensions in history and science. In addition, this investigation attempted (5) to determine, when relationships were discovered, the area of the population responsible for these relationships.

The forementioned specific purposes were means to more fundamental purposes. This study attempted to contribute to a more complete understanding of the relationships involved in the developmental reading process, and thus to aid in the determination of a better reading program in the public schools.

STUDENT POPULATION AND TESTS USED

The entire first term ninth-grade population of the Central Junior High School in Kansas City, Missouri, provided the student population. A total of 380 complete cases resulted. This group seemed

* Reprinted from *Journal of Educational Research*, Vol. 36, No. 8 (April 1943), pp. 584-93, by permission of the author and the publisher.

to be representative with respect to such factors of random sampling as socio-economic status, intelligence, reading ability, achievement, and educational experience. The nature of the statistical techniques employed in this study render unimportant possible selection with respect to relatively major factors of representativeness such as mental age and ability to read literature, science, and history.

Information was obtained with each of the tests in Table 1 for each of the 380 cases. These tests were administered under uniform testing conditions. No more than three weeks elapsed between the administration of any two tests.

METHOD

The statistical method employed in this investigation was a generalized approach to the matched-control type of research where the significance of a difference between means is found. Palmer Johnson and J. Neyman were responsible for the development of this generalized and more efficient method of analysis.[1] Good and poor groups [*][2] of readers with science and history materials were compared for differences in mean ability in each of the measured skills. Before each comparison the good and poor groups were rendered equivalent in mental age and ability to read literature. It was felt that with mental age uncontrolled, differences in level of mental development might account for differences between good and poor history or science readers in the various skills. Ability to read literature was controlled in order that discovered differences could not be explained by so-called factors of "general reading ability."

Since the difference in effects of the basic matching characters (mental age and ability to read literature) were determined before each comparison by

the regression of the skill on the matching characters, the need for individual matching of cases disappeared. Hence, the entire populations of good and poor readers of science and history were employed without the usual loss of cases in matching. The generalized method employed in this study offered still another advantage over the usual "matched-control" approach to research. It allowed not only the determination of significant differences between the good and poor science and history readers in separate skills, but also enabled determination of the section of the population with respect to the basic matching characters where these differences were significant. Through the use of this concept known as "regions of significance," limits of mental age and ability to read literature may be set whereby it is possible to say that the discovered difference is a significant one within these limits. That is, a significant difference may be found between good and poor history readers in ability to use the index. Through the use of "regions of significance" it is found that this difference is a reliable one only for those pupils with average mental age and average to slightly superior ability to read literature.

RESULTS

The results of this investigation are summarized in Table 2. When enumerated, they are as follows:

1. In the first analysis, groups of good and poor science readers were compared for significant differences in their mean ability in each of the measured skills. The ability to read science was found significantly related to the following skills and abilities: (1) history comprehension, (2) science vocabulary knowledge, (3) general vocabulary knowledge, (4) ability to read graphs, charts, and tables, (5) under-

---

* Kelley has found that the upper and lower twenty-seven per cent offers the most rigorous and efficient division. This division was closely approximated in the present study.

Table 1: Information Concerning Tests Used

Name of Test	Author	Date	Reliability Coefficient *	Admin. Time	Publisher
Iowa Every-Pupil Tests of Basic Skills Test A: Silent Reading Comprehension	Horn, Ernest; McBroom, M.; Spitzer, H. F.; Greene, H. A.; Knight, F. B.;	1939	.90	Approx. 85 min. (or two 45 min. periods)	Bureau of Educational Research and Service, Extension Division, University of Iowa, Iowa City, Iowa.
Part I Paragraph Comprehension			.67		
Part II Understanding of Details			.80		
Part III Organization of Ideas			.70		
Part IV Grasp of Total Meaning			.57		
Total—Parts I to IV			.90		
Part V Vocabulary			.91		
Iowa Every-Pupil Tests of Basic Skills Test B: Basic Study Skills	Same as above	1939	.95	Approx. 90 min. (or two 45 min. periods)	Same as above.
Part I Maps			.79		
Part II Graphs, Charts			.79		
Part III References			.87		
Part IV Index			.84		
Part V Dictionary			.83		
Total			.95		
Reading Scales in Literature	Van Wagenen, M. J.	1922 † (1939)	+ P. E. 3 to 8.5 C—score points	Approx. 45 min.	Educational Test Bureau, Educational Publishers, Inc. Minneapolis, Minn.
Reading Scales in Science	Van Wagenen, M. J.	1938	Same as above	Approx. 45 min.	Same as above
Reading Scales in History	Van Wagenen, M. J.	1938	Same as above	Approx. 45 min.	Same as above
Meaning of Words Used in Science	Swenson, E. J.	1938	.79	Approx. 20 min.	Unpublished, E. J. Swenson, College of Education, University of Minnesota, Minneapolis
Meaning of Words Used in History	Shores, J. H.	1938	.72	Approx. 20 min.	Unpublished, J. H. Shores, College of Education, University of Minnesota, Minneapolis
California Test of Mental Maturity— Advanced Battery (Total Score)	Sullivan, E. T. Clark, W. W. Tiege, E. W.	1937	.95	Two periods of approx. 45 to 50 min. each	California Test Bureau, 3636 Beverly Blvd., Los Angeles, California

* Reliability coefficients for the Iowa tests and for the Van Wagenen tests were secured from the authors.
† Published in 1922. Published in 1939 with changes from 1922 publication only in format and scoring method. On advice of the author the 1922 tests and 1939 scoring methods were used.

Table 2: Relationships Between Ability To Read Science and History and Various Reading Abilities *

| | Science Relationships | | | History Relationships | | |
| | Approximate percentiles in Region of Significance | | | Approximate percentiles in Region of Significance | | |
Abilities	Mental Age	Literature Compre-hension	Level of Signifi-cance	Mental Age	Literature Compre-hension	Level of Signifi-cance
Science Comprehension	0—100	0—100	Upper	10— 95	10— 85	Upper
History Comprehension	30—100	25—100	Upper	0—100	0—100	Upper
Science Vocabulary	10—100	10—100	Upper	0— 95	0— 85	Upper
History Vocabulary	60—100	45—100	Lower	15—100	15—100	Upper
General Vocabulary	35— 85	40— 80	Upper	15—100	5— 95	Upper
Understanding of Details	30— 90	40— 90	Upper	0— 95	0— 85	Upper
Organization of Ideas	10— 90	45—100	Lower	10— 80	10— 70	Upper
Grasp of Total Meaning			None	0— 55	0— 45	Upper
Paragraph Comprehension			None	0— 75	15— 90	Upper
Total Score: Silent Reading Comprehension	30— 65	45— 80	Upper	0— 90	0— 85	Upper
Reading Graphs, Charts, and Tables	0— 75	0— 75	Upper	0— 80	0— 75	Upper
Use of Basic References			None	10— 70	30— 90	Upper
Use of Index			None	30— 70	40— 75	Upper
Use of Dictionary			None	0—100	0—100	Upper
Comprehension of Maps	0— 60	30— 80	Lower			None
Total Score: Basic Study Skills			None	5—100	0—100	Upper

* Table 2 is as follows: The relationship between understanding of details and ability to read science is reliably established at the upper (.01) level of significance for those pupils whose co-ordinates in mental age and literature comprehension locate points between the thirtieth and nine-tieth percentiles in mental age and also between the fortieth and ninetieth percentiles in literature comprehension. Understanding of details is related at the upper level of significance to ability to read history for all pupils except those in the upper five per cent of the total mental age distribu-tion and also in the upper fifteen per cent of the total distribution in literature comprehension.

standing of details, and (6) the total score on the measured skills of silent reading comprehension. The relation-ship between ability to read science materials and the three following skills approached significance: (1) history vocabulary knowledge, (2) facility in the organization of ideas, and (3) ability to comprehend maps.

2. The ability to read history was found significantly related to all of the measured skills and abilities with the exception of ability to comprehend

maps. Factors of mental age and ability to read literature were again controlled. History reading ability was significantly related to the following skills: (1) sci-ence comprehension, (2) history vocab-ulary, (3) general vocabulary, (4) science vocabulary, (5) paragraph comprehension, (6) grasp of the total meaning of a reading passage, (7) or-ganization of ideas, (8) understanding of details, (9) the total score on the measured skills of silent reading com-prehension, (10) reading of graphs, charts and tables, (11) use of the index, (12) use of the dictionary, (13) use of basic references, and (14) the total score of the measured basic study skills.

3. All of the skills not found significantly related to ability to read science materials were significantly related to ability to read historical materials. These skills are: (1) paragraph comprehension, (2) grasp of the total meaning of a reading passage, (3) use of the index, (4) use of the dictionary, (5) use of basic references, (6) the total score of the measured basic study skills, (7) history vocabulary knowledge, and (8) organization of ideas. The relationship of the latter two abilities to history comprehension is firmly established, while their relationship to science comprehension only approaches significance.

4. The only measured skill not shown to hold a significant relationship to history reading ability, comprehension of maps, approached a significant relationship to science reading ability.

5. Several of the skills and abilities were found significantly related to ability to read both scientific and historical materials. These are as follows: (1) science comprehension, (2) history comprehension, (3) science vocabulary, (4) general vocabulary, (5) reading graphs, charts, and tables, (6) understanding of details, and (7) the total score of the measured skills of silent reading comprehension.

6. In general, the areas of the student population, with respect to the basic matching criteria (mental age and literature comprehension), wherein the established relationships may be said to be significant, are larger with the history reading relationships than with the science. That is, the relationships between history reading ability and the various skills seem to be reliably established for more students than do the science relationships.

7. The location of the areas of relationship between science reading ability and the various skills shown to be related to ability to read science indicates that these relationships are generally reliable for all students with average or superior, but not very superior, mental age and ability to read literature. The significant relationships between ability to read historical materials and the various skills tend to be reliable for all students except those with very high mental age or very superior ability to read literature. Thus, with few exceptions, superiority in ability to read science must be accompanied by average or superior mental age and ability to read literature before these better science readers are specifically and reliably better in certain related skills. On the other hand, with few exceptions, superiority in ability to read history indicates superior ability in the related skills for all students who do not have exceptionally high mental age and ability to read literature.

8. In no instance was a significant negative relationship discovered between ability to read science or history and a particular skill. That is, there was no comparison where the poorer readers of science or history were significantly superior to the better science or history readers in a particular ability. The poorer readers of science tended to be slightly superior to the better science readers in use of the index and use of references but these negative relationships fell far short of statistical significance.

CONCLUSIONS

The analysis of the data in the present study suggests the following conclusions:

1. By the time students have reached the ninth grade their reading proficiency is to a considerable extent specific to the content field in which the reading is done. To speak of "general reading ability" of ninth-grade students, without description of the content field in which

the reading is done, is unwarranted in overlooking this specificity. The ability to read scientific and historical materials holds unique and different relationships to a number of reading skills. Ability to read effectively in the materials of science or history probably requires combinations of skills either not related to or not as closely related to ability to read literature as these skills are to ability to read science and history.

2. Since the results of this study offer rather conclusive evidence in refutation of the concept of a general reading ability in the ninth grade, tests devised to measure reading ability at this level should take steps to control the type of materials with which the measurement is taken. The fact that various reading abilities tend to be associated with the reading of one type of content reading material does not assure that a similar association will hold with materials of another content field. Certain reading skills are significantly related to ability to read history and science materials in a manner not explained by ability to read literature.

3. The skills measured in this study seem, in general, to be more reliably related to ability to read historical materials than to ability to read scientific materials. With a single exception, these skills are concomitants of ability to read history. The unproved implication here is that the teaching of these skills should be, at least in part, the responsibility of teachers of history. Implications such as this one are subject to change with change in the nature of the instructional program. Under different instruction the relationship between these skills and ability to read history might be altered considerably.

4. Certain of the measured reading abilities were found significantly related to ability to read history materials and not to ability to read science materials. The implication here, while needing further substantiation through additional research, is that science teachers should probably be freed from specific responsibility for development of these skills. Again, this implication might change with change in the instructional program. The only skill tending to show significant relationship to science and not history reading ability (comprehension of maps) was established at a level of doubtful significance and therefore does not warrant dependable generalizations.

5. A number of the measured abilities present significant relationships to both ability to read scientific and historical materials in a manner not explained by ability to read literature. These skills seem to be specific concomitants of both ability to read science and history. Such findings seem to imply that since the ability to read science and history have a common close relationship to certain skills, the teaching of these skills should probably be the joint responsibility of at least the teachers of science and history. This implication needs further substantiation, and is subject to change with change in the instructional program. Such implications are also subject to practical application. For example, even though science vocabulary knowledge is significantly related to both ability to read science and history, practical considerations would tend to make the teaching of this skill largely the responsibility of the science teacher.

6. The skills and abilities measured in this study tend to divide themselves into several groups. There are those concerned with power of silent reading comprehension in the materials of several content fields, measures of specific and general vocabulary knowledges, skills concerned with the general significance or general meaning of a reading passage, skills where very exacting reading is required, and skills employed in the location of information. The skills tending to show a specific relationship to comprehension of scientific

materials are those calling for power of reading comprehension, vocabulary knowledge, or a very exact type of reading. There was no established relationship between science reading ability and the skills which require facility in either location of information or ability to comprehend the general meaning of a reading passage. On the other hand each of these groups of reading abilities tended to be a concomitant of ability to read historical materials.

The good readers of science tend to be also superior in more detailed and exacting skills of reading. The good history readers tend to be also superior in all the measured types of reading responses. Neither of these trends is the resultant of ability with the type of reading required with literary materials.

7. In general, the size of the areas of relationship seems to suggest that the association between ability to read history and the various skills will be a reliable one for a larger percentage of ninth-grade students than will the established science reading relationships. The history relationships tend to be firmly established for wider ranges of values of mental age and ability to read literature.

8. The data present a noticeable trend for the relationships between history reading ability and the various skills found significantly related to history reading to be reliably established for all pupils except those with very superior mental age and ability to read literature. In contrast, the trend with science reading ability and the related skills, was for these relationships to be firmly established for pupils with average or superior, but not extremely high, values of mental age and literature comprehension.

While the analysis of the data only presents and does not explain this condition, an hypothesis as to its meaning may be offered. Assuming that the relationship between ability to read his-

tory and a particular skill is a causal one, it may be said that ability in the skill is important for good readers of history. However, it may be that ability in the skill beyond that normally achieved by pupils of high mental age and very superior ability to read literature is not necessary to efficient reading of history. Good reading ability in literature and high mental age, with their accompanying excellence in the particular skill, may be adequate for effective reading of history. Hence, additional development of the skill at this level would not be functional in discriminating good from poor readers of history.

Reasoning in like manner, a higher excellence in the particular skill is required in science than in history reading before the skill becomes a significant factor to good reading of science. It has been hypothesized that as values of mental age and ability to read literature are higher, there is an accompanying increase in the amount of the skill. Thus, it may be that only those pupils with average or superior mental age and ability to read literature have enough of the skill necessary for effective reading of science. However, ability in the skill normally achieved by pupils of extremely high mental age and very superior ability to read literature may be adequate for effective reading of science, and any additional development of the skill for these pupils would not function to discriminate good from poor readers of science.

9. The fact that ninth-grade teachers should be concerned with the teaching of reading in the content materials of science and history is plainly indicated. The data suggest some of the skills that it might be well to teach in these subjects. Further research is needed to substantiate this contention.

10. These data strengthen the viewpoint that reading in the ninth-grade is neither a simple nor general ability. Reading at this level shows varying

degrees of relationship to several aspects of reading skill, depending at least in part upon the content field in which the reading is done.

PROBLEMS SUGGESTED FOR FURTHER STUDY

The results of this investigation indicate that study of the relationships between reading and study skills and reading proficiency in materials of various content fields should be a fruitful field for further research. Studies similar to the present one should be conducted in additional grades, with the reading materials of other content fields, and with additional measures of reading and study skills. It would be interesting to know the effects of reading and working rate on these relationships. The effects of varied instructional programs and methods on these relationships should also be of value.

Teachers in the content fields should conduct controlled studies to determine the effect on both achievement and reading ability in the materials of a given content field of specific instruction in the skills found related to ability to read the materials of that field. It should be valuable in studies of this nature to employ several control groups. In one group the teacher would continue in traditional manner with little specific instruction in reading. In another group an attempt would be made to teach all work-type reading skills. In a third control group, the teacher would attempt to teach those skills believed to be important to efficient reading ability and achievement in the particular subject.

Studies should be made of the effects of difficulty of materials, interest and motivation, reader's purpose, and meaning background on reading proficiency with the materials of the various content fields.

REFERENCES

1. Johnson, Palmer O., and Neyman, J., *Tests of Certain Linear Hypotheses and Their Applications to Some Educational Problems.* London, England: Department of Statistics, University of London, University College, June 1936.
2. Kelley, Truman L., "The Selection of Upper and Lower Groups for Valida-tion of Test Items," *Journal of Educational Psychology,* Vol. 30 (January 1939), pp. 17-24.
3. *The Teaching of Reading: A Second Report,* Thirty-sixth Yearbook of the National Society for the Study of Education, p. 6.

39: Some Psychological Factors in the Reading of Fiction *

LEE O. THAYER and N. H. PRONKO

A. INTRODUCTION

Look at a page of fiction in an unfamiliar language. Nothing happens. Now look at a printed page of a particularly appealing "story" in English. What happens? We "see" the characters, we have feelings for them, or with them. We are happy or sad with the fortunes of the hero.

* Reprinted from *The Journal of Genetic Psychology,* Vol. 93, First Half (September 1958), pp. 113-17, by permission of the senior author and the publisher.

How does it happen that certain words and phrases, put together in a certain way, can elicit in a reader a "living picture" of the story being revealed by its author?

Furthermore, we don't *see* the same picture. It would seem that there must be contributing factors beyond the linguistic. We seem not to *"perceive"* identical cues from which to construct our images, and we seem to *"project"* into this image something of our own creation.

Since reading plays such an important rôle in our daily lives, an understanding of the processes involved is warranted.

B. THE PRESENT STUDY

This exploratory study was designed and conducted to provide data necessary to the design of future studies. For this reason the present study is meant to emphasize the relative significance of a wide variety of contributing factors rather than the rôle of any one factor. The final objective is to determine the fundamental psychological factors involved in the reading of prose fiction.

C. PROCEDURE

One hundred twelve college students (31 female, 81 male) of varying ages and classifications, in beginning psychology and English courses, were asked to read five fiction excerpts, each of about one-half page in length. Then the students were asked to answer the following questions about the central character in each of the excerpts:

1. Did you have a good mental picture of _____?
2. Did you like _____? Why?
3. Describe _____ in your own words, in any manner you wish.
4. Upon what details or ideas in the passage have you based your answer to number 3 above?

5. Why do you suppose you selected those "cues" which you did, and possibly overlooked others?

The students were then asked to check a personality profile chart for the central character in each excerpt. The profile consisted of 25 selected personality "traits": aggressiveness, anxiety, argumentativeness, bashfulness, business-like, cheerfulness, decisiveness, confused, coöperative, dullness, easygoing, egotistic, friendliness, hesitant, impulsiveness, introspective, laziness, meekness, quietness, resourcefulness, self-confidence, self-consciousness, shyness, talkativeness, energetic.

Fundamental to the investigation was the fact that none of the characters was described in any manner in any of the excerpts. None of the students had seen any of the excerpts before. The excerpts were unrelated, except that each dealt with some phase of a love situation, a general theme of interest to most college students. Each of the excerpts was chosen as being representative of a different narrative technique.

D. RESULTS

1. The reported clearness of mental images varied from the 59 per cent who saw the third character clearly to the 91 per cent who reported "seeing" the second character clearly.

2. Not all of the characters were equally "liked." The first character, for example, was "liked" by 80 per cent; the second character was "liked" by only 20 per cent of the students.

3. Character descriptions were free and unlimited by the design of the experiment. For each of the five characters, there was a community of responses for both physical and personality descriptions. Concurrence of opinion about the appearance and personality of each character was marked. Deviations were isolated.

4. The personality profile for each of the characters showed marked clustering of opinion, representing a high degree of concurrence or similarity of impressions.

E. INTERPRETATIONS

Certainly many determining factors are at play in producing an individual reader's reactions to his reading—social and cultural patterns, linguistic habits and preferences, reading abilities, "tastes," and so forth. Evidence of these factors was apparent in the responses to the fictional situations imposed in this study. The clearest evidence, however, isolated the *processes* rather than the content of imagining. What, then, seems to happen when we read fiction?

1. One approach to the results of this investigation suggests that the reading of fiction involves both perceptive and projective processes. Without the operation of *structural* factors in perception of these fictional characters, concurrence of opinion among students would have been at a minimum. Clustering of opinion in describing the characters would have been negligible.

Deviations from the general concurrence of eidetic impression cannot alone be accounted for by structural factors in perception. *Functional* factors—the present needs, wants, and feelings of the reader—in apperceiving these fictional characters are apparent. Though one of the characters may have appeared to a reader as young and pleasant (structural factors dependent upon past experience with the general type of fiction situation, the mood, tone, or language of the excerpt, and the similarity of that fictional character to other fictional characters), the same character may have appeared to another reader as young but unpleasant (functional factors, dependent upon the reader's present mood, feelings, wants, etc.). The second reader's apperception of that character as unpleasant is a deviation from the concurrence of the majority of readers that the same character is pleasant, and thus suggests the stronger influence of functional factors in perceiving the character. One of the most pertinent discussions of the definition and meaning of structural and functional perception is to be found in Hallowell.[3]

Since no description of the characters appears in the excerpts, those details of description by the readers in which there is a significant concurrence may be considered to be dependent upon structural factors. In other words, those readers who concurred in their impressions were perceiving cues identified with common or similar past reading or other experiences. Those details of readers' descriptions in which there is a significant non-concurrence may be considered to be dependent upon functional factors. Those readers who did not concur in their impressions were perceiving cues which were identified with subjective feeling states or dissimilar personal experiences.

2. The results of this study also suggest that mental images in the reading of fiction are largely dependent upon the reader's projection of subjective interpretations into the situation.

If the fictional character is "liked," this seems to suggest, then, that character is endowed by the reader with the personality traits of what that reader would consider to be a "likable" person. If the fictional character is "disliked," then the reader seems to endow that character with what that reader would consider to be "undesirable" personality traits. If the reader neither "likes" nor "dislikes," then the mental image of the fictional character seems not to be clear to the reader, and the description provided by the author may thus be automatically accepted. Where an excerpt, by implication, intimates to the intelligent reader that the character is a "pleasant guy," then the reader, particularly if he neither "likes" nor "dislikes" the character, will be inclined to accept this implied description.

But if the reader "likes" or "dislikes" a fictional character, these results suggest, then the reader's image of that character will be relatively independent of the author's direct or implied descriptions of that character, and at the same time relatively more dependent upon the reader's projection into the fiction material what are to that reader the physical and personality traits most suitable to that reader's likes and dislikes in real people. In other words, if a reader really "hates" a fictional character, then that character is likely to appear to that reader with physical and personality traits considered "hate-able" by that reader, and this impression will be fairly impervious to the author's own description of the character.

Projection in the reading of fiction would seem to be, based upon the evidence of this study, dependent to some extent upon past reading experiences. It would seem probable that this is true because a certain number of reading experiences are required to establish the ability to identify and thus to discern those one likes from those one dislikes in fiction. A person who has read much and widely, for example, may be less likely to project a stereotyped pattern for a "villain" or a "hero" than will the person who has read little.

Another possible interpretation of the results discussed above is in terms of an interbehavioral theory of language as developed by Kantor.[4] Whereas most of our responses, such as throwing a ball, are unistimulational, language reactions are bistimulational. Whether we talk or listen to someone's speech, we react to two things concurrently. When we ourselves speak, we are obviously reacting to the person listening to us and to the "thing" we wish to tell him about. When we listen, we react to the speaker's utterance and to the "thing" he is talking about.[5]

Now, to come to our results. Since to a certain degree each individual's psychological history is unique and specific to him, to that degree will he react individualistically to the reading matter and its references. To the degree that our subjects had common backgrounds with the language and experiences "tapped" by the reading excerpts, to that degree did they show a concurrence of responses. This is an alternative way of explaining *both* the specificity and mutuality of the subjects' reactions in our experimental situation.

3. Students could not give answers to Questions 4 and 5. According to the one theory, this may indicate the inaccessibility of the perceptive and projective processes in the reading of fiction. Often, to support a descriptive detail, completely imaginary "cues" were "perceived" in the excerpt. Such behavior may reflect the complicated interplay of perceptive and projective processes in reading fiction.

Hallowell's study [2] suggested to him that the important element in the study of literature as a mirror of culture is the implicit rather than the manifest content. The same principle is true, it would seem, of the results of the present study. Manifest content of student responses to fictional situations is only a result of implicit "meanings" or reactions. For example, there is reason to believe, as pointed out particularly by Erickson and Lazarus,[1] that some degree of perceptual defense may be operating in the structuralization of mental images from the printed page of fiction.

An interbehavioral explanation for the failure of subjects to isolate the linguistic variables that called out their responses would stress the relatively greater rôle of the reader's reactional biography and the incidental rôle of the reading matter. In other words, the experiences that the reader brings to his readings are more important than the black marks on white paper. Language can "trigger" a host of the individual's interrelated responses. In Emerson's terms, "He who would bring home the wealth of the Indies, must first take with him the wealth of the Indies."

We offer the above alternative approaches to the results of the present exploratory study of what goes on when we read fiction.

REFERENCES

1. Erickson, C. W., and Lazarus, R. S., "Perceptual Defense and Projective Tests," *Journal of Abnormal and Social Psychology,* Vol. 47 (1952), pp. 302-8.
2. Hallowell, A. I., "Myth, Culture, and Personality," *American Anthropologist,* Vol. 49 (1947), pp. 544-56.
3. ———, "Cultural Factors in the Structuralization of Perception," in J. H. Rohrer, and M. Sherif (eds.), *Social Psychology at the Crossroads.* New York: Harper, 1951.
4. Kantor, J. R., *A Survey of the Science of Psychology.* Bloomington, Ind.: Principia Press, 1933.
5. Pronko, N. H., "Language and Psycholinguistics: A Review," *Psychological Bulletin,* Vol. 43 (1946), pp. 189-239.

40: Machines and Reading: A Review of Research *

ROBERT KARLIN

The use of mechanical devices in teaching reading has achieved acceptance in several quarters. Their popularity is great in the area of speed or rate of reading. In fact, the general public readily expects the reading "clinic" or "center" to possess these instruments, a situation which has grown out of very favorable reports in the press and popular magazines. Many public schools have either purchased these devices or are seriously considering them in developmental and remedial reading classes.

THE THREE CATEGORIES OF MACHINES

Flashmeters. Some flashmeters are called overhead projectors or tachistoscopes. One projects an image on a blackboard or screen for periods of from one or two seconds to perhaps one one-thousandth of a second. The length of projection is controlled by a timing device which is manually set for the appropriate time duration. Glass slides which contain lists of individual words, phrases, sentences, or paragraphs and columns of digits may be purchased or prepared by the user.

A second type is intended for individual use: The viewer releases a timed light which illuminates a printed card that contains a series of digits or phrases and sentences. In each instance the viewer records what he sees and then verifies it.

Pacers. The pacer contains a movable screen or bar under which the printed material is placed. The speed at which

* Reprinted from *The Clearing House,* Vol. 32, No. 6 (February 1958), pp. 349-52, by permission of the author and the publisher.

the screen or bar descends over the printed lines is regulated in terms of a given number of words per minute. Thus, if the reader is able to keep pace with the descending bar or screen, he knows that his rate of reading is equal to the predetermined setting. Specially prepared reading material with corresponding questions is available with some pacers.

Films. The third type of device consists of a series of films which are ordinarily designed to be used with sixteen-millimeter projectors. These films permit the viewer to see portions of a line of text in succession; what has preceded it and what is to follow are occluded. The rate at which the text appears is built into the film, and questions accompany each.

Tachistoscopic drills may be found on film which is projected by a machine of a different type.

The first and third types—flashmeters and films—are recommended to the student who desires to increase his perceptual span. It has been suggested that pacers assist the eyes to move more rapidly over the printed lines. All three have been introduced to bring about an increase in reading rate.

Our purpose here is not to evaluate the rationale upon which the design of these instruments is based. Such a discussion would largely be theoretical in nature. Nor is it the purpose of this writer either to exhort or deprecate use of them in reading programs. What is suggested is a dispassionate evaluation of these mechanical devices in terms of existing research. Perhaps some conclusion regarding the desirability of using them may be drawn after such an examination. The literature affords some opportunity to inquire into reading programs which utilized these machines and provides some data that have been obtained under controlled conditions. This review will be limited to investigations that have been undertaken in the last two decades.

A further limitation is the removal from consideration of reports which merely describe the use of mechanical instruments in reading programs. There is no way of knowing to what extent the use of such devices has contributed to reading growth unless there is some control over the variables which can influence the outcomes. Marked improvement in reading rate has been reported for groups which had not received any special training over a given period of time.[1, 5, 9, 12]

RESULTS AT FOUR LEVELS

Elementary Level. Practically all investigations which deal with machines have been undertaken on the secondary, college, and adult levels. Very few have been initiated in the elementary schools. One study has been reported by Cason,[3] whose sample was drawn from the third grade. Fifty-one children were divided into two groups: one received phrasing training without the use of any instrument, while the other was exposed to the same material with the metronoscope (a type of tachistoscope). Equated groups spent an equal amount of time in free library reading. Cason reported no significant differences between the two groups in reading phrases or improving eye movements. Also, there were no clear-cut gains in either programs over those secured through free reading.

Secondary Level. Barry and Smith [1] divided 2,166 ninth-grade pupils from the Rochester, New York, public schools into eight groups, each containing above-average, average, and below-average boys and girls. Some groups read only timed articles, others saw only the reading films and answered questions, while still others had some combinations of both. Seven hundred twenty-nine pupils received no special treatment. The investigators found that the gains in reading made without the use of films were similar to those made by the groups that did see films. The group which received no help made as much improvement as did most of the other pupils who received some training.

Blough [2] made available to 324 students of an Indianapolis high school reading training in the form of pacers, films, and specially prepared reading materials. These students participated in fourteen actual teaching sessions. Two hundred eighty-three students served as a control group. The experimental group experienced gains of 24.6 per cent in reading rate and 7.5 per cent in comprehension, while the control group had gains of 7.5 per cent and 3.1 per cent, respectively.

Leavell and Wilson [6] tested the relative merits of tachistoscopic and pacer exercises, direct approaches to reading skills through means other than mechanical devices, guided free reading, and a prescribed English course of study. Two hundred ninety sophomores of a Dallas, Texas, high school participated in the study. The data from one reading test did not favor any specific method within either the normal or superior I.Q. range of students. The results of a second test favored the groups that had tachistoscopic, pacer and tachistoscopic training, the direct approach, and the prescribed course of study over the groups that had pacer training and guided free reading.

College Level. Westover [12] divided ninety college freshmen into two equal groups. One was given practice in reading selected exercises; the second read the same content in phrases through a device for controlling eye movements. An additional fifty students received no special exercises in reading. At the end

of five weeks, reading tests were administered to all three groups. Westover found that both experimental groups made significant gains in speed of comprehension and rate of reading. However, there was no significant difference between the two. The control group also gained significantly in speed and level of comprehension.

Henry and Lauer [5] evaluated four methods of reading instruction with 274 college students. One group received verbal instruction without definite practice; a second received practice on the metronoscope; the third did practice exercises from mimeographed material, the text for which was the same as that used for the metronoscope; the last group followed self-improvement instructions on texts read at home. The group that did the practice exercises from mimeographed material made the largest percentage gains—18.3 per cent —with the home reading group a close second.

One hundred fifty college freshmen, matched for intelligence and reading ability, were divided into three sections by Wedeen.[11] Section A read with a pacer and section B read the same material under stop-watch conditions. Section C received no training. Section A exceeded B in rate but the latter was equal to A in comprehension growth. While the control group made gains in speed and comprehension, these gains were exceeded by both experimental groups.

To three groups of freshmen at the State University of Iowa, Sutherland [9] gave tachistoscopic word and phrase training, films and reading exercises, and no training in reading, respectively. The gains which were made by the films and reading exercises group exceeded those of the tachistoscopic group. The young men and women who did not receive any reading instruction made gains which were statistically significant.

Glock [4] selected 135 college freshmen who needed remedial reading. Some saw phrase reading films, others saw films that used the same text but which exposed two consecutive lines simultaneously, while the rest read the same material in pamphlet form. Glock realized results which showed improvement in rate and rate of comprehension with all three instructional methods. Some teachers obtained better results from one method than from another.

Wooster [13] tested the value of pacer training in a course of effective study. Two groups of six unmatched students each received 345 minutes and 315 minutes, respectively, of pacer training. A third group of forty-eight students served as a control. The investigator did not find any significant differences in rate or comprehension among the three groups.

Adult Level. Thompson [10] carried out an investigation with 438 officers of the Air Command and Staff School of Air University, Maxwell Air Force Base. The officers were placed through random selection into two experimental groups and one control group. Group I was organized as book centered. Group II used a pacer to read selections on military subjects, biography, and social studies. Group III did not experience any special reading instruction. On the basis of test results the book-group mean was fifty words a minute faster than the mean of the machine group. Very slight changes in comprehension occurred as a result of training.

Manolakes [8] tested the relative value of tachistoscopic training and pacer training with thirty-four officers of the Marine Corps. Both groups received additional help in vocabulary and comprehension skill. The group which had pacer training alone exceeded the other (pacer and tachistoscope) by 238 words

a minute. Both made significant gains in rate of reading.

A mixed group of high-school and college graduates, matched for reading speed, was divided into two sections by Lewis.[7] One section received training with the flashmeter and metronoscope and other eye-movement exercises; the other practiced reading timed selections and discussed what it had read. The eye-movement group made an average improvement in speed of 24.7 per cent; the practice reading group achieved an increase of 69.1 per cent.

CONCLUSIONS

From some of these studies it appears that gains in rate of reading can be achieved through the use of a mechanical device. To what extent credit may be given to such a device for such achievement is unknown. Few, if any, of these studies were sufficiently tight to minimize the influences of extraneous variables upon the outcomes.

A second conclusion may be reached: In eleven of the twelve investigations which measured natural reading against machine reading, the groups that received training in the former either equaled or surpassed the machine groups in rate of reading. From these data it can be said that outcomes in speed of reading similar to those achieved through the use of special instruments may be expected from suitable reading instruction which does not include these same instruments.

Of course all of the answers have not yet come into the hopper of truth. However, it is reasonable to suggest from what information is presently available that perhaps the monies which might be spent for the purchase of reading machines be used for other purposes.

REFERENCES

1. Barry, R. F., and Smith, P. E., "An Experiment in Ninth-Grade Reading Improvement," *Journal of Educational Psychology,* XLV (1954), 407-14.
2. Blough, Richard, "The Developmental Reading Laboratory: a Training and Proving Ground for Readers," *Bulletin of the National Association of Secondary-School Principals,* XL (1956), 38-41.
3. Cason, Eloise B., *Mechanical Methods for Increasing the Speed of Reading.* Columbia University: Teachers College Contributions to Education, No. 878, 1943.
4. Glock, M. D., "The Effect upon Eye-Movements and Reading Rate at the College Level of Three Methods of Training," *Journal of Educational Psychology,* XL (1949), 93-106.
5. Henry, I. K., and Lauer, A. R., "A Comparison of Four Methods of Increasing the Reading Speed of College Students," *Proceedings of the Iowa Academy of Science,* XLVI (1939), 273-6.
6. Leavell, U. W., and Wilson, G. E., "Guided Free Reading Versus Other Methods in High School English," *Peabody Journal of Education,* XXXIII (1956), 272-80.
7. Lewis, Norman, "An Investigation into Comparable Results Obtained from Two Methods of Increasing Reading Speed Among Adults," *College English,* XI (1949), 152-6.
8. Manolakes, George, "The Effects of Tachistoscopic Training in an Adult Reading Program," *Journal of Applied Psychology,* XXXVI (1952), 410-12.
9. Sutherland, Jean, "The Relationship between Perceptual Span and Rate of Reading," *Journal of Educational Psychology,* XXXVII (1946), 373-80.
10. Thompson, W. C., "A Book-Centered Course Versus a Machine-Centered Course in Adult Reading Improvement," *Journal of Educational Research,* XLIX (1956), 437-45.
11. Wedeen, S. U., "Mechanical Versus Non-Mechanical Reading Techniques for College Freshmen," *School and Society,* LXXIX (1954), 121-3.
12. Westover, F. L., *Controlled Eye Movements Versus Practice Exercises in Reading.* Columbia University: Teachers College Contributions to Education, No. 917, 1946.
13. Wooster, G. E., "An Experimental Study of the Reading-Rate Controller," *Journal of Educational Psychology,* XLV (1954), 421-6.

41: A Reading Program That Did Not Work *

WALTER B. BARBE

It may appear to be a strange coincidence that virtually all reports on various types of special reading programs give evidence of success. Why do not reports appear on programs which began with the optimistic hope that they would be successful but which failed for one reason or another? The most obvious answer is, of course, that school people caught with a reading program which is a failure are not so eager to spread the word as are those who have successful programs. But there is another answer, which is not so obvious. Most special reading programs are successful. The main reason

* Reprinted from the *Journal of Developmental Reading,* Vol. 1, No. 1 (October 1957), pp. 17-21, by permission of the author and the publisher.

for this is that any special program arouses interest on the part of both teachers and students. As a result, teachers do a better job of teaching and students do a better job of learning. The reading program is not the important factor; those putting the plan into practice—in this case the teachers —are the determining factor.

Being unable to find a single report in the literature on a plan which failed, the author decided to write up one such failure with which he is familiar. But rather than leave the program as a failure, certain suggestions as to why the program appeared to fail and what should be done about it seem necessary. Unfortunately, the accompanying bad attitude toward the program probably makes any new undertaking in this particular situation most unlikely in the near future. All of which probably brings us to basic principle number 1— *Begin a special program in reading only when there is certainty that it will succeed; for the resulting bad effects of a failure may block any future attempts.*

In the particular school, unnamed for obvious reasons, grades nine through twelve are taught. The results of a standardized reading test, along with teacher judgments, verified the fact that many ninth-graders were far below grade level in reading. This brings us to rule number 2—*Establish the need for some type of special reading program.* If the faculty does not agree that such a program is needed, there is little likelihood that it will be successful. And even if it is successful, the chances that it will continue are also unlikely. Our particular school followed this rule.

In order to demonstrate the value of a reading program, the entire ninth grade class was split into two parts. Since there were eight ninth-grade classes, this meant four classes in each group. Four classes were assigned to a teacher who would teach "reading," while the remaining classes were assigned to the traditional English class teacher. The plan was to swap the groups at the end of the first semester, providing the program was successful.

Standardized tests in reading were administered to all of the students in each group. The groups proved to be very similar in reading level, not only between the two larger groups, but also between the classes within each group. This was at least an attempt to do what becomes rule number 3—*Determine the reading levels of the students.* The author would strongly recommend grouping the students within each larger group by achievement level, not only for the reading classes but also for the English classes. This being a very traditional school, however, such an "undemocratic" practice would never be tolerated.

All went well during the first semester. The English teacher reported usual progress with his four English classes; the reading teacher reported progress with his reading groups. Just before the end of the semester, an alternate form of the same reading test was administered to the reading classes and the English classes. This brings us to another rule, which for the time being will remain unnumbered—*Evaluate at the end of the program to determine progress.*

If the results obtained were to be as expected, there would clearly be a difference in the progress made by the reading group from that made by the English group. The group which had been receiving instruction had a mean gain of about seven months. Since six months had elapsed, this was discouraging but not fatal to the program. Not fatal, that is, until it was discovered that the English classes had made nearly eight months progress in reading. Actually, there was probably no significant difference in the two scores. Nevertheless, in order to prove the value of the program, the scores of the reading classes would have had to be far above the scores of the English classes. Since they were not, the reading class idea was done away with and all ninth-grade classes took traditional English the second semester. The program was chalked up as a failure. The usual, "I knew it all the time," 's were heard, along with a few, "I don't understand it," 's. Very few of the latter were actually expressed: many of the former were.

Now, we come upon the scene of the failure. The "why" is the perplexing question. Certainly one thing is always a possibility. The English teacher, knowing that his students were to be checked on reading at the end of the semester, may have turned his classes into reading sessions, either consciously or unconsciously. Upon being approached with this interpretation, he strongly denied the possibility by saying, "I taught just as I always have." The usual way of teaching, it turned out, involved a great deal of isolated learning of vocabulary words. So much for the English class. Still we have no definite answer to why the reading program did not do well.

The reading teacher reported knowing something about teaching reading, admittedly not a great deal. He stated as his objective of the classes, "to improve reading ability." Nice sounding, but very vague. Specifically, he intended to do this by improving rate and comprehension.

The English teacher taught vocabulary and literature, primarily. The reading teacher worked on reading rate and comprehension. Let us now turn back to the original test which was administered before and after the program. A quick glance at the test revealed two major categories—vocabulary and comprehension. Now we seem to be getting somewhere.

It was very clear that neither teacher had been teaching for the test. But the very organization of the reading program itself did not lend itself favorably to this particular test. If the aim of the program was to be the improvement of rate and comprehension, then it should have been made certain that the yardstick used to judge progress measured these two skills. Vocabulary is the easiest score to raise, comprehension is more difficult. Actually, the English teacher just happened to be teaching the skill upon which most weight was placed on the test used, while the reading teacher was not. Any progress the reading teacher made in rate was not measured by this particular test.

An examination of the subtest scores revealed this problem. The English classes had made a much greater gain than even the eight months in vocabulary, but had actually made only several months progress in comprehension. The reading class, on the other hand, had made only a slight amount of progress in vocabulary and really remarkable gains in comprehension. And so we come to the question, "Why did this program fail?" The answer is that it did not fail. Actually, no measure was ever made to see if it failed or not. Since the specific objectives of the instruction were not decided before the program began, it was impossible to determine which test would be the best measure. The rule should therefore be—*Determine the specific objectives of the program*. Then the next rule will follow— *Select a measuring stick in terms of the objectives of the program*.

Before leaving this particular point, however, it should be stated that the decision to have as objectives of a ninth-grade reading program the improvement of reading rate and comprehension, when many of the students are probably reading below grade level, does not seem wise. To emphasize reading rate to poor readers is drawing attention away from the basic reading skills and encouraging the student to become an even more careless reader. A wiser program for ninth-grade students would have been to have as objectives: improved vocabulary, better facility in attacking new words, improving comprehension, and increasing interest in reading.

The real tragedy of this case is that it will be cited by opponents of the program as proof that reading classes are not effective. Instead of being better off for having tried something, the school is now in a worse spot than before. At present, there is little likelihood that a reading program can be started until this attitude changes.

SUMMARY AND CONCLUSIONS

Not all reading programs can possibly succeed, but a review of the literature reveals actually hundreds of successful

approaches and not a single report of one that failed. As important as knowing what to do is also knowing what not to do. An examination of a reading program that did not work, and why it did not, seemed to have merit. It has been the purpose of this paper to examine a program that did not work and to determine just why it failed.

The program failed because the objectives of the program were not clearly defined, and a test was used to measure progress in areas which were not taught in the program. The resulting failure will hinder the possible success of every future reading program. With more careful preplanning, this failure could have been avoided.

CHAPTER X

Diagnosis and Correction of Reading Problems

42: Remedial Reading Practices in the Secondary School *

PAUL WITTY and WILLIAM BRINK

Formal instruction in silent reading is usually discontinued by the time the child completes the fifth or sixth grade. It is thought that, at this stage, pupils will have acquired the fundamental skills in silent and oral reading and will have developed attitudes which will lead them to read extensively. The failure of the typical school program to accomplish these objectives is revealed by the decrease in reading among older elementary-school pupils, and by the inadequate skills and needlessly slow reading of many upper elementary- and high-school students.

Even more noticeable and serious, perhaps, are the reading limitations of an unnecessarily large number of pupils who enter the secondary school. One study shows that 2169 out of 7380 eighth-grade graduates read at or below norms for the sixth grade.[2]

It is generally granted that because of the amount and severity of reading retardation, remedial instruction should be offered for the most seriously retarded pupils. The value of such efforts has been repeatedly demonstrated.[4]

Perhaps the clearest proof of the educability of most persons retarded in reading skill is found in the Army's effort to teach the three R's. Among the draftees for World War II there were large numbers of illiterate and non-English-speaking men. Special training units were organized to give these men the academic training they needed to become useful soldiers.

By applying tested and established methods, the Army succeeded in developing an amazingly efficient program, one that enabled the average illiterate man to acquire in eight weeks' time the basic academic skills needed in Army life.

The outstanding characteristics of the Army program are found in good remedial reading programs in the public schools. There is the same concern for diagnosing carefully the reading levels and needs of the pupils, for providing useful and stimulating materials, and for offering systematic instruction for a long enough time to assure genuine improvements in literacy.

The amount, nature, and severity of poor reading in the secondary school necessitates the establishment of special classes. The impetus given to learning through membership in a participating

* Reprinted from *The Journal of Educational Psychology*, Vol. 40, No. 4 (April 1949), pp. 193-205, by permission of the senior author and the publisher.

group and the gains resulting from strict adherence to an expertly directed program make possible the rehabilitation of large numbers of retarded secondary-school students. Not the least important among the concomitants of such work is the stimulating effect it has in extending and enriching out-of-school experiences —a condition which seems to contribute greatly to the mental hygiene and personality adjustment of the pupils. However, special classes should be looked upon as temporary expedients. And it should be recognized that the provision of remedial programs alone is inadequate to meet the needs of the modern high school. Such an effort should be associated with a broader concern aiming to offer every boy and girl the educational opportunities essential for his full development. The great needs at present seem to be: remedial work for some and developmental reading programs for all pupils.[3]

In spite of our knowledge of desirable practices to follow with seriously retarded readers, relatively few schools have established programs. As a result, public school administrators frequently refer to reading retardation as the largest obstacle to efficient instruction today.

A STUDY OF REMEDIAL READING PRACTICES

In this paper, it is our purpose to examine the extent to which remedial reading programs are being offered in American high schools. In addition, we shall present facts concerning: the objectives sought, the way the needs of pupils are diagnosed, the materials and methods of instruction employed, and the procedures used in evaluating outcomes.

Data were collected by means of questionnaires and interviews. Letters were addressed to five hundred school systems throughout the United States which had, in 1947, one or more secondary schools enrolling seven hundred or more students. Those schools which had remedial classes were invited to cooperate in the study. Questionnaires were sent to the schools. Replies were received from one hundred nine schools. Ninety-seven schools indicated that remedial reading was carried on in the English department by a regular teacher who gives part of his time to the reading program. Credit in English is usually given for satisfactory completion of the course.

OBJECTIVES OF REMEDIAL CLASSES

The Committee which directed the preparation of the *47th Yearbook of the National Society for the Study of Education* agreed that reading programs of the high school and college should emphasize: (a) skill in reading and studying different types of subject-matter, (b) reading experience to help the student understand himself better and to satisfy with increasing success his personal needs, (c) reading experience to assist him in becoming a more effective citizen in and out of school, and (d) experience that will result in a more enjoyable and profitable pattern of leisure reading.[3]

The questionnaire listed somewhat similar objectives and requested that respondents indicate whether each objective was stressed very much, somewhat, a little, or not at all. Space was provided for addition of objectives not mentioned. Table 1 presents some results of the study.

Seventy-five of the schools stated that they emphasized the development of basic habits and skills in reading. Eighty-six stressed greatly the development of interest and enjoyment to be obtained through guided reading. Sixty-six sought to provide reading experience more nearly in accord with pupils' abilities; and the same number also stressed the development of efficient study habits. Only twenty-three schools emphasized greatly improvement of students' ability

Table 1: Objectives of Remedial Reading Classes

	Frequency		
Objectives	Stressed Very Much	Stressed Some-what	Stressed Little or Not at All
To help students in developing basic reading abilities and skills	75	9	
To help students by means of guided reading experiences to develop greater interest and enjoyment in reading	86	19	
To provide for students who are unable to profit from the regular courses experiences more nearly in accord with their abilities	66	23	8
To assist students in the study and reading of materials of instruction of regular high-school classes	23	45	25
To help students to develop efficient and economical study habits	66	28	7

to read and study the materials of the various subject areas of the high school. Accordingly, it appears that most of these schools provide classes taught by the teacher of English and aim primarily to improve general skill in reading and to develop interest and pleasure in reading.

SELECTION AND STUDY OF PUPILS

The two methods utilized most frequently in the selection of pupils are: (1) recommendation of supervisors, administrators, and teachers, and (2) consideration of scores on standardized reading tests. Intelligence tests were employed in half of the schools. It is of interest that in forty-four per cent of the schools the students' requests for help were given primary consideration, while in fifty-three per cent, previous school rcords were similarly employed. The *Iowa Silent Reading Test* was the most widely used educational achievement test, while the general intelligence test most frequently given was the *Otis Group Test of Mental Ability*. Many

of the schools reported a somewhat comprehensive diagnostic program (including study of interests, background of experience, home relationships, and attitude toward reading). Table 2 reveals the emphasis given to various methods of diagnosing student need.

METHODS AND INSTRUCTIONAL MATERIALS USED

In approximately sixty per cent of the schools, a room library of easy reading material was provided, and direction to reading was given also in the central school library. Only twenty-nine per cent of the schools made a special effort to correlate the work in remedial reading with the endeavor in other subject fields, such as science or social studies. However, there was a rather large number of activities through which these schools sought to improve the students' ability to obtain greater meaning from the printed page. Table 3 presents these activities and indicates the emphasis given to each of them. It is clear that the major emphasis is accorded skills

Table 2: Methods Used in Diagnosis and Study of Pupil Need

	Frequency		
Activity	Empha-sized Greatly	Some Empha-sis	Little or No Em-phasis
Diagnosis by means of standardized tests	70	32	2
Acquainting pupils with their present reading status	58	44	4
Discovering the nature and extent of reading interests and activities	75	22	4
Stimulating informal discussions of reading interests and activities	46	47	7
Testing for possible visual defect	39	43	14
Testing for possible auditory defect	35	40	21
Obtaining information concerning experiential backgrounds of pupils	38	48	13
Locating instances of lip movements and other symptoms of vocalization in reading	47	48	5
Discovering interests in hobbies, movies, social activities, constructions, collecting, and vacations	51	41	8
Studying emotional characteristics of pupil	50	42	8
Discovering attitudes toward reading	72	28	1

Table 3: Activities for Developing Meaning Through Reading

	Frequency		
Activity	Empha-sized Greatly	Some Empha-sis	Little or No Em-phasis
Aiding pupils in interpreting the meaning of words in reading materials	87	18	0
Providing practice in comprehending central points in paragraphs	86	17	0
Helping pupils in methods of locating information in textbooks	58	42	5
Giving practice in predicting the outcomes of events	27	51	22
Teaching pupils how to follow directions in reading	83	20	1
Reporting to entire class on books read	27	46	25
Writing brief reports of materials read	22	50	22
Teaching pupils how to read the newspaper	26	41	33
Study of formal grammar	6	30	61
Enlarging vocabularies by means of word drills independent of reading materials	28	35	37
Providing practice in letter-writing	20	38	37
Writing short stories	5	23	65
Using practice books in reading	51	39	13
Teaching pupils how to draw conclusions from materials read	61	38	9

Table 4: Activities Designed To Promote Rapid Reading

	Frequency		
Activity	Empha-sized Greatly	Some Empha-sis	Little or No Em-phasis
Extensive rapid reading of easy, interesting material	68	27	2
Reading exercises under pressure of time control	36	53	15
Attention to lip movement and excessive vocalization	35	57	10
Keeping a record of pupils' progress in rate of reading	50	41	12
Increasing span of recognition by means of short exposure exercises, flashcards, etc.	25	38	39
Providing training in rapid word recognition	42	30	21
Helping pupils to adjust rate to purpose	62	37	4
Reading and discussing classics	21	33	43

such as comprehending the central thought of a paragraph, following directions, and obtaining the meaning of the words used in various selections.

Table 4 presents the various activities designed to promote rapid silent and oral reading. The frequency with which extensive rapid reading of easy materials is reported as a major emphasis and the high citation of activities designed to help pupils adjust their rates of reading to different kinds of materials are heartening features of this study. They show that these schools are making considerable progress in attacking the poblem in remedial reading. However, it should be kept in mind that (as shown in Table 1) relatively little attention is being given to reading in the various subject fields.

Wide use of visual and auditory aids was reported by these schools. Several of these aids are designed to help the student improve his rate of reading by developing rapid recognition of words and phrases. Other aids are employed for diagnosis of the condition of the pupils' vision and hearing. Table 5 lists the frequently used aids.

Materials of instruction that stress the visual approach were generally employed. Table 6 gives a list of these materials. The use of films in twenty-seven schools represents a distinctly new trend in remedial instruction.

The practice materials most widely used include *Reading Skill-texts* of Charles Merrill Company; *Reading for Meaning* of J. B. Lippincott Company; *Practice Readers* of Webster Publishing Company; *Getting the Meaning* of J. B. Lippincott Company, and *Practice Exercises in Reading* of Teachers College, Columbia University. These practice books were cited by fifteen, thirteen, eleven, ten, and ten schools, respectively. By far the most popular magazine was the *Reader's Digest,* reported by forty-seven schools. *Life* was employed in ten schools. Twenty-six schools indicated that newspaper reading was greatly stressed. It was noticeable from the replies that the remedial program is not usually correlated closely with the broader objectives of the secondary school. Little use was made of related aspects of the language arts, such as writing and discussion techniques, to reinforce and strengthen reading skills. Thus, it appeared that improvement in communication was infrequently the broad goal of the remedial classes.

Table 5: Devices Used To Diagnose Pupil Need or To Improve Reading Skills

Name of Device or Instrument	Frequency
Ophthalmograph	4
Metronoscope	4
Tachistoscope	3
Telebinocular	20
Audiometer	26
Flashmeter	1
Buswell Reading Board	2
Opaque projector	2

Table 6: Visual and Auditory Instructional Aids Employed in Remedial Reading Classes

Name of Aid	Frequency
Board work	3
Book jackets	2
Card sets—charts	1
Dolch cards	2
Drawings, pictures, picture books	7
Durrell Word Wheels	1
Films	27
Filmstrips	4
Flash cards	11
Games and contests	1
Maps	1
Oral reading records	1
Radio news and drama	1
Recordings	7
Slides	3
Stereoscope	1
Tachistoscope	11
Tape recorder	4

APPRAISAL OF PROGRESS IN READING

The students' progress was evaluated in the various schools by a number of methods. Table 7 presents the procedures reported. Fifty schools reported a strong emphasis on standard tests; teacher records of reading activity were used similarly by fifty-five, while records kept by the students were emphasized in forty-nine of the schools. It is worth noting that only twelve schools indicated that improvement of reading in various subject areas was seriously stressed in evaluating gains in reading.

THE ROLE OF THE TEACHER

Administrators cited the need for more adequately prepared teachers. Concern was expressed again and again regarding the teachers charged with remedial

Table 7: Method of Evaluation

	Frequency		
	Empha-sized Very Much	Empha-sized Some-what	Little or No Em-phasis
Standardized tests	50	41	6
Records of reading activities kept by students, book report cards, etc.	49	46	6
Oral reports given in class on books and other materials read	29	54	19
Records kept by teacher of reading activities of pupils	55	35	4
Report on reading improvement by teachers of other subjects	12	35	42
Subjective evaluation by teacher	37	44	5
Grades in English	23	42	3

work; for example: "We have no teachers who are specifically trained for this type of class; therefore, the responsibility falls upon a few who are interested and have shown some ability in teaching reading." And again, "We have no specially trained teachers for such courses, and have had to depend upon volunteers who were willing to undertake it."

Of the one hundred twenty-six teachers who were reported to be teaching remedial reading courses in these school systems, only twenty-eight were full-time specialists. The other ninety-eight were regular teachers who volunteered or were drafted for the work. A majority of them had no special preparation for the work. Seventy-five schools used the same teachers as long as the program had been in operation; twenty-one schools "passed the classes around." The latter expression, used by one respondent, discloses the feeling among a significant number of teachers that remedial reading classes are undesirable or a special burden. The feeling is further revealed by comments such as: "I have been stuck with these classes for two years now." On the other hand, the vital need for really effective teaching is shown by the comments of many administrators. The following is a typical comment: "We have one teacher doing this special work. She was chosen because of her preparation, wide experience, unusual wisdom and success in working with pupils, and her faith that they can succeed. I would not want such a course unless the 'right teacher' could be found."

CONCLUDING STATEMENT

Although this survey shows that considerable gains are being made in organizing and developing remedial reading classes, much more comprehensive programs need to be undertaken and correlated with developmental reading programs. Unfortunately, little is being done to provide such a correlation. Perhaps a fairly reliable indication of the status of reading in the typical high school may be obtained from William R. Wood's account entitled "Typical Programs of High School Reading Instruction" in *The North Central Association Quarterly* for April, 1947: [5]

"From a study of the survey reports, a procedure pattern emerges. The typical school does a good deal of objective testing to determine reading deficiencies. On the basis of the test results and previous scholastic records, pupils are homogeneously grouped. Those who are two or more years retarded are placed in special remedial sections where progress is determined largely by the individual teacher's enthusiasm and special knowledge. Periodically, additional reading tests are given to measure progress, and pupils are transferred to classes at their own grade level if the test results and other factors warrant. The remedial class may be an extra assignment for after-school hours or a replacement of the usual activities hour. Ordinarily, however, it is simply a substitution for the regular English course offered by the school. In a few instances schools which do not have specially trained teachers of reading are fortunate in being able to utilize the services of a private reading clinic.

"No one is satisfied with the typical procedures that have been outlined. The whole problem of the developmental program for average and superior students is not handled in an effective way. The remedial work seldom accomplishes as much as it should. For the ambitious teacher there are unusual opportunities ahead for discovery of new methods, for the production of better materials, and for the creation of an over-all reading instruction plan."

It is evident that there is a need for remedial reading as a temporary expedient in the junior and senior high school. One of the most significant aspects of modern remedial programs is the attention thus made possible to the needs of individuals and small groups. It should be pointed out that, wherever possible, individual guidance and help should be given to the poor reader. In every attempt to offer assistance, there should be a conscientious effort to diagnose carefully the reading levels and needs of the pupils, to provide useful and stimulating materials, and to offer systematic instruction for a long enough time to assure improvement.[1] In public schools where such programs have been developed, high-school students almost invariably have been found to improve their ability to read for many important purposes. However, such remedial efforts should be regarded as one part only of a larger program designed to improve reading in all subject areas and to make instruction in reading a responsibility of every teacher.

REFERENCES

1. Gray, William S., *The Teacher of Reading: A Second Report, Thirty-sixth* Yearbook of the National Society for the Study of Education, Part I. Bloomington, Ill.: Public School Publishing Company, 1937, Chapters I and III.
2. Kottmeyer, William, "Improving Reading Instruction in the St. Louis Schools," *Elementary School Journal*, Vol. 45 (September 1944), pp. 33-8.
3. Witty, Paul, *Reading in High School and College* (W. S. Gray, editor), 47th Yearbook of the National Society for the Study of Education. Chicago: University of Chicago Press, 1948, Chapter II.
4. ————, and Kopel, David, *Reading and the Educative Process*. Boston: Ginn and Company, 1939.
5. Wood, William R., "A Second Attack on Reading Problems in Secondary Schools," Chapter III, in "Typical Program of High School Reading Instruction," Report of Subcommittee on Reading, *The North Central Association Quarterly*, Vol. 21 (1947), pp. 481-3.

43: Certain Basic Concepts in Remedial Reading *

RUSSELL G. STAUFFER

An eight-year-old boy with above-normal intelligence, who had spent a year in kindergarten and two and one-half years in school, had not learned to read. It is the purpose of this article to report how he acquired an initial reading vocabulary and started to read books. The discussion that follows gives a brief summary of the results obtained by a clinical analysis, describes a "learning-to-read" process, and presents certain concepts considered basic to differentiated reading instruction.

CLINICAL FINDINGS

The boy, whose assumed name for this report is Paul, was referred by his third-grade teacher to the Temple University Reading Clinic. The referral was made in January, after five months of renewed efforts in a large classroom situation had been unsuccessful.

An extensive analysis was made.[1, 16] Through interviewing the parents, the teacher, and Paul himself a case history was obtained. Previous health-service records were examined. Tests of vision and hearing were used. Data concerned with emotional development and social adjustment were obtained by interview, observation, and standardized measures. Psychological tests of capacity, memory, memory span, associative learning, laterality, and discrimination were given. Achievement in reading and related areas was measured.

Paul's chronological age was eight years and four months; his mental age, nine years and eight months. On the Gates Primary Reading Tests, he attained a reading grade of 2.10 on the test of word recognition; of 2.20 on the tests of sentence-reading and paragraph-reading. A word-recognition test (based on Betts Reading Vocabulary Study) showed poor ability in word recognition above the preprimer level. On a spelling test, he spelled correctly 65 per cent of the first-grade words but only 15 per cent of the second-grade words. His visual and auditory discrimination skills were inadequate.

The boy had not assumed some of the ordinary personal responsibilities, such as dressing himself. Enuresis was reported. Emotional immaturity was evidenced by over-dependence on adults who ministered to his needs and in his social relations with his peers. He had had difficulty with reading since Grade I.

Use of an experience approach (pedagogically) and of the kinesthetic-tactile technique (psychologically) was recommended. It was indicated that progress would be dependent on improved social and emotional adjustments, as well as on remedial instruction.

A "LEARNING-TO-READ" PROCESS

Differentiated Instruction. The program of instruction required adjustment to certain time limitations. Paul was to receive instruction four hours a week, two hours on Thursday mornings from nine to eleven o'clock and two hours on Friday mornings at the same time. More desirable programs

* Reprinted from the *Elementary School Journal,* Vol. 51, No. 6 (February 1951), pp. 334-42, by permission of the author and the publisher.

would have been arranged if circumstances had not required a compromise.

Instruction was begun by the writer, using the techniques recommended. The first word Paul wanted to learn was *dictionary*. The meaning of the word was briefly discussed, and he was asked to tell the number of parts he heard. The teacher located the word in Webster's *Elementary Dictionary*, [17] and the pupil identified the number of syllables. The teacher then wrote the word in large, cursive style on a sheet of paper three inches by twelve inches, saying each part without distortion as he started the first letter of each part. The tracing technique was demonstrated, and the pupil was instructed to trace the word and say the parts until he felt that he could write the word without looking at it. The following illustrates how Paul learned the word:

dictionary: 4_w 10_w 7_w 1_w 2_w $1 - C$

The digits indicate the number of tracings needed up to one perfect reproduction. The letter w indicates attempts at writing which resulted in failure. C indicates correct reproduction. In other words, Paul traced the word four times and then felt he could write it. When he failed, he traced again—a total of ten times—and so on. In all, he needed twenty-five tracings to achieve one perfect reproduction.

Next he wanted to learn the word *book*. The procedure described above was used, with the following results:

book: 1_w 2_w 1_w $2 - C$

Six tracings were needed. Much of the difficulty in this word was with the letter k.

Then he wanted to learn *dog*, which he traced four times:

dog: 2_w $2 - C$

At this point the teacher suggested that he might want to keep a list of the words he had learned or perhaps write something in which he used the words. Paul preferred the latter and decided to write, "A dictionary is a book." In writing the word *dictionary* again, he found it necessary to trace it after an attempt at writing indicated inadequate recall. The learning proceeded as follows:

dictionary: $_w1_w$ $1 - C$

The word *is* was learned after two tracings. The word *book* needed no retracing. Already the saving in the number of tracings and the ease of reproduction were fostering security and confidence.

Now he suggested the sentence, "A dog bites and it barks." The words were learned as follows:

dog: $_w$ 1_w 1_w 1_w 1_w 1_w $1 - C$
bites: 3_w $1 - C$
and: 1_w 1_w $1 - C$
barks: 2_w 1_w 2_w $1 - C$

Dog needed six retracings, largely because of reversal of the *d*. The boy had no difficulty with the letter *k* this time and was particularly pleased.

Paul's sentences were typed. The next day he read the typed sentences, first silently and then orally. While his voice was somewhat high pitched and the reading was not rhythmical, he needed no help with word recognition. He was eager to continue.

Evidence of his maturity level, the extent to which he was influenced by immediate experiences, and the lack of consistency in his interests may be noted in this day's activities. First he wrote the sentence, "It is snowing." Next he wrote, "I go skiing and sledding and skating." He learned the words as follows:

snowing: 2_w 6_w 1_w $1 - C$
I: 1_w 1_w 2_w 4_w 3_w 5_w $3 - C$
skiing: 1_w $1 - C$ *and:* $_w$ $1 - C$
sledding: 2_w 1_w $2 - C$ *skating:* $1 - C$

Shifting his interest, he wrote, "I can box." Then, showing sensitivity to semantic shifts, he wrote, "I got a box." He had no difficulty with *I* and learned the other words as follows:

box: ₩ 1ᵥᵥ 1ᵥᵥ 2ᵥᵥ 1 — C
got: 3ᵥᵥ 1ᵥᵥ 2ᵥᵥ 1ᵥᵥ 1ᵥᵥ 2 — C

After four hours of help, he had learned to recognize, and to reproduce in writing, fifteen words. However, not all of each two-hour period was devoted to word-learning. As part of the program, Paul participated in group activities. He helped to prepare plans and learned to think of group goals. He learned to adjust to other pupils with reading difficulties and observed how they reacted to him. He listened to radio programs and group discussions and participated in oral-language activities.

By the time Paul had received fourteen hours of instruction, he had learned forty-nine words, which are listed below:

and	for	one
are	fox	paste
baby	George	pictures
barks	he	president
big	his	run
birthday	hobby	scrap
bites	horses	skating
book	I	skiing
box	important	sledding
brown	is	snowing
collecting	likes	some
dictionary	little	terrier
died	more	was
dog	my	Washington
February	need	white
fill	Norman	
first	of	

By this time Paul was also writing stories and relating events in sequence. The length of each "story" had increased, and it was all about one topic. Titles had been added—an indication of an appreciation for a central theme. Word-learning showed fewer tracings,

and some words were reproduced without tracing. The following is one of his "stories."

MY DOG

I got my dog for my birthday.
He is a little fox terrier.
He is brown and white.
He likes to run.

Paul learned the words as follows:

Dog: 3 — C	*fox:* 2 — C
I: 5 — C	*terrier:* 4ᵥᵥ K — C
got: K — C	*brown:* 2ᵥᵥ 2ᵥᵥ K — C
for: ᵥᵥ 1 — C	*white:* 1ᵥᵥ K — C
birthday: 5 — C	*likes:* Kᵥᵥ 1ᵥᵥ K — C
He: 2ᵥᵥKᵥᵥ 3ᵥᵥ K — C	*run:* 1 — C
little: 3ᵥᵥ K — C	

The boy had difficulty with the capital letters in *Dog* and *He*. An explanation for the learning of the word *He* follows: two tracings, a wrong writing. He then felt that he did not need to trace but could write the word correctly after looking at it and saying it. (This is referred to as *K*, representing visual-auditory-kinesthetic.) Then there followed: a wrong writing, three tracings, a wrong writing, a *K* response, and correct reproduction.

Progress in Word-Learning Ability. The boy's progress in word-learning ability and language structure may be noted in the following story, which was written after Paul had received forty hours of training.

HORSEBACK RIDING

I go horseback riding every Saturday. The first time I went riding the man let me go around alone.

He reproduced all these words, except *horseback,* by the kinesthetic technique, and he needed to study the words only once. *Horseback* required one tracing. The legibility and the rate of his handwriting were also much improved.

Table 1: Per Cent of the 192 Words Learned by Paul Which Are Found in Various Word Lists *

Word List	Per Cent	Word List	Per Cent
Gates Reading Vocabulary	82	International Kindergarten Union List	82
Horn Spoken Vocabulary to Six Years	66	Thorndike, Teacher's Word Book of 20,000 Words	92
Horn Basic Writing Vocabulary (Adults)	88	Thorndike, Teacher's Word Book of 20,000 Words (first and second thousand only)	77
Horn Basic Writing Vocabulary (first and second thousand only)	71		

* The sources of the word lists used were vocabularies assembled in *A Combined Word List* [5] and in *A Reading Vocabulary for the Primary Grades*.[10]

By this time Paul had accumulated a number of stories concerning his dog, and he wanted to take home copies of them. He became enthusiastic when it was suggested that he might like to arrange the stories in book form. Research was necessary, for a title-page, a table of contents, and story organization were needed. Paul carried through the project successfully.

Using Basal Readers. By this time, Paul had acquired a total reading vocabulary of 169 words through the experience approach. Because of his mounting interest in books, he was, at this point, introduced to basal readers, although experience stories were also continued. The preprimer was used, and he completed its activities in one session. He devoted two sessions each to the first and second primers, learning all the words by the visual-auditory method. The reading vocabulary acquired by the "basal-reader approach" totaled 31 words. A word-recognition recheck, with the 31 words presented in isolation, indicated 100 per cent accuracy.

Paul had received forty-five hours of training over a period of sixteen weeks. He had missed some lessons because of absence. The regular school term ended, and remedial instruction was discontinued. It may be noted that this program was irregular to the extent that both lesson days fell at the end of the week. Thus five days elapsed before the next two days of training were given. Retention was greatly taxed by delayed recall.

Commonness of Words Learned. Paul's reading vocabulary, acquired from the use of the experience approach, totaled 192 words. To determine the extent to which use of this technique encouraged the learning of common words, the list was checked against vocabulary studies.

Table 1 indicates that, even though no formal effort at vocabulary control was made, high percentages of agreement were obtained between the words learned and several vocabulary lists. The highest percentages of agreement are evident when comparisons are made with adult lists. The importance of the 192 words for retention as parts of a permanent reading vocabulary, and as a possible basis for the development of word-analysis skills, could be readily determined.

In Table 2 the words that are common to the Gates *Reading Vocabulary* are rated according to placement in the first, second, third, or fourth five hundred. This further emphasizes the value of the words as part of a permanent reading vocabulary.

Table 2: Words Learned by Paul Which Are Common to Gates Reading Vocabulary Rated According to Placement in First, Second, Third, or Fourth Five Hundred

Placement in Gates Vocabulary	Words Acquired by Paul	
	Number	Per Cent
1-500	110	70
500-1,000	29	18
1,001-1,500	9	6
1,501-2,000	9	6

BASES FOR DIFFERENTIATING INSTRUCTION

The procedure for remedial-reading instruction reported in this study has been found effective in many instances. It involves an "experience-approach" technique in teaching and a "kinesthetic-tactile" technique psychologically.[3, 8] Certain generalizations basic to remedial-reading instruction stand out.

Remedial Instruction. Use of the experience approach as a teaching method follows a precept basic to teaching: going from the known to the unknown. In this approach, the "known" was represented by the oral language used by Paul, and the "unknown" was represented by the printed symbols.

The reading vocabulary was obtained from Paul's speaking vocabulary. It reflected the mental constructs which his interests and attitudes had initiated. In addition, familiarity of the concepts facilitated fixation and retention of the reading vocabulary.

The kinesthetic-tactile technique followed many of the principles basic to the psychology of learning. As Paul learned to associate meaning with the printed symbols, his acquisition process may have been facilitated by the several afferent pathways that were stimulated: the visual-auditory-kinesthetic-tactile. The amount of concentration necessary for accurate tracing, and the co-ordinated pronunciation of each syllable as the initial letter of the part was being traced, required him to fix his attention on the task at hand. The accurate reproduction of the word without copying, which was demanded for two consecutive perfect trials became a measure of learning.

Retention was enhanced by filing the words in a vocabulary "word box" and by rereading them at intervals in the original learning context, in other contexts, and in isolation. Re-use of the words learned for retention purposes was encouraged by pursuing a series of related stories and a project. Psychologically, the association between the word and its meaning has been established for an individual when, in future instances, the printed symbols elicit appropriate experiences.[13]

Developmental Instruction. Since differentiated instruction has been receiving merited attention, ideas concerning reading retardation have been modified. Teachers are understanding that human variability exists at all grade levels.[6] A norm on a reading test is no longer being interpreted as a standard to which all pupils must conform. Individuals in a grade are not all being confined to the same book. Adjustments are viewed as varied and continuous rather than regimented and static.[11] As a result, many pupils who at one time might have been labeled "retarded" are now considered to need instruction at their present level of attainment, regardless of the premium placed on grade conformity. Acceptance of this viewpoint is especially encouraged since authorities agree that, in most instances, remedial instruction begins with good first teaching.[9]

An instructional program which is designed to develop an initial reading vocabulary will capitalize on a pupil's total assets: his mental age, social and emotional maturity, experiences, interests, language facility, and methods of work.[13] The program not only will take advantage of the abilities the pupil already possesses but will also refine and extend them. The statement made by Dora Smith about interests could be adapted to almost each area listed:

The reading interests with which pupils come to school are our opportunity, but the reading interests with which they leave school are our responsibility.[15]

While consideration of a pupil's "funds" is advocated at all levels, this is especially necessary at the reading-readiness stage. Readiness programs direct attention to social and emotional adjustment. The shift from "being read to" to "learning to read" requires a certain matureness. A mental age of six or six and one-half is suggested by research as an optimum time at which to start reading instruction. Pedagogically, grouping as a means of adjusting instruction is encouraged. Language factors (vocabulary, sentence structure, etc.) and typography (type size, leading, etc.) of reading materials are considered.[12]

In the beginning reading program, strong emphasis is placed on the acquisition of an initial reading, or "sight," vocabulary. Authors of basal series of readers attempt to capitalize on that which is known to pupils. Studies of vocabulary development, especially speaking vocabularies, are consulted. This is done so that oral-language skills may form the "known language" from which printed language may be developed.[2] New words are gradually introduced and are maintained by frequent repetition. The language structure is simple and direct, only gradually becoming more complex. The content is built on the common experiences of children within their immediate environment and is slowly expanded. Pictures and illustrations are generously utilized.[14] All

this is done in the beginning phase to facilitate for the pupil the transition from manipulating familiar concepts by oral language to manipulating the same concepts by printed language.

Reading is a process whereby the individual reorganizes his experiences, as a result of stimuli received from printed symbols which represent the writer's experiences. The concepts that the reader brings to the printed page are based on his previous experiences and the extent to which he has acquired a language to represent them. In this respect, the individual's supply of labels for experiences may be indicative of his attitudes and interests.[7]

"Concepts" in the generic sense are abstractions developed within, by, and from symbol-experience relationships.[4] When a person is not articulate about his concepts, functional differences may result. He may use words to represent experiences with which conventional usage does not agree. Or he may use words and, if challenged, be unable to index or abstract the experiences represented. While these statements may have connotations that might be questioned, it can hardly be doubted that they denote the existence of individuals who have either a "language deficiency" or an "experience deficiency."[3]

Involving an initial reading vocabulary through developmental or remedial instruction, the constructs used should be simple and should require the pupil to do little reorganization of previous experience. In this way, the major emphasis will fall on acquiring a reading vocabulary and not on the experiences the symbols represent.

Résumé. The use of procedures such as the experience approach and the kinesthetic-tactile technique possesses the decided advantage of newness and thus avoids many of the antagonisms of a tried, but unsuccessful, technique. The concepts used (words learned) are obtained from the pupil's experiences and require little, if any, reorganization. Instruction is given either individually or in a group of two or three pupils who need similar help. In this way, unfair competition is kept at a minimum, identification with the group and group therapy may be utilized, and any attention that is needed from the teacher is available. Finally, it appears evident that, when instruction is differentiated, it is adjusted pedagogically, psychologically, and psychotherapeutically, and individual differences are appropriately considered. As a consequence, in many instances, the distinction between developmental and remedial instruction appears to be general and relative rather than absolute and specific.

CONCLUSIONS

The extent to which such a program of differentiated instruction has succeeded may be attributed to a number of pedagogical and psychological adjustments. The concept development, semantic sensitivity, and language facility of the pupil served as the foundation for the reading vocabulary. Recognition of printed symbols was aided when "known" oral language was employed functionally by the pupil. Thus, meaning and use facilitated recognition and retention. Of the words learned through the experience approach, a large percentage is common to different word lists. This facilitated the introduction of basal readers and the subsequent development of word-recognition skills. The additional technique of tracing aided recall and helped concentration on the task at hand.

The stories which the pupil prepared demonstrated that his attitudes and interests had been considered in the instruction. The attention given to his habits of work, ego status, peer relations, and creative abilities probably facilitated progress and adjustment. Continued success, evidenced in the growing reading vocabulary and in the ease of control over vocabulary, gave needed security and confidence.

REFERENCES

1. Betts, Emmett Albert, *Classification of Reading Disabilities.* Philadelphia: Reading Clinic, Temple University [n.d.]. (Reprinted from *Visual Digest,* IX [Summer 1945], 36-44.)

2. ———, *Foundations of Reading Instruction with Emphasis on Differentiated Guidance.* New York: American Book Co., 1946.

3. ———, *Foundations of the Reading Program.* Philadelphia: Reading Clinic, Temple University [n.d.]. (Reprinted from *Education,* LXVII [March 1947], 399-41.)

4. Brownell, William A., and Hendrickson, Gordon, "How Children Learn Information, Concepts, and Generalizations," *Learning and Instruction,* pp. 92-128, Forty-ninth Yearbook of the National Society for the Study of Education, Part I. Chicago: Distrib-

uted by the University of Chicago Press, 1950.

5. Buckingham, B. R., and Dolch, E. W., *A Combined Word List.* Boston: Ginn & Co., 1936.

6. Cook, Walter W., *Grouping and Promotion in the Elementary School,* Series on Individualization of Instruction, No. 2. Minneapolis, Minnesota: University of Minnesota Press, 1941.

7. Dewey, John, *Context and Thought,* pp. 203-24, Publications in Philosophy, Vol. XII, No. 3. Berkeley, California: University of California Press, 1931.

8. Fernald, Grace M., *Remedial Techniques in Basic School Subjects.* New York: McGraw-Hill Book Co., Inc., 1943.

9. Gates, Arthur I., *The Improvement of Reading.* New York: Macmillan Co., 1947 (3rd edition).

10. Gates, Arthur I., *A Reading Vocabulary for the Primary Grades*. New York: Teachers College, Columbia University, 1935 (revised).
11. Gray, William S., "Reading as an Aid in Learning," *Reading in the Elementary School*, pp. 233-53, Forty-eighth Yearbook of the National Society for the Study of Education, Part II. Chicago: Distributed by the University of Chicago Press, 1949.
12. Gray, William S., and Leary, Bernice E., *What Makes a Book Readable?* Chicago: University of Chicago Press, 1935.
13. Horn, Ernest, "Language and Meaning," *The Psychology of Learning*, pp. 377-43, Forty-first Yearbook of the National Society for the Study of Education, Part II. Chicago: Distributed by the University of Chicago Press, 1942.

14. Russell, David H., *The Basic Reading Program in the Modern School*, Ginn and Company Contributions in Reading, No. 1. Boston: Ginn & Co., 1947.
15. Smith, Dora V., "Current Issues Relating to Development of Reading Interests and Tastes," *Recent Trends in Reading*, pp. 297-306, compiled and edited by William S. Gray, Supplementary Educational Monographs, No. 49. Chicago: University of Chicago Press, 1939.
16. Stauffer, Russell G., *Certain Psychological Manifestations of Retarded Readers*. Newark, Delaware: Reading Clinic, University of Delaware [n.d.]. (Reprinted from *Journal of Educational Research*, XLI [February 1948], 436-52.)
17. *Webster's Elementary Dictionary*. New York: American Book Co., 1941.

PART FIVE

Issues in Reading Instruction

If the 1960's are an exciting time to live in, education in general and reading instruction in particular dramatically reflect this excitement. Never before has there been more controversy about the teaching of reading, experimental programs, new approaches and techniques, and an ever increasing quantity of excellent material. The teacher of reading may be under pressure to do an ever better job, but she is being given methods and materials by which this can be done. Pleas of the 1950's for fewer children per classroom and a delay in formal instruction have fallen from their position of pre-eminent major issues into relative obscurity. The issues are so numerous today that it would be impossible to list them all. Upon one feature of the reading program are all teachers agreed: children must learn to read better than ever before if they are to keep up with the vast amount of knowledge being acquired in all fields.

CRITICISM OF READING INSTRUCTION

Educators have long been concerned about how reading instruction can most effectively be practiced. The early yearbooks of the National Society for the Study of Education devoted solely to reading [12] are a major indication of this interest. The rapid growth of the International Reading Association, a professional group of teachers concerned with reading, from its establishment a decade ago to its huge membership today is another indication of the great interest. Educators and the lay public are interested in the teaching of reading. The appearance in 1957 of *Why Johnny Can't Read*,[8] which stirred up controversy that has not yet subsided, clearly indicates the interest.

Flesch's book capitalized on a latent interest of the general public in reading.

In a series of grossly exaggerated statements—although true in some situations —Flesch claimed reading instruction was poorer than ever before. From his attack upon the methods used in reading instruction, he proposed as a simple cure the teaching of a specific phonic approach. The book served a major purpose in drawing the attention of educators and the general public to reading instruction, and to phonic instruction specifically, so that it can be considered a major contribution in this sense. The fact that it implied incompetency on the part of teachers is unfortunate, for the confidence of the lay public in the sincere dedication of teachers is essential.

Numerous other books (such as, *What Ivan Knows that Johnny Doesn't,* [13] and *Tomorrow's Illiterates* [14]) continue to attack the methods of instruction that are being used in the public schools. Not reserved entirely to lay people, the ranks of criticism are frequently joined by professional educators. If reading were a simple process of learning word-attack skills, the critics' solutions to the problems might be justified. Reading is, however, a complicated function involving a variety of processes of which the ability to analyze new words is only one part.

It is probably true that more direct teaching including phonic instruction was needed in some situations and for some children. It is also probably true that more time needs to be devoted to formal reading instruction at all levels. The program in the public schools directly reflects what the general public wants, and increased interest and attention to reading instruction by the general public has undoubtedly resulted in more attention to teaching reading in the public schools.

The critics are wrong when they claim that reading instruction in the public schools is poor; but they are correct in demanding that reading instruction improve. With more and more financial support for public education, better trained teachers, and more supplies, reading instruction must be better than ever before.

CHANGES AND INNOVATIONS

The changes and innovations involving the teaching of reading that are taking place in the public schools are nothing less than revolutionary. Causes for these changes are many, not least of which are the concern of the general public about reading instruction, the threat of Russian superiority in scientific areas, the resulting improvement of instruction at all levels, and the major breakthroughs in a wide variety of areas. A partial list of the recent innovations in reading would include the following:

1. Instruction in reading using non-basal materials
2. Linguistics in the teaching of reading
3. Teaching reading to pre-school children
4. The Augmented Roman Alphabet

An interesting aspect of virtually every new proposal, either in administration or in methodology, is that it apparently works better than methods previously used. This might lead some to believe that previous methods were so bad that any innovation would be an improvement, but in actuality the key is probably the teacher's enthusiasm for new methods and materials. Without question, the method is not nearly so important as the teacher who employs it. It is not unlikely that the teachers who were most successful with methods used previously will be the ones most successful in any new venture.

Individualized reading is currently receiving a great deal of attention, although there are conflicting reports as to its effectiveness.[6] Undoubtedly, one of the central problems is the lack of an adequate definition of the program. The word "personalized" has been suggested as a compromise between a completely unstructured program and the more traditional basal text approach.[1]

The idea of teaching children to read from materials that have been specifically selected to meet their particular needs is certainly not new. Leading authorities in the field of reading long ago advocated this.[3] There can be no question but that the basal text has provided the teacher with a guide, and that to completely remove this guide may result in less efficient instruction. In the "personalized" program, an interest approach is generally advocated with direct teaching of specific skills. By means of skills check-lists for each grade level, the teacher in an individualized or personalized program can make certain that skills are being mastered.[2] The real value of the individualized or personalized program is not that it offers an entirely new method of teaching reading, but rather that it offers the teacher yet another technique so that the reading program may be more flexible.

Linguistics has come to be almost a magic word in the field of reading. Beginning with Bloomfield's approach,[5] efforts have been made to adapt the linguistics movement to the teaching of reading. Two recent books have made major contributions in this direction.[9, 10] Betts has been a leader in translating the linguistics movement into practical procedures for classroom teachers.[4]

The notion that pre-school-aged children can be taught to read has gradually gained widespread acceptance. A variety of methods are being advocated, but there is little evidence to date that merely because it can be done there is any real justification for such earlier teaching. Such magazines as the *Ladies' Home*

Journal and *Harper's* have joined in the discussion. The *Journal* has even marketed a set of materials that parents may use to teach their "tiny children" to read.[7] In an article entitled "How Three-Year-Olds Teach Themselves To Read—and Love It," *Harper's* magazine described an ingenious "learning machine." Essentially the machine is a "talking typewriter" which teaches the child the letters and sounds simultaneously.[11] The methods are indeed novel and deserve attention of those concerned with teaching young children to read.

The question resolves itself into whether or not children should learn to read earlier, and, if so, who should teach them. The role of the parents in the formal reading program has frequently been debated, but it is generally agreed that where possible the parents should play a supportive role rather than an active one. Of the many types of things necessary for parents to teach their children, reading is one better left to those who understand both the methods of teaching reading and the way in which children learn to read.

REFERENCES

1. Barbe, Walter B., "Personalized or Individualized Reading Instruction?", *Education*, Vol. 81, No. 9 (May 1961), pp. 537-9.

2. ———, *Skills Check Lists,* Grade Levels: Readiness, First, Second, Third, Fourth, Fifth, and Sixth. Kent, Ohio: Special Education Department, Kent State University, 1960, 7 pp.

3. Betts, Emmett A., *Foundations of Reading Instruction.* New York: American Book Company, 1954, p. 715.

4. ———, "Reading: Linguistics," *Education*, Vol. 83, No. 9 (May 1963), pp. 515-26.

5. Bloomfield, Leonard, and Barnhart, Clarence, *Let's Read.* Detroit: Wayne State University Press, 1961.

6. Cutts, Warren G., *Research in Reading for the Middle Grades,* Bulletin 1963, No. 31. Washington, D.C.: Department of Health, Education, and Welfare, Office of Education, 1963, pp. 66-8.

7. Doman, Glenn, Stevens, George L., and Orem, Reginald C., "You Can Teach Your Baby To Read," *Ladies' Home Journal* (May 1963), pp. 62, 124, 126.

8. Flesch, Rudolph, *Why Johnny Can't Read.* New York: Harper and Brothers, 1957.

9. Fries, Charles C., *Linguistics and Reading.* New York: Holt, Rinehart and Winston, 1963.

10. Lefevre, Carl A., *Linguistics and the Teaching of Reading.* New York: McGraw-Hill Company, 1964.

11. Pines, Maya, "How Three-Year-Olds Teach Themselves To Read—and Love It," *Harper's Magazine,* Vol. 226, No. 1356 (May 1963), pp. 58-64.

12. *Report of the National Committee on Reading,* Twenty-fourth Yearbook of the National Society for the Study of Education, Part I. Bloomington, Ill.: Public School Publishing Company, 1925. *A Second Report,* Thirty-sixth Yearbook of the National Society for the Study of Education, Part I. Bloomington, Ill.: Public School Publishing Company, 1937.

13. Trace, Arthur S., Jr., *What Ivan Knows that Johnny Doesn't.* New York: Random House, 1961.

14. Walcutt, Charles C., *Tomorrow's Illiterates: The State of Reading Instruction Today.* Washington, D.C.: Council for Basic Education, 1961.

CHAPTER XI

Linguistics

44: A Linguist Looks at Reading: Leonard Bloomfield and the Phonemic Criterion *

B. ROBERT TABACHNICK

Reading instruction in the public schools comes under periodic attack from professional educators and from interested citizens outside the profession. In part, this is caused by the position of central importance which professionals and nonprofessionals alike tend to assign to teaching children to read. "Some subjects are more important than others. Reading is the most important of all," writes John W. Gardner.[6]

Overwhelmingly, the teaching of reading in elementary schools is organized in such a way as to utilize basal reading textbooks. Two kinds of charges, not necessarily related to each other, have been leveled at basal reading instruction: the first charge argues that most reading texts are based on an inadequate understanding of the mechanics of language and of reading, causing initial reading instruction to be inappropriate and productive of a large percentage (rarely specified) of failures; the second charge challenges the content of the readers on the grounds that controlling reading vocabulary has produced vacuous selections which are inadequate to the task of introducing children to our literary heritage.

Leonard Bloomfield's essay, "Teaching Children to Read," finds reading instruction wanting in the way in which it confronts children with the task of learning to read, and goes on to present an alternative based on a linguistic, essentially a phonemic, analysis of English. Although parts of the late Professor Bloomfield's essay have appeared earlier,[1] the manuscript, originally completed in 1937, appears in its entirety for the first time in *Let's Read*.[2]

Bloomfield believes that any reader performs two separate tasks: letters in words represent sounds to a reader; getting the sounds from the page, the reader performs the second task of trying to understand what these sounds mean. It is only the first of these, transforming written symbols into sounds, which Bloomfield accepts as defining reading. Making sense out of sounds is a task common to responding adequately to any use of language.[4] This kind of restriction on the domain of the reading teacher is consistent with the linguist's usual restriction of his own domain, language.

Defining language as "an arbitrary system of articulated sounds made use

* Reprinted from *Elementary English*, Vol. 39, No. 6 (October 1962), pp. 545-8, 561, by permission of the National Council of Teachers of English and the author.

of by a group of humans as a means of carrying on the affairs of their society," [5] linguists have discovered that of the vast range of sounds possible to any human speaker, each culture selects a small number of distinct and separate sounds out of which to build a language. Each member of this finite set of irreducible speech sounds is called a phoneme if using it in place of another sound changes a word's meaning. For example, substituting the phoneme /p/ for the phoneme /b/ at the beginning of the word "bit" changes the word's meaning; interchanging the initial and final phonemes of the word "tap" creates a completely new word "pat." Interchanging the initial and final phonemes of the word "pop" does *not* make a difference in English, although these sounds (or phones) are different from one another. In some languages they are separate phonemes; in English they are variants of the same phoneme, /p/.

It should be emphasized that phonemes are sounds. Written symbols, often called graphemes, may represent phonemes or they may represent words or they may represent ideas (as does the symbol "3," regardless of the word used by speakers of different languages in referring to it). Alphabetic writing uses written symbols to represent speech sounds. English, although it is "extremely imperfect and arbitrary" (Bloomfield's description), is an alphabetic system. Since an English writer transforms speech sounds into written symbols, a reader of English has the task of using the written symbols to help him recreate the original speech sounds.

Since Bloomfield's analysis stresses the substitution of emphasis on word-form for preoccupation with word-meaning, and since the relationship of letter(s)-to-sound is central, some readers may be tempted to equate this approach with phonic approaches to teaching reading. Bloomfield is uncompromisingly explicit in rejecting such a link.

The letters of the alphabet are signs which direct us to produce sounds of our language. A confused and vague appreciation of this fact has given rise to the so-called "phonic" method of teaching children to read. . . .[1]

Believing that children at six are quite facile in using their mother tongue, Bloomfield suggests that they "have no need whatever of the drill which is given by phonic methods."

Phonics errs not only in confusing writing with speech, but also in isolating speech sounds. It expects the child to produce on cue the sounds of letters isolated from any word in which they appear. Children practice making the "t-sound," for example, either alone or followed by an obscure vowel sound.

English speaking people . . . are not accustomed to making that kind of noise. Learning to pronounce such things is something in the nature of a stunt, and has nothing to do with learning to read. We intend to apply phonetics to our reading instruction; this does not mean that we are going to try to teach phonetics to young children. In this absurdity lies the greatest fault of the so-called phonic methods.[1]

It is important to remember that Bloomfield's description is of practices which he believed were common in the mid-1930's, although Graves [8] has recently described a way of teaching phonics which seems to have characteristics of the "phonic methods" which Bloomfield attacked. Some of Bloomfield's sharpest criticisms are reserved for nonphonic, presumably basal, reading instruction. The flat assertion that "actual instruction in our schools consists almost entirely of . . . the word method," precedes the suggestion that only a child's lucky (and independent) discovery of symbol-to-sound relationships saves him from the burden of learning separately all of the words he must know. If this purported to describe current reading instruction, it would be tempting to label it absurd.

Even a cursory look at the teachers' manuals of current reading texts reveals that the first formal teaching of letter-to-sound relationships occurs typically during the first grade. Attention is directed even earlier to aural discrimination of sound contrasts, especially in initial consonants. Unfortunately, we have little assurance that the readers are being used as their authors intend them to be used, which underscores the difficulty of speaking with confidence about "what the schools are doing." The discussion in *Let's Read* exercises little caution in this respect.

If a word method is one which tells children what word each group of letters represents, rather than forcing them to "work it out" for themselves, then Bloomfield's is itself a type of word method. (". . . teacher says, 'Now we have spelled the word. Now we are going to *read* it. This word is *can*. Read it; *can*.' ") [1] It is a word method with this difference: the words are presented in such a way that the contrasts in sound may be easily identified with differences in the letters used to form the contrasting words. Particularly in the earliest stages of instruction, vocabulary is controlled with great care so that each letter represents only one sound and each sound is represented by only one letter. (Strangely enough Bloomfield finds it necessary to violate this axiom on the very first page of his reader where, in such phrases as "a can, a fan, a pan," *a* has both the regular sound as in "can" and, when it is a word by itself, the irregular sound as in "bake." It is difficult to understand why this pronunciation was chosen since, as Bloomfield points out, this is rarely the pronunciation of the word "a" in normal speech.)

The difference in sound between "Dick" and "dill," between "dill" and "din," between "Dick" and "din," is in each case the smallest difference in sound which can occur between two words which have different meanings in English. The fact that the phoneme /k/ is spelled "ck" in one word, or that the phoneme /l/ is spelled "ll" in another, is irrelevant to the task of discovering differences in *sound*.* [9] However, controlling these "irregular" spellings is very relevant to introducing children to the relationship between grapheme (written or printed symbol) and phoneme. From Bloomfield's point of view they should be carefully screened out of initial reading instruction. This procedure for controlling the introduction of words simply extends to reading instruction the linguist's method of compiling lists of words with minimal differences in sound in order to discover those speech sounds which serve as phonemes in a language. Bloomfield's thesis is that such a presentation, by stressing the correspondence of phonemes and graphemes (written or printed symbols), builds the ability to read upon what is basic to the expressive structure of a language, and insures children a greater measure of success, achieved more quickly and easily, under conditions which allow them to become independent readers more readily.

Applying a phonemic criterion to the control of vocabulary suggests a number of intriguing hypotheses with respect to teaching reading and especially with respect to the beginning stages of reading instruction. One group of hypotheses would aim at making clear the nature of the relationship between reading and correspondences between phonemes and their spellings. A group at

---

* At least one linguist would have objected to our earlier definition of a phoneme as "a member of a set of sounds" with the statement, "The phonological system of a language is . . . not so much a 'set of sounds' as it is *network of differences between sounds*. In this frame of reference, the elements of a phonological system cannot be defined positively in terms of what they 'are' but only negatively in terms of what they are *not*, what they *contrast* with." In Charles F. Hockett, *A Course in Modern Linguistics*, New York: Macmillan, p. 24.

Cornell is currently investigating these relationships as they exist in adult readers.[7] Davis and Diman,[3] of the University of Wisconsin have conducted preliminary attempts to use Bloomfield-like materials with beginning readers in public school classrooms.

A second set of hypotheses includes those aimed at discovering the function and causes of motivation in learning to read. Some critics of the basal reading texts have argued that controlled vocabularies should not play as important a role as they do in determining content. Bloomfield attacks the *lack of control* (with respect to phoneme-grapheme correspondence) which characterizes the presentation of words to beginning readers. Does the even stricter control of vocabulary, needed to avoid ambiguity in the spelling of many English phonemes, increase initial reading success? Or do the limits on content imposed by this control produce material so empty of meaning as to make reading impossibly tedious?

Bloomfield predicts that the motivating factor of content is very likely irrelevant and possibly harmful to a beginning reader. The child beginning to read is too busy changing the printing into sounds to have energy or interest left for listening to the message. Knowing that he has responded to symbols with appropriate sounds is motivating enough to keep a reader working, even if the product is a nonsense syllable, according to Bloomfield.

Highly meaningful material may be reinforcing in ways that nonmeaningful material is not. It may provide a reader with the opportunity independently to estimate the correctness of a response. This opportunity is denied him to the extent that the content of his reading is unpredictable. Whether the content of basal reading texts is significantly more meaningful, in this respect, than the Bloomfield materials is, at least, open to question.

To present "the accurate calling of words" and "getting meaning from the printed page" as mutually exclusive alternatives seems to be something less than productive. Quite clearly we are interested in children's learning to call words correctly to the extent that this skill is crucial to their being able to understand and think about what they read. Whether making sense out of sounds is not (by definition) a part of reading, or whether it is the most important part of reading, it is certainly appropriate for schools to teach children to use and respond to language effectively. Can this skill develop most efficiently if it is taught as part of the teaching of reading? Is reading only one context in which this skill can profitably be developed? Does emphasis on meaning increase success in learning to call words correctly? We have only partial answers to many of these questions and no answers at all for others.

One can logically defend the statement: since phonemes represent the basic elements of a structure by which an adult comes to understand the expressive part of a language, the primary criterion in teaching children to read should be to introduce them to symbols which represent these elements. The questions: "What is reading?" and "How does a child most readily learn to read?" are separate questions. One answer may suffice for both; two answers, related to one another, may be needed; that two distinct and separate answers are required for these two questions, is also logically possible. Since the prediction that one alternative is superior to another is empirically verifiable, a reasonable expectation is that we will soon see the results of experiments replace the results of logical dispute.

REFERENCES

1. Bloomfield, Leonard, "Linguistics and Reading," *The Elementary English Review*, 19 (April 1942), pp. 125-30, and 19 (May 1942), pp. 183-6.
2. Bloomfield, Leonard, and Barnhart, Clarence L., *Let's Read*, Detroit: Wayne State University Press, 1961.
3. Davis, David C., and Diman, Roderic, *Phonemic Structual Approach to the Teaching of Reading*, 6 pp. mimeographed.
4. Dawkins, John, "Reading Theory—An Important Distinction," *Elementary English*, 38 (October 1961), pp. 389-92.
5. Francis, W. N., *The Structure of American English*, New York: Ronald Co., 1958.
6. Gardner, John W., "National Goals in Education" in *Goals for Americans*, the report of the President's Commission on National Goals, New York: Prentice-Hall, 1961.
7. Gibson, E. J., Gibson, J. J., Danielson, Anne, Osser, Harry, and Hammond, Marcia, *The Role of Grapheme—Phoneme Correspondence in Word Perception*, 29 pp. mimeographed.
8. Graves, William H., Jr., "A Blueprint for Reading," *Elementary English*, 39 (March 1962), pp. 246-9, 255.
9. Hockett, Charles F., *A Course in Modern Linguistics*, New York: Macmillan.

45: Linguistics and Reading *

LYNN GOLDBERG and DONALD RASMUSSEN

For three years we have used a linguistic or *phonemic-word* approach to teach beginning reading to first and second grade pupils at the Miquon School. We feel that although we have not had enough experience to evaluate one approach to reading as against another, certain of our experiences and observations may be worth reporting at this early stage. Following is a brief statement of the theory of our approach, a description of our efforts to use it, and a few of the conclusions that we feel may be drawn at this time.

We label our approach to teaching beginning reading *linguistic* because certain of its basic principles are derived from or are an application of the data and conclusions of the rapidly growing science of language analysis called linguistics. We also label our approach a *phonemic-word* approach because it is based on an analysis of our language according to the elemental speech sound called *phonemes*. The main characteristic of the approach is to teach the relationship of phonemes to their corresponding letter symbols or *graphemes*. We add *word* to the label in order to emphasize the linguistic principle that there are no isolated sounds for such letters as *b* or *c* or *d;* there are only names for them. The phonemes represented by these letters do not exist in isolation; they exist only in combination with other phonemes in words. Therefore, we teach the symbol-sound correspondence within words and

* Reprinted from *Explorations in Reading*, Lehigh University, Conference Proceedings, Vol. 2 (June 1962), pp. 22-7, by permission of the senior author and the publisher. This article also appeared in *Elementary English*, Vol. 49, No. 3, March 1963, pp. 242-7.

call this approach a *phonemic-word* approach. The main principles of this approach have been developed and described by such linguists as Leonard Bloomfield,[2] Robert Hall,[6] Henry Lee Smith, Jr.,[8] C. C. Fries [4] and others.

Some of the basic findings of linguists and their implications for teaching reading are as follows:

1. English is a language represented in a written form by an alphabet. It is thus distinguished from such a language as Chinese which is represented by characters that represent whole words. The problem of learning to read the symbols that represent the Chinese language is prodigious because one has to memorize a symbol-sound correspondence for each word in the language. Reading an alphabetic language is greatly simplified because one has only to learn the more limited relationships between letters or combinations of them and the sounds they represent. Of course, the more consistent or regular the relations of letters and sounds are, the more easily one can learn to read the language. One can actually learn to read without knowing the names of letters. However, because we have very frequent recourse to naming the letters as we teach the sounds which correspond to them, we find it necessary to teach the alphabet before attempting to teach a child to read. It is not necessary to have a perfect knowledge of the entire alphabet. (If this seems to belabor a very elementary point, one has only to be reminded that learning the names of letters is not considered a prerequisite to reading by the most popular of the current teaching methods.)

2. Linguists are agreed that there are approximately forty-six elemental speech sounds or phonemes in the English language. Each of these phonemes is represented in writing by one or more letters. Some letters represent two or more phonemes. There is, therefore, not complete regularity or perfect correspondence in the symbol-sound relationships of English. It follows that in attempting to teach a beginner to read an inconsistently spelled language by showing him the correspondence of symbol and sound, it is necessary to separate those words of the language which

are represented consistently, *i.e.*, according to patterns, from those which are exceptionally or irregularly represented. Once words are classified according to the regularity of their spelling, (and this linguists have done) the consistently spelled words can be presented by patterns while the irregularly spelled words may be considered exceptions to the patterns. It is therefore not necessary to memorize every word of the language. And one would also not confront a child with such words as *come* and *home* on an introductory page as is done in currently used texts. The reading materials of a linguistic approach would be based upon the very careful analysis of the consistency in patterns of symbol-sound relationships. In general, words with regular correspondences of symbol and sound, *i.e.*, words belonging to patterns, would be separated in presentation from irregularly spelled words. Learning to read words which belong to consistent patterns of symbol-sound relations can be based upon a full appreciation of the alphabetic nature of our language. One must learn to read irregularly spelled words differently depending on the parts of the word which may belong to a pattern.

3. A fact elementary to linguists is that written symbols (which are what we read) are the representations of sounds, and sounds are in turn the representations of ideas or of realities. Languages were spoken before they were represented by written symbols. The main task in learning to read appears then to be able to produce the sounds of a language when one sees the written marks which conventionally represent these sounds. This does not obviate the fact that the aim of all reading is to derive meaning or understanding from written symbols. Even though one might insist that the derivation of meaning is a necessary element in the reading process, we feel that a separation of the skill of associating sound with symbol from the aim of deriving meaning is important for the reason that the presentation of the subject of reading to the very beginning reader is made much less complicated by concentrating on the skill rather than on the promotion of understanding. The problem of deriving meaning is, of course, practically eliminated by restricting the words in reading materials to those that

children commonly use in oral expression or to the language he knows. This is very considerable for a six or seven year old child. (Again, if this seems to belabor a perfectly obvious point, we can show that popular texts go to great lengths to prepare children for the problem of getting meaning from the pronunciation of *ride* or of *cow* and many other words which we assume that children know.)

RELATION TO SIGHT METHOD

In our discussion of some of the characteristics of a linguistic approach to reading, we intimated some points of comparison with other currently used methods. Let us compare in more detail a linguistic approach with the *sight* or *look-say* method as well as with the phonic methods. Although we speak of the linguistic approach as distinctive from other approaches, it actually incorporates certain elements of the sight method *and* of phonics which we feel are the essential and scientific aspects of these approaches. This is the reason that under the pressure of improving the standards of reading of American children, we feel it is unfortunate to limit the choice of answer to either the phonics method or the sight method. Historically the sight method emerged as a correction of phonics. It would be a mistake to return to the phonic method as it was or even as it has been slightly modified in recent times. We need a new approach which will incorporate the sound principles of current practice as well as the new scientific findings of linguists.

With the sight method, a child learns to read by memorizing words he sees over and over again. The more words he can visually memorize, the more he can read. The beginning reader can only learn a new word by being told what it is. In order to promote independent reading he is taught to use context clues which help him guess words. To be certain that he is correct, however, he must still ask someone who knows the word. Without an actual check on his accuracy, the child remains with a doubtful guess and the possible cultivation of a habit of reading incorrectly. While he is memorizing words to the point of becoming confused, inaccurate phonic principles are introduced with the hope of helping him to begin to analyze words and to correct wrong habits. This is well illustrated in the process of helping a child to read correctly the simple sentence "Tom went to the store." We have heard children guess this sentence as "Tom wants to go to the store," "Tom won't go to the store," and "Tom wants the store." Each of these guesses might be expected from confusing the general appearance of the words. These guesses may also be due to the way phonic principles are introduced in the sight method. The sound of *w* may have been taught in the context of the word *water*. This ill prepares one to attempt to "figure out" the pronunciation of *went*. It doesn't work and before order is restored, the pupil has tried several possibilities. For some children the habits of mispronouncing and of guessing and of reading inaccurately are introduced at this time and are very difficult to change at any later stage.

Relation to Phonics

It would seem to us that the most effective way to learn to read some words such as *wad* or *put* would be to read them as whole words and to memorize them by sight. We state this because the sounds of *a* and *u* in these words are different from the sounds of these letters in all other three letter words in which these letters connect two consonants. With the help of linguists who know very precisely the patterns and frequencies of symbol-sound relations, we designate *wad* and *put* as irregular words. They are by our definition the exceptions to some rule. What we illustrate in the cases of these two words applies in a general way to all unphonetic words or to those words which do not belong to patterns of symbol-sound relations. Thus, the linguistic approach to reading may be said to use the sight method to teach the unphonetic words or parts of such words in our language. Because the linguistic approach teaches phonemes in the context of words, it may also be said that it uses the sight method in initiating the process of reading. Children have to know a few words (which they can only memorize by sight) before they can begin to discover and then to appreciate patterns of symbol-sound relationships. It is apparent that we feel the alphabetic nature of our language and the relationship of letters with speech sounds is not properly assumed, especially in teaching children to read the great portion of our language which is phonetic.

The phonics method recognizes the alphabetic structure of our language and attempts to relate a letter or letters to corresponding speech sounds. From sounds the reader may derive meaning and thus achieve the aim of reading. By relating letters with sounds the phonics method attempts to give the pupil an analytic tool by which he can "figure out" many words and thus become a reasonably independent reader. In these respects the phonics method resembles our linguistic approach.

Because linguistics is a science using precise concepts and tools of analysis, its data make the classifications and characterizations of the symbol-sound relationships of traditional phonics appear very crude and inconsistent. One could give many examples of such linguistic inaccuracies from any of the current phonics texts. Some linguist is soon going to report on the many inaccuracies of the phonics method. Although associating sounds with isolated letters is not an inherent aspect of the traditional phonic method, it is a prac-

tice commonly used by phonics teachers and, of course, in doing thus, they violate a linguistic principle. If we teach *C* as *Kuh*, *A* as *Aa*, and *T* as *Tuh*, C-A-T becomes Kuh-Aa-Tuh. This practice certainly can confuse the child's response to printed symbols.

To our knowledge one does not find any sequential order in organizing patterns of symbol-sound relationships in any phonics system. As a result, the words used to illustrate one symbol-sound pattern invariably contain contradictory elements of other patterns— many of which have not been taught yet. In other words there isn't any accurate programming of the principles in the phonic methods. For this reason we suspect that after decades of trial, it has not produced any literature or quantity of reading materials based upon a careful build-up of phonic principles. The linguistic approach is therefore like the phonic methods in using the patterns of symbol-sound correspondence, but the linguistic approach is based upon a more valid, refined, systematic analysis of the sounds of our language than one finds in phonic methods.

There are two general ways of associating symbol with sound in a language that is not represented consistently by regularly spelled words. One can use either symbol or sound as a variable. Thus, one can (1) classify the symbols or spellings and show the different ways in which the same letters or combinations of them may be pronounced, or, (2) one can classify sounds and show the different ways in which they may be represented. The reading system described in the *Phonetic Keys to Reading* [5] illustrates the first approach. In an explanation to teachers it is stated that the series "is devoted primarily to the development of skill in phonetic analysis. A step-by-step method of presenting the sounds of the letters and the phonetic principles is followed throughout the series." [7] The similarity of this approach to the linguistic approach is obvious. The difficulties found in the method, however, are similar to those found in phonic methods. There is no systematic approach to the element of sound nor even an attempt to see that all phonemes represented by particular letter combinations are presented. Certain pronunciations of letters are presented without a clear basis of selection. Some pronunciations of letter combinations are omitted altogether. There are, for example, thirteen spellings for the speech sound corresponding to *ee*. It is easy to see the difficulties in trying to systematize and to program such an approach.

In addition to the theoretic points which constitute its viewpoint, the linguistic approach is dependent upon a classification of our language according to phonemes. One can imagine many classifications and orders of words, and as the linguistic approach is further developed, undoubtedly new word arrangements will emerge. To date, however, the work of Leonard Bloomfield remains as the outstanding analysis of our language according to speech sounds. In 1942 Bloomfield outlined the main features of his system [1] and recently in collaboration with Clarence Barnhart they were published in detail. Our program at the Miquon School can be seen most clearly in contrast to the work of Bloomfield.

We can look back to three stages in the history of our project: (1) an introductory period of formulating our point of view and searching for materials; (2) an experiment with the Bloomfield word list and materials we prepared in conjunction with; and (3) the current period during which we are developing our own word list and are continuing to prepare our own materials to be used with this list.

It is very difficult to embark upon a new reading method without a literature that accompanies it. The stories and exercises of *The Royal Road* series by Daniels and Diack [3] and the publica-

tions of *Linguistica* by Frances Hall [5] came close to our viewpoint but did not adequately serve our needs. We used these materials with some children having difficulties in learning to read and we also used them in starting to teach a group of beginning readers. We ended this first stage of our project when we decided it was best to turn to the word list of regular and irregularly spelled words devised by Bloomfield. For one year we followed rather slavishly the prescriptions of Bloomfield on how to teach reading. We thought that we had at last found the appropriate materials to teach a child to read. We found that it was possible to teach children to read with a linguistic method, but we also found that we had to devise and to write totally new materials before the approach could be used successfully in the classroom. We did not have enough children to be able to draw conclusions about the effectiveness of a linguistic approach. We were encouraged to go on with the ideas we had in mind. Naturally the new materials we have developed since this experiment take note of the inadequacies we found in the Bloomfield-Barnhart materials.

IN CONTRAST TO BLOOMFIELD

Our principal effort during the past two years has been to write materials suitable for children and consistent with the linguistic theory described earlier. Although we recognize the importance of Bloomfield's classification of words according to the regularity of their spelling, we have found it quite unnecessary to introduce all the regularities in spelling before we could begin to introduce any irregularly spelled word. We have introduced some irregularly spelled words much earlier than Bloomfield prescribes. The important points are (1) that the beginning reader have a consciousness of regular and irregular words, and (2) that the different types of words should be introduced with such care that learning a word of one type does not interfere or handicap a reader in learning a word of another type. We have made our own selection of words on the basis of our classroom experience and a number of factors have affected our decisions. While it is not our main reason for doing so, we think that with an earlier use of certain irregular words, we can get a more readable literature without sacrificing the linguistic point of view.

Bloomfield begins his word list with simple two and three letter phonetic words. We agree that beginners should not use the length of a word in order to guess its pronunciation. It is also relatively easy in words of this length to illustrate most of the basic patterns in which sounds are represented by particular letters. However, among the introductory words used by Bloomfield are nonsense words. We do not use nonsense words, because we found that children learn meaningful words more easily than nonsense words. We had enough meaningful words to illustrate the patterns of symbol-sound relations we wanted to teach.

Although there is a general control of length of word in Bloomfield's list, our experience tells us length of word is a factor in reading that is even more significant than Bloomfield realized. Using the term *phonemic word length* as a more useful measuring concept than number of letters, we make a much more serious attempt than does Bloomfield to control this factor. We do not control the factor in the sense that we introduce words in the exact order of their phonemic length. It is rather that we are very conscious of the length of our words and have introduced longer words in our list only after careful consideration of our classroom experience.

As a result of our experience we found that consonant blends used at the end of a word are much easier for children to learn than blends used at

the beginning of a word. Bloomfield presents what in our experience have been the more difficult words to learn first. We follow the principle of introducing the easier words first. Continued experience in using the linguistic approach will probably uncover many additional alterations which we feel do not sacrifice the linguistic point of view while increasing the ease and effectiveness with which children can use the materials.

At the end of this year we shall have used our materials with approximately one hundred children of greatly varying abilities. Our principal interest thus far has been in the improvement of materials rather than in any attempt to draw conclusions about the merits of one reading approach as against another. Not until there are adequate quantities of attractive linguistic reading materials used by teachers trained in the method can we get any real measure of its success. We ourselves are sustained in our efforts by our theory as well as by our observations of the growth of individual children.

NO EVALUATION OF METHOD

Under the conditions of a completely individualized classroom organization, some of our children have learned to read in a remarkably short time. In cases of a few children who had "taught themselves to read" before entering first grade, we observed that they had actually learned regularly spelled words and the more simple irregular ones. As a result, these children had a reading vocabulary which fitted rather well into the cumulative word list we had used. On the other hand, we were not able to teach a few children to read who were handicapped by emotional difficulties. Other methods tried later with these children also failed to get results. We think that eventually linguistic reading materials ought to be of special value in remedial cases because the growth of word recognition is (1) developed in a very logical sequence, and (2) proceeds from easy to more difficult materials. This will have to be proved by experience. Most children have learned to read it at a pace we feel is more than satisfactory. Even here one must be reminded that in a changing field, the criteria for evaluating are also changing and much controversy will occur over these kinds of evaluations.

The materials for any approach to reading are built on a vocabulary that is gradually accumulative. With adult standards of taste, we wonder how children can be motivated through the beginning stages of any reading series when the vocabulary is small. We had this feeling when we approached children with man, fan and Dan. We have found that the "thrill of reading," of being able to say meaningful sounds consistent with written symbols, carries children through the very early period. By the time motivation from this source begins to wane, the vocabulary is large enough to compose stories and poems with a stimulating content. We observe in our present beginning pupils a high level of interest.

Our objective in trying a new approach to beginning reading was not to assume that we had a cure-all to solve all reading problems. We ourselves are wary of any panacea for the problems in this field. Our aim is to teach children to be more independent and accurate in their reading than they are commonly trained to be. We think we observe the accomplishment of this aim in the large majority of our children. We think this success is in large measure a result of our attempt to base our materials upon the findings of linguists —who are the scientists investigating language. We think the facts they give us will help us to deal with the realities of a very difficult problem. We cannot ignore the facts uncovered in the rapidly growing science of linguistics any more than we can abandon or ignore the findings of physiologists and psychologists which have a bearing on reading. The teacher of beginning reading today cannot decide whether or not she wants to use a linguistic approach. The question now is—What is *your* linguistic approach and how do you balance the linguistic facts with the other scientific facts *you* put into *your* reading program?

REFERENCES

1. Bloomfield, Leonard, "Linguistics and Reading," *The Elementary English Review,* Vol. 19 (April 1942), pp. 125-30, and Vol. 30 (May 1942), pp. 183-6.
2. ————, and Barnhart, Clarence, *Let's Read,* Detroit: Wayne State University Press, 1961.
3. Daniels, J. C., and Diack, Hunter, *The Royal Road Readers,* London: Chatto and Windus, Ltd., 1960.
4. Fries, Charles C., *The Structure of English: An Introduction to the Construction of English Sentences,* New York: Harcourt, Brace, 1952.
5. Hall, Frances Adkins, *Sounds and Letters* (preliminary edition), Ithaca, New York: Linguistica, 1956.
6. Hall, Robert A., *Leave Your Language Alone,* Ithaca, New York: Linguistica, 1950.
7. Sloop, Cornelia Brown, Garrison, Harrell E., and Creekmore, Mildred, *Phonetic Keys to Reading,* Oklahoma City: The Economy Company, 1952.
8. Smith, Henry Lee, Jr., *Linguistic Science and the Teaching of English,* Cambridge, Mass.: Harvard University Press, 1956.

CHAPTER XII

Individualized Reading

46: Individualized Reading—Myths and Facts *

N. DEAN EVANS

Most educators would agree that individualized instruction to some extent in all subject areas is a worthy goal. Today there are those who claim that an individualized reading program in the elementary school is the only feasible way of teaching Johnny to read effectively. It is the purpose of this article to examine the research and experimentation of the last eight years and to draw some conclusions regarding the validity of this claim.

THE THEORY OF INDIVIDUALIZED READING

Primarily, the reading program is organized so that all pupils read independently rather than in regular reading groups. Trade books chosen by the pupils are the basic reading materials. Self-selection of books is a key feature of individualized reading. Each child reads at his own pace and keeps a record in his notebook of the books he reads.

After the pupils are oriented to the program and understand that they are to have a book of their own choice in their possession at all times, the follow-

ing activities are carried out during the reading period:

1. Individual conferences, averaging five minutes, are held between the teacher and a child. At this time the student's reading list is checked to note progress and some of the books are discussed. The child may read orally to the teacher, and any difficulties can be corrected. A comprehension check is often made. A notebook sheet or card is kept for each pupil so that progress and deficiencies can be noted by the teacher during or immediately after the conference. Help may be given in the selection of books suitable to the child's reading level and interests.

2. When not in conference or otherwise engaged, the child reads independently at his seat or selects a new book from the shelf.

3. Teaching sessions with small, flexible groups are held from time to time to teach skills. The composition of these groups depends upon the teacher's conference notes, diagnostic reading test data, and observations.

4. Some of the earlier writers [3] suggested occasional use of basal readers for skill and basic vocabulary teaching.

* Reprinted from *Elementary English*, Vol. 39, No. 7 (October 1962), pp. 580-83, by permission of the National Council of Teachers of English and the author.

However, most present-day advocates are violently opposed to any use of the basal, which is criticized as too "dull" and restrictive.

5. Short periods are set aside for the sharing of reading experiences among the members of the class. Motivation for future reading takes place here.

6. Some children will work on their reading lists in their notebooks or will be adding words to their vocabulary lists.

7. Creative work, growing out of common reading experiences, may be going on in small groups. For example, some children may be preparing a play.

The following advantages have been claimed for individualized reading programs:

1. Children are purported to have made greater gains than control groups in vocabulary, comprehension, and total reading completed.

2. Children are much more interested in the reading program when they can select their own books.

3. As children mature, their interests, needs and abilities become much more diverse. Individualized reading meets these growing diversities more effectively, say its advocates.[4]

4. The amount of class time spent actually reading is increased; consequently more words are learned through context.

5. The psychological effect of the program on the child is favorable. Pressures and tensions to meet the standards of a traditional reading group are eliminated. Group competition is minimized, according to proponents.

WHAT DOES RESEARCH SAY?

Let us see now if research and critical classroom experience validate the enthusiastic claims made for individualized reading by its supporters.

First, there is relatively little controlled research data available. This fact, however, has not deterred various enthusiasts, (including the author in his earlier writings) from making extreme and unsubstantiated statements in favor of complete individualization of reading instruction.

Sartain reports on one of the very few valid studies: "In summary, because this study and others that have been carefully controlled show that the individualized method does not produce better reading gains than a strong basal program, there is no reason to forfeit the advantages of a well-planned basic system. Instead the benefits of the individual conferences should be obtained by their addition to the basic reader plan." [7] In another conclusion based on a summary of the limited research, Witty, Coomer and Sizemore write: "It may be readily concluded that available experimental data do not justify the recommendation of sole dependence on individualized reading. The experiments appear generally to be inconclusive and to lack sufficient provision for variable factors which may influence results." [9]

Various features of the program should now be examined in detail, in light of the experimental evidence available.

1. *The Individual Conference.* A salient feature of the individualized program, the conference definitely has its limitations. A teacher with a class of 25 pupils and one reading hour per day, will be fortunate to manage one five minute conference (average time) per pupil per week. In this short period she is expected to check the student's reading progress in his trade books, diagnose his reading deficiencies through oral and/or silent reading with a comprehension check, teach some reading skills, and assist him in selecting new books on his instructional and interest level. During or immediately after the conference she must record what has transpired for later reference. As Robinson has reported, "The fact that the

teacher is expected to assess progress in all aspects of reading, determine attitudes, and plan to help each child in five minutes implies that the teacher has superior training and insight." [5] Most reading teachers will agree that diagnosis is one of our most difficult problems, both in terms of reading level and skills. It is impossible for a teacher to know all the trade materials on her reading shelf. Yet in an individualized program she is expected to keep her pupils on the proper instructional level with each child reading a different book.

2. Assuming that the child happens to be reading a book on his instructional level, how much guidance does he receive in the extensive silent reading time? When not in conference or otherwise engaged, the teacher moves around the room to assist with problems. But how does she know when a pupil is having difficulty? Only when the student becomes aware of a word attack or vocabulary problem and asks for assistance. It is therefore quite likely that the child will learn incorrect pronunciations and inaccurate meanings in the course of his reading. He will then practice these errors unless they happen to show up in the sample he reads to the teacher during his conference or in his answers to the brief comprehension questions. [6] And yet this is represented as systematic instruction. For example, Veatch says, "I believe in systematic instruction, but of the type that develops with each child as he reads through increasingly challenging materials." [8]

3. When are skills taught? According to teachers who have experimented with individualized reading, skills are taught as needed during silent reading, or in the individual conference, or in small groups formulated according to diagnosed needs. In actual practice, little or no skill work is done. As discussed previously, the teacher can hardly identify word recognition problems during the silent reading period. It is extremely difficult, if not impossible, to form groups almost daily on the basis of individual conference notes. And the record-keeping required to maintain a systematic skills program for each child is overwhelming, even for the experienced reading teacher. From the vague discussions about reading skills in the literature, it can safely be concluded that they are taught sporadically, if at all, in most individualized programs. Furthermore, the extremists decry grouping for any purpose whatsoever.

HOW SHOULD READING BE TAUGHT?

Individualization of instruction is a worthy goal and it can be achieved to a great extent by some experienced, dedicated, master teachers, operating under very favorable circumstances. However, in the modern elementary school, there are many practical considerations:

1. The number of children in a class and their ranges of ability and interest.
2. Teacher skill and experience varies widely. The inexperienced teacher is lost in a completely individualized program and so are the children.
3. Teacher time for preparation, record-keeping and actual teaching is a big factor. An elementary teacher must plan seven or eight subject periods per day.

And so, despite the cries of those who insist that there can be no compromise —that every teacher must completely individualize, there are some level heads. It would surprise some of the tub-thumpers to know that Betts reported various individualized reading plans many years ago, including Lethal Kiesling's first grade experiment in 1938. [1] Betts has said, "There are few, if any, educators who would question the value of individualized instruction. However, there are many who would advance substantial reasons against any plan for . . . complete individualization. . . ."

Botel has advanced a most sensible proposal for the teaching of reading:

"What is needed . . . is a 'total approach' to reading . . . a plan to integrate the finest materials, methods, organizational plans, and in-service education into a unified package." [2]

A balanced program will include, therefore, the following:

1. Sequence and continuity of skill and vocabulary development, involving basal readers and other aids two or three days per week, with the children diagnosed and grouped by levels. (Experienced teachers may use co-basals or other materials.) Reader stories need not be dull. Good motivation depends on the teacher at any time.
2. Wide reading. A good library is essential, with each child having a book of his own choice at all times. Free reading at the independent level is important, but it assumes that skills have been taught which enable the child to unlock new words and to understand what he is reading. Each child should read as widely as possible in books he selects himself.
3. Some individual and small group activities, such as teacher-pupil conferences, sharing of reading experiences, independent work on vocabulary and reading lists, and literature appreciation.

Thus, all of the purported advantages of the individualized reading program can be combined with the proven benefits of good group instruction, where there is much learning in the sharing of ideas and in group interaction. A good, well-balanced reading program is not *either* individualized *or* group-oriented. It is both. As teachers grow in experience and competence in the skills of reading instruction, they should individualize their programs as much as possible, considering all of the problems discussed.

REFERENCES

1. Betts, Emmett A., *Foundations of Reading Instruction,* American Book Company, 1946, pp. 56-61.
2. Botel, Morton, "We Need a Total Approach to Reading," *The Reading Teacher* (April 1960), p. 254.
3. Evans, N. Dean, "An Individualized Reading Program for the Elementary Teacher," *Elementary English* (May 1953), p. 278.
4. Johnson, Eleanor M., "Individualized Reading," *Curriculum Letter No. 35,* Elementary School Services, Wesleyan University, Middletown, Conn., p. 1.
5. Robinson, Helen M., "Individualized Reading," *Elementary School Journal* (April 1960), p. 412.
6. Ibid. p. 417.
7. Sartain, Harry W., "The Roseville Experiment with Individualized Reading," *The Reading Teacher* (April 1960), p. 281.
8. Veatch, Jeannette, "In Defense of Individualized Reading," *Elementary English* (April 1960), p. 227.
9. Witty, Paul, Coomer, Ann, and Sizemore, Robert, "Individualized Reading —A Summary and Evaluation," *Elementary English* (October 1959), p. 408.

47: Research on Individualized Reading *

HARRY W. SARTAIN

The recent surge of interest in individualized reading has resulted in the publication of dozens of reports of experimentation.[20] Most of these consist of descriptions of procedures developed by individual teachers and offer little or no comparative data. With objectivity as a goal, this summary of research will limit itself to those studies which have involved more than one teacher and have provided a quantity of comparative data.

INDIVIDUALIZED-TEACHING MOVEMENT

Years ago investigations produced evidence that instruction becomes more effective as it is more adequately adjusted to the child's level of achievement.[16] Teachers devised a number of approaches to differentiated teaching,[4] and soon there was an increased emphasis on individualized reading.

The individualized approach requires that all children be taught separately, whether they are achieving at the same level or not.

Every child reads in books which he selects from a large collection. Reading skills are taught during a couple of brief individual conferences with the teacher each week. Occasional group work occurs when a few children need to learn a new skill at the same time, or when the class share what they have been reading from varied texts and trade books available to them.

ACTION RESEARCH

Most experiments have been of the action-research type, where there are no control groups and the data are not subjected to statistical tests of significance. This kind of informal experimentation increases the instructor's understanding of the complexity of learning and of his own capabilities in improving the process. However, results of informal experiments, which are not designed to provide randomization, replication, and statistical analysis, can be accepted only as the observer's well-considered opinions. Several informal studies of a more complicated nature deserve mention.

In one case, two principals disagreed on whether the individualized work had resulted in greater progress.[15] In another, achievement tests showed that first-grade children, following the individualized approach, made no greater growth than those in classes organized in the traditional manner.[14] A third experiment, involving especially capable primary reading groups, revealed that growth through the individualized plan was not significantly greater than under a basic reading plan.[8] In most situations the teachers observed that the experimental method resulted in greater pupil enthusiasm for reading.

In another study, individualized reading was initiated gradually during several years.[11] After three years, a fifth-grade class achieved a median reading score of 6.2 on the California Achievement Test, although the pupils' median mental-grade equivalent on the California Test of Mental Maturity was 5.2.

There were no control groups with which to make comparisons, and data for the other four participating classes were not listed.

FORMALLY DESIGNED EXPERIMENTS

Somewhat different findings were obtained in a study which incorporated control groups.[17] The third-grade classes in two California communities were taught by individualized and basal programs. Basal reading groups made slightly better progress in vocabulary and comprehension, but the teachers of the experimental classes were satisfied with the individualized approach.

Another study compared gains of pupils in a laboratory school's individualized program with those of pupils in a school where basal-reading instruction was given in groups.[2] Despite an average IQ handicap of ten points, far more children in the control group achived a reading age of 84 months than did those in individualized reading. This difference was eliminated when the children reached the age of 132 months.

An entirely different kind of study involved the detailed observation of twenty second-, third-, and fourth-grade teachers who had been recommended because of their work in individualized reading.[10] It was found that individualized teaching provided numerous valuable opportunities for utilizing principles of child development, but that such opportunities were not always utilized. Although the skills programs used were especially strong in word analysis and reading for different purposes, they gave little attention to meaning clues, work-study skills, and adapting rate of reading.

To evaluate progress made with individualized reading in New York, data were collected by structured interviews with teachers and principals.[9] Of the forty-six participating classes, thirty-one were described by their teachers as "bright" groups rather than as "average" or "slow" groups. It was observed that the teachers were more conscious of skills than they had been previously, but skills instruction was still one of their major concerns.

The supervisors of the program felt that teachers having special qualities of attitude, flexibility, resourcefulness, and creativity were needed to guarantee the program's success. The survey included a list of favorable reactions of teachers, pupils, and parents.

A few additional studies have been encouraging to the proponents of individualized reading. One investigator made a conscientious effort to set up the controls and statistical analysis required of formal research.[1] He matched 156 children in fourth-, fifth-, and sixth-grade classes on a number of standard tests and educational characteristics. After nine months of work the achievement of individualized classes was significantly better than that of the basal reader classes in silent-reading comprehension, oral reading, and number of books read. There was no great difference on vocabulary-test achievements of the classes.

Although only skilled teachers were involved, it is difficult to estimate how much the unobservable differences in their capabilities might have contributed to the findings. Also, the school system involved had a regulation prohibiting classroom libraries; this restriction could have had a limiting effect on the extent of supplementary reading done by children in the basic program.

In another situation, student teachers initiated an individualized reading program for intermediate grades.[12] Pupils were randomly assigned to the five experimental and five control sections, where the study ran from October 10 to January 4. Professional observers agreed that the reading skills were taught meaningfully.

Equivalent forms of the Standard Achievement Test revealed an average gain of six months for the control groups compared with two months for the basic reading groups. The respective subtests showed eight months' and four months' gain in word meaning, three months' gain and one month's loss in paragraph comprehension. The differences in favor of individualized reading were significant at the .01 level, and the pupils were enthusiastic about this approach.

This researcher, however, wisely pointed out several serious limitations on these conclusions. The individualized program enjoyed the advantage of teacher enthusiasm, longer daily reading periods, and the presence of regular and student teachers. No mention was made of whether or not the basic groups had as many extension readers available as were used in the individualized program. Also, one wonders what kind of teaching the basic groups received to make possible a loss in comprehension ability as was indicated.

SOME DOUBTS

A doctoral study involved intermediate-grade pupils who were matched on reading ability, IQ, and socio-economic status.[23] Student teachers were trained and supervised in teaching half of the groups by the individualized method and half by the basal-reader method. The children doing the individualized work seemed more interested and read more books than the children who studied by the basal-reader method; tests of significance showed no sure differences between the gains in reading abilities of the two groups. Very similar results were reported in another situation.[3]

In California an investigator took particular pains to guard against the possible salutory effect of placement in an experimental group.[19] He discovered that seven classes in the district had been taught reading according to principles of individualized self-selection during the preceding three years. Using the critical-ratio method, he found that the mean IQ (California Short-Form Test) of the 183 students was not significantly different from the mean of 117 for the district.

He then studied the available data from an achievement-test battery which had been administered to all pupils in October of the preceding two years. During the twelve-month period between tests, the average reading gain for the district was 1.25 years.

During the same year, the mean reading gains of the seven classes practicing self-selection were as follows: .43, .63, .51, .16, .28, .68, and .79. Only 26.7 per cent of the experimental pupils achieved one year's growth, and considerably fewer reached the district's average level. Gains of superior students were not significantly different from those of the average people; there were too few below-average youngsters to make any valid comparison.

In Minnesota an experiment was designed to provide that the same instructors teach with both methods, that the same students act as both the experimental and control groups, and that the same types and quantities of books be available in both the control and experimental classrooms.

These controls focused attention on comparative *pupil* growth, rather than on what different *teachers* could accomplish. Ten second-grade classes were randomly chosen from among those whose teachers volunteered to participate. The one beginning teacher in the group had conducted individualized reading as a student teacher. The other teachers were prepared by special study plus a great deal of experience in supervising self-selected reading activities as a part of their supplementary reading program.

Five classes were randomly selected

to begin individualized reading, while the other five classes engaged in a strong basal program. After three months, all classes rotated to the opposite method, and work was continued for another three months.

The basal reading program involved at least three reading groups in each room with a separate set of basal materials for each. One hundred or more different books at various difficulty levels were kept in both the experimental and the control classrooms. During the weeks of basic instruction the children were encouraged to read extensively and to record their supplementary books.

At the beginning, and again at the end, of both the first and second three-month periods, standardized tests of vocabulary, paragraph reading, and recognition of visual elements were administered. The analysis of variance treatment revealed no significant difference between the mean gains of the *capable* pupils when using the individualized or the basal group methods.

The *less capable pupils,* however, while using the basal group method, achieved a mean gain in word-recognition that was enough superior to their mean gain under the individualized method to be significant at the .05 level.

The teachers observed that the children were highly motivated through the individual conferences, and that they read more books as a result. These teachers decided to abandon the totally individualized plan because of its failure to include readiness activities, its instructional inefficiency, and its creation of undue time pressures on the conscientious teacher. Instead they planned to add individual conferences through the self-selected supplementary reading.

WHAT HAS BEEN LEARNED

Why have these research studies seemed to lead to conflicting conclusions? Obviously they were not all carried out under the same circumstances. In addition, various experiments display the faults of inadequate sampling, lack of replication, and failure to control the all-important factor of differences in teacher capability.[6]

Persons reporting experiments with individualized reading have been especially prone to omit a careful definition of the basal-reader program offered to the control classes. What does "traditional" or "customary" mean as an adjective preceding "basal program"? Do all children read at the same place in the same reader? Are the rich extension-reading resources and the creative activities included, or does the program consist merely of around-the-room oral reading?

It is difficult to evaluate reports of experiments comparing basal and individualized reading, because thousands of teachers use the basal books and teach little or none of the program that is made to go with them.

After analyzing the strengths and the shortcomings of each study, one can offer some factual conclusions.

1. *The Individualized-Reading Approach Can Be Somewhat Successful Under Certain Circumstances.* In most of the experiments, the mean gains on general growth factors were satisfactory. Unfortunately, little attention has been focused on the many specific word-recognition skills, different comprehension abilities, and varied study skills that are required of the well-rounded reader.[5] Also, the faults in the preparation of standard-test norms may result in erroneous data.[7] It is disturbing to note that the individualized approach was strikingly unsuccessful in a situation where the teachers did not expect comparison to be made.[19]

2. *The Successful Teaching of Individualized Reading Requires Especially Competent Teachers.*[9, 18, 21] In the Minnesota study the most highly educated and experienced teachers achieved the

best results with both methods. A very capable beginning teacher who had done student teaching with individualized reading was inordinately more successful with the strong basal program. She found a good manual to be an absolute necessity.

3. *The Less Capable Pupils Are Less Likely To Achieve Success in an Individualized Situation.*[21] This seemed to be anticipated in two studies.[8, 9] Slower children's ability to profit from the careful adjustment of work to their level is counterbalanced by their inability to work independently for the long periods that come between individual conferences.

4. *Children Read More Books under the Plan of Self-Selection with Individualized Instruction.*[1, 9, 21, 23]

5. *The Personal Conference Between the Pupil and the Teacher Is of Particular Value.* The children respond to this display of special interest with great enthusiasm.[9, 14, 21, 23]

6. *Individualized Reading Does Not Allow Adequate Time for the Setting of Thought-Provoking Purposes for Reading, nor for the Introduction of*

New Vocabulary. Psychology has shown the importance of purpose for efficient learning and experimental studies some years ago proved the value of direct teaching of vocabulary.[13]

7. *The Lack of a Planned Sequential Skills Program Makes Teachers Uneasy about a Wholly Individualized Organization.*[9, 10, 21] This feeling seems justified. Although children read more through individualized self-selection, the majority of controlled studies indicate that this method does not result in greater achievement. In some of the single-class experiments with self-selection, teachers have commented that they found it necessary to set aside periods for common-skills lessons with the whole class; this procedure may enforce more of a lock step in growth than any grouping procedure.

8. *Teachers Using the Wholly Individualized Approach Are Constantly Pressed for Time To Provide the Conferences that Pupils Need.* Most of the reports mention that only a couple of conferences can be scheduled with each child each week, and sometimes these must be brief. Also, additional planning time is needed to prepare for many individual lessons.

REFERENCES

1. Acinapura, Philip, *A Comparative Study of the Results of Two Instructional Reading Programs,* Unpublished Doctoral Dissertation, Teachers College, Columbia University, 1959.
2. Anderson, Irving H., Hughes, Byron, A., and Dixon, Robert W., "The Relationship between Reading Achievement and the Method of Teaching Reading," *University of Michigan School of Education Bulletin No. 27* (April 1956), pp. 104-8.
3. Burdette, Eunice E., in "What Research Says," *Reading Teacher,* Vol. 11 (1958), p. 119.
4. Betts, E. A., "Approaches to Differentiated Guidance in Reading," *Education,* Vol. 70 (1950), pp. 582-99.
5. Betts, Emmett A., "Developing Basic Reading Skills Through Effective Class Organization," *Education,* Vol. 78 (1958).
6. ———, *Foundations of Reading Instruction,* New York: American Book Co., 1957, Chap. 25.
7. Betts, E. A., "Reading—Unfinished Business," *Reading Teacher,* Vol. 11 (1957), pp. 131-6.
8. Bohnhorst, Ben A., and Sellars, Sophia N., "Individual Reading Instruction vs.

Basal Textbook Instruction: Some Tentative Explorations," *Elementary English,* Vol. 36 (1959), pp. 185-96, 202.

9. Bureau of Educational Research, Board of Education of the City of New York. *Individualized Reading Interim Report* (1957).

10. Carr, Constance, *Individualized Development of Abilities and Skills in Reading: A Description and Critique of Emerging Practices,* Unpublished Doctoral Dissertation, Teachers College, Columbia University, 1959.

11. Cyrog, Frances, "The Principal and His Staff Move Forward in Developing New Ways of Thinking about Reading," *California Journal of Elementary Education,* Vol. 27 (1959), pp. 178-87.

12. Duker, Sam, "Research Report: Effects of Introducing an Individualized Reading Approach by Student Teachers," *Reading in Action,* Vol. 2 of IRA Conference Proceedings (1957), pp. 57-62.

13. Gray, William S., and Holmes, Eleanor, *The Development of Meaning Vocabularies in Reading: An Experimental Study,* Chicago: Department of Education, University of Chicago, 1938.

14. Hilson, Helen H., and Thomas, Glenn G., "Individualized Reading in First Grade," *Educational Leadership,* Vol. 16 (1959), pp. 319-22.

15. Jenkins, Marian, "Self-Selection in Reading," *Reading Teacher,* Vol. 11 (1957), pp. 84-90.

16. Jones, Daisy M., "An Experiment in Adaptation to Individual Differences," *Journal of Educational Psychology,* Vol. 39 (1948), pp. 257-72.

17. Kaar, Harold, "An Experiment with an Individualized Method of Teaching Reading," *Reading Teacher,* Vol. 7 (1954), pp. 174-7.

18. Robinson, Helen M., "News and Comment," *Elementary School Journal,* Vol. 60 (1950), pp. 411-20.

19. Safford, Alton L., "Evaluation of an Individualized Reading Program," *Reading Teacher,* Vol. 13 (1960), pp. 266-70.

20. Sartain, Harry W., "The Roseville Experiment with Individualized Reading," *Reading Teacher,* Vol. 13 (1960), pp. 277-81.

21. ———, "A Bibliography on Individualized Reading," *Reading Teacher,* Vol. 13 (1960), pp. 262-5, 270.

22. ———, "In Combining Sequential and Individualized Reading," *Sequential Development of Reading Abilities,* ed. Helen M. Robinson, Supplementary Educational Monograph No. 90, Chicago: University of Chicago Press, 1960, pp. 187-90.

23. Veatch, Jeannette, "In Defense of Individualized Reading," *Elementary English,* Vol. 27 (1960), pp. 227-34.

48: Heterogeneous, Homogeneous, or Individualized Approach to Reading? *

DAYTON G. ROTHROCK

Teachers have long argued the merits of homogeneous grouping versus heterogeneous grouping. The former method has come and gone and has been revived again.

A newer approach, perhaps, to the problem of organizing the class for instruction is the individualized approach. Much has been written in recent years about the merits of this approach in the teaching of reading. Other grouping patterns have also been tried over the

* Reprinted from *Elementary English,* Vol. 38, No. 4 (April 1961), pp. 233-5, by permission of the National Council of Teachers of English and the author.

years. Numerous claims have been made for the advantages of some of these plans and the rate of gain that can be expected if this or that method is used.

Since many school administrators and teachers are casting about for more effective ways of organizing their classes, the writer conducted an experiment to compare the effectiveness of three approaches in organizing the reading class. Admittedly, class organization is only a small part of the total reading program, but it does seem to present a real problem to many teachers. Because of large classes and the wide range of abilities among pupils, some teachers are prevented from doing an effective job of teaching.

In a controlled experiment, a heterogeneous, a homogeneous, and an individualized approach to the teaching of reading were compared. The heterogeneous approach was the traditional method of teaching a varied group of children with the possibility of using small intra-class groups. The homogeneous approach was the plan in which the children crossed grade levels and moved to the room that approximated their reading level. The individualized approach followed as closely as possible the interpretation of this method as described in current literature.

The fourth and fifth grades of the McPherson Public Schools, McPherson, Kansas, were selected for the experiment which was to run from September to May of one school year. A total of 186 cases were finally compared, with four classes in each of the three approaches being used.

Factors that were considered to be comparable were the socio-economic background of the pupils, the size of the classes, the materials available, and the experience and training of the teachers. Every possible effort was made to make the teaching design of the four teachers in each of the approaches uniform for that approach. It was considered essential in this experiment that three variables should be controlled through the statistical design of analysis of covariance. These variables were intelligence, previous reading achievment, and sex.

The Iowa Every-Pupil Tests of Basic Skills, Test A, Reading Comprehension, and Test B, Work-Study Skills were used to measure the reading achievement of the children. Eight months elapsed between the giving of Form L and Form M of these tests.

In analyzing the results of the tests it was found that at the 1 per cent level of confidence the homogeneous approach had made a significant gain in three of four divisions. Only in reading comprehension for the fifth grade had any one of the approaches failed to make a significantly superior gain. In both the fourth and fifth grades in study skills the homogeneous approach had made a superior gain. It also was significantly superior in reading comprehension at the fourth grade level. The individualized approach scored next high in the three significant tests.

Tables for Test A (reading comprehension) and Test B (work-study skills) at both the fourth and fifth grade levels are summarized in the following tables. Adjusted means are given for the three significant comparisons.

It became very obvious throughout the study that whenever good teaching was done with appropriate materials and children were stimulated, great improvement in reading achievement could result under each of the three methods. On some tests groups scored a 100 per cent gain above the expected gain; in other cases the gain was 20, 18, and 16 months' gain in an 8-month period. This was true of some groups in all of the plans. (A high I.Q. average probably accounted for part of this high gain.)

Schools or teachers within a school do not need to use the same organizational pattern to achieve good gains during a year. Some schools are seeking

Means for I.Q., Fall and Spring Test Scores for Test A, Fifth Grade

Approach	Number	I.Q.	Fall Test	Spring Test	Gain *
Heterogeneous	34	111.6	5.21	6.57	1.36
Homogeneous	34	111.9	5.78	7.14	1.36
Individualized	34	112.8	5.64	7.07	1.43

* By using the statistical design of analysis of covariance which controlled intelligence, previous reading achievement, and sex, it was found that there were no significant differences in the gains made by the three approaches.

Means for I.Q., Fall and Spring Test Scores for Test B, Fifth Grade

Approach	Number	I.Q.	Fall Test	Spring Test	Gain	Adj. Mean
Heterogeneous	34	110.9	5.25	6.37	1.12	6.56
Homogeneous	34	111.8	5.76	7.02	1.26	6.94 *
Individualized	34	113.1	5.72	6.79	1.07	6.69

* Significant at the 1 per cent level of confidence.

Means for I.Q., Fall and Spring Test Scores for Test A, Fourth Grade

Approach	Number	I.Q.	Fall Test	Spring Test	Gain	Adj. Mean
Heterogeneous	28	108.3	4.35	5.61	1.26	5.40
Homogeneous	28	111.4	4.46	6.13	1.67	6.02 *
Individualized	28	109.0	4.05	5.55	1.50	5.66

* Significant at the 1 per cent level of confidence.

Means for I.Q., Fall and Spring Test Scores for Test B, Fourth Grade

Approach	Number	I.Q.	Fall Test	Spring Test	Gain	Adj. Mean
Heterogeneous	28	108.3	4.15	5.21	1.06	5.25
Homogeneous	28	111.4	4.01	6.02	2.01	6.00 *
Individualized	28	109.0	4.11	5.58	1.47	5.60

* Significant at the 1 per cent level of confidence.

for easy answers to their reading problems, usually through some magic rearrangement of the teachers or pupils; they are not likely to find the answers in this way. A well-qualified teacher may still be by far the most important factor in any grouping plan.

Other conclusions that were drawn from the study tried to show some of the related values of the three approaches. Test results were also analyzed for the first and fourth quartiles of pupils. It was found that none of the plans was superior with the first quartile, but with the fourth quartile some form of grouping or individualizing of instruction was found to be more effective, especially with the work-study skills.

In another analysis of the results it was found that individual pupils could make good gains under all of the approaches. Some pupils made over two years' gain under each of the plans; likewise some pupils showed a loss under each of the plans.

A reading attitude test was given at the beginning of the year and was repeated again at the end of the school year. The individualized approach showed the greatest gain in favorable attitudes toward reading as indicated by both the pupils' and teachers' ratings.

There was some indication from a survey of the number of books read by the pupils that the individualized participants had done the most outside reading during the year.

While the writer made every possible effort to control all the major variables in the experiment, he is not convinced that teacher motivation and competence were equal in all of the methods. The heterogeneous plan was carried over from former years in one school, and

the teachers of individualized reading were inexperienced in this approach.

The writer hopes that teachers and administrators will be very careful in changing their reading method because of the reported research of this experiment or even several experiments. A real weakness in most of these experiments is that few standardized reading tests are designed to measure some very important parts of the reading program. Most standardized tests fail to measure such important areas as reading attitudes, carry-over values, oral interpretation, critical reading skills, word attack skills, etc. Also, for years the social and emotional effects of class groupings have been discussed, but little research has been done in this area.

The organizational pattern for the teaching of reading and other subjects must take into account many factors, not just the gain made on a teacher-made or standardized achievement test.

CHAPTER XIII

Teaching Reading:
When and by Whom

49: An Earlier Start in Reading *

DOLORES DURKIN

Today the subject of reading and the preschool child is attracting much attention. It is provoking controversy too —or at least differences of opinion. Reactions of kindergarten teachers, for example, tend to fall into three categories. Some spurn any kind of reading instruction for the five-year-old. Others seem too eager to rush to a work-book curriculum. Somewhere in the middle is another group that recognizes the inadequacy of typical kindergarten programs for some five-year-olds and does not interpret the asking of questions about these programs as a prelude to inevitable and unfriendly criticism.

Parents of young children show other differences in reaction. At one extreme are the Harvard-conscious parents who seriously believe that three years of age is none too soon to develop good study habits and at least a small amount of achievement in reading. At the other extreme are those parents who consciously heed educators who continue to maintain that preschool help with reading results in confusion and leads to problems when a child enters first grade.

Meanwhile, nationwide publicity is being given to the Denver schools as they attempt to develop TV programs on reading for parents of preschool children. Attention is also being focused on Omar Moore, at Yale University, who is using complicated machinery to introduce pre-first-grade children to written language. Whitby School in Connecticut, too, is attracting attention as it demonstrates the learnings of three- and four-year-olds when a Montessori curriculum is followed.

Many different groups, then, are examining, proposing, and opposing the idea that children start to learn to read before the age of six. Consequently, it becomes important to step outside the controversy to look carefully at the questions that are being raised and at those that ought to be raised.

Among the important questions, certainly, is that of the future value of an early start in reading. If a child gets a head start in reading, will he remain ahead? If a child enters first grade with the reading ability of an average second- or third-grader will he, over the years, continue to remain ahead of children who are of equal mental ability

* Reprinted from the *Elementary School Journal,* Vol. 63, No. 3 (December 1962), pp. 147-51, by permission of the author and the publisher.

but could not read when they started first grade?

This article is directed to these questions. It is a report on one part of a longitudinal study of children who could read when they entered first grade.[1]

In September, 1958, all the beginning first-graders in a California public school system were individually tested to identify those who had learned to read at home.[2] From this group of 5,103 children, forty-nine were found to have some ability in reading. At the time of the first testing, their reading achievement ranged from 1.5 to 4.5, according to grade-level norms. The median grade level was 1.9. Intelligence quotients derived from the Revised Stanford-Binet Scale ranged from 91 to 161, with a median quotient of 121. The coefficient of correlation for intelligence and reading achievement was +0.40.

To examine the future value of an early start in reading, the plan was to compare, at the end of third grade, the reading achievement of the forty-nine early readers with the reading achievement of children who had started school with them, who had had the same teachers as they for the first three grades, and who were of comparable mental ability but who were not able to read when they started first grade. Mental ability was to be assessed in terms of intelligence quotients derived from the Kuhlmann-Anderson Intelligence test, which was administered by the school system when the children were in second grade.

As it turned out, even a cursory look at these intelligence quotients showed that they were anything but realistic. There was no apparent relationship, for example, between a child's intelligence, as measured by the Kuhlmann-Anderson Intelligence test, and his achievement score in reading.

For the children who were not early readers, the intelligence quotients hov-ered narrowly around 100. For the early readers the Kuhlmann-Anderson scores consistently underestimated the intelligence of the brighter children, as it had been measured by the Revised Stanford-Binet Scale.

It was decided, therefore, to include in the control group only those children who had been given the Revised Stanford-Binet Scale by a school psychometrist. This decision necessitated other changes and, in a sense, compromises in the research plan. These will be noted indirectly in the description of what finally constituted the experimental group and the control group.

The experimental group included twenty-five of the forty-nine early readers. The remaining twenty-four had either transferred to other schools or had been double-promoted during the three-year period. Although the experimental group was reduced to twenty-five children, the intelligence quotients based on results of the Revised Stanford-Binet Scale still ranged from 91 to 161. The median intelligence quotient for the group was 114.8. Reading scores based on tests administered by the schools toward the end of Grade 3 showed grade levels ranging from 4.4 to 6.0, with a median of 5.0.

The control group was made up of 201 children who had entered first grade with the twenty-five preschool readers but who could not read when they started school. They had remained in the same schools as these early readers for Grades 1, 2, and 3. They had also been given the Revised Stanford-Binet Scale. For this control group, intelligence quotients ranged from 70 to 191, with a median of 110.2. Reading achievement scores based on school-administered tests ranged from 2.0 to 6.0, with a median grade level of 4.3.

A scatter diagram, in which reading scores for both the experimental and the control groups were plotted, revealed the inadequacy of the school-administered reading tests in establishing upper limits of achievement for the brighter children.[3] Consequently, a twofold comparison was made between the achievement of the early readers and the achievement of children who were not early readers. The first comparison focused on children who had intelligence quotients of 120 or less. The second comparison considered children who had intelligence quotients of 121 or higher.

Of the children who were not early readers 129 had intelligence quotients of 120 or less. A first step in examining the value of a head start in reading was to calculate coefficient of correlation between the intelligence as masured by the Revised Stanford-Binet Scale and the reading achievement of these children who were not early readers. The coefficient of correlation was found to be +0.61.

Next, the regression equation for predicting reading achievement on the basis of intelligence was formulated. The equation was then used to calculate predicted reading scores for each of the fifteen early readers who also had intelligence quotients of 120 or less.

When these predicted scores were calculated, it was found that for all the children who were early readers actual scores in reading were greater than would have been predicted for them on the basis of their intelligence, as measured by the Revised Stanford-Binet Scale. The greatest single difference, in terms of years of reading achievement, was 1.3. The smallest single difference was 0.2. Group differences, according to intelligence level, are shown in Table 1.

Because the groups were small, no statement can be made at this time about children who are early readers in general. Two observations can be made concerning these fifteen early readers who had intelligence quotients of 120 or less. First, they appear to have profited from their early start. Second, the lower the child's intelligence quotient, the greater seems to be the advantage of starting early.

What can be said about the children who had intelligence quotients higher than 120? As I pointed out earlier, the school-administered reading tests were not difficult enough to establish the upper limits of achievement for the brighter children in either the control group or the experimental group. As a result, the coefficient of correlation between the intelligence quotients of the seventy-two children who were not early readers and their reading scores was only +0.17.

With such a low coefficient of correlation it is not too meaningful to ask: As derived from the relationship between reading achievement and intelligence, what would be the predicted reading score for each of the early readers who had intelligence quotients of 121 or more? Nonetheless the question was asked, and the answer appears in Table 1.

Table: 1: Deviation of Achievement of Early Readers from Expected Achievement on the Basis of Intelligence Quotients

Intelligence Quotient	Number of Pupils	Average Deviation in Years
91-100	5	+0.92
101-110	6	+0.68
111-120	4	+0.35
121-130	3	+0.30
131-140	4	−0.33
141-161	3	+0.43

Probably the most appropriate comment to make at this point is to express the hope that when more appropriate reading tests are used with the control and the experimental groups at the end of Grade 6, more meaningful and more significant findings will be available, especially for the brighter children in both groups.

Meanwhile, it seems appropriate to attempt some kind of summary of conclusions or, to be more accurate, some kind of summary of ideas and feelings that resulted from this longitudinal study of precocious readers.

Certainly, one persistent feeling is that many parents of preschool children are confused and uncertain about their role, or lack of it, in the matter of their child's learning to read. Frequent contacts with parents, through interviews and correspondence, repeatedly point to the need for home-school communication that gives parents, first, at least a general understanding of their role as educators of the preschool child and, second, specific help on how they, as parents, can advance the language skills of young children without putting uncomfortable pressures on them.

These same contacts with parents also suggest that educators have been encouraging parents, perhaps unintentionally, to put a child's questions about words into a do-not-touch category on the assumption that what a child learns about reading before he enters school interferes with subsequent school instruction. This study of early readers does not verify this assumption.

In fact, what is tentatively suggested is that children of relatively lower intelligence especially benefit from an early start. Should this finding be duplicated in a second study recently begun in another school system, it might well mean that slower children need contact with learning to read that is spread out over time. Instead of a postponement of reading instruction, they need an earlier start with it. This thinking, to be sure, is in contrast to much current thinking on reading readiness. But it is a possibility that deserves attention.

One final comment on kindergarten children and kindergarten programs. I urge that the schools pay some attention to the five-year-olds who are already reading and to those who are so close to it that even less than mediocre help would turn them into readers. If we really believe that good education begins where the child is, then kindergarten teachers ought to feel obligated to give certain children help with reading.

Out of this new concern might eventually come not only achievement in reading but, in addition, a really fresh approach to the teaching of beginning reading. It might well be that those of us who are interested in teaching methods and materials have for too long been greasing a squeaky wheel when we should have been looking for a genuinely new one.

REFERENCES

1. This article is based on a paper read at a meeting of the American Educational Research Association in Atlantic City, February 1962.
2. Durkin, Dolores, "Children Who Learned To Read at Home," *Elementary School Journal,* LXII (October 1961), pp. 15-18.
3. A carefully planned testing procedure has been followed for all the forty-nine early readers. In this particular part of the study, data from school-administered reading tests had to be used because these were the only data available for the control group.

50: Should Parents Teach Reading? *

RUTH STRANG

This one question raises a cluster of related questions: *Do* some children learn to read before they come to school? *Should* they? *Can* preschool children learn to read? *How* do they learn to read? Does teaching a child to read during his preschool years make him a better reader later on? How *can* a parent help a young child to become a good reader?

SOME READ; SOME DON'T

If you visit a first grade at the beginning of the next school year, you will probably find that one out of four of the pupils can already read a number of words. Some in this group will be children of average ability, but more of them will be bright. Almost all will be from homes where parents think reading is very important and answer their youngsters' questions about words and reading.

Some children seem to "catch on" to reading by themselves in some mysterious way. Reading comes naturally to them. If asked later on how they learned to read they will say, "I don't know; I just learned." Others will remember being encouraged and helped at home by parents who responded to their curiosity about what lies between the covers of books. Some children who have been in kindergarten score high on reading readiness tests. During the summer before they enter first grade they may begin to read.

On the other hand, there are children who become confused or resentful when someone tries to teach them words that they do not want or need to know. One boy, thinking back over his early reading experiences, described his feelings about being forced to read before he was ready:

"I was about four years old when my mother tried to teach me to read. She would take a card and write a word on it and then say it. This took a very long time, and after a while I became very tired of reading."

Learning to read is an exciting experience for a child, and many youngsters can be taught to read before the age of six. The psychologist O. K. Moore has reported startling results with very young children. Picture a group of three-to-five-year-olds sitting at electric typewriters. They begin hitting the letter keys at random. As each letter pops up, an obliging adult says the name of the letter. Soon of their own accord they begin to write these letters on the blackboard. From writing the letters they progress to typing little stories they have dictated and then to reading words and sentences. This they do on their own initiative. No one urges or pushes them; they teach themselves. No one praises them; they get their satisfaction from the activity itself. Learning is sufficient reward.

Next, visit a kindergarten in Whitby, Connecticut. Some of the children are only three years old. The classroom has a wealth of teaching material that stimulates children to read and write. The children take the initiative. When they need help, the teacher is there to give the needed instruction.

* Reprinted from the *P.T.A. Magazine,* Vol. 57, No. 7 (March 1963), by permission of the author and the publisher.

Now go to a home in Denver where a parent has been watching a television program that tells how to teach reading to preschoolers. The parent has a booklet of sixteen lessons in phonics that teach children to identify and discriminate sounds in words, to associate sounds with letters, and, by using a combination of initial letter sounds and context, to recognize words in sentences. The television program guides the parent in teaching these lessons to his children.

By these and other methods preschool children do learn to read. But—should parents use such formal methods? Is the early teaching of reading advantageous in the long run? Is it worth the effort?

Let's see what evidence there is against the formal teaching of reading to preschool children.

Children must learn to hear and speak words clearly and correctly before they can read successfully. Language development should precede reading.

Noting small details such as letters in words is difficult for children five and six years of age or younger. They tend to see words as a meaningless jumble of letters.

Scottish children who were taught to read at the age of five were no better readers at eight years of age than a comparable group of English children taught to read at six.

Premature instruction in word-analysis skills often results in confusion and failure.

Parents' pressure and impatience when a preschool child does not respond well to such instruction may cause him to dislike or resist reading.

MAKING READY FOR READING

Instead of attempting to teach a preschool child to read, most parents can make a greater contribution by developing his readiness for reading. Here are some important ways of doing this:

Creating the Desire To Read. A child

must want to read before he can learn to read. Sometimes this desire develops simply from being with people who like to read. Jerry recalls that when he was still in his crib he used to see his mother reading and eating cherry-filled chocolates. Both seemed delightful. He thought, "When I grow up, I'm going to read a lot." Billy sees Daddy reading the newspaper, so he makes believe he is also reading it, though he may hold it upside down. Five-year-old Janey looks on the book her seven-year-old sister is reading and wishes that she too could find out what the characters are saying and what they will do next.

Reading Aloud. In addition to creating a desire to read, reading aloud has many other values. When parent and child share a book that they both enjoy, a good relationship develops. Listening to children's literature familiarizes children with the vocabulary and language of published material and with the rhythm, sound, and picture-forming quality of words. They learn to hear words accurately and use them grammatically.

What shall we read to preschool children? Little children enjoy rhythm and repetition. The sound of words fascinates them. And there are many excellent books, in verse and prose, that have this appeal. Remember "James James Morrison Morrison Weatherby George Dupree"? Or "the great grey-green, greasy Limpopo River"?

"All the world, real and unreal," says Anne Thaxter Eaton, "lies before the child who reads." Preschool children, like their older brothers and sisters, seek information as well as entertainment in books and television programs. Their physical and social world is changing dramatically, and they enjoy books that present facts about this changing world in a clear and meaningful way.

Children need realistic books that help them understand their experiences and interpret their partly formulated thoughts. *A Friend Is Someone Who Likes You* by Joan Walsh Anglund is a book of this kind. It helps small children learn to love the objects and animals around them. *The Important Book* by Margaret Wise Brown stimulates children to think about what is most important in the everyday things and people of their environment. One little child told what she thought was the important thing about a mother. "The most important thing about a mother," she said, "is that she loves you."

Little children need reassuring books. They are comforted when the Mother Bear in Else H. Minarik's *Little Bear* says, "Of course I didn't forget your birthday and I never will." They are reassured when Peter Rabbit's mother still loves him even after he has been naughty.

Children need books that evoke laughter and tears. Books that show genuine feelings are especially necessary today to counteract the indifference to suffering and violence that may be engendered by many TV and radio programs.

Children need stories and poems that give them wings, that stir the imagination. Some years ago certain psychologists objected to fairy tales. Now we feel sure that children need fanciful stories to bring reality more sharply into focus.

Children need books that help them to understand themselves and other people. Many books now on the market tell about children with various backgrounds, in other cultures and other lands. These books show children how much alike the whole human family is.

The best approach to reading aloud is to observe the interests and needs of your child and try to find books he will like. Different books appeal to youngsters at different stages of development. One father who was very fond of Kenneth Grahame's *The Wind in the Willows* was disappointed when his five-year-old was not interested in it. But three years later when he read it aloud, the child was enchanted.

Listening to a story may not lead to any visible or audible activity; it may make a silent impression on the mind and heart. Each child selects from a story something he needs at that particular time.

Providing Picture Books. Picture books also create a desire to read—linen books for two-year-olds, more grown-up picture books for children who have learned to treat books as friends. There are classics such as Randolph Caldecott's *Collection of Pictures and Songs,* originally published in 1878-85, and Kate Greenaway's *Under the Window* (1868). These were both reprinted by Frederick Warne in 1962. Your librarian will introduce you to a wealth of modern picture books like Katharina Barry's *A Is for Anything* (Harcourt, Brace and World, 1961); Doris Van Lieuw Foster's *A Pocketful of Seasons* (Lothrop, 1961); or Georgia Tufts' *The Rabbit Garden* (Lothrop, 1961).

Picture books are for children to enjoy, look at, wonder about, and use as a stimulus to telling their own stories. They also help children to learn to look for meaningful details and identify pictures with familiar objects.

Providing First-Hand Experiences. Experience makes reading meaningful and interesting. Preschool children may obtain valuable experiences near home. They may explore the seashore, lake, or river; learn much about airplanes at the airport; visit a farm, a dairy, a factory, a museum, or a zoo. On each excursion they should have plenty of time to look and listen, handle when handling is permitted, ask questions, and talk about what they have seen and heard and done.

Share and Tell. Telling about their adventures helps them to learn new words, to use language correctly as a tool of thinking, to relate events in sequence, to discover cause-and-effect relationships. At first Billy may stumble over words just as he stumbled when he was learning to walk. He may often repeat a word, as we all do when we are groping for the right one. He is especially likely to stutter and stumble when he is excited about something he wants to tell you. "And I saw-saw a g-great big ele-ele-phant!" This is not the time to stop him and insist that he tell what he saw in a more connected way. Let him get his story out in his own fashion—often vivid, sometimes poetic. Then help him to tell it with better sequence and sentence structure.

Since speaking comes before reading and writing, the child who enters school with habits of clear, distinct, coherent speech has a decided advantage.

All these—the desire to read, curiosity, background of experience, familiarity with the language patterns of literature, the ability to communicate in speech—are prerequisites for success in reading. Should parents go a step further and attempt to teach a child to read before he enters school?

Certainly parents should respond to a child's questions about words and about reading. When the child looks on while being read to and says, "Daddy, where does it say 'little black lamb'?" Daddy should point out the words. When the child wonders about the meanings of words and sentences in road signs, labels, and other things in his environment, some obliging older person should of course tell him.

Word games are a good way of increasing children's ability to recognize and distinguish sounds in words—beginning sounds and ending rhymes. It is fun for a child to anticipate Mother's meaning when she leaves out an important word in a sentence, such as "I'm going to call Daddy to———." Whatever the child says that makes sense is acceptable, though Mother may have had the word "dinner" in mind.

ONE STEP MORE?

Alphabet books and blocks teach a child the letters of the alphabet, if someone is near to name the letters as the child looks at them. There is a difference of opinion about children's need to learn the alphabet before they begin to read, but the child who knows the names of the letters has an advantage. He will find this knowledge useful later.

If a child has of his own accord learned a number of words by sight and mastered enough sound-letter associations to puzzle out the meaning of many unfamiliar words, he is definitely on the road to reading. In fact, he can read, and there is no reason why he should be denied the pleasure and excitement of his newly acquired ability. We can leave a few carefully selected beginning-reading books around the house for him to dip into on his own initiative. If the child says, "Mommy, let me read to *you*," we can listen and take advantage of this opportunity to approve his effective reading skills and help him to change any poor reading habits he may have.

It is more important that a child build a firm foundation for reading during the preschool years than that he learn to read certain words or pronounce a few simple sentences in a book. It is not hard to tell when a child is ready to read. He is trustful, curious, and eager to explore. He *wants* to learn to read. He has become familiar with the language patterns of literature by hearing books read aloud from his earliest years. His experiences have taught him meaningful speaking vocabulary, and he can communicate his thoughts in language appropriate to his age. When a child has had these preschool, prereading experiences, not only is he ready to read—he will learn quickly.

CHAPTER XIV

Teaching Reading:
A Re-examination

51: Why Do Students Bog Down on the First R? *

JOHN HERSEY

All over the country, this month and next, most of the 28,800,000 pupils in the public schools are being given standardized year-end achievement tests. A question that both educators and parents will want to see answered by those tests is: Are our young citizens learning to use our language well enough?

This question has been more and more frequently asked in recent years. Parents have cried in dismay that their children could not read out loud, could not spell, could not write clearly enough to read their own pen tracks. Business-men have complained that they could not find stenographers to write grammatical letters. Employers have said that mechanics could not read simple directions.

Many a college has blamed high schools for passing on students with average or better I.Q.s who could not read adequately to study college subjects; high schools have had to give remedial reading instruction to boys and girls who did not learn to read properly in elementary schools; the sixth-grade teacher has blamed the

fourth-grade teacher; the fourth, the first; and all the teachers have now and then blamed parents, and with justice.

Two years ago the Citizens' School Study Council of Fairfield, Conn., a residential community with a population of 33,000, appointed a committee to confront this question so far as the children of the town were concerned. We of the committee read technical books, consulted experts, attended our local schools to observe the teaching of reading, and during two school years argued among ourselves to late hours.

The intelligence quotient of the median student in Fairfield—half rank higher than the median, half lower—is 102, or two points higher than the national norm. Results of the nation-wide Metropolitan Achievement Tests administered in the first six grades show that our median students run just slightly ahead of the national norms. So Fairfield's accomplishments and trou-bles, if not typical, are pretty close to those of the average American com-munity. In any case it became obvious to us early in our discussions that read-ing problems could not be solved in a

* Reprinted from *Life*, Vol. 36, No. 21 (May 24, 1954), pp. 136-40, 142, 144, 147-8, 150, by permission of the author.

vacuum in Fairfield or any other single community in our country. These problems are built into prevailing educational philosophy, into teacher-training schools, into textbooks, into homes, into television sets and into American folkways of the present time.

This is why we presume to share our investigation and our findings with others in this article drawn from the committee's report. Our work convinces us that it will be possible for parents to support educators in solving these nationwide problems only if they attack them together in many communities in many states, with prolonged study and without undue excitement. Surely neither apathy nor hysteria—extremes with which our citizenry has long honored the public schools—will solve them.

There is very little in this field that is measurable. The experts disagree. The best of them admit that they still have much to find out about the mysterious and magical process of learning to read. So the committee's findings are necessarily intuitive. Here are the main ones:

Our public schools have done a heroic job, during a period of enormous expansion and in the face of ever-tightening budgets, to maintain standards in the teaching of reading. The seriousness of purpose, the selflessness and the integrity of public-school teachers are manifest. Some children read very well indeed.

However, grave reading problems exist. Educators are aware of them and are working hard to solve them.

One sort of problem arises from unwitting misuse and abuse of some of the widely accepted philosophical assumptions now underlying American public education—such as the aim of "teaching the whole child," of making school a happy place and of teaching children through experiences they have had in common. The end results of

these distortions have been that some children have not mastered essential skills; that many children understandably prefer lurid comic books and television shows to insipid, goody-goody school readers; and that pupils are taught to conform rather than to be individuals.

Another kind of problem comes from the fact that some current teaching techniques have shown serious weaknesses. The most serious of all are complications of the desirable practice of taking each child at his or her own natural speed in learning. Others are a consequence of the battle, beloved by parents, between "Grunt-and-Groan" and "Look-and-Say"—that is, between phonetics and sight reading. Others have brought the puzzling result that many more boys than girls hate reading and do poorly in it. And many reading troubles come from a failure to help children to *want* to read, a failure to which parents have generously contributed.

A third group of problems comes from the competition these days between words and images—especially between reading and television.

It must be said that in urging a close look at these three kinds of problems, we do not urge a blind turning back of the clock. We repudiate the angry shouts of certain American primitives who have lately set themselves up as judges of all things American, including education, and whose oversimplified battle cry in this field is "Back to the Three R's!" We cannot, in our day, go back to primitive ways—to the hornbook, that wooden board like a Ping-pong paddle from which colonial children learned the alphabet, or to the watchpocket-sized *New England Primer* with its microscopic print and moralistic sayings, or to the high-minded McGuffey's Readers, or to the birch rod, the dunce's cap and the Franklin stove. Nor will reading problems be solved by any single, simple panacea, such as "going back to phonetics."

Now let us examine each of the three kinds of problems.

THE CULT OF ENTERTAINMENT

From the sound principle that a happy child takes more easily to learning than an unhappy child, there may come the unsound result that school is turned into something like pure entertainment.

The pre-primer teachers' manual used in Fairfield is used in every state in the country; it is typical of such manuals used in most American schools. In listing objectives of the first-grade reading program, it gives as the first of 36 objectives: "To create a feeling of pleasure and satisfaction from reading humorous, surprising, and interesting stories." Two thirds of the way down the list, in 21st place, stands this objective: "To develop the ability to read short sentences with understanding, both orally and silently."

Is it not misplaced emphasis, to say the least, when the objective of deriving pleasure from an act is put so far ahead of the objective of learning to perform the act?

Is not the point that pleasure in itself is not an objective of the school curriculum at all, that learning is the main objective, and that pleasure may be an aid, a motivation, a means toward the realization of the true objective and a wonderfully desirable by-product of its attainment?

There is, besides, a possibility that not happiness but its very opposite may result from the creation of an image of life, or a pretense of that image, that does not correspond at all with reality. Stories of happy play, helping others, cheerful good-hearted neighbors, and so on, describe things that are desirable, but they do not exactly offer a slice of life. A small child who through accident or parents' carelessness one afternoon

watches on television not Howdy Doody but a documentary moving picture about unspeakable degradations in a Nazi prison camp goes to school the next day and is given reading readiness, but perhaps not life readiness, in an antiseptic little sugar-book showing how Tom and Betty have fun at home and school.

This is not to advocate a pre-primer of horrors. Far from it. It is simply to ask: if our educators are to make pretensions to psychological understanding, should they not earnestly and continuously study the gap between the reality of life and the ideal image of it they may be creating?

Must they not look closely to see why many children resist the textbooks they are given? Is not revulsion against namby-pamby school readers perhaps a reason why they like lurid comic books so much? Are age-old fairy tales so unwholesome after all that they must be given happy endings in the manner of slick magazines? Is it a guarantee of happiness to end a retelling of *The Sorcerer's Apprentice* in a sixth-grade reader, in which the apprentice, who has turned himself into a hen, has just gobbled up the sorcerer, who has turned himself into a kernel of grain, with these pious words: "And wasn't it fine that all the powers and brews, which had been used for evil by the sorcerer, were now in the hands of a boy who would use them only for the good of man and beast?" Must we carry into the schoolroom those classic oversimplifications of our time: the Good Guys and the Bad Guys?

As parents we accept the charge that it is really for *us* to seek the kind of understanding that may help our children to find true happiness: we have, indeed, enormous work to do. Having said that, we may add that we believe that the wide gap between schoolbook ideality and life's reality deserves close study on the part of educators.

THE CULT OF WHOLENESS

Much emphasis in recent years has
properly been placed on integration:
on the whole child, the whole of learning. This emphasis is also applied to
curriculum. Educators tend to speak
not of elements—reading, writing, spelling, grammar and so on—but of the
whole: "language arts."

Our committee has come to believe
that an individual's sense of wholeness
and wholesomeness follows, and cannot
precede, a sense of accomplishment. In
order to integrate there must be solid
materials to be brought together. We
speak with respect of "a man of parts";
we admire the whole of this man because certain of his diverse talents, or
of the elements of his character, or of
his intellectual gifts have been highly
and separately developed.

A paradox, and a harmful one, may
come from misapplied "integration." It
is this: a constant effort is made to
touch on all the parts of the whole
subject: the consequence is a scattering
of effect, the opposite of integration.
This may be true of teachers' use of
time; it may be true of texts. As one
Fairfield teacher remarked of a certain
textbook not long ago, "It jumps around
too much."

In the name of variety, the content
of many reading textbooks is higgledy-
piggledy and is often entirely unrelated
either to the children's actual interests
or to the material in other subjects being tackled at the same time.

Similarly, textbooks introduce skills,
such as grammar and phonetic analysis,
piecemeal at various times, and this too
may result not in integration but in
diffusion.

Should not schools reapply themselves to the problem of how children
can learn the troublesome fundamentals
early enough and well enough to become well-rounded readers—readers,
that is, who not only understand and
remember what they read but also are

discriminating and skeptical about it?
Otherwise may we not stand in danger
of producing the "whole" but empty
child?

THE CULT OF UNIFORMITY

It is natural that our hard-pressed
teachers should tend to "teach by the
book"—that is, lean to a large extent
on the teachers' manuals that are supplied nowadays with almost all reading
textbooks. Indeed it is a good thing they
have manuals to help them organize
their busy days. But what does "the
book" say?

Let us quote briefly from a typical
manual, the one supplied for the reading-readiness book, *Fun with Tom and
Betty*: " 'Today [the teacher is told to
say] you are each going to have a new
book like this one.' Hold the book so
that the class may see the cover and
say, 'The name of our book is *Fun with
Tom and Betty*.' With the hand indicate
the title of the book, with a left to right
sweep across the cover. 'Tom and Betty
are two children who are going to
school, just as you are. They do the
same things you do. . . .' "

These instructions—for they are instructions, not suggestions—are doubtless good ones; the methods have presumably been tested; these acts and
words may in fact be the best of all
possible acts and words—for many
schoolrooms.

But these instructions leave a kind
of distress in the mind. They conjure a
picture of an automatic teacher. Worse,
one sees on a September morning
thousands, perhaps hundreds of thousands, of teachers all over the country
giving a left to right sweep of the hand
across the cover and saying, "Tom and
Betty are two children. . . ." The next
picture is of the teacher gesturing and
handing out books while a loudspeaker
does the talking for her. And finally we
have a scene from George Orwell's
nightmarish novel, *1984,* in which the

teacher has disappeared and the citizen, as child and man, learns everything from a loudspeaker, out of which voices retell history to suit convenience and cultivate the mental process known as "doublethink"—everything means its exact opposite.

Now this is, of course, going absurdly far from the simple and wise directions in the manual. And it goes without saying that experienced teachers grow away from manuals. It is evident, however, that both the reading texts and the manuals used in our schools do tend to encourage uniformity and discourage individuality.

Teachers have discovered that in learning to read and in understanding what they read, children must bring to the printed page their own experience. Therefore most texts use children's experiences that may be assumed to have been shared as a basis for teaching. This in itself is a tremendous force for uniformity. The key sentence in the paragraph we have quoted is, "They do the same things you do." Throughout the reading textbooks of the primary grades our children build their whole structure of reading upon a foundation of uniformity—a mass-produced prefab of life, so to speak. The ideal image, presented both through texts and illustrations, is of a happy middle-class family in ever-clean clothes, straight out of the ads in the magazines.

Should not the authors of textbooks and the teachers who use them reevaluate the theory of learning through shared experience in the light of this undeniable influence toward uniformity? Teachers should not be passive and automatic but should bring to their work those great American virtues of originality, individuality and independence, and the same qualities should be developed to the utmost in our children; particularly in a period when one of the most disturbing elements in our national life is the pressure for uniformity and conformity.

FOUR PRACTICAL PROBLEMS

1. Each at His Own Speed

In any given public school classroom there is a range of talent and achievement of about five years. In a fourth-grade classroom, for instance, there will be children unable to read at anything better than a second-grade level of achievement and there will also be children who have progressed far enough to be able to read at a sixth-grade level. In some classes the range is even wider.

A basic principle of present-day public school education is that each child should be taken along at his own most suitable rate of speed in learning. This principle is based on the sound premises that the fastest-moving pupils should not be held down to the rate of progress of the slowest, and conversely the slowest should not be deprived of the rudiments of education just because they cannot keep up with brighter children.

This is both the strongest and the weakest point in modern American public education. It is strong because it is based on the noble promise of equal opportunity for all, rich and poor, favored and handicapped, bright and slow; weak because it has produced complications that seem not yet to have been thought through.

Children do not progress at the same speed in all subjects. A pupil who is slow in reading may be faster in arithmetic.

The confusion resulting from this basic fact shows itself sharply for the first time in the fourth grade, where relatively complicated work-reading is met as never before, in social studies, arithmetic, science and other subjects. Children are then given textbooks *in the subject of reading* at various levels of difficulty, depending on their various levels of accomplishment, but they are given textbooks *in the other subjects* all of which are uniformly set at the fourth-grade level, or perhaps slightly below it. The slow readers may not be able to read these texts; the fast ones may be bored by them.

Another confusion comes when the child, not the teacher, sets the individual's rate of progress. This is a matter for teacher education. It comes about when a child's inclinations, interest and motivation are allowed to determine his rate of progress, rather than the only proper determinant: his capacity to learn.

Confusion also comes from the fact that the principle of learning "each according to his talents" has not been applied logically in all areas of the so-called "language arts" program. Pupils in a fourth grade read in sections, using three or four different reading textbooks set at various grade levels, yet all study spelling together out of the same textbook at the same rate of speed. This means either that slow pupils are trying to learn to spell words they have not even encountered as readers, or that the grade's spelling vocabulary is alarmingly more primitive than its standard reading vocabulary, to say nothing of that of its fast readers.

There is, besides, sheer physical confusion. For reading instruction the typical classroom is divided up into three, or sometimes four, groups. The teacher can give direct instruction to only one section at a time. The other two or three groups are kept busy with written work (which incidentally means an appalling waste of time and efficiency), and they are supposed to carry on this written work under the noise of oral classroom instruction being given in another part of the room. Members of our committee who visited reading classes came away understanding at last how our children not only can abide studying homework with the radio or television going but seem to prefer it to silent work. It is their habit to work clothed in noise. Sometimes, where the caliber of teaching was especially fine, we who visited were treated to the spectacle of children who were ostensibly working hard at written problems raising their hands to answer oral questions put to another section. Such division of attention does not develop work habits of concentration.

In the fourth grade and up, retarded readers may be quite incapable of reading the standard textbooks in science, social studies, arithmetic and other subjects. Thus, having fallen behind in reading, they fall even further behind in other subjects. They develop a habit of failure and begin to assume that they will fail in anything to do with the mind.

One of the fourth-grade teachers whose classes our committee attended had had a visit from an excited mother who had been horrified to find that her son was unable to read the arithmetic problems he had been given for homework. The mother blamed the teacher, stated that she was at fault for letting the boy lag in reading and insisted that she concentrate on bringing him up to grade in reading as quickly as possible. What was the teacher to do? She had inherited from the third grade a reader who, going at his own speed, had become retarded; she *had* been trying to help him and he had been making good progress, but the boy was, after all, only one of 30 pupils. Was she to drop everything and bring him up to grade? Or was she to refrain from trying to teach him arithmetic out of the only available textbook—or at least from giving him any homework?

Reading retardation can be largely prevented, can be detected early and can be remedied. But in order that these things may be done, we need vastly greater understanding on the part of parents and taxpayers, for the job takes time and it certainly takes money. It requires above all enough superior supplemental teachers—particularly remedial and guidance teachers.

In "each at his own speed" there is a hazard for bright children too. It is mediocrity.

Educators do not believe students should be given textbooks *above* the level of the grade in which the students find themselves. Instead of pushing bright students ahead into more difficult material, our teachers give them what is called "enrichment"—that is, more work, in ever-widening circles, at the grade level of difficulty. Enrichment is something all pupils are supposed to get, only the bright ones are supposed to get more of it than the others—as when a bright child finishes his assignment ahead of others, goes to the bookshelf and gets supplementary reading on his own. The teacher may also give him extra assignments in looking up, delving into hobbies and so on.

We believe that the enrichment theory is unsatisfactory in three ways:

In a public school classroom with from 25 to 40 pupils, the teacher simply does not have time to devote to special enrichment for advanced pupils; she has a hard enough time getting through the basic material for all.

The fast learners are not always the fast performers; indeed they are prominent among the dawdlers, daydreamers and out-the-window-gazers, and enrichment depends on speed of dispatch of the basic work.

Most important of all, is the theory that students should not venture into more difficult texts really sound? It seems to be based on a feeling long favored in this country that precocity if too much encouraged turns children into worms. But where are we to get future leaders of science, politics and the arts if we do not urge some minds to press forward with all the eagerness they can muster? Can we conceive a Mozart, a Darwin, an Einstein emerging from a public school classroom that puts a ceiling on the difficulty of study materials?

The number of badly retarded readers is generally small compared with the number who might be able to move above grade level, yet the two groups get equal instruction time. In classes visited by this committee, the total size of which was about 30 each, the slowest-reading group consisted of six children or less, and in some cases consisted of only two or three. The group of best readers averaged from 10 to 12 in number. In extreme cases, therefore, two pupils are given a full half-hour reading period, then 12 pupils are given a half hour—equal class time but one sixth the individual instruction. Even the middle mass of average students suffers relatively in this situation.

WHO GETS THE WORST OF A BAD DEAL?

Thus children at both ends of the scale —the potential leaders and the potential handicapped of our society—are not getting anywhere near the attention they need and deserve. Of this bad deal the bright ones are getting the worst.

Why are slow learners less badly off than fast learners?

By and large, reading textbooks and teachers' manuals concern themselves far more with retarded than with advanced students. The pre-primer manual used in Fairfield asserts, "The teaching plans are based upon the principle of differentiating instruction to fit individual abilities." But how is this implemented? "Special provision," the manual says, "is made for the slow learner under the heading, 'Helping the Individual Child.' " No mention at all is made of the gifted child. In manuals of the middle grades, fourth through sixth, it is claimed that the gifted child "will be by no means the neglected child in this basal reading program." Yet in the introductory pages of these manuals, a section of 625 words is devoted to slow learners, one of only 90 words to bright pupils.

There are other reasons why slow learners are less badly off. One is a compassion we all feel for those who obviously need help. Another is the natural anxiety a teacher has to keep her record good: a visible blot on it will not be made by a bright pupil who just coasts along but will be made by a failure. A final and most obvious reason is the inadequacy of the average remedial-guidance teaching staff—the citizenry's fault, not the schools'.

2. Sight Reading vs. Phonetics

This is the famous battle of Grunt-and-Groan vs. Look-and-Say.

Early in the century the phonetic method of teaching was overdone. Innocent little children were taught to put the diacritical marks of pronunciation over words, as if the magic book of reading had turned into a monstrous dictionary. Beginners sounded out words and parts of words by the hour, so that during the revolt against this excess, the system was nicknamed by some people the Grunt-and-Groan method. It was then combined with the sight-reading system, alias the Look-and-Say method.

In concern over reading failures and mediocrities, parents in many parts of the country have begun to blame sight reading and to clamor for a "return to phonetics."

Our committee is satisfied that we cannot, in the light of what has been learned about how children's minds work, go back to the alphabet method or to the excessive phonetic method or to over-done oral reading; that we cannot, indeed, abandon the sight-reading method, which works well for most beginners.

We do believe that when reading readiness has been definitely and clearly established, sight vocabulary could be given to beginners more quickly than it now is. Some educators now believe beginners could absorb as many as 200 words in the first six months provided words are used that the children want to learn. We tend to side with those who argue that the rudiments of pho-

netic training, which are generally introduced at about that point, could then also be given at a somewhat faster rate than now prevails and that relatively more attention could be given phonetics in the second and third grades.

We further believe that if phonetic training is to be withheld until children are ready for it, they must be taught it well when they are given it. What alarms parents, and rightly, is the sight of fourth- and fifth-grade children who still have a very shaky grasp on the relationship between combinations of letters and the sounds for which they stand. It is undeniable that there are such children aplenty.

3. Backward Boys

Boys become retarded readers much more often than girls. The main theory to account for this is that during the kindergarten and primary years boys tend to mature somewhat more slowly than girls and hence are often pushed into actual reading training before their readiness for it has been completely established.

There is also a possibility that the pallid content of pre-primers and early readers may have something to do with their trouble. Little boys trying to learn to read in Fairfield witness a lone boy named Tom condemned to play endlessly, and with unnatural control of his manners, with two syrupy girls, Betty and Susan. This frightful life that poor Tom leads is bound up inextricably with the crucial first stages of reading. It is not entirely surprising that some boys draw back from the experience.

Our committee feels that boys' special problems deserve more study than they have had.

4. The Urge To Read

Neither schools nor parents do enough about fostering their children's inner urge to learn to read. This is what school people call motivation. A child who really wants to learn something usually learns it.

This is the area in which parents do the most harm and could do the most good. We believe that parents should create in the home an atmosphere that is conducive to reading. They should have good books and magazines at hand. Parents should read to children. They should try to entertain them with reading and make reading a pleasure, as television is a pleasure. If school is where learning to read belongs, home is where happiness in reading belongs.

Wrongful pressure on the part of both schools and parents does more than anything else to kill the inner urge to read. Why is it that boys who are retarded readers are very quick to learn subtle points about baseball? An interesting experiment with these boys, which we fear will never be conducted, would be to make baseball a school subject with tests, textbooks, homework, compulsory daily practice and angry parental pushing; and turn them loose for recess in the library to read anything they want, just for fun, with the librarian urging them please, for heaven's sake, to take it easy and not read so much.

COMPETITION WITH READING:
THE IMAGE

Reading has to compete for the interest of children with television, radio, movies, comic books, magazines and sports. Above all, with television. The printed word has to compete at every turn with pictures, on both screens and printed pages. This is hard competition because most commonplace pictures demand an act of imagination.

Considering the outside pressure of images on the consciousness of our children, our schools may have begun to lean too heavily on pictures in teaching to read. Furthermore, the caliber of pictures generally used in reading textbooks may have something to do with poor reading, or at least with unimaginative reading.

At the reading-readiness and pre-primer levels the child is given far more pictures than words. For beginners the textbook manufacturers provide "dictionary cards" showing a picture on one side and a word on the other. In primary grade readers, pictures on each page give clues to virtually everything in the text. This is both good and bad. The child is helped to visualize words, but he is helped by pictures that are uniform, bland, idealized and terribly literal. Why should they not have pictures that widen rather than narrow the associative richness the children give to the words they illustrate—drawings like those of the wonderfully imaginative geniuses among children's illustrators, Tenniel, Howard Pyle, "Dr. Seuss," Walt Disney?

TELEVISION, THE ENEMY

Through a survey of 230 fourth-grade children in Fairfield Public Schools, our committee has satisfied itself that television presents serious competition to reading—and probably to other things too, but our topic is a limited one.

In the first place nearly everyone in our town has a television set. Only 15 of the 230 children indicated that there is no set in their homes.

The amount of time spent on television by these children is appalling. By their own calculation they spend, on the average, 3 hours, 8 minutes and 24 seconds per child-day in front of their television sets. Of course this is what 10-year-old children say they do; from a scientific and statistical point of view, their answers must be taken with salt. There was, however, a high enough degree of correlation between their answers on time spent and number of programs watched to justify as a positive assertion the first sentence in this paragraph.

Fascinating answers, many of which have a bearing on the competition reading suffers, were elicited by the question: "What do you like about television?" Some children stress the instructive nature of TV: ". . . because I learn lots of interesting things." "I like to see things that happened in the past." Entertainment is of course cited: music, comedy, old movies and "I like to watch good acting." One child wrote, "I like it because on radio you can't see and I never knew what Guy Lombardo looked like until I got television." Interplanetary space and bad spelling both figured in many answers: "I can learn abough Outer speast." Some answers highlighted the passive aspect of TV viewing: "You can rest while watching it." A few hinted at the hypnotic effect of the screen: "Because it sits there and looks at you." Other answers: "It gives you a feeling that you are in there." "Good programs." "You don't have to go there. All you have to do is turn a handle." "Because instead of your mother hitting you, you have something to do." "You can get real fantashed things." "You don't have to pay for every movie you see." Most concise answer: "It works."

THE CRUX: THE TEACHER

There can be, and there are, reading failures under any system of teaching, whether extremely progressive or extremely traditional. These failures can also be avoided and remedied by various, and very different, methods of teaching. The most important single factor in the whole reading program then is not the method but the teacher.

Just as we have a feeling that sometimes our schools expect too little of our schoolchildren, we are almost certain that we expect too much of most of our schoolteachers.

It has become a commonplace that the rewards, both social and financial, of teaching in the U.S. are meager. Last year the average income of all teachers in the country was $3,605. The life of all teachers is cluttered; a recent National Education Association survey showed that the average teacher works 48 hours a week at her many-faceted job. These are tiresome facts that everyone knows and does nothing about.

On top of all her other duties, the teacher who tackles reading is expected to be a psychologist, a literary tourist guide, a charming storyteller, a perfect grammarian, a steady workhorse with the mass of average pupils, and one with a special knack for bringing out the best in geniuses and morons. If she is not all these things, a ton of angry parenthood falls on her.

What does she do in the face of such demands? She does what one of the teachers we visited does. "I like the manual," she says. "If you follow that, you can't go far wrong."

But what does the manual urge? It urges a multiplicity of techniques and procedures that simply cannot be followed. The reading-readiness manual used by our teachers urges the keeping of a notebook containing a continuing checklist on the readiness of individual pupils. This checklist contains 52 items. A teacher who has 30 children in her class is therefore expected to keep running track of 1,560 items. She is also, incidentally, supposed to teach. In higher grades the manual divides teaching instructions for every single lesson into the following sections: "Developing Readiness for Reading," "Guide Reading," "Purposeful Re-reading Activities," "Related Reading Activities," "Language and Special Activities," "Enrichment Activities," "Evaluating Activities," "Helping the Individual Child." The teacher with three or four sections of pupils working in different textbooks is lucky if she can struggle each day through one of the first three of these items, which taken out of pedagogical gobbledygook simply means preparation, reading and review.

What is the consequence of this bewildering multiplicity? It is that teachers are obliged to pick and choose methods and activities according to their instincts. And so we are at last pretty much at the mercy of the teacher. She has to be good.

All this leads to the hope that our school systems will make, more than ever before, an effort to acquire teachers who understand the complexity of the reading act, are cultivated readers, enthusiasts for good language and great writing, graduates of liberal arts colleges as well as teacher-training schools. Above all they should be lovers of books, not lovers of method.

We of the Fairfield committee do not pretend to offer simple remedies for these widespread reading problems: for the most part we have been able only to pose questions. But of one thing we are sure. These questions address themselves to every parent in the country, for teachers cannot answer them alone. In meeting them the schools need the support of an informed citizenry. Who can begrudge this support? It is, after all, for the benefit of our children.

52. The Teaching of Reading—Objective Evidence versus Opinion *

ARTHUR I. GATES

The November 13, 1961, issue of *Newsweek* comments as follows: "If there's anything guaranteed to rouse the fears of the modern parent, it's an article or book which sweepingly insists that American children are growing up unable to read. The latest example of this sort of alarmist literature is . . . called *Tomorrow's Illiterates* . . . in which Professor Charles C. Walcutt and six associates estimate that three out of four young Americans are not reading as well as they should or could.

"Without citing any statistical source of this estimate, Walcutt, who teaches English at New York City's Queens College, blames the situation on the 'word recognition' method . . ." which "necessarily limits the reading vocabulary of young children. . . ."

Newsweek states that although Mr. Walcutt's "arguments have some validity for the few schools that still rely solely on word recognition, . . . the overwhelming majority of children today are being taught to read with a variety of methods. . . ."

Another book, *What Ivan Knows That Johnny Doesn't,* by Arthur S. Trace, Jr., appeared at almost the same time and presents views similar to those of Mr. Walcutt. It also offers no objective evidence. It consists of opinions based on a comparison of several characteristics of American and Russian basal readers, such as the number of different words introduced in the two series of books.

EVIDENCE THAT
CHILDREN READ BETTER TODAY

Mr. Walcutt states correctly that intensive phonic methods were employed by most schools from 1900 to 1925, when

* Reprinted from *Phi Delta Kappan*, Vol. 43, No. 5 (February 1962), pp. 197-205, by permission of the author and the publisher.

transition to the less formal and less time-consuming procedure was getting under way. This newer program which he attacks had been adopted by most schools by 1930.

These authors present no relevant objective evidence to support their assertion that American children read less well today than comparable youngsters did prior to 1930. The available objective data indicate that the opposite is true. For example, a study reported by D. A. Worcester and Anne Kline, *Reading Achievement in Lincoln, Nebraska, Schools: 1921 and 1947,* a booklet published by the University of Nebraska Teachers College in 1947, showed that a marked improvement had been made during the quarter century preceding 1947. Pupils in grade five in 1947 made an average reading point or "raw" score of 93.1, as compared with 78.9 for the 1921 fifth-grade pupils. In 1947 there were fewer poor and failing readers: 4.1 per cent achieved a test score of 30 or less in 1947, compared with 23.7 per cent in 1921.

In my recent study, *Reading Attainment in Elementary Schools: 1957 and 1937,*[2] based on a comparison of test scores obtained from approximately 107,000 children in 1937 and 31,000 in 1957 (both groups selected as fair representatives of American schools in general and used in developing norms for the tests), less spectacular but clearly substantial improvement was shown. In tests of vocabulary, speed and accuracy of reading, and level or power of reading comprehension, 1957 children surpassed 1937 youngsters of the same age and scholastic aptitude (intelligence) in grades five and six by at least a half grade. I do not know of any objective evidence which shows that children tested in the last two decades are less able readers than youngsters of equivalent age and intelligence tested prior to 1930.

An important fact that is often not taken into account is that many poor readers who would have dropped out of school prior to 1925 are now kept in school. The study cited in the preceding paragraph presents evidence supporting this statement. Equally important is the fact that children at each of the grade levels, such as those in the middle of the fourth grade (grade position or grade status 4.5), are appreciably younger today than they were a third of a century ago. The recent policy of promoting children who would then have been required to repeat a grade means that the average reading ability of those at any particular grade level today would be much lower were it not compensated for by gains in ability.

EVIDENCE THAT INTENSIVE PHONICS IS NOT MORE EFFECTIVE

The claim is made in both books, but with more emphasis and detail in Mr. Walcutt's volume, that the one indispensable way of developing ability to recognize words and to read in general is to teach phonics in certain ways. The authors further claim that instruction in reading in American schools today is a "word guessing," or "look-and-say," or "word recognition" method which does not include training in phonics except possibly in the most incidental way. The first of these statements is unproved and the second one is untrue.

The methods of teaching phonics which Mr. Walcutt and his colleagues approve are essentially the same as various systems in wide use between 1900 and 1925. In fact, one system which he warmly recommends was published in 1913. Mr. Walcutt insists that other methods of teaching children to use the sounds of letters and letter combinations are really not *phonic* methods. The fact that children today read appreciably better than children of equivalent age and scholastic aptitude twenty-five or more years ago implies that the old type of phonic training is not in fact superior to the method of teaching phonics now widely used.

The prevailing method of teaching from 1900 to 1925 required a large amount of time and drill on the mastery of phonics—on teaching children to recognize, name, and sound letters and various letter combinations (phonograms) and to combine the sounds of the parts into a total word sound. The children were taught the names and sounds of the letters and some letter combinations before they learned to recognize words and read meaningful material. Typically, the child was laboriously taught one of the formal systems of phonics. In the last chapter of his book, Mr. Walcutt recommends and gives a brief sketch of a number of the systems.

Although Mr. Walcutt states that other reading programs depend entirely upon "look-and-say" methods, the fact is that all of those in wide use today also teach phonics. In nearly all of these systems, the child is taught from the beginning to read words. Soon he starts to learn the name and sound the letters and letter combinations (blends, phonograms, syllables). This study is kept up until the child can use word sounds along with a number of other techniques of word recognition. Although the amount and kind of phonic instruction recommended by the authors of the programs now in use vary considerably, most of them differ mainly from the phonic programs approved by Mr. Walcutt by introducing phonics more gradually, by teaching other useful methods of figuring out words, and by enabling the child to read from the beginning instead of delaying real reading until an extended period of drill on phonics is completed. The typical programs now in use do teach phonics quite thoroughly, as anyone can discover by examining the teachers' manuals.

During the twenty-five years in which the general type of phonic teaching recommended in these two books was used in most schools, it did not work the magic that Mr. Walcutt and his colleagues now claim for it. It was tried out during more than a quarter century with growing discontent because the load of narrow phonic drill was extremely heavy and it did not work well with many pupils. Contrary to the claims of these authors, the evidence indicates that there were more serious reading failures and general retardation prior to 1925 than there are now. It was for this reason that a number of psychologists and other persons began to study reading disabilities.

Around 1910 Psychologist Augusta F. Bronner began to investigate youngsters retarded or failing in reading. She published an important book on reading difficulties in 1916. Another psychologist, Grace M. Fernald, responding to appeals for help from schools, moved into the field and spent the rest of her life developing methods of teaching nonreaders by kinesthetic or motor tracing procedures, which included relatively little phonic training. These methods were remarkably successful with large numbers of children who had failed to learn by phonic and also by "look-and-say" methods. Between 1915 and 1920 Leta S. Hollingsworth, William S. Gray, and many others began to study numerous forms of reading disability. When I first came to Teachers College in 1917, I was told by Edward L. Thorndike (and others) how numerous and serious reading difficulties were. Following Thorndike's suggestion, I soon began to work in this field. My first studies were reported in 1922 in a small book, *The Psychology of Reading and Spelling with Special Reference to Disability*. It describes the many reading difficulties found among the students of superior intelligence in a private school. A report by Walter P. Percival pointed out the seriousness and frequency of reading disability during the years preceding 1925. He found that 99.2 per cent of the failures in grade one, 90 per cent in grade two, 70 per cent of those in grade three, and so on down to 40 per cent in grade five were due to failures in reading.[3]

EXPERIMENTAL STUDIES OF PHONIC METHODS

Such experiments as were done prior to 1920 consisted mainly of a comparison of a heavy phonic program with a pure look-and-say or unguided learning procedure. The phonic groups seemed usually to do no better than those trained by look-and-say. For example, a study by Lillian B. Currier and Oliver C. Duguid, published in the *Elementary School Journal* in 1916, showed that phonic training confused many pupils and had a "discouraging" influence on many other pupils, even many who became quite good readers. The latter learned to read without much enthusiasm for reading.

Karl D. Waldo reported in the *Elementary School Journal* for January, 1915, that youngsters trained by the Ward system of phonic instruction became no better readers than children taught by any one of several other methods. In 1919 and later, Gray reported studies in which he found no consistent difference between schools using the time-consuming phonic method and those using other methods. The studies which I carried out between 1920 and 1930 revealed weaknesses both in the phonic systems popular at that time and in extreme look-and-say methods.

In the final section of my report on my first studies of reading difficulty (*The Psychology of Reading and Spelling with Special Reference to Disability*, 1922), I said:

Learning wholly by the "natural" method or "word" method or otherwise without training in visual perception or analysis results frequently in inappropriate methods of observing words.

In a later report based on many additional studies (*New Methods in Primary Reading*, 1928) is the following statement:

The "natural method" is really an unabridged trial and error or trial and accidental success procedure, the limitations of which are recognized in the learning of other skills. The frequency of failure, of difficulties of various sorts, and of probable unnecessarily low accomplishment by many whose deficiencies were overcome or compensated for after struggles is sufficient reason for seeking definite methods of instruction which make the development of the basal perceptive skills a definite objective of teaching.

The method which gradually developed and is now most widely used starts off by teaching the children to recognize a few individual words which they begin at once to read in simple narrative selections. Many of these selections are not very exciting, but the child finds it very thrilling to be able to read them. Soon the child will be reading material in the classroom and elsewhere as well as in his basal reader. The modern plan is based squarely on the assumption that the child from the earliest possible moment reads widely both in school and elsewhere.

As soon as a youngster learns a few words, a good teacher begins to attract his attention to the similarities and differences among them. As new words are introduced in the basal readers, the teacher helps the pupil examine them. The teacher shows the child how to study these words, by moving the eyes over them always from left to right and by observing the successive parts of the word. He is then taught to read and sound the letters and many combinations of letters. Skill in recognizing letters and letter combinations and translating them into sounds and blending the sounds into whole-word sounds are carefully developed, but the teaching is not restricted to these devices. Many others, as anyone can easily discover by reading a modern teacher's manual, are taught. The aim is to give the pupil a kit of many tools, not just one, with which to deal with all the types of word recognition problems that he will encounter.

Efforts to compare experimentally this general procedure with those which depend upon more exclusive and extensive phonic approaches are difficult to carry out because it is so hard to control all the variables. I believe, however, that an appraisal of the studies reported within recent years will not support the contention that the more extended and intensive concentration on phonic instruction gives any better results than a typical modern procedure. Mr. Walcutt's book is full of assertions to the contrary. He lists a number of schools in which, he maintains, very superior results have been achieved by the phonic programs. For example, he is especially enthusiastic about one system which is designed to be introduced in the kindergarten and maintained all the way through grade eight. John A. McCollum, in a report issued by the Office of the Director of Elementary Education, Berkeley, California, June, 1961, recently compared the test results obtained from a few of these schools with those secured from comparable public schools in Berkeley. In no instance did Mr. Walcutt's preferred phonic methods groups excell those taught by means of other typical American programs.

In the course of standardizing a series of reading tests in 1957, these tests were given to the pupils in a school near New York City which had used one of Mr. Walcutt's favorite phonic programs for more than a decade. The average of the grade scores obtained from tests of vocabulary, speed and accuracy of reading, and level of reading comprehension for 243 pupils examined near the end of the school year, and the mental ages of these pupils, computed from the school records of intelligence test scores and converted into mental grades in the usual manner, were as follows:

	Mental Grade	Reading Grade	Difference
Grade 3.9	5.30	4.86	0.44
Grade 4.9	6.10	5.97	0.13
Grade 5.9	7.00	6.88	0.12

The reading grades shown in the above table do not quite equal the mental grades. This means that the youngsters who received the very extensive phonic training provided by this system were doing no better, if indeed they did quite as well, as the average child of the same mental ability who had been taught in the average American school under average conditions by a teacher of average ability.

The intelligence quotients (IQ's) and consequently the mental ages and grades of the pupils in this school were high. Many of the schools which Mr. Walcutt praises for producing outstanding results are in similar suburban areas near New York City. It is precisely in such schools that one usually finds a relatively large number of children of high IQ, superior teachers, better school facilities, and equipment including books and library services. Since these children are likely also to come from homes of better than average educational, social, and economic status, they should be superior readers. Almost any reading system, even a very inferior one, when taught to intellectually superior children by superior teachers will make a very good showing.

The fact that the extreme phonic method used in these schools did not always produce superior readers can be shown by comparing the mental grades and reading grades of individual pupils. Following are the data for fifteen fifth-grade pupils who had received the extreme form of phonic training during their entire school career:

Reading Grade	Mental Grade	Difference (R.G.—M.G.)
1.	3.8	6.2	−2.4
2.	4.4	6.2	−1.8
3.	5.9	7.5	−1.6
4.	6.1	7.3	−1.2
5.	4.0	5.0	−1.0
6.	5.5	6.4	−0.9
7.	6.6	7.4	−0.8
8.	6.6	7.0	−0.4
9.	5.3	5.7	−0.4
10.	7.6	7.9	−0.3
11.	6.4	6.3	+0.1
12.	6.6	6.5	+0.1
13.	6.4	6.3	+0.1
14.	6.6	6.2	+0.4
15.	10.0	7.5	+2.5

The figures for five students who were given no training by this particular phonic method, mainly transfers from other schools, are as follows:

Reading Grade	Mental Grade	Difference R.G.—M.G.
7.2	8.7	−1.5
3.2	4.2	−1.0
7.4	7.1	+0.3
6.0	5.4	+0.6
7.4	5.6	+1.8

In another school in the same city, a fifth-grade class contained ten children who had had the same phonic systems during their entire school career, and five, mainly transfers from various other schools, who had had none. The following list gives the amount, in grade scores, by which the mental grade exceeds the reading grade of each of these children. A minus sign (−) means that the reading grade is lower than the mental grade, a plus (+) that it is higher.

Pupils taught four years by phonic method: −2.7, −1.5, −0.6, −0.4, −0.2, −0.2, +0.6, +0.9, +1.1, +1.3

Pupils taught by other methods: −0.9, +0.5, +0.6, +1.3, +1.3

In another fifth-grade class the same figures for individual children are:

Pupils taught four years by phonic method: −1.6, −1.5, −1.2, −1.2, −1.1, −0.8, −0.8, −0.7, −0.3, −0.2, +0.2, +0.4, +0.5, +0.8, +1.0, +2.3

Pupils taught by other methods: +0.2, +0.2, +0.4, +1.2

These differences between the reading grade scores and the mental grade scores are low in reliability in the case of an individual child, but the above list gives no support to the claim that the particular phonic method used in this school produced fewer unfavorable scores than the procedures followed in other American schools.

EVIDENCE OF LARGE READING VOCABULARIES AMONG CHILDREN

The assertion made in both books that children in today's schools do not learn how to figure out unfamiliar words or words not taught in the basal readers deserves the most serious consideration. Both authors point out correctly that typical series of basal readers now in use include selections which are less difficult and based on fewer different words than those which were most widely employed during the first quarter of the present century. Mr. Trace's book compares the American program unfavorably with the Russian basal readers in these respects. The two authors state that because of this relatively light basal reader vocabulary, children do not learn to read nearly as many words today as they did a quarter of a century ago in American schools, or as many as the Russian children now learn in their program. Both authors assume that the only words children can read are those found in their basal reader, as illustrated in the following quotation from Mr. Trace's book:

There can be no question, then, that all students who are taught to read from these basal readers are being seriously short-changed. Most students begin to study history and geography and science in the fourth grade, and if the texts for these subjects are good texts, they are bound to have a vocabulary of between 6,000 and 8,000 words; and yet fourth-grade students inherit a reading knowledge of only about 1,000 words from their third-grade readers. One wonders how many students really succeed in overcoming the handicap which these basal readers place them under in learning other subjects. . . .

Mr. Trace's major recommendation is to develop new basal readers "that have three to five times the vocabulary and at last twice as much text as the typical reader series now has. . . ." He states that "second-grade readers must have a 2,000-word vocabulary" and "fourth-grade readers should have no less than a 5,000-word vocabulary" and a "sixth-grade reader must have an absolute minimum of a 10,000-word vocabulary." Both authors recommend that this increase in vocabulary in the basal books be accomplished by using the extreme type of phonic drill which they favor.

The purpose of the modern basal reader program is to help the youngsters develop the basic reading skills necessary to enable them to enlarge their vocabulary as well as to enrich their understanding by wide reading in a great variety of other materials. It is assumed that if they develop good methods of working out the recognition, pronunciation, and meaning of unfamiliar words they will be able to read a large amount of literature with understanding and thereby continuously increase their reading vocabulary. The crucial question is whether today's children are limited to the relatively small number of words introduced in their basal reading program. Fortunately, there are objective data bearing on this issue. I shall give only a few examples.

Records are available which show how many words American public school children on the average can pronounce of those included in a word pronunciation test. The test used consists of eighty words, beginning with such words as *so, we, as,* and ending with such words as *superstition, affectionate, philosopher, treacherous, lamentation.* The table of scores based on tests of a large sampling of public school children shows that before he reaches the middle of the sixth grade, the average child recognizes and pronounces correctly all the words in the test without a single error. (See Table XIII, page 35, of the *Manual of Directions for Gates Reading Diagnostic Tests,* Teachers College Bureau of Publications, 1953.)

In another study, published in the November, 1961, issue of *The Reading Teacher,* 75 per cent of the children in grade three in New York City public schools read and understood, in a multiple-choice test, 17 out of 21 words previously studied in their basal readers and nearly as many (16.5 out of 20) which are introduced for the first time in the fourth-grade basal reader. In this and a later study, to be published in the May, 1962, issue of the same journal, second-grade children read and understood 91 per cent as many untaught words from the third-grade readers and 88 per cent from the fourth-grade "new" words as they did of the words previously taught to them in their first- and second-grade basal readers. These children had developed marked ability to tackle untaught words successfully. Using these techniques in a program of wide reading, they learned to read a great many words not encountered in their basal readers.

In another study, by Arthur I. Gates, Guy L. Bond, and David H. Russell, published in the *Journal of Educational Research,* November, 1938, 600 children in grades two to six inclusive in New York City public schools were tested for the sole purpose of comparing the relative difficulty of the successive thousand words comprising the

Thorndike list of 20,000 words. By taking every thirty-third or thirty-fourth word, a random sampling of 600 words from this list was secured, making it possible to compute the number of words the children would have read successfully had they been given all twenty thousand. The total number of words pronounced correctly when each was shown alone, or in a sentence, was approximately the same. The number correctly pronounced was, for grade six (second term), 13,800 words; grade four (second term), 10,000; grade three (second term), 7,200; grade two (second term), 3,200. In a test given later to a smaller number of similar pupils, it was found that of the words the children were able to pronounce correctly they could also demonstrate a reasonable understanding of 86 per cent in grade six, 80 per cent in grade four, and 77 per cent in grade three. Grade two was not tested in this study. Applying these percentages to the number of words correctly pronounced (given above), the numbers of words both pronounced and understood are for the sixth grade 11,868, the fourth grade 8,000, and the third grade 5,544.

The Thorndike list of 20,000 words is not a childish list, as some writers have implied. It is heavily loaded with words from the Bible, English classics, and adult reading in all fields. Following are words which appear in the indicated thousand:

6th thousand—*abominable, admonish, apprehension*
8th thousand—*adaptation, adversity, allurement, analysis*
10th thousand—*acquiescence, adjunct, apostolic*
12th thousand—*alluvial, avaunt, Archimedes*
14th thousand—*archipelago, Aurelius, aboriginal*
16th thousand—*alliteration, appanage, asseveration, avoirdupois*
18th thousand—*acrimonious, Aeschylus, manuensis, anathematize, apotheosis*
20th thousand—*abnegation, agaric*

The finding that the children were almost as successful on a test in which words were shown alone as when they were contained in a sentence is significant in the light of the assertion that since 1925 children have depended so much on "guessing" on the basis of the context that they are helpless when a word is shown alone. The average sixth-grade pupil demonstrated ability to pronounce approximately 14,000 words from the Thorndike list when they were shown alone without context clues of any sort.

It should not be assumed that the only words a child can read are those contained in the Thorndike list of 20,000 words. The *Thorndike Century Senior Dictionary*, a convenient book for adults, contains "more than 30,000" additional words. Even this is a comparatively small dictionary. Average public school youngsters certainly learn to read many words in this additional 30,000. Among the words in it which are not in the Thorndike 20,000 list are *abacus, abaft, abeam, abrasion, absinthe, acidosis, acne, acoustic, activate, actuary, acuity, adaptable, addiction, ad lib, aeronautics, ageratum, aglitter, agnostic, agog, Akron, Alamo, à la mode, Albany, Alcatraz, alienist, alimony, allergic, altimeter*. These words do not appear to be more difficult than many of the words from the latter part of the Thorndike list.

One needs only to walk through a modern department store or glance through a mail order catalogue to realize how many words a youth runs into, many of them frequently, which are not in the Thorndike lists or in many dictionaries. For example, new words such as *television, electronic, hi-fi, transistor, stereo, feedback, diesel, radar, helicopter, octane, airlift, airline, neutron, proton, aspirin, pencillin, antibiotics, Coca-Cola, Pepsicola, detergent*, and *tabloid* do not appear in the Thorndike list. *Polaroid, Prestone, Brillo, Flako, Kleenex, Kelvinator, Frigidaire*, and many others do not appear. If one spends a few minutes with a Sears catalogue, one will encounter many words not in the Thorndike lists which most sixth-grade youngsters can read today; for example, *bra, orlon, abrasive, acrilan, adapter, additive, aerator, anklet, antifreeze, antihistamine, ascorbic acid,* and scores of trade names.

Edgar Dale and Gerhard Eichholz of Ohio State University began in 1954 to assemble lists of words which were known by 67 per cent or more of the pupils in grades four, six, eight, ten, and twelve. At intervals since that time additional words have been tried out by giving students multiple-choice tests. The latest interim report, published in March, 1960 (*Children's Knowledge of Words,* Bureau of Educational Research and Service), lists the words, the meanings of which were correctly indicated by 67 per cent or more children (except for a few for which the percentage was slightly lower) in several grades. The number for the fourth grade was 4,302 and for the sixth grade was 10,430 words.

The Dale-Eichholz list falls short of the total number known by fourth- and sixth-grade children. It is limited to words which these investigators have thus far tested. Additions will be made as additional words are tested in future years. There are many thousands of words not as yet tested. The multiple-choice tests such as those used in these studies are often unexpectedly difficult and subtle, even for adults. This list will doubtless be extended greatly in future years. Even in its present incomplete form, it shows that a high percentage of our grade four children know at least 4,302 words (or four times as many as Mr. Trace gives them credit for knowing). Sixth-grade children (tested throughout the school year, and thus representing on the average mid-sixth-grade performance) know well at least 10,430 words. This is more than the total of 8,000 words found in

all of Milton's writings and close to the 15,000 in the works of Shakespeare.[2] Indeed, the Dale-Eichholz incomplete lists shows for mid-eighth-grade pupils a total of nearly 15,000 words—14,992, to be exact.

JUSTIFICATION OF MODERN METHODS OF TEACHING READING

During the period 1915 to 1925 a number of persons began to experiment and theorize about the then-popular phonic method. Efforts were made to find less time-consuming methods. It was felt that unless the extensive phonic drill produced clearly better results, any method which enabled children to do some genuine reading would be preferred. Shortly before 1920 suggestions began to appear. One was that the youngster be equipped to read as soon as possible and that the major activity should be actual reading. This led to efforts to provide more and better reading materials in each classroom, as well as in the school library, and much more time for reading outside of the basal readers. In a general way the teacher of reading was advised to adopt the plan used by most of the best golf instructors, who after a brief and vigorous lesson in techniques and procedures, would recommend that the learner go out and play golf as much as he could, then return for a later lesson period during which his abilities would be diagnosed again and additional instruction provided.

During the years between 1915 and 1930 many studies were launched in the hope of developing a program of this sort. There was an immediate call for a great increase in suitable reading material for use in the classroom, in the school library, and in the home as a necessary part of the new program. More and better books and magazines, and even children's newspapers, were soon available for all grades from the first up—books on history, science, practical arts, travel, and other fields. New bookcases soon to be filled with attractive new volumes appeared in the typical classroom. A recent survey shows that the average primary grade classroom now contains eighty to one hundred books, intermediate grade classrooms one hundred or more.

In the new program the basal reader is devoted frankly to the task of teaching the abilities and skills needed to read well and to enjoy it. It is understood that this will occupy only a small part of the time devoted to reading in the school program. The basal books are designed to contribute as much help as possible. The teacher must provide the remainder of the guidance needed to enable the pupil to learn how to recognize words and acquire all the other basal skills. Teachers' manuals are prepared to help the teacher round out the program by means of individual and group demonstration and instruction.

The modern basal reader program is designed primarily to teach reading, not literature or science or history or geography or any other subject. It undertakes to develop the skills needed to read books and other material. The teacher is advised to encourage and supervise this wide program of reading as much as necessary. This policy is based in part on a conviction growing out of many observations and studies such as those of James F. Hosic, *Empirical Studies in School Reading,* Teachers College Bureau of Publications, 1921; Theodore W. Irion, *Comprehension Difficulties of Ninth-Grade Students in the Study of Literature,* Teachers College Bureau of Publications, 1925; and May Lazar, *Reading Interests, Activities, and Opportunities of Bright, Average, and Dull Children,* Teachers College Bureau of Publications, 1937.

These studies show that appreciation of literature is more likely to be frus-

trated than encouraged by using it as a means of laboring through the analyses and practice needed to enable a child to learn to read well. The basal book and the instruction carried on in connection with it should take care of this type of instruction, leaving literature and other materials to be read and studied without the interruptions and distractions which the teaching of reading techniques usually requires.

Authors of basal readers have since 1920 gradually reduced the vocabulary burden, the complexity, and the amount of basal reading material. Teachers found these easier basal books more satisfactory for use in developing the many complex skills involved in reading. It is exceedingly difficult to determine the ideal number of words to introduce in the basal books for the reason that the optimum varies for different pupils and teachers. Current basal readers consequently vary considerably. Some are better for classes of brighter children, others for the less able learners. Each teacher must adjust the kind and amount of teaching to suit very different children. This can be done by cutting down on formal work with a basal reader in some cases and increasing it in others by using other suitable books and practice material. Herein lies the advantage of individual instruction and "remedial" teaching which typically are limited to one child or so few at a time that the teacher is able to teach according to individual needs.

THE NATURE OF READING READINESS

Mr. Walcutt and others condemn reading readiness. Yet judging reading readiness and acting upon it are merely doing what everyone does in many other areas. Is little Johnny "ready" to carry in the milk bottles, or should he have more practice carrying blocks? Is teen-age Johnny "ready" to drive a car on the public highway? Is grown-up John "ready" to take command of a bank or battleship? The idea and practice of "reading readiness" are exactly the same as those employed in other fields. Critics of today's reading methods make capital of mistakes which teachers sometimes commit. Of course they make some mistakes, but so do Casey Stengel and other shrewd persons.

POSSIBILITIES OF FUTURE IMPROVEMENT

Mr. Trace and Mr. Walcutt seem to feel that reading is now taught and should continue to be taught as it was in 1900. At that time the teacher often had little or nothing but a single basal reader in each grade with which to teach reading, literature, manners and morals, and American ideals. The basal readers therefore had to be big, complex, and for most pupils discouragingly difficult. As I saw for myself as a ten-year-old in 1900, the results were not happy. This was shown in a report, *Laggards in Our Schools,* Russell Sage Foundation, 1909, by Leonard P. Ayers. He found that children were required to repeat grades and dropped out of school with great frequency. For example, he states that in 1906 the "general tendency of American city school systems is to carry" only "half . . . to the final elementary grade, and only one in ten to the final year of high school."

In 1900 books suitable for use in the primary grades were hard to come by. I do not recall having seen a bookcase in the first six classrooms I attended. The "revolution of the Twenties" was due in large measure to recognizing that more and better books and other forms of reading material would be published if they were asked for. The little red school and the big basal reader were passing out of existence. The new world visible in 1920 called for a program based on reading many books, beginning in the first grade. Mr. Trace and

Mr. Walcutt seem not to have discovered this change. Mr. Trace bases his major assertions on the assumption that reading skill and vocabulary, literary taste, and an understanding of the American way of life will not be acquired unless they are taught in the basal readers. He has completely missed the point of the educational program prevailing in American schools since 1930.

In spite of several decades of work by many persons, some youngsters still have trouble with reading and the common cold. I hope it will soon be possible to prevent both. I feel, however, that a look toward the future is more promising than a return to the program of the American past or the Russian present. Another new day is dawning now; it promises to be more revolutionary than the one which began in 1920. At times I feel as if I were in a hurricane of new types of electronic devices, teaching machines, television programs, audio-visual devices, scrambled textbooks, minutely detailed printed "programs," and practice materials which were not dreamed of in 1920.

This hurricane contains threats as well as promises. One threat was portrayed a few years ago in a *Punch* cartoon which pictured a half-dozen youngsters and a few parents sitting before a television set. All of the children were looking at the screen, except one little fellow who sat off at the side absorbed in a book. The mother of this child, as she directed another mother's attention to him, exclaimed, "I am really getting terribly worried about Johnny."

The new age has already brought incredible mechanical inventions and great improvements in printed materials. They promise many types of aid for the reading teacher. If they do no more than save time a teacher must now spend in routine activities and laborious oral instruction, they will be of enormous value. The outstanding need today is to provide the time and facilities to enable every teacher to become a more insightful and skilled instructor and to permit her to spend far more time in individual work with her pupils.

It will be advisable also to study the sociological factors which play a vital role in determining the reading activities of old and young alike. Dean E. G. Trotzig, head of the Department of Journalism of the University of South Dakota, stated in the June, 1957, PHI DELTA KAPPAN that "children cannot be expected to do any more reading

than their elders." The home which is supplied with a television set, several radios, a phonograph, an automobile or two, and a host of mechanical gadgets and toys but no shelves of books or magazines is not likely to house persons who care much about reading. If Johnny comes home each day to find a conspicuous array of good reading materials and his parents absorbed in reading and in discussing what they have read, he will tend to share this happy home enterprise and make it a permanent part of his pattern of life.

REFERENCES

1. See Edwin W. Dorin, "A Study of Vocabularies," The Pedagogical Seminary, 1907, pp. 401-38.
2. New York: Teachers College Bureau of Publications, 1961.

3. Percival, Walter P., A Study of the Causes and Subjects of School Failure, Unpublished Dissertation, Teachers College, 1926.

53: Reading Instruction—A Forward Look *

PAUL WITTY

During the past decade we have had in the United States much adverse criticism of reading methods and materials of instruction. The strictures have emphasized the inadequacy of repetitious and uninteresting presentations in textbooks and associated materials. Critics have stressed too the school's failure to make extensive use of films, filmstrips, and other aids. Some have cited the neglect of interest and motive and have deplored an insufficient emphasis on phonics. Others have pointed to the unjustifiably high per cent of reading failures among children and to the lack of

reading skill and interest on the part of many youth and adults today. Still others have cited the school's failure to treat reading as a thinking process. Undeniably there is ample reason for criticism, but the wholesale condemnation of our schools and the over-simplification of causes and cures are not only unjustifiable but deplorable.

A most insistent criticism has centered about the teaching of phonics, a topic which persists as a controversial issue. This criticism and a related one directed toward oral reading were in part justified by the neglect of phonics

* Reprinted from Elementary English, Vol. 38, No. 3 (March 1961), pp. 151-64, by permission of the National Council of Teachers of English and the author.

in some schools and by the abandonment of instruction in oral reading in others. Inconceivable as it may now appear, a group of educators at one time sponsored a nonoral reading program. Few schools adopted nonoral methods, and phonic instruction was usually offered, although the procedures and the extent of the emphasis varied widely. A few critics attributed all or almost all poor reading to lack of phonic training and appeared to believe that the inauguration of particular "approaches" would provide a cure-all for every kind of reading failure or problem. This unfortunately is not the case.

A critical study of the literature will demonstrate the significance of a number of factors which contribute to poor reading, including unfavorable home conditions, lack of readiness, emotional disturbances, few and unsuitable materials, and so forth. Of course, lack of phonic ability is sometimes associated with poor reading, but so too are other factors in various combinations. This fact has been well established by studies of the past. At the present time, several investigations are yielding additional valuable insights concerning causation as attention is being given in extreme cases to the significance of brain damage and other factors inadequately explored in earlier studies. The role played by attitude and emotion is receiving renewed attention, and interest and motivation are also being investigated. The future will bring, we hope, a greatly reduced tendency to overemphasize single items in studying causation. Moreover, we hope that the prevention of reading difficulties will receive greater attention in the coming years.

PHONICS AS A CURE-ALL

Some writers, however, continue to oversimplify the problem of effective reading instruction and attack with vehemence current educational practices. Perhaps

the most exaggerated position was represented by Rudolph Flesch,[8] who stated: "Teach the child what each letter stands for and he can read." Moreover, Mr. Flesch recognized no limitation in the phonic approach—in teaching children to read or in remedial reading. Thus he stated: "The reading 'experts' of course will say that such a program of remedial reading is much too simple. What about Johnny's emotional troubles, what about such nervous habits as reversals, what about correcting his eye movements? But my answer to all of that is phonics. Phonics is the key."[9]

Mr. Flesch's book reiterates the statement that children "never really learn to read" in our schools. . . . Parents therefore must take over since "the teaching of reading is too important to be left to the educators." Two other writers have examined current problems a little more realistically, but have arrived at a similar conclusion concerning the role of phonics. It is stated on the bookjacket of *Reading Chaos and Cure* that the authors, Sybil Terman and C. C. Walcutt "advocate an application of the phonics method as opposed to the 'reading readiness' and 'word configuration' program now widely in use."[33] In the book the following statements are found: "It is absurdly easy to teach a child to read with the proper method. Most of the children in America could be taught in a few weeks or months at the age of five. We shall tell you about various schools, now functioning, where a problem reader is virtually unheard of. . . ."

Some critics, like Mr. Flesch, are apparently interested chiefly or solely, it appears, in mere pronunciation of words. They have a very limited appreciation of reading as an intelligent, meaningful act by which thinking is promoted. Mr. Flesch makes this position abundantly clear in a story he tells:

I once surprised a native of Prague by reading aloud from a Czech newspaper,

"Oh, you know Czech?" he asked. "No, I don't understand a word of it," I answered. "I can only read it." [10]

Later, he describes a group of first grade children reading a newspaper and states: "But the fact is, and I testify to it, that those children read what was in the paper. They were perfectly able to pronounce words they had never seen before." In describing one child, he continues: "Needless to say, that six-year-old child hadn't the slightest idea of what the word meant. How could he?" Certainly pronunciation without understanding is not the aim of modern reading instruction. Nor is meaningless pronunciation thought of as reading. Reading is considered by some as a thinking process through which meaning is obtained from printed symbols. It is recognized that we do not get the meaning of a word—invariably or generally—from its spelling or from its pronunciation. To some of us, failure to obtain meaning is the most significant and unfortunate outcome of faulty or inadequate reading instruction. The child who is not encouraged to find appropriate meanings in various ways, such as by examining the context, is not being taught to read effectively. Rather, he is engaging merely in a parrot-like, routine exercise. It is recognized, too, that reading is both oral and silent; and that it is a two-way thinking process involving the individual's reaction to the symbol or statement and his interpretation of it in terms of his experience.

Some critics ignore and ridicule much that experimentation has divulged in the past 20 or 30 years about child growth and development in relation to effective instruction in reading. For example, they categorically deny that there is such a thing as readiness for the various steps in the process of learning to read. They discount, too, the importance of the interest factor and of goals, purposes, and needs in the reading process.

Phonics and Interest

Criticisms assume various guises. A few advocates of simple procedures such as phonic instruction recognize the possibility that other factors also cause or contribute to poor reading. For example, Glenn McCracken has some reservations about the complete adequacy of phonic approaches. He states that interest should come first:

I do not agree with Dr. Flesch, however, that phonics constitutes the only important teaching technique necessary for producing superior readers. The maintenance of interest must always come first. If interest is low, success will be lower. Particularly among slower learners better results will accompany accelerated interest.[20]

We should like to stress the fact that "accelerated interest" also will foster learning among average and rapid learners. To obtain interest, McCracken recommends heartily the presentation of materials in filmstrip form:

Another value associated with the textfilm approach is its facility for promoting class discussion. We have found this feature to be particularly pertinent to reading growth. Avid group conversation brings out many ideas. It stimulates interest and is helpful to pupils with good as well as weak mental abilities. When there is only one object of interest to look at in the room and when all children can see it equally well, conversation naturally ensues. It is common practice in these classes for the pupils guided by the teacher, to arrive at group decisions. This is learning in its finest form.[20]

This group approach is coordinated with the use of a basal text, and outstanding results are reported.

The filmstrip approach undoubtedly has merits. It was used with remarkable success in the Army's program for functionally illiterate men during World War II. Concerning the problem of illiteracy, Terman and Walcutt state:

When the Army launched the great draft at the beginning of World War II, it discovered that between ten million (over twenty-five years old) and sixteen million (over twenty years old) Americans were unable to read up to fourth grade level! By 1943 a million draftees had been rejected for illiteracy and three-quarters of a million had been accepted who read at or below a fourth-grade level. These millions could not all have come from Al Capp's mythical communities in the Southern mountains.[34]

But it should be pointed out that analyses of the origin of these men *did* disclose a meager background of educational experience. The majority of the men *did* come from educationally deprived areas. Moreover, the poor reading was not attributable primarily to inadequacies in their education but instead to lack of education. Terman and Walcutt also fail to indicate that we developed and used an unusually efficient program of instruction based upon research in child development and education.

THE ARMY PROGRAM FOR FUNCTIONALLY ILLITERATE MEN

In order to satisfy the need for manpower in the Armed Forces, it was necessary to induct large numbers of illiterate and non-English-speaking men. Special Training Units were organized to give the academic training these men needed to become useful soldiers. In these units they participated in an educational program characterized by (a) definite objectives, (b) high motive and interest, (c) careful study and proper grouping of individuals, (d) use of functional methods and materials in small classes, (e) wide application of visual aids, (f) hygienic conditions insuring a sense of security and general well-being, (g) provision for success from the start and for steady progress, and (h) the use of thoroughly trained, enthusiastic instructors.

Under the above conditions, it became possible for functionally illiterate and non-English-speaking men to acquire the reading skills needed in the Army in the short period of eight weeks. The writer of this article has described the steps in this accomplishment elsewhere and he has indicated some of the implications for the classroom teacher. He has outlined too his concept of a well-rounded reading program for the elementary school. Such a program is similarly characterized by (a) definite objectives, (b) provision for an orderly mastery of basic habits and skills, (c) application of appropriate techniques in appraising pupils' needs and in evaluating their growth, (d) the use of functional materials and methods of instruction, (e) the appropriate use of visual and auditory materials, and (f) the maintenance of hygienic conditions for learning under skilled teachers.[36] In this program, individual and group instruction are judiciously combined, and reading is looked upon as a process which helps pupils meet their problems with success and understanding.

THE ROLE OF INTEREST

Again and again the writer has referred to the value of ascertaining and utilizing children's interests.[37] In this emphasis, he has found support in research which provides convincing evidence that the curriculum should be developed in accord with the children's needs, interests, and problems if it is to have maximum significance and application. For years capable teachers have utilized children's interests as strong motives for learning. Committees engaged in curriculum development or reconstruction have also given recognition to the interests of boys and girls at different ages.

Specialists in reading too sometimes recommend that teachers utilize existing interests as a starting point in remedial endeavor. These workers are aware that some interests are transitory and that others are unworthy of extension. Therefore it has been suggested that teachers aim to modify old patterns, create new interests, and raise the level of pupils' tastes. In fact, the interests of boys and girls on coming to school may be thought of as constituting a unique opportunity for teachers. The interests of pupils at the time they leave a class or school may reflect the extent to which the teacher has accepted responsibility for directing pupil growth. Thus in a balanced reading program the study of children's interests becomes a primary consideration.

It is recognized also that learning to read with meaning increases the child's sense of power and opens the doors to new satisfactions and new sources of knowledge. Throughout all stages of the learning process, the child's satisfaction in real achievement and progress is a primary concern. This is the logical corollary to the foregoing emphasis on the interest factor. This dual approach guarantees the child the chance to follow worthwhile interests in a program characterized by systematic guidance and continuous evaluation. In such a program, successful achievement and disciplined growth are objectives.

In the Army program widespread use was made of films and filmstrips, as motivational and instructional devices. Following World War II, filmstrips were gradually introduced and employed successfully in certain phases of reading instruction. And films, too, were used with outstanding success in association with reading materials. For example, in an experiment conducted by James Fitzwater and the writer, films were employed to present simple narratives of strong appeal to second-grade children.[39] After the children had seen each film and had listened to the commentary, they read the story in a film-reader. Then they developed their own story which was reproduced and heard by them *via* the magnetic sound track. This experiment, combining reading with listening and discussion, was demonstrably successful. Under these conditions, the acquisition of concepts and of skill in interpreting presentations was greatly enhanced. The film played an important role in this program; however, it was recognized that the use of the film was one factor only in effecting success. Similarly, the use of filmstrips has been found to foster the development of reading skills.

It is the hope of the writer that the future will bring increased use of films and filmstrips soundly articulated in a developmental program with full recognition of their motivational and instructional worth. The value of visual and auditory devices is unquestionably great; their use should not be looked upon as a panacea but rather as a way of facilitating learning when they are employed in appropriate context or used as a part of a balanced program of instruction. These statements apply also to the use of tachistoscopes, reading accelerators, and "teaching machines." Similarly the use of "closed circuit TV" should not be looked upon as a cure-all device, nor regarded as a substitute for the teacher and as *the* way to solve the teacher shortage. The worth of each of these devices and approaches should be acknowledged and research should be undertaken to ascertain when and how they can be employed most advantageously.

THE ROLE OF INTEREST IN A DEVELOPMENTAL PROGRAM

Although many authorities in reading have recommended the use of interests in motivating instruction, relatively few studies of the interest factor have been made during the past fifteen or twenty years. During this period the emergence of TV has altered greatly the recreation of boys and girls and has deeply affected their interests. A recent comprehensive study reveals that the impact of TV and the mass media has altered children's interests greatly and has probably increased the need for guidance.[38] We believe that in the future, knowledge concerning the interests of pupils will be regarded as essential in planning the reading curriculum and in guiding each pupil. We hope the principle of interest will receive greater recognition not only in the elementary school but also in the high school and in the college.

THE ROLE OF TEXTBOOKS

There are, of course, various ways to teach children to read. Some teachers have succeeded through the conventional textbook approach; others have utilized an "individualized method"; some have employed films and film-readers with success; and still others have combined effectively group and individual approaches. It has become clear that various means may be used to establish and improve reading skills. Although reading skills may be achieved by different approaches, we should observe that there are different outcomes and relationships associated with each. Increasingly, educators are recommending a comprehensive program of instruction which stresses meaningful reaction and reading as thinking. Accordingly, greater recognition is being given to the effects of reading experience upon the pupil.[35] In efforts to provide a more valid evaluation than that reflected only by the acquisition of skill, teachers are asking questions such as: Do pupils read more widely? Are they more interested in and better able to read the materials of the subject fields? Have they obtained competency in using the library to satisfy interests and meet re-

curring needs? Have they developed, as a result of instruction, a strong interest in reading and independence in the selection of materials?

Recently we have had our attention directed to certain inadequacies of the instructional program that follows the typical textbook pattern to achieve the objectives implied by the foregoing questions. Criticisms have centered in some cases on the content of elementary school textbooks. Indeed, the first-grade reading program has become a subject for ridicule or scorn on the part of some critics, and the textbook has served as the special object of attack. The assumption that children may obtain maximum benefits from the presentation of words in highly repetitious contexts woven about trivial situations *is* highly questionable. Certainly more meaningful materials closely related to children's current experiences are essential in a sound program of reading instruction.

The design for textbooks of the future (and the instructional guides and practice materials) will, we hope, provide for greater flexibility and make more ingenious provision for individual differences through the inclusion of richer and more varied content. It is hoped that greater attention will be given to concept building rather than to repetition of words in routine patterns. Reading in the content fields, critical reading, and reading to satisfy personal and social needs, deserve, and should receive far greater attention. There will be too, we hope, a much needed enrichment for superior pupils, as well as provision for wide use of materials to afford opportunities for pupils to apply reading skills in the subject fields. The elementary school of the future will, we hope, have a central library and a school librarian. The school librarian, like the teacher, will be thoroughly trained in child study. The librarian will encourage teachers and pupils in the use

of the library aids, reference books, cat-
alogs, indexes, and bibliographies, and
will also keep teachers informed as to
new books and visual and auditory materials as well. Through the foregoing
steps, we shall see the diffusion of developmental practices throughout our
schools.

A developmental reading program
will recognize the value of continuous,
systematic instruction, utilization of interests, fulfillment of developmental
needs, and the articulation of reading
experience with other types of worthwhile activity. The chief aim of this
program will be to help pupils *become* skillful, self-reliant, and independent readers, who will continue to enrich
their understandings and satisfactions
throughout their lives by reading. At all
stages, reading as a thinking process
will be cultivated.

INDIVIDUALIZED READING

The above objectives will be conceded
to be desirable. But how they are to be
achieved is a matter of controversy.

With some of these in mind, one
group of educators and teachers is advocating what is called "Individualized
Reading." This term means many things
to differe .t persons who advocate the
practice. Leland Jacobs, in a practical
manner, discusses the topic and states:

In the first place, "individualized reading"
is not a single method with predetermined
steps in procedure to be followed. It is not
possible to say that every teacher who
would individualize guidance in reading
must do this or that. It is not feasible or
desirable to present a simple, single meth-
odological formulation of what is right
in "individualized reading" which every
teacher shall follow.[11]

Certain writers have attempted to define "individualized reading" as a unique
program and have emphasized its value
as a method of instruction. We would

agree with the persons who recommend "individualized reading" if the following conditions were recognized. Individualized reading should be accepted
as a *part* of (not a subordinate to,
or an adjunct of) the basal program,
but not as *the* program. We see little
need for calling the program "individualized" and designating this approach
as "the method" to be followed. May
Lazar in a generally admirable discussion states: "Individualized Reading is
not subordinate to or an adjunct of the
basic reading program." However, she
adds *"it is the basic program."* [14] Why
can't we recognize that neither group
nor individual practices alone constitute
the reading program? Why can't we
grant the importance of both approaches
and cease to think of them as mutually
exclusive practices? Isn't it possible to
find a way by which agreement can be
reached so as to utilize the undeniably
desirable features of both approaches
in a program which encourages thinking,
independent choice, and self-directed
behavior? Admittedly, this will necessitate the abandonment of some practices
associated with the typical textbook pattern of instruction; it will necessitate
too the disavowal of belief in a single
pattern to be followed by all children
in a class. Adaptations, revisions, and
extensions of current practices will be
necessary.

CHARACTERISTICS OF INDIVIDUALIZED READING

Various persons have described the distinguishing features of "individualized
reading." For example, Dorothy M.
Dietrich emphasized some of the characteristics of individualized reading as
follows:

Presently, numerous articles have been
written concerning the individualized approach to the teaching of reading. Although
these reports vary as to the organization
and methods used, they do agree that the

elements necessary for conducting an individualized reading program include: (1) a large classroom library made up of basal and supplementary readers, books brought from home by the children and/or materials borrowed from public or school libraries; (2) a free choice by the children of the reading materials depending upon interest and/or readability; (3) a follow-up activity which may be a series of questions devised by the teacher pertaining to each book, a general report of the book read, a visual presentation of the highlights of the book to the class as a whole, or a discussion with other children concerning characters, plots, etc.; (4) a conference between each child and the classroom teacher, the number of conferences depending upon class size and individual need; (5) a reading skill program which may be taught to the class as a whole, or in some cases, on a flexible small group basis depending upon the emerging needs of the individual.[6]

May Lazar and two members of the Bureau staff, after visiting about 50 classes and making a survey of current practices in the schools where individualized reading had been started, found that "although no two teachers worked exactly in the same way even in the same school, there emerged a general picture of their procedures."

Teachers generally gave some directions to the class as a whole. A time was given when all children read independently from self-selected material. Teachers held sessions or "conferences" with individual children or with a small group. Teachers kept records of children's abilities, needs, and interests.

The children kept simple records and reports of their readings.

There was class or group discussion or sharing of books read.[15]

It will be found that most teachers who have tried the individualized approach are enthusiastic about its results.[7] Some schools have reported that a combination of the individualized approach with the traditional basic method has proved more satisfactory. Several writers have concluded that the most desirable procedure is to adapt the best features of individualized and of group instruction to the reading situation and the needs existing in different schools.

Both strengths and weaknesses in the individualized method have been noted. H. W. Sartain reports the results of an experiment "to determine whether second-grade groups would make greater progress in reading skills when taught for three months by the method of individualized self-selection or when taught for an equivalent period by the method of ability grouping using basic readers plus a variety of supplementary books." [26] He drew the following conclusions from his study:

In summary, because this study and others that have been carefully controlled show that the individualized method does not produce better reading gains than a strong basal program, there is no reason to forfeit the advantages of a well-planned basic system. Instead the benefits of the individual conferences should be obtained by their addition to the basic reader plan.[27]

Sartain notes some strengths and weaknesses of the individualized method as listed by the the teachers who participated in the study:

STRENGTHS OF THE METHOD OF INDIVIDUALIZED SELF-SELECTION

1. Individual conferences provide a valuable personal relationship with pupils.
2. Children are motivated to read more extensively.
3. There is a keen interest in sharing.
4. There is a strong motivation for individual improvement.
5. Top readers are especially responsive.

WEAKNESSES OF THE INDIVIDUAL METHOD

1. All slow pupils and others who cannot work well independently become restless and tend to waste time.

2. There is no opportunity to teach new vocabulary and concepts needed before reading.
3. It is impossible to provide a systematic program of word attack skills.
4. It is exceedingly hard to identify pupils' difficulties in short infrequent conferences.
5. There is some doubt about the permanence of skills taught so briefly.
6. The method is inefficient because of the time required to teach skills to individuals instead of teaching groups who are progressing at a similar rate.
7. The conscientious teacher becomes frustrated in attempting to provide individual conferences for all pupils who need them each day.[28]

Eleanor Johnson, too, in evaluating the individualized reading approach, lists the following values and limitations:

Values. Individualized reading allows a pupil to read at his own level without being frustrated by those of differing reading ability. A child can follow his own reading interests. Tensions are reduced. Pupils enjoy the personal attention they receive in teacher-pupil conferences.

Limitations. The individualized approach to basic reading has at least four important limitations. (1) *Readiness.* For maximum achievement, every child on every level needs readiness for reading any story. Individualized reading appears to ignore the principle of readiness. (2) *Skills.* Reading skills are many and complex. A child does not learn them merely by reading. Leaving them to individual teaching can open a Pandora's Box of reading deficiencies. (3) *Purpose.* Reading is a thinking process. Skill in thinking needs more guidance than can be given in a brief conference. (4) *Efficiency.* It is a waste of time to do individually what can be done more efficiently on a group basis.[12]

May Lazar also points to some values of and some items of concern about the individualized approach.

This approach: Really provides for individual differences; satisfies children's needs of seeking, self-selection, and pacing.

Better integration with other language arts—more creative thinking and critical reading; wide increase in vocabulary; motivation for listening, writing, and spelling; strong desire to communicate ideas.

Decided carry-over to homes; more self-initiated reading; extensive use of public library.

Social interaction—good relationships within the class; acceptance of one another's contributions; "caste system" is broken down.

The child has a better sense of his own worth—self-understanding; he is a participating member of the group;—he relies on his own self-management; he feels that he is a real part of the program and is learning from his own efforts and not always because of what the teacher wants him to learn.

Child actually reads; learns to cherish and handle books; respects authors and their ideas.[16]

May Lazar mentions some problems that were encountered.

The teachers and principals expressed concern about:

Materials—there are not enough books as yet to fit the needs of the classes; administration and organization of the books are serious factors.

Children's Ability in Selection—some children may need special guidance that the teacher does not foresee.

Teacher Attitude—fear of something new.

Teacher Effectiveness—would all teachers be able to handle this approach?

Supervision—flexibility makes procedures more difficult to assess. If the supervisor understands and has the same objectives, evaluation will not be too difficult. He may, however, have to employ evaluative measures somewhat different in nature from the existing ones.

Parents' Reactions—skepticism about changing procedures.[17]

Although some of the writers on individualized reading do not recommend dropping basal textbooks, Sartain states that "most of the enthusiasts recommend dropping the basal reader program entirely, but several teachers have found that a combination of basal and individualized reading is more desirable.[24]

We have noted some examples of effective combination of group and individual approaches. Thus, Maida Wood Sharpe describes an ingenious program in which the teacher worked "one or two days each week in the basal readers for systematic study and instruction in basic reader skills," and used on the other days an individualized reading program.[29] Also Louise G. Carson reports that in her school district the teachers were "not yet convinced that a completely individualized program" was "necessary or advisable," but that they were interested in the idea. She thought that were she to embark on such a program, she "would retain reading groups of basal reading" and "would individualize all supplementary reading."[1] This suggestion has been made by a number of writers including John J. DeBoer.[4]

Another distinct innovation is suggested by Margaret Kirby who described a program in which reading skills are presented and demonstrated to the children. For three days each week the children work independently and on the other two days they work together. An important feature of this program is in the arrangement for books. Six to eight books of like levels are placed on shelves covered with varying colors of shelf paper. Kirby thus describes the use of these books by the children:

Each child is told to choose the book he wants from a shelf of a particular color. No book may be put back on the shelf until checked by the teacher. A move to another shelf is determined by the child's own progress. When a new shelf is started, the basic book is required reading. In this way every child is getting the basic vocabulary.

If a child asks for a book from another shelf, I let him try. In most cases the child has come back and asked to go back to the shelf he had originally been assigned. This gives the child a chance to make an evaluation of his own ability. One child read a book much below his reading level. Together teacher and child evaluated this

reading experience and decided that sometimes a book is worthwhile because of the enjoyment it gives or the information it presents. Another child wanted a book from a more advanced level and proved that she was capable of handling this level because she was willing to put forth the extra effort it required.

During the independent reading period I work with one child at a time at my desk. Theoretically each child has one ten-minute conference each week.[13]

Esther Dornhoefer,[23] after following for several weeks an individualized program with her children, has "some problems" to solve:

... selective reading also involved some problems. Many of the children were in primers and first readers. The stories were longer and it took more time to read. It was now impossible to read with each child every day. I had tried taking half the group one day and the other half the next day but the children didn't like it. "I didn't get to read today" was the complaint. Again I thought, "Oh joy, they really do like to read. This is what I have been working for."

By this time, of course, I was almost sold on individualized reading except for one thing. There is a certain sense of pleasure in sharing a story with your classmates—in other words, group reading. But if I added group reading to our individual reading the day would be heavily overbalanced with language arts. And yet —the next teacher might prefer to use group reading and it seemed only fair that the children should have the experience. . . .

The longer I teach the more I feel that there isn't any *one* approach—rather a combination that ultimately shapes the results. This past year has been one of experiment, mistakes, and problems. But next year with some changes, I shall use a variety of approaches—group reading, the newspaper, the reading table with the freedom of choosing books to take home—but the backbone will be individualized reading.

We would most certainly concur with the conclusion of this excellent teacher in recognizing that there isn't any *one* approach to efficient instruction. Moreover, we believe that we should continue exploration to determine which combination of approaches is most effective. We admire greatly the courageous efforts of teachers to solve this problem and we agree too with the following statements of John Marcatante about possible reactions to the *Individualized Reading Program:*

... One teacher may attribute panacea-like powers to it, while another will maintain that it is a waste of time. Both these extremists may stand in error.[19]

This is precisely the point we attempted to make in an article published in *Elementary English,* October, 1959. In this article, we tried to give a rather representative summary of investigations and to evaluate the results. This summary was criticized as incomplete (which it was intentionally). Since that time, additional summaries have been published, such as that by Harry W. Sartain who concludes that because his own study and others "that have been carefully controlled" show that the "individualized method does not produce better reading gains than a strong basal program, there is no reason to forfeit the advantages of a well-planned basic system." [25] However, he does recognize some of the strengths of the individualized approach. Several other accounts demonstrate clearly some of the distinct values of individualized reading. One of these, by Helen F. Darrow and Virgil M. Howes, gives examples of effective reading instruction.[2] In the preface, the authors state that "The individualized method is no panacea, no quick trick to solve all reading problems," and that "At best it is a means to achieve the major goals of reading instruction." We were most impressed in this account with the care and success of the teachers in studying the interests of boys and girls and in associating interests with reading materials. Called by either name (individualized or developmental) this is an admirable

practice. We were greatly pleased too with the consideration of skills and the various methods used to establish them. Perhaps the greatest strength of this admirable pamphlet lies in the ingenious provisions for recording development and evaluating growth through reading. The title of this booklet is *Approaches to Individualized Reading.* We believe that this monograph could just as appropriately be entitled *Approaches to Developmental Reading* as we have described the latter.

It seems to us that it is idle to debate whether individualized *or* group approaches are preferable. Common sense as well as some of the studies would support the use of both approaches in effective combinations and not with one subservient to the other. In doing this, we should, of course, recognize the need for the abandonment of the routine *basal* approach in using a single reading series; but this would not rule out systematic instruction in which reading textbooks in various combinations are used as needed.

Ruth Strang and Donald M. Lindquist also recognize this point of view in their interpretation of individualized reading. They state:

Individualized reading is an essential part of the developmental reading program. Children should be guided in selecting books of interest to them and at their reading level, and teachers should give them individualized help with their chosen reading.[32]

They point out that there are many ways of individualizing reading. "The most common method of individualization on all educational levels is subgrouping within a class." Other procedures are discussed and are followed by this conclusion; "These and other methods of individualization do not constitute the whole reading program. They are features of a classroom procedure that provide for both group and individual instruction and practice."

NEED FOR MORE DEFINITIVE RESEARCH

It is difficult indeed to appraise scientifically a "method" which is interpreted in so many and such varied ways as is "individualized reading." And, we should hasten to add that developmental reading has many interpretations, one of which is found in this article. Similarly, instruction using the *basal* materials is difficult to evaluate since many plans are employed; in some, multiple texts and varied practice materials are used in different combinations; in others *a* basal reader and its accompanying materials are meticulously followed. Perhaps it would be well to admit these facts and abandon trying to ascertain the value of "individual" versus the textbook approach. Instead we might try to agree upon common objectives and seek to evaluate some aspects of both approaches, such as when and how pacing may be utilized successfully, when and how self-selection may be engendered and practiced most effectively, when and how skills under-emphasized in most textbooks can be most advantageously developed, and under what conditions films and filmstrips can be most efficiently utilized. The role of self-teaching devices should also be explored.

In summarizing the results and implications of studies and experiments to discover ways of improving reading achievement through the means of program organization, methods and materials, Lofthouse comments thus on some of the pitfalls to be avoided in making comparisons:

Individuals who undertake experimentation should try to control or at least take account of the numerous factors which might bias their findings. Pitfalls to avoid include comparing results achieved by teachers who are of unequal ability, experience, preparation, or motivation or who used classes of different socio-economic backgrounds. The amount of time spent and the emphasis placed on the subject being taught should be equivalent when plans of organization or procedures are being evaluated.[18]

And Clare B. Routley makes the following recommendations for reading practices and materials for the future:

Teachers in the future must pay more attention to individualized reading programs. Grouping must be planned to meet the needs of all pupils. Even gifted children may be retarded readers. Other gifted children may be reading below their potentialities. . . .

To meet the unprecedented demands in reading which the changing characteristics of our age will demand, there must be more research, more experimentation, more testing and increased use of clinical procedures. The best of the New Castle Plan, the Joplin Plan, and all other plans must be made available for teachers in order that a sound developmental program may be followed.[22]

With the foregoing statements we are in full agreement. Moreover, we find in the following conclusions of John De-Boer and Martha Dallman an interesting commentary on needs in today's schools.

While it is true that some children learn to read well without any systematic instruction, acquiring all needed skills through abundant and highly motivated reading, the vast majority of children need instructional assistance if they are to learn to read at their best. The regularly scheduled reading period and the basal reader will continue to be indispensable for most teachers and with most children if essential skills are to be developed. Extensive reading may be sufficient for bright children under the guidance of skillful teachers, and it is likely to produce rapid readers, readers who readily grasp the total meaning of a passage. For most pupils, however, it should be supplemented with intensive instruction for the continuous development of increasingly difficult skills such as word recognition, comprehension of sentence meaning, and following directions.

DeBoer and Dallman make the following suggestions for modifying conventional textbook practice:

Certain general cautions should be observed in the planning of a basal reading program. These cautions grow out of facts and principles developed earlier in this book. For example, reliance should not be placed upon a single basal reader for the whole class; indeed it should not be placed upon an entire single series. In any given class, basal readers designed for many levels of reading ability and containing many different kinds of material should be provided. Basal readers should not be labeled according to grade level of difficulty, although the publisher's estimate of difficulty level may be indicated by some code device. All basal readers should be amply supplemented with general reading materials on many subjects and representing many levels of reading difficulty.[5]

A provocative point of view is also expressed by Russell G. Stauffer who states:

It is recommended, then, that a modified basic reader approach be used. To do this effectively one must, first, drop the notion that a basic reader program in and of itself is final and sacred. It is not. Second, one must drop the notion that time can be equated with equality. Not every group must be met every day for the same length of time. Third, the idea that a basic book recommended for a grade level must be "finished" by all pupils in a grade before they can be promoted must be discarded. Fourth, teaching reading as a *memoriter* process by presenting new words in advance of the reading and then having pupils tell back the story must be stopped. If reading is taught as a thinking process, even short basic-reader stories will be read with enthusiasm. . . . Sixth, effective skills of word attack must be taught. Basic reading books do not provide for such skill training; neither do trade books.[30]

Following is an illustration, again from Darrow and Howes, of the way textbooks and group instruction have been combined effectively.

On certain days, instead of sharing individual reading, children worked on skills in small groups. For practicing certain skills, the children worked from a common reader; for others, they used workbooks, their individual reading books, and other aids. All kinds of skills were practiced: speed, word meanings, dictionary skills, word analyses, use of indexes and tables of content, and others. The teacher checked frequently with the county course of study in reading and in other books so as to keep in mind the range of reading skills.[3]

It will be granted that some widely followed basal programs are inflexible. Other programs and textbooks are more flexible. It is clear that we need new designs for texts and related materials. When these are developed, they will, we hope, stress reading as a thinking process to a greater extent. In the meantime, it is desirable to follow a flexible program using the best texts available and combining group with individualized reading, as DeBoer and Dallman have suggested. Stauffer, too, makes a distinctive recommendation.

. . . the reading program should be divided so as to allow about half of the time for each approach—a basic reader program and an individualized program. This might be done by using the group approach with basic readers for about a week or two, and then the individualized or self-selection approach for a similar period of time. When a pupil is free to select day after day for two or three weeks, he is almost forced to examine his interests and decide more carefully about what he wants to do.[31]

The suggestions given above seem plausible. It would be desirable for teachers to try out these approaches. What outcomes will they yield? Similarly we might through cooperative efforts seek answers to other questions, such as:

a. How can children be best prepared for self-selection and for successful silent reading experiences? What is the role of readiness? How can phonic skills be best acquired?

b. What combination of individual and of group endeavor is most advantageous in various situations?

c. What provision should be made for "conferences" between pupil and teacher in classes of various sizes? How often should conferences be held in various situations?

d. How can we use films, filmstrips, and film readers more effectively to promote pleasure and success in reading?

e. What provision should be made for the acquisition of skill in oral reading? In story-telling? In creative endeavor of various kinds?

f. How can individual and group interests be best ascertained? And how can individual and group interests be best provided for?

g. What is a desirable combination of group and individual practices to follow in the subject areas? How can such practices be encouraged and evaluated?

h. What is the best combination of group and individual practice to follow in guiding exceptional children? In encouraging creativity?

i. In what ways can we encourage reading as a thinking process? How can we foster critical reading most effectively?

One of the values of individualized reading insufficiently stressed, is the opportunity it offers the creative child or the gifted pupil to explore his interests and to develop his background through reading. The principle of self-selection has special relevance here since its use may permit the expression or the development of gifts.

The above questions and others can be answered best through various types of classroom endeavor accompanied by research. They are not questions at present to be answered primarily by debate. Certainly we have few dependable answers at present to most of these questions. New and bold departures are necessary if we are to make the most of our present opportunities. During World War II, we demonstrated the value of films and filmstrips in teaching reading. And after World War II, the value of films associated with film readers was shown in the development of habits and skills in reading. Schools have been remiss by neglecting to incorporate such approaches in the teaching of reading. We should recognize, however, that some teachers are at present courageously making efforts to depart greatly from established practice and to test new approaches. With the unparalleled opportunities today for the use of new approaches and devices to foster enjoyment and success in reading, it is hoped that in the future we shall extend these efforts greatly and shall not be forced to acknowledge our neglect with its far-reaching consequences.

REFERENCES

1. Carson, Louise G., "Moving Toward Individualization—A Second Grade Program," *Elementary English,* Vol. 34 (October 1957).

2. Darrow, Helen F., and Howes, Virgil M., *Approaches to Individualized Reading.* New York: Appleton-Century-Crofts, Inc., 1960.

3. Ibid., p. 16.

4. DeBoer, John J., Address given at Northwestern University, Summer Reading Conference, 1959.

5. ———, and Dallman, Martha, *The Teaching of Reading.* New York: Henry Holt and Company, 1960.

6. Dietrich, Dorothy M., *Reading in a Changing Society,* edited by J. Allen Figurel, Part V, "Experimental Procedures Significant for Future Trends in Reading Instruction, 9. For Reading Supervisors; a, In Methods and Materials," International Reading Association Conference Proceedings, Vol. 4, 1959, p. 233. Published and distributed by Scholastic Magazines, 33 West 42nd St., New York 36.

7. For the individual approach, see the essays in Jeannette Veatch's *Individualizing Your Reading Program.* New York: Putnam, 1959.

8. Flesch, Rudolph, *Why Johnny Can't Read.* New York: Harper and Brothers, 1955, p. 3.
9. Ibid. p. 116.
10. Ibid.
11. Jacobs, Leland, "Individualized Reading Is Not a Thing," in *Individualizing Reading Practices,* edited by Alice Miel. New York: Bureau of Publications, Teachers College, Columbia University, 1958.
12. Johnson, Eleanor M., "The Trend Toward Individualized Reading," *My Weekly Reader,* Vol. 29 (May 2-6, 1960), Teacher's Edition, 2. Section 1 of two sections.
13. Kirby, Margaret, "Tête-à-tête Lessons Develop Independent Readers," *Elementary English,* Vol. 34 (May 1957), pp. 302-3.
14. Lazar, May, "Individualized Reading: A Program of Seeking, Self-Selection, and Pacing," Chapter 15 in Jeannette Veatch, *Individualizing Your Reading Program.* New York: Putnam, 1959.
15. Ibid. p. 198.
16. Ibid. pp. 200-201.
17. Ibid. pp. 199-200.
18. Lofthouse, Yvonne M. (Mercy College, Detroit, Michigan), *Reading in a Changing Society,* edited by J. Allen Figurel, Part V, "Experimental Procedures Significant for Future Trends in Reading Instruction, I. In Primary Grades; a, In Methods and Materials," International Reading Association Conference Proceedings, Vol. 4, 1959, p. 177. Published and distributed by Scholastic Magazines, 33 West 42nd St., New York 36.
19. Marcatante, John (Junior High School 126, Queens), "The Programmatic Fallacy and Individualized Reading," *High Points* (May 1960), pp. 47-50.
20. McCracken, Glenn, *The Right To Learn.* Chicago: Henry Regnery Company, 1959, p. 156.
21. Ibid. p. 171.
22. Routley, Clare B. (Supervisor of Professional Development, Ontario). *Reading in a Changing Society,* op. cit. Part IV, "Implications of a Changing Society for Future Practices in Reading Instruction, 9. For Reading Supervisors; a, In Practices and Materials," pp. 144-5.
23. Rowe, Ruth, and Dornhoefer, Esther, "Individualized Reading," *Childhood Education,* Vol. 34 (November 1957), pp. 118-22.
24. Sartain, Harry W., "A Bibliography on Individualized Reading," *The Reading Teacher,* Vol. 13 (April, 1960), p. 262.
25. Ibid.
26. ———, "The Roseville Experiment with Individualized Reading," *The Reading Teacher,* Vol. 13 (April 1960), p. 277.
27. Ibid. p. 281.
28. Ibid. p. 279.
29. Sharpe, Maida Wood, "An Individualized Reading Program," *Elementary English,* Vol. 35 (December 1958), pp. 507-12.
30. Stauffer, Russell G., "Individualized and Group Directed Reading Instruction," *Elementary English,* Vol. 37 (October 1960), p. 381.
31. Ibid.
32. Strang, Ruth, and Lindquist, Donald M., *The Administrator and the Improvement of Reading.* New York: Appleton-Century-Crofts, Inc., 1960, pp. 14-16, 86.
33. Terman, Sybil, and Walcutt, Charles Child, *Reading Chaos and Cure.* New York: McGraw-Hill Book Company, 1958. Quotes are from the book jacket.
34. Ibid. p. 19.
35. Witty, Paul (Chairman), *Development in and Through Reading,* Sixtieth Yearbook, National Society for the Study of Education. Chicago: University of Chicago Press, 1961.
36. ———, *Reading in Modern Education.* Boston: D. C. Heath, 1949, p. 10.
37. Ibid.
38. Witty, Paul, *The Effects of the Mass Media,* Golden Anniversary White House Conference on Children and Youth, Washington, D.C., 1960. See also *A Study of the Interests of Children and Youth,* a co-operative research project between Northwestern University and the Office of Education, U.S. Department of Health, Education, and Welfare, directed by Paul A. Witty, Northwestern University, 1960.
39. ———, and Fitzwater, James, "An Experiment with Films, Film Readers, and the Magnetic Sound Track Projector," *Elementary English* (April 1952).

Author Index

Subject Index

Achievement, measurement of, 134-6
California Tests, 251, 281, 378-9
Iowa Every-Pupil Test, 326, 384
Metropolitan Tests, 88-94, 95, 207, 217-19, 222, 395
Stanford Test, 380
Acquisition of generan information, 140-41
Action research, 378
Activities and preferences, 265-6
Activity program, 41, 42
Adults, correlation of measures for, 254
machines and reading, 338
scores for, 256
Age, of first graders, 212-20
groups, and phonics, 199
Alphabetical approach, 5, 208-9
Alton, Illinois, 214-5
American Association for the Advancement of Science, 38
American Book Company, 103, 151
Analytical method, 222
Appreciation, tastes and, 296-7
Arithmetic, Courtis Tests, 38
achievement in, 139-40
Army program, 419
Associative learning, 12
Attitudes, 51-3, 141-3
Auditory aids, 348
Average pupils, reading accomplishments, 281-4
Ayres-Buckingham word list, 138
Dolch word list, 108, 112
spelling scale, 38

Basal readers, 58, 150-53, 210, 222, 275, 354, 375, 418, 428
Beginning reading, 16, 26, 40, 189-90
factors in, 203-4
Betts Reading Vocabulary Study, 351
Book behavior, 75-81
Brooklyn, New York, 203
Buckingham-Ayres word list, 138

California tests of achievement, 251, 281, 378-9
mental maturity, 95, 215, 223, 251, 281, 326, 379
Characteristics of the reader, 314
Chicago, 202, 205, 266-7
Child Study Center, 65
Clark's reading readiness, 95
Cleveland Public Schools, 3
College level, 304-10
instructor, 10
Comprehension, developing, 186-7, 233-45, 282, 292-4
determinants of, 233-45
factors in, 233-45, 293
listening, 248
measuring, 235, 246-8
or memory, 246
and mispronunciation, 203
oral and silent, 248
and speed, 249
test, 250
Concepts, in remedial reading, 40, 351-8
mathematical test, 233
Conscious teaching of language, 173-4
Consonants, 192-3
Content, implicit and manifest, 334
Context, word meaning through, 101, 115-20, 121-5, 291
clues, 99-100, 119-21
and word form, 99-100, 291
meaning of, 115, 116
Contextual aids, 116-19
pictorial representatives, 118
Core words, 105-7
Correlation of intelligence, reading achievement, and readiness, 85, 86
Courtis Arithmetic Tests, 38
Creative responses, 240
Creative writing, 58
Critical reading, 67, 277-80, 405-46